PENNSYLVANIA MARRIAGES PRIOR TO 1790

Names of Persons
for whom
MARRIAGE LICENSES
Were Issued in the Province of Pennsylvania
Previous to 1790

Compiled Under the Editorial Supervision of
John B. Linn and William H. Egle

REPRINTED WITH SUPPLEMENTARY MATERIAL FROM
the Pennsylvania Magazine of History and Biography
and The Pennsylvania Genealogical Magazine

CLEARFIELD

Originally published as Volume II, Second Series,
Pennsylvania Archives
Harrisburg, 1890
Reprinted by Genealogical Publishing Co., Inc.
Baltimore, 1963, 1968

Reprinted with the Following Supplements:

"Pennsylvania Marriage Licenses, 1742-1748," excerpted
from the *Pennsylvania Magazine of History and Biography*,
Volume XXXIX, Nos. 2, 3, 4 (1915)

"Pennsylvania Marriage Licenses, Issued by Governor
James Hamilton, 1748-1752," excerpted from
the *Pennsylvania Magazine of History and Biography*,
Volume XXXII, Nos. 1, 2, 3, 4 (1908)

"List of Marriage Licenses Issued in the Secretary's
Office from August 1755 through April 1759,"
excerpted from *The Pennsylvania Genealogical Magazine*,
Volume XXI, No. 4 (1960)

Genealogical Publishing Co., Inc.
Baltimore, 1976, 1979, 1984, 1994
Library of Congress Catalogue Card Number 75-37471

Reprinted for Clearfield Company by
Genealogical Publishing Company
Baltimore, Maryland
2011

13-digit ISBN: 978-0-8063-0709-1

Made in the United States of America

INTRODUCTORY.

Among the laws agreed upon in England by the Proprietary for the government of the Province of Pennsylvania, was one providing for a registry of marriages, births and deaths. By virtue of this law licenses were issued by the authorities. Although the Assembly frequently declared it "the opinion of this House that the Proprietary or his Deputy Granting Lycenses to marry is not Incident to any authority Granted them by the Royal Charter, nor warranted thereby, nor by any power that we understand they have; but the Granting of such Lycenses is Contrary to Law, & of an Evil Tendency;" the practice did not fall into total desuetude until some years after the formation of the Constitution of the Commonwealth of 1790. Four volumes of these records are in existence, covering a period of not quite forty years. What has become of the earlier registers and those also kept during the Revolution, it has been impossible to ascertain.

The license was issued from the Provincial Secretary's office, and the date prefixed to each name is that of the issuing the same, not that of the marriage. Ministers and others performing the ceremony sent forward the penal bond properly signed, whereupon the license was issued. Accounts were kept with these persons, and from the records we glean the following names. The reader may look, perchance, for some of the celebrated clergymen of the old-time; but many of these procured their licenses through the civil magistrate, and hence do not appear in the books referred to :

1760. Alricks, Hermanus, Esq., Cumberland county.
1767. Andrews, Rev. John, Lewestown, Sussex county.
1762. Alsentz, George, Germantown.
1742. Backhouse, Reverend.
1763. Barton, Rev. Thomas, Lancaster.
1742. Beckert, Rev. William.
1759. Borell, Rev. Andrew, Rector at Wilmington.
1760. Bordenlied, Rev. Mr.
1767. Bucher, Rev. Conrad, Carlisle.
1742. Chew, Samuel, Esq.
1742. Cookson, Thomas, Esq.
1762. Craig, Rev. George, Chester.

INTRODUCTORY.

1744. Currie, Rev. William, at the Great Valley, Chester County.
1742. Franberg, Rev. Peter.
1768. Gircelius, Rev. Lawrence, Wilmington.
1762. Gordon, Lewis, Esq., Northampton county.
1766. Graham, Henry Hale, Esq., Chester.
1762. Griffith, Rev. Abel, "Baptist Minister in West Bradford Township, Chester County."
1744. Grffith, Timothy, "in Penn Cador Hund'd, New Castle County."
1762. Growden, Lawrence, Esq., Bucks county.
1763. Hall, David, Esq., Sussex county.
1743. Holt, Ryves, Esq., Lewes Town, Sussex county.
1764. Huston, Rev. Alexander, "Mushmellion Hund'd, Kent county."
1762. Inglis, Rev. Charles, Dover.
1764. Johnston, Samuel, Esq., York county.
1743. Legat, John.
1768. Long, Rev. James, "of Connecocheague in Cumberland county."
1767. McGaw, [Magaw,] Rev. Mr., Dover.
1762. McKannon, Rev. William, "of White Clay Creek, New Castle county."
1762. McWilliams, Richard, Esq., New Castle county.
1743. Mackay, John, New Castle.
1760. Miller, Rev. John, "near Dover."
1763. Murray, Rev. Alexander, Reading, Berks county.
1763. Neal, Rev. Mr., "of Oxford, Germantown."
1742. Noxon, Thomas, Esq.
1762. Parker, Joseph, Esq., Chester.
1765. Peters, Rev. Richard, "of the city of Philadelphia."
1743. Pugh, Rev. John.
1762. Read, James, Esq., Berks county.
1762. Reading, Rev. Philip, "Appoquinimink Hundred, New Castle county."
1760. Reeger, Rev. Mr., Lancaster.
1744. Ridgley, Nicholas, Esq.
1762. Rodgers, Rev. John, "at St. George's, New Castle county."
1743. Ross, Rev. Æneas, Oxford.
1762. Schlatter, Rev. Michael, near Germantown.
1762. Shippen, Edward, Esq., Lancaster county.
1766. Spencer, Rev. Elihu, "at St. George's, New Castle county."
1762. Steel, Rev. John, "Carlisle in Cumberland county."
1762. Stevenson, George, Esq., York county.
1762. Stover, Rev. Casper, Lebanon Township, Lancaster county.

1760. Sturgeon, Rev. Mr.
1762. Thompson, Rev. William, " Commissionary at York county."
1759. Unander, Rev. Mr.
1768. Van Buskirk, Rev. Jacob, Germantown.
1762. Vining, John, Esq., Kent county.

Severe laws were passed in the early days of the Province against clandestine marriages, and an act of the Assembly of 1683 proposed a law for "young Men's Marrieing at such an age." The issuing of a license was not obligatory, but was intended for those cases where the banns were not published or the marrying in church dispensed with, and as a protection to ministers and others performing the ceremonies.

PENNSYLVANIA MARRIAGES.

A.

Date.		Names.
1773, Aug.	7.	Aaron, Hannah, and Jonathan Jones.
1767, Sep.	4.	Aaron, Rachel, and John Kelly.
1764, Aug.	1.	Abbett, Jonathan, and Abigail Sidders.
1774, Dec.	3.	Abbott, Ezekiel, and Elizabeth Williams.
1783, June	21.	Abel, John.
1768, Apr.	18.	Abel, Matthias, and Jane Elliart.
1771, Dec.	11.	Abel, Sarah, and Samuel Shaw.
1774, M'ch	17.	Abel, Susannah, and John Anderson.
1763, Apr.	18.	Abercromby, Elizabeth, and Hugh Bower.
1765, May	9.	Abercrummey, Judith, and Robert Malcolm.
1774, Jan.	1.	Aberdeen, Joseph, and Susanna Leacock.
1774, May	25.	Abraham, James, and Hannah George.
1773, Dec.	18.	Abraham, Margaret, and Benjamin Eastburne.
1766, May	23.	Abrams, Elizabeth, and John Lancaster.
1771, Jan.	14.	Abreeken, Mary, and Jacob Shafer.
1767, May	16.	Aburn, Hannah, and Richard Hughes.
1765, Oct.	17.	Ackles, Susannah, and Andrew Wade.
1762, Dec.	22.	Acred, John, and Hannah Ireland.
1774, Dec.	21.	Adair, Thomas, and Eleanor Jones.
1764, Dec.	5.	Adams, Alexander, and Martha Galer.
1775, Oct.	12.	Adams, Ann, and Thomas Conyngham.
1770, Sep.	25.	Adams, Catharine, and George McKowan.
1772, July	10.	Adams, Catharine, and Patrick Robertson.
1764, Nov.	1.	Adams, Elizabeth, and George Willson.
1770, Dec.	1.	Adams, Elizabeth, and John Hewitt.
1764, Feb.	29.	Adams, Elizabeth, and William Lang.
1764, Nov.	1.	Adams, Elizabeth, and William Smith.
1768, Oct.	17.	Adams, Hannah, and John Wilkie.
1748, Jan.	—.	Adams, James, and Sarah Jones.
1763, July	27.	Adams, Jane, and George Nimmen.
1745, Dec.	—.	Adams, John.
1772, Aug.	20.	Adams, John, and Catharine Hummer.
1775, Nov.	15.	Adams, John, and Elizabeth Walker,
1764, Dec.	24.	Adams, John, and Martha Hamilton.
1775, Feb.	3.	Adams, John, and Mary Davis.
1776, M'ch	9.	Adams, John, and Phœbe Winn.
1769, Dec.	28.	Adams, Jonathan, and Susannah Flower.

1762, Feb. 16. Adams, Joseph, and Ann Morrow.
1769, M'ch 16. Adams, Margaret, and Samuel Webster.
1762, Sep.   6. Adams, Mary, and Gabriel Dolbow.
1763, Aug. 10. Adams, Mary, and Gideon Vore.
1765, June 26. Adams, Mary, and James Urch.
1774, Dec.   8. Adamson, Alexander, and Mary Groce.
1748, M'ch —. Adamson, Anthony, and Dorothy Haines.
1746, Jan. —. Adamson, Philip.
1748, July 13. Adamson, Susanna, and John Parsons.
1765, Aug. 29. Adamson, William, and Elizabeth Story.
1767, June 8. Adams, Patience, and William Watson.
1766, M'ch 26. Adams, Peter, and Mary Rick.
1762, Nov.   6. Adams, Rachael, and James Black.
1762, July 23. Addidle, Charity, and George Elliott.
1771, Feb. 16. Addis, Martha, and Joseph Harding.
1767, Nov. 12. Addis, Mary, and Jacob Duffield.
1748, Feb. —. Addis, Richard, and Susanna Haslet.
1769, Dec. 27. Adudell, John, and Eleanor Hanse.
1764, Sep. 14. Adudel, Sarah, and William Harding.
1763, Sep. 24. Agen, Alexander, and Agnes Morrison.
1763, Aug. 11. Aglee, John, and Rosanna Weaver.
1770, Oct. 24. Agnew, Margaret, and Joseph Price.
1768, Dec. 12. Aires, Stephen, and Hester Wells.
1786, Dec. 15. Airs, Elizabeth, and Arnol Baker.
1771, Dec. 3. Akerly, Keziah, and William Carlisle.
1768, May 26. Akin, Hannah, and Joseph Nicholson.
1774, Feb. 19. Akins, Hannah, and John Caldwell.
1764, May 7. Alberger, Mary, and John Bernholt.
1767, July 16. Alberry, Adam, and Elizabeth Mouse.
1747, M'ch —. Alberton, Catharine, and Jacob Beezens.
1761, Oct. 29. Albertson, Jonathan, and Jemima Thomas.
1771, June 1. Albertson, Sarah, and William Flennigan.
1770, May 10. Albertson, Susannah, and William Edwards.
1762, July 26. Albright, Hannah, and Anthony Wright.
1747, Oct. —. Albright, Mary, and Alexander Guthrie.
1762, Aug. 31. Albright, Mary, and Charles Barber.
1775, Feb. 20. Albright, Michael, and Juliana Dowterman.
1748, Nov. 11. Albrighton, Xhia, and Nicholas Hicks.
1769, Oct. 6. Aldworth, William, and Hannnah Coffing.
1764, Sep. 24. Alee, Elizabeth, and Jno. Reynolds.
1770, Sep. 6. Alexander, Adam, and Hannah Bailes.
1764, Dec. 6. Alexander, Charles, and Eleanor Johnston.
1773, Jan. 13. Alexander, David, and Elizabeth Cochran.
1762, Sep. 22. Alexander, Elizabeth, and William Bunn.
1776, Jan. 6. Alexander, Hannah, and James McCrea.
1766, Apr. 17. Alexander, Henry, and Hester Rush.

1772, Oct. 17. Alexander, James, and Jane Parker.
1760, July 8. Alexander, James, and Lydia Porter.
1767, Jan. 10. Alexander, James, and Mary Thompson.
1771, July 17. Alexander, James, and Rachel Craven.
1761, July 25. Alexander, John. and Marg't Johnson.
1764, July 31. Alexander, Margaret, and Lewis Grant.
1766, Dec. 18. Alexander, Sarah, and Jennings Stevenson.
1764, Nov. 14. Alexander. Thomas. and Catharine Simpson.
1775, Apr. 5. Alexander, Thomas, and Mary Smith.
1768, Jan. 6. Alison, Benjamin, and Sarah Chambers.
1768, Aug. 11. Allardice, Joseph, and Elizabeth Ashton.
1768, Apr. 24. Allen, Andrew, and Sarah Cox.
1768, Dec. 7. Allenby, James, and Elizabeth Snow.
1774, Dec. 20. Allen, Elizabeth. and Isaac Oakman.
1774, Aug. 30. Allen, Elizabeth, and Thomas Magee.
1773, Sep. 28. Allen, George, and Esther Bowen.
1748, Jan. —. Allen, George, and Mary Harding.
1772, Oct. 7. Allen, Hannah, and Robert Gill.
1774, Nov. 2. Allen, Hannah, and William Little.
1769, Dec. 20. Allen, Isaac, and Sarah Campble.
1765, Jan. 15. Allen, James, and Catharine Christy.
1769, May 6. Allen, James, and Elizabeth Hull.
1768, M'ch 9. Allen, James, and Elizabeth Lawrence.
1773, Oct. 11. Allen, James, and Margaret Fitzgerald.
1760, Nov. 12. Allen, Jane, and Henry Ewing.
1767, Dec. 12. Allen, Jedediah, and Ruth Nicholson.
1774, M'ch —. Allen, John.
1764, M'ch 13. Allen, Joseph, and Sarah Plumley.
1747, Nov. —. Allen, Margaret, and Adam Burk.
1767, Feb. 22. Allen, Margaret, and John Lockhart.
1763, May 3. Allen. Mary, and Joseph Rodman.
1771, M'ch 2. Allen, Mary, and Thomas Coates.
1773, June 28. Allen, Mary, and William Price.
1773, Apr. 21. Allen, Nathaniel, Jr., and Mary Dean.
1768 Apr. 6. Allen, Patience, and Josiah Clark.
1743, Dec. —. Allen, Patrick.
1762 Jan. 7. Allen, Peter, and Rebecca Holth.
1765, Jan. 26. Allen. Richmond, and Mary Farmer.
1761, June 6. Allen, Sarah, and Thomas Jones.
1748, Sep. —. Allen, Susanna, and Jacob Spike.
1744, May —. Allen, Ulrich.
1748, Apr. 13. Allen, William, and Jane Reed.
1764, May 3. Allen, William, and Martha Brooks.
1748, June 16. Allen, Woolrick, and Mary Mandlin.
1763, Jan. 13. Allibone, William, and Sarah Gauthony.
1774, Oct. 19. Allison, Aaron, and Elizabeth Phipps.

1761, Feb.   4. Allison, Elizabeth, and David Briggan.
1743, Oct.   —. Allison, James.
1769, May   27. Allison, Jane, and Philip Jenkins.
1761, May   5. Allison, Patrick, and Catharine Hamilton.
1766, Apr.   23. Allison, Robert, and Margaret Thompson.
1766, Dec.   2. Allison, Robert, and Rachel Gunning.
1760, June   28. Allison, Thomas, and Elizabeth White.
1763, Dec.   11. Allison, William, and Grace Caldwell.
1748, July   13. Allison, William, and Mary Pennington.
1760, July   9. Allis, Phebe, and James McMicken.
1760, May   17. Allman, Elizabeth, and Michael Younkman.
1769, Feb.   15. Allman, Lawrence, and Hannah Thomas.
1769, Apr.   15. Allman, Rachel, and John Harrison.
1772, July   10. Alloway, Marsena, and Catharine Davis.
1767, July   4. Allyn, Adam, and Ann Scott.
1760. Jan.   1. Allyn, Adam, and Sarah Foulquier.
1772, June   19. Alricks Mary, and Thomas Scully.
1770, June   22. Alsentz, Barbara, and Jacob Wentz.
1770, Feb.   10. Alston, Joseph, Jun'r, and Mary Berry.
1768, Apr.   13. Altemus, John, and Catharine Hopple.
1765, M'ch   19. Alverse, Catharine, and John Cruger.
1763, June   16. Aman, Jacob, and Mary Lee.
1743, Apr.   9. Ambler, Nathan.
1772, July   4. Ames, Elizabeth, and William Wellman.
1761, Sep.   25. Amos, Juliana, and William Empson.
1768, Jan.   26. Ampmaning, Catharine, and John Bender.
1776, May   8. Anderholdt, Leveace, and Ludowick Staigner.
1766, Apr.   29. Anderson, Abraham, and Hannah Price.
1774, Nov.   30. Anderson, Ann, and John Patterson.
1765, Sep.   5. Anderson, Ann, and Joseph Thacker.
1762, Sep.   20. Anderson, Christopher, and Elizabeth Sears.
1767, May   26. Anderson, Elijah, and Mary West.
1746, July   —. Anderson, Elizabeth, and Abram Nutt.
1773, Apr.   10. Anderson, Elizabeth, and John Middleton.
1774, M'ch   5. Anderson, Elizabeth, and Matthew Clugston.
1768, .Jan.   6. Anderson, Elizabeth, and Samuel Breese.
1765, Sep.   5. Anderson, Evan, and Esther Bowen.
1774, Sep.   3. Anderson, George, and Sarah Strong.
1769, July   12. Anderson, Gilbert, and Mary Doggad.
1769, Aug.   15. Anderson, Hannah, and Job Harvey.
1774, July   26. Anderson, Hannah, and John Morrison.
1765, Sep.   24. Anderson, Isaac, and Sarah Pearson.
1774, July   29. Anderson, James, and Margaret Francis.
1771, Dec.   18. Anderson, Jane, and James Sample.
1743, M'ch   19. Anderson, John.
1761, June   20. Anderson, John, and Elizabeth Miller.

1747, Aug —. Anderson, John, and Jane White.
1769, Nov. 15. Anderson, John, and Sarah Flack.
1771, Jan. 2. Anderson, John, and Sarah Jenkins.
1743, Jan. 26. Anderson, Lawrence.
1761, Oct. 1. Anderson, Margaret, and Ellis Hughes.
1762, Nov. 29. Anderson, Margaret, and Thomas McHarg.
1775, June 20. Anderson, Mary, and Alexander Henderson.
1761, Aug. 17. Anderson, Mary, and Benjamin Thackray.
1766, Aug. 18. Anderson, Mary, and Jacob Hill.
1774, Dec. 2. Anderson, Mary, and William Knowles.
1762, May 22. Anderson, Nancy, and Henry Jones.
1775, Apr. 19. Anderson, Rachel, and Bryan Lafferty.
1762, July 19. Anderson, Robert, and Ann Jones.
1774, Nov. 11. Anderson, Samuel, and Ann Nelson.
1776, Apr. 23. Anderson, William, and Jane Rodgers.
1773, Aug. 19. Andreas, Michael, and Anna Eliz. Cloninger.
1768, Dec. 10. Andreas, Zacharias, and Mary Sinsfelder.
1769, Sep. 5. Andres, Adam, and Anne Derling.
1766, Dec. 18. Andrew, John, and Ann Sharpless.
1762, Aug. 17. Andrews, John, and Mary Encey.
1765, Nov. 2. Angila, Sarah, and Joshua Hemmenway.
1775, Apr. 19. Angus, John, and Hannah Approwen.
1774, M'ch 17. Annedown, John, and Susannah Abel.
1746, Nov. —. Annis, John, and Mary Hollin.
1763, Sep. 3. Annis, Mary, and Dennis McGrah.
1743, Dec. —. Annis, William.
1772, Aug. 18. Anson, John, and Sarah Cassel.
1748, June 16. Anstill, Ann, and Charles Pearce.
1760, Sep. 30. Answorth, Ann, and William Howa.
1776, Jan. 9. Antes, Christiana, and Jacob Mercley.
1772, July 9. Anthony, Abigail, and William Turner.
1766, Dec. 8. Anthony, Ann, and Thomas Guy.
1747, June —. Anthony, Stephen, and Susanna Boerman.
1775, M'ch 8. Antis, Elizabeth, and John Schuller.
1775, July 22. Antis, Frederick, and Catharine Shuler.
1767, Dec. 8. Antis, Henry, and Sophia Snyder.
1772, June 13. Aple, Ann, and Frederick Place.
1773, Feb. 13. Aple, Susannah, and Jacob Good.
1771, Apr. 19. Appleby, Anne, and William Brown.
1769, Oct. 25. Appleby, Elizabeth, and John James.
1771, June 15. Applegate, George, and Mary Lazalier.
1764, June 28. Appleton, Josiah, and Rebecca Gilbert.
1760, July 5. Appleton, William, and Mary Ripton.
1775, Feb. 1. Appowen, John, and Mary Mason.
1774, Oct. 27. Appowen, Mary, and William Jackson.
1764, Dec. 10. Archdearon, Patrick, and Jane Quin.
2—Vol. II.

1763, July 13. Archer, Benjamin, and Experience Middleton.
1775, Feb. 28. Archey, Elizabeth, and Charles Finney.
1775, June 14. Archibald, Elizabeth, and John McGee.
1760, Aug. 7. Arcle, Mary and Jno. Brown.
1776, June 3. Ardla, Philip, and Barbara White.
1773, Nov. 18. Argyle, Eleanor, and Joseph Young.
1766, June 5. Aries, Sarah, and Philip Benezet.
1767, Jan. 10. Aris, Mary, and David Potts.
1767, Aug. 7. Armitage, Dorcas, and Robert Montgomery.
1743, Jan. 1. Armitage, Enoch.
1768, Apr. 26. Armour, John, and Catharine Swain.
1772, May 5. Armstrong, Catharine, and John McCleane.
1760, Oct. 21. Armstrong, Ephraim, and Margaret Brennan.
1766, Apr. 7. Armstrong, George, and Martha Turner.
1760, May 22. Armstrong, James, and Ruth Bastian.
1766, Apr. 26. Armstrong, Jane, and Simon Armstrong.
1746, Nov. —. Armstrong, John, and Rebecca Armstrong.
1772, Apr. 23. Armstrong, Mary, and Francis Willson.
1762, Apr. 3. Armstrong, Mary, and John Folk.
1765, M'ch 23. Armstrong, Mary, and John Oliver.
1770, July 3. Armstrong, Rachel, and Robert Willson.
1746, Nov. --. Armstrong, Rebecca, and John Armstrong.
1775, Jan. 11. Armstrong, Samuel, and Elizabeth Gibson.
1766, Apr. 26. Armstrong, Simon, and Jane Armstrong.
1762, July 6. Armstrong, Thomas, and Sarah McHenry.
1762, Feb. 1. Arnell, Barbara, and Edmund Butler.
1764, Apr. 2. Arney, John, and Martha Paxton.
1769, Sep. 21. Arnold, Agnes, and Dennis Ryan.
1746, Oct. —. Arnold, Jonathan, and Elizabeth McCollock.
1773, Oct. 16. Arnold, Margaret, and John Sandon.
1764, May 10. Arrele, Catharine, and Jesse Carey.
1746, July —. Artis, Mary, and Jonathan Bebor.
1748, Jan. —. Arts, John, and Martha Morgan.
1770, M'ch 7. Arup, Henry Christopher, and Sophia Beering.
1763, M'ch 17. Ashard, Margaret, and Joseph Lefever.
1774, Dec. 26. Ash, Barbara, and Daniel Carsner.
1775, Feb. 20. Ashburnham, Joseph, and Rachel Griffin.
1765, Jan. 9. Ashburn, John, and Elizabeth Gottier.
1767, May 9. Ash, Caleb, and Rebecca Lowns.
1774, Feb. 28. Ashenfelder, Ludowick, and Sarah Schunk.
1769, Feb. 7. Asherfelder, Thomas, and Anna Hendricks.
1743, Oct. —. Asherton, Isaac.
1760, Nov. 15. Ash, Hannah, and John Marle.
1770, May 23. Ash, Henry and Philippine Miller.
1774, Feb. 22. Ash, James, and Mary Lindsay.
1771, May 18. Ash, James, and Sarah Hinchman.

1769, M'ch 18. Ash, Joshua, and Abigail Evans.
1761, May 27. Ash, Law, and Martha Kownland.
1768, July 15. Ashman, Lewis, and Hannah Cooper.
1773, Oct. 26. Ash, Mary, and James Craig.
1770, Apr. 6. Ashmead, Jacob, and Mary Naglee.
1768, Feb. 13. Ashmead, Rachel, and James Hood.
1771, Nov. 25. Ash, Samuel, and Martha Pearson.
1766, M'ch 24. Ashton, Andrew, and Rachel Thomas.
1763, Feb. 8. Ashton, Daniel, and Elizabeth Ritchie.
1768, Aug. 11. Ashton, Elizabeth, and Jos. Allardice.
1772, Oct. 28. Ashton, Elizabeth, and Sampson Davis.
1773, Oct. 13. Ashton, Isaac, and Rachel Northrop.
1767, Apr. 2. Ashton, Isaac, and Rebecca Powel.
1764, Sep. 17. Ashton. James, and Ann Delavan.
1774, Dec. 29. Ashton, Joseph, and Letetia Cooper.
1760, M'ch 3, Ashton, Joseph, and Rachel Northop.
1774, Feb. 19. Ashton, Martha, and Samuel Swift, jun.
1773, Apr. 28. Ashton, Mary, and Jacob Garrigues.
1767, M'ch 24, Ashton, Susannah, and John Johnson.
1744, May —. Ashton, Thomas.
1761, July 29. Askton, William, and Phœbe Hutchinson.
1748, April 13. Aspbens, Mary, and Henry Harrison.
1775, Feb. 28. Assheton, Esther, and Caleb Coburn.
1767, M'ch 10. Assheton, Frances, and Stephen Watts.
1773, June 17. Assheton, Mary, and Boas Walton.
1776, Feb. 7. Assheton, Mary, and Isaac Troth.
1775, Oct. 25. Assheton, Thomas, and Esther Johnston.
1767, Nov. 14. Assheton, Thomas, and Hannah Flower.
1763, Nov. 5. Aston, George, and Hannah Phipps.
1766, Dec. 9. Atherholdt, Wilhelmina, and John Leise.
1747. M'ch, —. Atkins, John, and Phœbe Phillpott.
1775, Oct. 2. Atkinson, Isaac, and Elizabeth Toy.
1769, Nov. 18. Atkinson, John, and Margaret Whitehead.
1766, Jan. 22. Atkinson, Joseph, and Elizabeth Croxford.
1770, Feb. 10. Atkinson, Samuel, and Elizabeth Conaroe.
1774, May 11. Atkinson, William, and Ann Lawrence.
1759, Nov. 20. Atkinson, William, and Catharine Kreemer.
1771, M'ch 28. Atkinson, William, and Charity Hayes.
1763, Sep. 1. Atlee, William, and Esther Sayre.
1768, Sep. 21. Attmore, Jonathan, and Rachel Mason.
1769, Aug. 21. Atwell, Anne, and Richard Tyson.
1766, M'ch 17. Aubery, Ann, and William Norris.
1762, Feb. 10. Audley, Eleanor, and Paul Hemings.
1771, May 21. Austin, Jane, and Daniel Vancourt.
1744, Nov. —. Austin, John.

1748, Feb. —. Austin, John, and Martha Morgan.
1748, Oct. 18. Austin, Samuel, and Widow Stilly.
1761, Jan. 5. Austin, Thomas, and Mary Thomas.
1772, Nov. 20. Aves, John, and Rachel Clark.
1774, Aug. 25. Avrin, Margaret, and Samuel Ford.
1769, M'ch 4. Awlman, John, and Abigail Vanhorn.
1773, Oct. 26. Ax, Ann, and John Fries.
1773, Aug. 21. Axford, Elizabeth, and William Wilkins.
1726, Feb. 23. Ayers, William, and Elizabeth Rust.
1760, Oct. 25. Ayres, John, and Mary Bennett.
1772, Dec. 12. Ayres, Samuel, and Deborah Yerkes.

B.

1773, Jan. 8. Baar, Jacob, and Anna Margaret Reamer.
1760, Oct. 11. Baby, William, and Mary Haggins.
1761, Mch. 21. Baccorth, John, and Mary Payne.
1766, Sept. 11. Bracer, Mary, and Casper Welsh.
1747, Dec. —. Bachston, Rebecca, and William Ghiselin.
1769, Nov. 2. Backhouse, Richard, and Mary Williams.
1772, Oct. 28. Backman, Abraham, and Phebe Graff.
1743, Sept. —. Backman, Jacob.
1763, Jan. 18. Backman, Samuel, and Rachel Owen.
1767, Mch. 24. Bacon, Catharine, and Wendan Zerban.
1766, Nov. 1. Bacon, Elizabeth, and Morto O'Brian.
1771, Dec. 21. Badcock, John, and Christiana King.
1768, Apr. 21. Badger, Daniel, and Ann Doughty.
1761, Dec. 19. Badger, Edm., and Mary Harding.
1773, May 12. Badger, Sarah, and Thomas Coombe, Jun.
1761, Nov. 19. Bagnall, William, and Elizabeth Sulton.
1770, Sep. 6. Bailes, Hannah, and Adam Alexander.
1761, Aug. 31. Bailey, Ann, and Richard Jones.
1746, June —. Bailey, Hannah, and Walter Brown.
1748, Sep. —. Bailey, James, and Rebecca Davis.
1775, Apr. 19. Bailey, John, and Isabella Simpson.
1761, Sep. 5. Bailey, Mary, and Thomas Shavley.
1765, Dec. 23. Bail, Robert, and Margaret Potter.
1763, Apr. 18. Baily, Rebecca, and Jane Carroll.
1773, July 28. Baily, Susannah, and Enoch Morgan.
1773, Apr. 16. Baily, William, and Mary Campbell.
1760, Apr. 1. Baines, Matthew, and Sarah Irwin.
1760, Oct. 1. Bainghurst, George, and Sarah Trump.
1746, Aug. —. Baird, Eliz., and Samuel Wallace.
1767, Apr. 18. Baird, Hannah, and Robt. Jamison.
1766, May 12. Baird, Jane, and William Richards.
1763, June 25. Baird, John, and Elizabeth Diamond.
1761, Nov. 21. Baird, Joseph, and Sarah Smith.

1745, May —. Baird, Thomas.
1766, May 2. Bait, Rebecca, and Job Thomas.
1772, Nov. 6. Bakely, Elizabeth, and Valentine Grouse.
1773, Mch. 15. Baker, Adam, and Elizabeth Neff.
1768, Dec. 15. Baker, Arnol, and Elizabeth Airs.
1774, June 21. Baker, Christopher, and Catharine Kreider.
1776, Mch. 4. Baker, Civel, and Thomas Cumpton.
1759, Dec. 27. Baker, Elizabeth, and Benjamin Evan.
1765, Jan. 3. Baker, George, and Mary Preston.
1770, Mch. 9. Baker, Hannah, and Adam Shetzland.
1764, Jan. 21. Baker, Hannah, and Joseph Barker.
1774, Feb. 18. Baker, Henry, and Sarah Jones.
1769, Nov. 23, Baker, Isaac, and Hannah Pacay Cook.
1761, Apr. 6. Baker, Jacob, and Catharine March.
1774, Apr. 8. Baker, Jacob, and Hannah Smith.
1762, Jan. 12. Baker, Jacob, and Mary Miller.
1768, May 12. Baker, James, and Martha Neill.
1774, Dec. 6. Baker, James, and Mary White.
1764, Jan. 16. Baker, John, and Eleanor Wheeler.
1767, Oct. 1. Baker, John, and Elizabeth Roberts.
1775, Feb. 28. Baker, John, and Elizabeth Schreiner.
1775, Nov. 9. Baker, John, and Susannah Bonner.
1770, Sept. 27. Baker, Lidia, and John Richardson.
1773, Jan. 25. Baker, Mary, and John Sowder.
1770, Oct. 12. Baker, Mary, and Lambert Wilmer.
1769, July 3. Baker, Samuel, and Susannah Wallace.
1772, June 18. Baker, Susannah, and Daniel James.
1766, Jan. 27. Baker, William, and Sarah Neave.
1774, Feb. 19. Bakin, Catharine, and Conrod Devetter.
1764, June 23. Balderston, Bartholomew, and Sarah Johnson.
1761, Mch. 5. Baldwin, John, and Sarah Hampton.
1747, Dec. —. Baldridge, Thomas, and Ann Bell.
1768, Mch. 5. Baldwin, Hannah, and John Marshall.
1775, Nov. 27. Baldwin, John, and Jane Downing.
1774, Feb. 24. Baldwin, John, and Jane Farringdon.
1763, Mch. 30. Baldwin, John, and Massey Sotcher.
1744, June 7. Baldwin, William.
1748, Nov. 11. Bale, Joseph, and Ann Smith.
1776, May 29. Balfour, James, and Hannah Morgan.
1773, Nov. 18. Ballard, Elizabeth, and Isaac Watson.
1763, Apr. 20. Ballard, Peter, and Barbara Haggerty.
1761, Jan. 30. Ball, Eleanor, and John Watson.
1769, Jan. 12. Ball, Elizabeth, and William Moore.
1769, Oct. 2. Ball, Hannah, and George Powell.
1764, July 16. Ballinger, Rebecca, and Joseph Jones.
1764, Aug. 22. Ball, Mary, and Andrew May.

1772, Mch. 20. Ball, Rachel, and John Rice.
1775, July 20. Ball, Sarah, and John Daniels.
1773, Nov. 12. Ball, William, and Ann Gilbert.
1771, June 11. Ball, William, and Elizabeth Byles.
1769, Jan. 11. Balson, John, and Elizabeth Prince.
1769, Sep. 14. Baltiwine, Catharine, and Frederick Ublevy.
1766, Dec. 1. Baltzer, Susannah, and Jacob Creig.
1747, May. —. Balwin, Mary, and Samuel Mennan.
1771, Jan. 21. Bamberger, Eliz., and Michael Stamber.
1773, Sep. 16. Bamford, John, and Ann Lehman.
1769, Apr. 1. Bamford, Mary, and William Dogharty.
1761, M'ch 11. Banard, Mary, and Benj'n Lusher.
1760, Apr. 23. Banart, Hannah, and Derrick Krausen.
1773, Oct. 16. Bane, Abigail, and Thomas Butler.
1748, May 16. Bane, Rachel, and Hugh M'Clone.
1766, Feb. 21. Banks, Ann, and Henry Stiles.
1767, May 25. Bank, Sarah, and Anthony Noble.
1776, Feb. 10. Banks, Joseph, and Ann Lee.
1771, Oct. 3. Bankson, Andrew, Jun., and Mary Tallman.
1745, July —. Bankson, Daniel.
1760, Nov. 19. Bankson, Elinor, and Nathaniel Pillet.
1743, Jan. 15. Bankson, Henry.
1767, Dec. 28. Bankson, Hester, and James Channel.
1744, Apr. —. Bankson, Jacob.
1770, Sep. 13. Bankson, Margaret, and Augustine Tallman.
1765, Aug. 17. Bankson, Mary, and Jacob Hanse.
1766, April 17. Bankson, Mary, and Samuel Taylor.
1743, Oct. —. Bankson, Peter.
1769, June 21. Banks, Sarah, and Andrew Cape.
1763, May 4. Banks, Sarah, and Nathan Dykes.
1772, July 15. Banks, Susannah, and Joseph Oliver.
1767, Nov. 3. Banks, Thomas, and Francis Lovekin.
1773, Jan. 21. Bantick, Ann, and Thomas Glenn.
1768, Sept. 21. Barber, Ann, and David Ware.
1762, Aug. 13. Barber, Charles, and Mary Albright.
1762, Sept. 25. Barber, Hannah, and Daniel White.
1762, Oct. 25. Barber, Margaret, and Laughlin Curry.
1763, Aug. 8. Barber, William, and Mary Stoops.
1772, M'ch 3. Barclay, Ann, and Andrew Dennison.
1760, Feb. 13. Barclay, Elinor, and John Chevalier.
1761, Dec. 31. Barclay, Gilbert, and Ann Ingliss,
1765, Aug. 24. Barclay, Hannah, and Rich'd Palmer.
1766, Nov. 12. Barclay, Jane, and William Craig.
1766, M'ch 29. Barclay, Mary, and Rob't Miller.
1776, M'ch 20. Barclay, Mary, and Thomas Barr.
1770, Oct. 18. Barclay, Thomas, and Mary Hoops.

1771, Apr. 16. Barcroft, Ambrus, and Phebe Quimby.
1771, Apr. 16. Barcroft, Hannah, and Edward Rice.
1768, Nov. 12. Barcroft, Martha, and William Hamilton.
1743, Aug. 26. Bardier, Joseph.
1773, June 22. Bardon, Stephen, and Catharine Smith.
1774, Aug. 15. Barge, Elizabeth, and Jacob Whiteman.
1774, Oct. 12. Barge, Joseph, and Dorothy Ottinger.
1767, Aug. 27. Barker, Auther, and Sarah Smith.
1745, Jan. —. Barker Benjamin.
1770, July 10. Barker James, and Mary Weir.
1769, July 13. Barker, John, and Mary Nelson.
1764, Jan. 21. Barker, Joseph, and Hannah Baker.
1776, Jan. 13. Barker, Mary, and John Miller.
1772, M'ch 11. Barker, William, and Elizabeth Wallis.
1748, Apr. 13. Barkely, Elizabeth, and John Blakely.
1761, July 31. Bark, Mary, and Joseph Roberts.
1760, Dec. 17. Barlow, John, and Hannah Savage.
1761, April 22. Barnard, Sarah, and David Bilderback.
1762, July 10. Barndollar, Peter, and Margaret Wilkinson.
1775, Apr. 10. Barnes, James, and Ann Davis.
1772, Nov. 4. Barnes, Mary, and Benjamin Loxley, Jun.
1766, Apr. 18. Barnes, Mary, and John Packard.
1760, July 30. Barnes, Robert, and Sarah Colbert.
1768, Sept. 8. Barnes, William, and Ruth Mott.
1772, Aug. 26. Barnet, Agnes, and John Evans.
1768, May. 30. Barnet, Margaret, and Francis Lewis.
1774, Nov. 26. Barnet, Sarah, and John Brice.
1748, July 13. Barnet, Sarah, and Samuel Crispin.
1775, May 30. Barnet, Simon, and Margaret Sidell.
1763, Apr. 18. Barnett, Ann, and Samuel Burchett.
1761, Dec. 2. Barnett, Elizabeth, and Samuel Crawford.
1761, Feb. 12. Barnett, Sarah, and Andrew Boyd.
1771, Oct. 24. Barnet, William M., and Elizabeth Stone.
1745, Aug. —. Barney, Valentine.
1769, Aug. 9. Barnhill, Isabella, and John Taylor.
1769, Feb. 14. Barnhill, Margaret, and Henry Brubst.
1770, Dec. 22. Barnhill, Margaret, and Samuel Henry.
1768, June 17. Barns, Lambert, and Elizabeth Hay.
1772, May 5. Barnsley, John, and Elizabeth Vancourt.
1772, May 23. Barrell, Francis, and Elizabeth Harrison.
1762, July 8. Barrents, Ann, and William Singleton.
1764, Oct. 13. Barret, Enoch, and Mary De Normandie.
1769, July 14. Barret, Enoch, and Rachel Simmonds.
1768, Apr. 25. Barret, Mary, and John Winter.
1770, Dec. 22. Barret, Richard, and Elizabeth Trapnal.
1747, M'ch —. Barret, Richard, and Mary Evanson.

1761, June 2. Barret, Jane, and John Floyd.
1772, Apr. 8. Barr, George, and Mary Eakan.
1760, Oct. 31. Barr, Jennet, and Griffith Jones.
1774, July 11. Barr. John, and Sarah Thompson.
1775, May 18. Barr, Margaret, and Henry Kreps.
1770, Dec. 6, Barr, Martha, and Matthias Orrick.
1774, Jan. 3. Barrow, John, and Mary Roberts.
1764, Nov. 5. Barr, Rachel, and Josiah Forster.
1776, M'ch 20. Barr, Thomas, and Mary Barclay.
1765. Jan. 1. Barry, Elizabeth, and William Wild.
1767, Oct. 31. Barry, John, and Mary Clary.
1768, Apr. 6. Barry, Judith, and John Shaw.
1772, Oct. 10. Barry, Patrick, and Mary Farrell.
1746, June —. Barr, Zachariah, and Jane Griffin.
1772, May 18. Barthket, William, and Catharine Delany.
1744, May —. Bartholomew, Andrew.
1773, M'ch 4. Bartholomew, Benjamin, and Elizabeth Bull.
1771, Oct. 10. Bartholomew, Catharine, and Benjamin Griffith.
1766, Aug. 21. Bartholomew, Gaynor, and David Kinsey.
1766, June 4. Bartholomew, Hannah, and Archibald Thompson.
1768, May 3. Bartholomew, Mary, and Abel Pearson.
1772, June 26. Barthot, Hannah, and Nathaniel Ricketts.
1773, Oct. 1. Barthurst, Elizabeth, and James Rowland.
1774, Aug. 6. Bartlet, Ambrose, and Alice Willand.
1770, May 3. Bartling, Christlet, and Elizabeth Honogrot.
1765, Jan. 17. Bartling, Emanuel, and Elizabeth Etter.
1762, July 15. Bartly, Grace, and James Stuart.
1773, May 8. Bartolet, William, and Elizabeth Holmes.
1760, Jan. 1. Barton, Andrew, and Stanch Robinson.
1767, Dec. 26. Barton, Elias, and Ann Blair.
1762, Sep. 8. Barton, Elizabeth, and Jonathan Ewer.
1761, Aug. 19. Barton, Hannah, and William Gorely.
1761, May 20. Barton, Job, and Lucretia West.
1763, Nov. 23. Barton, Joseph, and Elizabeth Griffith.
1760, Dec. 2. Barton, Samuel, and Jane Tallas.
1767, M'ch 23. Barton, Sarah and Joseph Jones.
1767, Feb. 16. Barton, Sarah, and Richard Doyle.
1775, Apr. 8. Barton, Susannah, and Levi Evans.
1766, May 19. Barton, Thomas, and Patience Eldridge.
1768, June 23. Bartow, Thomas, Jun., and Sarah Benezet.
1767, Jan. 14. Bartram, Alexander, and Jane Martin.
1771, Aug. 2. Bartram, Elizabeth, and William Wright.
1767, Dec. 1. Bartram, William, and Mary Fisher.
1746, M'ch —. Barwick, John.

1761, M'ch 19. Bass, Elizabeth, and Thomas Findal.
1763, Oct. 12. Bassonet, Martha, and Richard Johnson.
1760, May 22. Bastian, Ruth, and James Armstrong.
1762, Dec. 18. Bastine, Benjamin, and Elizabeth Stewart.
1763, Jan. 27. Bastone, Henry, and Mary Hazleton.
1768, Oct. 27. Batchelor, Edward, and Frances Henry.
1773, Nov. 10. Bate, Elizabeth, and Martin Wilson.
1747, Sep. —. Bateman, Susannah, and Andrew Geary.
1769, Apr. 20. Bateman, Thomas, and Sarah Moore.
1773, Sep. 21. Bateman, William, and Margaret Porter.
1769, Sep. 20. Bate, Ruth, and Amos Thomas.
1774, Oct. 31. Bates, Hannah, and Andrew Stillman.
1776, Feb. 27. Bates, Sarah, and Jacob Holmes.
1764, July 21. Bate, William, and Phebe Holmes.
1769, July 5. Bathkill, William, and Catharine Williams.
1773, June 23. Baths, William, and Elizabeth Trace.
1770, Apr. 26. Bathurst, Mary, and Thomas Steele.
1760, June 28. Bateman, Thomas, and Frances Burk.
1766, Nov. 27. Baton, Catharine, and John Pennel.
1768, May 19. Batson, Thomas, and Catharine Jones.
1748, Oct. 18. Battin, Dorothy, and Benjamin Peters.
1768, Aug. 27. Battin, Enoch, and Rebecca Jones.
1744, May —. Battin, Thomas.
1765, June 22. Battle, Susannah, and Phineas Massey.
1769, Jan. 2. Batton, Mary, and James Brown.
1771, Jan. 10. Batt, Thomas, and Catharine McCall.
1775, Apr. 17. Bauer, Susannah, and John Truckenmiller.
1772, May 7. Baulby, Rachel, and Samuel Wigfall.
1773, Oct. 6. Baxter, James, and Ann Brown.
1760, Dec. 16, Baxter, James, and Elizabeth Turner.
1770, May 30. Baxter, John, and Eleanor Tape.
1762, Apr. 8. Baxter, Nancy, and Richard James.
1766, June 16. Baxton, Daniel, and Catharine Fling.
1769, Feb. 28. Bayman, Anne, and Anthony Hart.
1768, M'ch 24. Bayne, Eliazbeth, and George Syng.
1772, Dec. 13. Baynton, Elizabeth, and Abraham Markoe.
1770, Dec. 5. Baynton, Esther, and Joseph Bullock.
1764, Oct. 18. Baynton, Mary, and George Morgan.
1748, Apr. 13. Bay, Rebecca, and John Windell.
1743, Jan. 10. Bay, Thomas.
1769, Jan. 10. Bazelee, Mary, and Humphrey Fullerton.
1761, July 4. Bazelee, Sarah, and Joseph Marsh.
1767, Aug. 17. Beach, Edward, and Elizabeth Osburn.
1763, June 14. Beakler, John, and Christiana Romeck.
1772, Jan. 31. Beaks, Jane, and Joseph Smith.
1761, June 11. Beaks, John, and Deboro Macy

1767, July 29. Bealert, David, and Mary Fultz.
1762, Jan. 23. Bealert, Jacob, and Lydia Edwards.
1763, Dec. 24. Beale, William, Jun., and Edith Pennald.
1761, Feb. 13. Beal, John, and Jane Lloyd.
1743, July 27. Beaman, William.
1769, Oct. 28. Beam, Thomas, Jun., and Mary Tillyer.
1773, May 5. Beanes, Elizabeth, and Seth Beanes.
1773, May 5. Beanes, Seth, and Elizabeth Beanes.
1772, Dec 5. Beanor, Mary, and Charles Pennington.
1772, Nov. 21. Beanes, Thomas, and Elizabeth Hollingshead.
1776, Oct. 1. Beard, Ann, and James Fitsimmons.
1762, Sep. 1. Bearding, Amberus, and Sarah Waters.
1769, Apr. 26. Beardin, Sarah, and Samuel Woodbridge.
1746, Oct. — Beard, James, and Elizabeth Newby.
1768, July 22. Beard, Rosanna, and Joshua Groves.
1746, June —. Beason, Mary, and James Smith.
1744, Apr. —. Beaton, Daniel.
1767, Feb. 2. Beaty, James, and Catharine Smith.
1771, July 10. Beaven, William, and Mary Greenway.
1746, July —. Bebor, Jonathan, and Mary Artis.
1747, June —. Beckor, Frederick, and Christ. Lazarcen.
1773, M'ch 3. Beck, George Henry, and Elizabeth Ernst.
1764, Oct. 15. Beckin, Margaretta, and Erhard Scheeck.
1743, Feb. 1. Beck, Jeoffrey.
1768, Aug. 15. Beckely, Samuel, and Margaret Caulson.
1776, Feb. 15. Beck, Thomas, and Amelia Vandegrift.
1748, Oct. 18. Beddon, Joseph, and Elizabeth Sallows.
1762, May 6. Bedford, Mary Ann, and John Young.
1764, Feb. 18. Beedby, William, and Deborah Springer.
1760, Dec. 24. Bee, Elizabeth, and Andrew Long.
1746, Nov. —. Beegle, Barbara, and John Gibbons.
1770, Dec. 6. Beekman, John, and Elizabeth Renandet.
1768, Dec. 6. Beere, Jonathan, and Mary Wilson.
1770, M'ch 7. Beering, Sophia, and Henry Christopher Arup.
1761, M'ch 19. Beesley, Jno., and Ann Scoghan.
1747, M'ch —. Beezens, Jacob, and Catharine Alberton.
1765, Oct. 31. Beezley, Stephen, and Abigail Harrison.
1765, Dec. 28. Behlin, Anna Maria, and Casper Shell.
1772, Nov. 4. Belangee, Hannah, and Thomas Naglee.
1766, May 26. Belangee, Sarah, and David Loggan.
1772, May 14. Belford, Mary, and Richard Neeld.
1775, June 10. Belkenbine, Catharine, and Daniel Gilbert.
1771, Jan. 24. Bellamy, William, and Anne Whitebread.
1772, Oct. 6. Bellamy, William, and Elizabeth Pines.
1747, Dec. —. Bell, Ann, and Thomas Baldridge.
1764, June 16. Bell, Ann, and William Smith.

1774, Jan. 1. Bell, Edward, and Ann Philaby.
1746, July —. Belless, Sarah, and Thomas Dodd.
1767, May 6. Bell, George, and Hannah Davis.
1760, May 20. Bell, Hannah, and Cornelius McCleas.
1774, Oct. 12. Bell, Hannah, and Edmund Dare.
1774, Nov. 18. Bellingee, John, and Hannah Bonsall.
1761, Nov. 19. Bell, James, and Jane Roe.
1763, Apr. 27. Bell. John, and Anna Tilden.
1774, Nov. 23. Bell, John, and Ann McGinnis.
1774, June 15. Bell, John, and Mary McFarlane.
1767, Apr. 20. Bell, Joseph, and Rebecca Worrell.
1761, Oct. 21. Bell, Margaret, and John Winter.
1775, Jan. 28. Bell, Margaret, and Peter Lewis.
1772. Feb. 11. Bell, Margaret, and Thomas Neal.
1763, May 21. Bell, Margaret, and William Marshall.
1771, Feb. 13. Bell, Mary Ann, and Joseph Brown.
1763, Oct. 13. Bell, Mary Ann, and Robert Bell.
1776, June 29, Bell, Mary, and Dennis Collins.
1769, Dec. 1. Bell, Mary, and Gabriel McClann.
1765, Apr. 10. Bell, Peter, and Mary Williamson.
1771, July 11. Bell, Richard, and Sarah Coulter.
1763, May 6. Bell, Robert, and Elizabeth Fullerton.
1763, Oct. 13. Bell, Robert, and Mary Ann Bell.
1774, Aug. 27. Bell, Sarah, and Jacob Le Gay.
1768, M'ch 26. Bell, Sarah, and Nicholas Bird.
1745, Oct. —. Bell, Thomas.
1765, Sep. 5. Bell, Thomas, and Rosanna Shirley.
1743, Apr. 6. Bell, William.
1770, M'ch 3. Bell, William, and Margaret Stonematz.
1770, Sep. 5. Belsford, Timothy, and Hannah Hedley.
1773, Sep. 16. Bem, John, and Mary Bradshaw.
1768, Jan. 26. Bender, John, and Catharine Ampmaning.
1768, Apr. 9. Bener, Isaac, and Latitia Helton.
1776, Feb. 17. Bener, Lydia, and Benjamin Butcher.
1774, June. 9. Benezet, Anthony, Jun., and Catharine Graff.
1745, Feb. —. Benezet, Daniel.
1745, Apr. —. Benezet, Daniel.
1747, June —. Benezet, James, and Ann Hasell.
1775, Oct. 26. Benezet, John, and Hannah Bingham.
1766, June 5. Benezet, Philip, and Sarah Aries.
1768, June 23. Benezet, Sarah, and Thomas Bartow, Jun.
1767, Nov. 5. Benhart, Martin, and Catharine Hines.
1770, Oct. 10. Benn, Chloe, and Abraham Haiket.
1771, Aug. 5. Bennet, Abraham, and Martha White.
1769, July 19. Bennet, Agnus, and Andrew Coupland.
1766, Nov. 12. Bennet, Charity, and Joseph Vanpelt.

1768, Dec. 21. Bennet, Edith, and Derrick Hogeland.
1768, Aug. 3. Bennet, Elizabeth, and Henry Huddleston.
1768, Aug. 11. Bennet, Jacob, and Hannah Hogeland.
1769, July 11. Bennet, James, and Christiana Rainholt.
1761, Dec, 9. Bennet, John, and Ann Jones.
1765, May 20. Bennet, John, and Margaret Redmond.
1774, Oct. 25. Bennet, Margaret, and John Harper.
1760, Oct. 25. Bennet, Mary, and John Aymes.
1770, M'ch 6. Bennet, Matthew, and Sarah Scattergood.
1761, M'ch 2. Bennet, Sophia, and Garret Dungan.
1775, Nov. 28. Benneville, Mary, and John Lennington.
1770, Oct. 24. Benning, Elizabeth, and Jonathan Brown.
1763, May 17, Bensel, Mary, and William Steele.
1762, Apr. 10. Bensel, Samuel, and Sarah Challen.
1771, May 1. Benson, Margaret, and John Jones.
1763, Dec. 6. Benson, Margery, and Charles Prior.
1762, Oct. 25. Benson, Thomas, and Hannah Helspy.
1772, Nov. 20. Bentley, Eli, and Mary Hunter.
1747, Dec. —. Benton, John, and Elizabeth Chevalier.
1764, M'ch 22. Benton, Parthenia, and George Stewart.
1770, Dec. 1. Berends, John Michael, and Barbara Schott.
1775, June 21. Berghartin, Magdalena, and Frederick Brock.
1748, Oct. 18. Berkman, Hannah, and William Moritz.
1768, Aug 17. Berndollar, Ann, and Daniel Snyder.
1748, Aug. 15. Berney, James.
1765, Oct. 29. Bernhold, Henry, and Anna Nelson.
1764, May 7. Bernholt, John, and Mary Alberger.
1765, Apr. 10. Bern, John, and Mary Brooks.
1783, June 1. Berriman, Duncan.
1773, Oct. 18. Berry, Abraham, and Mary McCallister.
1764, May 4. Berry, Adam, and Sophia Johnson.
1773, Aug. 12. Berry, Elizabeth, and Benjamin Scull.
1773, Sep. 1. Berry, Hannah, and John Timmons.
1763, Sep. 5. Berry, James, and Rachael Philips.
1743, June 2. Berry, John.
1773, M'ch 9. Berryman, Joseph, and Prudence Hammet.
1783, June 1. Berry, Martin.
1770, Feb. 10. Berry, Mary, and Joseph Alston, Jun.
1764, Dec. 29. Berry, Theodorah, and Francis Coattam.
1769, Apr. 24. Beson, Jesper, and Mary Smith.
1746, Nov. —. Bessat, Elizabeth, and Hugh Liney.
1763, Sep. 24. Bess, Elizabeth, and Mark Burnett.
1764, May 31. Bessonet, Daniel, and Sarah Johnson.
1748, Sep. —. Bessonet, Sarah, and James Bodine.
1772, July 6. Best, Mary, and James Donaldson.
1775, Aug. 25. Betagh, Thomas, and Margaret Blanchard.

1774, Sep. 19. Bethell, Robert, and Elizabeth Rush.
1761, Aug. 7. Bethrat, Doro, and John Tippet.
1769, Apr. 24. Betson, Samuel, and Elizabeth Malone.
1773, Jan. 29. Betson, Samuel, and Hannah Richardson.
1771, Sep. 12. Betterton, Rachel, and James Smithers.
1771, M'ch 28. Betterton, Martha, and Joshua Collins.
1763, Feb. 12. Betting, Anthony, and Martha Poe.
1761, Aug. 22. Betts, Arthur, and Eleanor Clary.
1747, M'ch —. Betty, Ann, and Joseph Brown.
1747, June —. Betty, Thomas, and Hannah Fabes.
1767, Nov. 4. Bevan, Ann, and John Ferguson.
1774, Nov. 8. Bevan, Ann, and Simon Ellison.
1764, Aug. 25. Bevan, Mary, and Samuel Guilkey.
1768, Jan. 9. Bevan, Mary, and William Forbes.
1775, Nov. 7. Bewly, George, and Hannah Paul.
1766, May 21. Bewman, Roger, and Margaret Johnson.
1762, Sep. 14. Beyer, Elizabeth, and Jacob Ummensetter.
1761, Apr. 1. Beynon, James, and Margaret Manson.
1775, Dec. 1. Bickham, Caleb, and Mary Hunn.
1761, Nov. 23. Bickham, Sarah, and Thomas Tawson.
1773, May 7. Bickley, Catharine, and George Taylor.
1768, June 8. Bickley, Mary, and John Jarmon.
1765, Apr. 25. Biddle, Abigail, and Nich's Burtrow.
1761, June 26. Biddle, Edward, and Eliz. Ross.
1772, Dec. 5. Biddle, Rachael, and Jonathan Izard.
1766, M'ch 15. Biddle, Sarah, and James Penrose.
1760, Apr. 17. Biddle, Thomas, and Abigail Scull.
1766, Oct. 9. Bidel, Catharine, and Law Brant.
1763, Sep. 24. Bidgood, Esther, and Benjamin Palmer.
1774, July 12. Biggs, Ann, and David Lowry.
1771, Sep. 4. Biggs, Peter, and Sarah Holland.
1764, July 17. Bigler, George, and Ann Miller.
1761, Apr. 22. Bilderback, David, and Sarah Barnard.
1769, May 2. Biles, Ann, and Asher Mott.
1767, Nov. 12. Biles, Jonathan, and Latitia Galbraith.
1764, May 12. Biles, Sarah, and Daniel Lovett.
1774, M'ch 24. Biles, Sarah, and John Harvey.
1766, June 21. Biles, William, and Hannah Kirkbride.
1769, Apr. 8. Billen, Ann, and Joseph Folwell.
1766, Dec. 24. Billew, Ann, and Thomas Mitchiner.
1767, Dec. 22. Billew, Daniel, and Priscilla Wood.
1768, Jan. 9. Billew, Daniel, and Rebecca Vansant.
1772, Feb. 1. Billew, Jacob, and Elizabeth Jones.
1773, Jan. 27. Billew, Rachel, and John McSwerry.
1766, M'ch 26. Billow, Elizabeth, and John Folwell.
1769, Feb 15. Bilyere, Eve, and Thomas Leech.

1767, July 27. Binder, Jacob, and Mary Wisebaugh.
1775, Oct 26. Bingham, Hannah,.and John Benezet.
1745, Sep. —. Bingham, William.
1763, Dec. 2. Bingley, Edward, and Mary Taylor.
1773, Oct. 30. Binington, Robert, and Elizabeth Rambo.
1772, Sep. 23. Binks, Christopher, and Mary Siddon.
1762, M'ch 3. Bird, John, and Mary Stilley.
1762, Dec. 31. Bird, Mark, and Mary Ross.
1768, M'ch 26. Bird, Nicholas, and Sarah Bell.
1762, Dec. 31. Bird, Rebecca, and Peter Turner.
1748, May. 14. Bird, ——, and —— Shippy.
1776, Jan. 16. Birsban, John, and Elizabeth Boyd.
1773, Dec. 28. Bisey, Charles, and Elizabeth Krips.
1767, Dec. 29. Bishop, Hannah, and Job Briggs.
1767, Sep. 14. Bishop, Sarah, and Joseph Griffith.
1763, Nov. 3. Bishop, Thomas, and Elizabeth Wood.
1744, Jan. —. Bispham, Joshua.
1773, Feb. 16. Bissel, John, and Letitia Philips.
1747, Oct. —. Bittew, Isaac, and Rachel Britton.
1745, Jan. —. Bitting, Henry.
1767, Aug. 15. Bizzey, Elizabeth, and Richard Campain.
1761, Aug. 15. Black, Abram, and Catharine Smith.
1775, May 8. Black, Elizabeth, and Edward Bowring.
1775, Aug. 9. Black, Eliza, and Charles Scoby.
1761, Sep. 5. Black, Hugh, and Margaret Morgan.
1762, Nov. 6. Black, James, and Rachel Adams.
1775, M'ch 4. Black, John, and Magdalena Holton.
1770, Oct. 26. Blackleage, Mary, and Francis Cruzen.
1774, Dec. 24. Blackledge, Esther, and George Newell.
1774, June 16. Blackledge, Rachel, and John Kelly.
1765, Sep. 18. Blacklidge, Mary, and John Climmer.
1743, Sep. —. Blackman, Henry.
1768, Oct. 7. Black, Margaret, and David Register.
1772, Jan. 2. Black, Margaret, and Edward James.
1772, Dec. 16. Black, Martha, and Robert Miller.
1772, Apr. 22. Black, Mary, and John Farran.
1774, Dec. 21. Black, Mary, and Thomas McMinn.
1762, Apr. 19. Black, Sarah, and John Tomlinson.
1765, Sep. 12. Blackston, Prisley, and Sarah Warwick.
1769, Apr. 6. Black, Susannah, and Murdoch Kennedy.
1769, M'ch 1. Blackwood, Mary, and Christian Fiss.
1774, Nov. 29. Blair, Alexander, and Rachel Carson.
1767, Dec. 26. Blair, Ann, and Elias Barton.
1773, Feb. 1. Blair, Elizabeth, and William Jenkins.
1771, Feb. 6. Blair, Jennet, and Jacob Verity.
1766, Sep. 2. Blair, Margaret, and Geo. Fullerton.

1774, Jan. 10. Blair, Rebecca, and William Linn.
1767, Sep. 23. Blair, Samuel, and Susannah Shippen.
1770, Apr. 14. Blake, John, and Catharine Stephens.
1748, Apr. 13. Blakely, John, and Eliz Barkley.
1748, Sep. —. Blakeney, John, and Jane Parker.
1773, Aug. 2. Blake, Roger, and Alice M'Carty.
1775, Aug. 25. Blanchard, Margaret, and Thomas Betagh.
1762, July 3. Blanchfield, Mary, and John Poskell.
1775, Aug. 5. Blanchflower, Charles, and Mary Clarke.
1766, July 12. Blanch, Mary, and David Houlton.
1769, Aug. 30. Blaylock, Jane, and John Montgomery.
1769, Feb. 17. Blazedell, Catharine, and Robert Shannon.
1763, Dec. 1. Blazer, Maria Eliazbeth, and John Jacob Schweitzer.
1771, May 18. Blaze, Rosana, and Andrew Tyce.
1765, Apr. 4. Blencone, Nath'l, and Kezia Heretage.
1765, Jan. 14. Bloomer, Elizabeth, and Jacob Huber.
1771, Oct. 24. Bloomfield, Catharine, and John Sutton.
1776, June 12. Bloomfield, Elisha, and Margaret Johnston.
1768, Dec. 12. Bloom, Margaret, and Thomas Meyer.
1763, Oct. 10. Bluewhite, Sarah, and Matthew Collins.
1776, Apr. 5. Blyth, John, and Mary Jones.
1765, May 16. Blyth, Mary, and William Skilling.
1762, July 31. Boardin, Ann, and William Rodin.
1747, Aug. —. Boardman, George, and Mary Wyson.
1747, June —. Boardman, Mary, and James Lindsay.
1775, May 30. Boardman, Philip, and Mary Guy.
1775, Feb. 27. Boast, Sarah, and Samuel Gothrop.
1760, Sep. 11. Boatman, Dorothy, and James Smith.
1763, Dec. 28. Boatman, Philip, and Burges Bromingham.
1748, Feb. —. Bobkin, Mary, and Joseph Lane.
1746, Nov. —. Bocke, Susannah, and Peter Wells.
1776, Jan. 22. Bockius, Francis, and Susannah Miller.
1766, Nov. 28. Boden, Hugh, and Jane Kelso.
1748, Sep. —. Bodine, James, and Sarah Bessonet.
1771, Dec. 24. Bob, John, and Hannah Morgan.
1769, Oct. 4. Bodlev, Isabella, and Matthew Willson.
1772, Feb. 5. Boehne, Charles Lewis, and Catharine Moser.
1747, June —. Boerman, Susannah, and Stephen Anthony.
1769, Oct. 29. Bogart, Geisbart, and Catharine Seiburn.
1772, Nov. 14. Bogart, John, and Mary Jameson.
1764, June 22. Bogar, William, and Esther Johnson.
1768, Feb. 9. Boggs, Agnes, and Davidson Filson.
1772, Dec. 10. Boggs, Alexander, and Ann Hemphill.
1760, Nov. 26. Boggs, Alice, and Alexander Johnson.
1774, Nov. 24. Boggs, Elizabeth, and Isaac Githin.

1746, June —. Boggs, James, and Catharine Knoble.
1770, Jan. 23. Boggs, Margaret, and David Buchanan.
1762, Aug. 16. Boggs, Margaret, and John Hemphill.
1761, Dec. 2. Boggs, Margaret, and William Watson.
1761, Jan. 15. Boggs, Mary, and Robert Cook.
1772, Apr. 30. Boggs, Rebecca, and Charles Risk.
1766, July 12. Boggs, William, and Sarah McIntire.
1763, Aug. 14. Bogt, Christiana, and ——— Grey.
1761, June 20. Boirs, William, and Elizabeth Williams.
1768, Sep. 14. Boise, Martha, and Cornelius Brian.
1763, Oct. 26. Boley, John, and Sophia Shellcock.
1744, M'ch —. Bolitho, John.
1772, May 2. Bolton, Anne, and Isaac Cooper.
1762, Nov. 13. Bolton, Anthony, and Martha Roberts.
1764, Feb. 13. Bolton, Everhard, and Deborah Griscomb
1764, May 3. Bolton, Rebecca, and Abraham Jones.
1762, June 1. Bolton, William, and Sarah Graham.
1763, July 27. Bome, Barbara, and John Bryan.
1768, Aug. 1. Bomin, Christiana, and John Phillips.
1761, M'ch 5. Bonham, Ephraim, and Margaret Garrat.
1765, May 8. Bond, Elizabeth, and John Martin.
1771, Nov. 27. Bond, Elizabeth, and Richard Sands.
1761, July 24. Bond, Mary, and Nathan Hendricks.
1768, Sep. 21. Bond, Rebecca, and Thomas Lawrence.
1773, July 21. Bond, Sarah, and Clement Dungan.
1748, Feb. —. Bond, Susannah, and William McKnight.
1764, May 10. Bond, Thomas, and Ann Morgan.
1763, Aug. 8. Boned, Sarah, and Daniel Wilkinson.
1763, May 5. Bone, John, and Rebecca Lewis.
1760, Jan. 1. Boneringh, Margaret, and Adam Sharrer.
1773, Aug. 16. Bonfield, Elizabeth, and Nicholas Brehant.
1771, Nov. 30. Bonham, William, and Elizabeth Taggart.
1768, Aug. 29. Bonner, John, and Elizabeth Staddleman.
1775, Nov. 9. Bonner, Susannah, and John Baker.
1774, Nov. 18. Bonsall, Hannah, and John Bellingee.
1762, Apr. 7. Bonsel, Nathaniel, and Hannah Gamble.
1764, Nov. 8. Bonum, Mary, and Robert Harrison.
1771, M'ch 6. Booce, Jacob, and Barbara Harman.
1763, Jan. 10. Boockhan, Gedradt, and Peter Keider.
1765, M'ch 20. Boon, Andrew, and Elizabeth White.
1763, Apr. 13. Boone, Andrew, and Martha Gurion.
1763, July 25. Boone, Ann, and John Linkon.
1763, Aug. 20. Boone, Garrat, and Eleanor Moreton.
1766, Nov. 28. Boone, Samuel, and Jane Hughes.
1766, Feb. 28. Boor, Elizabeth, and Charles Jervis.
1764, Nov. 20. Boore, Hannah, and Amos Davis.

1743, Jan. 18. Boore, Joseph.
1763, July 21. Boore, Rebecca, and John Pierce.
1762, June 5. Booth, Thomas, and Catharine Farmer.
1774, Feb. 28. Booz, John, and Ann Keller.
1762, Feb. 3. Boram, William, and Deborah Drake.
1747, Nov. —. Bord, John, and Ann Bryant.
1761, Aug. 28. Bornhill, Sarah, and Archibald Finley.
1770, Oct. 18. Borradiall, Susannah, and John Rodman.
1761, June 15. Boshan, Catharine, and John Henry.
1742, Dec. 31. Boss, Elisha.
1763, Aug. 20. Bottomly, Catharine, and Robert Gill.
1771, Oct. 19. Boucher, Joseph, and Rachel Watson.
1748, July 13. Boucher, Thomas, and Mary Farrell.
1774, Jan. 26. Bouden, Sarah, and James Cabean.
1761, Nov. 23. Boughton, Dorothy, and John Gibbs.
1770, Feb. 21. Boulby, Mary, and John Hamilton.
1774, May 12. Boulter, Benjamin, and Ann Hamilton.
1767, Feb. 28. Boulter, Mary, and John Hennessy.
1746, June —. Bound, Susanna, and John Cornway.
1768, Dec. 7. Bourdmanning, Rachel, and Michael Wild.
1762, Apr. 22. Bourin, Mary, and John Remberger.
1767, Apr. 1. Bourk, William, and Elizabeth Tomkins.
1744, Feb. —. Bourne, Daniel.
1743, Nov. —. Bourne, Patrick.
1743, Dec. —. Bourne, Thomas.
1764, Nov. 1. Bourns, John, and Jane Wilson.
1746, Sep. —. Bowan, John, and Margaret Hill.
1767, Dec. 15. Bowde, Sarah, and William Osborne.
1765, Sep. 5. Bowen, Esther, and Evan Anderson.
1773, Sep. 28. Bowen, Esther, and George Allen.
1764, Sep. 1. Bowen, Hannah, and Jacob Learney.
1747, Jan. —. Bower, Conrad, and Philipina Keylwein.
1763, Apr. 18. Bower, Hugh, and Elizabeth Abercromby.
1774, May 10. Bower, John, and Jane Oliver.
1771, Nov. 28. Bower, Sabina, and Leonard Wright.
1761, June 13. Bower, Thomas, and Ann Cummings.
1774, Apr. 20. Bower, Thomas, and Sarah Yerkus.
1760, May 14. Bower, Valentine, and Hannah Hippard.
1760, Nov. 15. Bowes, Esther, and John Cox.
1745, Aug. —. Bowes, Hugh.
1767, Nov. 12. Bowes, Margaret, and James Montgomery.
1761, Sep. 22. Bowies, Angus, and Rachel Rush.
1766, Nov. 24. Bowldin, Thomas, and Elizabeth Kemp.
1743, June 22. Bowler, John.
1776, Feb. 10. Bowler, Joseph, and Elizabeth Indicot.
3—VOL. II.

1773, Feb. 12. Bowler, Mary, and Zachariah Nieman.
1761, Oct. 6. Bowles, Susanna, and Isaac Taylor.
1747, June —. Bowlin, ——, and James Murray.
1768, Oct. 29. Bowlsby, Martha, and William Harrison.
1770, Nov. 19. Bowman, Anne, and John Michael Price.
1770, May 5. Bowman, Charles, and Mary Nerry.
1760, Apr. 1. Bowman, James, and Martha McKee.
1760, Feb. 25. Bowman, Susannah, and Rudolph Fress.
1761, Aug. 6. Bowne, Sarah, and Jesse Roe.
1745, Nov. —. Bowney, Patrick.
1775, May 8. Bowring, Edward, and Elizabeth Black.
1762, Sep. 20. Boyce, Margaret, and William Wood.
1767, Sep. 17. Boyce, Samuel, and Mary Granville.
1773, July 1. Boyd, Adam, and Catharine Jenkins.
1761, Feb. 12. Boyd, Andrew, and Sarah Barnett.
1769, Jan. 10. Boyd, Anna, and David Cloyd.
1769, Feb. 20. Boyd, Anne, and John McDougle.
1776, Jan. 15. Boyd, Elizabeth, and John Brisban.
1745, Oct. —. Boyd, Hugh.
1766, Sep. 3. Boyd, John, and Sarah Miller.
1761, July 4. Boyd, Margaret, and David Harrald.
1763, April 2. Boyd, Mary, and John Dunlap.
1765, July 30. Boyd, Phebe, and David McCullogh.
1747, June —. Boyers, David, and Elizabeth Byers.
1769, Oct. 24. Boyers, Rebecca, and John Pillager.
1772, Dec. 4. Boyes, Mary, and James McNaught.
1776, Jan. 3. Boyle, Alexander, and Hannah Cross.
1768, Feb. 16. Boyle, Hannah, and Joseph Dean.
1745, July —. Boyle, Uriah.
1763, Nov. 12. Boys, Ann, and Nathaniel Mercer.
1748, Oct. 18. Boyse, James, and Mary Grimes.
1767, Sep. 5. Boys, Elizabeth, and Martha Scull.
1759, Dec. 29. Boys, John, and Mary Eaton.
1763, Nov. 16. Boys, Mary, and John Stilla.
1760, July 11. Boys, Samuel, and Mary Winter.
1769, Nov. 29. Boyte, Hester, and Benjamin George Eyre.
1775, Sep. 13. Brackley, Mary Ann, and Charles McKenzie.
1775, Jan. 25. Braddock, John, and Anne Green.
1763, Feb 26. Braden, Rebecca, and Abraham Charlesworth.
1772, Apr. 22. Bradfield, Abner, and Phebe West.
1774, M'ch 17. Bradford, Joseph, and Sarah Hood.
1765, Nov. 18. Bradford, Martha, and Samuel Hall.
1760, M'ch 15. Bradford, Mary, and Sampson Harvey.
1770, Aug. 18. Bradford, Susannah, and Robert Welch.
1773, Aug. 3. Bradford, Tace, and Joshua Maddox Wallace.
1768, Nov. 23. Bradford, Thomas, and Mary Fisher.

1775, Apr.   1. Bradin, Elizabeth, and James Sharshwood.
1747, June —. Bradley, Esther, and Jacob Dutchee.
1743, Oct.   —. Bradley, George.
1771, June 13. Bradshaw, David, and Patience Farmer.
1773, Sep.   16. Bradshaw, Mary, and John Bem.
1747, Apr   —. Brady, Catharine, and Edward Williams.
1775, Aug. 10. Brady, Mark, and Priscilla Gaddle.
1772, Dec.   19. Brady, Mary, and Thomas Short.
1769, Mch. 31. Brady, Michael, and Mary Lobb.
1767, Apr.   10. Brady, Patrick, and Mary Davidson.
1763, Jan.   7. Brady, Robert, and Mary Trump.
1765, Sep.   5. Braford, Mary, and William Peterkin.
1774, M'ch   5. Braithwait, Elizabeth, and Robert Threlfal.
1773, Jan.   29. Brakell, Mary, and Thomas Rose.
1770, Sep.   11. Brakell, Richard, and Mary Jones.
1767, Jan.   3. Bralsford, William, and Sarah Brown.
1775, Nov.   16. Bramall, Thomas, and Mary Miller.
1744, July 21. Bramhall, Samuel.
1764, Nov.   11. Brandollas, Nicholas, and Catharine Stone.
1772, Dec.   29. Brandt, Catharine, and Conrad Myerly.
1767, Aug.   26. Branin, Ann, and Charles Read.
1770, June   6. Branin, Hannah, and John Torr.
1774, Aug.   4. Branin, Mary, and David Gallagher.
1773, Aug.   16. Branon, Mary, and Robert Galbraith.
1766, Jan.   16. Brannum, Edward, and Margaret Collings.
1771, Nov.   28. Branson, Henry, and Mary Knight.
1761, May   18. Branson, Michael, and Christ. Humphreys.
1776, Jan.   13. Branson, Samuel, and Mary Wood.
1771, M'ch   4. Branston, Samuel, and Annie Hopper.
1768, June 10. Brant, John, and Amelia Turner.
1765, Dec.   5. Brant, John, and Elizabeth Frazier.
1766, Oct.   9. Brant, Lawrence, and Catharine Bidel.
1764, Oct   10. Bratten, Elizabeth, and John James.
1769, Sep.   13. Bray, John, and Judith Cotter.
1764, Aug.   15. Bray, Robert, and Johanna Leader.
1764, Aug.   11. Brazil, Mary, and Henry Bruster.
1771, Sep.   9. Breatherton, Eleanor, and Joseph Chatham.
1775, June 21. Breck, Frederick, and Magdalena Berghartin.
1774, June —. Bredin, Elizabeth, and James Collins.
1763, May   17. Breese, Hannah, and Abel Stockhouse.
1768, Jan.   6. Breese, Samuel, and Elizabeth Anderson.
1773, Aug.   16. Brehant, Nicholas, and Elizabeth Bonfield.
1771, May   22. Breintnall, Joseph, and Jane Ham.
1771, Dec.   18. Brelsford, Benjamin. Jun., and Martha Gillmer.
1762, Nov.   29. Bremar, Sarah, and Samuel Weatherby.
1760, Oct.   21. Brennan, Margaret, and Ephraim Armstrong.

1746, Oct. —. Brenneman, Elizabeth, and Frederick Walder.
1764, Dec. 29. Brenneman, Jacob, and Susannah Evans.
1776, Feb. 7. Breton, Paul Casper, and Susannah Kryder.
1766, June 12. Brewton, Robert, and Eleanor Toy.
1768, Sep. 14. Brian, Cornelius, and Martha Boise.
1763, June 13. Brian, Judea, and William McKey.
1776, Nov. 26. Brice, John, and Sarah Barnett.
1775, Sep. 27. Brick, Grace, and George Hunter.
1769, Dec. 23. Brick, Hannah, and James Collins.
1769, Sep. 1. Bridges, Robert, and Jemima Shepherd.
1761, Feb. 4. Briggan, David, and Elizabeth Allison.
1761, Jan. 27. Briggs, Edmond, and Rachael Groom.
1773, Jan. 7. Briggs, Hannah, and Timothy Knowles.
1767, Dec. 29. Briggs, Job, and Hannah Bishop.
1774, Feb. 26. Briggs, John, and Charlotte Howell.
1765, Sep. 19. Briggs, Margaret, and Stephen Field.
1775, Nov. 9. Briggs, Sarah, and John Dyer.
1775, Nov. 27. Brighdehen, Christiana, and Henry Lochman.
1743, Feb. 4. Bright, Anthony.
1772, Dec. 23. Bright, Barnaby, and Cornelia Evans.
1765, Apr. 3. Bright, Christiana, and Christopher Pechin.
1774, Apr. 28. Bright, George, and Mary Moulder.
1747, M'ch —. Brimbo, Cully, and Alexander Crookshank.
1772, June 8. Brindley, Francis, and Rebecca Garwood.
1769, June 1. Bringhurst, William, and Mary Norris.
1764, July 17. Brintnell, Sarah, and Gabriel Wilson.
1746, May —. Brisbem, Hugh.
1747, May 10. Bristol, Isaac, and Mary Jenkins.
1769, Sep. 25. Bristol, Jacob, and Sarah Loyd.
1772, Aug. 24. Britman, Thomas, and Margaret Neumannin.
1767, M'ch 28. Briton, John, and Eleanor Waters.
1748, May 14. Briton, Mary, and Benjamin Parker.
1775, Jan. 17. Briton, Sarah, and Daniel Thomas.
1763, Aug. 9. Briton, Sarah, and Jesse Williamson.
1763, June 3. Briton, Thomas, and Sarah Harvey.
1760, Apr. 14. Brittain, Frances, and James Woolard.
1763, Sep. 11. Britton, Abraham, and Kezia Vansant.
1761, Aug. 22. Britton, John, and Elizabeth Stephens.
1775, July 14. Britton, Mary, and Robert Gibson.
1747, Oct. —. Britton, Rachel, and Isaac Bittew.
1770, Dec. 15. Britton, Sarah, and John Ridge.
1768, Sep. 21. Britton, Thomas, and Catharine Forbes.
1762, Aug. 3. Broades, Arthur, and Catharine Rinard.
1769, May 6. Broadnecks, Rebecca, and Thomas Cabe.
1771, M'ch 30. Broadnicks, Mary, and Thomas Fleming.
1768, M'ch 3. Brockden, Mary, and Thomas Patterson.

1760, Apr. 19. Brockden, E., and William John.
1769, Sep. 1. Brockington, Anne, and Patrick Reiley.
1761, Nov. 28. Brock, John, and Martha Jones.
1771, Nov. 23. Broderick, Richard, and Mary Sinnot.
1773, Oct. 6. Broderick, Richard, and Susannah Evey.
1747, Aug. —. Brobrick, Edmund, and Mary Cahoon.
1763, Dec. 28. Bromingham, Burges, and Philip Boatman.
1768, Sep. 17. Brouse, Henry, and Ann Craven.
1747, M'ch —. Brookbank, Richard, and Mary Rosindell.
1767, Aug. 22. Brooke, Bowyer, and Hannah Reese.
1762, May 21. Brooke, John, and Elizabeth May.
1763, Nov. 9. Brookhouse, Samuel, and Mary Duncan.
1760, M'ch 17. Brook, J. P., and Conrad Ring.
1769, Jan. 3. Brook, Mary, and David Jones.
1771, Jan. 16. Brook, Mary, and James Evans.
1772, Oct. 15. Brook, Owen, and Elizabeth Hammer.
1760, M'ch 13. Brooks, Andrew, and Mary Burk.
1762, Oct. 23. Brooks, Anna, and Daniel Evans.
1769, June 21. Brooks, Anne, and Thomas Murfin.
1762, Nov. 18. Brooks, Ann, and Isaac Morton.
1760, Jan. 11. Brooks, Elizabeth, and John Lloyd.
1767, July 22. Brooks, Elizabeth, and William Murfin.
1774, May 2. Brooks, Hannah, and Jesse Sturgus.
1773, M'ch 16. Brooks, Hannah, and Thomas Tremble.
1776, Apr. 22. Brooks, Jacob, and Mary Burk.
1763, Jan. 31. Brooks, Jane, and William Murdock.
1776, May 11. Brooks, John, and Catharine Roberts.
1762, Aug. 21. Brooks, John, and Hannah Craven.
1747, Oct. —. Brooks, Jonathan, and Rebecca Hayes.
1763, June 4. Brooks, Joseph, and Anna Mashawn.
1764, May 3. Brooks, Martha, and William Allen.
1765, Apr. 10. Brooks, Mary. and John Bern.
1774, June 18. Brooks, Sarah, and George Randle.
1765, Nov. 6. Brooks, Sarah, and Thomas Coulter.
1768, Oct. 21. Brooks, William, and Rachel King.
1769, M'ch 22. Broom, Elizabeth, and John Pyne.
1772, Oct. 9. Brown, Alexander, and Ann Peel.
1769, Dec. 19. Brown, Alexander, and Mary Shotsland.
1773, Oct. 6. Brown, Ann, and James Baxter.
1764, Nov. 8. Brown, Ann, and William Knight.
1748, Jan. —. Brownback, Elizabeth, and Richard Custard.
1773, June 9. Brownbash, Benjamin, and Rachel Parker.
1768, May 23. Brown, Catharine, and James Jenkins.
1760, July 1. Brown, Catharine, and William Horack.
1763, Dec. 2. Brown, Clark, and Christine Hinkle.
1763, Jan. 22. Brown, Daniel, and Mary Donaldson.

1767, May 12. Brown, David, and Elizabeth Higgins.
1762, Apr. 15. Brown, David, and Susannah Paul.
1769, Apr. 20. Brownfield, Mary, and Jacob Levering.
1766, Dec. 17. Brown, Gilbert, and Jane McMullen.
1761, Mc'h 16. Browning, Joseph, and Sarah Rowand.
1748, Jan. —. Browning, William, and Abigail Custard.
1776, June 7. Brown, Isabella, and Conrad Hanse.
1770, Oct. 29. Brown, James, and Catharine McCormick.
1769, Jan. 2. Brown, James, and Mary Batton.
1761, Sep. 30. Brown, James, and Mary Wall.
1763, July 16. Brown, James, and Roe Roe.
1762, May 24. Brown, James, and Sarah Marin.
1762, Nov. 11. Brown, Jane, and Hugh Tomland.
1762, June 21. Brown, Jane, and James Cannon.
1768, Sep. 9. Brown, Jane, and John King.
1745, Feb. —. Brown, John.
1765, Sep. 10. Brown, John Alexander, and Sarah Hatton.
1766, June 19. Brown, John, and Ann Seans.
1768, Apr. 28. Brown, John, and Ann Wilson.
1773, Sep. 16. Brown, John, and Eleanor Saunders.
1775, June 1. Brown, John, and Margaret Thomas.
1760, Aug. 7. Brown, John, and Mary Arcle.
1774, June 13. Brown, John, and Mary Chambers.
1772, Apr. 14. Brown, John, and Sarah Levering.
1770. Oct. 24. Brown, Jonathan, and Elizabeth Benning.
1747, M'ch —. Brown, Joseph, and Ann Betty.
1771, Feb. 13. Brown, Joseph, and Mary Ann Bell.
1747, June —. Brown, Joseph, and Mary Waln.
1761, June 6. Brown, Leah, and John Ellicott.
1772, May 11. Brown, Lucy, and Thomas Chesson.
1747, June 18. Brown, Margaret, and Andrew M'Glone.
1768, Jan. 14. Brown, Margaret, and Daniel Neal.
1766, Aug. 13. Brown, Margaret, and John Edwards.
1761, M'ch 27. Brown, Margaret, and Patrick McGuffuck.
1773, Feb. 24. Brown, Margaret, and Paul Dowlin.
1768, Jan. 13. Brown, Mary, and Daniel Meredith.
1748, Sep. —. Brown, Mary, and Edward Williams.
1771, Nov. 28. Brown, Mary, and Frederick Hitner.
1763, Aug. 2. Brown, Mary, and George Roxby.
1764, Oct. 11. Brown, Mary, and James Russel.
1773, Sep. 24. Brown, Mary, and Richard Hazard.
1748, Sep. —. Brown, Peserue, and Elizabeth Tell.
1773, Apr. 28. Brown, Peter, and Sarah Dutton.
1775, M'ch 8. Brown, Richard, and Rachel Wickward.
1764, Aug. 14. Brown, Robert, and Hannah Stevens.
1775, Apr. 22. Brown, Samuel, and Elizabeth Tyson.

1764, Nov. 7. Brown, Sarah, and John Mason.
1767, Jan. 3. Brown, Sarah, and William Bralsford.
1765, Feb. 23. Brown, Themisine, and John Marris.
1744, Oct. —. Brown, Thomas.
1783, June 14. Brown, Thomas.
1775, July 3. Brown, Thomas, and Ann Sherwood.
1771, June 13. Brown, Thomas, and Mary Dunn.
1769, May 17. Brown, Thomas, and Sarah Daniels.
1763, Jan. 26. Brown, Thurston, and Elizabeth Dowsey.
1774, Apr. 30. Brown, Thurston, and Mary Porpus.
1746, June. —. Brown, Walter, and Hannah Baily.
1771, Apr. 19. Brown, William, and Anne Appleby.
1775, Apr. 1. Brown, William, and Ann McSeeny.
1763, July 27. Brown, William, and Lelies Hart.
1769, Feb. 14. Brubst, Henry, and Margaret Barnhill.
1759, Dec. 31. Bruce, Ann, and John Halding.
1748. Sept. —. Bruce, Isabel, and John Pine.
1766, June 27. Bruce, Rebecca, and William McEwen.
1775, Nov. 6. Bruellhet, Maria Catharine, and Noel Barnaby
                 Veyrant Denstellance.
1760. Oct. 24. Brumfield, Joseph, and Dorothy Glenson.
1763, Jan. 15. Brumfield, Margaret, and Daniel Craig.
1762, Oct. 6. Brumfield, Mary, and Thomas Jones.
1762, Feb. 18. Brummage, Ann, and Benjamin Randolph.
1760, June 30. Brunner, Ann M., and Christian Smith.
1761, Apr. 29. Brunnery, Mary, and George Powel.
1765, M'ch 9. Bruno, Susannah, and Richard Fry.
1774. Oct. 7. Brunston, Barefoot, and Agnes White.
1771, Dec. 4. Bruse, John, and Susannah Cooper.
1768, June 6. Brusster, Peter, and Elizabeth Townsend.
1763, Oct. 29. Brusster, Samuel, and Rebecca Taber.
1765, Sep. 5. Bruster, Benjamin, and Rebecca Tatlow.
1764, Aug. 11. Bruster, Henry, and Mary Brazil.
1768, Jan. 23. Brustrum, Ann, and James Fullerton.
1760, May 7. Brustrum, Mary, and William Styles.
1775, Apr. 24. Bryan, Catharine, and Thomas Page.
1774, Nov 21. Bryan, Effy, and Philip Miller.
1775, Sep. 7. Bryan, Eleanor, and Michal O'Daniel.
1762, Feb. 3. Bryan, Elizabeth, and William Butterfield.
1763, July 27. Bryan, John, and Barbara Boone.
1762, Nov. 8. Bryan, John, and Catharine Burker.
1762, Jan. 26. Bryan, John, and Elizabeth Cloud.
1747, Feb. 5. Bryan, Joseph, and Jehosheba Wells.
1765, Dec. 5. Bryan, Josiah, and Elizabeth McHenry.
1762, Oct. 25. Bryan, Mary, and Henry Gill.
1774, Aug. 27. Bryan, Rebecca, and Samuel Tingle.

1773, Apr. 13. Bryan, Sarah, and Peter Peters.
1747, Nov. —. Bryant, Ann, and John Bord.
1763, Jan. 10. Bryant, Margaret, and Andrew Stewart.
1744, Jan. —. Bryson, Walter.
1747, June. —. Bubb, William, and Martha Thomson.
1764, Oct. 15. Buber, Hannah, and John Huff.
1770, Jan. 23. Buchanan, David, and Margaret Boggs.
1746, May —. Buchanan, James.
1767, M'ch 20. Buchanan, William, and Rachel Harman.
1761, Sep. 30. Buchan, Caleb, and Hannah Pierce.
1748, Sep. —. Buchan, Mary, and Morris Evans.
1775, Jan. 13. Buchwater, Esther, and Jacob Zigler.
1760, Sept. 13. Buckham, Patience, and Samuel Skill.
1766, Aug. 5. Buck, Henry, and Elizabeth Kirts.
1776, May 8. Buckin, Sarah, and Henry Valentine.
1775, May 7. Buck, Isaac, and Hannah Hicks.
1761, Dec. 9. Buckley, Deborah, and Charles Fagan.
1769, July 1. Buckley, Isaac, and Elizabeth Graham.
1763, Sep. 15. Buckley, Isaac, and Mary Knowles.
1774, Dec. 20. Buckley, James, and Mary Campbell.
1748, Oct. 18. Buckley, Jane, and Solomon Helliard.
1745, May —. Buckley, John.
1760, July 28. Buckley, Thomas, and Mary Twiner.
1769, Jan. 12. Buckman, Hester, and John Cooper.
1771, July 4. Buckman, James, and Mary Hart.
1774, Sep. 3. Buck, Philip, and Ann Stamp.
1767, Dec. 29. Budden, Mary, and John Duffield.
1762, Nov. 25. Budd, Levy, and Elizabeth Shields.
1771. Dec. 1. Budd, Thomas, and Susannah Coburn.
1763, Jan. 10. Buffington, Jane, and Jacob Dieter.
1766, M'ch 26. Buffington, Mary, and John Snow.
1768, Mch. 7. Bulger, Thomas, and Lean Harvey.
1773, Mch. 4. Bull, Elizabeth, and Benjamin Bartholomew.
1770, Dec. 26. Bull, Elizabeth, and Benjamin Rittenhouse.
1771, Nov. 27. Bull, Elizabeth, and Peter Byrch.
1762, Jan. 5. Bulley, Sarah, and William Sellers.
1762, Sep. 10. Bullis, James, and Catharine Ellis.
1764, June 16. Bullman, Frances, and Dunin Irwin.
1772, Dec. 5. Bull, Micah, and George Meredith.
1774, Feb. 9. Bullock, Elizabeth, and William Innes.
1772, May 25. Bullock, Isabella, and William Wright.
1770, Dec. 5. Bullock, Joseph, and Esther Baynton.
1763, Apr. 13. Bullock, Mary, and Thomas Hall.
1769, Dec. 11. Bull, Rebecca, and Henry Pawling.
1775, June 3. Bull, Sarah, and James McKenzie.
1771, Apr. 24. Bull, Thomas, and Sarah Grow.

1766, Sept. 4. Bumberry, Christopher, and Mary Stoops.
1768, May 19. Bunberry, Robert, and Mary Iveson.
1760, Dec. 16. Bunison, Catharine, and Benjamin Fordham.
1770, Dec. 19. Bunner, Andrew, and Sarah Fisher.
1772, M'ch 5. Bunner, Jacob, and Elizabeth Moser.
1762, Sep. 22. Bunn, William, and Elizabeth Alexander.
1760, Feb. 21. Bunting, Marmaduke, and Mary Dinslow.
1762, Dec. 29. Bunting, Samuel, and Esther Syng.
1761, Dec. 2. Bunting, Timothy, and Elizabeth Hedley.
1771, Oct. 8. Bur, Ann, and Gabriel Coxe.
1773, M'ch 18. Burchardt, Daniel, and Catharine White.
1763, Apr. 18. Burchett, Samuel, and Ann Barnett
1760, Feb. 15. Burch, Mary, and John Marriage.
1772, Sep. 23. Burch, Mathias, and Susannah Wooland.
1769, Sep. 13. Burden, George, and Hannah Roe.
1764, M'ch 10. Burd, Jacob, and Sarah Wright.
1770, Jan. 10. Burchet, Anne, and John Dick.
1770, Aug. 9. Burgess, Francis, and Mary MacNamara.
1748, May 14. Burghard, Nicholas, and Hannah Frederica Pessbear.
1774, June 9. Burghy, Henry, and Elizabeth Kreider.
1761, Nov. 14. Burhau, Nicholas, and Albina Carpenter.
1747, Nov. —. Burk, Adam, and Margaret Allen.
1769, Jan. 29. Burk, Ann, and Philip Ryan.
1765, June 12. Burk, Elizabeh, and John Clark.
1761, Oct. 12. Burkels, Jacob, and Martha Green.
1765, Oct. 15. Burkensha, Daniel, and Susannah Crockfurd.
1762, Nov. 8. Burker, Catharine, and John Bryan.
1763, Jan. 7. Burket, Jacob, and Barbara Fisher.
1769, Aug. 29. Burkey, Henry, and Mary Chamberlain.
1760, June 28. Burk, Frances, and Thomas Batman.
1768, Jan. 25. Burkhart, Daniel, and Elizabeth Mock.
1764, Nov. 19. Burkhart, Margaret, and Thomas Whaland.
1761, Jan. 12. Burk, Margaret, and Michael Gate.
1760, M'ch 13. Burk, Mary, and Andrew Brooks.
1769, Jan. 28. Burk, Mary, and George Enser.
1776, Apr. 22. Burk, Mary, and Jacob Brooks.
1775, Nov. 1. Burk, Mary, and William Huston.
1769, Jan. 16. Burk, Ruth, and Hugh Frazer.
1764, Nov. 19. Burk, Susanna, and John McDonald.
1760, July 5. Burley, John, and Jane Spear.
1762, Oct. 28. Burman, Edward, and Mary Craven.
1765, Dec. 11. Burnet, Henry, and Mary Reiley.
1767, Feb. 27. Burnet, John, and Jane McDowel.
1763, Sep. 24. Burnett, Mark, and Elizabeth Bess.
1762, Feb. 3. Burnett, William, and Margaret Royall.

1762, May   12. Burney, Alexander, and Margaret Dickey.
1766, Dec.   2. Burns, Joseph, and Jane Lowns.
1767, May   4. Burr, Hudson, and Phebe Lippincott.
1761, Apr.   8. Burrough, Isaac, and Abigail Hulard.
1773, Dec. 27. Burrow, John, and Hannah Meony.
1767, Oct.   7. Burrow, Rachel, and John Pine.
1763, Oct. 31. Burrows, Arthur, and Mary Morgan.
1768, Aug. 13. Burrows, John, and Margaret Sherlock.
1759, Dec.   1. Burrows, Mary, and George Robotham.
1766, Apr.   7. Burrows, Mary, and John McGibbons.
1769, Nov.   4. Burrow, Thomas, and Catharine Stretch.
1769, July 29. Burry, Martin, and Martha Skrouse.
1761, Oct. 29. Burtholt, Elizabeth, and Barnabas Neaus.
1769, Nov. 14. Burton, John, and Mary Matthew.
1760, Oct.   9. Burton, Margaret, and William Martin.
1771, Feb.   6. Burton, Robert, and Hannah Goslin.
1765, Apr. 25. Burtrow, Nicholas, and Abigail Biddle.
1771, Sept. 30. Busby, William, and Mary Hooper.
1748, May   14. Busly, Richard, and Elizabeth Richardson.
1748, Feb.   —. Bussard, Caspar, and Deborah Vocum.
1774, Feb.   2. Bustard, Elizabeth, and John Steward.
1776, Feb. 17. Butcher, Benjamin, and Lydia Bener.
1768, July 25. Butcher, Job, and Mary Shepherd.
1770, Oct. 30. Butcher, John, and Anne Evans.
1770, Apr. 18. Butcher, John, and Anne Thomas.
1762, Dec. 24. Butcher, Mary, and John Hufty.
1772, Apr. 10. Butler, Abiah, and Elizabeth Thomas.
1760, Feb. 13. Butler, Ameron, and Felix Vershon.
1765, M'ch 20. Butler, Ann, and Thomas Merris, Jun.
1768, Nov. 21. Butler, Barbara, and Joseph Kauffman.
1762, Feb.   1. Butler, Edmund, and Barbara Arnell.
1764, Jan. 13. Butler, Elizabeth, and Samuel Cartwright.
1763, Dec. 17. Butler, Henry, and Sarah Thompson.
1761, Aug. 14. Butler, James, and Mary Thomas.
1774, Feb. 24. Butler, John, and Mary McLaughlan.
1770, Dec. 19. Butler, John, and Susannah English.
1763, Jan. 27. Butler, Joseph, and Rebecca Main.
1768, Dec.   6. Butler, Margaret, and Nathan Matthew.
1747, June   —. Butler, Mary Ann, and John Hunt.
1767, June 12. Butler, Mary, and Barney Campbell.
1768, Sep.   8. Butler, Mary, and James Skinner.
1775, Jan. 30. Butler, Mary, and Michael Clarke.
1771, July 30. Butler, Mary, and William Johnson.
1764, June   4. Butler, Matthew, and Sarah Gardner.
1766, May   23. Butler, Peter, and Ann Nell.
1773, Oct. 16. Butler, Thomas, and Abigail Bane.

1764, May 10. Butner, Elias, and Elizabeth Edwards.
1762, Feb. 3. Butterfield, William, and Elizabeth Brian.
1762, Oct. 8. Butterworth, Elizabeth, and John Clark.
1767, Dec. 24. Butterworth, Mary, and Alexander Power.
1770, Sep. 8. Butts, Richard, and Margaret Davis.
1745, Nov. —. Buxon, John.
1764, Nov. 5. Buzby, Grace, and William Evans.
1762, May 5. Buzby, Samuel, and Mary Ward.
1760, July 29. Byard, James, and Agnes Hodge.
1766, Feb. 18. Byerly, Christopher, and Elizabeth Clymer.
1747, June —. Byers, Elizabeth, and David Boyers.
1747, Nov. —. Byers, Samuel, and Elizabeth Calwell.
1771, June 11. Byles, Elizabeth, and William Ball.
1760, July 17. Bylish, Thomas, and Sarah Green.
1771, Nov, 27. Byrch, Peter, and Elizabeth Bull.
1771, May 29. Byrne, Patrick, and Mary Murphy.
1774, Oct. 18. Byrnes, John, and Elizabeth Furrow.
1773, Sep. 28. Bywater, Elizabeth, and Nathaniel Hunter.
1761, Nov. 16. Bywater, William, and Margaret Harper.

C.

1774, Jan. 26. Cabean, James, and Sarah Bouden.
1769, May 6. Cabe, Thomas, and Rebecca Broadnecks.
1761, Sep. 9. Cadman, Anthony, and Ruth Ross.
1772, May. 19. Cadwalader, Margaret, and Samuel Meredith.
1774, Oct. 20. Cadwalader, Martha, and John Dagworthy.
1767, July 14. Cadwalader, Mary, and Philemon Dickinson.
1760, Jan. 29. Cadwallader, Jane, and Peter Lukins.
1773, Nov. 19. Cahan, Frances, and Patrick Finney.
1764, Jan. 30. Cahange, Thomas, and Ann Reily.
1766, Dec. 1. Cahill, John, and Catharine Smith.
1762, Jan. 15. Cahoone, Isabella, and William Maddock.
1747, Aug. —. Cahoon, Mary, and Edmund Brodrick.
1766, June 10. Cails, Margaret, and Daniel McPherson.
1746, July —. Cain, Hugh, and Sarah Klainkoof.
1765, M'ch 4. Cain, John, and Eleanor McDonald.
1763, Sep. 19. Cain, John, and Sarah McMullan.
1745, Sep. —. Cain, Roger.
1775, Jan. 18. Cake, David, and Margaret Cowger.
1775, Dec. 8. Calam, Margaret, and John Henry Stout.
1766, Sep. 2. Calder, John, and Judah Huston.
1762, Dec. 18. Caldwell, Andrew, and Jane Mitchell.
1763, Dec. 17. Caldwell, Grace, and William Allison.
1772, Sep. 21. Caldwell, James, and Sarah Mitchell.
1774, Feb. 19. Caldwell, John, and Hannah Atkins.
1766, M'ch 28. Caldwell, Mary, and David Cather.

1766, M'ch 19. Caldwell, Mary, and Enoch Morris.
1773, Oct. 21. Caldwell, Mary, and John McFaddon.
1774, Apr. 28. Caldwell, Rachel, and Benjamin Kelly.
1770, June 25. Caldwell, William, and Elizabeth Edgar.
1766, Dec. 2. Calhoun, James, and Elizabeth Wilson.
1760, Nov. 20. Callagher, Catharine, and Patrick Ryan.
1774, Nov. 24. Callahan, Ann, and Barnabas McMahon.
1761, Jan. 15. Callahan, Dennis, and Elizabeth Wright.
1773, Aug. 7. Callahan, Patrick, and Margaret Daulton.
1760, Nov. 10. Callander, Thomas, and Margaret Roak.
1766, Dec. 18. Callen, Edward, and Jane McIllroy.
1762, May 12. Calley, Sarah, and Richard Leedom.
1763, Aug. 31. Call, Hannah, and William Parker.
1771, May 4. Callwellin, Mary, and William Hughes.
1762, Feb. 3. Cally, Mary, and Thomas Tynard.
1773, Sep. 18. Calvan, Lydia, and David Dunn.
1774, Oct. 12. Calvely, William, and Elizabeth Reeve.
1747, Nov. —. Calwell, Elizabeth, and Samuel Byers.
1768, Oct. 27. Camalin, Thomas, and Barbara Russell.
1764, Feb. 8. Camble, Mary, and Peter McDowel.
1765, Aug. 8. Camel, Margaret, and John McCool.
1767, Feb. 20. Camel, Mary, and George McKay.
1769, Feb. 27. Cameron, Elizabeth, and Thomas Carr.
1763, Nov. 29. Cameron, Finley, and Jane Hamilton.
1761, Aug. 29. Cammeck, John, and Isabell McKnight.
1766, Sep. 1. Cammel, Catharine, and John Preston.
1766, Aug. 18. Cammel, Elizabeth, and Alexander St. Clair.
1765, Jan. 15. Cammel, Jane, and Francis Stewart.
1766, Aug. 7. Cammel, Mary, and Michael Davenport.
1747, M'ch —. Cammel, Thomas.
1767, Aug. 15. Campain, Richard, and Elizabeth Bizzey.
1770, Aug. 21. Campbell, Alexander, and Martha McNealy.
1774, Nov. 18. Campbell, Ann, and Henry O'Neill.
1772, Apr. 1. Campbell, Ann, and Hugh Hamilton.
1771, Apr. 13. Campbell, Arthur, and Eleanor Hurley.
1767, June 12. Campbell, Barney, and Mary Butler
1770, Apr. 9. Campbell, Catharine, and Henry Kreps.
1765, Aug. 13. Campbell, Catharine, and Richard Johnson.
1764, Sep. 8. Campbell, Edward, and Rachael Conyngham.
1775, Oct. 19. Campbell, Elizabeth, and William Thompson.
1770, Dec. 12. Campbell, George, Esq., and Helen Donaldson.
1770, Dec. 18. Campbell, George, and Mary Cavert.
1760, Jan. 29. Campbell, Hugh, and Mary Hanna.
1773, M'ch 29. Campbell, Jane, and Charles Costlee.
1770, May 9. Campbell, Jane, and John Eve.
1744, Apr. —. Campbell, John.

1771, Nov.   1. Campbell, John, and Mary Wood.
1770, Mch.   7. Campbell, Margaret, and Peter Norie.
1761, June   3. Campbell, Martha, and John Robeson.
1774, Dec. 20. Campbell, Mary, and James Buckley.
1773, Aug. 11. Campbell, Mary, and John Henderson.
1763, Jan. 22. Campbell, Mary, and Thomas Grant.
1762, Oct. 23. Campbell, Mary, and Thomas Ward.
1773, Apr. 16. Campbell, Mary, and William Baily.
1773, Aug. 14. Campbell, Sarah, and Thomas Robins.
1764, May   16. Campbell, William, and Anna Philips.
1773, Jan. 21. Campbell, William, and Hannah Crane.
1769, Dec. 20. Campble, Sarah, and Isaac Allen.
1774, M'ch 26. Camper, Mary, and William Saunders.
1761, May   12. Campton, Mary, and Robert Cowen.
1760, July 17. Canady, Abigail, and Samuel Smith.
1774, May   25. Cane, Catharine, and Jesse Coast.
1776, Jan.   5. Cane, Peter, and Mary Martin.
1761, Feb.   4. Cannady, Mary, and Joseph Williams.
1763, Feb. 21. Cannaedy, William, and Hannah Smith.
1779, Nov. 21. Cannan, Mary, and Robert Gray.
1768, June 21. Cannon, James, and Jane Brown.
1774, July 27. Cannon, Margaret, and John Motherral.
1775, Aug.   2. Cannon Margaret, and John Shields.
1771, Oct. 26. Cannon, Mary, and John Wood.
1771, Sep. 23. Cannon, Patrick, and Phebe Howell.
1761, Feb.   9. Canons, Benjamin, and Mary Sharp.
1761, Nov. 30. Canthorn, David, and Hannah Simpson.
1769, June   6. Cape, Andrew, and Sarah Banks.
1770, Aug.   3. Capock, Edward, and Margaret Gale.
1762, Aug.   2. Capont, Peter, and Dority Coupin.
1762, Mch.   3. Cardwell, Matthew, and Hannah Creemer.
1769, Sep.   1. Care, Barbara, and Peter White.
1765, July 27. Care, Peter, and Barbara Butterfoss.
1774, Sep.   8. Carey, John, and Catharine Lawrence.
1773, Feb. 11. Carker, Catharine, and Albertus Henfelstein.
1772, Apr. 10. Carl, Conrad, and Mary Waggoner.
1763, Oct. 10. Carle, Martha, and John George.
1762, Apr. 12. Carlisle, Alexander, and Mary Gordon.
1770, M'ch 20. Carlisle, Anne, and Mark Cullan.
1764, Nov. 11. Carlisle, Elizabeth, and John McKinstry.
1771, Dec.   3. Carlisle, William, and Keziah Akerly.
1775, July 27. Carmack, Gilbert, and Elizabeth Reinhold.
1771, July   9. Carmack, Isabella, and Ephraim Davis.
1773, May   3. Carmalt, Martha, and Edward Gabriel.
1771, Sep. 13. Carmalt, Susannah, and John Linington.
1759, Nov. 22. Carman, Ephraim, and Mary Lisby.

1761, Nov. 5. Carman, Mary, and Sellwood Griff.
1764, Feb. 27. Carmick, Margaret, and John Potts.
1770, Oct. 15. Carnaghan, John, and Elizabeth MacLean.
1767, M'ch 28. Carncross, William, and Ann Wigmore.
1768, Apr. 30. Carnelly, Johanna, and William Selly.
1764, Nov. 17. Carpenter, Abraham, and Eleanor Hillyard.
1761. Nov. 14. Carpenter, Albina, and Nicholas Burhaw.
1768, June 16. Carpenter, Benjamin, and Grace Morgan.
1772, Aug. 10. Carpenter, Benjamin, and Mary Morgan.
1743, May 3. Carpenter, John.
1743. Dec. —. Carpenter, Joshua.
1765. May 9. Carpenter, Mary, and John Watson.
1772, Aug. 6. Carpenter, Mercy, and Amos Wilkinson.
1763, M'ch 2. Carpenter, Miles, and Mary Steer.
1775, Feb. 11. Carpenter, Sarah, and Llewellyn Joe Taylor.
1746, Nov. —. Carpenter, Stephen, and Rebecca Collins.
1763, Feb. 1. Carpenter, Thomas, and Esther Squirrell.
1744, May 28. Carpenter, William.
1774, Feb. 28. Carr, Ann Agnes, and John Wright.
1763, Dec. 19. Carrel, Eleanor, and John Hart.
1765, Apr. 11. Carr, Elizabeth, and William Kirkpatrick.
1747, Oct. —. Carrighan, Patrick, and Margaret Douglass.
1765, Jan. 10. Carr, John, and Elizabeth Linmire.
1766, Nov. 27. Carr, Magnus, and Isabella Sutor.
1774, Oct. 27. Carrol, Ann, and Roger McGeary.
1764, Sep. 5. Carrol, Elizabeth, and Joseph Dungan.
1775, May 17. Carroll, Daniel, and Julian Powers.
1763, Apr. 18. Carroll, James, and Rebecca Baily.
1772, Nov. 12. Carroll, Margaret, and John Dawson.
1773, July 19. Carr, Patrick, and Mary Foreman.
1769, Feb. 27. Carr, Thomas, and Elizabeth Cameron.
1770, Oct. 18. Carr, William, and Frances McGrath.
1769, June 7. Carsen, William, and Martha Hare.
1774, Dec. 26. Carsner, Daniel, and Barbara Ash.
1769, M'ch 1. Carson, Andrew, and Jane Hall.
1775, Apr. 26. Carson, Ann, and John McFeteridge.
1769, M'ch 6. Carsonbury, Catharine, and Jonathan Redhead.
1770, Dec. 19. Carson, Esther, and Nathaniel Maxwell.
1760, May, 12. Carson, Grace, and Mayham Southwick.
1748, June 16. Carson, James, and Mary Espy.
1771, Aug. 20. Carson, Jane, and William Edwards.
1748, Nov. 11. Carson, John, and Ann Pywell.
1765, Apr. 2. Carson, Joseph, and Mary Correy.
1764, July 18. Carson, Margaret, and Joseph Rankin.
1770, Oct. 22. Carson, Mary, and Isaac Ely.
1774, Nov. 29. Carson, Rachel, and Alexander Blair.

1769, M'ch 2. Carson, Robert, and Elizabeth Moore.
1773, M'ch 10. Carson, Samuel, and Hannah Price.
1770, M'ch 21. Carson, William, and Mary Hamilton.
1769, Dec. 28. Carswell, James, and Anne Grove.
1769, Aug. 4. Carswell, James, and Elizabeth McCracken.
1760, Aug. 13. Carter, Elizabeth and Jeremiah Heaton.
1761, Dec. 24. Carteret, Daniel, and Elizabeth Jones.
1763, Feb. 15. Carter, James, and Rebecca Lincoln.
1744, Nov. —. Carter, Joseph.
1761, May 27. Carter, Margaret, and James Taylor.
1768, May 17. Carter, Margaret, and Solomon Stainer.
1765, Oct. 26. Carter, Rebecca, and David Jones.
1764, Oct. 6. Carter, Richard, and Agnes Yeates.
1774, Oct. 27. Carter, Sarah, and Jeremiah Dickinson.
1744, May —. Carter, Stephen.
1772, May 18. Carter, Thomas, and Mary Shadaker.
1769, May 29. Carter, Thomas, and Mary Ward.
1747, May —. Carthy, Patrick, and Ann Meredith.
1760, Feb. 29. Cartland, Catharine, and Anthony McCarty.
1774, May 5. Cartwright, John, and Margaret Yokee.
1764, Jan. 13. Cartwright, Samuel, and Elizabeth Butler.
1773, July 3. Cartwright, Sarah, and Peter Finnemore.
1762, June 9. Carty, Isaac, and Rachael Cosswell.
1745, Dec. —. Carty, Thomas.
1748, Aug. 15. Caruther, John.
1761, June 4. Caruthers, Isabella, and Allen Jack.
1769, Nov. 10. Caruthers, James, and Sarah May.
1767, June 14. Caruthers, Samuel, and Elizabeth Elliot.
1760, Nov. 22. Carver, Martha, and Isaac Washington.
1773, Dec. 6. Carver, Mary, and Benjamin Taylor.
1767, Jan. 24. Carver, Mary, and Joseph Worthington.
1774, Oct. 8. Carver, Phebe, and Thomas Tomlinson.
1761, Apr. 25. Carver, Sarah, and George Such.
1747, Apr. —. Carvour, Ann, and Robert Heaton.
1747, Apr. —. Carvour, John, and Rachel Naclor.
1766, Sep. 2. Cary, Ann, and John McGonish.
1764, May 10. Cary, Jesse, and Catharine Arrcle.
1772, Apr. 9. Casdrop, Jane, and James Pickering.
1748, Oct. 18. Case, Jonathan, and Elizabeth Durborow.
1775, July 3. Casey, Catharine, and Darby Sullivan.
1774, June 27. Casey, Margaret, and Robert Francis.
1773, May 11. Cash, Jane, and Simon Murray.
1772, July 28. Cash, Rebecca, and George Thompson.
1765, Aug. 23. Cassady, Hugh, and Rachel Richards.
1768, Apr. 30. Cassen, Robert, and Mary Spencer.
1744, June 5. Cassell, Nicholas.

1776, M'ch 13. Cassell, Sarah, and William Whitpaine.
1772, Aug. 18. Cassel, Sarah, and John Anson.
1763, Oct. 27. Cassett, Joseph, and Mary Evans.
1762, Nov. 27. Cassey, Rebecca, and John Starr.
1775, June 6. Cassin, Ann, and James Mullins.
1771, M'ch 7. Cass, Mary, and John Dunbar.
1763, April 13. Casswell, Jacob, and Mary Davis.
1774, July 25. Castelow, Phebe, and William McCord.
1760, M'ch 28. Caster, Elizabeth, and John Fallwell.
1762, Sep. 20. Caster, Paul, and Elizabeth Gasehlick.
1760, Dec. 19. Caster, William, and Rebecca Sirl.
1762, July 15. Castle, Deborah, and Francis Harper.
1769, June 20. Castle, Joy, and Jane Reed.
1760, Oct. 24. Castle, Margaret, and William Robinson.
1776, Jan. 16. Castle, Sarah, and John Scott.
1766, Aug. 19. Castle, Thomas, and Margaret Honeygroat.
1773, Sep. 10. Castle, Thomas, and Margaret Shelling.
1762, July 29. Castoley, Paul, and Phebe Longacre.
1776, May 15. Castor, Abraham, and Elizabeth Hendricks.
1763, M'ch 24. Caswell, Mary, and Anthony Moore.
1769, June 17. Catan, Catharine, and Thomas Willson.
1744, May —. Catharinger, John.
1766, M'ch 20. Cather, David, and Mary Caldwell.
1764, Aug. 1. Cather, Elizabeth, and James Reed.
1764, Oct. 17. Catman, Esther, and Benjamin Dungan.
1767, Nov. 6. Caton, George, and Mary Hines.
1768, Aug. 15. Caulson, Margaret, and Samuel Beckley.
1748, Apr. 13. Cavannaugh, Daniel, and Hannah Demsey.
1775, Nov. 7. Cavel, William, and Margaret Ross.
1776, M'ch 23. Cavener, Timothy, and Hannah Toy.
1770, Dec. 18. Cavert, Mary, and George Campbell.
1773, June 17. Cawley, Sarah, and John Fenton.
1773, Apr. 3. Cawley, Sarah, and Joshua Dungan.
1760, Feb. 28. Cæser, and Hagar.
1766, Aug. 11. Ceeseman, Samuel, and Sarah Tennant.
1746, Aug. —. Celfrey, John, and Frances Dukemaneer.
1772, Sep. 26. Cell, Elizabeth, and Philip Leicester.
1762, July 29. Cenon, Ann, and Alexander Mills.
1762, Dec. 29. Cetman, Benjamin, and Susannah Leech.
1771, Nov. 2. Chaband, James, and Elizabeth Russell
1763, Sep. 24. Chadwick, Sarah, and Andrew Sims.
1744, Nov. —. Chairman, Edward.
1762, Apr. 10. Challen, Sarah, and Samuel Bensel.
1767, Apr. 20. Chalmers, Mary, and John Kimble.
1747, Oct. —. Chalmler, Isabel, and William Edwards.
1763, Sep. 5. Chamber, Ann, and John Mathews.

1768, Aug. 27. Chamberlain, Mary, and Daniel Green.
1769, Aug. 29. Chamberlain, Mary, and Henry Burkey.
1762, Dec. 25. Chamberlain, Benjamin, and Sarah Collins.
1746, July —. Chambers, Alexander, and Ann Fox.
1783, June 10. Chambers, Benjamin.
1744, Sep. —. Chambers, David.
1760, Apr. 30. Chambers, David, and Anne McGie.
1762, May 21. Chambers, Easter, and Robert Johnston.
1761, Dec. 11. Chambers, Elizabeth, and William Read.
1766, Oct. 22. Chambers, Mary, and George Tallman.
1774, June 13. Chambers, Mary, and John Brown.
1761, June 24. Chambers, Rebecca, and John Wharton.
1768, Jan. 6. Chambers, Sarah, and Benjamin Alison.
1766, Nov. 6. Chambers, William, and Henrietta Cozens.
1762, Aug. 12. Champshear, Elizabeth, and Benjamin Ramshear.
1745, Nov. —. Chancellor, David.
1762, Nov. 19. Chancellor, Letthea, and Benjamin Spring.
1769, Oct. 25. Chandler, Jane, and James Welsh.
1773, Jan. 30. Chandler, John, and Anna Jones.
1768, May 12. Chandler, Mary, and William Smith.
1767, Dec. 28. Channel, James, and Hester Barkson.
1747, Jan. —. Channel, Samuel, and Catharine Offinger.
1775, Sep. 28. Channel, Samuel, and Susannah Robinet.
1746, July —. Channell, James, and Rebecca Key.
1770, May 11. Channell, Rebecca, and George Pickering.
1761, Oct. 15. Chapman, James, and Agnes Thwaits.
1763, July 16. Chapman, James, and Jane Reynolds.
1747, Dec. —. Chapman, Samuel, and Martha Moore.
1769, Feb. 11. Chapman, Sarah, and James Hill.
1770, July 14. Chapman, William, and Mary Comeley.
1767, Apr. 25. Chappel, Elizabeth, and James Miller.
1760, Jan. 30. Charce, Mary, and William Yarnal.
1746, Nov. —. Chares, John, and Jane Coffin.
1763, Feb. 26. Charlesworth, Abraham, and Rebecca Braden.
1748, May 14. Charlesworth, James, and Ann Cruiss.
1762, Feb. 11. Charlesworth, Rebecca, and Wm. McClean.
1763, M'ch 22. Charlesworth, Sarah, and Moses McClean.
1775, Nov. 21. Chatham, John, and Elizabeth Willson.
1764, June 13. Chatham, John, and Margaret Francis.
1764, Oct. 3. Chatham, John, and Tacy Thomas.
1771, Sep. 9. Chatham, Joseph, and Eleanor Breatherton.
1772, June 24. Chattell, Benjamin, and Mary McCall.
1776, May 1. Cheeseman, Elizabeth, and Abraham Du Bois.
1767, Aug. 31. Cheeseman, Mary, and Edward Ireland.
1770, Oct. 4. Cheeseman, Thomas, and Sarah Wiles.

1760, Apr. 19. Cheeseman, Martha, and Joshua Couzins.
1743, Sep. —. Cheeseman, Peter.
1744, Sep. —. Cheesman, Samuel.
1744, June 20. Chepman, James.
1760, June 5. Cherry, James, and Margaret Logan.
1772, May 11. Chesson, Thomas, and Lucy Brown.
1760, Apr. 19. Chester, John, and Elizabeth Cousins.
1747, Dec. —. Chevalier, Elizabeth, and John Benton.
1760, Feb. 13. Chevalier, John, and Elinor Barclay.
1764, May 27. Chew, Edward, and Mary Thomas.
1774, May 25. Chew, Elizabeth, and Edward Tilghman.
1760, Oct. 20. Chew, Jesse, and Mary Richards.
1768, May 17. Chew, Mary, and Alexander Wilcocks.
1770, Nov. 19. Chew, Mary Ann, and David Morris.
1770, Dec. 5. Chew, Michael, and Mary Robinson.
1743, Dec. —. Chew, Nathan.
1776, June 24. Chew, Sarah, and William Coxe.
1765, Sep. 16. Chigney, Richard, and Mary Hannum.
1774, Dec. 12. Chilcot, Dorothy, and Edward Stone.
1767, Oct. 31. Child, Catharine, and John Waters Martindale.
1764, July 27. Childerstone, John, and Frances Knox.
1761, Dec. 5. Chilleat, George, and Dorothy Talbert.
1760, June 24. Chland, James, and Jane McCullough.
1772, Nov. 16. Chresoman, Nicholas, and Susannah Shaneholtz.
1775, May 18. Chreissler, Barbara, and Lawrence Sickles.
1772, Apr. 29. Christian, Frederick, and Elizabeth Hodgkinson.
1775, May 17. Christian, Mary, and John Osborne.
1748, Aug. 15. Christie, Archibald.
1776, Jan. 25. Christie, John, and Mary Harding.
1773, Sep. 23. Christopher, Rachel, and Charles Farrier.
1765, Jan. 15. Christy, Catharine, and James Allen.
1760, Dec. 18. Christy, Margaret, and John Hamilton.
1769, Feb. 6. Christy, Mary, and Walter Stephens.
1764, May 29. Christy, William, and Sarah Laughrey.
1767, Feb. 18. Chrystie, John, and Mary Paine.
1763, Apr. 9. Church, Ann, and Thomas Maloney.
1761, Apr. 29. Church, Dorothy, and William Davis.
1761, Sep. 3. Church, Edward Henry, and Sarah Swanson.
1763, M'ch 3. Churchman, Hannah, and John Woods.
1761, Apr. 18. Church, Mary, and George McCalla.
1775, Jan. 18. Church, Samuel, and Anne Justice.
1767, Aug. 10. Church, Thomas, and Martha Lane.
1763, Feb. 1. Church, William, and Elizabeth Moore.
1772, Dec. 12. Cipple, Elizabeth, and Louis Guionnet.
1772, Jan. 4. Clady, Mary, and John Jager.
1775, Feb. 14. Clampffer, Adam, and Mary Kerlin.

1769, M'ch 30. Clampffer, Anna, and William Will.
1769, Sep. 30. Clampffer, Elizabeth, and Bernard Lawersuyler.
1773, Jan. 20. Clancy, Susannah, and Patterson Doyle.
1770, Oct. 10. Clanderman, Margaret, and James Kelley.
1770, Oct. 3. Claney, William, and Frances Shippey.
1766, Nov. 1. Clare, Elizabeth, and Joseph Perkins.
1764, Jan. 21. Clare, Esther, and Jacob Vansciver.
1760, Jan. 3. Clark, Abner, and Hannah Gilbert.
1772, Nov. 25. Clark, Ann, and Patrick Hamilton.
1767, Nov. 12. Clark, Ann, and Samuel Wilson.
1763, June 14. Clark, Catharine, and Robert Thecker.
1768, M'ch 3. Clark, Catharine, and Wallaston Redman.
1745, May —. Clarke, Henry.
1769, Dec. 28. Clarke, Joel, and Phebe Ward.
1772, June 17. Clarke, John, and Margaret McIlvain.
1763, Apr. 7. Clark, Elizabeth, and Robert Wilkinson.
1764, Sep. 24. Clark, Elizabeth, and Thomas Hartley.
1775, Aug. 5. Clarke, Mary, and Charles Blanchflower.
1775, Jan. 30. Clarke, Michael, and Mary Butler.
1769, Apr. 29. Clarke, Rebecca, and John Wiliot.
1766, Nov. 27. Clark, George, and Ann Sutor.
1774, Oct. 12. Clark, Heman, and Sarah Mitchell.
1764, Feb. 10. Clark, James, and Ann Donaldson.
1764, Apr. 9. Clark, James, and John Duche.
1765, June 12. Clark, John, and Elizabeth Burk.
1762, Oct. 8. Clark, John, and Elizabeth Butterworth.
1768, Jan. 28. Clark, Joseph, and Mary Durvey.
1768, Apr. 6. Clark, Josiah, and Patience Allen.
1773, July 23. Clark, Mary, and James French.
1772, Nov. 20. Clark, Rachel, and John Aves.
1776, Jan. 18. Clark, Richard, and Ann Owen.
1774, Aug. 27. Clark, Sampson, and Mary Sutton.
1775, Nov. 18. Clark, Sarah, and Charles Richards.
1768, June 8. Clark, Sarah, and Lawrence Johnson.
1761, May 13. Clarkson, Ann, and Samuel Finley.
1761, May 13. Clarkson, Gerardus, and Mary Flower.
1761, June 29. Clarkson, Rachael, and John Mullen.
1764, Dec. 22. Clark, Sylla, and James Davis.
1760, May 23. Clark, Thomas, and Katherine Walton.
1763, Feb. 23. Clark, Thomas, and Rebecca Clary.
1762, June 21. Clark, William, and Ann Kappock.
1746, Oct. —. Clark, William, and Buleah Coats.
1764, Dec. 17. Clark, William, and Susannah Falkler.
1763, Dec. 20. Clark, William, and Susanna Young.
1761, Aug. 22. Clary, Elean, 'and Arthur Betts.
1767, Oct. 31. Clary, Mary, and John Barry.

1763, Feb. 23. Clary, Rebecca, and Thomas Clark.
1764, Sep. 15. Claxton, Ann, and Richard Sewel.
1773, Dec. 27. Claxton, Jane, and Ebenezer Massey.
1768, Nov. 3. Clay, Curtis, and Margaret Wood.
1774, Nov. 19. Claypoole, Elizabeth and Norris Copper.
1746, Jan. —. Claypoole, George.
1770, Sep. 11. Claypoole, George, and Catharine Dowers.
1763, M'ch 8. Claypoole, James, and Lucretia Garwood.
1773, May 13. Claypoole, Mary, and Walter Fitzgerald.
1763, Nov. 29. Claypoole, Sarah, and Alwood Cowman.
1775, Sep. 21. Claypoole, Sarah, and James Withey.
1769, July 12. Clayton, Andrew, and Margaret Shockressy.
1761, Sep. 9. Clayton, Ann, and Ebenezer Harper.
1773, M'ch 6. Clayton, Asher, and Susannah Parker.
1765, June 27. Clayton, John, and Elizabeth Leech.
1773, Sep. 23. Clayton, Mary, and Herman Yerkus.
1773, Aug. 5. Clayton, Parnel, and Mary Grimes.
1767, Feb. 3. Clayton, Richard, and Elizabeth Sands.
1772, June 16. Clayton, Thomas, and Mary Walker.
1772, M'ch 10. Cleaver, Hannah, and Jacob Wyncoop.
1773, May 17. Cleaver, Joshua, and Margaret Nelson.
1775, July 15. Cleland, Jane, and John White.
1776, Jan. 18. Clelan, James, and Rachel Logan.
1771, Sep. 14. Clemens, Jacob, and Ann Updegraff.
1767, Aug. 20. Clement, John, and Jane Hervey.
1767, June 6. Clement, Rebecca, and George Hudson.
1767, Dec. 24. Clements, James, and Elizabeth Smith.
1770, May 26. Clements, John, and Catharine Mertle.
1774, Sep. 15. Clements, Mary, and Henry Leary.
1769, Nov. 8. Clendennon, Thomas, and Lydia Heslet.
1775, Oct. 7. Clevenstine, Henry, and Mary Emrecken.
1770, Apr. 2. Clews, Ruth, and Daniel Morris.
1773, Jan. 26. Clifford, Ann, and Zachariah Goforth.
1775, Aug. 30. Clifford, Thomas, and Eleanor Smith.
1763, Aug. 11. Cliffton, Thomas, and Martha James.
1762, Dec. 6. Clift, Jonathan, and Christiana Helviston.
1774, Oct. 12. Clifton, James, and Sarah Harris.
1765, M'ch 22. Climer, George, and Elizabeth Meredith.
1765, Sep. 18. Climmer, John, and Mary Blacklidge.
1772, Sep. 23. Cline, Ann, and Anthony Martin.
1768, Nov. 4. Cline, Catharine, and Henry Rutter.
1769, May 10. Cline, Mary, and John Lamb.
1744, Nov. —. Cline, Mathias.
1766, July 30. Cline, Philip, and Mary White.
1767, Oct. 31. Cline, Rosannah, and John Hay.
1775, May 27. Clingman, Barbara, and Thomas Young.

1775, Feb. 25. Clingman, Elizabeth, and Philip Miser.
1774, June 7. Clinton, Catharine, and Isaac Heston.
1775, Nov. 15. Clinton, John, and Ann Fivey.
1775, July 15. Clinton, Samuel, and Elizabeth Williams.
1765, Dec. 2. Clinton, Sarah, and William Noblitt.
1761, Nov. 13. Clisston, Hannah, and Charles Monk.
1766, M'ch 10. Clogg, Michael, and Catharine Woodcock.
1773, Aug. 19. Cloninger, Anna Elizabeth, and Michael Andrews.
1762, Jan. 6. Cloud, Elizabeth, and John Bryan.
1776, May 17. Cloud, John, and Elizabeth Patterson.
1776, Apr. 18. Clowser, Elizabeth, and Henry McCormick.
1769, Jan. 10. Cloyd, David, and Anna Boyd.
1769, Apr. 5. Club, James, and Margaret Lamont.
1764, M'ch 27. Clue, John, and Anna Johnson.
1762, Jan. 23. Clues, Abigail, and Evan Harry.
1774, M'ch 5. Clugston, Matthew, and Elizabeth Anderson.
1766, Feb. 18. Clymer, Elizabeth, and Christopher Byerly.
1762, Dec. 28. Clyme, Peter, and Ann Dennins.
1775, M'ch 23. Coakley, Ann, and James Spencer.
1775, Apr. 20. Coale, Samuel Stringer, and Ann Hopkinson.
1768, May 21. Coarsen, Richard, and Rachel Noles.
1774, May 25. Coast, Jesse, and Catharine Cane.
1765, Nov. 6. Coates, Alice, and John Langdale.
1747, M'ch —. Coates, Hannah, and Richard Dennis.
1770, Sep. 8. Coates, Hester, and Alexander Rickey.
1771 Nov. 7. Coates, Jonathan, and Jane Stinson,.
1774, Aug. 23. Coates, Mary, and Paine Newman.
1774, Sep. 7. Coates, Mary, and Robert Cumming.
1771, Jan. 9. Coates, Susannah, and Joseph Gladan.
1771, M'ch 2. Coates, Thomas, and Mary Allen.
1775, May 11. Coates, William, and Jane Dupice.
1769, Dec. 30. Coatham, Mary, and John Savadge.
1767, Oct. 3. Coat, Hannah, and John Fromberger.
1746, Oct. —. Coats, Buleah, and William Clark.
1765, May 1. Coats, Lindsay, and Ruth Hughes.
1747, Jan. —. Coats, Martha, and William Sheed.
1762, Aug. 13. Coats, Mary, and Thomas Plumsted.
1764, Oct. 9. Coats, William, and Martha Davis.
1762, Nov. 2. Coats, William, and Susannah Loupler.
1764, Dec. 29. Coattam, Francis, and Theodorah Berry.
1764, Jan. 26. Cobb, Susannah, and Henry Grubb.
1771, Aug. 26. Cobham, Mary, and John May.
1775, Dec. 2. Coburn, Ann, and William Humphreys.
1775, Feb. 25. Coburn, Caleb, and Esther Assheton.
1773, June 24. Coburn, Elizabeth, and David Rees.
1769, Apr. 14. Coburn, Jacob, and Sarah Evans.

1775, Jan.   23. Coburn, James, and Sarah Hayes.
1747, Dec.   —. Coburn, Rachel, and John McFarland.
1774, Dec.   1. Coburn, Susannah, and Thomas Budd.
1764, M'ch 28. Cochan, John, and Elizabeth Titeem.
1773, Jan.   13. Cochran, Elizabeth, and David Alexander.
1763, Jan.   14. Cochran, James, and Alice Kearns.
1767, Dec.   10. Cochran, James, and Elizabeth Faries.
1768, Nov.   29. Cochran, Jane, and Alexander Mitchell.
1765, Jan.   15. Cochran, Jane, and Robert Work.
1766, Apr.   14. Cochran, Margaret, and John Wrighton.
1776, May   21. Cochran, Mary, and Adam Watts.
1775, June   28. Cochran, Mary, and Michael McCarty.
1765, Dec.   9. Cochran, Matthew, and Eleanor Gilmore.
1744, Oct.   —. Cock, Andrew.
1771, Dec.   30. Cock, John, and Sarah Heslet.
1766, Oct.   21. Cockle, Mary, and Humphrey Robinson.
1775, Jan.   24. Cockshott, John, and Sarah Rivers.
1746, Nov.   —. Cody, Margaret, and Henry Krier.
1761, Feb.   14. Coffee, James, and Mary Sisson.
1768, May   28. Coffee, James, and Rebecca Winterton.
1769, Aug.   30. Coffin, Anne, and John Yerkus.
1771, June   13. Coffin, Elizabeth, and Samuel Powel.
1769, Oct.   6. Coffing, Hannah, and William Aldworth·
1771, M'ch 23. Coffing, William, and Abigail Potts.
1746, Nov.   —. Coffin, Jane, and John Chares.
1767, Oct.   23. Coffin, Margaret, and John Nice.
1763, M'ch 1. Coffin, Sarah, and Solomon Willson.
1775, Feb.   22. Coffman, John, and Mary Gitling.
1763, Sep.   13. Coggins, Ann, and Ebenezer Tomlinson.
1775, Nov.   21. Coggins, Lydia, and John Hanley.
1772, July   23. Cohen, Abraham, and Mary Garman.
1773, Nov.   15. Cokley, Mary, and Israel Shreve.
1770, July   30. Colbert, Mary, and George Reinholdt.
1760, July   30. Colbert, Sarah, and Robert Barnes.
1760, M'ch 15. Colbin, Mary, and Fredrick Lunds.
1761, July   24. Cole, Ann, and Robert Hunter.
1766, Oct.   1. Cole, Balzer, and Elizabeth Reily.
1775, Aug.   22. Cole, Hannah, and Peter Strine.
1765, July   30. Cole, John, and Ann Shute.
1765, June   24. Cole, John, and Esther Merry.
1760, Jan.   10. Cole, John, and Grace Dwyt.
1763, Dec.   5. Cole, John, and Margaret Lock.
1761, Apr.   25. Cole, John, and Mary McFarrand.
1747, Oct.   —. Cole, John, and Sarah Stinson.
1773, Dec.   9. Coleman, Anne, and Joseph Power.
1776, Apr.   16. Coleman, Elizabeth, and David DeBerholt.

1773, Dec. 15. Coleman, Elizabeth, and William Mintz.
1768, May 26. Coleman, Jane, and Isaac Quigley.
1766, Dec. 10. Coleman, John, and Martha Long.
1771, Feb. 13. Cole, Rachel, and Joseph Roward.
1770, Feb. 21. Coles, Grace, and John Doughton.
1760, Nov. 6. Coleson, Sarah, and James Kelly.
1768, Apr. 28. Coleston, John, and Elizabeth Wentz.
1765, June 12. Colleck, Alice, and John Green.
1775, Apr. 17. Collet, Ann, and John Wormington.
1765, M'ch 14. Collet, Hannah, and Anthony Mahony.
1748, Nov. 11. Collet, Thomas, and Lydia Vanhorne.
1776, Mch. 18. Collet, Isabella, and Thomas Millard.
1761, July 30. Collet, Thomas, and Mary Lyken.
1748, Nov. 11. Colliday, Mary, and Melchor Manny.
1760, Jan. 7. Colliday, Sarah, and Dollore Ming.
1767, Jan. 21. Collings, Hannah, and George Marshall.
1766, Jan. 18. Collings, James, and Eleanor McDonnell.
1766, Jan. 16. Collings, Margaret, and Edward Brannum.
1745, Apr. —. Collins, Abraham.
1774, June 25. Collins, Abraham, and Catharine Cuthbert.
1772, May 20. Collins, Abraham, and Catharine Taylor.
1770, Oct. 8. Collins, Charity, and Joseph Garret.
1745, Aug. —. Collins, Charles.
1776, June 29. Collins, Dennis, and Mary Bell.
1763, Jan. 26. Collins, Edward, and Margaret Shovelin.
1746, June —. Collins, Elisah, and Benjamin Street.
1748, Oct. 18. Collins, Elizabeth, and John Stockerd.
1766, July 29. Collins, Hannah, and Cornelius Conolly.
1746, June —. Collins, James, and Ann Wells.
1747, June —. Collins, James, and Elizabeth Bredin.
1769, Dec. 23. Collins, James, and Hannah Brick.
1771, M'ch 28. Collins, Joshua, and Martha Betterton.
1772, July 27. Collins, Margaret, and Michael McMullan.
1763, Oct. 10. Collins, Matthew, and Sarah Bluewhite.
1765, Nov. 28. Collins, Mercy, and Samuel Thomas.
1771, Oct. 31. Collins, Nathan, and Catharine Dobbins.
1762, June 12. Collins, Rachael, and Joseph Falconer.
1774, May 28. Collins, Rebecca, and James Jackson.
1746, Nov. —. Collins, Rebecca, and Stephen Carpenter.
1748, May 14. Collins, Rebecca, and William Ellis.
1769, Aug. 24. Collins, Richard, and Elizabeth McCormick.
1770, June 4. Collins, Robert, and Rachel Maskell.
1762, Dec. 25. Collins, Sarah, and Benjamin Chamberlin.
1770, M'ch 17. Collins, Sophia, and John Rabhoorn.
1773, June 25. Collins, Thomas Wharton, and Mary Hinton.
1768, Apr. 14. Collins, William, and Mary Lurdon.

1766, Sep. 17. Collister, Elizabeth, and Thomas Tompkin.
1761, Aug. 28. Collitt, Robert, and Hannah Durmady.
1763, Oct. 5. Colloby, Catharine, and Balser Reser.
1769, May 10. Collum, Elizabeth, and Demas Worrall,
1743, Sep —. Collum, James.
1775, Nov. 14. Collum, Jesse, and Jane Francis.
1773, Oct. 20. Collum, Mary, and Eli Hibbs.
1745, Apr. —. Collum, William.
1762, June 23. Colston, William, and Ann Taylor.
1761, Jan. 12. Colton, Lucy, and Benjamin Coster.
1760, Nov. 26. Colton, Mary, and Eleazer Turning.
1764, Aug. 23. Colton, Phebe, and Edward Robinson.
1772, Feb. 25. Comb, Margaret, and Benjamin Harbeson.
1744, Apr. —. Comdon, Daniel.
1763, Sep. 19. Comfort, Jacob, and Margaret Gold.
1769, Nov. 23. Comley, Benjamin, and Elizabeth Dungan.
1775, July 1. Comley, Isaac, and Elizabeth Moore.
1769. Nov. 6. Comley, Jacob, and Rachel Comley.
1775, M'ch 25. Comley, Joseph, and Rachel Edwards.
1775, M'ch 31. Comley, Mary, and John Robinson.
1769, Nov. 6. Comley, Rachel, and Jacob Comley.
1768, Oct. 1. Comley, Rebecca, and James Vansant.
1767, June 10. Comly, John, and Mary Hellings.
1766, July 24. Comly, Joshua, and Catharine Willet.
1763, Nov. 5. Comron, Elizabeth, and Manan Kennard.
1772, Apr. 27. Comron, Mary, and John Shaw.
1770, Feb. 10. Conorroe, Elizabeth, and Samuel Atkinson.
1763, Apr. 14. Conarroe, Rebecca, and Samuel Conarroe.
1763 April 14. Conarroe, Samuel, and Rebecca Conarroe.
1775, Sep. 5. Condon, Michael, and Elizabeth Fitzpatrick.
1768, Aug. 5. Conger, Martha, and Samuel Scarsborough.
1744, Sep. —. Congers, Joseph.
1761, Oct. 5. Coningham, Simpson, and Rachael Lampley.
1775, July 25. Conly, Mary, and James Otis.
1761. Nov. 7. Connady, Mary, and Farguson McGuey.
1766, Feb. 15. Connaway, Margaret, and Thomas Haley.
1761, June 6. Connaway, Mary, and Robert Tieft.
1769, Feb. 25. Connell, Alice, and William Paul.
1775, June 8. Connell, Donald, and Margaret Tobin.
1770, Feb. 16. Connell, Eleanor, and James Kirkpatrick
1769, Oct. 7. Connell, Elizabeth, and John Harrison.
1767, Apr. 22. Connell, William, and Sarah Richards.
1762, Oct. 14. Connely, Sarah, and Daniel Rees.
1760, Feb. 25. Conner, Mary, and John Wilson.
1765, Apr. 6. Conner, William, and Agnes Read.
1765, Aug. 12. Conner, William, and Susannah Power.

1771, Feb.   7. Conn, Letitia, and Hugh Willson.
1765, Oct. 18. Connody, William, and Hannah Pastorius.
1772, Feb. 15. Connoly, Isabella, and John McAimoyei.
1773, July 19. Connoly, Rebecca, and Abraham Robinson.
1773, Apr. 26. Connoly, Robert, andBridget Dunn.
1760, July 31. Cannon, Sarah, and George Stevenson.
1771, Aug.   2. Connor, John, and Judith Kennedy.
1774, Jan.   8. Connor, Michael, and Mary Cottinger.
1763, M'ch 17. Conn, Robert, and Margaret Fletcher.
1766, July 29. Conolly, Cornelius, and Hannah Collins.
1745, ——   —. Conolly, Michael.
1767, Sep.   1. Conolly, Robert, and Ann McMullan.
1747, Dec. —. Conrad, James, and Jane Hatfield.
1772, Dec. 28. Conrad, John, and Margaret Fry.
1760, Oct.   1. Conrad, Margaret, and Thomas White.
1766, Apr. 12. Conser, George, and Sarah Wolfganger.
1773, Apr. 26. Consor, George, and Barbara Fridley.
1775, May   8. Conyngham, Elizabeth, and Nathaniel Donnell.
1773, Oct. 23. Conyngham, Gustavus, and Ann Hockley.
1764, Sep.   8. Conyngham, Rachael, and Edward Campbell.
1775, Oct. 12. Conyngham, Thomas, and Ann Adams.
1770, Sep. 20. Cook, Amelia, and John Keen.
1770, July 28. Cook, Catharine, and Michael Rainbow.
1766, Nov. 25. Cook, Elizabeth, and Frederick Stuber.
1776, May   16. Cooke, Mary, and Peter Sutter.
1769, Nov. 23. Cook, Hannah Pacay, and Isaac Baker.
1766, Apr. 16. Cook, John, and Mary Robinson.
1770, Feb. 21. Cook, Lawrence, and Catharine McCarty.
1761, Jan.   8. Cook, Mary, and Nathan Ferryby.
1746, Sep. —. Cook, Nathan, and Mary Rogers.
1761, Jan. 15. Cook, Robert, and Mary Boggs.
1772, M'ch 14. Cook, Rosanna, and James Morris.
1769, Oct   30. Cook, Rose, and Francis Ryans.
1765, May   22. Cook, Sarah, and Archibald Hamilton.
1760, Sep. 30. Cookson, Hannah, and Joseph Galloway.
1766, Jan. 30. Cookson, Mary, and John Shellenberg.
1747, May   —. Coole, Elizabeth, and Peter White.
1773, May   12. Coombe, Thomas, Jun., and Sarah Badger.
1775, May   22. Cooper, Ananias, and Bridget Dwir.
1744, July 21. Cooper, Edmond.
1769, Oct.   4. Cooper, Elizabeth, and James Hartley.
1763, Dec.   5. Cooper, Elizabeth, and Joseph Correy.
1768, July 15. Cooper, Hannah, and Lewis Ashman.
1765, May   28. Cooper, Hugh, and Mary Fowler.
1772, May   2. Cooper, Isaac, and Anne Bolton.
1762, Dec. 14. Cooper, James, and Ann Hims.

1769, M'ch 30. Cooper, James, and Sarah Mullan.
1763, M'ch 29. Cooper, Jane, and George, Kennedy.
1769, Jan. 12. Cooper, John, and Hester Buckman.
1776, Feb. 13. Cooper, John, and Jane McKibbin.
1761, Dec. 2. Cooper, Keziah, and Moses Long.
1774, Dec. 29. Cooper, Letitia, and Joseph Ashton.
1748, Sep. —. Cooper, Lydia, and Cadwallader Morgan.
1763, Dec. 24. Cooper, Mary, and Joseph Wilson.
1771, Oct. 21. Cooper, Mary, and Robert Maxwell.
1763, Apr. 7. Cooper, Robert, and Mary Crawford.
1776, June 15. Cooper, Sarah, and Hugh Lenox.
1771, Dec. 4. Cooper, Susannah, and John Breese.
1763, May 25. Cooper, Susannah, and Thomas Sealock.
1774, Apr. 27. Cooper, William, corker, and Rebecca Evans.
1764, Nov. 1. Cooper, William, and Eleanor Helmes.
1769, Jan. 7. Cope, John, and Hannah Edwards.
1764, Sep. 4. Cope, John, and Martha Darts.
1774, Nov. 19. Copper, Norris, and Elizabeth Claypoole.
1747, M'ch —. Copp, Henry, and Susannah Lamplugh.
1774, Oct. 27. Coran, Mary, and John Knight.
1748, Oct. 18. Corbet, John, and Mary Todd.
1761, Oct. 31. Corbett, Mary, and Hugh Long.
1771, Dec. 14. Corbett, Phebe, and John Dungan.
1771, May 27. Corbett, William, and Sarah Phipps.
1745, M'ch —. Corbetz, Christopher.
1747, Aug. —. Corbit, Patrick, and Ann Donavon.
1771, Oct. 16. Corbman, Elizabeth, and Philip Kline.
1764, Dec. 8. Corbut, Sarah, and Charles Crossley.
1775, M'ch 23. Cordien, John, and Catharine Kranston.
1763, May 16. Cordrey, Henry, and Mary Wildman.
1769, Sep. 4. Coren, Elizabeth, and Richard Robinson.
1773, Jan. 20. Corgae, Thomas, and Ann Elliot.
1769, Sep. 9. Cornelius, Christopher, and Elizabeth Roberts.
1760, May 8. Cornelius, Joseph, and Christina Magdalin.
1761, Aug. 13. Cornelland, William, and Ann Williams.
1760, Oct. 18. Cornell, Simon, and Adrian Cruzen.
1770, July 14. Cornely, Mary, and William Chapman.
1767, May 21. Cornman, Deborah, and George May.
1760, Sep. 2. Cornman, John, and Elizabeth Goor.
1767, May 22. Cornog, Daniel, and Sarah Jones.
1766, Nov. 4. Cornog, Mary, and John Davis.
1775, Nov. 25. Cornwall, Robert, and Sarah Rankin.
1746, June —. Cornway, John, and Susannah Bound.
1771, June 19. Correy, Henry, and Elizabeth Flick
1763, Dec. 5. Correy, Joseph, and Elizabeth Cooper.
1765, Apr. 2. Correy, Mary, and Joseph Carson.
1771, July 8. Correy, Samuel, and Ann Singleton.

1775, Apr. 20. Correy, Walter, and Bridget Downey.
1769, June 23. Corris, George, and Elizabeth Gordon.
1769, Dec. 23. Corry, Hannah, and Thomas Mills.
1762, June 8. Corsan, Christian, and Elizabeth Cruzer.
1765, Apr. 29. Corse, Jacob, and Hannah Prigg.
1775, M'ch 8. Corson, Mary, and Enoch Marple.
1766, Jan. 22. Corssen, Ann, and William Maynard.
1767, Aug. 26. Corssen, Jeminine, and James Forrester.
1761, Jan. 12. Corter, Benjamin, and Lucy Colton.
1745, Apr. —. Cortes, Warwick.
1760, Oct. 31. Cosner, Rebecca, and Benjamin Fell.
1762, June 9. Cosswell, Rachael, and Isaac Carty.
1747, Dec. —. Coster, Samuel, and Ann Thomas.
1769, M'ch 16. Costigan, Lewis Johnston, and Mary Lockhar.
1773, M'ch 29. Costlee, Charles, and Jane Campbell.
1773, Dec. 3. Costolo, Richard, and Alice Swaine.
1762, June 16. Cotnam, Ann, and Michael Davis.
1761, Jan. 9. Cotter, Eleanor, and John Cummings.
1769, Sep. 13. Cotter, Judith, and John Bray.
1761, June 10. Cotton, Thomas, and Elean Flack.
1774, Jan. 8. Cottringer, Mary, and Michael Conner.
1776, Jan. 3. Couch, Samuel, and Ann Quigg.
1743, Nov. —. Couch, William.
1774, Aug. 8. Coulay, Patrick, and Elizabeth Osborne.
1760, Jan. 10. Coulston, Sarah, and John Landerman.
1747, June —. Coutlas, Margaret, and William Newbald.
1771, July 11. Coulter, Sarah, and Richard Bell.
1765, Nov. 6. Coulter, Thomas, and Sarah Brooks.
1770, Apr. 12. Coupar, Robert, and Mary Dunlap.
1762, Aug. 2. Coupin, Dority, and Peter Capont.
1769, July 19. Coupland, Andrew, and Agnus Bennet.
1768, May 19. Courtney, Hercules, and Mary Shute.
1760, Apr. 19. Cousins, Elizabeth, and John Chester.
1760, Apr. 19. Couzins, Joshua, and Martha Cheesman.
1769, June 9. Cover, Powell, and Barbara Herman.
1774, Sep. 26. Covinger, Jane, and John Pake.
1767, Sep. 4. Cowan, William, and Susannah Kite.
1762, May 4. Coward, Sarah, and John Field.
1747, Feb. —. Cowe, Jane, and George Landers.
1761, May 12. Cowen, Robert, and Mary Campton.
1775, Jan. 18. Cowger, Margaret, and David Cake.
1767, M'ch 26. Cowgill, Martha, and Robert Hardy.
1773, May 18. Cowgill, Nehemiah, and Mary Middleton.
1763, Nov. 29. Cowman, Alwood, and Sarah Claypoole.
1769, June 3. Cowman, Atwood, and Amy Sharald.
1746, June —. Cowper, James, and Rebecca Edwards.

1768, Apr. 25. Cowperthwaite, Joseph, and Susannah Hulings.
1774, Sep. 8. Cowperthwaite, Mary, and John Kille.
1772, May 11. Cowpland, William, and Jane Parkinson.
1770, Feb. 26. Cowsan, Elizabeth, and John Eyrich.
1767, Oct. 19. Cox, Abel, and Ann Cunningham.
1769, M'ch 30. Cox, Altha, and Peter Wikoff.
1769, Apr. 8. Cox, Ann, and Thomas Marshall.
1765, June 26. Cox, Catharine, and James How.
1764, Apr. 5. Cox, Catharine, and Joseph Element.
1759, Dec. 6. Cox, Charles, and Rebecca Wells.
1771, June 5. Coxe, Daniel, and Sarah Redman.
1765, M'ch 4. Coxe, Eleanor, and Andrew Yorke.
1774, July 27. Coxe, Elizabeth, and Robert Graham.
1771, Oct. 8. Coxe, Gabriel, and Ann Bur.
1767, Feb. 4. Cox, Elizabeth, and John Heathcoate.
1767, M'ch 25. Cox, Elizabeth, and William Moore.
1774, Oct. 26. Coxe, Margaret, and Stephen Morris.
1746, Oct. —. Coxe, Rebecca, and John Jacob Wyse.
1775, M'ch 21, Coxe, Robert, and Jane Watkins.
1774, Dec. 21. Coxe, Thomas, and Ann Peterson.
1776, June 24. Coxe, William, and Sarah Chew.
1762, M'ch 25. Cox, Francis, and Juno. (Two negroes of this City.)
1760, Nov. 15. Cox, John, and Ester Bowes.
1769, Aug. 16. Cox, John, and Mary McCalla.
1760, Aug. 11. Cox, Joseph, and Mary Sutton.
1747, June —. Cox, Margaret, and Francis Manny.
1766, Jan. 8. Cox, Martha, and Isaac Wikoff.
1764, Feb. 8. Cox, Mary, and John Winter.
1765, Feb. 21. Cox, Mary, and Joseph Marshall.
1770, M'ch 1. Cox, Mary, and Robert Jones.
1764. M'ch 14. Cox, Nicholas, and Rebecca Potts.
1767, Nov. 11. Cox, Rachel, and Francis Ilbingworth.
1763, Dec. 21. Cox, Rebecca, and John Stinson.
1775, Oct. 9. Cox, Samuel, and Priscilla Holmes.
1768, Apr. 24. Cox, Sarah, and Andrew Allen.
1773, Mch. 27. Cox, Sarah, and Enous Scallinger.
1747, May —. Cox, Susannah, and Andrew Torten.
1773, Jan. 11. Cox, William, and Phebe Duffield.
1772, Jan. 18. Coyl, John, and Ann Maddin.
1762, Dec. 7. Coyl, Mary, and William Mahanoy.
1761, Dec. 21. Cozens, Amy, and Samuel Scott.
1767, Sep. 5. Cozens, Daniel, and Elizabeth Shivers.
1776, M'ch 7. Cozens, Elijah, and Ann Moffat.
1766, Nov. 6. Cozens, Henrietta, and William Chambers.
1774, Dec. 26. Cracker, Hannah, and Daniel Mackey.

1762, Sep.   1. Craddock, James, and Hester Price.
1764, Dec.   6. Craft, Mary, and Thomas Hadley.
1763, Nov. 24. Craft, Mary, and Thomas Wilkinson.
1748, M'ch 11. Crafts, Henry, and Mary Fowler.
1774, Oct. 15. Crafts, James, and Jemima House.
1774, Oct. 15. Crager, Mary, and William Moore.
1769, Jan. 21. Craig, Alexander, and Sarah Thompson.
1763, Jan. 15. Craig, Daniel, and Margaret Brumfield.
1775, Aug.   8. Craig, Isabella, and John Hethrington.
1772, Dec. 22. Craig, Isabella, and Matthew Knox.
1773, Oct. 26. Craig, James, and Mary Ash.
1775, M'ch 27. Craig, John, and Ann Driscoll.
1760, Nov.   1. Craig, John, and Elizabeth Elder.
1769, Jan. 16. Craig, John, and Rebeck Stevens.
1763, May   4. Craig, John, and Sarah Hale.
1766, Dec   1. Craig, Jacob, and Susannah Baltzer.
1763, Aug. 12. Craig, Martha, and George Wilson.
1771, June 15. Craig, Martha, and James Hanlon.
1766, Oct. 22. Craig, Rebecca, and Hugh Stevenson.
1771, July 20. Craig, Robert, and Sarah Gardiner.
1760, Oct. 30. Craig, Samuel, and Jane Morgan.
1764, M'ch 24. Craig, Thomas, and Grace Morris.
1775, June 26. Craig, Thomas, and Lydia Jackson.
1766, Nov. 12. Craig, William, and Jane Barclay.
1759, Dec. 21. Craig, William, and Jane Small.
1774, Apr. 28. Craig, William, and Mary Johns.
1763, Jan.   6. Cramrine, Catharine, and Henry Ports.
1773, Jan. 21. Crane, Hannah, and William Campbell.
1744, Sep. —. Cranfield, Michael.
1775, Feb. 27. Crann, John, and Sarah Souder.
1764, June 22. Crason, Eve, and Christopher Krafley.
1760, Aug. 16. Crathorne, Jonathan, and Mary Keen.
1771, Oct. 12. Crathorne, Mary, and Thomas Roker.
1764, June 16. Craton, Elizabeth, and John Rambo.
1768, Sep   17. Craven, Ann, and Henry Brouse.
1762, Aug. 21. Craven, Hannah, and John Brooks.
1762, Oct. 28. Craven, Mary, and Edward Burman.
1771, July 17. Craven, Rachael, and James Alexander.
1766, Dec.   6. Craven, Thomas, and Eleanor Huff.
1770, Nov. 19. Crawford, Andrew, and Judith Smith.
1761, Oct. 10. Crawford, Andrew, and Sarah James.
1763, Feb.   1. Crawford, Ann, and William Shaw.
1769, Dec. 23. Crawford, Christopher, and Mary Culp.
1766, Aug.   5. Crawford, David, and Lydia Lloyd.
1778, May   1. Crawford, Elijah, and Elizabeth Stout.
1774, Feb. 10. Crawford, Elizabeth, and James Shannon.

1761, Dec.   2. Crawford, Samuel, and Elizabeth Barnett.
1770, Dec.   1. Crawford, Frances, and James Kelly
1762, M'ch 2. Crawford, James, and Catharine Howell.
1768, Oct.   4. Crawford, James, and Ruth Doyle.
1772, Nov. 24. Crawford, Jane, and Robert Poke.
1773, Sep. 29. Crawford, Martha, and Robert Dodds.
1763, Apr.   7. Crawford, Mary, and Robert Cooper.
1767, M'ch 12. Crawford, Moses, and Jane Jamison.
1746, Apr. —. Crawford, Peter.
1771, Dec.   4. Crawford, William, and Ann Hines.
1746, Dec. —. Craypeel, Nicholas, and Margaret Feghlyn.
1774, Sep.   1. Creagh, Thomas, and Ann Nelson.
1764, July 30. Creag, James, and Elizabeth Wilkinson.
1767, July   8. Creddock, Elizabeth, and William Hawkins.
1762, M'ch 3. Creemer, Hannah, and Matthew Cardwell.
1766, Feb.   6. Creen. Eleanor, and John Shepard.
1769, June 9. Creesmer, Mary, and Jacob Hill.
1760, Sept. 23. Creighton, Ann, and Cornelius Tucker.
1772, Oct. 10. Creighton, James, and Catharine McCann.
1776, M'ch 6. Creps, Mary, and John Kungils.
1764, Aug.   6. Cressap, Michael, and Mary Whitehead.
1769, Oct. 31. Cresse, Lydia, and Daniel Styles.
1771, May 14. Cresserin, Elizabeth, and Thomas Tisdale.
1767, June 9. Cressman, Elizabeth, and Jacob Kilpack.
1761, Sep.   1. Cribb, John, and Sarah Swanson.
1769, Aug.   8. Criles, Eve, and Andrew Woolf.
1747, Oct. —. Crimmen, Thomas, and Elizabeth Edwards.
1767, Sep. 26. Crippin, Thomas, and Elizabeth Midwinter.
1764, June 29. Cripps, John Adam, and Catharine Wikenerin.
1765, Aug. 28. Crips, Barbara, and George Warner.
1760, Aug. 19. Crishman, Felix, and Rebecca Milchant.
1776, Jan. 13. Crisp, Adam, and Mary Moore.
1762, Sep. 14. Crispan, Joseph, and Elizabeth Owen.
1770, Feb. 19. Crispin, Anne, and John Russell.
1771, Aug. 20. Crispin, Hester, and Joseph Green.
1769, Dec. 30. Crispin, Mary, and Warwick Hale.
1764, Sep. 29. Crispin, Paul, and Rebecca Hewlins.
1748, July 13. Crispin, Samuel, and Sarah Barnett.
1773, Apr. 19. Crispin, Thomas, and Ann Kitchen.
1763, Feb.   7. Crisp, William, and Mary Parr.
1771, Jan. 24. Crist, Casper, and Catharine Lyng.
1761, Jan.   1. Croce, Adam, and Barbara Harts.
1765, Oct. 15. Crockford, Susannah, and Daniel Berkensha.
1774, July   6. Crohan, Dennis, and Margaret Malaby.
1775, Aug. 26. Cromby, Thomas, and Mary McCallister.
1763, Dec.   9. Crone, Ann, and Thomas Flint.

1765, Oct. 14. Croney, John, and Catharine Hasand.
1773, Feb. 26. Cronin, James, and Bridget Sherlock.
1774, July 4. Cronin, John, and Mary Yosset.
1775, Aug. 17. Crook, Frances, and Thomas Ellison.
1746, Oct. —. Crook, John, and Beata Hoffman.
1747, M'ch —. Crookshank, Alexander, and Cully Brimbre.
1768, Dec. 8. Crookshank, Clementina, and John Ross.
1766, Sep. 13. Crosby, John, and Elizabeth Culin.
1763, Dec. 12. Crosby, Richard, and Esther Phipps.
1747, May —. Crosly, John, and Alice Mahlen.
1770, Jan. 3. Cross, Anne, and William Pinkerton.
1771, M'ch 4. Crossby, Alice, and George Spear.
1761, M'ch 26. Cross, George, and Hannah Franks.
1776, Jan. 3. Cross, Hannah, and Alexander Boyle.
1764, July 20. Crossier, Ann, and Richard Garaty.
1764, Dec. 8. Crossley, Charles, and Sarah Corbut.
1766, Nov. 3. Cross, Margaret, and William McIlvaine
1774, July 7. Cross, Robert Richardson, and Mary Wallace.
1770, Nov. 22. Crosstan, Anne, and John Sprogell.
1743, June 11. Cross, Westema.
1765, Sep. 11. Croston, Margaret, and Henry Naglee.
1770, Dec. 11. Crousen, Barbara, and George Orffar.
1761, M'ch 21. Crousen, Lamakeer, and Cornelius Wikoff.
1768, Oct. 12. Crowley, David, and Mary Lamb.
1767, Oct. 8. Crowley, Mary, and Robert Martin.
1762, Apr. 24. Crowley, Thomison, and Henry Lanaway.
1745, Jan. —. Crows, John.
1776, Jan. 22. Croxford, Elizabeth, and Joseph Atkinson.
1771, Jan. 8. Crozier, Anne, and Hugh Morton.
1769, Sep. 13. Crozier, James, and Catharine Peterson.
1771, Jan. 19. Crozier, Margaret, and John Ringrose.
1763, Nov. 11. Crozier, Samuel, and Jane Thomas.
1774, Feb. 23. Crozius, Margaret, and Peter Wells.
1748, Jan. —. Crue, Dorothy, and John Stagg.
1765, M'ch 19. Cruger, John, and Catharine Alverse.
1744, Oct. —. Cruikshank, Alexander.
1748, May 14. Cruiss, Ann, and James Charlesworth.
1774, M'ch 7. Crumby, Ralph, and Catharine Van Horn.
1775, Nov. 6. Cruse, Paul, and Mary Ruden.
1760, Oct. 18. Cruzen, Adrian, and Simon Cornell.
1770, Oct. 26. Cruzen, Francis, and Mary Blackledge.
1762, June 8. Cruzer, Elizabeth, and Christian Corsan.
1764, Nov. 2. Cuff, and Judith. (Two negroes belonging to Messrs. Mifflin & Elves.)
1761, M'ch 26. Culbertson, John, and Sarah Denny.
1769, M'ch 22. Culin, Daniel, and Rebecca Hendrickson.

1766, Sep. 13. Culin, Elizabeth, and John Crosby.
1763, Jan. 8. Culing, Martha, and Andrew Lycans.
1763, July 28. Culin, William, and Rebecca Justice.
1774, Nov. 23. Cullam, John, and Elizabeth Peeling.
1770, M'ch 20. Cullan, Mark, and Anne Carlisle.
1764, July 4. Culp, Barbara, and William Will.
1769, Dec. 23. Culp, Mary, and Christopher Crawford.
1760, Feb. 29. Cummerford, Ann, and Nathaniel Donnel.
1774, Sep. 7. Cumming, Robert, and Mary Coates.
1761, June 13. Cummings, Ann, and Thomas Bower.
1748, May 14. Cummings, David, and Sarah Jobson.
1747, Oct. —. Cummings, Elizabeth, and Charles Shea.
1760, Jan. 22. Cummings, Grace, and Alexander Lindsey.
1760, Nov. 7. Cummings, Jane, and William Marshall.
1761, Jan. 9. Cummings, John, and Eleanor Cotter.
1766, May 27. Cummings, John, and Eleanor Thompson.
1767, May 15. Cummings, John, and Margaret McPherson.
1765, Sep. 26. Cummins, Ann, and Alexander Stewart.
1764, Aug. 17. Cummins, Eleanor, and William Philips.
1762, M'ch 31. Cummins, James, and Jane Cummins.
1762, M'ch 31. Cummins, Jane, and James Cummins.
1763, Dec. 23. Cummins, John, and Margaret Johnston.
1771, Dec. 3. Cummins, Mary, and David Jones.
1763, June 22. Cummins, Mary, and James Marsh.
1748, Jan. —. Cummins, Matthew, and Elizabeth Warren.
1767, May 28. Cummins, William, and Catharine Jones.
1776, M'ch 4. Cumpston, Thomas, and Civel Baker.
1746, Nov. —. Cumree, Elizabeth, and George Righter.
1783, June 22. Cunard, Abraham.
1747, Dec. —. Cunningham, Agnes, and James Curry.
1767, Oct. 19. Cunningham, Ann, and Abel Cox.
1746, July —. Cunningham, Ann, and John Philpot.
1773, Nov. 27. Cunningham, Elizabeth, and Peter McIntire.
1774, Sep. 1. Cunningham, Mary, and Alvery Hodgson.
1744, Jan. —. Cunningham, William.
1771, July 15. Cunrad, Samuel, and Susannah Foulks.
1775, Aug. 30. Curpman, Margaret, and Isaac Kendricks.
1771, Aug. 22. Currey, Ann, and Joseph Rice.
1770, July 9. Currey, Susannah, and James Read.
1759, Dec. 5. Currie, Elizabeth, and James Dieman.
1765, M'ch 14. Currie, James, and Margaret Haley.
1747, Dec. —. Curry, James, and Agnes Cunningham.
1762, Oct. 25. Curry, Laughlin, and Margaret Barber.
1770, Aug. 15. Curry, Martha, and Richard Wells.
1770, Oct. 24. Curry, Mary, and George Dunn.
1764, Jan. 2. Curtain, James, and Hannah Rush.

1766, M'ch 29. Cuspin, Rachel, and Jesse Roe.
1763, Feb. 3. Cuss, Elizabeth, and John Dawson.
1748, Jan. —. Custard, Abigale, and William Browning.
1760, Aug. 20. Custard, John, and FrancesThomas.
1748, Jan. —. Custard, Richard, and Elizabeth Brownback.
1768, May 24. Custer, Mary, and Mathias Pennebecker.
1746, July —. Custis, George, and Sarah Mukins.
1770, Sep. 3. Cutbush, Edward, and Anne Marriot.
1775, M'ch 1. Cuthbert, Anthony, and Sarah Dixon.
1774, June 25. Cuthbert, Catharine, and Abraham Collins.
1744, May —. Cuthbert, Thomas.
1773, June 22. Cuthbert, Thomas, and Sarah Latimer.
1768, Oct. 29. Cyder, Mary, and Hugh Pugh.
1775, M'ch 23. Cypher, Mary, and John Lip.

D.

1746, Aug. —. Dagger, Mary, and John Turner.
1774, Oct. 20. Dagworthy, John, and Martha Cadwalader.
1763, June 8. Daily, Ann, and Alexander Ross.
1763, May 29. Daily, Cornelius, and Elizabeth Krewsen.
1773, Apr. 17. Daily, John, and Elizabeth Masterson.
1774, May 18. Daily, Sarah, and Benjamin Leigh.
1747, Jan. —. Dalbo, Andrew, and Catharine Van Culm.
1760, Dec. 19. Daley, William, and Ann Edwards.
1772, May 29. Dalrymple, John, and Eleanor Williams.
1769, Nov. 10. Dalton, Margaret, and Daniel Delany.
1761, Apr. 4. Daly, Owen, and Catharine McGrough.
1761, May 20, Damdlespeck, John, and Margaret Kilgarine.
1783, June 1. Daniel, Charles.
1766, Sep. 16. Daniel, Daniel, and Martha Sutton.
1776, Feb. 24. Daniel, Elizabeth, and Andrew Stone.
1760, Apr. 29. Daniel, George, and Elizabeth Hanse.
1770, Jan. 29. Daniel, Mary, and Silas Hart.
1775, July 20. Daniels, John, and Sarah Ball.
1769, May 17. Daniels, Sarah, and Thomas Brown.
1761, Nov 11. Darbyshire, John, and Mary Reckey.
1774, Oct. 12. Dare, Edmund, and Hannah Bell.
1748, Jan. —. Dark, Ann, and Alexander Sage.
1763, Nov. 28. Dark, Mary, and Ralph Moore.
1768, Oct. 4. Darling, Nathan, and Esther McCoskry.
1762, June 29. Darlington, Mary, and Samuel Mackelduff.
1775, July 19. Darrock, Thomas, and Margaret Gregory.
1748, May 14. Darrough, Agnes, and John Davis.
1763, Apr. 1. Darry, Hannah, and John Richardson.
1764, Sep. 4. Darts, Martha, and John Cope.
1772, Oct. 6. Dashner, Mary, and James Glenn.

1762, July 21. Daugan, Mary, and Henry Wetley.
1765, Jan. 22. Daullis, George, and Mary Vaughan.
1773, Aug. 2. Daulton, Margaret, and Patrick Callahan.
1773, Oct. 5. Davald, Alexander, and Elizabeth Johnston.
1770, Nov. 13. Davenport, Anne, and Samuel Kating.
1771, Sep. 5. Davenport, Eleanor, and Thomas Lathbridge.
1774, Aug. 27. Davenport, Margaret, and Maurice Hennessy.
1769, Feb. 24. Davenport, Mary, and Conyers Stokeld.
1766, Aug. 7. Davenport, Michael, and Mary Cammel.
1769, Sep. 23. Davenport, Rebecca, and John Davis.
1767, June 29. Daverau, William, and Rose Hanlan.
1774, May 5. Davey, Amos, and Mary Rowland.
1772, Nov. 18. Davey, William, and Rachel Snowden.
1760, Oct. 22. David, Enoch, and Elizabeth Harrison.
1762, July 26. David, George, and Mary Morgan.
1766, Dec. 1. David, John, and Deborah Williams.
1764, May 16. David, John, and Mary Thomas.
1748, Sep. —. David, Mary, and John Parkinson.
1773, May 30. Davids, Hannah, and Joseph Jenks.
1771, June 22. Davidson, Grace, and Elizabeth Stratton.
1767, Apr. 10. Davidson, Mary, and Patrick Brady.
1769, Feb. 27. Davidson, Rachel, and James Goudy.
1743, Aug. 20. Davie, Hugh.
1774, Oct. 8. Davie, Richard, and Martha Hall.
1767, May 13. Davies, Charles, and Hannah Levy.
1747, Aug. —. Davies, Elizabeth, and James Milner.
1748, Apr. 13. Davies, Margaret, and Thomas Reid.
1745, Nov. —. Davies, Samuel.
1769, July 1. Davis, Abigail, and William Faris.
1759, Nov. 29. Davis, Agnes, and William Knowles.
1764, Nov. 20. Davis, Amos, and Hannah Boore.
1768, Nov. 26. Davis, Amy, and John Elliot.
1766, July 23. Davis, Ann, and Alexander Guy.
1770, May 1. Davis, Anne, and William Weston.
1775, Apr. 10. Davis, Ann, and James Barnes.
1769, Apr. 17. Davis, Ann, and John Davis.
1764, May 10. Davis, Ann, and John Turk.
1769, June 29. Davis, Arthur, and Elizabeth Murray.
1768, Apr. 18. Davis, Benjamin, and Catharine Pugh.
1776, Jan, 3. Davis, Benjamin, and Jane Meredith.
1766, M'ch 18. Davis, Benjamin, and Mary Neiss.
1768, Dec. 16. Davis, Catharine, and David Davis.
1772, July 10. Davis, Catharine, and Marsena Alloway.
1771, Dec. 30. Davis, Conrad, and Mary Hart.
1773, Sep. 23. Davis, Curtis, and Ann Gayman.
1748, Aug. 15. Davis, David.

1768, Dec. 16. Davis, David, and Catharine ———.
1764, June 20. Davis, David, and Elizabeth Rambo.
1761, Aug. 27. Davis, Elijah, and Elizabeth Jones.
1768, M'ch 28. Davis, Elisha, and Susannah Castlebury.
1771, Apr. 12. Davis, Elizabeth, and Carpenter Wharto'
1768, Feb. 8. Davis, Elizabeth, and Edward Jones.
1763, Apr. 13. Davis, Elizabeth, and Edward Stretcher.
1765, Jan. 2. Davis, Elizabeth, and Isaac Somers.
1772, M'ch 3. Davis, Elizabeth, and Robert Gordon.
1762, Oct. 23. Davis, Elizabeth, and Thomas Penny.
1761, Dec. 29. Davis, Enoch, and Elizabeth Jervis.
1771, July 9. Davis, Ephraim, and Isabella Carmach.
1745, July —. Davis, Evan.
1783, June 21. Davis, George.
1769, June 10. Davis, George, and Catharine Jordan.
1748, Apr. 13. Davis, George, and Elizabeth James.
1763, July 9. Davis, Grace, and David Terry.
1775, M'ch 22. Davis, Hannah, and Francis McKay.
1767, May 6. Davis, Hannah, and George Bell.
1775, Nov. 11. Davis, Hannah, and William Todd.
1776, May 22. Davis, Isabella, and Abel Owens.
1765, Aug. 22. Davis, James, and Ann McFall.
1771, June 19. Davis, James, and Elizabeth Parkes.
1761, Oct. 15. Davis, James, and Elizabeth Savage.
1771, July 1. Davis, James, and Franey Wyson.
1768, M'ch 3. Davis, James, and Margaret Miller.
1764, Dec. 10. Davis, James, and Mary Hall.
1761, May 8. Davis, James, and Mary Thomas.
1764, Dec. 22. Davis, James, and Sylla Clark.
1773, May 19. Davis, Jemimah, and Peter Wells.
1771, Dec. 16. Davis, Jesse, and Catharine Humphreys.
1748, May 14. Davis, John, and Agnes Darrough.
1769, Apr. 17. Davis, John, and Ann Davis.
1776, May 16. Davis, John, and Ann Kemble.
1760, June 9. Davis, John, and Hannah Oblebee.
1760, Aug. 20. Davis, John, and Hannah Rogers.
1766, Nov. 4. Davis, John, and Mary Cornog.
1769, Sept. 23. Davis, John, and Rebecca Davenport.
1771, Aug. 29. Davis, Jonathan, and Sybilla Philips.
1771, Nov. 28. Davis, Josiah, and Priscilla Robinson.
1747, June —. Davis, Lewellin, and Elizabeth Pritchard.
1772, Apr. 23. Davis, Lydia, and Isaac Haines.
1773, Apr. 22. Davis, Lydia, and Isaac Reily.
1775, Apr. 20. Davis, Lydia, and William Harp.
1770, Sept. 8. Davis, Margaret, and Richard Butts.
1765, Jan. 24. Davis, Margaret, and Robert McMullen.

1773, Dec.   7. Davis, Margaret, and Thomas Davis.
1771, Apr.   16. Davis, Margaret, and William Evans.
1769, Feb.   6. Davis, Martha. and Benjamin Harris.
1764, Oct.   9. Davis, Martha, and William Coats.
1763, Apr.   13. Davis, Mary, and Jacob Casswell.
1772, Jan.   21. Davis, Mary, and James Robinson.
1775, Feb.   3. Davis, Mary, and John Adams.
1764, June   6. Davis, Mary, and Leonard Harwood.
1764, Feb.   1. Davis, Mary, and Levy Dungan.
1765, Dec.   28. Davis, Mary, and Lewis German.
1762, Apr.   17. Davis, Mary, and Robert Wilson.
1775, May   9. Davis, Mary, and Thomas Harper.
1748, Sept. —. Davis, Mary, and Thomas Nevell.
1747, May   —. Davis, Mary, and Thomas Rooke.
1762, June   16. Davis, Michael, and Ann Cotnam.
1764, Sept.   1. Davis, Morris. and Abigail Rork.
1745, Aug.   —. Davis, Myrick, Jun.
1746, M'ch   —. Davis, Nathaniel.
1761, June   25. Davison, David, and Mary Simonson.
1765, July   30. Davison, Gaine, and Mary Fitzgerald.
1762, Sept. 30. Davison, John, and Rachael Liggit.
1761, Sept. 23. Davison, Samuel, and Catharine Ferguson.
1774, Dec.   22. Davison, Thomas, and Ann Read.
1748, M'ch   11. Davison. William, and Esther Deverix.
1762, May   11. Davis, Patrick, and Elizabeth Williams.
1775, Oct.   11. Davis, Priscilla, and Andrew Heucks.
1762. Jan.   9. Davis, Rachel, and Benjamin Drake.
1748, Sep.   —. Davis, Rebecca, and James Bailey.
1747, Nov.   —. Davis, Rebecca, and Joshua Mitchell.
1775, Jan.   24. Davis, Richard, and Ruth Marshall.
1771, June   6. Davis, Richard, and Sarah Moore.
1744, Dec.   —. Davis, Robert.
1772, Oct.   28. Davis, Sampson, and Elizabeth Ashton.
1771, Dec.   18. Davis, Samuel, and Hannah Price.
1768, Aug.   17. Davis, Samuel, and Margaret Philips.
1770. M'ch   27. Davis, Sarah, and Joshua Phillipps.
1748, May   14. Davis, Sarah, and William Davis.
1766, Apr.   10. Davis, Sarah, and William Ogilby.
1771, June   7. Davis. Sarah, and William Shedaker.
1766, May   7. Davis, Sophia, and George McAlhaney.
1765, June   26. Davis. Susannah, and John Roberts.
1761, Apr.   8. Davis, Thomas, and Jane McKillop.
1773, Dec.   7. Davis, Thomas, and Margaret Davis.
1763, Dec.   21. Davis, Thomas, and Mary Grayman.
1760, July   5. Davis, Thomas, and Susannah Holly.
1772, Oct.   10. Davis, ——, and Thomas Terry.

1748, June 16. Davis, Truston, and Isabel Jemison.
1743, Feb. 28. Davis, William.
1770, Sep. 13. Davis, William, and Ann King.
1776, Mch. 21. Davis, William, and Catharine Whitman.
1761, Apr. 29. Davis, William, and Dorothy Church.
1762, Feb. 15. Davis, William, and Eleanor Smith.
1747, M'ch —. Davis, William, and Martha Jemmison.
1767, Dec. 17. Davis, William, and Mary Griffith.
1772, Nov. 7. Davis, William, and Mary McNeal.
1747, Oct. —. Davis, William, and Rachel Purce.
1748, May 14. Davis, William, and Sarah Davis.
1776, Jan. 31. Davis, Zachariah, and Mary Evans.
1771, Apr. 3. Dawkins, Henry, and Mary McDowell.
1769, Oct. 9. Dawny, Sarah, and Michael Haines.
1771, June 13. Dawser, Paul, and Mary Pass.
1764, July 6. Daws, Meriam, and Gerrard Hopkins.
1773, Sep. 3. Dawson, Charlotte, and William Lawrence.
1768, June 24. Dawson, Henry, and Margaret Elliot.
1762, Oct. 29. Dawson, James, and Mary Hamilton.
1763, Feb. 3. Dawson, John, and Elizabeth Cuss.
1772, Nov. 12. Dawson, John, and Margaret Carroll.
1761, Dec. 30. Dawson, Mary, and Robert Moore.
1745, Apr. —. Dawson, Robert.
1775, Aug. 1. Day, Mary, and Samuel Simpson.
1772, Dec. 10. Daymon, Francis, and Ann White.
1771, Sep. 12. Deacon, Rebecca, and Joseph Rigley.
1768, Sep. 13. Deacon, Robert, and Sarah Shedaker.
1769, May 11. Deacon, Sarah, and Peter Sutter.
1776, Jan. 24. Deakin, Elizabeth, and Robert Stevenson.
1761, Oct. 28. Dean, Elizabeth, and John Jervis.
1763, June 22. Dean, Elizabeth, and John McClure.
1744, Sep. —. Dean, James.
1771, Feb. 23. Dean, James, and Mary Gilbert.
1774, Apr. 11. Dean, Jemima, and Samuel Wallace.
1775, Jan. 5. Dean, John, and Catharine Hall.
1764, Dec. 13. Dean, John, and Mary Rose.
1762, Apr. 5. Dean, Joseph, and Frances McCrakin.
1768, Feb. 10. Dean, Joseph, and Hannah Boyle.
1770, Jan. 17. Dean, Joseph, and Rachel Morris.
1769, May 19. Dean, Mary, and John Fulton.
1773, April 21. Dean, Mary, and Nathaniel Allen, Jun'r.
1772, Dec. 31. Dean, Mary, and Thomas Thomas.
1760, Jan. 24. Dean, Sarah, and Hugh McHenry.
1776, Apr. 16. DeBertholt, David, and Elizabeth Coleman.
1760, Dec. 18. Debtford, Agnes, and William Williams.

1775, Nov. 6. Decastellane, Noel Barnaby Veyrant and Maria Catharine Bruellhet.

1774, Dec. 20. Decator, Stephen, and Ann Peni.

1766, Oct. 23. Decony, Susannah, and Arthur Gordon.

1769, Oct. 4. Dederer, Christian, and Elizabeth Harling.

1774, May 11. Dederick, Margaret, and Adam Schneider.

1748, Oct. 18. Deel, Eve, and Peter Harper.

1775, Apr. 22. Dehaven, Hugh, and Sarah Holstein.

1769, Feb. 17. Dehaven, Mary, and Nicholas Schneider.

1763, Jan. 18. Dehaven, Peter, and Elizabeth Knight.

1743, June 16. Deigner, Peter.

1772, Sep. 21. Deilman, Mary, and Erhart Sheidle.

1763, Jan. 12. Deiter, Jacob, and Jane Buffington.

1775, Oct. 20. Deklyn, Mary, and Samuel Kirk.

1774, Oct. 25. Delabar, Catharine, and Adam Nees.

1772, May 18. Delany, Catharine, and William Barthket.

1769, Nov. 10. Delany, Daniel, and Margaret Dalton.

1774, Sep. 27. Delany, Jeremiah, and Sarah Thomas.

1774, Jan. 20. Delany Mary, and Richard Johnston.

1766, Aug. 18. Delany, Sarah, and Hiram Gihon.

1762, Sep. 21. Delap, John, and Catharine Scott.

1760, Dec. 29. Delaplaine, Hannah, and John Price.

1775, Feb. 3. Delaplaine, James, and Mary Keen.

1768, July 9. Delaplaine, Phebe, and John Knox.

1748, M'ch 11. Delaplain, Hannah, and Robert Thomson.

1763, June 16. Delaplan, Sarah, and Gerrard Vandegrift.

1764, Sep. 17. Delavan, Ann, and James Ashton.

1760, July 28. Delavan, Elizabeth, and William Preston.

1760, July 23. Delavan, Hannah, and William Roberts.

1774, July 6. Delavan, John, and Barbara Krozer.

1767, Aug. 1. Delavan, Joseph, and Mary Dougherty.

1767, M'ch 18. Delaven, Isaac, and Hannah Grovian.

1747, May —. Delays, James, and Mary Moore.

1745, July —. Dele, Philip.

1761, Jan. 6. Deling, Catharine, and James Harter.

1760, Feb. 15. Delworth, William, and Lettice McDaugh.

1774, Aug. 19. Dempsey, James, and Mary Russel.

1748, Apr. 13. Demsey, Hannah, and Daniel Cavannaugh.

1769, Jan. 26. Demsy, Joseph, Jun'r, and Mary Finny.

1763, June 4. Denald, Jane, and James Freeling.

1772, Aug. 21. Denham, Elizabeth, and Matthias Garret.

1770, Aug. 18. Dennaughey, Hannah, and Samuel Harper.

1762, Dec. 28. Dennins, Ann, and Peter Clyne.

1773, July 20. Dennis, Ann, and John Scott.

1768, Feb. 4. Dennis, Catharine, and John McIlvaine.

1761, July 21. Dennis, Elizabeth, and John Duff.

1774, Apr. 5. Dennison, Agnes, and John Shannon.
1772, M'ch 3. Dennison, Andrew, and Ann Barclay.
1746, Dec. —. Dennison, Catharine, and William Rumsey.
1761, May 7. Dennison, James, and Mary Sims.
1763, Apr. 13. Dennison, Mary, and John Scott.
1763, Feb. 14. Dennison, Mary, and Leonard Johnson.
1763, May 18. Dennison, Sarah, and Thomas Lytle.
1747, M'ch —. Dennis, Richard, and Hannah Coates.
1771, Sep. 27. Dennis, Sarah, and Thomas Edward Wallace.
1774, M'ch 19. Denny, Mary, and James Lang.
1769, May 31. Denny, Mary, and Nathan Posset.
1761, M'ch 26. Denny, Sarah, and John Culbertson.
1748, M'ch 11. Denny, Sarah, and John Evans.
1775, June 3. Denormandie, Elizabeth, and George Gillispie.
1764, Oct. 13. Denormandie, Mary, and Enoch Barret.
1745, July —. Denormandy, John Abram.
1745, July —. Denormandy, William.
1775, Sep. 10. Dent, Hannah, and James Gilmer.
1763, Sep. 15. Dent, John, and Jane Morrison.
1748, July 13. Denton, John, and Mercy Roberts.
1765, Oct. 28. Denton, Massey, and Samuel Hastings.
1746, Dec. —. DeNyce, John, and Jane North.
1774, Nov. 19. Depperwin, Adam, and Elizabeth Swaine.
1771, Sep. 25. Depui, Nicholas, and Lana Shoemaker.
1744, July 21. Derborov.
1769, Sep. 4. Derling, Anne, and Adam Andres.
1762, Aug. 31. Derragh, Ann, and Blair McClenachen.
1775, Aug. 31. Derrick, Mary, and James Morris.
1775, Nov. 8. Derringen, Elizabeth, and Martin Zahar.
1764, Dec. 11. Derringer, Elizabeth, and Samuel Walker.
1773, May 8. Derringer, Hannah, and Richard Fordham.
1760, Aug. 13. Derrock, Henry, and Ann Jemmison.
1760, Feb. 12. Derrock, William, and Rebecca Thompson.
1768, Feb. 18. Derry, Joseph, and Hannah Greenway.
1772, Feb. 24. Dersey, Michael, and Mary Skepwith.
1775, July 22. Derwett, Susannah, and John Hercules.
1768, July 12. Deshler, Ann, and Jacob Roush.
1774, Feb. 19. Deshler, Elizabeth, and Thomas Dowman.
1767, Oct. 27. Deshong, Henry, and Catharine Fite.
1774, Dec. 15. Deshung, Peter, and Susannah Gillman.
1775, Sept. 2. Detchevery, Bethrend, and Hannah Rodgers.
1764, Oct. 9. Deuring, Catharine, and James Jackson.
1762, Dec. 27. Devan, John, and Ann Oliver.
1746, July —. Devereux, James, and Esther James.
1748, Mar. 11. Deverix, Esther, and William Davison.
1774, Feb. 19. Devetter, Conrad, and Catharine Bakin.

1748, July 13. Devit, Joseph, and Agnes Nise.
1766, Dec. 8. Devo, Benjamin, and CatharineWalker.
1776, June 18. Dewar, Susannah, and John Paplay.
1743, Nov. —. Dewees, Henry.
1769, Nov. 15. Dewees, William, and Sarah Waters.
1748, Oct. 18. Dewer, David, and Susanna Thornhill.
1764, May 30. Dewers, John, and Mary Thornhill.
1768, June 17. Dewey, Elizabeth, and John Stancliff.
1774, July 28. Dewick, Thomas, and Ann Moore.
1775, Dec. 7. Dewies, Elizabeth, and James McDowell.
1763, Jan. 15. Dew, John, and Ann McCall.
1763, June 22. Diamond, Elizabeth, and John Baird.
1763, April 14. Diana, ——, and Robert Venable, (negroes.)
1760, Aug. 9. Dibo, Catharine, and Andrew Thess.
1772, Dec. 3. Dick, Elizabeth, and Jacob Graff.
1762, May 12. Dicky, Margaret, and Alexander Burney.
1775, Mar. 28. Dickinson, Ann, and Robert Plunket.
1761, Nov. 21. Dickinson, Cadwall, and Mary Draper.
1768, Jan. 12. Dickinson, Elizabeth, and George Weed.
1768, Oct. 1. Dickinson, James, and Elizabeth Myers.
1774, Oct. 27. Dickinson, Jeremiah, and Sarah Carter.
1766, Jan. 11. Dickinson, John, and Sarah McGlaughlin.
1762, Jan. 20. Dickinson, Mary, and Joseph Head.
1767, July 14. Dickinson, Philemon, and Mary Cadwalader.
1748, Oct. 18. Dickinson, Rebecca, and George Stevenson.
1765, Sept. 19. Dickinson, Thomas, and Mary Lort.
1771, Dec. 18. Dick, Jane, and William McFarlan.
1770, Jan. 10. Dick, John, and Anne Burehet.
1776, June 2. Dick, Mary Ann, and John Gorely.
1783, June 4. Dick, Philip.
1766, Sept. 6. Dickson, Henry, and Rebecca Robinet.
1767, Jan. 27. Dickson, Martha, and Thomas Walker.
1767, Nov. 19. Dickson, Mary, and Samuel Green.
1748, Jan. —. Dicks, Sarah and Thomas Ely.
1759, Dec. 5. Diemen, James, and Elizabeth Currie.
1748, Feb. —. Dilks, Thomas, and Rhody Langly.
1775, May 3. Dillon, John, and Margaret Watkins.
1761, Dec. 23. Dillon, Jonathan, and Mary Yeates.
1766, Sep. 3. Dill, Robert, and Margaret Stall.
1776, M'ch 27. Dillworth, Amos, and Hannah Taylor.
1773, Oct. 20. Dilworth, John, and Hannah Hunter.
1763, Sep. 14. Dimsey, Joseph, and Sarah Jones.
1760, Feb. 21. Dinslow, Mary, and Marmaduke Bunting.
1760, July 22. Dinsman, Catharine, and George Sheitz.
1769, Oct. 24. Dittmars, Catharine, and John Roman.
1762, Feb. 24. Dixey, Margaret, and Joseph Lukens.

1772, July 28. Dixey, William, and Martha McHenry.
1747, May —. Dixon, Ann, and Alexander McBride.
1771, Nov. 8. Dixon, John, and Catharine Harpin.
1748, June 16. Dixon, John, and Mary Wilson.
1774, M'ch 1. Dixon, Sarah, and Anthony Cuthbert.
1762, Dec. 10. Dixon, Sarah, and Peter Spence.
1765, Aug. 8. Dixon, Thomas, and Dorothy Hungary.
1768, Oct. 25. Doach, Mary, and James Pack.
1764, Jan. 26. Doach, Susannah, and William Kennedy.
1769, July 25. Doane, Ephraim, and Susannah Griscom.
1769, May 24. Doan, Mary, and Benjamin Scott.
1747, Dec. —. Dobbings, Martha, and Christopher Finny.
1771, Oct. 31. Dobbins, Catharine, and Nathan Collins.
1763, Jan. 29. Dobbins, Joseph, and Mary Forster.
1771, Oct. 31. Dobbins, Mary Ann, and John Williams.
1765, July 18. Dobbins, Rebecca, and George Moore.
1762, June 2. Dobins, Rachael, and James Russell.
1763, Dec. 9. Dobson, Ann, and David Stille.
1773, Sep. 29. Dodds, Robert, and Martha Crawford.
1746, July —. Dodd, Thomas, and Sarah Belles.
1765, Feb. 25. Dodge, Isaac, and Rebecca Wood.
1762, Aug. 25. Dod, Sarah, and Jonathan Nortin.
1745, Jan. —. Dodson, John.
1773, June 24. Doffield, Peter, and Margaret Finley.
1769, July 12. Doggad, Mary, and Gibert Anderson.
1773, Jan. 7. Dogharty, Catharine, and Fincher Hellings.
1769, Feb. 23. Dogharty, Michael, and Sarah Shilly.
1769, Apr. 1. Dogharty, William, and Mary Bamford.
1769, Jan. 11. Doil, Jonathan, and Ann Matthews.
1762, Sep. 6. Dolbo, Gabriel, and Mary Adams.
1775, June 10. Dolby, Daniel, and Mary Snow.
1774, Dec. 15. Dolby, Martha, and John Earle.
1770, July 19. Dolneck, Catharine, and Henry Dortsman.
1768, Dec. 5. Dominick, Henry, and Elizabeth Welsh.
1760, June 25. Donahew, Jane, and Joshua Kootolow.
1764, M'ch 29. Donalds, Hannah, and James Harvey.
1762, M'ch 23. Donaldson, Andrew, and Eleanor Toy.
1764, Feb. 10. Donaldson, Ann, and James Clark.
1763, Sep. 15. Donaldson, Arthur, and Elizabeth Keighan.
1765, Aug. 1. Donaldson, Eleanor, and William Fullerton.
1770, Dec. 12. Donaldson, Helen, and George Campbell, Esq.
1763, Dec, 12. Donaldson, James, and Hannah Jones.
1772, July 6. Donaldson, James, and Mary Best.
1763, Jan. 22. Donaldson, Mary, and Daniel Brown.
1770, Dec. 31. Donaldson, William, and Sarah Griscomb.
1762, Feb. 6. Donavan, Susannah, and George Thompson.

1747, Aug. —. Donavon, Ann, and Patrick Corbit.
1747, Feb. —. Donavon, Elizabeth, and Thomas Oliver.
1761, May 28. Donaway, Matthew, and Elizabeth Scout.
1767, M'ch 24. Done, Mahitable, and Samuel Kirk.
1761, Feb. 3. Done, Martha, and John Facundus.
1765, Apr. 22. Donnally, Elizabeth, and Joseph Mullen.
1775, May 18. Donnell, Nathaniel, and Elizabeth Conyngham.
1760, Feb. 29. Donnel, Nathaniel, and Ann Cummerford.
1765, Apr. 25. Donovan, Lydia, and George McClay.
1762, Dec. 15. Donovan, Rachel, and Patrick Flynn.
1761, Sep. 8. Doran, John, and Isabella McGorough.
1744, May, —. Doraugh, James.
1769, July 15. Dordes, Catharine, and Daniel Haley.
1773, July 5. Dorland, Catharine, and James Scott.
1770, Jan. 22. Dorland, Hermina, and Charles Hufty.
1773, Sep. 10. Dorohue, John, and Joanna Townsley.
1761, Dec. 12. Dorrel, Henry, and Ann Tosst.
1766, June 12. Dorsey, Elizabeth, and Owen McCarty.
1770, July 19. Dortsman, Henry, and Catharine Dolneck.
1766, May 2. Dorvill, John, and Elizabeth Kearnes.
1765, June 13. Double, Mary, and Nicholas Young.
1760, Oct. 30. Dougherty, Charles, and Sophia Price.
1764, Nov. 23. Dougherty, Dennis, and Margaret Murphy.
1761, M'ch 21. Dougherty, Dudley, and Ann Kelsey.
1767, June 25. Dougherty, James, and Mary Wilson.
1767, Jan. 20. Dougherty, Mary, and Jacob Lobb.
1767, Aug. 1. Dougherty, Mary, and Joseph Delevan.
1764, Oct. 10. Dougherty, Susannah, and Israel Taylor.
1770, Feb. 21. Doughton, John, and Grace Coles.
1772, Apr. 16. Doughty, Abigail, and Benjamin Towne.
1768, Apr. 21. Doughty, Ann, and Daniel Badger.
1745, Dec. —. Doughty, Ebenezer.
1772, Feb. 6. Doughty, James, and Margaret Young.
1775, July 15. Doughty, Rebecca, and Cornelius Farrin.
1763, Jan. 13. Doughty, Robert, and Elizabeth Garrigues.
1773, Oct. 13. Douglass, Alexander, and Margaret Porterfield.
1767, Dec. 8. Douglass, George, and Elizabeth Howel.
1772, Aug. 10. Douglass, John, and Ann Jones.
1747, Oct. —. Douglass, Margaret, and Patrick Carrighan.
1763, Jan. 28. Douglass, Mary, and David Howell.
1774, June 16. Douglass, Mary, and Richard Graham.
1762, Sep. 20. Doulbear, Sophia, and George Smith.
1764, Oct. 23. Dove, Robert, and Isabella Hunton.
1768, Feb. 24. Dowdishle, Jacob, and Barbara Taylor.
1764, May 9. Dowdney, Nathaniel, and Sarah Loanan.
1773, Apr. 8. Dow, Elijah, and Rebecca Jones.

1776, Feb. 26. Dowell, Grace, and William Parr, Esq.
1769, Aug. 24. Dowell, Mary, and Hugh Read.
1762, May 18. Dowell. William, and Grace Peel.
1770, Sep. 11. Dowers, Catharine, and George Claypoole.
1764, Apr. 20. Dowig, George Christophel, and Margaretta Holliday.
1761, Aug. 5. Dowins, Francis, and Jane Grimes.
1773, Feb. 24. Dowlin, Paul, and Margaret Brown.
1774, Feb. 19. Dowman, Thomas, and Elizabeth Deshler.
1773, M'ch 11. Downes, Sarah, and William Fletcher.
1775, Apr. 1. Downes, William, and Ann Gerrard.
1775, Apr. 20. Downey, Bridget, and Walter Correy.
1775, Apr. 6. Downey, John, and Ann Elizabeth Yeates.
1775, Nov. 27. Downing, Jane, and John Baldwin.
1769, Apr. 14. Down, Mary, and William Tennant.
1746, Feb. —. Down, Robert.
1762, Aug. 21. Downs, Francis, and Sarah Grimes.
1765, Oct. 4. Downey, Thomas, and Mary Robinson.
1743, May 27. Dowree.
1763, Jan. 26. Dowsey, Elizabeth, and Thurston Browne.
1775, Feb. 20. Dowterman, Juliana, and Michael Albright. .
1766, Dec. 24. Dowthaitt, Mary, and Thomas Wall.
1743, June 13. Dowthwaits, Samuel.
1762, July 8. Doyle, John, and Hannah Wister.
1762, Apr. 8. Doyle, Deborah, and Bartholomew Sutton.
1767, July 25. Doyle, Hannah, and Thomas Magrah.
1774, Oct. 7. Doyle, Martha, and Robert Gill.
1770, M'ch 2. Doyle, Mary, and Elisha Griffith.
1773, Jan. 20. Doyle, Patterson, and Susannah Clancy.
1767, Feb. 16. Doyle, Richard, and Sarah Barton.
1768, Oct. 4. Doyle, Ruth, and James Crawford.
1775, Nov. 1. Doyl, Mary, and John Tipler.
1745, M'ch —. Dracord, Ralph.
1767, June 6. Drake, Affa, and George Smith.
1762, Jan. 9. Drake, Benjamin, and Rachael Davis.
1762, Feb. 3. Drake, Deborah, and William Boram.
1771, Jan. 22. Drake, Jacob, and Elizabeth Neely.
1761, July 20. Drake, Mary and Japeth Thomas.
1760, Oct. 14. Drake, Thomas, and Uriah Humphrey.
1776, M'ch 14. Draper, Jonathan, and Edith Gardner.
1761, Oct. 21. Draper, Mary, and Cadwall Dickinson.
1763, Sep. 10. Draper, Sarah, and Jacob Potts.
1767, Nov. 28. Drew, Joseph, and Margaret May.
1767, Sep. 27. Drewry, William, and Sarah Wolley.
1773, Jan. 23. Drift, Catharine, and John Moss.
1773, Feb. 18. Drinker, Deborah, and Thomas Harper.

1775, M'ch 27. Driscoll, Ann, and John Craig.
1746, Sep. —. Driver, Lydia, and Abram Worthington.
1768, Dec. 1. Dubbing, Edward, and Elizabeth Masho.
1776, May 1. DuBois, Abraham, and Elizabeth Cheeseman.
1774, Aug. 31. Dubre, Susannah, and Thomas Palmer.
1761, July 4. Dubrey, John, and Margery Hall.
1763, Apr. 28. Duche, Ann, and John Moyer.
1770, Apr. 24. Duche, Anthony, and Sarah Falconer.
1760, June 18. Duchee, Jacob, and Elizabeth Hopkinson.
1747, June —. Duchee, Jacob, and Esther Bradley.
1764, Apr. 9. Duche, John, and Jane Clark.
1774, July 19. Duche, Lydia, and Richard Paul.
1763, Oct. 8. Duddle, Thomas, and Catharine Forrest.
1762, Nov. 10. Dudley, Thomas, and Martha Evens.
1774, Jan. 25. Duer, John, Jun., and Jane Hollingshead.
1763, Apr. 16. Duff, Ann, and Matthew Moore.
1763, May 19. Duffey, John, and Anna Murfey.
1774, Feb. 1. Duffield, Hannah, and Thomas Groom.
1767, Nov. 12. Duffield, Jacob, and Mary Addis.
1767, Dec. 29. Duffield, John, and Mary Budden.
1773, May 29. Duffield, Joseph, and Deborah Ingle.
1768, June 13. Duffield, Mary, and Jonathan Gostelow.
1773, Jan. 11. Duffield, Phebe, and William Cox.
1760, M'ch 5. Duffill, Mary, and Thomas Humphreys.
1761, July 21. Duff, John, and Elizabeth Dennis.
1774, Dec. 8. Duffy, Patrick, and Margaret Miller.
1776, Jan. 24. Duffy, Peter, and Phebe Williams.
1776, June 29. Dugan, Jane, and Peter Purser.
1764, Aug. 1. Dugan, Samuel, and Elizabeth Watson.
1770, Feb. 9. Dugan, Walter, and Jane Thomas.
1776, June 19. Duguis, Agnes, and Thomas Emerson.
1746, Aug. —. Dukemancer, Frances, and John Celfrey.
1774, Sep. 23. Duke, Thomas, and Catharine Hartley.
1774, Sep. 6. Dull, Casper, and Hannah Mathews.
1770, Oct. 31. Dunbar, Martha, and Alexander Ramsay.
1771, Aug. 29. Dunbar, Eleanor, and William Kemble.
1771, M'ch 7. Dunbar, John, and Mary Cass.
1765, Aug. 13. Dunbar, Thomas, and Hannah Higgins.
1767, Oct. 19. Duncan, Elliot, and Jane McGruger.
1743, July 1. Duncan, Francis.
1745, Nov. —. Duncan, John.
1763, Nov. 9. Duncan, Mary, and Samuel Brookhouse.
1767, Feb. 3. Duncan, Thomas, and Eleanor Malone.
1776, Apr. 10. Duncan, William, and Rosanna Gallagher.
1770, Oct. 24. Dungan, Ann, and George Vanada.
1764, Oct. 17. Dungan, Benjamin, and Esther Cetman.

1773, July 21. Dungan, Clement, and Sarah Bond.
1762, Feb.   1. Dungan, Daniel, and Martha Lockley.
1769, Nov. 23. Dungan, Elizabeth, and Benjamin Comley
1760, Nov. 15. Dungan, Enoch, and Elizabeth Hufty.
1761, M'ch   2. Dungan, Garret, and Sophia Bennet.
1773, Nov. 12. Dungan, Hannah, and Benjamin Marple.
1774, June   6. Dungan, James, and Catharine Jones.
1762 Nov.   24. Dungan Jeremiah, and Mary Witton.
1744, May —. Dungan, John.
1771, Dec. 14. Dungan, John, and Phebe Corbett.
1772, Dec.   8. Dungan, Jonathan, and Agnes Kelton.
1764, Sep.   5. Dungan, Joseph, and Elizabeth Carrol.
1773, Apr.   3. Dungan, Joshua, and Sarah Cawley.
1764, Feb.   1. Dungan, Levy, and Mary Davis.
1775, Dec. 30. Dungan, Nathan, and Jane Gouly.
1761, Oct. 17. Dungan, Sarah, and Benjamin Fisher.
1761, Apr.   7. Dunging, Hannah, and Richard Johnson.
1761, July 11. Dunging, Massey, and Jacob Fisher.
1768, Sep. 16. Dungin, Lucretia, and Richard Rundle.
1765, Sep. 16. Dunkin, Robert, and Ann Henry.
1763, April 9. Dunklit, Elizabeth, and William Woodward.
1773, Feb.   3. Dunlap, John, and Elizabeth Ellison.
1763, Apr.   2. Dunlap, John, and Mary Boyd.
1770, Apr. 12. Dunlap, Mary, and Robert Coupar.
1765, July 25. Dunlap, Robert, and Sarah Hood.
1773, Feb.   4. Dunlap, Samuel, and Mary Ann Howey.
1762, Aug. 26. Dunlap, William, and Elinor McCoughen.
1775, June 23. Dunn, Archibald, and Mary Maher.
1764, June   1. Dunnawin, Mary, and Benjamin Rawlins.
1773, Apr. 26. Dunn, Bridget, and Robert Connoly.
1773, Sep. 18. Dunn, David, and Lydia Calvan.
1770, July 23. Dunn, Elizabeth, and Hugh McKinley.
1770, Oct. 24. Dunn, George, and Mary Curry.
1747, Dec. —. Dunn, Henry, and Hannah Totten.
1763, M'ch 12. Dunning, Elizabeth, and Peter Staets.
1768, June 17. Dunn, James, and Isabella Jordan.
1762, Sep.   8. Dunn, John, and Ann Hopewell.
1771, Aug. 19. Dunn, John, and Mary Sowder.
1775, Dec   9. Dunn, Margaret, and James Johnston.
1768, Sep. 12. Dunn, Martha, and Samuel Johnson.
1771, June, 13. Dunn, Mary, and Thomas Brown.
1768, Nov. 26. Dunn, Patrick, and Ann McKee.
1744, Dec. —. Dunn, Ralph.
1766, Sep. 13. Dunn, William, and Bridget Wigmire.
1772, May 14. Dunton, William, and Mary Statler.
1761, Dec.   8. Dunwick, William, and Catharine Williams.

1774, Nov. 29. Dunwoody, Susannah, and William Hamble.
1775, May 11. Dupice, Jane, and William Coates.
1771, Oct. 2. Dupree, Ann, and Stephen Tucker.
1746, Sep. —. Dupuy, Daniel, and Eleanor Dylander.
1748, Oct. 18. Durborrow, Elizabeth, and Jonathan Case.
1765, Oct. 16. Durborrow, Isaac, and Elizabeth Newton.
1744, May 28. Durell, Jonathan.
1770, Nov. 7. Durf, William, and Christiana Holtzhouser.
,1746, Dec. —. Durham, Stephen, and Jane Wilson.
1761, Aug. 28. Durmady, Hannah, and Robert Collitt.
1764, Apr. 5. Durows, Jane, and Robert Martin.
1772, Jan. 17. Durrow, John, and Elizabeth Kelly.
1768, Jan. 28. Durvey, Mary, and Joseph Clark.
1760, M'ch 3. Dushane, Eleanor, and Henry Tuder.
1767, Feb. 2. Dushong, Frederick, and Margaret Keplering.
1772, Feb. 20. Dutton, Elizabeth, and Nicholas Pump.
1775, Sep. 23. Dutton, James, and Lydia Kimler.
1773, Apr. 28. Dutton, Sarah, and Peter Brown.
1746, Jan. —. Duysbrugh, George.
1768, Dec. 1. Dwine, Nicholas, and Susannah Kearney.
1775, May 22. Dwir, Bridget, and Ananias Cooper.
1768, Sep. 29. Dwyer, Catharine, and Arthur Haggin.
1760, Jan. 10. Dwyt, Grace, and John Cole.
1748, Oct. 18. Dyer, Dennis, and Abigail Edwards.
1775, Nov. 9. Dyer, John, and Sarah Briggs.
1772, Oct. 20. Dyer, Mary, and Archibald Morrison.
1766, Oct. 8. Dyer, Mary, and Patrick Lesley.
1773, Jan. 21 Dyer, Sarah, and Benjamin Thomas.
1746, Oct. —. Dyke, Nathan, and Sarah Johnson.
1763, May 4. Dykes, Nathan, and Sarah Banks.
1746, Sep. —. Dylander, Eleanor, and Daniel Dupuy.

E.

1775, Sep. 4. Eachus, William, and Mary Richard.
1772, Apr. 8 Eakan, Mary, and George Barr.
1771, Apr. 19 Earhottin, Barbara, and Adam Wertman.
1774, Dec 15 Earle, John, and Martha Dolby.
1745, June —. Early, Stephen.
1745, Sep. —. Early, Stephen.
1773, Dec. 18. Eastburn, Benjamin, and Margaret Abraham.
1769, Feb. 18. Eastburn, Benjamin, and Mary Newall.
1771, June 10. Eastburn, Joseph, and Anne Owen.
1763, M'ch 29. Eastburn, Mary, and Samuel Roberts.
1769, Feb. 14. Easterd, Anne, and Henry Van Reed.
1767, June 11. Eastlack, Hannah, and Aaron Kemble.
1762, Nov. 18. Eastlack, John, and Sarah Hampton.
1763, Oct. 27. Eastlack, Reuben, and Ann Flemings.

1768, Oct. 25. Eastlack, Samuel, and Hannah Ellis.
1760. Jan. 7. Eaton, Benjamin, and Miziam Lowber.
1760, Sep. 25. Eaton, David, and Mary Eaton.
1766, June 14. Eaton, Edith, and John James.
1773, M'ch 27. Eaton, Edward, and Hester Kinnerd.
1762, Sep. 25. Eaton, Elizabeth, and James James.
1772, Apr. 14. Eaton, Martha, and Stephen Watts.
1760, Sep. 25. Eaton, Mary, and David Eaton.
1774. Oct. 19. Eaton, Mary, and Isaac Williams.
1759, Dec. 29. Eaton, Mary, and John Boys.
1773, Aug. 12. Eaton, Peter, and Margaret Evans.
1768, Aug. 27. Eavenson, Richard, and Mary Johnson.
1761, Jan. 17. Eckhart, William, and Mary Streighkan.
1761, M'ch 7. Eckleson, Sarah, and George Russel.
1748, M'ch 11. Ecoff, Mary, and Thomas Kennard.
1771, Apr. 2. Ecroyad, Elizabeth, and Samuel Young.
1756, Aug. 10. Edes, Edith, and John Oliver.
1761, June 27. Edgar, Elizabeth, and Benjamin Pyne.
1760, July 23. Edgecombe, Elizabeth, and Stephen Reeves.
1776, Apr. 8. Edgar, Martha, and John Murray.
1745, July. —. Edge, Robert.
1769, July 21. Edminston, Hannah, and William Jamison.
1770, Nov. 20. Edmiston, John, and Sarah Edmiston.
1770. Nov. 20. Edmiston, Sarah, and John Edmiston.
1748, Oct. 18. Edwards, Abigail, and Dennis Dyer.
1759, Nov. 28. Edwards, Andros, and Rachel Parmel.
1772, Nov. 5. Edwards, Alexander, and Eliza Morgan.
1771, Feb. 13. Edwards, Anne, and William McDowell.
1748, June 16. Edwards, Ann, and John Williams.
1760, Oct. 28. Edwards, Ann, and Joseph Russel.
1760, Dec. 19. Edwards, Ann, and William Daley.
1773, Nov. 2. Edwards, Catharine, and Jacob Bentson Tested.
1767, M'ch 13, Edwards, David, and Mary Evans.
1760, June 10. Edwards, Edward, and Mary Grace.
1747, Apr. —. Edwards, Eleanor, and Griffy Evans.
1764, May 10. Edwards, Elizabeth, and Elias Butner.
1761, May 12. Edwards, Elizabeth, and John Roberts.
1747, Oct. —. Edwards, Elizabeth, and Thomas Crimmen.
1746, Jan. —. Edwards, Evan.
1769, Jan. 7. Edwards, Hannah, and John Cope.
1772, Mar. 11. Edwards, Jemima, and Charles Wharton.
1746, Jan. —. Edwards, John.
1765, April 1. Edwards, John, and Ann Griffith.
1766, Aug. 13. Edwards, John, and Margaret Brown.
1771, Aug. 8. Edwards, John, and Martha Moore.
1774, July 2. Edwards, John, and Mary Hallowell.

1765, June 19. Edwards, John, and Rachel Gregory.
1761, Nov. 11. Edwards, Joseph, and Hannah Register.
1762, July 10, Edwards, Joseph, and Margaret Read.
1762, Jan. 23. Edwards, Lydia. and Jacob Bealert.
1768, Oct. 13. Edwards, Marshall, and Martha Holmes.
1763, Oct. 31. Edwards, Mary, and George Wright.
1768, June 9. Edwards, Mary, and Isaac Taylor.
1761, Mar, 7. Edwards, Mary, and Miles Helborn.
1771, May 3. Edwards, Morgan, Rev., and Elizabeth Singleton.
1768, July 2. Edwards, Rachel, and John Lucken.
1771, Mar. 25. Edwards, Rachel, and Joseph Comely.
1746, June —. Edwards, Rebecca, and James Cowper.
1761, June 24. Edwards, Tamar, and Thomas James.
1772, Aug. 14. Edwards, Thomas, and Hannah Roberts.
1768, Mar. 14. Edwards, William, and Hannah Hall.
1747, Oct. —. Edwards, William, and Isabel Chalmler.
1771, Aug. 20. Edwards, William, and Jane Carson.
1768, Aug. 1. Edwards, William, and Mary White.
1770, May 10. Edwards, William, and Susannah Albertson.
1772, Mar. 17. Egan, Nicholas, and Ann Seymore.
1770, June 25. Egdar, Elizabeth, and William Caldwell.
1747, Nov. —. Eggar, Thomas, and Elizabeth Ellis.
1759, Dec. 15. Egle, Margaret, and Robert Kennedy.
1763, Mar. 30. Eichus, Michael, and Alice Kaplin.
1768, Jan. 26. Ekins, Jane, and Charles Lindsay.
1760, Nov. 1. Elder, Elizabeth, and John Craig.
1748, Feb. —. Elder, Elizabeth, and Peter Matthew.
1744, Aug. 13. Elder, John.
1774, June 23. Elder, Joseph, and Ann Folger.
1762, Nov. 10. Eldridge, James, and Hannah Evans.
1766, May 19. Eldridge, Patience, and Thomas Barton.
1761, Nov. 6. Eldridge, William, and Deboro Mayland.
1763, April 5. Element, Joseph, and Catharine Cox.
1762, July 23. Eliott, George, and Charity Addidle.
1762, Jan. 16. Elizabeth, Mary, and George Frank.
1748, June 16. Elleson, Margaret, and Charles Geltoy.
1747, Nov. —. Ellet, Thomas, and Bridget Peters.
1768, April 18. Elliart, Jane, and Matthew Abel.
1760, May 29. Ellick, John, and Katharine Walner.
1761, June 6. Ellicot, John, and Leah Brown.
1744, April —. Ellin, John.
1774, Sept. 15. Elliot, Anne, and Henry Hanvest.
1773, Jan. 20. Elliot, Ann, and Thomas Corgal.
1765, May 10. Elliot, Barbara, and Matthew Henderson.
1772, Oct. 31. Elliot, Binkey, and Daniel Huger.
1775, Oct. 10. Elliot, Chloe, and George Forsyth.

1767, Jan. 14. Elliot, Elizabeth, and Samuel Caruthers.
1768, Nov. 26. Elliot, John, and Amy Davis.
1762, Feb. 13. Elliot, John, and Mary Thomas.
1770, Jan. 1. Elliot, Levina, and William Gillilan.
1768, June 24. Elliot, Margaret, and Henry Dawson.
1762, Sep. 10. Ellis, Catharine, and James Bullis.
1747, Nov. —. Ellis, Elizabeth, and Thomas Eggar.
1768, Oct. 25. Ellis, Hannah, and Samuel Eastlack.
1745, May —. Ellis, John.
1764, Apr. 9. Ellis, Joseph, and Sarah Hugg.
1767, Aug. 29. Ellis, Mary, and Henry McBride.
1770, Nov. 22. Ellis, Mary, and Peter Long.
1773, Feb. 3. Ellison, Elizabeth, and John Dunlap.
1774, Nov. 8. Ellison, Simon, and Ann Bevan.
1775, Aug. 17. Ellison, Thomas, and Frances Crook.
1764, Aug. 10. Ellis, Reuben, and Hannah Schrach.
1744, Jan. —. Ellis, Richard.
1744, Nov. —. Ellis, Richard.
1745, Sep. —. Ellis, Richard.
1760, Dec. 19. Ellis, Rowland, and Hannah Whitebread.
1765, M'ch 28. Ellis, Thomas, and Sarah Stinson.
1748, May 14. Ellis, William, and Rebecca Collins.
1772, Dec. 16. Elton, Mary, and Jacob Schreck.
1763, Apr. 6. Elton, Robert, and Margaret Hart.
1774, Nov. 10. Elton, Thomas, and Susannah Wood.
1744, Oct. —. Elwis, Henry.
1770, Oct. 22. Ely, Isaac, and Mary Carson.
1748, Jan. —. Ely, Thomas, and Sarah Dicks.
1747, May —. Emerson, Ann, and William McIlvain.
1764, Sep. 12. Emerson, Reuben, and Joyce Palmer.
1748, July 16. Emerson, Lambert.
1776, June 19. Emerson, Thomas, and Agnes Duguis.
1747, Nov. --. Emmerson, Mary, and James Kappock.
1773, Apr. 20. Emmes, John, and Mary Mitchell.
1748, July 13. Emmit, Hannah, and David Griffith.
1771, May 20. Empson, Judith, and Nicholas Rash.
1761, Sep. 25. Empson, William, and Juliana Amos.
1775, Oct. 7. Emricken, Mary, and Henry Clevenstine.
1774, Dec. 3. Emrick, Balthazer, and Mary Reese.
1763, Jan. 5. Emson, Mary, and Jonathan Hulings.
1762, Aug. 17. Encey, Mary, and John Andrew.
1761, Aug. 13. Endt, Mary, and George Miller.
1772, Oct. 19. England, Cornelia, and James King.
1773, Sep. 10. England, Martha, and Joseph Miley.
1774, Feb. 24. England, Mary, and William Justice.
6—Vol. II.

1745, Aug. —. Engle, Peter
1765, Jan. 10. Engles, Silas, and Mary Trent.
1770, M'ch 22. English, Anne, and Jedediah Snowden.
1763, Jan. 1. English, Elizabeth, and John Little.
1770, Dec. 19. English, Susannah, and John Butler.
1764, Nov. 5. Ennery, William, and Martha Naugle.
1763, May 14. Ennis, James, and Jane Johnson.
1775, June 7. Ennis, Richard, and Mary Rinedollar.
1769, Jan. 28. Enser, George, and Mary Burk.
1746, Dec. —. Ernest, George, and Elue Mary Sneider.
1773, M'ch 3. Ernest, Elizabeth, and George Henry Beck.
1775, Dec. 5. Erwin, Alice, and Francis Johnston.
1771, July 27. Erwin, Arthur, and Mary Kennedy.
1774, Dec. 7. Erwin, Eleanor, and Conrad Hoober.
1764, Feb. 28. Erwin, Elizabeth, and Richard Templin.
1764, Feb. 20. Erwin, Elizabeth, and Samuel Lowry.
1774, June 27. Erwin, Margaret, and Matthew Henderson.
1760, Apr. 1. Erwin, Sarah, and Matthew Baines.
1761, Sep. 7. Eshbaugh, Margaret, and David Levy.
1772, Oct. 5. Eshinbaugh, John, and Rebecca Zimmerman.
1774, Sep. 17. Esler, Henry, and Ann John.
1776, May 21. Eslick, Sarah, and George Swanton.
1748, June 16. Espy, Mary, and James Carson.
1769, June 24. Esserwine, John, and Abigail Roberts.
1767, Apr. 29. Estlack, Ann, and Ebenezer Turner.
1763, Aug. 17. Estlack, William, and Diana Shute.
1765, Jan. 17. Etter, Elizabeth, and Emanuel Bartling.
1773, June 21. Eustace, Charles, and Rachel Fitz Randolph.
1759, Dec. 27. Evan, Benjamin, and Elizabeth Baker.
1769, M'ch 18. Evans, Abigail, and Joshua Ash.
1771, May 30. Evans, Abraham, and Sarah Price.
1763, May 11. Evans, Amy, and Samuel Pugh.
1770, Oct. 30. Evans, Anne, and John Butcher.
1771, Oct. 5. Evans, Bernard, and Ann Kelly.
1761, Jan. 9. Evans, Catharine, and Mordecai Evans.
1772, Dec. 23. Evans, Cornelia, and Barnaby Bright.
1762, Oct. 23. Evans, Daniel, and Anna Brooks.
1776, Apr. 19. Evans, Daniel, and Elizabeth Guest.
1760, M'ch 28. Evans, Daniel, and Martha James.
1761, Aug. 15. Evans, David, and Mary Hutton.
1764, M'ch 9. Evans, David, and Susannah Morris.
1775, Nov. 6. Evans, Edward, and Ann Ladd.
1770, May 17. Evans, Eleanor, and Hugh James.
1745, Apr. —. Evans, Eliazer.
1766, Apr. 7. Evans, Elizabeth, and Daniel Phile.
1772, Apr. 10. Evans, Elizabeth, and Josiah James.

1771, May 22. Evans, Elizabeth, and Manassah Thomas.
1747, Nov. —. Evans, Elizabeth, and Nathaniel West.
1761, M'ch 14. Evans, Elizabeth, and Richard Gardner.
1761, Aug. 21. Evans, Elizabeth, and Thomas Pugh.
1767, Jan. 21. Evans, Evan, and Hannah Simcocks.
1764, Jan. 23. Evans, George, and Elizabeth North.
1747, Apr. —. Evans, Griffy, and Eleanor Edwards.
1762, Nov. 10. Evans, Hannah, and James Eldridge.
1773, Aug. 11. Evans, Hannah, and Joseph Huddle.
1761, Dec. 17. Evans, Hannah, and Nathaniel Richards.
1764, June 21. Evans, Hannah, and Samuel Robins.
1771, M'ch 14. Evans, Jacob, and Hannah Morris.
1771, Jan. 16. Evans, James, and Mary Brook.
1764, May 22. Evans, Jane, and John Thomas.
1772, Aug. 26. Evans, John, and Agnes Barnet.
1760, Feb. 2. Evans, John, and Hannah Griffiths.
1748, M'ch 11. Evans, John, and Sarah Denny.
1770, Nov. 27. Evans, Jonathan, and Mary Matthias.
1764, Nov. 19. Evans, Jonathan, and Sarah Kirk.
1764, Dec. 12. Evans, Joshua, and Mary Thomas.
1775, April 8. Evans, Levi, and Susannah Barton.
1744, Jan. —. Evans, Lewis.
1747, Nov. —. Evans, Lot, and Jane Patterson.
1773, Aug. 12. Evans, Margaret, and Peter Eaton.
1765, May 13. Evans, Martha, and Jacob Jackson.
1766, June 11. Evans, Martha, and Samuel McKinstry.
1762, Nov. 10. Evans, Martha, and Thomas Dudley.
1774, Sept. 6. Evans, Mary, and Charles Ferguson, Jr.
1767, Mar. 13. Evans, Mary, and David Edwards.
1772, April 10. Evans, Mary, and George Sheed.
1746, Oct. —. Evans, Mary, and James Scot.
1763, Oct. 27. Evans, Mary, and Joseph Cassett.
1767, Aug. 5. Evans, Mary, and Mungrel Peters.
1772, Nov 11. Evans, Mary, and William Peyton.
1776, Jan. 31. Evans, Mary, and Zachariah Davis.
1761, Jan. 9. Evans, Mordecai, and Catharine Evans.
1748, Sep. —. Evans, Morris, and Mary Buchan.
1747, M'ch —. Evanson, Mary, and Richard Barret.
1746, May —. Evanson, Nathaniel.
1761, Nov. 21. Evanson, Richard, and Sarah Micham.
1761, Apr. 22. Evans, Peter, and Rachel Evans.
1776, Jan. 31. Evans, Phebe, and George Priest.
1775, June 10. Evans, Priscilla, and Samuel Thomas.
1761, Apr. 22. Evans, Rachel, and Peter Evans.
1768, Feb. 7. Evans, Rebecca, and David Swain.
1760, Apr. 30. Evans, Rebecca, and Garret Vanzant.

1774, Apr.   27. Evans, Rebecca, and William Corker Cooper.
1761, Jan.   29. Evans, Rees, and Hannah Nedham.
1764, M'ch   27. Evans, Robert, and Jane Pugh.
1771, Dec.   19. Evans, Robert, and Martha Taylor.
1773, Jan.   9. Evans, Ruth, and Abraham Free.
1769, Aug.   2. Evans, Ruth, and John Scotton,
1773, Sep.   2. Evans, Ruth, and Moses Peters.
1772, Jan.   21. Evans, Sarah, and Adam Hubley.
1771, May   13. Evans, Sarah, and Charles Humphrey.
1763, Apr.   11. Evans, Sarah, and George Geary.
1769, Apr.   14. Evans, Sarah, and Jacob Coburn.
1765, Apr.   25. Evans, Sarah, and James Megettigen.
1744, Apr.   ---. Evans, Simons.
1764, Dec.   29. Evans, Susannah, and Jacob Brenneman.
1748, Aug.   15. Evans, Thomas.
1767, May   4. Evans, Thomas, and Elizabeth Moore.
1774, Apr.   28. Evans, Thomas, and Mary Morris.
1764, Nov.   5. Evans, William, and Grace Buzby.
1771, Apr.   16. Evans, William, and Margaret Davis.
1770, May   9. Eve, John, and Jane Campbell.
1773, Oct.   14. Even, John, and Elizabeth Few.
1744, May   28. Eve, Oswald.
1770, Feb.   16. Everard, George, and Mary Myers.
1773, M'ch   24. Everhart, John, and Catharine Mouse.
1762, Sep.   20. Everly, Catharine, and John Smith.
1764, Aug.   13. Eves, Jane, and Moses Gurlin.
1766, Sep.   3. Evitt, William, and Elizabeth Palmer.
1773, Oct.   6. Evry, Susannah, and Richard Broderick.
1770, Nov.   26. Evy, Mary, and John Williams.
1747, May   ---. Ewalt, Charles, and Catharine Pezoman.
1767, Oct.   27. Ewer, Ann, and Jenkins Jones.
1762, Oct.   13. Ewer, John, and Sarah Gladny.
1762, Sep.   8. Ewer, Jonathan, and Elizabeth Barton.
1761, Jan.   21. Ewer, Mary, and Thomas Jones.
1772, Oct.   3. Ewer, Robert, and Mary Kelsey
1760, Nov.   12. Ewing, Henry, and Jane Allen.
1747, May   ---. Ewres, Mary, and John Smallwood.
1769, Nov.   29. Eyre, Benjamin George, and Hester Boyte.
1761, Dec.   28. Eyre, John, and Lydia Wright.
1761, Jan.   8. Eyre, Manuel, and Mary Wright.
1773, May   24. Eyres, Richard, and Sophia Nicholson.
1770, Feb.   26. Eyrick, John, and Elizabeth Cowsan.
1747, Oct.   ---. Eyris, Rebecca, and Joseph Friend.

F.

1766, Dec.   24. Faber, Henry, and Mary Stulberger.
1747, June —. Fabes. Hannah, and Thomas Betty.
1761, Feb.   3. Facundus, John, and Martha Done.
1761, Apr.   27. Faedley, Esther, and George Grush.
1761, Dec.   9. Fagan, Charles, and Deborah Buckley.
1763, Jan.   29. Fagan, Elizabeth, and Adam Seishols.
1772, Apr.   2. Fagan, Henry, and Rebecca Vandegrift.
1760, Feb,   19. Fagan, John, and Elizabeth Holme.
1764, M'ch   3. Faines, Jacob, and Catharine Past.
1769, Apr.   10. Fairbuttle, Elizabeth, and Cuthbert Landreth.
1760, Apr.   28. Fairchild, Isabella, and Skinner Sarrup.
1760, Nov.   26. Faires, Zacharias, and Margaret Knox.
1774, Nov.   20. Fairland, Samuel, and Hannah Richardson
1769, Aug,   16, Fairy, James, and Elizabeth Kale.
1770, Apr.   12. Falconer, Ephraim, and Mary Shafford.
1762, June   12. Falconer, Joseph, and Rachel Collins.
1743, June   30. Falconer, Magnus.
1770, Apr.   24. Falconer, Sarah, and Anthony Duche.
1768, Feb.   15. Falconer, Sarah, and James Thompson.
1771, Oct.   15. Falkenstein, Jacob, and Catharine Hart.
1763, Apr.   14. Falkner, Elizabeth, and Francis Faries.
1764, M'ch   1. Falkner, Lester, and Sarah Penrose.
1763, Nov.   26. Falkner, Mary, and Thomas Robison.
1764, Dec.   17. Falkner, Susannah, and William Clark.
1748, Nov.   11. Falkner, William, and Abigail Harcob.
1762, M'ch   30. Falkner, William, and Heclace Ganard.
1760, M'ch   28. Fallwell, John, and Elizabeth Caster.
1772, Dec.   3. Fandlin, Barbara, and Samuel Poole.
1763, Apr.   4. Fanendus, Marie Margaretta, and Jacob Glows.
1771, Jan.   1. Fanning, Joseph, and Lydia Grice.
1773, Jan.   26. Fanning, Joshua, and Ann Read.
1770, Jan.   10. Farguson, Charles, and Anne Musgrove.
1767, Dec.   10. Faries, Elizabeth, and James Cochran.
1763, Apr.   14. Faries, Francis, and Elizabeth Falkner.
1766, Feb.   8. Faries, James, and Elizabeth Stevens.
1774, M'ch   7, Faries, Margaret, and Tobias Rambo,
1764, June   27. Faries, William, and Mary Forster.
1769, July   1. Faris, William, and Abigail Davis.
1771, June   13. Farmar, Patience, and David Bradshaw.
1762, June   5. Farmer, Catharine, and Booth Thomas.
1765, Apr.   13. Farmer, James, and Margaret Messner.
1768, M'ch   7. Farmer, Martha, and John Vance.
1765, Jan.   26. Farmer, Mary, and Richmond Allen.
1764, Apr.   20. Farmer, Sarah, and Andrew Purfield.
1743, Oct. —. Farmer, Thomas.

1765, Feb. 23. Farns, John, and Themisine Brown.
1764, July 16. Farnsworth, Rachel, and Josiah Jenkins.
1772, Apr. 22. Farran, John, and Mary Black.
1768, M'ch 24. Farrel, Catharine, and Gabriel Simpson.
1774, Feb. 28. Farrel, Elizabeth, and Martin Worknot.
1743, May 19. Farrel, James.
1772, Oct. 10. Farrel, Marv, and Patrick Barry.
1748, July 13. Farrel, Mary, and Thomas Boucher.
1746, Dec. —. Farrel, Michael, and Marv Moran.
1761, M'ch 24. Farrel, Rose, and James Welch.
1743, Oct. —. Farrey, John.
1773, Sep. 23. Farrier, Charles, and Rachel Christopher.
1775, July 15. Farrin, Cornelius, and Rebecca Doughty.
1774, Feb. 24. Farrington, Jane, and John Baldwin.
1766, May 19. Farr, Isaac, and Mary Musgrove.
1760, Aug. 20. Farris, William, and Mary Ranbury.
1761, July 29. Farr, John, and Catharine Myers.
1760, June 9. Farr, Mary, and Richard Kinton.
1774, Oct. 31. Fa_lin, Hans Adam, and Elizabeth Haines.
1760, Dec. 1. Fauntz, John, and Margaret Pauston.
1775, July 1. Favell, William, and Jane Hay.
1773, Apr. 17. Fawkes, John, and Sarah Lane.
1761, July 15. Fawset, Nathan, and Abba Wilkins.
1764, May 4. Feagan, Elizabeth, and James Garnick.
1768, Sep. 8 Fearis, Bernard, and Hannah White.
1766, May 10. Featherhead, George, and Hannah Stengis.
1770, Oct. 27. Feathers, Deborah, and Samuel Titus.
1762, June 1. Fechlman, Christopher, and Rebecca Kitts.
1774, M'ch 28. Fechter, John, and Catharine Hoffman.
1774, Apr. 22. Fegan, John, and Mary Kanan.
1746, Dec. —. Feghlvn, Margaret, and Nichols Craypeel.
1763, Oct. 10. Feiss, Peter, and Anna Maria Stocking.
1773, Apr. 1. Feit, Jacob, and Eleanor McCallaghan.
1746, May. —. Felby, Sebastian.
1760, Sep. 30. Fell, Benjamin, and Rebecca Cosner.
1770, Nov. 24. Fell, Mary, and William Marshall.
1761, M'ch 18. Fell, Thomas, and Mary Tay.
1762, Dec. 23. Felson, Mary, and Benjamin Shoemaker.
1771, June 29. Felton, Sarah, and John Sowder.
1764, May 21. Felwell, Thomas, and Elizabeth Watts.
1762, Sep. 3. Fendeberry, Derrick Cornelius, and Hannah
Ledlson.
1765, May 15. Fenimore, William, and Martha Mott.
1774, Dec. 20. Fennikle, Mary, and Baltzer Foggs.
1760, May 2. Fenny, George, and Sarah Whitefield.
1760, June 5. Fentle, Frederick, and Elizabeth Myer.

1773, June 17. Fenton, John, and Sarah Cawley.
1772, May 23. Fenton, Mary, and William Gilbert.
1760, Dec. 24. Fergeson, James, and Jane McFarrel.
1768, Feb. 11. Fergison, Hugh, and Ann Gibbs.
1761, Sep. 23. Fergueson, Catharine, and Samuel Davison.
1766, May 29. Fergunton, Abram, and Sarah Harrison.
1761. Aug. 1. Fergurson, John, and Rose McDavit.
1766, July 19. Ferguson, Agnes, and John Shaw.
1774, Sep. 6. Ferguson, Charles, Jun., and Mary Evans.
1767, Nov. 4. Ferguson, John, and Ann Bevan.
1768, Feb. 27. Ferguson, John, and Elizabeth McGill.
1765, May 15. Ferguson, John, and Margaret Mitchell.
1771, May 14. Ferguson, John, and Mary Magee.
1748, Sep. —. Ferguson, Joseph, and Martha Walner.
1770, Oct. 31. Ferguson, Margaret and, Francis Gottier.
1764, Apr. 24. Ferris, Esther, and William Ross.
1761, Jan. 8. Ferryby, Nathaniel, and Mary Cook.
1770, Aug. 15. Ferten, Matthias, and Rachel Hardy.
1773, M'ch 25. Fetter, George, and Hannah Righter.
1764, July 16. Fetter, Hannah, and Archibald McCormick.
1776, Jan. 30. Fetters, Mary, and Andrew Vanbuskirk.
1773, Oct. 14. Few, Elizabeth, and John Even.
1768, Feb. 22. Feyring, Julianna, and John Schneider.
1772, July 23. Fians, William, and Mary Rice.
1745, June —. Field, John.
1763, June 3. Field, John, and Mary Field.
1762, May 4. Field, John, and Sarah Coward.
1763, June 3. Field, Mary, and John Field.
1765, Oct. 22. Field, Robert, and Mary Peel.
1765, Sep. 19. Field, Stephen, and Margaret Briggs.
1764, Nov. 16. Filgeren, Catharine, and Lewis Senn.
1765, June 20. Filpot, Isabella, and George Kerr.
1768, Feb. 9. Filson, Davidson, and Agnes Boggs.
1761, M'ch 19. Findal, Thomas, and Elizabeth Bass.
1763, Nov. 2. Findley, Martha, and Alexander Henderson.
1747, Apr. —. Finley, Agnes, and Matthew Jackson.
1761, Aug. 28. Finley, Archibald, and Sarah Bornhill.
1775, Aug. 17. Finley, Elizabeth, and Philip Winemore.
1762, May 4. Finley, John, and Sarah Todd.
1744, July 21. Finley, Joseph.
1773, June 24. Finley, Margaret, and Peter Duffield.
1761, May 13. Finley, Samuel, and Ann Clarkson.
1765, Oct. 31. Finley, William, and Susannah Skinner.
1774, Aug. 30. Finnegen, Catharine, and Philip James.
1773, July 3. Finnemore, Peter, and Sarah Cartwright.
1770, Apr. 28. Finney, Anne, and Thomas Whitton.

1775, Feb. 28. Finney, Charles, and Elizabeth Archey.

1747, Dec. —. Finney, Christopher, and Martha Dobbing.

1745, May —. Finney, John.

1772, Dec. 3. Finney, John, and Elizabeth Jackson.

1769, Jan. 26. Finney, Mary, and Joseph Demsy, Jun.

1767, Nov. 7. Finney, Mary, and Thomas Skillman.

1773, Nov. 19. Finney, Patrick, and Frances Cahan.

1763, M'ch 21. Finney, Rebecca, and John Jones.

1746, Sep. —. Finney, Robert, and Diana Spencer.

1774, Dec. 6. Fishbourne, Elizabeth, and Thomas Wharton, Jun.

1767, July 3. Fisher, Ann, and William Watkins.

1783, June 25. Fisher, Archibald.

1763, Jan. 7. Fisher, Barbara, and Jacob Burket.

1761, Oct. 17. Fisher, Benjamin, and Sarah Dungan.

1771, May 16. Fisher, Charles, and Anne Peirce.

1761, Dec. 4. Fisher, Christian, and Barbara Omensetter.

1774, Apr. 8. Fisher, Daniel, and Margaret Krees.

1761, July 11. Fisher, Jacob, and Massey Dunging.

1774, June 3. Fisher, John, and Esther Tybout.

1767, Apr. 10. Fisher, Lucy, and William Williams.

1773, Nov. 6. Fisher, Martin, and Catharine Shallus.

1766, May 23. Fisher, Mary, and Benjamin Korster.

1772, Feb. 17. Fisher, Mary, and Hermanus Johnston.

1768, Nov. 23. Fisher, Mary, and Thomas Bradford.

1767, Dec. 1. Fisher, Mary, and William Bartram.

1760, Feb. 20. Fisher, Michael, and Elizabeth Winter.

1761, June 2. Fisher, Michael, and Mary Kearney.

1760, June 17. Fisher, Rachel, and William Lesher.

1770, Dec. 19. Fisher, Sarah, and Andrew Bunner.

1744, Aug. 13. Fisher, Thomas.

1762, Nov. 3. Fish, Isaac, and Grace Young.

1760, Sep. 24. Fish, John, and Sarah Scott.

1775, Sep. 9. Fisler, Mary, and James Guy.

1769, M'ch 1. Fiss, Christian, and Mary Blackwood.

1763, July 7. Fiss, John, and Ann Amelia How.

1762, Aug. 23. Fister, Elizabeth, and Richard Smith.

1767, Oct. 27. Fite, Catharine, and Henry Deshong.

1763, June 30. Fithing, Anna Maria, and Michael Sarlix.

1746, Oct. —. Fitswater, Elizabeth, and Joseph House.

1773, Sep. 4. Fitzgerald, Catharine, and Godfrey Hawker.

1773, May 13. Fitzgerald, Eleanor, and Peter Smick.

1773, Oct. 11. Fitzgerald, Margaret, and James Allen.

1765, July 30. Fitzgerald, Mary, and Gains Davison.

1774, Sep. 29. Fitzgerald, Mary, and William Gregory.

1776, M'ch 21. Fitzgerald, Mary, and William McIlvaine.

1768, Nov. 21. Fitzgerald, Robert, and Elizabeth Harris.
1771, Dec. 19. Fitzgerald, Robert, and Kesiah Scott.
1773, May 13. Fitzgerald, Walter, and Mary Claypoole.
1767, Oct. 28. Fitzgerrald, Phebe, and John Fling.
1776, Apr. 13. Fitzpatrick, Daniel, and Margaret Lynch.
1775, Sep. 5. Fitzpatrick, Eliza, and Michael Condon.
1776, Feb. 6. Fitzpatrick, John, and Eleanor Pryor.
1775, Oct. 9. Fitzpatrick, William, and Mary Graham.
1770, July 25. Fitzrandolph, Edward, and Mary Sims.
1773, June 21. Fitzrandolph, Rachel, and Charles Eustace.
1765, Oct. 30. Fitzsimmons, Andrew, and Ann Rearden.
1761, Oct. 1. Fitzsimmons, James, and Ann Beard.
1774, Apr. 15. Fitzsimmons, Mary, and William Toy.
1761, Nov. 23, Fitzsimmons, Thomas, and Catharine Mead.
1775, Nov. 15. Fivey, Ann, and John Clinton.
1761, June 10. Flack, Eleanor, and Thomas Cotton.
1768, May 11. Flack, Robert, and Mary Weir.
1769, Nov. 15. Flack, Sarah, and John Anderson.
1774, Jan. 15. Flahaven, Ann, and James Gallagher.
1768, Apr. 2. Flahavan, Roger, and Catharine Swan.
1766, Apr. 3. Fleeson, Ann, and Samuel Penrose.
1763, Sep. 8. Fleeson, Esther, and Samuel Leacock.
1745, June —. Fleming, Joseph.
1744, May 28. Fleming, Robert.
1771, M'ch 30. Fleming, Thomas, and Mary Broadnicks.
1766, Jan. 27. Flemming, Mary, and Samuel McBean.
1767, June 26. Flemming, Mary, and William McClay.
1763, Oct. 27, Flemmings, Ann, and Reuben Eastlack.
1771, June 1. Flennigan, William, and Sarah Albertson.
1767, Apr. 25. Fletcher, Elizabeth, and Isaac Garner.
1774, M'ch 21. Fletcher, Jane, and Peter Woglom.
1744, May 28. Fletcher, John.
1762, M'ch 17. Fletcher, Margaret, and Robert Conn.
1773, Feb. 1. Fletcher, Mary, and Jacob Greswold.
1775, M'ch 25. Fletcher, Mary, and Jonathan Giddens.
1776, May 16. Fletcher, Samuel, and Elizabeth Watson.
1773, M'ch 11. Fletcher, William, and Sarah Downes.
1764, Dec. 8. Flet, John, and Catharine Webber.
1771, June 19. Flick, Elizabeth, and Henry Corry.
1775, Sep. 14. Flick, Philip, and Mary Lowry.
1747, June —. Fling, Ann, and George Vincent Daws.
1766, June 16. Fling, Catharine, and Daniel Baxton.
1767, Oct. 28. Fling, John, and Phebe Fitzgerrald.
1774, Dec. 15. Fling, William, and Sarah Vaughan.
1767, Aug. 15. Flin, Margaret, and Anthony Hammond.
1772, Feb. 17. Flinn, John, and Susannah Tatnall.

1743, Sep. —. Flinn, Martin.
1762, June 24. Flinthem, John, and Margaret Steel.
1763, Dec. 9. Flint, Thomas, and Ann Crone.
1771, Sep. 14. Flood, Jane, and Henry Leaight.
1765, Nov. 26. Flower, Ann, and Samuel Wheeler.
1771, Feb. 6. Flower, Benjamin, and Sarah Pickles.
1760, Sep. 6. Flower, Enoch, and Mary Pemberton.
1771, Feb. 12. Flower, Hannah, and John Wall.
1767, Nov. 14. Flower, Hannah, and Thomas Assheton.
1761, May 13. Flower, Mary, and Gerardus Clarkson.
1772, Oct. 27. Flower, Mary, and Joseph Gamble.
1769, Dec. 19. Flower, Rachel, and Samuel Saunders.
1762, May 5. Flower, Rebecca, and William Young.
1762, May 19. Flower, Samuel, and Sarah Ann Williams.
1769, Dec. 28. Flower, Susannah, and Jonathan Adams.
1767, May 7. Floyd, Jane, and Neal McIntire.
1761, June 2. Floyd, John, and Jane Barrett.
1761, July 23. Fluellen, Elizabeth, and Jacob Warrick.
176:, M'ch 3. Fluellen, John, and Elizabeth Norton.
1762, Dec. 15. Flynn, Patrick, and Rachael Donovan.
1776, Jan. 18. Flyn, Patrick, and Christiana Malaby.
1769, Feb. 6. Flysher, Elizabeth, and Peter House.
1769, Oct. 31. Foaring, Christian Frederick, and Margaret Miller.
1774, Dec. 20. Foggs, Baltzer, and Mary Fennikle.
1774, Nov. 15. Fogle, Frederick, and Elizabeth Kupin.
1774, June 23. Folger, Ann, and Joseph Elden.
1762, Apr. 3. Folk, John, and Mary Armstrong.
1762, June 14. Folk, Matthias, and Catharine Smith.
1766, M'ch 26. Folwell, John, and Elizabeth Billow.
1769, Apr. 8. Folwell, Joseph, and Ann Billen.
1768, June 28. Foly, Catharine, and Thomas Jewson.
1771, June 10. Fonnerden, Adam, and Martha McCannan.
1769, Jan. 23. Foos, Nicholas, and Eleanor Martin.
1768, Feb. 27. Forbes, Catharine, and Thomas Britton.
1764, May 30. Forbes, Margaret, and Thomas York.
1768, Jan. 9. Forbes, William, and Mary Bevan.
1767, June 1. Ford, Ann, and John Studham.
1761, M'ch 21. Ford, Ann, and Philip Lawrence.
1761, June 1. Ford, Battice, and Mary Strawcutter.
1772, M'ch 2. Ford, Elizabeth, and Joseph Welcome.
1760, Dec. 16. Fordham. Benjamin, and Catharine Bunnison.
1773, May 8. Fordham, Richard, and Hannah Derringer.
1774, Aug. —. Ford, Mary, and James Waldrick.
1770, Apr. 19. Ford, Mercy, and Jacob Hymer.
1774, Aug. 25. Ford, Samuel, and Margaret Avrin.

1769, Aug. 30. Foreman, Catharine, and David Jenkins.
1776, Jan. 31. Foreman, Ezekiel, and Peggy Neilson.
1773, July 19. Foreman, Mary, and Patrick Carr.
1746, July -- Forest, William, and Sarah Hall.
1760, M'ch 12. Ferguson, Joseph, and Mary Jones.
1763, Oct. 8. Forrest, Catharine, and Thomas Duddle.
1775, M'ch 14. Forrester, Elizabeth, and David Lyons.
1767, Aug. 26. Forrester, James, and Jeminine Corssen.
1770, Jan. 9. Forrest, John, and Margaret Harkens.
1771, May 20. Forrest, Mary, and John Symes.
1772, Dec. 9. Forrest, Sarah, and Sturges Shoveler.
1770, Apr. 28. Forrest, Thomas, and Anne Whitepaine.
1746, Oct. --. Forstar, George, and Mary Philips.
1763, July 15. Forster, Henry, and Mary Montgomery.
1783, June 17. Forster, Joseph.
1764, Nov. 5. Forster, Josiah, and Rachel Barr.
1776, May 21. Forster, Mary, and John Stonemetz.
1763, Jan. 29. Forster, Mary, and Joseph Dobbins.
1764, June 27. Forster, Mary, and William Faries.
1761, Feb. 6, Forster, Samuel, and Mary Haeps.
1761, Apr. 22. Forster, Samuel, and Sara Norris.
1761, Oct. 30. Forst, Henry, and Lidya White.
1767, Apr. 15. Forst, Henry, and Sophia Susannah Izelorin.
1769, Dec. 5. Forst, John, and Hannah Williams.
1771, Apr. 22. Forsyth, Andrew, and Elizabeth Williams.
1775, Oct. 10. Forsyth, George, and Chloe Elliot.
1770, Nov. 7. Forsyth, Isaac, and Sarah Williams.
1760, June 7. Fortion, Margaret, and James Smith.
1771, Sep. 28. Fortune, Anthony, and Mary Yates.
1775, Jan. 12. Fortune, Richard, and Amelia Maxwell.
1747, June --. Fotheringham, John, and Margaret Shoemaker.
1776, Jan. 25. Fought, Mary, and Godfrey Hawger.
1776, Jan. 30. Foulckrod, Elizabeth, and Christian Troutman.
1763, Sep. 7. Foulke, Mary, and Peter House.
1771, July 15. Foulkes, Susannah, and Samuel Cunrad.
1760, Jan. 7. Foulquier, Sarah, and Adam Allyn.
1764, Oct. 2. Fouracres, John, and Elizabeth Stedham.
1770, July. 2. Fowl, Catharine, and Joseph Insee.
1775, Feb. 10. Fowler, Isaac, and Margaret Heiggins.
1773, Apr. 8. Fowler, James, and Hannah Swanson.
1748, M'ch 11. Fowler, Mary, and Henry Crafts.
1765, May 28. Fowler, Mary, and Hugh Cooper.
1748, Sep. --. Fowler, William, and Susannah Jones.
1774, Sep. 25. Fox, Abraham, and Sophia Wasseman.
1746, July --. Fox, Ann, and Alexander Chambers.
1775, June 28. Fox, Catharine, and Jeremiah Much.

1775, June 20. Fox, Francis, and Sarah Thomson.
1744, M'ch —. Fox, John.
1772, M'ch 17. Fox, John, and Elizabeth Gardner.
1762, Nov. 13. Fox, John, and Judah Lanniell.
1774, July 6. Fox, Mary, and John Rasberry.
1766, Dec. 31. Fox, Mary, and Thomas Procter.
1762, Dec. 8. Fox, Mary, and Thomas Roberts.
1771, Nov. 18. Fox, Peter, and Catharine Jones.
1748, Aug. 15. Fox, Thomas.
1775, M'ch 13. Foy, John, and Hoppee Hewett.
1775, Nov. 3. Fræme, Eliazbeth, and John Hanna.
1769, May 13. Fraley, Henry, and Susannah Rice.
1762, Aug. 25. Fraily, Ragina, and Jacob Gardner.
1764, Dec. 29. Francis, Arnold, and Elizabeth Hamstred.
1765, Feb. 1. Francis, Elizabeth, and Harman Umsted.
1775, Nov. 14. Francis, Jane, and Jesse Cullum.
1759, Dec. 12. Francis, Joseph, and Mary Parry.
1774, July 29. Francis, Margaret, and James Anderson.
1764, June 13. Francis, Margaret, and John Chatham.
1763, Oct. 1. Francis, Mary, and James Williams.
1760, M'ch 3. Francis, Rachel, and John Relf.
1774, June 27. Francis, Robert, and Margaret Casey.
1762, Feb. 8. Francis, Tench, and Ann Willing.
1766, Apr. 9. Francis, Thomas, and Hannah Martin.
1770, Sep. 26. Francis, Turbutt, and Sarah Mifflin.
1762, Jan. 16. Frank, George, and Mary Elizabeth.
1772, Jan. 9. Frank, Jacob, and Mary Magdalan Schlosser.
1768, Jan. 6. Franks, Abigail, and Andrew Hamilton.
1744, Oct. —. Franks, David.
1761, M'ch 26. Franks, Hannah, and George Cross.
1760, June 15. Franks, John, and Appollonia Seymore.
1762, June 10. Franks, John, and Margaret Philmeyer.
1773, Sep. 15. Frazer, Alice, and Timothy Sloan.
1769, Jan. 16. Frazer, Hugh, and Ruth Burk.
1766, Sep. 30. Frazer, Persifor, and Mary Worrel Taylor.
1765, June 7. Frazier, Alexander, and Sarah King.
1765, Dec. 5. Frazier, Elizabeth, and John Brant.
1764, Apr. 10. Freak, Rebecca, and Charles Willson.
1747, May —. Freame, Elizabeth, and Jacob Good.
1746, Aug. —. Freame, Letitia, and Daniel Taylor.
1763, Nov. 10. Fredrica, Catharine, and Thomas Hyser.
1746, Sep. —. Frederick, Elizabeth, and William Killpatrick.
1765, Apr. 22. Frederick, Philip, and Elizabeth Kennedy.
1773, Jan. 16. Fredericks, Christiana, and John Lycon.
1773, Jan. 9. Free, Abraham, and Ruth Evans.
1774, M'ch 3. Fread, Salome, and Gabriel Swatzlander.

1763, June 4. Freeling, James, and Jane Denald.
1760, Sep. 19. Freeman, John, and Sarah Mason.
1774, M'ch 30. Freeman, Sarah, and Jonathan Thomas.
1761, Nov. 4. Freeman, Sarah, and Lewis Webster.
1744, June 11. Freeman, William.
1765, Sep. 20. Freid, Abraham, and Sarah Stout.
1770, Dec. 3. Freight, Anne, and George Riddell.
1773, July 23. French, James, and Mary Clark.
1772, July 23. French, Robert, and Mary Ker.
1775, Nov. 11. French, Samuel, and Mary Wayne.
1760, Feb. 25. Fress, Rudolph, and Susannah Bowman.
1748, July 13. Frewin, Selia, and William Henderson.
1746, Sep. —. Freys, Rachel, and Joseph Johnson.
1773, Apr. 26. Fridley, Barbara, and George Consor.
1747, Oct. —. Friend, Joseph, and Rebecca Eyres.
1773, Oct. 26. Fries, John, and Ann Ax.
1761, June 18. Frin, Cecily, and William Pitt.
1772, Oct. 20. Fritts, Sarah, and Samuel Potts.
1773, May 5. Fritz, Elizabeth, and Leonard Reed.
1763, Dec. 22. Fritz, Jacob, and Sarah Jones.
1767, Oct. 3. Fromberger, John, and Hannah Coat.
1767, Nov. 19. Frump, Jonathan, and Ann Wellden.
1763, Jan. 7. Frump, Mary, and Robert Brady.
1744, Oct. —. Fruston, John.
1768, Oct. 5. Fryan, Abalan, and Nicholas Light.
1759, Dec. 29. Fry, Jacob, and Mary Griffltts.
1771, Oct. 16. Fry, Joseph, and Elizabeth Hoffman.
1772, Oct. 15. Fry, Joseph, and Martha Hurrie.
1772, Dec. 28. Fry, Margaret, and John Conrad.
1772, Oct. 17. Fry, Mary, and Henry Hook.
1765, M'ch 9. Fry, Richard, and Susannah Bruno.
1763, Dec. 28. Fry, Thomas, and Elizabeth Greenwood.
1760, Apr. 24. Fry, William, and Elizabeth Gore.
1744, Nov. —. Fudge, George.
1772, Feb. 27. Fudge, George, and Margaret Griffits.
1769, Sep. 1. Fudge, Mary, and John Gater.
1773, May 31. Fullan, Philip, and Letitia Hendricks.
1770, Jan. 26. Fuller, Mary, and James Roberts.
1763, May 6. Fullerton, Elizabeth, and Robert Bell.
1766, Sep. 2. Fullerton, George, and Margaret Blair.
1769, Jan. 10. Fullerton, Humphrey, and Mary Bazelee.
1768, Jan. 23. Fullerton, James, and Ann Brustrum.
1764, Feb. 27. Fullerton, Jane, and John Huston.
1769, Oct. 26. Fullerton, John, Jun., and Elizabeth Wincheles.
1768, July 9. Fullerton, Mary, and Robert Pew.
1746, Aug. —. Fullerton, Rose, and Edward Magennis.

1765, Aug. 1. Fullerton, William, and Eleanor Donaldson.
1766, July 21. Fullerton, William, and Mary Skellman.
1748, Sep. —. Fulton, Elizabeth, and William Stanley.
1768, Sep. 6. Fulton, James, and Sarah Vancourt.
1769, May 19. Fulton, John, and Mary Dean.
1765, Jan. 30. Fulton, John, and Mary Goo.
1744, Dec. —. Fulton, Richard.
1761, Sep. 12. Fulton, Westes, and Adam Middleton.
1767, July 29. Fultz, Mary, and David Bealert.
1763, May 14. Funk, John, and Elizabeth Lewis.
1768, M'ch 17. Furman, Moore, and Sarah White.
1766, Sep. 25. Furnis, William, and Margaret Holmes.
1774, Oct. 18. Furrow, Elizabeth, and John Byrnes.
1763, Sep. 8. Fust, Ann, and Peter Waters.

G.

1773, Jan. 16. Gaa, Hannah, and Robert Magee.
1760, Jan. 4. Gaa, William, and Mary Rouse.
1773, Nov. 10. Gabb, Sarah, and Nicholas Smith.
1767, Aug. 11. Gabb, William, and Elizabeth Moore.
1764, Feb. 20. Gable, David, and Catharine Rhinehart.
1773, May 3. Gabriel, Edward, and Martha Carmalt.
1775, Aug. 10. Gaddle, Priscilla, and Mark Brady.
1768, Aug. 10. Gaff, Catharine, and Benjamin James.
1767, Nov. 12. Galbraith, Latitia, and Jonathan Biles.
1773, Aug. 16. Galbraith, Robert, and Mary Brannon.
1765, Aug. 28. Galbraith, Samuel, and Margaret Miloy.
1774, June 16. Galbreath, Archibald, and Mary Galbreath.
1766, July 9. Galbreath, Catharine, and Charles Tennant.
1771, Nov. 16. Galbreath, Jane, and Edward Lawrence.
1760, M'ch 5. Galbreath, Jennet, and Patrick Work.
1774, June 16. Galbreath, Mary, and Archibald Galbreath.
1770, Aug. 3. Gale, Margaret, and Edward Capock.
1764, Dec. 5. Galer, Martha, and Alexander Adams.
1775, Oct. 30. Gallagher, Andrew, and Jane Shannon.
1771, Feb. 19. Gallagher, Catharine, and Henry Treen.
1774, Jan. 15. Gallagher, James, and Ann Flavahen.
1765, Jan. 8. Gallagher, John, and Ann Ingland.
1765, Jan 29. Gallagher, John, and Eleanor Huffey.
1764, Feb. 10. Gallagher, John, and Sarah Mires.
1774, Aug. 4. Gallagher, Michael, and Mary Brannin.
1776, Jan. 20. Gallagher, Peter, and Elizabeth Lusher.
1776, Apr. 10. Gallagher, Rosanna, and William Duncan.
1764, Apr. 19. Gallagher, William, and Mary McCoy.
1762, Aug. 17. Galley, Jane, and Richard Miller.
1761, Oct. 5. Galloway, Henry, and Elizabeth Merchant.

1762, Nov. 4. Galloway, John, and Mary Harrison.
1760, Sep. 30. Galloway, Joseph, and Hannah Cookson.
1761, Apr. 9. Galt, Nathaniel, and Ann Spafford.
1759, Dec. 21. Gambies, Samuel, and Elinor Robinson.
1762, Apr. 7. Gamble, Hannah, and Nathaniel Bonsel.
1772, Nov. 26. Gamble, Joseph, and Mary Flower.
1763, Apr. 19. Gamble, Samuel, and Elizabeth Johnson.
1764, Nov. 19. Gamble, William, and Ann McDonald.
1760, Jan. 3. Gamper, Mary, and Nicholas Schriner.
1760, Oct. 6. Gandawit, Catharine, and Robert Way.
1760, July 16. Gandousel, Lucy, and James McDaniel.
1761, Oct. 28. Ganthony, James, and Sarah Greenway.
1763, Jan. 13. Ganthony, Sarah, and William Allibone.
1764, Aug. 28. Garaud, Jacob, and Mary McKee.
1764, July 20. Garaty, Richard, and Ann Crossier.
1747, Feb. —. Gardener, Hannah, and Doughty Jones.
1773, July 22. Gardiner, Frances, and Abraham Mitchell.
1773, June 28. Gardiner, Hannah, and William Rogers.
1774, Feb. 1. Gardiner, Sarah, and John Reynolds
1771, July 20. Gardiner, Sarah, and Robert Craig.
1743, Apr. 9. Gardmer, Joseph.
1768, Dec. 13. Gardner, Alexander, and Elizabeth Hoover.
1760, Nov. 11. Gardner, Archibald, and Mary Patterson.
1776, M'ch 14. Gardner, Edith, and Jonathan Draper.
1764, Sep. 22. Gardner, Eleanor, and James Hunter.
1772, M'ch 17 Gardner, Elizabeth, and John Fox.
1764, July 6. Gardner, Elizabeth, and John Harrison.
1769, June 22. Gardner, Hannah, and Francis Trumble.
1762, Aug. 25. Gardner, Jacob, and Ragina Fraily.
1774, M'ch 31. Gardner John, and Mary Scott.
1772, Oct. 15. Gardner, Mary, and Jacob Utre.
1764, Jan. 16. Gardner, Matthew, and Mary Little.
1761, M'ch 14. Gardner, Richard, and Elizabeth Evans.
1764, June 4. Gardner, Sarah, and Matthew Butler.
1773, Jan. 13. Gardner, Thomas, and Letitia Stevens.
1767, M'ch 13, Gardner, William, and Sarah Holton.
1768, Nov. 3. Garland, George, and Ruth Terry.
1764, June 5. Garlick, Abigail, and Ezekiel Hand.
1765, Dec. 2. Garlin, John, and Mary Smith.
1772, July 23. Garman, Mary, and Abraham Cohen.
1761, Apr. 13. Garnal, Nathan, and Hannah Penner.
1767, Apr. 25. Garner, Isaac, and Elizabeth Fletcher.
1764, Nov. 24. Garner, Joseph, and Hannah Thornhill.
1764, May 4. Garnick, James, and Elizabeth Feagan.
1762, M'ch 30. Garrard, Heclace, and William Falkner.
1762, Jan. 2. Garrat, John, and Hannah Bond.

1761, M'ch 5. Garrat, Margaret, and Ephraim Bonham.
1763, M'ch 29. Garren, Elizabeth, and Christian Lauer.
1772, Apr. 16. Garret, Abraham, and Mary Taylor.
1775, Feb. 22. Garret, Adam, and Christiana Hysel.
1770, Oct. 8. Garret, Joseph, and Charity Collins.
1764, M'ch 1. Garret, Lydia, and Edward Hawes.
1775, Sep. 12. Garret, Margaret, and Joseph Johnston.
1765, Dec. 23. Garret, Mary, and Robert Tucker.
1772, Aug. 21. Garret, Matthias, and Elizabeth Denham.
1761, July 24. Garret, Sarah, and Henry Stuart.
1744, Oct. —. Garretson, Cornelius.
1762, Dec. 1. Garretson, John, and Hannah Smith.
1774, M'ch 26. Garrett, Ann, and John Thompson.
1761, Oct. 10. Garrett, Mary, and John Pyewell.
1747, June —. Garrigue, Sarah, and George Howell.
1763, Jan. 13. Garrigues, Elizabeth, and Robert Doughty.
1766, Feb. 12. Garrigues, Elizabeth, and William Smith.
1747, Jan. —. Garrigues, Francis, and Mary Knoxly.
1763, July 1. Garrigues, Isaac, and Hester Taylor.
1773, Apr. 28. Garrigues, Jacob, and Mary Ashton.
1766, Sep. 9. Garrigues, Rebecca, and Henry Robinson.
1759, Dec. 22. Garrigues, Sarah, and Charles Wolfall.
1746, July —. Garwood, Esther, and Nicholas Quinn.
1772, Aug. 15. Garwood, John, and Sarah Neithermark.
1763, M'ch 8. Garwood, Lucretia, and James Claypoole.
1772, June 8. Garwood, Rebecca, and Francis Brindly.
1743, July 11. Garwood, William.
1774, June 14. Garytie, Ann, and Robert McCrea.
1762, Sep. 20. Gasehlick, Elizabeth, and Paul Caster.
1762, Oct. 26. Gaskin, Thomas, and Mary Heany.
1761, Jan. 12. Gate, Michael, and Margaret Burk.
1769, Sep. 1. Gater, John, and Mary Fudge.
1766, Dec. 8. Gauff, Martha, and John Tufft.
1764, Nov. 28. Gaw, Margaret, and Alexander Adams.
1769. M'ch 24. Gaylor, Dorothy, and William Keen.
1773, Sep. 23. Gayman, Ann, and Curtis Davis.
1763, Dec. 21. Gayman, Mary, and Thomas Davis.
1744, May 28. Gayner, Henry.
1770, M'ch 10. Geaff, Catharine, and Valentine Welch.
1763, July 9. Gear, Ann, and Mathew Longwood.
1764, Feb. 1. Gearheart, Frederick, and Ann Maria Mullendore.
1747, Sep. —. Geary, Andrew, and Susannah Bateman.
1763, Apr. 11. Geary, George, and Sarah Evans.
1763, Feb. 24. Ged, Dougaldus, and Margery Thomas.
1763, Apr. 13. Geerion, Martha, and Andrew Boone.
1766, Dec. 31. Geer, Mary, and Thomas Inkester.

1746, Dec. —. Gelhard, Ann, and Joseph Thompson.
1775, M'ch 13. Genger, Hannah, and William Hood.
1774, Dec. 22. Genn, Thomas, and Mary Smith.
1775, Nov. 20. George, Eleanor, and Joseph Marsh.
1775, Aug. 8. George, Elizabeth, and Benjamin Myers.
1774, May 25. George, Hannah, and James Abraham.
1765, Sep. 11. George, Hannah, and Samuel Parker.
1760, July 29. George, John, and Catharine Pingard.
1763, Oct. 10. George, John, and Martha Carle.
1761, Nov. 27. George, Lilly, and Robert Wallis.
1768, Dec. 28. George, Margaret, and Henry Shriver.
1765, June 19. George, Margaret, and Hugh Maxwell.
1761, Jan. 27. George, Margaret, and Matthew McGlathery.
1764, Sep. 8. George, Martha, and Henry McClelland.
1774, Nov. 16. George, Susannah, and Henry Stoop.
1761, Oct. 7. George, William, and Jane Richardson.
1765, June 11. Geraud, Mary, and James Paulkill.
1760, Jan. 21. Gerehard, Catharine, and Jacob Maag.
1765, Dec. 28. German, Lewis, and Mary Davis.
1744, Apr. —. German, Lodowyck.
1771, Oct. 12. Germ, Hannah, and Samuel Snowden.
1770, Jan. 13. Gerrard, Agnes, and Matthew Strong.
1775, Apr. 1. Gerrard, Ann, and William Downes.
1748, Apr. 13. Gerrard, Elizabeth, and Balthaser Kramer.
1775, Apr. 4. Gestling, Frederick, and Elizabeth Seffrons.
1747, Dec. —. Ghiselin, William, and Rebecca Bachston.
1743, July 11. Gibbins, Henry.
1764, Feb. 29. Gibbon, Abel, and Eleanor John.
1770, May 16. Gibbons, Eliazbeth, and Edward Jones.
1746, Nov. —. Gibbons, John, and Barbara Beegle.
1765, Dec. 4. Gibbs, Alexander, and Ann Parker.
1768, Feb. 11. Gibbs, Ann, and Hugh Fergison.
1774, Feb. 2. Gibbs, Benjamin, and Hannah Shewell.
1761, Nov. 23. Gibbs, John, and Dorothy Boughton.
1764, July 17. Gibbs, Rebecca, and Samuel Patrick.
1761, Sep. 12. Gibbs, Sarah, and Justice Rivercome.
1775, Jan. 11. Gibson, Elizabeth, and Samuel Armstrong.
1764, Dec. 25. Gibson, James, and Isabella Sergeant.
1762, Feb. 16. Gibson, John, and Sarah McGraugh.
1775, July 14. Gibson, Robert, and Mary Britton.
1763, July 18. Gibson, Sarah, and Isaac Hart.
1762, Aug 31. Gibson, Thomas, and Elizabeth Williams.
1762, Sep. 4. Gibson, William, and Ruth Johnson.
1775, M'ch 25. Giddens, Jonathan, and Mary Fletcher.
1769, Apr. 14. Giffin, David, and Mary Skinner.
1771, Apr. 17. Giffin, James, and Priscilla Shaw.

7—VOL. II.

1775, Feb. 20. Giffin, Rachel, and Joseph Ashburnham.
1770, May 31. Giffins, John, and Anne Roberts.
1766, Aug. 18. Gihon, Hiram, and Sarah Delany.
1764, M'ch 27. Gilben, Abigail, and George Tomkins.
1766, Oct. 30. Gilbert, Adam, and Mary Zienining.
1773, Nov. 12. Gilbert, Ann, and William Ball.
1743, Aug. 16. Gilbert, Benjamin.
1760, Aug. 18. Gilbert, Benjamin, and Elizabeth Pert.
1770, Aug. 1. Gilbert, Christiana, and Samuel Rusk.
1775, June 10. Gilbert, Daniel, and Catharine Belkenbine.
1770, Jan. 1. Gilbert, Elizabeth, and Joseph Hart.
1766, June. 18. Gilbert, Elizabeth, and Samuel Prior.
1775, M'ch 14. Gilbert, Francis, and Margaret Nelson.
1760, Jan. 3. Gilbert, Hannah, and Abner Clark.
1775, Apr. 26. Gilbert, Hannah, and Robert Norris.
1762, Aug. 31. Gilbert, Hannah, and Thomas Norris.
1761, Aug. 20. Gilbert, John, and Mary Storry.
1770, Dec. 1. Gilbert, Joseph, and Euphæmia Rees.
1772, Feb. 19. Gilbert, Joshua, and Priscilla Shrigby.
1773, Dec. 7. Gilbert, Mary, and Daniel Mouse.
1771, Feb. 23. Gilbert, Mary, and James Dean.
1773, Dec. 18. Gilbert, Mary, and John Lort.
1775, Nov. 17. Gilbert, Nathan, and Elizabeth Scout.
1746, Jan. —. Gilbert, Nicholas.
1775, Jan. 25. Gilbert, Rachel, and John Pogue.
1764, June 28. Gilbert, Rebecca, and Josiah Appleton.
1761, Sep. 1. Gilbert, Sarah, and Daniel Walton.
1770, Jan. 31. Gilbert, Sarah, and Elias Hughes.
1765, Nov. 16. Gilbert, Sarah, and Lewis O'Bryan.
1772, May 23. Gilbert, William, and Mary Fenton.
1760, May 29. Giles, Edward, and Margaret Yeo.
1775, June 3. Gillespie, George, and Elizabeth Denormandie.
1762, Oct. 28. Gill, Henry, and Mary Bryan.
1771, Jan. 1. Gillilan, William, and Levina Elliot.
1773, July 8. Gillin, Daniel, and Catharine Haughan.
1761, Dec. 1. Gillis, Alexander, and Jane Jenkins.
1771, Dec. 31. Gillis, Ann, and John Mears.
1773, Dec. 6. Gillis, Mary, and Arthur Kirk.
1766, Aug. 8. Gill, John, and Sarah Hazell.
1774, Feb. 14. Gillman, Adolph, and Eva Strome.
1774, Dec. 15. Gillman, Susannah and Peter Deshung.
1767, M'ch 21. Gill, Mary, and Jacob Roberts.
1771, Dec. 18. Gillmer, Martha, and Benjamin Brelsford, **Jr.**
1774, Dec. 6. Gill, Philip, and Mary Quirk.
1763, Aug. 20. Gill, Robert, and Catharine Bottomly.
1772, Oct. 7. Gill, Robert, and Hannah Allen.

1774, Oct.   7. Gill, Robert, and Martha Doyle.
1775, Feb.   28. Gill, Samuel, and Jemima Hughes.
1770, Dec.   4. Gillyan, Catharine, and John Murphy.
1764, Aug.   30. Gillyatt, Jane, and Matthew Potter.
1775, Sep.   10. Gilmer, James, and Hannah Dent.
1765, Dec.   9. Gilmore, Eleanor, and Matthew Cochran.
1763, June   3. Gilmore, Jean, and David Minsor.
1744, Apr.   —. Gilpin, Thomas.
1748, June   16. Gilfoy, Charles, and Margaret Elleson.
1759, Dec.   17. Gisler, Moses, and Eleanor McCoy.
1774, Nov.   24. Githin, Isaac, and Elizabeth Boggs.
1775, Feb.   23. Gitling, Mary, and John Coffman.
1764, Apr.   21. Givin, Joseph, and Elizabeth Turbury.
1771, Jan.   9. Gladan, Joseph, and Susannah Coates.
1770, Dec.   5. Gladding, David, and Rebecca Ratcliff.
1760, Feb.   2. Gladney, Joseph, and Elizabeth Smith.
1762, Oct.   13. Gladny, Sarah, and John Ewer.
1760, Sep.   17. Glascowstine, Joseph, and Sarah Reynold.
1775, May   1. Glasgow, James, and Elizabeth Lee.
1770, Aug.   11. Glasgow, Jane, and James Harnet.
1771, July   18. Glassow, Ann, and Christian Smith.
1772, Sep.   28. Glayer, John, and Elizabeth Rice.
1745, Oct.   —. Gleave, Matthew.
1761, Jan.   24. Gledith, Charles, and Margaret Reinherd.
1773, Jan.   21. Gleen, Thomas, and Ann Bantick.
1772, Nov.   26. Gleeves, Rebecca, and Everard McClees.
1772, Oct.   6. Glenn, James, and Mary Dashner.
1760, Oct.   24. Glenson, Dorothy, and Joseph Brumfield.
1764, Nov.   29. Glentworth, George, and Margaret Linton.
1761, Sep.   25. Glidding, Garrat, and James Ratelis.
1770, Aug.   7. Glory, Mary, and James Murray.
1770, June   16. Glouse, Barbara, and Christopher Mintz.
1765, June   15. Glover, Esther, and Hugh Jones.
1773, Apr.   29. Glover, William, and Letitia Tittermary.
1763, Apr.   4. Glows, Jacob, and Maria Margretta Fanendus.
1760, Oct.   21. Godfrey, George, and Mary Margant.
1746, Dec.   —. Godfrey, Hannah, and James Stewart.
1775, May   13. Godfrey, Jane, and John Hamilton.
1764, June   28. Godfrey, Jane, and John Spine.
1762, July   19. Godlove, John, and Rachel Rouford.
1770, Dec.   18. Godshalk, Jacob, and Elizabeth Owen.
1773, June   17. Goff, Margaret, and Arthur O'Neil.
1773, Jan.   26. Goforth, Zachariah, and Ann Clifford.
1762, Aug.   3. Golden, Daniel, and Catharine Kilback.
1773, Feb.   27. Gold, Joseph, and Abigail Kerr.
1763, Sep.   19. Gold, Margaret, and Jacob Comfort.

1761, M'ch 13. Gold, Margaret, and William Miller.
1743, Apr. 9. Goldy, Joseph.
1760, May 5. Good, George, and Margaret Kison.
1744, Dec. —. Goodin, John.
1747, May —. Good, Jacob, and Elizabeth Freame.
1773, Feb. 13. Good, Jacob, and Susannah Aple.
1767, Dec. 17. Goodman, Hannah, and William Niles.
1772, Oct. 1. Goodman, Samuel, and Martha Kerr.
1769, Nov. 11. Goodshires, Jacob, and Mary Smith.
1760, Oct. 1. Goodwin, George, and Elizabeth Pearson.
1772, Dec. 7. Goodwin, George, and Susannah Rockwell.
1745, July —. Goodwin, Richard.
1764, Aug. 18. Goodwin, Sarah, and William Kerlin.
1774, Aug. 3. Goodwin, Susannah, and David Supplee.
1765, Jan. 30. Goo, Mary, and John Fulton.
1760, Sep. 2. Goon, Elizabeth, and John Cornman.
1762, July 15. Gordan, Elizabeth, and Charles Spackman.
1766, Oct. 23. Gordon, Arthur, and Susannah Decony.
1769, Nov. 29. Gordon, Dorothy, and Lawrence Saltar.
1769, June 23. Gordon, Elizabeth, and George Corris.
1774, Dec. 29. Gordon, Elizabeth, and John Saltar.
1771, Mar. 26. Gordon George, and Elizabeth Williams.
1774, Feb. 19. Gordon, Henry, and Elizabeth Lacy.
1783, June 5. Gordon, John.
1762, Apr. 12. Gordon, Mary, and Alexander Carlisle.
1772, M'ch 3. Gordon, Robert, and Elizabeth Davis.
1764, Nov. 24. Gordon, Thomas, and Hannah Jenkins.
1768, July 18. Gordon, William, and Barbara Springer.
1763, Dec. 30. Gordwin, Mary, and Jacob Miller.
1760, Apr. 24. Gore, Elizabeth, and William Fry.
1775, Dec. 30. Gorely, Jane, and Nathan Dungan.
1776, June 2. Gorely, John, and Mary Ann Dick.
1761, Aug. 19. Gorely, William, and Hannah Barton.
1768, Feb. 20. Gorton, Daniel, and Mary Stewart.
1771, Feb. 6. Goslin, Hannah, and Robert Burton.
1761, Dec. 14. Goss, Mary, and Justin McCarty.
1768, June 13. Gostelow, Jonathan, and Mary Duffield.
1747, Nov. —. Goterd, Jane, and John Morris.
1747, Sep. 10. Gotchill, Ann Margaret, and Garnet Hughes.
1775, Feb. 27. Gothrop, Samuel, and Sarah Boast.
1768, Aug. 2. Gottier, Edward, and Mary Wells.
1765, Jan. 9. Gottier, Elizabeth, and John Ashburn.
1770, Oct. 31. Gottier, Francis, and Margaret Ferguson.
1776, Feb. 7. Gottier, James, and Abigail Smith.
1769, June 23. Goucher, Jane, and Thomas Rouch.
1769, Feb. 27. Goudy, James, and Rachel Davidson.

1775, Aug.   7. Goveren, Mary, and William Wood.
1774, M'ch   8. Grace, Elizabeth, and John Strimbeck.
1760, June 10. Grace, Mary, and Edward Edwards.
1775, April 1. Grace, Susannah, and John Shepherd.
1774, June   9. Graff, Catharine, and Anthony Benezet, Jun.
1775, Dec. 28. Graff, George, and Sarah Nicholson.
1772, Dec.   3. Graff, Jacob, and Elizabeth Dick.
1774, Sep. 19. Graff, Jacob, and Mary Shinkle.
1776, Jan.   8. Graff, Jasper, and Suannah Mouse.
1771, Feb. 15. Graffley, Elizabeth, and Conrod Leutner.
1770, Dec. 10. Graffley, Ozella, and William Stutz.
1772, Oct. 28. Graff, Phebe, and Abraham Backman.
1770, July 19. Graff, Phebe, and Valentine Welsh.
1744, Jan. —. Graft, John Valentine.
1769, July   1. Graham, Elizabeth, and Isaac Buckley.
1761, July   8. Graham, Innes, and Jane McFarland
1775, Oct.   9. Graham, Mary, and William Fitzpatrick.
1747, Nov. —. Graham, Nathaniel, and Susannah.
1774, June 16. Graham, Richard, and Mary Douglass.
1774, July 27. Graham, Robert, and Elizabeth Coxe.
1762, Oct.   9. Graham, Samuel, and Hannah Vestine.
1762, June   1. Graham, Sarah, and William Bolton.
1773, June 17. Graham, Susannah, and William Main.
1764, June 21. Grant, Jane, and James McGinnnis.
1765, Aug.   4. Grant, John, and Deborah Montgomery.
1770, July 18. Grant, John, and Orminella Hall.
1764, July 31. Grant, Lewis, and Margaret Alexander.
1775, Feb. 11. Grant, Robert, and Sarah Tercas.
1771, Nov.   7. Grant, Sarah, and Andrew Yoacum.
1744, Feb. —. Grant, Thomas.
1763, Jan. 22. Grant, Thomas, and Mary Campbell.
1745, M'ch —. Grantsers, Peter.
1773, Dec. 11. Grantum, William, and Sarah Morton.
1767, Sep. 17. Granville, Mary, and Samuel Boyce.
1748, Jan. —. Gratehouse, Elizabeth, and John Arts.
1748, Jan. —. Gratis, Laycosh, and David Hall.
1747, Feb. —. Graydon, Alexander, and Rachel Marks.
1767, Mar.   9. Gray, Elizabeth, and William Jones.
1760, Nov. 20. Gray, Elizabeth, and William Killgore.
1775, Aug.   7. Gray, Hannah, and Allen Moore.
1744, M'ch —. Gray, Henry.
1763, Nov. 23. Gray, Isabella, and William Prichard.
1769, Feb. 10. Gray, John, and Pamelo Leonard.
1772, July 16. Gray, John, and Rachel Miller.
1769, M'ch   8. Gray, Mary, and Matthias Lukens.
1769, Nov. 21. Gray, Robert, and Mary Cannan.

1764, Oct. 15. Graysburg, James, and Sarah Hart.
1776, Apr. 25. Grayson, John, and Mary Hoffman.
1747, Nov. —. Gray, William, and Elizabeth Jones.
1774, Dec. 14. Gready, Eleanor, and James Merchant.
1772, Sep. 15. Grear, Frances, and William Little.
1761, June 16. Grebble, David, and Susan Reinwalton.
1775, Jan. 25. Green, Anna, and John Braddock.
1745, Dec. —. Green, Christopher.
1776, June 7. Green, Daniel, and Martha Oat.
1768, Aug. 27. Green, Daniel, and Mary Chamberlain.
1774, Dec. 27. Green, Edward, and Ann Stephenson.
1765, June 12. Green, John, and Alice Colleck.
1760, M'ch 27. Green, John, and Elizabeth Story.
1771, Aug. 20. Green, Joseph, and Hester Crispin.
1767, June 15. Green, Margaret, and John McCarty.
1765, Aug. 20. Green, Margaret, and Joshua Proctor.
1761, Oct. 12. Green, Martha, and Jacob Burkels.
1776, Feb. 19. Green, Mary, and John Turner.
1765, Sep. 11. Green, Mary, and William Pollard.
1775, Dec. 19. Green, Mary, and William Reed.
1744, Sep. —. Green, Pyre.
1760, Oct. 27. Green, Rachel, and John Pritchard.
1767, Nov. 19. Green, Samuel, and Mary Dickson.
1771, Sep. 25. Green, Sarah, and James Irvin.
1765, Jan. 1. Green, Sarah, and James O'Neal.
1760, July 17. Green, Sarah, and Thomas Bylish.
1771, Nov. 27. Green, Thomas, and Catharine Nelson.
1773, Jan. 12. Greenland, Sarah, and Edward Jackson.
1766, Apr. 10. Greenlaw, Mary, and Alexander Mitchell.
1773, May 13. Greenfield, Jesse, and Elizabeth Holliday.
1760, July 21. Greenough, Daniel, and Elizabeth Vaughan.
1774, Sep. 2. Greenway, Elizabeth, and James Ince.
1775, July 31. Greenway, Hannah, and James McGlew.
1768, Feb. 18. Greenway, Hannah, and Joseph Derry.
1771, June 10. Greenway, Mary, and William Beaven.
1761, Oct. 28. Greenway, Sarah, and James Ganthony.
1774, Feb. 1. Green, William, and Elizabeth Stackhouse.
1775, July 15. Green, William, and Margaret Grogan.
1772, Dec. 12. Green, William, and Mary Lewis.
1763, Dec. 28. Greenwood, Elizabeth, and Thomas Fry.
1770, Oct. 6. Greenwood, John, and Margaret Morrison.
1772, Jan. 29. Greer, Joseph, and Susannah Greer.
1768, Dec. 2. Greer, Martha, and John Jamison.
1769, Sep. 21. Greer, Peter, and Elizabeth Halkerston.
1772, Jan. 29. Greer, Susannah, and Joseph Greer.
1747, Dec. —. Greesbury, Ann, and Joseph Warner.

1770, Oct. 17. Gregg, Margaret, and Matthew McHenry.
1765, Sep. 25. Gregg, Robert, and Jennett O'Neal.
1767, Feb. 28. Gregory, Abraham, and Elizabeth Scott.
1773, Apr. 29. Gregory, Dougal, and Ann McIlharan.
1773, Aug. 13. Gregory, Elizabeth, and William Lyell.
1744, July 21. Gregory, James.
1763, July 7. Gregory, James, and Margaret Liniom, (free-negroes.)
1775, July 19. Gregory, Margaret, and Thomas Darrock.
1765, June 19. Gregory, Rachel, and John Edwards.
1776, May 15. Gregory, Rachel, and Peter Morgan.
1745, Oct. —. Gregory, William.
1774, Sep. 29. Gregory, William, and Mary Fitzgerald.
1773, Feb. 1. Greswold, Jacob, and Mary Fletcher.
1760, Aug. 6. Grewes, John, and Sarah Hamilton.
1764, Feb. 9. Grew, Louisa, and Hugh Williams.
1747, Oct. —. Grew, Theophilus, and Rebecca Richards.
1774, Oct. 28. Grey, Ann, and William Grey.
1763, Aug. 13. Grey, ———, and Christiana Boyt.
1765, M'ch 11. Grey, Darues, and James Huston.
1763, Nov. 28. Grey, Frederick, and Sarah Peppert.
1768, June 17. Grey, Hannah, and Enoch William.
1774, Oct. 28. Grey, William, and Ann Grey.
1764, Feb. 15. Greyger, Barbara, and George Stamer.
1775, Aug. 26. Gribble, Casper, and Sarah Merchant.
1771, Jan. 1. Grice, Lydia, and Joseph Fanning.
1768, Jan. 9. Grier, Jane, and Joseph Thomas.
1773, Oct. 7. Grier, Matthew, and Catharine Kelly.
1747, June —. Griffet, Sarah, and Levy Potter.
1768, Apr. 2. Griffey, Benjamin, and Margaret Patterson.
1762, Jan. 17. Griffin, Comfort, and James Wattkins.
1746, June —. Griffin, Jane, and Zachariah Barr.
1743, May 27. Griffin, Mary.
1775, Apr. 20. Griffin, Patrick, and Mary Nelson.
1761, Nov. 14. Griffin, Samuel, and Jane Toff.
1762, Apr. 28. Griffith, Ann, and Edward Middleton.
1765, Apr. 1. Griffith, Ann, and John Edwards.
1762, Apr. 28. Griffith, Ann, and William Morris.
1771, Oct. 10. Griffith, Benjamin, and Catharine Bartholomew.
1773, Dec. 2. Griffith, Benjamin, and Margaret Wilson.
1765, Oct. 14. Griffith, Benjamin, and Rachel Waters.
1775, Nov. 29. Griffith, Benjamin, and Sarah Stephens.
1771, Nov. 21. Griffith, Daniel, and Elizabeth Rodgers.
1748, July 13. Griffith, David, and Hannah Emmit.
1770, M'ch 2. Griffith, Elisha, and Mary Doyle.
1763, Nov. 23. Griffith, Elizabeth, and Joseph Barton.

1768, July   7. Griffith, George, and Rebecca January.
1760, Feb.   2. Griffith, Hannah, and John Evans.
1774, June   4. Griffith, Jane, and Evan Stephens.
1771, Apr.   14. Griffith, John, and Margaret Lewis.
1767, Sep.   14. Griffith, Joseph, and Sarah Bishop.
1767, Dec.   17. Griffith, Mary, and William Davis.
1771, Dec.   3. Griffith, Sarah, and Mordecai Massey.
1769, Nov.   15. Griffith, Sarah, and Robert Heaton.
1774, Oct.   8. Griffith, Sarah, and Thomas Matthew.
1744, Apr.   —. Griffith, Timothy.
1770, Oct.   20. Griffith, William, and Margaret Rodgers.
1761, Mar.   11. Griffith, William, and Martha Walton.
1765, Oct.   5. Griffiths, Amos, and Sarah Howel.
1760, Oct.   17. Griffiths, Mary, and John Sheffley.
1760, July   26. Griffiths, Rachel, and William Roberts.
1760, Sep.   24. Griffiths, Sarah, and James Hilton.
1772, Feb.   27. Griffits, Margaret, and George Fudge.
1770, M'ch   17. Griffits, Mary, and John Middleton.
1759, Dec.   29. Griffitts, Mary, and Jacob Fry.
1761, Nov.   7. Griffitts, William, and Hester Wenn.
1764, May   26. Griffitts, William, and Ruth Thomas.
1761, Nov.   5. Griff, Sellwood, and Mary Carman.
1762, M'ch   9. Grigg, James, and Hannah Plumly.
1764, Sep.   11. Grimes, Gilbert, and Martha Miller.
1761, Aug.   5. Grimes, Jane, and Francis Dowins.
1761, Dec.   24. Grimes, John, and Jane Smith.
1748, Oct.   —. Grimes, Mary, and James Boyse.
1773, Aug.   5. Grimes, Mary, and Parnel Clayton.
1761, June   3. Grimes, Rozanna, and Thomas Jones.
1762, Aug.   21. Grimes, Sarah, and Francis Downs.
1762, Sep.   10. Grimes, William, and Elizabeth Mann.
1764, Feb.   13. Griscomb, Deborah, and Everhard Bolton.
1770, Dec.   31. Griscomb, Sarah, and William Donaldson.
1769, July   25. Griscom, Susannah, and Ephraim Doane.
1747, Apr.   —. Griffy, Catharine, and Theophilus Williams.
1765, Jan.   28. Grizzle, Mary, and David Russel.
1774, Aug.   2. Groce, Elizabeth, and John Ute.
1774, Dec.   8. Groce, Mary, and Alexander Adamson.
1775, July   15. Grogan, Margaret, and William Green.
1747, Dec.   —. Grome, Ann, and Charles Stedman.
1771, Apr.   24. Grono, Sarah, and Thomas Bull.
1775, Mc'h   4. Groome Mary, and Joseph Siddell.
1761, Jan.   27. Groom, Rachel, and Edmund Briggs.
1774, Feb.   1. Groom, Thomas, and Hannah Duffield.
1747, May   —. Groom, Mary, and William Kenton.
1760, Dec.   3. Gross, Joseph, and Catharine Zimmerman.

1772, Nov. 6. Grouse, Valentine, and Elizabeth Bakely.
1769, Dec. 28. Grove, Ann, and James Carswell.
1773, Dec. 17. Grover, Elizabeth, and Michael Trites.
1765, July 1. Groves, John, and Ann Watson.
1768, July 22. Groves, Joshua, and Rosanna Beard.
1747, Dec. —. Grove, Morris, and Ann Roberts.
1767, M'ch 18. Grovian, Hannah, and Isaac Delavan.
1770, Jan. 19. Grubb, Catharine, and Peter Paul.
1770, May 26. Grubb, Henry, and Barbara Kinsley.
1761, Oct. 31. Grubb, Henry, and Sarah Wells.
1764, Jan. 26. Grubb, Henry, and Susannah Cobb.
1760, Aug. 9. Grudy, William, and Grace Kennedy.
1772, Apr. 17. Grugh, Charles, and Elizabeth Moore.
1761, Apr. 27. Grush, George, and Ester Faedley.
1743, Nov. —. Grymes, Michael.
1766, Apr. 19. Guest, Elizabeth, and Daniel Evans.
1743, May 27. Guest, John.
1761, Sep. 2. Guest, Simon, and Mary Wilcox.
1771, Nov. 12. Gugeny, John, and Rachel Stewart.
1772, Jan. 16. Guilden, Catharine, and Nicholas Holderman.
1763, Aug. 25. Guilkey, Samuel, and Mary Bevan.
1760, Jan. 19. Guinett, Rose, and John Quamany.
1772, Dec. 12. Guionnet, Louis, and Elizabeth Cipple.
1761, Feb. 21. Guir, Adam, and Jane Meakson.
1771, Aug. 30. Guirey, William, and Elizabeth Tavers.
1765, Oct. 11. Gullen, Henry, and Margaret Stinson.
1765, May 16. Gunning, Jane, and James Hunter.
1767, July 11. Gunning, Margaret, and Thomas Lee.
1761, Dec. 31. Gunning, Margaret, and Thomas Pretchard.
1766, Dec. 2. Gunning, Rachel, and Robert Allison.
1771, Nov. 15. Gunning, Rebecca, and John Thompson.
1764, Aug. 13. Gurlin, Moses, and Jane Eves.
1768, July 7. Gurney, Henry, and Catharine Ross.
1747, Oct. —. Guthrie, Alexander, and Mary Albright.
1762, Aug. 7. Guttier, Edward, and Mary Hartley.
1772, July 6. Guttier, James, and Margaret Kennedy.
1766, July 23. Guy, Alexander, and Ann Davis.
1774, June 16. Guy, Ann, and James Stuart.
1774, Oct. 28. Guy, Ann, and William Grey.
1771, Dec. 28. Guyer, Adam, and Mary Kearney.
1776, June 8. Guyer, Mary, and John David Sickle.
1746, June —. Guyger, Barbara, and Anthor Hyger.
1771, Jan. 31. Guyger, Casper, and Ann Pritchard.
1775, Sep. 9. Guy, James, and Mary Fisher.
1774, Jan. 22. Guy, Jane, and Edward McKegan.
1775, May 30. Guy, Mary, and Philip Boardman.

1766, Dec. 8. Guy, Thomas, and Ann Anthony.
1769, Feb. 14. Guy, William, and Margaret Townshend.
1748, June 16. Guy, William, and Mary Scot.

H.

1770, Mar. 17. Haas, Casper, and Catharine Sneck.
1776, May 13. Haas, Catharine, and Richard Walsh
1766, Dec. 1. Haas, John, and Barbara Heilman.
1770, June 30. Haas, Rachel, and Samuel James.
1776, Jan. 24. Hacket, Susannah and William Lewellin.
1761, Mar. 18. Hackett, Elizabeth, and Abram Thomas.
1764, June 27. Hackett, George, and Elizabeth McYoung.
1761, Oct. 9. Hadley, John, and Catharine Mauk.
1764, Dec. 26. Hadley, Thomas, and Mary Craft.
1763, Jan. 3. Haegner, Catharine, and Joseph Myer.
1761, Feb. 6. Haeps, Mary, and Samuel Forster.
1760, Aug. 11. Haetton, George, and Mary Moore.
1761, June 24. Haflick, Owen, and Mary Past.
1761, Sept. 1. Hagan, Cornelius, and Mary Potter.
1760, Feb. 28. Hagar, and Ceaser.
1763, Apr. 20. Haggerty, Barbara, and Peter Ballard.
1766, Dec. 18. Haggerty, Chlotilde, and James Wood.
1768, Sept. 29. Haggin, Arthur, and Catharine Dwyer.
1760, Oct. 11. Haggins, Mary, and William Baby.
1760, M'ch 24. Haig, Arthur, and Elizabeth Lykens.
1770, Oct. 10. Haiket, Abraham, and Chloe Benn.
1773, Sep. 29. Haild, Ruth, and Allan Langley.
1770, M'ch 19. Haines, Anthony, and Susannah Rohr.
1767, Dec. 11. Haines, Barzilla, and Hannah Young.
1748, Mar. 11. Haines, Dorothy, and Anthony Adamson.
1774, Oct. 31. Haines, Elizabeth, and Hans Adam Faulin.
1768, M'ch 8. Haines, Henry, and Elizabeth Thomas.
1772, April 23. Haines, Isaac, and Lydia Davis.
1769, July 24. Haines, Jane, and Alexander Russell.
1768, Nov. 16. Haines, John, and Sarah O'Neal.
1763, Oct. 3. Haines, Mary, and James Mullen.
1769, Oct. 9. Haines, Michael, and Sarah Downey.
1761, M'ch 24. Haines, Rebecca, and Andrew Morris.
1747, May —. Haines, Robert, and Jane Steward.
1768, June 2. Hainick, Francis, and Barbara Wentz.
1768, Apr. 20. Hair, Mary, and Edward Poole.
1759, Dec. 31. Halding, John, and Ann Bruce.
1768, July 13. Hale, Alexander, and Frances Yorkson.
1763, June 17. Hale, Jane, and James Riddle.
1763, May 4. Hale, Sarah, and John Craig.
1769, Dec. 30. Hale, Warwick, and Mary Crispin.

1769, July 5. Haley, Daniel, and Catharine Dordes.
1765, M'ch 14. Haley, Margaret, and James Currie.
1766, Jan. 15. Haley, Thomas, and Margaret Connaway.
1744, M'ch —. Haliday, James.
1769, Sep. 21. Halkerston, Elizabeth, and Peter Greer.
1762, July 23. Halkerston, Robert, and Elizabeth Hunt.
1767, Apr. 2. Hall, Aaron, and Hannah Hallowell.
1774, Sep. 1. Hall, Alice, and John Loe.
1761. Dec. 8. Hall, Alice, and Thomas Knox.
1760, Apr. 25. Hall, Andrew, and Ann M'Kendree.
1775, Jan. 5. Hall, Catharine, and John Dean.
1748, Jan. —. Hall, David, and Laycosh Gratis.
1762, Aug. 3. Hall, Elizabeth, and Michael Wain.
1775, May 25. Hall, Elizabeth, and Walter Oliver.
1768, M'ch 14. Hall, Hannah, and William Edwards.
1768, Apr. 3. Hall, Jacob, and Hermion Wood.
1764, Aug. 4. Hall, James, and Elizabeth Hill.
1772, Feb. 10. Hall, James, and Sarah Winn.
1769, M'ch 1. Hall, Jane, and Andrew Carson.
1760, Sep. 13. Hall, Jane, and George Hoops.
1763, Jan. 4. Hall, Jane and Jacob Vankirk.
1770, Oct. 4. Hall, Jane, and John Morrell.
1765, Dec. 24. Hall, Jane, and Patrick McGee.
1743, Oct. —. Hall, John.
1775, Dec. 14. Hall, John, and Isabella McConnel.
1746, June —. Hall, John, and Jane Patterson.
1760, Dec. 4. Hall, John, and Margaret Nesbitt.
1771, Oct. 12. Hall, John, and Mary Smith.
1747, Aug. —. Hall, John, and Sarah Parry.
1766, Nov. 1. Hall, Levin, and Christiana Hopman.
1759. Dec. 26. Hall, Margaret, and John Murray.
1747, Jan. —. Hall, Margaret, and Thomas Parkison.
1761, July 4. Hall, Margery, and John Dubrey.
1774, Oct. 8. Hall, Martha, and Richard Davie.
1764, Dec 10. Hall, Mary, and James Davis.
1761, Aug. 20. Hall, Mary, and John Gilbert.
1770, Dec. 20. Hall, Mary, and John Pyles.
1766, Dec. 18. Hall, Mary, and Samuel Laughlen.
1767, Apr. 9. Hall, Mary, and Thomas Ramsey.
1769, Apr. 1. Hall, Mary, and William Hans.
1770, July 18. Hall, Orminella, and John Grant.
1745, Aug. —. Hall, Richard.
1744, Feb. —. Hall, Robert.
1765, Nov. 18. Hall, Samuel, and Martha Bradford.
1775, Oct. 24. Hall, Sarah, and Richard Thomas.
1746, July —. Hall, Sarah, and William Forrest.

1775, M'ch   4. Hall, Thomas, and Margaret Sawyer.
1763, Apr. 13. Hall, Thomas, and Mary Bullock.
1767, Apr.   2. Hallowell, Hannah, and Aaron Hall.
1774, July   2. Hallowell, Mary, and John Edwards.
1760, Sep. 25. Halons, William, and Katharine Martin.
1763, M'ch   2. Halveston, Margaret, and Nicholas Marschar.
1772, Apr.   9. Hamble, John, Jun., and Judith Willson.
1775, Aug.   7. Hamble, Martha, and James Johnston.
1763, April 4. Hamble, William, and Elizabeth Schriner.
1774, Nov. 29. Hamble, William, and Susannah Dunwoody.
1768, Jan.   6. Hamilton, Andrew, and Abigail Franks.
1774, May   12. Hamilton, Ann, and Benjamin Boulter.
1764, Aug. 20. Hamilton, Ann, and Patrick Johnson.
1759, Dec. 22. Hamilton, Ann, and Robert Howard.
1765, May   22. Hamilton, Archibald, and Sarah Cook.
1762, Sep.   8. Hamilton, Benjamin, and Sarah Morrison.
1761, May   5. Hamilton, Catharine, and Patrick Allison.
1773, Nov. 13. Hamilton, Charles, and Elizabeth Richardson.
1774, M'ch 17. Hamilton, Charles, and Margaret Mitchell.
1761, July 14. Hamilton, David, and Margaret White.
1767, Aug. 20. Hamilton, Frances, and William Hunter.
1775, Aug. 16. Hamilton, Hannah, and Robert Williamson.
1772, April 1. Hamilton, Hugh, and Ann Campbell.
1776, M'ch   5. Hamilton, James, and Martha Willson.
1763, Nov. 29. Hamilton, Jane, and Finley Cameron.
1770, Dec. 27. Hamilton, Jane, and George Thompson.
1773, Oct.   1. Hamilton, John, and Deborah Shears.
1775, May   13. Hamilton, John, and Jane Godfrey.
1760, Dec. 18. Hamilton, John, and Margaret Christy.
1748, June 16. Hamilton, John, and Margaret Hamilton.
1770, Feb. 21. Hamilton, John, and Mary Boulby.
1763, Apr.   9. Hamilton, Margaret, and James Low.
1748, June 16. Hamilton, Margaret, and John Hamilton.
1760, May   6. Hamilton, Margaret, and John White
1764, M'ch 26. Hamilton, Margaret, and Lambert Tree.
1764, Dec. 24. Hamilton, Martha, and John Adams.
1760, Oct. 29. Hamilton, Mary, and James Dawson.
1760, May   6. Hamilton, Mary, and John Thornton.
1770, M'ch 21, Hamilton, Mary, and William Carson.
1772, Nov. 25. Hamilton, Patrick, and Ann Clark.
1772, June 11. Hamilton, Robert, and Mary Street.
1760, Aug.   6. Hamilton, Sarah, and John Grewes.
1761, Aug.   3. Hamilton, Tavenere, and Margaret Osborn.
1768, Nov. 12. Hamilton, William, and Martha Barcroft.
1771, June 15. Hamilton, William, and Rachel Herring.
1771, Apr. 20. Ham, James, and Hannah Jones.

1771, May 22. Ham, Jane, and Joseph Breintnall.
1774, May 10. Hamled, Godfrey, and Barbara Hartranfft.
1766, M'ch 31. Hammel, John, and Mary Kelly.
1772, Oct. 15. Hammer, Elizabeth, and Owen Brook
1774, June 29. Hammer, John, and Catharine Snyder.
1767, Aug. 29. Hammerly, August, and Mary Mulloy.
1775, May 6. Hammer, Mary, and Isaac Thomas.
1769, May 17. Hammerstane, Juliana, and Martin Lantz.
1773, M'ch 9. Hammet, Prudence, and Joseph Berryman.
1767, Oct. 19. Hammitt, Arody, and William Whitton.
1773, Feb. 13. Hammitt, Sarah, and John Wolohon.
1771, Sep. 25. Hammitt, Thomas, and Sarah Walker.
1765, Dec. 21. Hammon, Andrew, and Ann Manahon.
1767, Aug. 15. Hammond, Anthony, and Margaret Flin.
1760, M'ch 1. Hammond, William, and Susannah Patterson.
1767, M'ch 28. Hammon, Sarah, and Richard West.
1765, Apr. 24. Hampton, Elizabeth, and Jacob Vogdes.
1774, Nov. 2. Hampton, Elizabeth, and Jacob Williams.
1761, M'ch 5. Hampton, Sarah, and John Balding.
1762, Nov. 18. Hampton, Sarah. and John Estlack.
1762, July 6. Ham, Richard, and Elizabeth Kenard.
1767, Apr. 16. Hanbest, Robert, and Ann Thomas.
1766, July 26. Hance. Hannah, and George Syng.
1744. Jan. —. Hancock, Thomas.
1764, June 5. Hand, Ezekiel, and Abigail Garlick.
1744, Jan. —. Handlin, Valentine, and Sarah Russel.
1772, Oct, 7. Handschuckin, Henrietta Elizabeth, and **John**
Andrew Krug.
1762, Dec. 23. Handy, Mary, and Joseph Ritchie.
1765, Apr. 5. Haney, Elizabeth, and Samuel Honeyman.
1765, Sep. 4. Haney, Mary, and Edward Reynolds.
1768, Apr. 18. Hanlan, Ann, and John Livingston.
1767, June 29. Hanlan, Rose, and William Daverau.
1771, M'ch 13. Hanlin, Edward, and Elizabeth Stewart.
1771, June 15. Hanlon, James, and Martha Craig.
1775, Nov. 21. Hanly, John, and Lydia Coggins.
1775, Nov. 3. **Hanna,** John, and Elizabeth Froeme.
1768, Apr. 14. **Hanna,** John. and Phebe Wharton.
1775, Nov. 9. **Hanna,** John, and Rebecca Tanzer.
1760, Jan. 29. Hanna, Mary, and Hugh Campbell.
1775, Dec. 7. Hannes, Mary, and Johnston Smith.
1770, Apr. 3. Hannin, Susannah Regina, and Charles Hoffman.
1765, Sep. 16. Hannum, Mary, and Richard Cheyney.
1767, Feb. 4. Hansberger, Jacob, and Catharine Peel.
1776, June 7. Hanse, Conrad, and Isabella Brown.
1769, Dec. 27. Hanse, Eleanor, and John Adudell.

1760, Apr. 29. Hanse, Elizabeth, and George Daniel.
1765, Aug. 17. Hanse, Jacob, and Mary Bankson.
1763, Apr. 13. Hansel, Mary, and John Thomas.
1773, Jan. 20. Hansman, Elizabeth, and William Schriver.
1771, May 18. Hanson, Catharine, and Adam Rochaberger.
1760, Sep. 1. Hanson, Edward, and Susannah Powel.
1766, M'ch 26. Hanson, Jonathan, and Margaret Miller.
1773, Feb. 4. Hanson, Mary, and Henry McGee.
1768, Oct. 22. Hanson, Mary, and Thomas Robinson.
1769, Apr. 1. Hans, William, and Mary Hall.
1774, Sep. 15. Hanvest, Henry, and Anne Elliot.
1768, M'ch 17. Harbert, Ann, and James Willson.
1746, May —. Harbert, Benjamin.
1767, Aug. 3. Harbert, Michael, and Ellis Richards.
1772, Feb. 25. Harbeson, Benjamin, and Margaret Comb.
1748, Nov. 11. Harcob, Abigail, and William Falkner.
1760, Oct. 30. Hardin, Charles, and Jane Sheart.
1764, Oct. 26. Harding, Christiana, and William Moore.
1744, July 21. Harding, George.
1766, June 20. Harding, George, and Mary Nelson.
1775, M'ch 22. Harding, Jonathan, and Mary Randle.
1771, Feb. 16. Harding, Joseph, and Martha Addis.
1766, M'ch 18. Harding, Martha, and Walter Willet.
1766, M'ch 29. Harding, Mary, and Amos Strickland.
1761, Dec. 19. Harding, Mary, and Edmund Badger.
1766, Nov. 11. Harding, Mary, and Francis Simer.
1748, Jan. —. Harding, Mary, and George Allen.
1776, Jan. 25. Harding, Mary, and John Christie.
1765, July 18. Harding, Richard, and Martha Hust.
1771, Sep. 14. Harding, Thomas, and Sarah Kirk.
1774, July 11. Harding, William, and Jane Taylor.
1764, Sep. 14. Harding, William, and Sarah Adudel.
1761, Aug. 17. Hardly, Thomas, and Sarah Simon.
1764, May 11. Hardman, Peter, and Catharine Stone.
1770, Aug. 15. Hardy, Rachel, and Matthias Fertin.
1767, M'ch 26. Hardy, Robert, and Martha Cowgill.
1768, Oct. 1. Hare, Agnes, and Philip Terrapin.
1762, May 29. Hare, Edward, and Martha Wall.
1769, June 7. Hare, Martha, and William Carsen.
1775, Sep. 27. Hare, Patrick, and Mary Tool.
1775, Nov. 15. Hare, Robert, and Margaret Willing.
1770, Jan. 9. Harkens, Margaret, and John Forrest.
1761, Jan. 19. Harkes, James, and Elizabeth Hawkins.
1772, Oct. 27. Harlan, Abigail, and William Moran.
1769, Oct. 4. Harling, Elizabeth, and Christian Dederer.
1772, Aug. 10. Harlin, Sarah, and Joseph Snowden.

1759, Dec. 22. Harlin, Stephen, and Deborow Stroud.
1771, M'ch 6. Harman, Barbara, and Jacob Booce.
1761, Dec. 1. Harman, Isaac, and Rachel Stilley.
1767, M'ch 20. Harman, Rachel, and William Buchanon.
1748, Oct. —. Harmen, Sarah, and Matthew Ray.
1761, Oct. 12. Harmer, Hyd, and Frances Tavey.
1761, Oct. 29. Harman, Hannah, and George Jenkins.
1773, July 8. Harmonson, Ann, and John Magar.
1770, Aug. 11. Harnet, James, and Jane Glasgow.
1760, Nov. 28. Haro, Elizabeth, and James Henry.
1761, Sept. 1. Harper, Deboro, and John Studdert.
1761, Sept. 9. Harper, Ebenezer, and Ann Clayton.
1765, Oct. 21. Harper, Elizabeth, and Phineas Thomas.
1764, Nov. 23. Harper, Elizabeth, and William Smith.
1762, July 15. Harper, Francis, and Deborah Castle.
1763, Apr. 5. Harper, Hannah, and Bryan Kelly.
1774, Oct. 25. Harper, John, and Margaret Bennet.
1746, Dec. —. Harper, John, and Margaret Richy.
1763, Sep. 10. Harper, Josiah, and Catharine Luter.
1761, Nov. 16. Harper, Margaret, and William Bywater.
1747, June —. Harper, Margaret, and William Prigg.
1772, M'ch 7. Harper, Mary, and Anthony Yerkes.
1764, Sep. 6. Harper, Mary, and George Robinson.
1748, Oct. —. Harper, Peter, and Eve Deil.
1743, Aug. 20. Harper, Samuel.
1770, Aug. 18. Harper, Samuel, and Hannah Dennaughey.
1770, Jan. 30. Harper, Sarah, and John Wager.
1773, Feb. 18. Harper, Thomas, and Deborah Drinker.
1775, May 9. Harper, Thomas, and Mary Davis.
1760, June 25. Harper, William, and Elinor Smith.
1771, Feb. 25. Harper, William, and ―――― Kenton.
1768, Jan. 13. Harper, William, and Sarah Philips.
1747, May —. Harp, Henry, and Elizabeth Higgerbittom.
1771, Nov. 8. Harpin, Catharine, and John Dixon.
1775, Apr. 20. Harp, William, and Lydia Davis.
1770, Sep. 1. Harrae, Anne, and Patrick Stafford.
1761, July 4. Harrald, David, and Margaret Boyd.
1761, Feb. 24. Harral, Samuel, and Elizabeth Russell.
1769, Feb. 6. Harris, Benjamin, and Martha Davis.
1768, Nov. 21. Harris, Elizabeth, and Robert Fitzgerald.
1772, M'ch 10. Harris, Elizabeth, and William Hynes.
1744, Oct. —. Harris, George.
1764, Nov. 17. Harris, Isaac, and Edith Murray.
1771, Sep. 10. Harris, Isaac, and Mary White.
1774, Nov. 26. Harris, Margery, and Robert McFarland.
1765, Oct. 31. Harrison, Abigail, and Stephen Beezely.

1762, Apr. 14. Harrison, Charles, and Esther Shores.
1747, Sep. —. Harrison, Daniel.
1760, Oct. 22. Harrison, Elizabeth, and Enoch David:
1772, May 23. Harrison, Elizabeth and Francis Barrell.
1783, June 16. Harrison, Francis.
1760, June 26. Harrison, Frances, and John Knott.
1748, Apr. 13. Harrison, Henry, and Mary Aspden.
1747, June —. Harrison, Jane, and John McCalla.
1745, Jan. —. Harrison, John.
1769, Oct. 7. Harrison, John, and Elizabeth Connell.
1764, July 6. Harrison, John, and Elizabeth Gardner.
1764, Aug. 24. Harrison, John, and Elizabeth Hubbleston.
1769, Apr. 15. Harrison, John, and Rachel Allman.
1762, Nov. 4. Harrison, Mary, and John Galloway.
1773, Feb. 10. Harrison, Mary, and William White.
1764, Nov. 8. Harrison, Robert, and Mary Bonum.
1766, May 29. Harrison, Sarah, and Abram Ferguson.
1773, Dec. 11. Harrison, Thomas, and Sarah Hutton.
1764, Apr. 18. Harrison, Thomas, and Sarah Richards.
1768, Oct. 29. Harrison, William, and Martha Bowlsby.
1767, Sep. 23. Harris, Rebecca, and Abram Yocum.
1774, Oct. 12. Harris, Sarah, and James Clifton.
1776, M'ch 6. Harris. Thomas, and Elizabeth Stevens.
1744, Oct. —. Harris, William.
1774, Dec. 6. Harr, John, and Elizabeth Maddox.
1773, Sept. 25. Harrow, David, and Rebecca Wilkinson.
1762, Jan. 23. Harry, Edward, and Jane Lewis.
1762, Jan, 23, Harry, Evan, and Abigail Clues.
1769, Feb. 28. Hart, Anthony, and Anne Bayman.
1761, Jan. 1. Hart, Barbara, and Adam Croce.
1771, Oct. 15. Hart, Catharine, and Jacob Falkenstein.
1764, May 7. Hart, Charles, and Susannah McVaughn.
1761, Jan. 6. Harter, James, and Catharine Deling.
1762, Dec. 18. Hart, Felix, and Elizabeth Hosson.
1763, July 18. Hart, Isaac, and Sarah Gibson.
1770, May 19. Hart, John, and Catharine Knowles.
1763, Dec. 19. Hart, John, and Eleanor Carrel.
1770, Jan. 1. Hart, Joseph, and Elizabeth Gilbert.
1745, July —. Hartley, Benjamin.
1774, Sept. 23. Hartley, Catharine, and Thomas Duke.
1769, Oct. 4. Hartley, James, and Elizabeth Cooper.
1762, Aug. 7. Hartley, Mary, and Edward Guttier.
1768, Oct. 1. Hartley, Mary, and Richard Waddington.
1771, Feb. 17. Hartley, Richard, and Mary Welsh.
1764, Sep. 24. Hartley, Thomas, and Elizabeth Clark.
1767, Apr. 27. Hartley, William, and Elizabeth Legg.

1763, July 27. Hart, Lilies, and William Brown.
1765, Feb. 26. Hart, Margaret, and Christopher Yetter.
1763, Apr. 6. Hart, Margaret, and Robert Elton.
1771, Nov. 11. Hart, Margaret, and Robert Mitchell.
1746, Nov. —. Hart, Mary, and Abel Marpel.
1771, Dec. 30. Hart, Mary, and Conrod Davis.
1771, July 4. Hart, Mary, and James Buckman.
1747, Sep. —. Hart, Mary, and John Smallwood.
1774, June 14. Hart, Mary, and Stephen Porter.
1762, June 2. Hart, Phebe, and Robert Vernon.
1774, May 10, Hartranfft, Barbara, and Godfrey Hamled.
1783, June 1. Hartranfft, Christopher.
1761, Sep. 30. Hartrick, William, and Sarah Kelly.
1764, Oct. 15. Hart, Sarah, and James Graysbury.
1745, M'ch —. Hartshorn, James.
1770, Jan. 29. Hart, Silas, and Mary Daniel.
1769, May 8. Hartwell, Berry, and Martha Spencer.
1772, Oct. 21. Hartzell, Mary Magdalen, and Abraham Stout.
1748, Nov. 11. Harverd, Rachel, and John Mayhew.
1775, Oct. 27. Harvey, Catharine, and Elijah Philip.
1769, Nov. 6. Harvey, Elizabeth, and Benjamin Reeder.
1769, June 19. Harvey, George, and Dorothea Hunt.
1764, M'ch 29. Harvey, James, and Hannah Donalds.
1770, Aug. 18. Harvey, Jemima, and George Savadge.
1769, Aug. 15. Harvey, Job, and Hannah Anderson.
1761, M'ch 13. Harvey, John, and Jane Snodgrass.
1769, Sep. 28. Harvey, John, and Mary Jamison.
1774, Mc'h 24. Harvey, John, and Sarah Biles.
1768, Mar. 7. Harvey, Lean, and Thomas Bulger.
1769, Nov. 14. Harvey, Mary, and John Vicary.
1763, Sep. 29. Harvey, Mary, and Thomas McClean.
1760, M'ch 15. Harvey, Sampson, and Mary Bradford.
1769, July 31. Harvey, Samuel, and Catharine Tenbrook.
1763, June 3. Harvey, Sarah, and Thomas Briton.
1762, Oct. 23. Harvey, Susannah, and Daniel Rambo.
1772, Nov. 25. Harvey, Theodosia, and Thomas Quin.
1764, June 6. Harwood, Leonard, and Mary Davis.
1765, Oct. 14. Hasand, Catharine, and John Croney.
1772, Nov. 18. Hasenclever, Francis Gasper and Mary Melchoir.
1746, Oct. —. Hasleton, James, and Mary Wilkinson.
1748, Feb. —. Haslet, Susanna, and Richard Addis.
1760, Aug. 13. Haslet, William, and Jane Wilson.
1761, July 9. Hasloock, William, and Eve Pillages.
1762, Jan. 19. Hassard, Aaron, and Catharine Ritchel.

8—VOL. II.

1762, May   5. Hasselberg, Abraham, and Elizabeth Mets.
1747, June —. Hassell, Ann, and James Benezet.
1760, M'ch 18. Hasting, James, and Margaret Usher.
1748, June 16. Hastings, Mary, and George Plins.
1765, Oct. 28. Hastings, Samuel, and Massey Denton.
1747, Feb. —. Hastings, Sarah, and Swan Warner.
1775, July   7. Hastings, William, and Mary Lusad.
1747, Nov. —. Haston, Peter, and Margaret Hedges.
1774, M'ch 23. Hasty, Daniel, and Mary Hollingsworth.
1747, Dec. —. Hatfield, Jane, and James Conrad.
1767, Aug. 25. Hathorn, Daniel, and Elizabeth Willson.
1769, Feb. 24. Hathorn, James, and Martha Kerr.
1760, M'ch 19. Hatter, Richard, and Elizabeth Howe.
1773, July 26. Hattman, Henry, and Catharine Weising.
1776, Apr.   9. Hattner, Catharine, and John Otto.
1765, Sep. 10. Hatton, Sarah, and John Alexander Brown.
1743, Aug. 17. Haven, John.
1762, Nov. 23. Haverd, John, and Mary Lacey.
1783, June 25. Haward, Andrew.
1775, Feb. 25. Hawes, James, and Hannah Worrell.
1776, Jan. 25. Hawger, Godfrey, and Mary Fought.
1773, Sep.   4. Hawker, Godfrey, and Catharine Fitzgerald.
1767, Aug. 15. Hawke, Samuel, and Mary Main.
1746, Aug. —. Hawkins, Ann, and John Hutchins.
1761, Jan. 19. Hawkins, Elizabeth, and James Harkes.
1767, Sep.   1. Hawkins, Elizabeth, and Jonathan Montgomery.
1745, June —. Hawkins, George.
1766, May   8. Hawkins, Sarah, and Joseph Thompson.
1744, Jan. —. Hawkins, William.
1767, July   8. Hawkins, William, and Elizabeth Creddock.
1764, Aug.   2. Hawskin, William, and Martha Smith.
1771, May 29. Haycock, Hannah, and Nicholas Woollis.
1747, Jan. —. Haycott, David, and Mary Offinger.
1771, Dec. 10. Hay, Elizabeth, and David Shaffer.
1768, June 17. Hay, Elizabeth, and Lambert Barnes.
1771, M'ch 28. Hayes, Charity, and William Atkinson.
1760, Oct.   9. Hayes, Patience, and Edward Moor.
1747, Oct. —. Hayes, Rebecca, and Jonathan Brooks.
1766, Apr. 12. Hayes, Sarah, and Archibald Thompson.
1775, Jan. 23. Hayes, Sarah, and James Coburn.
1773, Nov.   1. Hayes, Thomas, and Margaret Summer.
1745, Nov. —. Hayhurst, William.
1775, July   1. Hay, Jane, and William Favell.
1767, Oct. 31. Hay, John, and Rosannah Cline.
1722, Oct. 15. Hayman, William, and Ann Wane.
1760, Dec. 20. Haynes, Charles, and Margaret Lockeridge.

1769, July 24. Hays, Casper, and Mary Ludwick.
1762, July 12. Hays, Conrad, and Charlotte Mousin.
1769, May 29. Hays, Elizabeth, and Amos Wickersham.
1776, June 1. Hays, Magdalen, and Samuel Smith.
1769, June 14. Hays, Martha, and Thomas Wright.
1763, Apr. 13. Hays, Rachel, and John Jones.
1770, Nov. 5. Hayward, John, and Anne Watson.
1773, Sep. 24. Hazard, Richard, and Mary Brown.
1766, Aug. 8. Hazell, Sarah, and John Gill.
1769, Apr. 25. Hazelhurst, Isaac, and Juliana Purviance.
1763, Jan. 27. Hazleton, Mary, and Henry Bastone.
1771, July 17. Hazlewood, John, and Hester Leacock.
1773, Feb. 22. Hazlewood, William, and Rachel Rouse.
1762, Jan. 20. Head, Joseph, and Mary Dickinson.
1765, June 8. Headley, Sarah, and Joseph White.
1769, June 12. Head, Margaret, and Philip Ross.
1761, Oct. 26. Heany, Mary, and Thomas Gaskin.
1761, July 16. Hearn, David, and Jennet Steel.
1746, Dec. —. Heass, George, and Mary Jacobs.
1764, Dec. 21. Heassley, Christiana, and John Young.
1769, July 12. Heatcorn, Elizabeth, and John Yeumans.
1767, Feb. 4. Heathcoate, John, and Elizabeth Cox.
1767, Feb. 4. Heatherington, Martha, and Roger Merrywhether.
1764, Jan 21. Heath, John, and Mary Taylor.
1763, May 17. Heath, John, and Sarah Reed.
1769, Dec. 16. Heaton Catharine, and Benjamin Vastine.
1761, Feb. 3. Heaton, Davis, and Susan Jones.
1760, Aug. 13. Heaton, Jeremiah, and Elizabeth Carter.
1747, Apr. —. Heaton, Robert, and Ann Carvour.
1769, Nov. 15. Heaton, Robert, and Sarah Griffith.
1761, M'ch 3. Heaton, Sarah, and John Walling.
1771, M'ch 21. Heblethwaite, Middleton, and Margaret Meskell.
1761, Dec. 2. Heddley, Elizabeth, and Timothy Bunting.
1747, Nov. —. Hedges, Margaret, and Peter Heston.
1770, Sep. 5. Hedley, Hannah, and Timothy Belsford.
1772, May 23. Heeny, John, and Elizabeth Hess.
1773, May 3. Heide, Mary, and Peter Smick.
1767, Aug. 17. Heiler, Sebastian, and Elizabeth Pillager.
1766, Dec. 1. Heilman, Barbara, and John Haas.
1747, Dec. —. Heine, Rebecca, and Isaac Hughes.
1767, Apr. 28. Heissel, Rebecca, and Christopher Young.
1761, Nov. 11. Heist, Henry, and Leah Peters.
1761, M'ch 7. Hellborn, Miles, and Mary Edwards.
1769, Feb. 20. Hellbourn, Thomas, and Margaret Johnson.
1775, Sep. 18. Heller, John, and Mary Jones.
1748, Oct. 18. Helliard, Solomon, and Jane Buckley.

1773, Jan.   7. Hellings, Fincher, and Catharine Dogharty.
1765, May   10. Hellings, John, and Elizabeth Titus.
1767, June   10. Hellings, Mary, and John Comly.
1747, May   —. Helm, Bretty, and John Holton.
1767, Jan.   8. Helm, Catharine, and Jacob Sutor.
1766, Apr.   8. Helm, Elizabeth, and Derrick Kuyper.
1764, Nov.   1. Helmes, Eleanor, and William Cooper.
1772, M'ch   12. Heim, John, and Elizabeth Thomas.
1765, Aug.   29. Helm, Peter, and Mary Wright.
1762, Oct.   25. Helspy, Hannah, and Thomas Benson.
1768, Apr.   9. Helton, Letitia, and Isaac Bener.
1762, Dec.   6. Helviston, Christiana, and Jonathan Clift.
1762, Feb.   10. Hemings, Paul, and Eleanor Audley.
1765, Nov.   21. Hemmenway, Joshua, and Sarah Angila.
1771, Nov.   13. Hemminger, John, and Catharine McCarty.
1772, Dec.   10. Hemphili, Ann, and Alexander Boggs.
1762, Aug.   16. Hemphill, John, and Margaret Boggs.
1770, May   18. Hencock, Sarah, and John Morgan.
1763, Nov.   2. Henderson, Alexander, and Martha Findley.
1775, June   20. Henderson, Alexander, and Mary Anderson.
1776, Feb.   19. Henderson, Ann, and Francis Procter.
1766, Dec.   20. Henderson, Eleanor, and John Ramsey.
1772, Sep.   24. Henderson, Elizabeth, and Martin Parkinson.
1769, Jan.   14. Henderson, Hannah, and Stokely Hosman.
1763, Sep.   10. Henderson, John, and Alice Watson.
1773, Aug.   11. Henderson, John, and Mary Campbell.
1766, May   15. Henderson, John, and Sarah Litle.
1748, Nov.   11. Henderson, Mary, and John Stevenson.
1765, May   10. Henderson, Matthew, and Barbara Elliot.
1774, June   27. Henderson, Matthew, and Margaret Erwin.
1773, Apr.   16. Henderson, Rosanna, and John Presly.
1748, July   13. Henderson, William, and Celia Frewin.
1747, Oct.   —. Henderson, William, and Mary Worrall.
1748, July   13. Hendrick, Michael, and Sarah Neil.
1773, M'ch   31. Hendricks, Catharine, and Samuel Long.
1776, May   15. Hendricks, Elizabeth, and Abraham Castor.
1764, Feb.   15. Hendricks, Elizabeth, and George Rife.
1773, May   31. Hendricks, Letitia, and Philip Fullar.
1761, July   24. Hendricks, Nathan, and Mary Bond.
1769, Oct.   31. Hendrickson, Isaac, and Margaret Nithermark.
1769, M'ch   22. Hendrickson, Rebecca, and Daniel Culin.
1772, Feb.   12. Hendricks, Samuel, and Abigail Umpstead.
1771, Oct.   24. Heneby, Richard, and Jane McKillup.
1773, Feb.   11. Henfelstein, Albertus, and Catharine Carker.
1771, Jan.   3. Henly, Eleanor, and John Hogan.
1768, Oct.   24. Henly, William, and Hannah Jenkins.

1767, Feb. 28. Hennessy, John, and Mary Boulton.
1774, Aug. 27. Hennessy, Maurice, and Margaret Davenport.
1769, Feb. 7. Henricks, Anna, and Thomas Asherfelder.
1762, Dec. 4. Henricks, Rachael, and Jacob Metz.
1765, Sep. 16. Henry, Ann, and Robert Dunkin.
1768, Oct. 27. Henry, Frances, and Edward Batchelor.
1774, Apr. 6. Henry, George, and Ann Usher.
1773, May 7. Henry, George, Jun., and Mary Sentzer.
1769, May 4. Henry, Hugh, and Phebe Morris.
1760, Nov. 28. Henry, James, and Elizabeth Haro.
1772, Nov. 26. Henry, Jane, and Richard Hodnott.
1761, June 15. Henry, John, and Catharine Bosham.
1746, Aug. —. Henry, John, and Elizabeth Smith.
1761, Feb. 6. Henry, Margaret, and James Stuart.
1764, Sep. 22. Henry, Mary, and John Honeyman.
1775, Oct. 11. Henry, Philip, and Margaret Thornburn.
1770, Dec. 22. Henry, Samuel, and Margaret Barnhill.
1774, Sep. 14. Hensliff, John, and Mary Sterret.
1773, Jan. 12. Hensman, Margaret, and George Zimmerman.
1743, Feb. 16. Henzy, Joshua.
1775, July 22. Hercules, John, and Susannah Derwett.
1765, Apr. 4. Heretage, Kezia, and Nathaniel Blencowe.
1762, Apr. 12. Herger, Margaret, and George Tannacker.
1747, Dec. —. Hering, Jennet, and John Moore.
1760, June 9. Herman, Barbara, and Powell Cover.
1748, Sep. —. Herman, Leonard, and Barbara Knepler.
1761, Apr. 13. Herring, ———, and Mary Ingliss.
1771, June 15. Herring, Rachel, and William Hamilton.
1745, Aug. —. Herr, John Adam.
1767, Aug. 20. Hervey, Jane, and John Clement.
1772, June 11. Herxe, Rachel, and Godfrey Slyhauff.
1769, Nov. 8. Heslett, Lydia, and Thomas Clendinnon.
1771, Dec. 20. Heslet, Sarah, and John Cock.
1772, May 23. Hess, Elizabeth, and John Heeny.
1762, Dec. 7. Hess, Michael, and Dorothy Spoone.
1746, Aug. —. Hesselius, Sarah, and Walker Porter.
1773, June 2. Hesser, Christiana, and Wigard Miller.
1774, June 7. Heston, Isaac, and Catharine Clinton.
1775, Aug. 8. Hetherington, John, and Isabella Craig.
1766, Oct, 15. Hewes, Caleb, and Deborah Potts.
1764, M'ch 1. Hewes, Edward, and Lydia Garrets.
1770, Oct. 9. Hewet, Charles, and Anne Pierce.
1775, M'ch 13. Hewett, Hoppel, and John Foy.
1770, Dec. 1. Hewitt, John, and Elizabeth Adams.
1764, Sep. 29. Hewlin, Rebecca, and Paul Crispin.
1747, June —. Hewlins, Abram, and Susannah Polgreen.

1773, Sep. 28. Hewster, Mary, and John Howe.
1768, Aug. 7. Heyl, George, and Dorothy Phyle.
1771, Sep. 18. Heyl, John, and Mary Stricker.
1771, Nov. 6. Heyl, Mary, and Philip Won.
1770, Aug. 29. Heynen, Elizabeth, and Caspar Taylor.
1763, June 16. Heyward, John, and Catharine King.
1762, Nov. 3. Hibbert, Esther, and Isaac Lobb.
1773, Oct. 20. Hibbs, Eli, and Mary Collum.
1761, Apr. 8. Hibbs, Hannah, and David Smith.
1761, Oct. 19. Hibbs, Jacob, and Elizabeth D. Young.
1761, Aug. 3. Hibbs, Jeremiah, and Richard Parsons.
1773, Jan. 28. Hickley, John, and Alice Tufft.
1744, Oct. —. Hickman, Benjamin.   (See note.)
1744, Oct. —. Hickman Joseph.   (See note.)
1768, June 6. Hickman, Margaret, and James Sanders.
1769, Nov. 8. Hicks, Edward, and Hannah Ratten.
1761, M'ch 13. Hicks, Elizabeth, and John Slicks.
1775, May 7. Hicks, Hannah, and Isaac Buck.
1748, Nov. 11. Hicks, Nicolas, and Christian Albrighton.
1767, May 12. Higgens, Elizabeth and David Brown.
1747, May —. Higgerbittom, Elizabeth, and Henry Harp.
1765, Aug. 13. Higgens, Hannah, and Thomas Dunbar.
1763, Oct. 27. Higgins, Ichabod, and Jemima Nowla.
1775, Feb. 10. Higgins, Margaret, and Isaac Fowler.
1770, June 11. Higgins, Patrick, and Dorothea Pennyfeather.
1768, Nov. 10. Higgins, Rachel, and James Robinson.
1775, June 5. Higgs, Elizabeth, and John Lee.
1769, June 28. Highle, John, and Elizabeth Tinney.
1769, Oct. 24. Hiley, Susannah, and Henry Taney.
1770, Dec. 22. Hill, Agnes, and Joseph Janvior.
1774, May 11. Hill, Ann, and Henry Norris.
1760, Dec. 4. Hillbo, Phebe, and Joseph Smith.
1767, Nov. 10. Hillburn, Christopher, and Mary Vansickle.
1768, Sep. 24. Hilldrup, Thomas, and Mary Ware.
1759, Dec. 8. Hill, Edward, and Catharine Mankin.
1765, Oct. 3. Hill, Edward, and Sarah Rue.
1767, Jan. 29. Hillegas, Susannah, and William Pitts.
1769, May 17. Hill, Elizabeth, and Hugh King.
1764, Aug. 4. Hill, Elizabeth, and James Hall.
1773, Jan. 20. Hiller, Frederick, and Catharine Kreese.
1773, June 1. Hill, Henry, and Anne Meredith.
1765, July 26. Hill, Henry, and Mary Purchess.
1747, Oct. —. Hillhouse, Mary, and John Reily.
1744, Oct. —. Hill, Hugh.
1768, Jan. 28. Hillings, Elizabeth, and Richard Watson.
1762, Aug. 25. Hillings, Susannah, and Robert Stackhouse.

1766, Aug. 18. Hill, Jacob, and Mary Anderson.
1769, June 9. Hill, Jacob, and Mary Cressmer.
1776, May 25. Hill, James, and Mary Huston.
1769, M'ch 11. Hill, James, and Sarah Chapman.
1767, Feb. 11. Hill, Jane, and Thomas Reed.
1761, Oct. 8. Hill, Josh, and Elizabeth West.
1774, May 3. Hillman, Cornelius, and Margaret Robinson.
1764, July 16. Hillman, Sarah, and Levy Peirce.
1746, Sep. —. Hill, Margaret, and John Bowan.
1764, July 7. Hill, Sarah, and James Middleton.
1767, May 14. Hill, Sarah, and John Kidd.
1768, Nov. 21. Hill, Susanna, and Charles Jones.
1747, Nov. —. Hill, Thomas, and Elizabeth McClellan.
1764, Nov. 17. Hillyard, Eleanor, and Abraham Carpenter.
1760, Sep. 24. Hilton, James, and Sarah Griffiths.
1761. M'ch 27. Hilton. Simon, and Tamson Lenox.
1762, Dec. 14. Hims, Ann, and James Cooper.
1763, June 6. Hinars, Mary, and Peter King
1771, May 18. Hinchman, Sarah, and James Ash.
1772, Sep. 11. Hine, Rachel, and William Polim.
1771, Dec. 4. Hines, Ann, and William Crawford.
1767, Nov. 5. Hines, Catharine, and Martin Benhart.
1774, July 14. Hines, Edward, and Elizabeth Pettit.
1767, Nov. 6. Hines, Mary, and George Caton.
1771, M'ch 20. Hines, Samuel, and Elizabeth Wright.
1744, Oct. —. Hinger, Christopher, Jun.
1760, Aug. 5. Hinkle, Catharine, and John Mannon.
1763, Dec. 2. Hinkle, Christian, and Clark Brown.
1767, Jan. 19. Hinsman, Mary, and Peter Schriver.
1747, Apr. —. Hinton, John, and Sarah Sherwood.
1773, Nov. 16. Hinton, Lydia, and William Wentworth.
1773, June 25. Hinton, Mary, and Thomas Wharton Collins.
1762, May 14. Hippard, Hannah, and Valentine Bower.
1765, Sep. 2. Hipple, Frederick, and Mary Rausbaughan.
1767, May 4. Hirman, Mary, and Ernst Schlosser.
1761, Apr. 25. Hirst, William, and Ann Thomas.
1765, Jan. 7. Hiser, John, and Annis Welch.
1761, May 2. Hitchcock, Elizabeth, and William Kaston.
1767, Jan. 17. Hitchcock, John, and Sarah Thomas.
1763, July 14. Hite, George, and Sophia Omensetter.
1775, Feb. 17. Hithal, John, and Margaret Huston.
1771, Nov. 28. Hitner, Frederick, and Mary Brown.
1763, Feb. 19. Hobbs, Hannah, and Anthony Wright.
1773, Oct. 23. Hockley, Ann, and Gustavus Conyngham.
1761, Nov. 5. Hockley, Thomas, and Eleanor Rogers.
1760, July 29. Hodge, Agnes, and James Bayard.

1761, Sep. 17. Hodge, Cassius, and Asfaa Jones.
1743, Sep. —. Hodge, Hugh.
1771, Oct. 31. Hodgkinson, Bethanath, and Catharine Simmons
1774, Sep. 1. Hodgson, Alvery, and Mary Cunningham.
1772, Nov. 26. Hodnot, Richard, and Jane Henry.
1773, June 2. Hoff, Elizabeth, and George Metzger.
1767, Oct. 24. Hoff, John, and Ruth Williams.
1746, Oct. —. Hoffman, Beata, and John Crook.
1774, M'ch 28. Hoffman, Catharine, and John Fechter.
1770, Apr. 3. Hoffman, Charles, and Susanna Regina Hannin.
1760, Aug. 14. Hoffman, Christian, and Catharine Hopen.
1771, Oct. 16. Hoffman, Elizabeth, and Joseph Fry.
1761, July 2. Hoffman, Elizabeth, and Joshua Leech.
1767, M'ch 12. Hoffman, John William, and Mary Wormly.
1775, Feb. 2. Hoffman, Mary, and Alexander Plunket.
1769, June 29. Hoffman, Mary, and Henry Miller.
1761, M'ch 18. Hoffman, Mary, and Isaac Slaughter.
1776, Apr. 25. Hoffman, Mary, and John Grayson.
1743, Apr. 9. Hoffman, Peter.
1764, Jan. 14. Hoffman, Rosanna, and George Young.
1771, Jan. 3. Hogan, John, and Eleanor Henly.
1766, Oct. 22. Hogeland, Catharine, and Herman Vansant.
1768, Dec. 21. Hogeland, Derrick, and Edith Bennet.
1767, June 20. Hogeland, George, and Mary Winecoop.
1768, Aug. 11. Hogeland, Hannah, and Jacob Bennet.
1774, M'ch 26. Hogeland, Johanna, and Simon Vanartsdalen.
1761, May 23. Hogland, Daniel, and Alice Krewson.
1762, Jan. 16. Holderman, Nicholas, and Catharine Guelden.
1764, June 13. Holder, Martin, and Catharine Tinsmanin.
1760, July 19. Holland, Hannah, and William Taylor.
1767, M'ch 10. Holland, Martha, and John Pickworth.
1761, M'ch 26. Holland, Robert, and Jane Price.
1771, Sep. 4. Holland, Sarah, and Peter Biggs.
1761, Apr. 20. Holland, Sarah, and Thomas May.
1743, May 4. Holland, William.
1764, M'ch 15. Holleback, Mary, and Jacobus Van Buskirk.
1763, Apr. 5. Hollen, Joseph, and Lilley Noblit.
1773, May 13. Holliday, Elizabeth, and Jesse Greenfield.
1764, Apr. 20. Holliday, Margretta, and George Christophel
        Dowig.
1772, Nov. 21. Hollingshead, Elizabeth, and Thomas Beans
1774, Jan. 25. Hollingshead, Jane, and John Duer, Jun.
1770, Feb. 20. Hollingshead, Nicholas, and Margaret Thompson.
1768, M'ch 9. Hollingsworth, Levi, and Hannah Paschall.
1770, M'ch 1. Hollingsworth, Lydia, and Samuel Wallis.
1774, M'ch 23. Hollingsworth, Mary, and Daniel Hasty.

1746, Nov. —. Hollin, Mary, and John Annis.
1774, June 14. Hollis, Abraham, and Martha Richi.
1744, Sep. —. Holl, John.
1767, Sep. 24. Holloway, Joseph, and Mary Jones.
1760, July 5. Holly, Susannah, and Thomas Davis.
1760, Feb. 19. Holme, Elizabeth, and John Fagon.
1760, Dec. 3. Holme, Johana, and Jonathan Rumford.
1773, May 8. Holmes, Elizabeth, and William Bartolet.
1760, Feb. 5. Holmes, Hannah, and Jacob Keen.
1776, Feb. 27. Holmes, Jacob, and Sarah Bates.
1743, Apr. 5. Holmes, John.
1773, Apr. 15. Holmes, John, Jun., and Hester Swift.
1766, Sep. 25. Holmes, Margaret, and William Furnis.
1768, Oct. 13. Holmes, Martha, and Marshall Edwards.
1772, Aug. 21. Holmes, Mary, and Benjamin Seyoe.
1764, July 21. Holmes, Phebe, and William Bate.
1775, Oct. 9. Holmes, Priscilla, and Samuel Cox.
1745, June —. Holmes, Samuel.
1773, Oct. 6. Holmes, Samuel, and Elizabeth Warwick.
1748, Oct. —. Holstein, Elizabeth, and Ezekiel Rambo.
1775, Apr. 22. Holstein, Sarah, and Hugh Dehaven.
1775, Jan. 5. Holsten, Ann, and Charles Robinson.
1775, M'ch 4. Holton, Magdalena, and John Black.
1762, Jan. 7. Holth, Rebecca, and Peter Allen.
1760, Jan. 15. Holton, Elizabeth, and James Scott.
1745, Jan. —. Holton, Francis.
1747, May —. Holton, John, and Bretty Helm.
1771, Sep. 26. Holton, Mary, and John Meredith.
1762, Aug. 13. Holton, Nathaniel, and Margaret Stuttle.
1773, Feb. 9. Holton, Ruth, and Isaac Rich.
1767, M'ch 13. Holton, Sarah, and William Gardner.
1770, Feb. 21. Holton, William, and Mary Smith.
1770, Nov. 10. Holtzhouser, Christiana, and William Durf.
1763, Jan. 28. Holwell, David, and Mary Douglass.
1763, Jan. 26. Holwell, Edward, and Eleanor Mason.
1743, July 2. Homer, Thomas.
1764, M'ch 13. Hommer, Esther, and William Watherington.
1767, Sep. 24. Honey, Christopher, and Catharine Stein.
1763, June 2. Honey, Mary, and Timothy Wallington.
1764, Sep. 22. Honeyman, John, and Mary Henry.
1765, Apr. 5. Honeyman, Samuel, and Elizabeth Heney.
1760, June 9. Honneur, John, and Sarah Stedham.
1770, May 3. Honorot, Elizabeth, and Christlet Bartling.
1772, May 21. Honyger, Justine, and Henry Horn.
1768, Feb. 13. Hood, James, and Rachel Ashmead.
1768, Nov. 25. Hood, Nicholas, and Sarah Young.

1774, M'ch 17. Hood, Sarah, and Joseph Bradford.
1765, July 25. Hood, Sarah, and Robert Dunlap.
1747, M'ch —. Hoodt, Thomas, and Sarah Robins.
1775, M'ch 13. Hood, William, and Hannah Genger.
1772, Oct. 17. Hood, Henry, and Mary Fry.
1776, Apr. 24. Hooman, John, and Mary Nagle.
1771, Sep. 30. Hooper, Mary, and William Busby.
1760, Sep. 13. Hoops, George, and Jane Hall.
1763, Jan. 10. Hoops, Isabella, and James Mease.
1768, Oct. 15. Hoops, Jane, and Joseph Robins.
1772, Sep. 16. Hoops, Margaret, and Thomas Walker.
1770, Oct. 18. Hoops, Mary, and Thomas Barclay.
1768, M'ch 17. Hoops, Sarah, and John Syme.
1771, July 3. Hoot, Gerart, and Mary Wentz.
1774, Dec. 7. Hoover, Conrad, and Eleanor Erwin.
1768, Dec. 13. Hoover, Elizabeth, and Alexander Gardner.
1760, Feb. 11. Hoover, Jacob, and Elizabeth Myersen.
1774, Jan. 13. Hoovis, Adam, and Mary James.
1759, Dec. 22. Hope, Adam, and Abigail Wheat.
1765, July 27. Hope, Mary, and Daniel Topham.
1760, Aug. 14. Hopen, Catharine, and Christian Hoffman
1762, Sep. 8. Hopewell, Ann, and John Dunn.
1745, Nov. —. Hopewell, John.
1764, July 6. Hopkins, Gerrard, and Meriam Daws.
1762, Aug. 26. Hopkins, Mary, and Henry Lenix.
1764, M'ch 14. Hopkins, Mary, and William Jackson, Jun.
1775, Apr. 20. Hopkinson, Ann, and Samuel Stringer Coale.
1760, June 19. Hopkinson, Elizabeth, and Jacob Duche.
1765, Sep. 3. Hopkinson, Mary, and John Morgan.
1766, Nov. 1. Hopman, Christiana, and Levin Hall.
1745, Sep. —. Hopman, Peter.
1771, M'ch 4. Hopper, Anne, and Samuel Branston.
1772, Nov. 30. Hopper, Isaac, and Sarah Leonard.
1768, Apr. 13. Hopple, Catharine, and John Altemus.
1760, July 17. Horack, William, and Catharine Brown.
1760, May 12. Horne, John, and Hannah Shurman.
1775, Sept. 28. Horn, George, and Sarah Jones.
1772, May 21. Horn, Henry, and Justine Honyger.
1761, Nov. 6. Horning, Catharine, and William Kirby.
1764, July 19. Horsing, Joseph, and Mary Yard.
1761, M'ch 3. Horton, Alice, and David Jones.
1769, Dec. 9. Horton, Charles, and Mary Tennis.
1769, Jan. 14. Hosman, Stokely, and Hannah Henderson.
1762, Dec. 18. Hosson, Elizabeth, and Felix Hart.
1762, May 18. Hoswell, Mary, and John Mitchel.
1764, Nov. 15. Houghead, Elizabeth, and James McDowell.

1764, Feb. 29. Hough, Elizabeth, and John Willet.
1774, Oct. 12. Hough, Elizabeth, and Samuel Lyons.
1766, July 12. Houlton, David, and Mary Blanch.
1773, July 21. Housard, Elizabeth, and John McAfee.
1765, Oct. 30. House, Catharine, and Thomas Little.
1774, June 10. House, Elizabeth, and Nicholas Trist.
1770, Oct. 20. Household, William, and Sarah Willson.
1774, Oct. 15. House, Jemima, and James Crafts.
1746, Oct. —. House, Joseph, and Elizabeth Fitswater.
1769, Feb. 6. House, Peter, and Elizabeth Flysher.
1763, Sep. 7. House, Peter, and Mary Foulke.
1760, Dec. 9. House. Rachel, and James Taylor.
1767, Oct. 10. Houston, James, and Catharine Quig.
1746, June —. Houton, John, and Esther Vandegrift.
1763, July 7. How, Ann Amelia, and John Fiss.
1760, Sep. 30. Howa, William, and Ann Answorth.
1744, Aug. 2. Howard, John.
1764, Dec. 28. Howard, John, and Bridget Osbern.
1763, Aug. 25. Howard, John Grimes, and Bridget Juda.
1769, M'ch 2. Howard, John, and Margaret Painter.
1748, June 16. Howard, Margaret, and Edward Ogle.
1746, Apr —. Howard, Peter.
1759, Dec. 22. Howard, Robert, and Ann Hamilton.
1769, Apr. 15. Howard, Theodosia, and Hugh Morton.
1760, M'ch 19. Howe, Elizabeth, and Richard Hatter.
1773, Sep. 28. Howe, John, and Mary Hewster.
1765, Oct. 9. Howel, Elizabeth, and Isaac Wood.
1765, Oct. 5. Howel, Sarah, and Amos Griffiths.
1762, M'ch 2. Howell, Catharine, and James Crawford.
1774, Feb. 26. Howell, Charlotte, and John Briggs.
1767, Dec. 12. Howell, Elizabeth, and Elias Thomas.
1767, Dec. 8. Howell, Elizabeth, and George Douglass.
1747, June —. Howell, George, and Sarah Garrigue.
1761, M'ch 13, Howell, Hannah, and Richard Shannon.
1761, Feb. 24. Howell, John, and Frances Paschall.
1769, Oct. 2. Howell, Mary, and Sebastian Jarret.
1771, Sep. 23. Howell, Phebe, and Patrick Cannon.
1762, Oct. 19. Howell, Prudence, and James Lucas.
1748, M'ch 11. Howell, Rees, and Sarah West.
1770, M'ch 5. Howell, Sarah, and Peter Stretch.
1765, June 26. How, James, and Catharine Cox.
1768, Feb. 20. How, Samuel, and Ann Yocum.
1775, Apr. 7. Howey, Ann, and Andrew Sigler.
1773, Feb. 27. Howey, Margaret, and Jonathan Richardson.
1773, Feb. 4. Howey, Mary Ann, and Samuel Dunlap.
1767, June 29. Howey, Rachel, and John McNeal.

1773, Oct. 4. Howtin, Elizabeth, and George Peeling.
1747, M'ch —. Hoy, Elizabeth, and Francis Kelly.
1759, Dec. 17. Huay, James, and Mary Miller.
1764, Aug. 24. Hubbleson, Elizabeth, and John Harrison.
1770, Dec. 8. Hubbs, Henry, and Sarah Lownes.
1767, Apr. 15. Hubbs, Sarah, and John Wing.
1765, Jan 14 Huber, Jacob, and Elizabeth Bloomer.
1772, Jan. 21. Hubley, Adam, and Mary Evans.
1775, Oct. 11. Huck, Andrew, and Priscilla Davis.
1763, Aug. 11. Huddle, Joseph, and Hannah Evans.
1768, Aug. 3. Huddleston, Henry, and Elizabeth Bennet.
1768, May 7. Huddleston, Joseph, and Margaret Thomas.
1773, Nov. 15. Huddleston, Nathaniel and Esther White.
1762, Oct. 9. Huddleston, Sarah and James Price.
1763, Aug. 19. Huddleston, Thomas, and Elizabeth Stiger.
1760, Sep. 18. Hudman, H. C., and Isaac Marshall.
1772, July 21. Hudner, William, and Catharine Inglis.
1767, Dec. 24. Hudson, Catharine, and Abel Lippincott.
1767, June 6. Hudson, George, and Rebecca Clement.
1763, Oct. 22. Hudson, James, and Ruth Powell.
1760, Aug. 7. Huevelston, Herman, and Mary Wilmingham.
1765, Dec. 24. Huff, Ann, and Simon Meredith.
1770, Apr. 14. Huffdale, John, and Elizabeth Yerkus.
1775, Jan. 25. Huff, Daniel, and Mary Sharp.
1766, Dec 6. Huff, Eleanor, and Thomas Craven.
1765, Jan. 29. Huffey, Eleanor, and John Gallagher.
1764, Oct. 15. Huff, John, and Hannah Buber.
1762, Jan. 13. Huffman, Mary, and Thomas Whitehead.
1773, Feb. 10. Huff, Oliff, and Francis Jodun.
1775, Oct. 2. Huffty, Catharine, and Anthony Rue.
1770, June 22. Hufty, Charles, and Hermina Dorland.
1760, Nov. 15. Hufty, Elizabeth, and Enoch Dungan.
1762, Dec. 24. Hufty, John, and Mary Butcher.
1765, Oct. 26. Hufty, Mary, and Samuel Robinson.
1772, M'ch 13. Hufty, Simon, and Rebecca Till.
1772, Oct. 31. Huger, Daniel, and Binkey Elliot.
1774, Aug. 16. Hugg, John, and Sarah West.
1764, Apr. 9. Hugg. Sarah, and Joseph Ellis.
1770, May 17. Hughes, Aaron, and Mary Pancoast.
1774, May 25. Hughes, Alexander, and Margaret Levering.
1764, Aug. 29. Hughes, David, and Elizabeth McCarnon.
1744, Sep. —. Hughes, Elias, and Rebecca Wright.
1770, Jan. 31. Hughes, Elias, and Sarah Gilbert.
1768, Jan. 9. Hughes, Elizabeth, and John North.
1771, May 17. Hughes, Elizabeth, and Thomas Jones.
1761, Oct. 1. Hughes, Ellis, and Margaret Anderson.

1768, Jan. 21. Hughes, Enoch, and Bathsheba Marshall.
1764, Sep. 10. Hughes, Garnet, and Ann Margaret Gotchill.
1747, Dec. —. Hughes, Isaac, and Rebecca Heine.
1764, Aug. 1. Hughes, Isabella, and Robert Walker.
1773, Nov. 24. Hughes, Jacob, and Ann Lawrence.
1770, June 4. Hughes, Jacob, and Sarah Richards.
1760, Aug. 26. Hughes, James, and Margaret McNealy.
1766, Nov. 28. Hughes, Jane, and Samuel Boone.
1775, Feb. 28. Hughes, Jemima, and Samuel Gill.
1767, June 11. Hughes, John, Jun., and Margaret Paschall.
1768, June 10. Hughes, Judith, and Joseph Prichard.
1763, Aug. 20. Hughes, Martha, and John Mathew.
1767, Nov. 12. Hughes, Mary, and Thomas Wood.
1773, M'ch 29. Hughes, Mary, and William Wilson.
1766, Dec. 4. Hughes, Matthew, and Jane Rogers.
1745, Jan. —. Hughes, Morgan.
1767, May 16. Hughes, Richard, and Hannah Aburn.
1746, Sep. —. Hughes, Robert, and Eve Price.
1765, May 1. Hughes, Ruth, and Lindsay Coats.
1744, Jan. —. Hughes, William.
1764, M'ch 2. Hughes, William, and Maria Shunberger.
1771, May 4. Hughes, William, and Mary Callwellin.
1760, Nov. 21. Hughes, William, and Susannah May.
1747, M'ch —. Hugh, Jonathan, and Elenor McClellan.
1770, Apr. 14. Hugh, Nicholas, and Anne Roberts.
1764, Feb. 16. Hugisheimer, George, and Rosanna Rumspeiger.
1761, Apr. 8. Hularg. Abigail, and Isaac Burrough.
1763, Jan. 5. Hulings, Jonathan, and Mary Emson.
1763, Dec. 27. Hulings, Marcus, and Willimine Skillings.
1768, Apr. 25. Hulings, Susannah, and Joseph Cowperthwait.
1769, May 6. Hull, Elizabeth, and James Allen.
1773 Aug. 4. Hull, Sarah, and Alexander Hunter.
1761, Oct. 29. Hultzheimer, Jacob, and Hannah Walker.
1770, Nov. 13. Hume, Robert, and Catharine McClennon.
1772, Dec. 21. Hume, Susannah, and James Kotter.
1772, Aug. 20. Hummer, Catharine, and John Adams.
1772, Dec. 24. Humphrevile, Parnel, and Benjamin McVeagh.
1768, Apr. 7. Humphrey, Charity, and Andrew Murray.
1771, May 13. Humphrey, Charles, and Sarah Evans.
1760, July 18. Humphrey, Hannah, and William Philipson.
1771, Dec. 16. Humphreys, Catharine, and Jesse Davis.
1761, May 18. Humphreys, Christi, and Muh. Branson.
1768, Nov. 24. Humphreys, Joshua, and Anna Jones.
1767, Nov. 26. Humphreys, Sarah, and Daniel Murphy.
1762, Sep. 6. Humphreys, Sarah, and John Thomas.
1760, M'ch 15. Humphreys, Thomas, and Mary Duffill.

1775, Dec. 2. Humphreys, William, and Ann Coburn.
1760, Oct. 14. Humphrey, Uriah, and Thomas Drake.
1775, Sep. 12. Humphries, Susannah, and Samuel Jeffrys.
1764, Dec. 29. Humstred, Elizabeth, and Arnold Francis.
1765, Aug. 8. Hungary, Dorothy, and Thomas Dixon.
1774, Nov. 30. Hungary, Mary, and James McCay.
1776, Feb. 14. Hunn, John, and Mary Silsby.
1775, Dec. 1. Hunn, Mary, and Caleb Bickham.
1770, Apr. 20. Hunnyger, Mark, and Christiana Lochlar.
1767, May 6. Hunt, Bridget, and Thomas Sutor.
1769, June 19. Hunt, Dorothea, and George Harvey.
1766, Aug. 5. Hunt, Edward, and Ann Watson.
1761, June 8. Hunt, Elizabeth, and John McCullough.
1747, Feb. —. Hunt, Elizabeth, and John Vaughan.
1762, July 23. Hunt, Elizabeth, and Robert Halkerston.
1771, Oct. 25. Hunter, Aaron, and Mary Shannon.
1773, Aug. 4. Hunter, Alexander, and Sarah Hull.
1764, Aug. 22. Hunter, Alice, and John Jones.
1775, Jan. 14. Hunter, Edward, and Hannah Maris.
1775, Sep. 27. Hunter, George, and Grace Brick.
1773, Oct. 20. Hunter, Hannah, and John Dilworth.
1759, Dec. 29. Hunter, Hannah, and Malachi Jones.
1764, Sep. 22. Hunter, James, and Eleanor Gardner.
1765, May 16. Hunter, James, and Jane Gunning.
1774, May 24. Hunter, James, and Mary Stewart.
1762, Jan. 7. Hunter, Lillis, and William Rutherford.
1772, Nov. 20. Hunter, Mary, and Eli Bentley.
1773, Sep. 28. Hunter, Nathaniel, and Elizabeth Bywater.
1761, July 24. Hunter, Robert, and Ann Cole.
1743, Feb. 4. Hunter, Thomas.
1767, Aug. 20. Hunter, William, and Frances Hamilton.
1772, Jan. 2. Hunter, William, and Susannah Rudderou.
1774, Sep. 5. Hunt, Esaias, and Elizabeth Stratton.
1767, June 17. Hunt, Isaac, and Mary Shewell.
1747, June —. Hunt, John, and Mary Ann Butler.
1761, May 7. Hunt, Joseph, and Ann Trigger.
1760, Oct. 24. Hunt, Mary Ann, and Thomas Nevill.
1764, Oct. 23. Hunton, Isabella, and Robert Dove.
1763, Oct. 24. Hunt, Peter, and Ann Weily.
1773, Nov. 12. Huntsberger, Catharine, and Adam Kern.
1765, June 19. Hunt, Thomas, and Mary Skelton.
1771, Apr. 13. Hurley, Eleanor, and Arthur Campbell.
1772, Oct. 15. Hurrie, Martha, and Joseph Fry.
1760, May 22. Hurst, Susannah, and James West.
1775, Dec. 27. Hussey, Sarah, and William McFadden.
1776, May 25. Hustin, Mary, and James Hill.

1762, Sept. 20. Hust, Lydia, and George Miers.
1765, July 18. Hust, Martha, and Richard Harding.
1745, Sep. —. Huston, Alexander.
1772, June 3. Huston, Ann, and John Taylor.
1765, M'ch 11. Huston, James, and Darius Grey.
1767, Feb. 25. Huston, James, and Elizabeth Killgore.
1764, Feb. 27. Huston, John, and Jane Fullerton.
1766, Sep. 2. Huston, Judah, and John Calder.
1775, Feb. 17. Huston, Margaret, and John Hithal.
1766, Jan. 8. Huston, Martha, and John Vandyke.
1762, Feb. 17. Huston, Mary ,and John Thompson.
1775, Nov. 1. Huston, William, and Mary Burk.
1760, Aug. 7. Huston, William, and Sarah Williams.
1776, Feb. 19. Huston, William, and Susannah Lentz.
1768, Feb. 3. Hutcheson, Mary, and Archibald McCoomb.
1746, Aug. —. Hutchins, John, and Ann Hawkins.
1768, Dec. 2. Hutchinson, Catharine, and Benjamin Ramshaw.
1766, July 3. Hutchinson, Ezekiah, and Eleanor Miller.
1771, May 30. Hutchinson, John, and Letitia Wright.
1771, Oct. 21. Hutchinson, Mary, and George Williams.
1762, July 29. Hutchinson, Phebe, and John West.
1761, July 29. Hutchinson, Phebe, and William Askton.
1760, Nov. 19. Hutchinson, Robert, and Jane Wallace.
1743, Oct. —. Hutchinson, William.
1762, Dec. 10. Hutchison, Ann, and John Mickesner.
1762, Dec. 28. Hutchison, Mary, and David Thompson.
1762, Dec. 14. Hutchison, Mary, and John Purdon.
1764, Oct. 6. Hutton, John, and Elizabeth Merriott.
1761, Aug. 15. Hutton, Mary, and David Evans.
1773, Dec. 11. Hutton, Sarah, and Thomas Harrison.
1744, Aug. 13. Hyat, John.
1776, Jan. 25. Hyder, Ann, and William Wiles.
1775, Sep. 27. Hyder, Rachel, and John Smart.
1772, Apr. 27. Hyde, Thomas, and Anna Herback.
1746, June —. Hyger, Anthor, and Barbara Guyger.
1762, June 10. Hyle, Philip, and Jacobina Zeiglerin.
1764, M'ch 13. Hyley, Frances, and John Stall.
1762, July 9. Hyman, Elizabeth, and John Widdifield.
1771, Apr. 10. Hyman, Jane, and Daniel Kinnicut.
1770, Apr. 19. Hymer, Jacob, and Mercy Ford.
1746, Sep. —. Hyneman, Peter, and Hester Meirs.
1772, M'ch 10. Hynes, William, and Elizabeth Harris.
1775, Feb. 22. Hysel, Christiana, and Adam Garret.
1763, Nov. 10. Hyser, Thomas, and Catharine Fredrica.

I.

1772, Dec.   3. Iann, Thomas, and Mary Piles.
1761, Aug.   20. Iden, John, and Mary Hall.
1767, Nov.   11. Ilbingworth, Francis, and Rachel Cox.
1771, Feb.   1. Iliff, John, and Margaret Williams.
1775, Jan.   9. Immel, George Michael, and Catharine Sidle.
1774, Sep.   2. Ince, James, and Elizabeth Greenway.
1776, Feb.   10. Indicot, Elizabeth, and Joseph Bowler.
1764, Nov.   1. Indicot, Samuel, and Elizabeth Roberts.
1770, May   3. Ingels, George, and Mary Rush.
1765, Jan.   8. Ingland, Ann, and John Gallagher.
1773, May   29. Ingle, Deborah, and Joseph Duffield.
1776, May   20. Ingle, Hannah, and Benjamin Thaw.
1746, Sep.   —. Ingle, Margaret, and Elias Shryver.
1772, July   21. Inglis, Catharine, and William Hudner.
1772, Nov.   21. Inglis, Hannah, and Thomas Waterman.
1767, Jan.   1. Inglis, James, and Mary January.
1765, Jan.   2. Inglis, John, and Eleanor Yocum.
1760, Nov.   28. Inglis, Rebecca, and John Swaine.
1761, Dec.   31. Ingliss, Ann, and Gilbert Barclay.
1761, Apr.   13. Ingliss, Mary, and ———— Herring.
1761, July   28. Ingram, George, and Rachel Talbert.
1743, Nov.   —. Ingram, John.
1747, Sep.   —. Ingram, ————, and Sarah Johnson.
1766, Dec.   31. Inkester, Thomas, and Mary Geer.
1774, Feb.   9. Innes, William, and Elizabeth Bullock.
1770, July   2. Insee, Joseph, and Catharine Fowl.
1761, Oct.   9. Insley, Sarah, and Charles Jenney.
1767, Aug.   31. Ireland, Edward, and Mary Cheeseman.
1775, Feb.   2. Ireland, Elizabeth, and George Millward.
1762, Dec.   22. Ireland, Hannah, and John Acred.
1762, Apr.   29. Ireland, Henry, and Elizabeth Osburn.
1760, Sep.   3. Irish, Ann, and Bradford Roberts.
1762, Apr.   24. Ironfield, Elizabeth, and Henry Peters.
1771, Sep.   25. Irvin, James, and Sarah Green.
1765, M'ch   18. Irwin, Ann, and Michael McIntire.
1764, June   16. Irwin, Dunin, and Frances Bullman.
1762, Jan.   1. Irwin, Gerrard, and Rachael Owen.
1765, Jan.   7. Irwin, James, and Elizabeth Yarborough.
1747, June   —. Irwin, Jane, and Allen McClean.
1775, Jan.   27. Irwin, Jennet, and Hughes Johnston.
1744, Sep.   —. Irwin, John.
1775, Oct.   21. Irwin, Mary, and John Shuhan.
1770, Jane   5. Irwin, Matthew, and Esther Mifflin.
1745, Dec.   —. Irwin, Robert.
1761, Mar.   18. Isaac, William, and Susannah Reading.

1765, M'ch 14. Isler, Mary, and Benjamin Thomlinson.
1765, Oct. 20. Ismaster, William, and Mary Stinson.
1746, Feb. —. Israel, Michael.
1767, Nov. 21. Iszard, Jane, and Joseph Saunders.
1770, Oct. 15. Iszard, Rachel, and Henry Test.
1768, May 19. Iveson, Mary, and Robert Bunbury.
1768, Mar. 31. Ivory, Douglass, and Mary Powell.
1766, Oct. 30. Iwyer, John, and Mary Rialt.
1776, Jan. 4. Izard, Barbara, and Peter Schung.
1772, Dec. 5. Izard, Jonathan, and Rachel Biddle.
1767, Apr. 15. Izelorin, Sophia Susannah, and Henry Forst.

J.

1761, June 4. Jack, Allen, and Isabella Caruthers.
1748, Sep. —. Jackman, Thomas, and Elizabeth Stapler.
1761, July 27. Jack, Negro, and Negro Phillis.
1762, May 1. Jackson, Ann, and Joseph Rhoads.
1770, Jan. 23. Jackson, Archibald, and Jane Millar.
1770, Feb. 26. Jackson, David, and Jane Jackson.
1773, Jan. 12. Jackson, Edward, and Sarah Greenland.
1772, Dec. 3. Jackson, Elizabeth, and John Finney.
1760, Apr. 29. Jackson, Hannah, and Garret Kruson.
1765, May 13. Jackson, Jacob, and Martha Evans.
1764, Oct. 9. Jackson, James, and Catharine Denning.
1774, May. 28. Jackson, James, and Rebecca Collins.
1770, Feb. 26. Jackson, Jane, and David Jackson.
1774, M'ch 24. Jackson, John, Jun., and Hannah Krewson.
1764, June 9. Jackson, John, and Martha Weaver.
1776, Jan. 23. Jackson, Josiah, and Deborah Johnson.
1775, June 26. Jackson, Lydia, and Thomas Craig.
1748, Apr. 13. Jackson, Mary, and Emanuel Rouse.
1767, M'ch 2. Jackson, Mary, and John Steward.
1747, Apr. —. Jackson, Matthew, and Agnes Finley.
1760, May 1. Jackson, Paul, and Jane Mather.
1770, July 21. Jackson, Phebe, and Cowley Wells.
1768, Oct. 27. Jackson, Rebecca, and Matthias Sandham.
1766, Oct. 9. Jackson, Samuel, and Sarah Voto.
1768, June 17. Jackson, Wesley, and Eleanor McKey.
1763, June 13. Jackson, William, and Margaret Lavingston.
1774, Oct. 27. Jackson, William, and Mary Appowen.
1764, M'ch 14. Jackson, William, and Mary Hopkins.
1769, Oct. 24. Jacobs, Christopher, Jun., and Mary Snyder.
1761, Dec. 15. Jacobs, Elizabeth, and Caleb Parry.
1772, Dec. 31. Jacobs, Hannah, and David Rittenhouse.
1746. Dec. —. Jacobs, Mary, and George Heass.

1772, Sep. 2. Jacobs, Mary, and James Miller.
1747, June —. Jacquett, Isabel, and Peter Stedham.
1772, Jan. 4. Jagar, John, and Mary Clady.
1762, June 28. Jaggard, Mary, and Thomas Wilkins.
1744, Sep. —. James, Abel.
1773, Sep. 22. James, Abiah, and Rachel Williams.
1772, Nov. 17. James, Ann, and Peter Rambo.
1768, Aug. 10. James, Benjamin, and Catharine Gaff.
1772, June 18. James, Daniel, and Susannah Baker.
1772, Jan. 2. James, Edward, and Margaret Black.
1748, Apr. 13. James, Elizabeth, and George Davis.
1771. June 17. James, Elizabeth, and John Robins.
1769, Apr. 26. James, Elizabeth, and Jonathan White.
1762. Apr. 29. James, Enoch, and Rachel Richards.
1746, July —. James, Esther, and James Devereux.
1761, Jan. 22. James, Hugh, and Christiana Lower.
1770, May 17. James, Hugh, and Eleanor Evans.
1771, M'ch 28. James, Isaiah, and Mary McKinney.
1763, Sep. 14. James, Jacob, and Christine Ryon.
1762, Sep. 25. James, James, and Elizabeth Eaton.
1775, M'ch 24. James, Jonathan, and Mary Latch.
1772, May 27. James, John, and Dorothy Jones.
1766, June 14. James, John, and Edith Eaton.
1769, Oct. 25. James, John, and Elizabeth Appleby.
1764, Oct. 10. James, John, and Elizabeth Bratton.
1762, Aug. 13. James, John, and Medelina Kishlen.
1772, Apr. 10. James, Josiah, and Elizabeth Evans.
1760, M'ch 28. James, Martha, and Daniel Evans.
1763, Aug. 11. James, Martha, and Thomas Cliffton.
1774, Jan. 13. James, Mary, and Adam Hoovis.
1767, Dec. 10. James, Mary, and Henry Kerr.
1760, Jan. 2. James, Mary, and Jeremiah Price.
1772, Apr. 4. James, Mary, and Timothy Roberts.
1776, M'ch 5. James, Mary, and William Shimin.
1765, Apr. 23. Jameson, Ann, and Alexander Robinson.
1775, May 4. Jameson, John, and Catharine Osborne.
1772, Apr. 1. Jameson, John, and Mary Ross.
1772, Nov. 14. Jameson, Mary, and John Bogart.
1772, Dec. 18. Jameson, Robert, and Sarah Mairns.
1774, Aug. 30. James, Philip, and Catharine Finnegen.
1774, Dec. 1. James, Rachel, and Robert Martin.
1762, Apr. 8. James, Richard, and Nancy Baxter.
1765, Apr. 8. James, Samuel, and Anna Keslurn.
1770, June 30. James, Samuel, and Rachel Haas.
1761, Oct. 10. James, Sarah, and Andrew Crawford.
1760, Aug. 30. James, Sarah, and Samuel Miles.

1746, M'ch —. James, Thomas.
1764, Nov. 6. James, Thomas, and Ann Page.
1747, June —. James, Thomas, and Mary Syng.
1761, June 24. James, Thomas, and Tamar Edwards.
1743, Jan. 7. James, William.
1767, May 8. James, William, and Ann Morris.
1769, Jan. 25. James, William, and Rebecca Williams.
1764, Aug. 29. Jamison, Alexander, and Isabell Poak.
1767, M'ch 12. Jamison, Jane, and Moses Crawford.
1768, Dec. 2. Jamison, John, and Martha Greer.
1768, Apr. 25. Jamison, Margaret, and James Roney.
1769, Sep. 28. Jamison, Mary, and John Harvey.
1767, Apr. 18. Jamison, Robert, and Hannah Baird.
1767, Dec. 15. Jamison, Thomas, and Jane Long.
1769, July 21. Jamison, William, and Hannah Edminston.
1772, Dec. 3. Jann, Thomas, and Mary Piles.
1763, Dec. 22. January, Ann, and Alexander McGriger.
1775, M'ch 16. January, Benjamin, and Hannah Langdale.
1762, Apr. 22. January, Elizabeth, and Benjamin Jenkins.
1747, June —. January, Isaac, and Ann Shubert.
1767, Jan. 1. January, Mary, and James Inglis.
1761, Apr. 23. January, Peter, and Mary Walton.
1768, July 7. January, Rebecca, and George Griffith.
1760, May 5. Janvier, Ann, and William Western.
1763, Apr. 14. Janvier, Isaac, and Elizabeth Renshau.
1770, Dec. 22. Janvier, Joseph, and Agnes Hill.
1747, Nov. —. Jaquet, Elizabeth, and Peter Jaquet.
1747, Nov. —. Jaquet, Peter, and Elizabeth Jaquet.
1768, June 8. Jarman, John, and Mary Bickley.
1746, Dec. —. Jarrant, Thomas, and Mary Radley.
1769, Oct. 2. Jarret, Sebastian, and Mary Howell.
1761, Sep. 28. Jeffreys, Sarah, and Alexander McKey.
1775, Sep. 12. Jeffrys, Samuel, and Susannah Humphries.
1748, June 16. Jemison, Isabel, and Trustram Davis.
1770, Jan. 30. Jemison, Mary, and John Pennington.
1760, Aug. 13. Jemmison, Ann, and Henry Derrock.
1747, M'ch —. Jemmison, Martha, and William Davis.
1747, Feb. —. Jenkings, Rachel, and Joseph Street.
1772, Feb. 4. Jenkins, Anna, and Thomas McFee.
1762, Apr. 22. Jenkins, Benjamin, and Elizabeth January.
1773, July 1. Jenkins, Catharine, and Adam Boyd.
1769, Aug. 30. Jenkins, David, and Catharine Foreman.
1767, June 25. Jenkins, Elizabeth, and Thomas Middleton.
1771, Oct. 8. Jenkins, Elizabeth, and William Sarnighausen.
1761, Oct. 29. Jenkins, George, and Hannah Harmon.
1764, Nov. 24. Jenkins, Hannah, and Thomas Gordon.

1768, Oct. 24. Jenkins, Hannah, and William Henly.
1772, Sep. 16. Jenkins, Israel, and Rosanna O'Neal.
1768, May 23. Jenkins, James, and Catharine Brown.
1761, Dec. 1. Jenkins, Jane, and Alexander Gillis.
1747, Aug. —. Jenkins, John, and Sidney Thomas.
1770, June 14. Jenkins, Josael, and Jane McGargy.
1763, Sep. 17. Jenkins, Joseph, and Ann Willard.
1764 July 16. Jenkins, Josiah, and Rachael Farnsworth
1761, May 20. Jenkins, Margaret, and John Thomas.
1774, May 10. Jenkins, Mary, and Isaac Bristol.
1769, May 27. Jenkins, Philip, and Jane Allison.
1771, Jan. 2. Jenkins, Sarah, and John Anderson.
1773, Feb. 1. Jenkins, William, and Elizabeth Blair.
1772, Nov. 14. Jenkins, William, and Sarah McLaughlan.
1776, May 30. Jenks, Joseph, and Hannah Davids.
1761, Oct. 9. Jenney, Charles, and Sarah Insley.
1764, Aug. 8. Jenney, Elizabeth, and Andrew Reed.
1746, Nov. —. Jennings, Mary, and Andrew McNare.
1765, Dec. 2. Jennings, Mary, and John Needham.
1760, Feb. 1. Jennings, Susannah, and James Scull.
1774, July 26. Jennings, William, and Elizabeth McCadames.
1748, Apr. 13. Jenny, Robert, and Jane Elizabeth Cummins.
1774, Sep. 5. Jerman, Mary, and Patrick McFall.
1766, Feb. 28. Jervis, Charles, and Elizabeth Boor.
1761, Dec. 29. Jervis, Elizabeth, and Enoch Davis.
1761, Oct. 28. Jervis, John, and Elizabeth Dean.
1762, July 10. Jessip, Samuel, and Elizabeth Neeld.
1766, Oct. 30. Jevyer, John, and Mary Rialt.
1761, M'ch 21. Jewell, Ann, and Samuel Roberts.
1745, Feb. —. Jewers, John.
1760, June 28. Jewson, Thomas, and Catharine Foly.
1769, Apr. 13. Jobs, Deborah, and Ezekiel Morriam.
1766, Oct. 4. Jobs, Rebecca, and William Price.
1748, May 14. Jobson, Sarah, and David Cumming.
1744, May —. Jodon, Francis.
1773, Feb. 10. Jodun, Francis, and Oliff Huff.
1764, Feb. 29. John, Eleanor, and Abel Gibbon.
1769, Jan. 4. John, Hester, and John Williams.
1774, Sep. 17. Johns, Ann, and Henry Esler.
1762, Nov. 25. Johns, Ann, and Whitehead Jones.
1767, June 13. Johns, Joseph, and Ann Maers.
1774, Apr. 28. Johns, Mary, and William Craig.
1761, Jan. 22. Johnson, Abram, and Mary Taylor.
1760, Nov. 26. Johnson, Alexander, and Alice Boggs.
1764, M'ch 27. Johnson, Anna, and John Clue.
1770, Nov. 15. Johnson, Anna Maria, and Christian Schneider.

1763, Sep. 10. Johnson, Benjamin, and Elizabeth Young.
1776, Jan. 23. Johnson, Deborah, and Josiah Jackson.
1763, Aug. 30. Johnson, Debora, and William Stubbs.
1760, Aug. 7. Johnson, Elizabeth, and James Ranton.
1763, Apr. 19. Johnson, Elizabeth, and Samuel Gamble.
1761, May 12. Johnson, Elizabeth, and Samuel Shimmer.
1764, June 22. Johnson, Esther, and William Bogar.
1767, M'ch 5. Johnson, Jacob, and Hannah Thomas.
1763, May 14. Johnson, Jane, and James Ennis.
1773, Dec. 9. Johnson, John, and Hannah Mitchell.
1764, June 26. Johnson, John, and Mary Seddons.
1767, M'ch 24. Johnson, John, and Susannah Ashton.
1746, Jan. —. Johnson, Joseph.
1746, Sep. —. Johnson, Joseph, and Rachel Freys.
1769, Dec. 20. Johnson, Joseph, and Sarah Morgan.
1768, June 8. Johnson, Lawrence, and Sarah Clark.
1763, Feb. 14. Johnson, Leonard, and Mary Dennison.
1766, Sep. 9. Johnson, Margaret, and Alexander McMichael.
1761, July 25. Johnson, Margaret, and John Alexander.
1762, Nov. 15. Johnson, Margaret, and John Reading.
1768, Apr. 18. Johnson, Margaret, and Joseph Wild.
1766, May 21. Johnson, Margaret, and Roger Bewman.
1769, Feb. 20. Johnson, Margaret, and Thomas Hillbourn.
1761, Aug. 31. Johnson, Mary, and Bryan Laferty.
1768, Aug. 27. Johnson, Mary, and Richard Eavenson.
1764, Aug. 20. Johnson, Patrick, and Ann Hamilton.
1748, Apr. 13. Johnson, Peter, and Sarah Vankirk.
1765, Aug. 13. Johnson, Richard, and Catharine Campbell.
1761, Apr. 7. Johnson, Richard, and Hannah Dunging.
1763, Oct. 12. Johnson, Richard, and Martha Bassonet.
1763, Feb. 1. Johnson, Robert, and Jane Graham.
1772, Sep. 4. Johnson, Ruth, and William Gibson.
1768, Sep. 12. Johnson, Samuel, and Martha Dunn.
1776, May 11. Johnson, Sarah, and Benjamin Towne.
1764, May 31. Johnson, Sarah, and Daniel Bessonet.
1747, Sep. —. Johnson, Sarah, and ———— Ingram.
1746, Oct. —. Johnson, Sarah, and Nathan Dyke.
1764, May 4. Johnson, Sophia, and Adam Berry.
1744, May —. Johnson, Thomas.
1763, M'ch 4. Johnson, William, and Margaret Powel.
1771, July 30. Johnson, William, and Mary Butler.
1767, Nov. 27. Johnson, William, and Mary Moore.
1774, Nov. 11. Johnston, Ann, and Thomas Williams.
1775, Sep. 19. Johnston, Christiana, and George McKeag.
1764, Dec. 6. Johnston, Eleanor, and Charles Alexander.
1773, Oct. 5. Johnston, Elizabeth, and Alexander Davald.

1764, Jan 21. Johnston, Elizabeth, and James McGill.
1773, Feb. 11. Johnston, Elizabeth, and Joseph Philips.
1775, Oct. 25. Johnston, Esther, and Thomas Assheton.
1775, Dec. 15. Johnston, Francis, and Alice Erwin.
1772, Feb. 17. Johnston, Hermanus, and Mary Fisher.
1775, Jan. 27. Johnston, Hughes, and Jennet Irwin.
1772, Dec. 28. Johnston, James, and Christiana Murray.
1775, Dec. 9. Johnston, James, and Margaret Dunn.
1775, Aug. 7. Johnston, James, and Martha Hamble.
1773, M'ch 6. Johnston, Jane, and Matthew Shepherd.
1760, Feb. 15. Johnston, John, and Margaret Robinson.
1770, Sep. 24. Johnston, John, and Mary Semple.
1770, Jan. 30. Johnston, John, and Mary Webster.
1776, Apr. 10. Johnston, Joseph, and Elizabeth McGill.
1776, June 12. Johnston, Margaret, and Elisha Bloomfield.
1763, Dec. 23. Johnston, Margaret, and John Cummins.
1775, Dec. 16. Johnston, Mary, and Isaac Larrew.
1774, Oct. 4. Johnston, Mary, and Phineas Waterman.
1770, Apr. 25. Johnston, Mary, and Thomas Rooke.
1774, Jan. 20. Johnston, Richard, and Mary Delany.
1762, May 21. Johnston, Robert, and Easter Chambers
1764, June 23. Johnston, Sarah, and Bartholomew Balderston.
1771, April 15. Johnston, Susannah, and John O'Neal.
1760, Apr. 19. John, William, and —— Brockdon.
1760, Nov. 21. Jolley, Ann, and John Woodward.
1774, Sep. 3. Jolly, Margaret, and John Lang.
1764, May 3. Jones, Abraham, and Rebecca Bolton.
1767, Dec. 30. Jones, Agnes, and John Read.
1773, Jan. 30. Jones, Anna, and John Chandler.
1768, Nov. 24. Jones, Anna, and Joshua Humphreys.
1764, May 2. Jones, Ann, and Charles Philips.
1761, Dec. 9. Jones, Ann, and John Bennet.
1772, Aug. 10. Jones, Ann, and John Douglass.
1762, July 19. Jones, Ann, and Robert Anderson.
1761, Sep. 17. Jones, Asfaa, and Cassius Hodge.
1769, July 24. Jones, Benjamin, and Tacy Roberts.
1743, Nov. —. Jones, Blaithwaite.
1762, May 29. Jones, Blaithwaite, and Mary Morris.
1774, June 6. Jones, Catharine, and James Dungan.
1776, June 4. Jones, Catharine, and John Lily.
1771, Nov. 18. Jones, Catharine, and Peter Fox.
1768, May 19. Jones, Catharine, and Thomas Batson.
1767, May 28. Jones, Catharine, and William Cummins.
1761, Aug. 10. Jones, Charles, and Catharine Real.
1768, Nov. 21. Jones, Charles, and Susannah Hill.
1761, June 4. Jones, Daniel, and Jeremiah Morris.

1761, M'ch   3. Jones, David, and Alice Horton.
1773, Dec. 27. Jones, David, and Letitia Powel.
1769, Jan.   3. Jones, David, and Mary Brook.
1771, Dec.   3. Jones, David, and Mary Cummins.
1765, Oct. 26. Jones, David, and Rebecca Carter.
1772, May   27. Jones, Dorothy, and John James.
1747, Feb. —. Jones, Doughty, and Hannah Gardiner
1770, Jan.   2. Jones, Ebenezer, and Rebecca Sturk.
1768, Feb.   8. Jones, Edward, and Elizabeth Davis.
1770, May   16. Jones, Edward, and Elizabeth Gibbons.
1767, Aug. 10. Jones, Edward, and Maria Sarah Rifflin.
1774, Dec. 21. Jones, Eleanor, and Thomas Adair.
1747, Sept. —. Jones, Eleanor, and Adam Lyn.
1761, Dec. 24. Jones, Elizabeth, and Daniel Carteret.
1761, Aug. 27. Jones, Elizabeth, and Elijah Davis.
1772, Feb.   1. Jones, Elizabeth, and Jacob Billew.
1762, June 26. Jones, Elizabeth, and John Smith.
1771, May   4. Jones, Elizabeth, and Nathaniel Jones.
1747, Nov. —. Jones, Elizabeth, and William Gray.
1773, July 14. Jones, Ephraim, and Rachel Richardson.
1745, Aug. —. Jones, Evan.
1745, Dec. —. Jones, Evan.
1775, June 15. Jones, Gibbs, and Margaret Moore.
1760, Nov. 29. Jones, Griffith, and Elizabeth ———— .
1765, Oct. 16. Jones, Griffith, and Hannah Loyd.
1760, Oct. 31. Jones, Griffith, and Jennet Barr.
1774, Dec.   9. Jones, Griffith, and Rebecca Morgan.
1772, June 17. Jones, Hannah, and Henry Moore.
1763, Dec. 12. Jones, Hannah, and James Donaldson.
1771, Apr. 20. Jones, Hannah, and James Ham.
1775, May   11. Jones, Hannah, and Robert Shields.
1746, Nov. —. Jones, Hannah, and Stephen Lewis.
1762, May   22. Jones, Henry, and Nancy Anderson.
1765, June 15. Jones, Hugh, and Esther Glover.
1743, Feb. 15. Jones, Isaac.
1776, M'ch 26. Jones, Isaac, and Ann Watkins.
1763, Apr. 26. Jones, Jacob, and Sarah Tomkins.
1771, Aug.   8. Jones, Jane, and Jacob Peters.
1767, Oct. 27. Jones, Jenkins, and Ann Ewer.
1743, Aug. 20. Jones, John.
1764, Aug. 22. Jones, John, and Alice Hunter.
1746, Dec. —. Jones, John, and Elizabeth Wilkinson.
1771, May   1. Jones, John, and Margaret Benson.
1747, Nov. —. Jones, John, and Mary Philips.
1771, Aug. 15. Jones, John, and Mary Rowland.
1763, Apr. 13. Jones, John, and Rachael Hays.

1763, M'ch 21. Jones, John, and Rebecca Finney.
1773, Aug. 7. Jones, Jonathan, and Hannah Aaron.
1764, July 16. Jones, Joseph, and Rebecca Ballinger.
1767, M'ch 23. Jones, Joseph, and Sarah Barton.
1763, June 29. Jones, Joshu, and Margaret McMaster.
1760, May 5. Jones, Lowry, and Daniel Wister.
1761, May 11. Jones, Lydia, and James Moorhead.
1770, June 7. Jones, Lydia, and John Smart.
1759, Dec. 29. Jones, Malachi, and Hannah Hunter.
1774, Apr. 7. Jones, Margaret, and Christian Rufcorn.
1773, June 23. Jones, Margaret, and James Martin
1764, May 30. Jones, Margaret, and John Shagney.
1761, Nov. 28. Jones, Martha, and John Brock.
1747, Sep. —. Jones, Mary, and Griffith Prichard.
1763, Nov. 9. Jones, Mary, and Henry Pugh.
1761, Jan. 19. Jones, Mary, and James Middleton,
1776, Apr. 5. Jones, Mary, and John Blyth.
1775, Sep. 8. Jones, Mary, and John Keller.
1765, Nov. 20. Jones, Mary, and John Lewis.
1765, Mar. 13. Jones, Mary, and John Wilder.
1760, M'ch 12. Jones, Mary, and Joseph Forguson.
1767, Sep. 24. Jones, Mary, and Joseph Holloway
1770, Sep. 11. Jones, Mary, and Richard Brakell.
1760, Aug. 23. Jones, Mary, and Richard Morgan.
1748, May 14. Jones, Mary, and Swan Justis.
1773, M'ch 29. Jones, Matthew, and Elizabeth Knowles.
1743, M'ch 26. Jones, Meredith.
1761, May 4. Jones, Nathaniel, and Elizabeth Jones.
1774, Jan. 4. Jones, Nathan, and Mary Proctor.
1745, June —. Jones, Neels.
1774, Sep. 24. Jones, Paul, and Phebe Robins
1744, July 4. Jones, Peter.
1769, M'ch 4. Jones, Peter, and Elizabeth Rose.
1747, May —. Jones, Priscilla, and Joshua Wooleston.
1773, M'ch 31. Jones, Priscilla, and William McElroy.
1773, April 8. Jones, Rebecca, and Elijah Dow.
1768, Aug. 27. Jones, Rebecca, and Enoch Battin.
1765, July 1. Jones, Rebecca, and John Mattingley.
1761, Aug. 31. Jones, Richard, and Ann Bailey.
1770, M'ch 1. Jones, Robert, and Mary Cox.
1774, Mc'h 22. Jones, Robert Strettell, and Ann Shippen.
1747, Nov. —. Jones, Samuel, and Hannah Rees.
1764, Nov. 9. Jones, Samuel, and Sylvia Spicer.
1767, May 22. Jones, Sarah, and Daniel Cornog.
1775, Sep. 28. Jones, Sarah, and George Horn.
1774, Feb. 18. Jones, Sarah, and Henry Baker.

1763, Sep. 19. Jones, Sarah, and Isaac Ott.
1763 Dec. 22. Jones, Sarah, and Jacob Fritz.
1748, Jan. —. Jones, Sarah, and James Adams.
1771, May 27. Jones, Sarah, and John O'Harra.
1763, Sep. 14. Jones, Sarah, and Joseph Dimsey.
1773, July 20. Jones, Sarah, and Whitehead Weatherby.
1761, Feb. 3. Jones, Susan, and Davis Heaton.
1748, Sep. —. Jones, Susanna, and William Fowler.
1774, M'ch 11. Jones, Thomas, and Alice Morris.
1761, Sep. 19. Jones, Thomas, and Ann Meridy.
1766, Nov. 27. Jones, Thomas, and Ann Murnix.
1771, May 17. Jones, Thomas, and Elizabeth Hughes.
1776, Apr. 4. Jones, Thomas, and Hannah Kyser.
1763, Oct. 22. Jones, Thomas, and Hannah Williams.
1767, Aug. 5. Jones, Thomas, and Jane Smith.
1762, Oct. 6. Jones, Thomas, and Mary Brumfield.
1761, Jan. 21. Jones, Thomas, and Mary Ewer.
1771, May 10. Jones, Thomas, and Mary Parker.
1761, June 3. Jones, Thomas, and Rozanna Grimes.
1761, June 6. Jones, Thomas, and Sarah Allen.
1762, Nov. 25. Jones, Whitehead, and Ann Johns.
1767, Mar. 9. Jones, William, and Elizabeth Grey.
1747, Sep. —. Jones, William, and Elizabeth Robinson.
1766, Sep. 4. Jones, William, and Jane Reeny.
1769, June 10. Jordan, Catharine, and George Davis.
1759, Dec. 26. Jordan, Francis, and Catharine Kendall.
1768, June 17. Jordan, Isabella, and James Dunn.
1760, Feb. 23. Jordan, Rachel, and William Lloyd.
1763, Jan. 15. Jordan, Robert, and Christiana McCammon.
1767, July 27. Jordan, Susannah, and Aaron Leadlie.
1767, Sep. 12. Joseph, ———, and Serene Thompson, (negroes.)
1776, Feb. 1. Josiah, Lydia, and Jeremiah Williamson.
1764, Dec. 13. Josiah, Margaret, and John Terras.
1760, Feb. 27. Josiah, Mary, and William Kemp.
1772, Feb. 27. Josiah, Robert, and Jemimah Moulder.
1761, Jan. 27. Joyce, Cornelius, and Sarah Longford.
1776, June 21. Joyce, Dominick, and Jennet Sibbald.
1748, Nov. 11. Joyce, Thomas, and Elizabeth Smith.
1746, June —. Joyner, Elenor, and Sopher Perry.
1763, Aug. 25. Juda, Bridget, and John Grimes Howard.
1764, Nov. 2. Judith, and Cuff. (Two negroes the property of Messrs. Mifflin & Elves.)
1745, June —. Jugs, Richard.
1767, M'ch 30. Junkins, Ann, and James Parkinson.

1762, M'ch 25. Juno. ———, and Francis Cox. (Two negroes of this city.)

1745, Nov. —. Junton, Joseph.

1775, Jan. 18. Justice, Anne, and Samuel Church.

1761, Jan. 14. Justice, Elizabeth, and Peter Main.

1774, June 1. Justice, James, and Hannah Wayne.

1763, July 28. Justice, Rebecca, and William Culin.

1774, Oct. 25. Justice, Rebecca, and William Weston.

1774, Feb. 24. Justice, William, and Mary England.

1775, Jan. 14. Justis, Charles, and Mary Morton.

1776, Apr. 6. Justis, Penelope, and Thomas Rice.

1748, May 14. Justis, Swan, and Mary Jones.

1762, Aug. 21. Juvil, Mary, and Daniel Minanti.

K.

1747. Feb. —. Kadd, Lewis, and Catharine Oylers.

1774, Apr. 7. Kaign, James, and Hannah Mason.

1766, Sep. 8. Kaldazer, Isabella, and John Sample.

1769, Aug. 16. Kale, Elizabeth, and James Fairy.

1774, Apr. 22. Kanan, Mary, and John Fegan.

1763, M'ch 30. Kaplin, Alice, and Michael Eichus.

1762, June 21. Kappock, Ann, and William Clark.

1747, Nov. —. Kappock, James, and Mary Emmerson.

1768, Nov. 15. Kaps, John, and Susannah Snyder.

1743, July 1. Karnes, David.

1761, M'ch 9. Karr, Margaret, and Thomas McCune.

1761, May 2. Kastor, William, and Elizabeth Hitchcock.

1770, Nov. 13. Kating, Samuel, and Anne Davenport.

1774, Nov. 22. Katter, Catharine, and Mark McCall.

1768, Nov. 21. Kauffman, Joseph, and Barbara Butler.

1765, July 11. Kaufman, Jacob, and Ann Wolferdin.

1766, M'ch 27. Kay, Joseph, and Judith Lippincot.

1762, Sep. 6. Keappock, Mary, and Samuel Sterrat.

1774, Sep. 8. Kearn, Elizabeth, and Anthony Lowdon.

1776, May 2. Kearnes, Elizabeth, and John Dorvill.

1772, Apr. 8. Kearnes, Mary, and Samuel Rogers.

1772, Dec. 22. Kearnes, Rosanna, and James Pyet.

1771, Dec. 28. Kearney, Mary, and Adam Guyger.

1761, June 2. Kearney, Mary, and Michael Fisher.

1768, Dec. 1. Kearney, Susannah, and Nicholas Devine.

1763, Jan. 14. Kearns, Alice, and James Cochran.

1771, Oct. 17. Keble, John, and Abigail Spicer.

1769, Dec. 28. Keegan, Joseph, and Hannah Walker.

1761, July 29. Keeler, Catharine, and George Reedder.

1765, Oct. 31. Keen, Hannah, and James Nevil.

1764, July 2. Keen, Hannah, and James Poole.

1760, Feb. 5. Keen, Jacob, and Hannah Holmes.

1770, Sep. 20. Keen, John, and Amelia Cook.
1768, July 15. Keen, John, and Rebecca Relin.
1775, Feb. 3. Keen, Mary, and James Delaplaine.
1760, Aug. 16. Keen, Mary, and Jonathan Crathorne.
1763, Sep. 14. Keen, Mary, and Joseph Strout.
1746, Apr. —. Keen, Matthias.
1760, M'ch 24. Keen, William, and Dorothy Gaylor.
1763, Jan. 10. Keider, Peter, and Gedradt Boochan.
1773, Sep. 15. Keighan, Elizabeth, and Arthur Donaldson.
1766, Apr. 10. Keigher, Christopher, and Mary Schatfer.
1765, Feb. 19. Keign, Henry, and Barbara Mulladore.
1775, Aug. 16. Keimer, James, and Sarah King.
1772, Aug. 6. Keiser, Sarah, and Christopher Will.
1776, May 18. Keissler, Sarah, and Jacob Whiteman.
1775, Dec. 26. Keiter, John, and Martha White.
1762, Sep. 20. Keith, Joseph, and Elizabeth Roberts.
1766, M'ch 12. Keith, Martha, and James McNair.
1770, May 31. Keith, William, and Jane Ormes.
1743, May 11. Keley, William.
1762, Sep. 4. Kellar, George, and Doriley Painter.
1774, Feb. 28. Keller, Ann, and John Booz.
1772, Dec. 1. Keller, Elizabeth, and Martin Knoll.
1771, Oct. 31. Keller, Mary, and Philip Wager.
1770, Oct. 10. Kelley, James, and Margaret Clanderman.
1775, July 13. Kellum, Ann, and Furgus Main.
1771, Oct. 5. Kelly, Ann, and Bernard Evans.
1776, June 3. Kelly, Ann, and Philip Lane.
1774, Apr. 28. Kelly, Benjamin, and Rachel Caldwell.
1763, Apr. 5. Kelly, Bryan, and Hannah Harper.
1769, May 24. Kelly, Catharine, and John Spear.
1773, Oct. 7. Kelly, Catharine, and Matthew Grier.
1764, Nov. 1. Kelly, Charles, and Martha Overend.
1772, Jan. 17. Kelly, Elizabeth, and John Durrow.
1770, Nov. 1. Kelly, Erasmus, and Mary Morgan.
1747, M'ch —. Kelly, Francis, and Elizabeth Hoy.
1771, Nov. 1. Kelly, George, and Mary Young.
1761, Nov. 17. Kelly, Hannah, and Jacob Titus.
1770, Dec. 1. Kelly, James, and Frances Crawford.
1761, Feb. 14. Kelly, James, and Mary Wright.
1760, Nov. 6. Kelly, James, and Sarah Coleson.
1761, Apr. 14. Kelly, John, and Elizabeth Newton.
1767, Sep. 4. Kelly, John, and Rachel Aaron.
1774, June 16. Kelly, John, and Rachel Blackledge.
1766, M'ch 31. Kelly, Mary, and John Hammel.
1765, July 25. Kelly, Miriam, and Joseph Potts.
1776, M'ch 4. Kelly, Sarah, and George Shinn.

1761, Sep. 30. Kelly, Sarah, and William Hartrick.
1747, Feb. —. Kelly, William, and Susannah Leonard.
1760, M'ch 21. Kelsee, John, and Mary Kern.
1761, M'ch 21. Kelsey, Ann, and Dubley Dougherty.
1769, Apr. 24. Kelsey, Elizabeth, and William Lollar.
1772, Oct. 3. Kelsey, Mary, and Robert Ewer.
1765, July 31. Kelso, Henry, and Agnes Kreiter.
1766, Nov. 28. Kelso, Jane, and Hugh Boden.
1761, July 30. Kelson, Ann, and Peter Tyshang.
1760, May 27. Kelso, Thomas, and Dorotha Lanterman.
1772, Dec. 8. Kelton, Agnes, and Jonathan Dungan.
1767, June 11. Kemble, Aaron, and Hannah Eastlack.
1776, May 16. Kemble, Ann, and John Davis.
1773, Dec. 19. Kemble, George, and Elizabeth Robinson.
1771, Aug. 29. Kemble, William, and Eleanor Dunbar.
1770, Sep. 20. Kemble, William, and Sarah Worthington.
1760, Dec. 19. Kemle, Elizabeth, and Anthony Miller.
1763, Aug. 23. Kemley, George, and Elizabeth Thimingen.
1770, Aug. 23. Kemmerer, Henry, and Catharine Sheetz.
1766, Dec. 24. Kemp, Elizabeth, and Thomas Bowldin.
1783, June 22. Kempert, John.
1770, M'ch 21. Kemp, George, and Susannah Levan.
1760, May 24. Kemp, William, and Mary Josiah.
1776, Apr. 24. Kenan, Margaret, and Patrick Tonry.
1762, July 6. Kenard, Elizabeth, and Richard Ham.
1759, Dec. 26. Kendall, Catharine, and Francis Jordan.
1766, June 16. Kendall, Jane, and Sarah Randall.
1762, Nov. 13. Kendordine, Rachel, and William Lukens.
1775, Aug. 30. Kendricks, Isaac, and Margaret Curpman.
1770, Oct. 18. Kendry, Barnabas, and Rachel Thomas.
1765, Aug. 7. Kennady, Mary, and William Sweetapple.
1763, Nov. 5. Kennard, Menan, and Elizabeth Cameron.
1748, M'ch 11. Kennard, Thomas, and Mary Ecoff.
1774, Feb. 17. Kennedy, Andrew, and Elizabeth Potts.
1772, Sep. 18. Kennedy, Catharine, and John Welsh.
1760, Sep. 18. Kennedy, Catharine, and William Millen.
1765, Apr. 22. Kennedy, Elizabeth, and Philip Frederick.
1763, M'ch 29. Kennedy, George, and Jane Cooper.
1760, Aug. 9. Kennedy, Grace, and William Grudy.
1765, Sep. 28. Kennedy, Jane, and Francis Quin.
1760, Mc'h 21. Kennedy, Jane, and William McEntire.
1771, Aug. 2. Kennedy, Judith, and John Connor.
1772, July 6. Kennedy, Margaret, and James Guttier.
1772, Nov. 11. Kennedy, Mary, and Alexander Willson.
1771, July 27. Kennedy, Mary, and Arthur Erwin.
1773, Dec. 2. Kennedy, Matthew, and Lucia Long.

1769, Apr.　6. Kennedy, Murdoch, and Susannah Back.
1745, June —. Kennedy, Richard.
1759, Dec. 15. Kennedy, Robert, and Margaret Egle.
1776, Jan. 16. Kennedy, William, and Mary Young.
1764, Jan. 26. Kennedy, William, and Susannah Doack.
1767, Oct. 28. Kennety, Thomas, and Dianna Piercal.
1775, Mc'h 17. Kenney, Margaret, and Robert Wallace.
1768, July 20. Kenny, Elizabeth, and William Koppock.
1770, M'ch 27. Kenny, Martha, and Samuel McCure.
1764, Dec.　3. Kenny, Rebecca, and John Moore.
1746, Aug. —. Kenoby, John, and Ann Roe.
1765, May　9. Kensinger, John, and Mary Wyven.
1764, Dec. 27. Kensley, Christian, and Rebecca Won.
1772, Dec　28. Kentee, Sarah, and John Price.
1769, June 17. Kenton, Mary, and Joseph Welden.
1747, Dec. —. Kenton, Moses, and Mary Leeds.
1771, Feb. 25. Kenton, ————, and William Harper.
1747, May —. Kenton, William, and Mary Grover.
1761, Sep.　2. Kenty, Mary, and John Williams.
1768, Apr. 11. Kepharting, Rachel, and John Strupe.
1767, Feb.　2. Keplering, Margaret, and Frederick Dushong.
1765, Apr. 18. Kepple, Catharine, and John Steinmetz.
1773, Jan. 14. Kepple, Susannah, and Adam Zantzinger.
1775, Feb. 14. Kerlin, Mary, and Adam Clampffer.
1764, Aug. 18. Kerlin, William, and Sarah Goodwin.
1772, July 23. Ker, Mary, and Robert French.
1773, Nov. 12. Kern, Adam, and Catharine Huntsberger.
1760, M'ch 21. Kern, Mary, and John Kelsee.
1773, Feb. 27. Kerr, Abigail, and Joseph Gold.
1764, Nov. 28. Kerr, Adam, and Jane Miller.
1765, June 20. Kerr, George, and Isabella Filpot.
1767, Dec. 10. Kerr, Henry, and Mary James.
1770, May 16. Kerr, James, and Mary Landy.
1775, Jan.　5. Kerr, James, and Rebecca Simpson.
1765, Jan. 22. Kerr, John, and Mary Shecon.
1769, Feb. 24. Kerr, Martha, and James Hathorn.
1772, Oct.　1. Kerr, Martha, and Samuel Goodman.
1770, Jan.　5. Kerr, Mary, and James Young.
1764, Nov. 15. Kerr, Thomas, and Martha Ritche.
1765, Jan. 23. Kerr, Walker, and Martha Palmer.
1765, Apr.　8. Keslurn, Anna, and Samuel James.
1768, M'ch 17. Kethcart, Mary, and Thomas West.
1771, Jan.　4. Keyler, Mary, and Edward Powel.
1762, Sep.　6. Keyll, John, and ———— McFurtricks.
1747, Jan. —. Keylwein, Philipina, and Conrad Bower.
1746, June —. Key, Rebecca, and James Channell.

1776, M'ch 11. Kidd, Ann, and Richard Sheepshanks.
1772, July 2. Kidd, George, and Mary Wolfe.
1773, Apr. 26. Kidd, Hugh, and Jane Rankin.
1768, Sep. 22. Kidd, John, and Ann Spencer.
1767, May 14. Kidd, John, and Sarah Hill.
1773, May 3. Kidd, Peter, and Jane Stone.
1763, May 12. Kidd, William, and Hannah Rodgers.
1772, Dec. 17. Kigings, Susannah, and James Miles.
1762, Aug. 3. Kilback, Catharine, and Daniel Golden.
1746, Sep. —. Kilcrease, Ann, and Richard Mosely.
1761, May 20. Kilgarine, Margaret, and John Damdelspeck.
1760, Nov. 7. Kilheart, Allen, and Elizabeth Rambo.
1770, Mch. 6. Kill, Catharine, and Henry Willock.
1772, Oct. 21. Killden, Thomas, and Isabella McClean.
1774, Sep. 8. Kille, John, and Mary Cowperthwaite.
1767, Feb. 25. Killgore, Elizabeth, and James Huston.
1760, Nov. 20. Killgore, William, and Elizabeth Gray.
1760, Feb. 29. Killinger, George, and Elizabeth Bennet.
1746, Sep. —. Killpatrick, William, and Elizabeth Frederick.
1771, June 12. Kilmagh, Eleanor, and Joseph Williams.
1767, June 9. Kilpack, Jacob, and Elizabeth Cressmore.
1764, Oct. 23. Kilpatrick, Frances, and Hugh Miller.
1767, Apr. 20. Kimble, John, and Mary Chalmers.
1761, M'ch 23. Kimble, Joseph, and Margaret Rogers.
1763, Aug. 10. Kimble, Margaret, and John McClelland.
1767, Oct. 22. Kime, Mary, and Patrick Lundy.
1775, Sep. 23. Kimler, Lydia, and James Dutton.
1773, Oct. 9. Kimmons, Hannah, and Philip Redmond.
1766, Aug. 13. Kimsey, Mary, and John Wood.
1760, Nov. 26. Kinderdine, Hannah, and, James Paul.
1770, Sep. 13. King, Ann, and William Davis.
1763, June 16. King, Catharine, and John Heyward.
1771, Dec. 21. King, Christiana, and John Badcock.
1769, Feb. 4. King, Hay, and Hannah Magraw.
1769, May 17. King, Hugh, and Elizabeth Hill.
1772, Oct. 19. King, James, and Cornelia England.
1774, Dec. 6. King, James, and Margaret Shannon.
1768, Sep. 9. King John, and Jane Brown.
1766, Sep. 29. King, John, and Mary Turner.
1763, June 6. King, Peter, and Mary Hinars.
1768, Oct. 21. King, Rachel, and William Brooks.
1765, June 7. King, Sarah, and Alexander Frazier.
1775, Aug. 16. King, Sarah, and James Keimer.
1773, Aug. 27. Kingrick, John, and Anne Barbara Kloninger.
1774, Nov. 15. Kingsley, Samuel, and Ann Test.
1765, Sep. 3. Kinkead, James, and Margaret Legit.

1773, Dec. 14. Kinnard, Jacob, and Mary Wallis.
1771, Aug. 12. Kinnard, Sarah, and William White.
1775, May 4. Kinnard, William, and Elizabeth Stockford.
1773, M'ch 27. Kinnerd, Hester, and Edward Eaton.
1765, Apr. 22. Kinnersly, Esther, and Joseph Shenell.
1771, Apr. 10. Kinnicut, Daniel, and Jane Hyman.
1760, Aug. 7. Kinsey, Ann, and Ezekiel Woorel.
1766, Aug. 21. Kinsey, David, and Gaynor Bartholomew.
1765, Apr. 29. Kinsey, George, and Phebe Smith.
1775, May 13. Kinsey, Philip, and Jane Morris.
1770, May 26. Kinseley, Barbara, and Henry Grubb.
1760, June 9. Kinton, Richard, and Mary Farr.
1768, July 18. Kion, Mary, and Matthew Mason.
1761, Apr. 14. Kiplinger, Peter, and Hannah Oyster.
1761, Apr. 28. Kirk, Ann, and Michael McNorth.
1773, Dec. 6. Kirk, Arthur, and Mary Gillis.
1775, May 24. Kirk, Philip, and Esther Worrell.
1767, M'ch 24. Kirk, Samuel, and Mahittable Done.
1775, Oct. 20. Kirk, Samuel, and Mary Deklyn.
1764, Nov. 19. Kirk, Sarah, and Jonathan Evans.
1771, Sep. 14. Kirk, Sarah, and Thomas Harding.
1765, Nov. 26. Kirk, William, and Mary Malone.
1766, June 21. Kirkbride, Hannah, and William Biles.
1773, Dec. 24. Kirkbridge, Mary, and Samuel Rogers.
1748, Sep. —. Kirkby, Margaret, and William Purcell.
1761, Nov. 6. Kirkby, William, and Catharine Horning.
1761, Dec. 22. Kirke, Sarah, and William Luffborrow.
1768, Nov. 7. Kirkpatrick, Isabella, and Peter McIntosh.
1770, Feb. 16. Kirkpatrick, James, and Eleanor Connell.
1764, Dec. 21. Kirkpatrick, Mary, and Joseph Moore.
1765, Apr. 11. Kirkpatrick, William, and Elizabeth Carr.
1764, May 4. Kirkpatrick, William, and Margaret Piper.
1764, Oct. 13. Kirks, Martha, and Seth Thomas.
1766, Aug. 5. Kirts, Elizabeth, and Henry Buck.
1762, Aug. 13. Kishlen, Medelina, and John James.
1760, May 5. Kison, Margaret, and George Good.
1774, Aug. 23. Kisselman, Frederick, and Susannah Van Reed.
1774, Apr. 9. Kissler, Margaret, and John Taylor.
1773, Apr. 19. Kitchen, Ann, and Thomas Crispin.
1773, Sep. 28. Kite, Mary, and Jonathan Mullan.
1774, Dec. 15. Kite, Mary, and Richard Pearce.
1767, Sep. 4. Kite, Susannah, and William Cowan.
1776, Apr. 10. Kithcart, Hannah, and John West.
1762, June 1. Kitts, Rebecca, and Christopher Fechlman.
1746, July —. Klainkoof, Sarah, and Hugh Cain.
1771, Oct. 16. Kline, Philip, and Elizabeth Corbman.

1773, Aug. 27. Kloninger, Anna Barbara, and John Kingrick.
1775, M'ch 18. Knees, Catharine, and John Specht.
1748, Sep. —. Knepler, Barbara, and Leonard Herman.
1760, Jan. 24. Knight, Ann, and Jonathan Warrington.
1775, Sep. 18. Knight, Deborah, and Henry Matthews.
1763, Jan. 18. Knight, Elizabeth, and Peter Dehaven.
1773, Sep. 29. Knight, Isaac, and Rebecca Lawrence.
1774, Oct. 27. Knight, John, and Mary Coran.
1771, Nov. 28. Knight, Mary, and Henry Branson.
1748, Sep. —. Knight, Nicholas, and Margaret Warner.
1762, Nov. 8. Knight, Rachel, and Jonathan Philips.
1762, June 14. Knight, Rachel, and Josiah Sharrald.
1768, June 14. Knight, Rebecca, and William Mann.
1764, Nov. 8. Knight, William, and Ann Brown.
1760, June 24. Knight, William Jacob, and Elizabeth Plannjer.
1746, June —. Knoble, Catharine, and James Boggs.
1772, Dec. 1. Knoll, Martin, and Elizabeth Keller.
1760, June 26. Knott, John, and Frances Harrison.
1761, May 27. Knowland, Martha, and Lau. Ash.
1770, May 19. Knowles, Catharine, and John Hart.
1773, M'ch 29. Knowles, Elizabeth, and Matthew Jones.
1770, M'ch 21. Knowles, John, and Hannah Preston.
1744, Sep. —. Knowles, John, Jun.
1773, Sep. 15. Knowles, Mary, and Isaac Buckley.
1743, July 5. Knowles, Samuel.
1773, Jan. 7, Knowles, Timothy, and Hannah Briggs.
1759, Nov. 29. Knowles, William, and Agnes Davis.
1774, Dec. 2. Knowles, William, and Mary Anderson.
1764, July 27. Knox, Frances, and John Childerstone.
1774, M'ch 9. Knox, Frances, and John Knox.
1771, Dec. 18. Knox, Hugh, and Catharine Lewis.
1773, July 30. Knox, Jane, and James McClenachan.
1771, Nov. 27. Knox, John, and Elizabeth Matlack.
1774, M'ch 9. Knox, John, and Frances Knox.
1768, July 9. Knox, John, and Phebe Delaplaine.
1747, Jan. —. Knoxley, Mary, and Francis Garrigues.
1760, Nov. 26. Knox, Margaret, and Zacharies Faires.
1772, Dec. 22. Knox, Matthew, and Isabella Craig.
1761, Dec. 8. Knox, Thomas, and Alice Hall.
1768, June 29. Kolb, Jacob, and Ann Yoder.
1762, Nov. 17. Kolleck, Hester, and Robert Sandelson.
1746, Jan. —. Kollosh, Philip.
1760, June 25. Kootolow, Joshua, and Jane Donahew.
1764, Feb. 6. Kopple, John, and Elizabeth Morrin.
1768, July 20. Koppock, William, and Elizabeth Kenny.
1766, May 23. Korster, Benjamin, and Mary Fisher.

1768, Oct. 25. Kostor, John, and Ann Pitt.
1773, M'ch 6. Kotman, Susannah, and John Quee.
1772, Dec. 21. Kotter, James, and Susannah Hume.
1764, June 22. Krafley, Christopher, and Eve Crason.
1761, July 7. Kramar, Samuel, and Ottilia Ludwick.
1775, M'ch 23. Kranston, Catharine, and John Cordien.
1760, Apr. 23. Krausen, Derrick, and Hannah Banart.
1748, Apr. 13. Kreamer, Balthaser, and Elizabeth Gerrard.
1759, Nov. 20. Kreener, Catharine, and William Atkinson.
1774, Apr. 8. Krees, Margaret, and Daniel Fisher.
1774, June 21. Kreider, Catharine, and Christopher Baker.
1774, June 9. Kreider, Elizabeth, and Henry Burgy.
1746, Nov. —. Kreir, Henry, and Margaret Coby.
1775, Aug. 26. Kreiser, John, and Rebecca White.
1765, July 31. Kreiten, Agnes, and Henry Kelso.
1765, Dec. 20. Kremer, Christian, and Margaret Waggoner.
1770, Apr. 9. Kreps, Henry, and Catharine Campbell.
1775, May 18. Kreps, Henry, and Margaret Barr.
1772, Dec. 2. Kreusen, Catharine Peter and Peter Wikoff.
1773, May 29. Krewson, Elizabeth, and Cornelius Daily.
1761, May 23. Krewsen, Alice, and Daniel Hogland.
1774, M'ch 24. Krewson, Hannah, and John Jackson, Jun.
1773, Dec. 28. Krips, Elizabeth, and Charles Bisey.
1772, Nov. 4. Kreps, John, and Sarah Murphy.
1763, Aug. 26. Krowle, Catharine, and Henry Sterner.
1774, July 6. Krozer, Barbara, and John Delavan.
1772, Oct. 7. Krug, John Andrew, and Henrietta Elizabeth. Handschuckin.
1773, Jan. 20. Kruse, Catharine, and Fredrick Hiller.
1760, Apr. 29. Kruson, Garret, and Hannah Jackson.
1776, M'ch 2. Kruzen, Garret, and Jane Vanosdow.
1776, Apr. 8. Kryder, Christiana, and Thomas McCormick.
1776, Feb. 7. Kryder, Susannah, and Paul Casper Breton.
1776, M'ch 15, Kugler, Paul, and Sarah Shrack.
1762, Feb. 19. Kuhl, George Frederick, and Susannah Kuhl.
1762, Feb. 19. Kuhl, Susannah, and George Frederick Kuhl.
1776, M'ch 6. Kungils, John, and Mary Creps.
1762, Oct. 25. Kun, Reynold, and Christina Stilley.
1774, Nov. 15. Kupin, Elizabeth, and Frederick Fogle.
1768, M'ch 4. Kurts, Catharine, and Conrad Shultz.
1773, Oct. 25. Kurtz, George, and Mary Pissant.
1770, July 2. Kurtz, Peter, and Sarah Younger.
1765, M'ch 4. Kurtzen, Catharine, and Christian Stadtler.
1766, Apr. 8. Kuyper, Derrick, and Elizabeth Helm,
1747, May. —. Kygher, Valentine, and Sarah Wittatue.

10—VOL. II.

1770, Sep. 21. Kyle, Barbara, and Christopher Shultz.
1776, Apr. 4. Kyser, Hannah, and Thomas Jones.
1775, Nov. 28. Kyser, Henry, and Mary Lush.
1767, Oct. 23. Kyser, Nicholas, and Anna Paul.

L.

1776, Apr. 24. Labbs, Joseph, and Elizabeth ———.
1762, Dec. 13. Labour, Elizabeth, and Joseph Williams.
1762, Nov. 23. Lacey, Mary, and John Haverd.
1763, Apr. 16. Lacon, Samuel, and Mary Slinton.
1774, Feb. 19. Lacy, Elizabeth, and Henry Gordon.
1775, Nov. 6. Ladd, Ann, and Edward Evans.
1748, July 13. Ladner, Robert, and Elizabeth Pyles.
1761, Aug. 31. Laferty, Bryan, and Mary Johnson.
1773. May 18. Lake, Catharine, and John Pringle.
1746, July —. Lake, Thomas, and Harriet Priscot.
1768, May 2. Lammany, Mary, and John William Read.
1769, May 10. Lamb, John, and Mary Cline.
1768, Oct. 12. Lamb, Mary, and David Crowls.
1772, May 14. Lamb, Mary, and Richard Grafton Preston.
1766, Nov. 10. Lamburgh, John, and Sarah Mentzer.
1769, Apr. 5. Lamont, Margaret, and James Club.
1761, Oct. 5. Lampley, Rachel, and Simpson Coningham.
1746, June —. Lamplugh, Martha, and James Steel Thomson.
1747, M'ch —. Lamplugh, Susannah, and Henry Copp.
1762, May 24. Lanaway, Henry, and Thornison Crowley.
1766, May 23. Lancaster, John, and Elizabeth Abrams.
1771, Oct. 2. Landee, James, and Elizabeth Suffrance.
1760, Jan. 10. Landerman, John, and Sarah Coulston.
1746, Nov. —. Landerman, Mary, and Arthur Nitcullues.
1747, Feb. —. Landers, George, and Jane Cowe.
1769, Apr. 10. Landreth, Cuthbert, and Elizabeth Fairbuttle.
1770, May 16. Landy, Mary, and James Kerr.
1772, Oct. 1. Lane, Elizabeth, and James Shannon.
1761, June 30. Lane, Isaac, and Zuba Wilkins.
1748, Feb. —. Lane, Joseph, and Mary Bobkins.
1767, Aug. 10. Lane, Martha, and Thomas Church.
1776, June 3. Lane, Philip, and Ann Kelly.
1773, Apr. 17. Lane, Sarah, and John Fawkes.
1745, June —. Lane, William.
1775, M'ch 16, Langdale, Hannah, and Benjamin January.
1765, Oct. 25. Langdale, John, and Alice Coates.
1773, July 17. Langdon, William, and Susannah Sanky.
1774, M'ch 19. Lang, James, and Mary Denny.
1774, Sep. 3. Lang, John, and Margaret Jolly.
1773, Sep. 29. Langley, Allen, and Ruth Haild.

1761, June 29. Langley, John, and Mary McAble.
1748, Feb. —. Langly, Rhody, and Thomas Dilks.
1764, Feb. 29. Lang, William, and Elizabeth Adams.
1762, Nov. 13. Lanniell, Judah, and John Fox.
1760, May 27. Lanterman, Dorotha, and Thomas Kelso.
1769, May 17. Lantz, Martin, and Juliana Hammerstane.
1773, Aug. 7. Laperty, Daniel, and Martha Lucas.
1776, June 6. Laps, Adam, and Mary Peters.
1769, Feb. 13. Laren, Abraham, and Elizabeth Praul.
1775, Jun. 7. Large, Ebenezer, and Dorothy Sparks.
1764, Aug. 3. Large, Jane, and Jonathan Thomas.
1775, June 6. Larimore, Elizabeth, and Benjamin Williamson.
1743, Sep. —. Larne, Isaac.
1770, Oct. 6. Larne, Isaac, and Gartree Stone.
1769, Apr. 25. Larne, Mary, and Richard Stillwill.
1768, May 28. Larrew, David, and Sarah Lazelere.
1775, Dec. 16. Larrew, Isaac, and Mary Johnston.
1775, May 3. Larriall, Hannah, and John Roberts.
1744, Nov. —. Larrymore, James.
1769, Oct. 19. Larue, Moses, and Catharine Lazalier.
1760, Dec. 24. Lasy, Mary, and John Perkins.
1775, M'ch 24. Latch, Mary, and Jonathan James.
1771, Sep. 5. Lathbridge, Thomas, and Eleanor Davenport.
1773, June 22. Latimer, Sarah, and Thomas Cuthbert.
1748, June 16. Latimore, Arthur, and Mary Wilson.
1765, Feb. 26. Latta, James, and Mary McCalla.
1767, Feb. 19. Lauderback, Christiana, and Henry Seckel.
1766, Nov. 6. Lauderbrun, Frederick, and Eleanor Thompson.
1763, M'ch 29. Lauer, Christian, aand Elizabeth Garren.
1775, May 22. Laughlan, Bryan, and Margaret McKone.
1766, Dec. 18. Laughlen, Samuel, and Mary Hall.
1771, Oct. 26. Laughran, Elizabeth, and John Rogers.
1764, May 29. Laughery, Sarah, and William Christy
1769, M'ch 7. Lavairr, Margaret, and Andrew Gotthard Lavin.
1769, Aug. 25. Lavan, Mary, and John Sitfreet.
1769, M'ch 7. Lavin, Andrew Gotthard, and Margaret Lavairr.
1763, June 13. Laviston, Maragret, and William Jackson.
1771, Jan. 17. Laversweiller, Mary, and Daniel Oldenburch.
1773, Feb. 12. Lawderburr, Frederick, and Rebecca Ulrick.
1769, Sep. 30. Lawersuyler, Bernard, and Elizabeth Clampffer.
1767, M'ch 4. Law, Matthew, and Margaret Snodgrass.
1773, Nov. 24. Lawrence, Ann, and Jacob Hughes.
1768, Oct. 20. Lawrence, Ann, and John McLaughan.
1776, May 2. Lawrence, Ann, and Owen Mullan.
1774, May 17. Lawrence, Ann, and William Atkinson.
1774, Sep. 8. Lawrence, Catharine, and John Garey.

1771, Nov. 16. Lawrence, Edward, and Jane Galbreath.
1768, M'ch 9. Lawrence, Elizabeth, and James Allen.
1775, Sep. 27. Lawrence, Elizabeth, and Joseph West.
1748, Aug. 15. Lawrence, Giles.
1764, Jan. 4. Lawrence, Jane, and Isaac Vaughan.
1764, Nov. 10. Lawrence, Martha, and Charles Moore.
1770, Apr. 9. Lawrence, Mary, and John McGlathery.
1761, M'ch 21, Lawrence, Philip, and Ann Ford.
1768, Jan. 7. Lawrence, Rachel, and John McCarston.
1763, Sep. 29. Lawrence, Rebecca, and Isaac Knight.
1775, Oct. 9. Lawrence, Richard, and Mary Miller.
1772, June 4. Lawrence, Susannah, and Jesse Moore.
1763, Jan. 1. Lawrence, Thomas, and Hannah Williamson.
1768, Sep. 21. Lawrence, Thomas, Jun., and Rebecca Bond.
1771, Oct. 12. Lawrence, William, and Ann Robinson.
1763, Jan. 24. Lawrence, William, and Barbara Robinson.
1773, Sep. 3. Lawrence, William, and Charlotte Dawson.
1776, Apr. 24. Lawther, Hannah, and John Rhodes.
1772, Apr. 1. Lawwell, Sarah, and Benjamin Weston.
1769, Oct. 19. Lazalier, Catharine, and Moses Larue.
1771, June 20. Lazalier, Hester, and Richard Mitchell.
1771, June 15. Lazalier, Mary, and George Applegate.
1747, June —. Lazarein, Christian, and Frederick Becker.
1768, May 28. Lazelere, John, and Margaret Vanhorn.
1768, May 28. Lazelere, Sarah, and David Larrew.
1771, July 17. Leacock, Hester, and John Hazlewood.
1772, Oct. 7. Leacock, John, and Martha Ogilby.
1763, Sep. 8. Leacock, Samuel, and Esther Fleeson.
1774, Jan. 1. Leacock, Susannah, and Joseph Aberdeen.
1766, M'ch 27. Leadbetter, Ann, and William Martin.
1746, Feb. —. Leadbetters, George.
1764, Aug. 15. Leader, Johanna, and Robert Bray.
1763, Apr. 14. Leadley, Jean, and Alexander McKervy.
1767, July 27. Leadlie, Aaron, and Susannah Jordan.
1771, Sep. 14. Leaight, Henry, and Jane Flood.
1764, Sep. 1. Learny, Jacob, and Hannah Bowen.
1774, Sep. 5. Leary, Henry, and Mary Clements.
1743, M'ch 8. Lease, John.
1748, Oct. 18. Leaver, Erasmus, and Catharine Meary.
1748, Sep. —. Le Blan, Francis, and Margaret Mallaby.
1762, July 14. Lecony, James, and Elizabeth McCay.
1774, July 18. Ledlie, William, and Elizabeth Wood.
1762, Sep. 3. Ledison, Hannah, and Derrick Cornelius Fen
    berry.
1767, Jan. 15. Ledru, Joseph, and Mary Wormly.
1776, Feb. 10. Lee, Ann, and Joseph Banks.

1774, Feb. 12. Lee, Catharine, and Daniel Fitz Patrick.
1762, Nov. 27. Lee, Catharine, and Jacob Shoemaker.
1769, Apr. 17. Leech, Eleanor, and Abraham Pastorius.
1769, June 27. Leech, Elizabeth, and John Clayton.
1748. Apr. 13. Leech, Ephraim, and Mary Nixon.
1765, May 7. Leech, Hannah, and Thomas Wagstaff.
1770, June 25. Leech, Hester, and Thomas Randal
1761, July 2. Leech, Joshua, and Elizabeth Hoffman.
1762, Dec. 24. Leech, Rebecca, and Boaz Walton.
1762, Dec. 29. Leech, Susannah, and Benjamin Cetman.
1769, Feb. 15. Leech, Thomas, and Eve Bilyere.
1765, M'ch 2. Leedom, Benjamin, and Alice Pearson.
1762, May 12. Leedom, Richard, and Sarah Calley.
1747, Dec. —. Leeds, Mary, and Moses Kenton.
1775, May 1. Lee, Elizabeth, and James Glasgow.
1768, Jan. 20. Lee, Hannah, and Joseph Scott.
1768, Dec. 6. Lee, Honour, and James Ramsay.
1775, June 5. Lee, John, and Elizabeth Higg.
1772, Sep. 15. Lee, Martha, and Nicholas Spencer.
1770, Nov. 5. Lee, Mary, and Charles Maclean.
1763, Jan. 31. Lee, Mary, and Charles West.
1763. June 16. Lee, Mary, and Jacob Amon.
1770, Oct. 22. Lee, Mary, and Thomas Powell.
1775, Oct. 1. Lees, Henry, and Elizabeth Styber.
1770, June 7. Lees, James, and Susannah Winnemore.
1763, Jan. 8. Lees, Sarah, and George Whitebread.
1767, July 11. Lee, Thomas, and Margaret Gunning.
1771, Oct. 4. Lee, Thomas, and Mary Spencer.
1763, M'ch 17. Lefever, Joseph, and Margaret Ashard.
1765, Apr. 20. Lefever, Sarah, and John Snowden.
1743, Feb. 15. Legay, Jacob.
1774, Aug. 27. Le Gay, Jacob, and Sarah Bell.
1776, Apr. 18. Legdey, Mary, and Casper Wack.
1767, Apr. 27. Legg, Elizabeth, and William Hartley.
1765, Sep. 3. Legit, Margaret, and James Kinkead.
1766, Sep. 2. Legit Ruth, and John Thompson.
1773, Sep. 16. Lehman, Ann, and John Bamford.
1772, Apr. 9. Leib, William, and Ann Salen.
1772, Sept. 26. Leicester, Philip, and Elizabeth Cell.
1762, Oct. 16. Leidam, Samuel, and Hannah Slaugts.
1774, May 18. Leigh, Benjamin, and Sarah Daily.
1746, Apr. —. Leipencutt, Jacob.
1766, Dec. 9. Leise, John, and Wilhelmina Atherholdt.
1760, Apr. 1. Lemont, John, and Margaret Fullerton.
1762, Aug. 24. Lenard, James, and Mary Smith.
1762, Aug. 26. Lenix, Henry, and Mary Hopkins.

1775, Nov. 28. Lennington, John, and Mary Benneville.
1776, June 15. Lenox, Hugh, and Sarah Cooper.
1761, M'ch 27. Lenox, Tamson, and Simon Hilton.
1776, Feb. 19. Lentz, Susannah, and William Huston.
1771, Apr. 11. Leonard, James, and Margaret Rigger.
1769, Feb. 10. Leonard, Pamela, and John Gray.
1768, Jan. 12. Leonard, Ruth, and Hugh Steward.
1772, Nov. 30. Leonard, Sarah, and Isaac Hopper.
1747, Feb. —. Leonard, Susannah, and William Kelly.
1748, M'ch 11. Leonard, Thomas, and Elizabeth Martgridge
1763, Sep. 10. Lepis, Thomas, and Hannah Taylor.
1769, Dec. 9. Lepper, Thomas, and Mary Toland.
1766, Oct. 30. Leseone, Isaac, and Hannah Noarth.
1760, June 17. Lesher, William, and Rachel Fisher.
1766, Oct. 8. Lesley, Patrick, and Mary Dyer.
1775, July 21. Lester, Daniel, and Catharine Weaver.
1773, July 24. Lettellier, Michael Joseph, and Mary Richardson
1770, Aug. 7. Letetiere, John, and Mary Rogers.
1772, Apr. 9. Letts, Ezekiel, and Hannah Palmer.
1771, Feb. 15. Leuttner, Conrod, and Elizabeth Graffley.
1773, June 22. Levan, Elizabeth, and John Waggoner.
1762, Dec. 7. Levan, Eve, and Peter Yoder.
1763, June 14. Levan, Jacob, and Susannah Ludwick.
1760, May 28. Levan, Judith, and Samuel Weiser
1770, M'ch 21. Levan, Susannah, and George Kemp.
1763, May 9. Levering, Aaron, and Ann Wrighter.
1771, Jan. 21. Levering, Deborah, and John Streper.
1765, Feb. 10. Levering, Enoch, and Mary Wrighter.
1769, Apr. 20. Levering, Jacob, and Mary Brownfield.
1774, May 25. Levering, Margaret, and Alexander Hughes.
1772, Apr. 14. Levering, Sarah, and John Brown.
1765, Oct. 30. Levis, Hannah, and Levy Lloyd.
1766, Oct. 14. Leviston, Neal, and Catharine McMullen.
1761, Sep. 7. Levy, David, and Margaret Eshbaugh.
1767, May 13. Levy, Hannah, and Charles Davis.
1776, Jan. 24. Lewellin, William, and Susannah Hacket.
1743, Aug. 24. Lewis, Henry.
1761, M'ch 2. Lewis, Ann, and James Smith.
1774, Sep. 1. Lewis, Ann, and Samuel Murdoch.
1771, Dec. 18. Lewis, Catharine, and Hugh Knox.
1744, Aug. 2. Lewis, David.
1747, Nov. —. Lewis, David, and Margaret Morris.
1763, May 14. Lewis, Elizabeth, and John Funk.
1768, May 30. Lewis, Francis. and Mary Barnet.
1746, M'ch —. Lewis, George.
1768, Apr. 18. Lewis, Henry, and Elizabeth Lownes.

1768, June 22. Lewis, Henry, and Sarah Lewis.
1762, May 29. Lewis, Isaac, and Elizabeth Rees.
1763, Feb. 19. Lewis, Isaac, and Mary McColly.
1748, Feb. —. Lewis, Isaac, and Mary Phipps.
1762, Jan. 23. Lewis, Jane, and Edward Harry.
1765, Nov. 20. Lewis, John, and Mary Jones.
1766, Dec. 2. Lewis, Joseph, and Eleanor Taylor.
1762, Jan. 7. Lewis, Lewis, and Deborough Richardson.
1748, M'ch 11. Lewis, Lewis, and Elizabeth Rees.
1771, May 14. Lewis, Margaret, and John Griffiths.
1765, Jan. 12. Lewis, Martha, and Thomas Smith.
1772, Apr. 10. Lewis, Mary, and James Thomas
1772, Feb. 29. Lewis, Mary, and John Miles.
1772, Dec. 12. Lewis, Mary, and William Green.
1774, M'ch 22. Lewis, Moses, and Elizabeth Owen.
1775, Jan. 28. Lewis, Peters, and Margaret Bell.
1763, May 5. Lewis, Rebecca, and John Bone.
1763, M'ch 11. Lewis, Richard, and Margaret Thomas.
1768, June 22. Lewis, Sarah, and Henry Lewis.
1775, Aug. 26. Lewis, Stephen, and Deborah Pleasenton.
1746, Nov. —. Lewis, Stephen, and Hannah Jones.
1760, Feb. 16. Lewis, Susannah, and Edward Middleton.
1744, Dec. —. Lewis, Thomas.
1775, Aug. 31. Lewis, William, and Elizabeth Ranstead.
1760, July 8. Lewton, Robert, and Ann Winter.
1775, Oct. 31. Lex, Andrew, and Mary Vackenhurst.
1775, M'ch 20. Librant, Conrod, and Hannah Sellers.
1765, May 15. Librant, George, and Elizabeth Schuack.
1775, Dec. 15. Librick, Mary, and Daniel Nauman.
1762, M'ch 13. Lickle, Susannah, and Henry Willibe.
1772, Nov. 6. Liggit, John, and Mary Shields.
1762, Sep. 30. Liggit, Rachael, and John Davison.
1768, Oct. 27. Lightbody, Robert, and Mary Logan.
1760, Nov. 19. Lightmenon, Mary, and John Wildmire.
1768, Oct. 5. Light, Nicholas, and Abalan Fryan.
1774, May 27. Likens, John, and Ann Torton.
1748, Oct. 18. Likens, Rachel, and Stacey Woodel.
1776, June 4. Lily, John, and Catharine Jones.
1775, Nov. 25. Lilly, Robert, and Lewis Ward.
1775, Jan. 7. Linch, John, and Ann Russel.
1764, Sep. 10. Linch, Samuel, and Elizabeth Vanneman.
1747, June —. Lincoln, Jacob, and Ann Rambo.
1763, Feb. 15. Lincoln, Rebecca, and James Carter.
1746, Dec. —. Lincon, Isaac, and Mary Shute.
1771, Nov. 28. Lincon, Sarah, and Samuel Pastorius.
1773, Nov. 13. Lind, John, and Catharine Naglee.

1766, Dec. 16. Lindley, Hannah, and John Murray.
1767, Jan. 13. Lindmire, Rebecca, and George Ord.
1771, June 8. Lindsay, Charles, and Anne Moore.
1768, Jan. 26. Lindsay, Charles, and Jane Ekins.
1747, June —. Lindsay, James, and Mary Boardman.
1769, Feb. 28. Lindsay, Jane, and John Rees.
1743, Oct. —. Lindsay, John.
1761, May 15. Lindsay, John, and Rose Matthews.
1764, May 27. Lindsay, Margaret, and Robert Porter.
1774, Feb. 22. Lindsay, Mary, and James Ash.
1764, Aug. 23. Lindsay, William, and Jane Marshall.
1760, Jan. 22. Lindsey, Alexander, and Grace Cummings.
1761, Apr. 18. Lindsey, John, and Rebecca Moore.
1746, Nov. —. Liney, Hugh, and Elizabeth Bessat.
1760, Dec. 27. Lington, Margaret, and John Webb.
1763, July 7. Limoin, Margaret, and James Gregory, (free negroes.)
1763, July 25. Linkon, John, and Anne Boone.
1770, Apr. 19. Linley, John, and Elizabeth Slack.
1765, Jan. 10. Linmire, Elizabeth, and John Carr.
1776, M'ch 25. Linnard, William, and Susannah McMullan.
1771, Sep. 13. Linnington, John, and Susannah Carmalt.
1761, July 21. Linn, Sarah, and John Richey.
1774, Jan. 10. Linn, William, and Rebecca Blair.
1764, Nov. 29. Linton, Margaret, and George Glentworth.
1775, M'ch 23. Lip, John, and Mary Cyphert.
1767, M'ch 27. Lippencot, Judith, and Joseph Kay.
1761, Sep. 29. Lippenket, Grace, and John Wilson.
1767, Dec. 24. Lippincott, Abel, and Catharine Hudson.
1767, May 4. Lippincott, Phebe, and Hudson Burr.
1759, Nov. 22. Lisby, Mary, and Ephraim Carman.
1762, Aug. 26. Lissa, Catharine, and Enos Weeton.
1743, May 27. Lister, Adam.
1746, M'ch —. Litle, James.
1774, M'ch 24. Litle, John, and Mary Williams.
1766, May 15. Litle, Sarah, and John Henderson.
1763, May 18. Litle, Thomas, and Sarah Dennison.
1771, Apr. 15. Litman, Henry, and Elizabeth Murrin.
1762, Oct. 29. Little, Abigail, and Fergus Purden.
1763, Jan. 1. Little, John, and Elizabeth English.
1762, May 22. Little, John, and Grace Nicholson.
1764, Jan. 16. Little, Mary, and Matthew Gardner.
1765, Oct. 30. Little, Thomas, and Catharine House.
1772, Sep. 15. Little, William, and Frances Grear.
1774, Nov. 2. Little, William, and Hannah Allen.
1768, Apr. 18. Livingston, John, and Ann Hanlan.

1772, Aug.   5. Llewellyn, Ariadna, and Llewellyn Young.
1766, Aug. 13. Lloyd, Abigail, and Edward Williams.
1747, Aug. —. Lloyd, Agnes. and Samuel Walker.
1747, Sep. —. Lloyd, Ann, and Abraham Mathews.
1761, Feb. 13. Lloyd, Jane, and John Beal.
1760, Jan. 11. Lloyd, John, and Elizabeth Brooks.
1765, Oct. 30. Lloyd, Levy, and Hannah Levis.
1747, Dec. —. Lloyd, Lydia, and Anthony McCue.
1766, Aug.   5. Lloyd, Lydia, and David Crawford.
1774, Oct. 20. Lloyd, Martha, and Daniel Morris.
1761, Sep. 28. Lloyd, Mary, and William Mathews.
1783, June 17. Lloyd, Nicholas.
1761, Oct. 17. Lloyd, Nicholas, and Grace Smith.
1766, Apr. 11. Lloyd, Philip, and Hannah Templin.
1772, Jan. 15. Lloyd, Ruth and Amos Thomas.
1762, Nov.   4. Lloyd, Susannah, and Thomas Wharton.
1760, Feb. 23. Lloyd, William, and Rachel Jordan.
1764, May   9. Loanan, Sarah, and Nathaniel Dowdney.
1762, Nov. 13. Lobb, Isaac, and Esther Hibbert.
1767, Jan. 20. Lobb, Jacob, and Mary Dougherty.
1769, M'ch 31. Lobb, Mary, and Michael Brady.
1770, Apr. 20. Lochlar, Christiana, and Mark Hunnyger.
1775, Jan.   7. Lock, Ann, and John Pluckrose.
1761, Nov. 28. Lockart, Francis, and Jane Wear.
1760, Dec. 20. Lockeridge, Margaret, and Charles Haynes.
1769, M'ch 16. Locklar, Mary, and Lewis Johnston Costigan.
1767, Feb. 22. Lockhart, John, and Margaret Allen.
1762, Feb.   1. Lockley, Martha, and Daniel Dungan.
1763, Dec.   5. Lock, Margaret, and John Cole.
1773, May   6. Lockridge, Jane, and John Taylor.
1776, May   2. Loder, Edward, and Ann Tustin.
1747, M'ch. —. Lodge, Abel, and Hannah Wood.
1763, Oct. 25. Lodge, Jane, and William Scull.
1747, Dec. —. Lodges, Margaret, and Dennis Sullevan.
1774, Sep.   1. Loe, John, and Alice Hall.
1775, Apr. 19. Lofferty, Bryan, and Rachel Anderson.
1772, Oct. 23. Loftus, Samuel, and Beulah Saylor.
1769, Aug. 31. Loftus, Sarah, Baulton, and David Provost.
1769, Jan. 28. Logan, Dorcas, and Alexander Millar.
1773, July 30. Logan, John, and Ann Talbert.
1760, June   5. Logan, Margaret, and James Cherrv.
1768, Oct. 27. Logan, Mary, and Robert Lightbody.
1776, Jan. 18. Logan, Rachel, and James Clelan.
1746, Jan. —. Logan, William.
1766, Sep. 15. Logan, William, and Margaret, Sterling.
1766, May 26. Loggan, David, and Sarah Belangee.

1769, Apr. 24. Lollar, William, and Elizabeth Kelsey.
1775, Sep. 2. Lombalter, Conrad, and Margaret Shallerin.
1762, July 29. Longacre, Phebe, and Paul Castoley.
1760, Dec. 24. Long, Andrew, and Elizabeth Bee.
1774, M'ch 15. Long, Ann, and Francis Roberts.
1761, Jan. 27. Longford, Sarah, and Cornelius Joyce.
1770, July 26. Longhman, Nicholas, and Mary Snyder.
1761, Oct. 31. Long, Hugh, and Mary Corbett.
1773, June 18. Long, Jane, and Elijah Parkhill.
1767, Dec. 15. Long, Jane, and Thomas Jamison.
1773, Dec. 2. Long, Lucia, and Matthew Kennedy.
1768, M'ch 6. Long, Margaret, and Robert Norris.
1766, Dec. 10. Long, Martha, and John Coleman.
1775, Mc'h 13, Long, Martha, and Robert Milnor.
1744, Sep. —. Long, Michael.
1761, Dec. 2. Long, Moses, and Keziah Cooper.
1770, Nov. 22. Long, Peter, and Mary Ellis.
1760, Apr. 12. Long, Peter, and Mary Margaret Euters.
1773, M'ch 11. Long, Samuel, and Catharine Hendricks.
1768, June 10. Long, Thomos, and Rachel Morgan.
1770, May 1. Long, William, and Hannah Maddock.
1763, July 9. Longwood, Matthew, and Ann Gear.
1765, Sep. 21. Loofbercugh, David, and Sarah Twining.
1774, Dec. 26. Loots, Michael, and Susannah Young.
1744, Nov. —. Lord, Oliver.
1744, June —. Lork, John.
1773, Dec. 18. Lort, John, and Mary Gilbert.
1765, Sep. 19, Lort, Mary, and Thomas Dickinson.
1773, Jan. 18. Lott, Zephania, and Alice Vanpelt.
1774, Nov. —. Louderman, William.
1762, Nov. 2. Loupler, Susannah, and William Coats.
1766, Oct. 6. Louttit, Henry, and Jane Mouret.
1762, July 10, Lovegrove, Mary, and Francis Skiverton.
1763, Jan. 18. Love, James, and Hannah Russel.
1760, M'ch 28. Love, John, and Jane Robinson.
1743, Jan. 27. Love, Joseph.
1767, Nov. 3. Lovekin, Frances, and Thomas Banks.
1770, Apr. 28. Lovell, John, and Mary Vinnest.
1764, May 12. Lovett, Daniel, and Sarah Biles.
1760, Jan. 7. Lowber, Miziam, and Benjamin Eaton.
1774, Sep. 8. Lowdon, Anthony, and Elizabeth Kearn.
1761, Jan. 22. Lower, Christiana, and Hugh James.
1763, Apr. 19. Low, James, and Margaret Hamilton.
1768, M'ch 18. Lownes, Elizabeth, and Henry Lewis.
1770, Dec. 8. Lownes, Sarah, and Henry Hubbs.
1766, Dec. 2. Lowns, Jane, and Joseph Burns.

1767, May 9. Lowns, Rebecca, and Caleb Ash.
1768, Nov. 22. Lowra, George, and Elizabeth Rhoads.
1774, July 12. Lowry, David, and Ann Biggs.
1767, Aug. 12. Lowry, Jacob, and Newill Quicksall.
1763, Apr. 28. Lowry, Mary, and Isaac Taylor.
1775, Sep. 14. Lowry, Mary, and Philip Flick.
1743, Nov. —. Lowry. Robert.
1764, Feb. 20. Lowry, Samuel, and Elizabeth Erwin.
1743, M'ch 28. Loxley, Benjamin.
1772, Nov. 4. Loxley, Benjamin, and Mary Barnes.
1765, Oct. 16. Loyd, Hannah, and Griffith Jones.
1769, Sep. 25. Loyd, Sarah, and Jacob Bristol.
1747, Feb. —. Lucars, Margaret, and Robert Roberts.
1762, Oct. 19. Lucas, James, and Prudence Howell.
1773, Aug. 7. Lucas, Martha, and Daniel Laperty.
1773, Dec. 14. Lucas, Mary, and Laughlan Maclean.
1774, May 8. Lucas, Robert, and Mary Rowan.
1768, July. 2. Lucken, John, and Rachel Edwards.
1769, Sep. 25. Ludlow, Margaret, and Patrick Neave
1769, July 24. Ludwick, Mary, and Casper Hays.
1773, Aug. 20. Ludwick, Otilla, and John Wilson.
1761, July 7. Ludwick, Ottilia, and Samuel Kramar.
1763, June 14. Ludwick, Susannah, and Jacob Levan.
1761, Dec. 22. Luffborrow, William, and Sarah Kirke.
1775, Jan. 19. Lukens, Elizabeth, and Joseph Jacob Wallace.
1771, Oct. 29. Lukens, Elizabeth, and Samuel Willis.
1762, Feb. 24. Lukens, Joseph, and Margaret Dixey.
1769, M'ch 8. Lukens, Matthias, and Mary Gray.
1762, Nov. 13. Lukens, William, and Rachael Kenderdine.
1760, Jan. 29. Lukins, Peter, and Jane Cadwallader.
1747, Nov. —. Lukins, Renier, and Jane Perry.
1765, Apr. 19. Lumbarder, Margaret, and Lawrence Mann.
1762, Apr. 6. Lumley, Rebecca, and Samuel Vickery.
1760, M'ch 15. Lunds, Frederick, and Mary Colbin.
1767, Oct. 22. Lundy, Patrick, and Mary Kime.
1774, Nov. 10. Lunt, Sarah, and John Many.
1760, Nov. 20. Luptan, Thomas, and Sarah Thomas.
1764, Dec. 11. Lupton, Elistre, and Daniel Stillwell.
1768, Apr. 14. Lurdon, Mary, and William Collins.
1775, July 7. Lusard, Mary, and William Hastings.
1761, M'ch 11. Lusher, Benjamin, and Mary Banard.
1776, Jan. 20. Lusher, Elizabeth, and Peter Gallagher.
1774, Nov. 21. Lusher, Mary, and David Murdock.
1759, Dec. 6. Lusherton, Cradle, and Henry Willoughby.
1775, Nov. 28. Lush, Mary, and Henry Kyser.
1769, Dec. 23. Lusk, Mary, and John Parker.

1767, July 14. Lusk, Thomas, and Mary McKinzey.
1763, Sep. 10. Luter, Catharine, and Josiah Harper.
1776, Apr. 6. Lutes, Jacob, and Susannah Weaver.
1774, Dec. 15. Lutsen, Catharine, and Martin Worknot.
1761, Apr. 30. Lutzin, Hannah, and Peter Shuck.
1763, Jan. 8. Lycans, Andrew, and Martha Culing.
1771, Feb. 5. Lycon, Elizabeth, and Edmund Richardson.
1773, Jan. 16. Lycon, John, and Christiana Fredericks.
1773, Aug. 13. Lyell, William, and Elizabeth Gregory.
1771, Aug. 26. Lykens, Patrick, and Mary Nicholson.
1761, July 30. Lyken, Mary, and Thomas Collett.
1760, M'ch 24. Lykins, Elizabeth, and Arthur Haig.
1747, Sep. —. Lyn, Adam, and Eleanor Jones.
1776, Apr. 13. Lynch, Margaret, and Daniel Fitzpatrick.
1776, Feb. 20. Lynch, Mary, and John McGrath.
1766, Dec. 2. Lyndall, Richard, and Susannah Townsend.
1760, June 1. Lyndmyre, Christiana, and George Melin.
1773, May 27. Lyne, John, and Mary Walker.
1771, Jan. 24. Lyng, Catharine, and Casper Crist.
1760, Apr. 23. Lyng, Susannah, and John McKilvie.
1748, Aug. 15. Lyn, David.
1774, Nov. 26. Lynn, Mercy, and Josiah Monger.
1744, Jan. —. Lyon, Charles.
1763, Feb. 19. Lyon, Charles, and Ann Vaughan.
1761, July 13. Lyon, Samuel, and Charlotte Morrison.
1775, M'ch 14. Lyons, David, and Elizabeth Forrester.
1774, Oct. 12. Lyons, Samuel, and Elizabeth Hough.
1761, Nov. 19. Lyttle, Elizabeth, and George Michael Rey.

M.

1769, May 6. Maag, Ann, and Robert Walker.
1764, Jan. 17. Maag, Barbara, and Samuel Sibert.
1775, Nov. 1. Maag, Henry, and Sarah Punket.
1768, Sep. 23. Maag, Jacob, and Barbara Stonemetz.
1760, Jan. 21. Maag, Jacob, and Catharine Gerehard.
1768, Oct. 5. Maain, Thomas, and Rachel Whitfield.
1773, Apr. 28. Maburry, William, and Ann Nicholson.
1761, June 29. McAble, Mary, and John Langley.
1764, July 19. McAdams, Henry, and Mary Robins.
1764, Oct. 17. McAddin, Elizabeth, and John McFall.
1773, July 21. McAfee, John, and Elizabeth Housard.
1766, May 7. McAlhaney, George, and Sophia Davis.
1775, Aug. 25. McAllister, Mary, and Thomas Cromby.
1772, Feb. 15. McAlmoyal, John, and Isabella Connelly.
1767, Nov. 11. McBane, Robert, and Rebecca Neb.
1766, Jan. 27. McBean, Samuel, and Mary Flemming.

1747, May —. McBride, Alexander and Ann Dixon.
1760, Nov. 13. McBride, Alley, and Archibald Nicholson.
1767, Aug. 29. McBride, Henry, and Mary Ellis.
1765, June 20. McBride, Margery, and Archibald McCorkel.
1764, Feb. 20. McBrier, Jane, and James Robinson.
1744, M'ch —. McBroom, Andrew.
1774, July 26. McCademes, Elizabeth, and William Jennings.
1772, Oct. 8. McCadden, Daniel, and Elizabeth Pollard.
1761, Apr. 18. McCalla, George, and Mary Church.
1773, Apr. 1. McCallaghan, Eleanor, and Jacob Frit.
1747, June —. McCalla, John, and Jane Harrison.
1761, May 27. McCalla, John, and Tamer Rich.
1765, Feb. 26. McCalla, Mary, and James Latta.
1769, Aug. 16. McCalla, Mary, and John Cox.
1763, Jan. 15. McCall, Ann, and John Dew.
1763, June 9. McCall, Ann, and Thomas Willing.
1762, Sep. 21. McCall, Catharine, and Patrick Malcom.
1770, Jan. 10. McCall, Catharine. and Thomas Batt.
1745, Oct. —. McCall, Gasper.
1745, Feb. —. McCall, George.
1761, June 8. McCall, Isabella, and John May.
1774, Nov. 2. McCall, Mark, and Catharine Katter.
1772, June 24. McCall, Mary, and Benjamin Chattell.
1763, M'ch 17. McCall, Mary, and Isaac Snowden.
1746, May —. McCall, Mary, and James Wilson.
1766, Dec. 19. McCall, Michael, and Hannah Row.
1743, Jan. 29. McCall, Samuel.
1773, Oct. 18. McCallister, Mary, and Abraham Berry.
1773, Feb. 16. McCameron, Elizabeth, and John McCameron.
1773, Feb. 16. McCameron, John, and Elizabeth McCameron.
1770, Aug. 11. McCamlin, Mark, and Elizabeth Sheed.
1763, Jan. 15. McCammon, Christiana, and Robert Jordan.
1773, May 1. McCammon, Jane, and Munro Pearson.
1771, June 10. McCannan, Martha, and Adam Fonnerden.
1772, Oct. 10. McCann, Catharine, and James Creighton.
1769, Dec. 1. McCann, Gabriel, and Mary Bell.
1769, Aug. 29. McCann, Mary, and Edward Minton.
1764, Aug. 29. McCarnon, Elizabeth, and David Hughes.
1773, Dec. 1. McCarracher, Alexander, and Mary Pritchard.
1768, Jan. 7. McCarston, John, and Rachel Lawrence.
1773, Aug. 2. McCarty, Alice, and Roger Blake.
1760, Feb. 29. McCarty, Anthony, and Catharine Cartland.
1771, Nov. 13. McCarty, Catharine, and John Hemminger.
1770, Feb. 21. McCarty, Catharine, and Lawrence Cook.
1771, Feb. 7. McCarty, Catharine, and William Walters.
1767, Aug. 8. McCarty, Edward, and Ann McGuire.

1767, Dec. 16. McCarty, Elizabeth, and Jacob Sewery.
1746, Oct. —. McCarthy, Gregory, and Sarah Stoaks.
1767, June 15. McCarty, John, and Margaret Green.
1761, Dec. 14. McCarty, Justin, and Mary Goss.
1775, June 28. McCarty, Michael, and Mary Cochran.
1766, June 12. McCarty, Owen, and Elizabeth Dorsey.
1766, Nov. 5. McCarty, Paul, and Kissander Williams.
1768, Oct. 4. McCaskry, Esther, and Nathan Darling.
1769, June 19. McCasland, Anne, and David Richardson.
1762, Aug. 26. McCaughen, Elinor, and William Dunlap.
1768, M'ch 24. McCaullay, Jane, and John Smith.
1762, July 14. McCay, Elizabeth, and James Lecony.
1763, Apr. 27. McCay, William, and Rachael Stroub.
1761, May 27. McClane, Joseph, and Rachael Wood.
1765, Apr. 25. McClay, George, and Lydia Donovan.
1763, July 8. McClay, William, and Margaret McCroskey.
1767, June 26. McClay, William, and Mary Flemming.
1763, Sep. 3. McClean, Alexander, and Jane Strawbridge.
1747, June --. McClean, Allen, and Jane Irwin.
1776, Apr. 11. McClean, Hannah, and David Marple.
1772, Oct. 21. McClean, Isabella, and Thomas Killden.
1763, M'ch 22. McClean, Moses, and Sarah Charlesworth.
1762, May 13. McClean, Patrick, and Elizabeth Young.
1763, Sep. 29. McClean, Thomas, and Mary Harvey.
1745, Apr. —. McCleane, Daniel.
1772, May 5. McCleane, John, and Catharine Armstrong.
1762, Feb. 11. McCleane, William, and Rebecca Charlesworth.
1767, Oct. 19. McClear, James, and Jane Sinclair.
1760, May 20. McCleas, Cornelius, and Hannah Bell.
1770, Sep. 25. McCleaster, Collins, and Sarah Yarnall.
1772, Dec. 31. McClees, Ann, and Andrew Macomson.
1772, Nov. 26. McClees, Everard, and Rebecca Gleeves.
1776, Feb. 26. McCleland, John, and Ann Willsford.
1771, Jan. 19. McCleland, Margaret, and Daniel Montgomery.
1764, Sep. 8. McClelland, Henry, and Martha George.
1763, Aug. 10. McClelland, John, and Margaret Kimble.
1747, M'ch —. McClellan, Elenor, and Jonathan Hugh.
1747, Nov. —. McClellan, Elizabeth, and Thomas Hill.
1744, Oct. —. McClellan. John, (see note.)
1773, July 30. McClenachan, James, and Jane Knox.
1762, Aug. 31. McClenachen, Blair, and Ann Derragh.
1763, June 11. McClenaghan, John, and Elizabeth Taylor.
1761, M'ch 19. McClenaghan, Mr.
1770, Nov. 13. McClennon, Catharine, and Robert Hume.
1768, Nov. 5. McClennon, Mary, and Thomas Piercy.
1763, May 28. McClinaghan, Reverend.

1744, Oct. —. McCloghlin, Dennis, (see note.)
1748, Sep. —. McClon, Susanna, and Patrick Miller.
1748, May 14. McClone, Hugh, and Rachel Bane.
1743, M'ch 3. McCluer, John.
1763, June 22. McClure, John, and Elizabeth Deal.
1770, M'ch 27. McClure, Samuel, and Martha Kenny.
1761, July 2. McClusky, Barnaby, and Frances Massey.
1745, June —. McColla, Wílliam.
1746, Oct. —. MCollock, Elizabeth, and Jonathan Arnold.
1745, Sep. —. McCollum, John.
1763, Feb. 19. McColly, Mary, and Isaac Lewis.
1768, Feb. 3. McComb, Archibald, and Mary Hutcheson.
1776, May 28. McConnel, Adam, and Jane McGiles.
1775, Dec. 14. McConnell, Isabella, and John Hall.
1771, M'ch 30. McConnell, Jane, and James Rowan.
1769, Oct. 11. McConnelly, Martha, and Andrew Sullivan.
1769, June 23. McCool, Catharine, and Josiah White.
1765, Aug. 8. McCool, John, and Margaret Camel.
1764, Nov. 22. McCord, Mark, and Catharine Miller.
1774, July 25. McCord, William, and Phebe Costilow.
1764, Apr. 19. McCorkel, Archibald, and Jane McMicken.
1765, June 20. McCorkel, Archibald, and Margery McBride.
1760, Jan. 23. McCorkle, Dorcas, and John White.
1775, July 29. McCormick, Andrew, and Agnes Race.
1764, July 16. McCormick, Arichibald, and Hannah Fetter.
1770, Oct. 29. McCormick, Catharine, and James Brown.
1769, Aug. 24. McCormick, Elizabeth, and Richard Collins.
1776, Apr. 18. McCormick, Henry, and Elizabeth Clowser.
1745, Oct. —. McCormick, John.
1772, July 13. McCormick, Samuel, and Abigail Philips
1776, Apr. 8. McCormick, Thomas, and Christiana Kryder.
1759, Dec. 17. McCoy, Eleanor, and Moses Gisler.
1768, June 3. McCoy, John, and Mary Yeates.
1769, May 4. McCoy, Joseph, and Eleanor Stewart.
1767, Apr. 24. McCoy, Mary, and John Murray.
1764, Apr. 19. McCoy, Mary, and William Gallagher.
1764, Nov. 29. McCoy, Rebecca, and Daniel Pearce.
1769, Aug. 4. McCracken, Elizabeth, and James Carswell
1768, Oct. 26. McCracken, Mary, and Allen Russell.
1762, Apr. 5. McCrackin, Frances, and Joseph Dean.
1767, Aug. 7. McCrackin, James, and Elizabeth Murray.
1771, Feb. 16. McCrackin, Samuel, and Elizabeth Murchland.
1776, Jan. 6. McCrea, James, and Hannah Alexander.
1774, May 27. McCrea, Jane, and Abner White.
1774, June 14. McCrea, Robert, and Ann Garytie.
1765, Feb. 16. McCree, James, and Jane Porter.

1745, July —. McCreagh, William.
1761, Dec. 31. McCroney, Margaret, and John Tweddle.
1760, May 29, McCrory, Jane, and John, McCrory.
1760, May 29. McCrory, John and Jane McCrory.
1763, July 8. McCroskey, Margaret, and William McClay.
1763, Oct. 21. McCrump, Eleanor, and Robert Ross.
1747, Dec. —. McClue, Anthony, and Lydia Lloyd.
1772, Jan. 2. McCulloch, William, and Margaret Palmer.
1765, July 30. McCullogh, David, and Phebe Boyd.
1743, M'ch 18. McCullogh, John.
1773, Aug. 31. McCullough, Ann, and David Williamson.
1747, Dec. —. McCullough, James, and Rachel Spencer.
1760, June 24. McCullough, Jane, and James Chland.
1761, June 8. McCullough, John, and Elizabeth Hunt.
1771, Aug. 17. McCullough, John, and Jennet Morrison.
1772, Nov. 6. McCullough, John, and Margaret Peters.
1774, Jan. 18. McCullough, Mary, and Finley McDonald.
1772, June 3. McCullough, William, and Hannah Williams.
1761, M'ch 9. McCune, Thomas, and Margaret Karr.
1775, Jan. 24. McDaniel, Edmund, and Mary Matson.
1763, Jan. 5. McDaniel, James, and Ann McNamaray.
1775, Dec. 14. McDaniel, James, and Eleanor Stuart.
1760, July 16. McDaniel, James, and Lucy Gandversil.
1761, Dec. 2. McDaniel, Jane, and George Young.
1770, Apr. 26. McDaniel, John, and Mary Whitebread.
1763, Oct. 16. McDaniel, Rose, and Oliver Williams.
1775, Jan. 23. McDaniel, Sarah, and Jacob Vernor.
1760, Feb. 15. McDaugh, Lettice, and William Delworth.
1761, Aug. 1. McDavel, Rose, and John Ferguson.
1743, Oct. —. McDonagle, Patrick.
1764, Nov. 19. McDonald, Ann, and William Gamble.
1765, M'ch 4. McDonald, Eleanor, and John Cain.
1774, Jan. 18. McDonald, Finley, and Mary McCullough.
1771, Sep. 23. McDonald, Jane, and Thomas More.
1764, Nov. 19. McDonald, John, and Susannah Burk.
1766, Jan. 18. McDonnell, Eleanor, and James Collings.
1768, Feb. 20. McDougle, John, and Anne Boyd.
1767, Feb. 27. McDowel, Jane, and John Burnet.
1762, Apr. 3. McDowel, Margaret, and Isaac Wood.
1764, Feb. 8. McDowel, Peter, and Mary Camble.
1771, Oct. 15. McDowell, Henry, and Mary Smith.
1775, Dec. 7. McDowell, James, and Elizabeth Dewees.
1764, Nov. 15. McDowell, James, and Elizabeth Houghead.
1771, Apr. 3. McDowell, Mary, and Henry Dawkins.
1771, Feb. 13. McDowell, William, and Anne Edwards.
1774, Dec. 19. McDonnough, John, and Mary Sands.

1773, M'ch 31. McElroy, William, and Priscilla Jones.
1760, Apr. 26. McEntire, John, and Ester Smith.
1760, M'ch 21. McEntire, William, and Jane Kennedy.
1766, June 27. McEwen, William, and Rebecca Bruce.
1775, Dec. 27. McFadden, William, and Sarah Hussey.
1773, Oct. 21. McFadden, John, and Mary Caldwell.
1765, Aug. 22. McFall, Ann, and James Davis.
1764, Oct. 17. McFall, John, and Elizabeth McAddin.
1774, Sep. 5. McFall, Patrick, and Mary Jerman.
1761, July 8. McFarland, Jane, and Innes Graham.
1773, Dec. 29. McFarland, John, and Margaret Remmey.
1747, Dec. —. McFarland, John, and Rachel Coburn.
1774, Nov. 26. McFarland, Robert, and Margery Harris.
1774, June 15. McFarlane, Mary, and John Bell.
1766, Dec. 22. McFarlan, Eve, and Solomon McFarlan.
1766, Oct. 10. McFarlan, Farlan, and Elizabeth Wood.
1761, Aug. 6. McFarlan, Margaret, and John Sloan.
1766, Dec. 22. McFarlan, Solomon, and Eve McFarlan.
1771, Dec. 18. McFarlan, William, and Jane Dick.
1763, July 30. McFarlan, William, and Elizabeth St. Clair.
1761, Apr. 25. McFarrand, Mary, and John Cole.
1760, Dec. 24. McFarrel, Jane, and James Fergeson.
1748, Sep. —. McFarson, John, and Margaret Rogers.
1776, Feb. 10. McFee, David, and Jane Triggs.
1765, June 8. McFee, Elizabeth, and William Moore.
1772, Feb. 4. McFee, Thomas, and Ann Jenkins.
1775, Apr. 26. McFeteridge, John, and Ann Carson.
1773, Jan. 5. McFunn, Mary, and Collison Read.
1762, Sep. 6. McFurtricks, Margaret, and John Kevll.
1770, June 14. McGargy, Jane, and Josael, Jenkins.
1764, Jan. 4. McGarragy, Elizabeth, and William Rupart.
1765, Oct. 29. McGarvol, Barbary, and Catharine Mitchell.
1774, Oct. 27. McGeary, Roger, and Ann Carrol.
1773, Feb. 4. McGee, Henry, and Mary Hanson.
1775, June 14. McGee, John, and Elizabeth Archibald.
1765, Dec. 24. McGee, Patrick, and Jane Hall.
1767, Dec. 9. McGeshan, James, and Mary Stenson
1766, Apr. 7. McGibbon, John, and Mary Burrows.
1760, Apr. 30. McGee, Anne, and David Chambers.
1776, May 28. McGiles, Jane, and Adam McConnel.
1768, Feb 27. McGill, Elizabeth, and John Ferguson.
1776, Apr. 10. McGill, Elizabeth, and Joseph Johnson.
1764, Jan. 21. McGill, James, and Elizabeth Johnson.
1774, Nov. 23. McGinnis, Ann, and John Bell.
1764, June 21. McGinnis, James, and Jane Grant.
11—VOL. II.

1775, Dec. 5. McGinnis, Mary, and Andrew Nelson.
1775, Apr. 8. McGlathery, Isaac, and Rachel McGlathery.
1770, Apr. 9. McGlathery, John, and Mary Lawrence.
1761, Jan. 27. McGlathery, Matthew, and Margaret George.
1775, Apr. 8. McGlathery, Rachel, and Isaac McGlathery.
1764, Dec. 19. McGlaughan, William, and Mary Pinley.
1765, Dec. 19. McGlaughlin, Elizabeth, and John Mann.
1763, Sep. 6. McGlaughlin, Mary, and Robert Turner.
1775, July 31. McGlew, James, and Hannah Greenway.
1767, M'ch 9. McGloachlon, Mary, and Daniel Robertson.
1766, June 2. McGlone, Andrew, and Frances Morris.
1774, June 18. McGlone, Andrew, and Margaret Browne.
1745, Oct. —. McGlone, Hugh.
1766, Jan. 11. McGloughlin, Sarah, and John Dickinson.
1766, Sep. 2. McGoresk, John, and Ann Cary.
1761, Sep. 8. McGorough, Isabella, and John Doran.
1763, Sep. 3. McGrah, Dennis, and Mary Annis.
1763, July 14. McGranger, James, and Jane Patton.
1774, Sep. 23. McGrath, Catharine, and Francis Wrighley.
1770, Oct. 18. McGrath, Frances, and William Carr.
1776, M'ch 20. McGrath, John, and Mary Lynch.
1762, Feb. 16. McGraugh, Sarah, and John Gibson.
1764, Dec. 1. McGraw, James, and Bridget Twyer.
1763, June 27. McGreger, Greger, and Jane Morrow.
1763, Dec. 22. McGriger, Alexander, and Ann January.
1761, Apr. 4. McGrough, Catharine, and Owen Daly.
1767, Oct. 19. McGruger, Jane, and Elliot Duncan.
1761, Nov. 7. McGuey, Farguson, and Mary Connady.
1761, M'ch 27. McGuffuck, Patrick, and Margaret Brown.
1773, Nov. 29. McGuire, Andrew, and Mary Rogers.
1767, Aug. 8. McGuire, Ann, and Edward McCarty.
1769, Sep. 30. McGuire, Eleanor, and William Newman.
1772, Sep. 29. McGuire, William, and Elizabeth Thomas.
1762, Nov. 29. McHarg, Thomas, and Margaret Anderson.
1765, Dec. 5. McHenry, Elizabeth, and Josiah Brian.
1760, Jan. 24. McHenry, Hugh, and Sarah Dean.
1772, July 28. McHenry, Martha, and William Dixey.
1770, Oct. 17. McHenry, Matthew, and Margaret Gregg.
1762, July 6. McHenry, Sarah, and Thomas Armstrong.
1773, Apr. 29. McIlharan, Ann, and Dougal Gregory.
1773, July 15. McIlhenny, William, and Hannah Woodside.
1775, July 3. McIlherring, Charles, and Mary McMullan.
1769, Apr. 29. McIlhose, Thomas, and Ann Scott.
1766, Dec. 18. McIllroy, Jane, and Edward Callen.
1772, June 17. McIlvaine, Margaret, and John Clarke.
1775, Dec. 12. McIlvaine, Mary, and William McIlvaine.

1775, Aug. 19. McIlvaine, Sarah, and John Stewart.
1747, May —. McIlvaine, William, and Ann Emerson.
1766, Nov. 3. McIlvaine, William, and Margaret Cross.
1776, M'ch 21. McIlvaine, William, and Mary Fitzgerald.
1775, Dec. 12. McIlvaine, William, and Mary McIlvaine.
1768, Feb. 4. McIlvane, John, and Catharine Dennis.
1769, Nov. 11. McIntire, Charles, and Anne Sullivan.
1776, Jan. 17. McIntire, Elizabeth, and Matthias Taylor.
1764, June 1. McIntire, Martha, and William Murray.
1765, M'ch 18. McIntire, Michael, and Ann Irwin.
1767, May 7. McIntire, Neal, and Jane Floyd.
1773, Nov. 27. McIntire, Peter, and Elizabeth Cunningham.
1766, July 12. McIntire, Sarah, and William Boggs.
1766, Aug. 6. McIntosh, Alexander, and Ann Shields.
1768, Nov. 7. McIntosh, Peter, and Isabella Kirkpatrick.
1766, Sep. 3. McIntosh, William, and Jane Morrison.
1762, May 10. McIntoss, Margaret, and Ralph Nuns.
1773, M'ch 23. McKahan, Ann, and Gilbert McKillup.
1773, Oct. 4. McKay, Daniel, and Abigail Philips.
1775, M'ch 22. McKay, Francis, and Hannah Davis.
1767, Feb. 20. McKay, George, and Mary Camel.
1774, Nov. 30. McKay, James, and Mary Hungary.
1775, Sep. 19. McKeag, George, and Christiana Johnston.
1768, Nov. 26. McKee, Ann, and Patrick Dunn.
1770, Nov. 8. McKee, Jane, and Samuel McMichan.
1760, Apr. 1. McKee, Martha, and James Bowman.
1764, Aug. 28. McKee, Mary, and Jacob Garaud.
1774, Jan. 22. McKegen, Edward, and Jane Guy.
1760, Apr. 15. McKendree, Ann, and Andrew Hall.
1746, Feb. —. McKenny, John.
1775, Sep. 13. McKenzie, Charles, and Mary Ann Brackley.
1773, June 3. McKenzie, James, and Sarah Bull.
1763, Apr. 14. McKervy, Alexander, and Jean Leadley.
1761, Nov. 30. McKessock, Archibald, and Elea Nelson.
1761, Sep. 28. McKey, Alexander, and Sarah Jeffreys.
1768, June 17. McKey, Eleanor, and Wesley Jackson.
1763, June 13. McKey, William, and Judea Brian.
1776, Feb. 13. McKibbin, Jane, and John Cooper.
1765, Jan. 8. McKichan, John, and Margaret McPherson.
1761, Apr. 8. McKillop, Jane, and Thomas Davis.
1773, M'ch 23. McKillup, Gilbert, and Ann McKahan.
1771, Oct. 24. McKillup, Jane, and Richard Heneby.
1763, Sep. 5. McKillup, Randall, and Jane Miller.
1760, Apr. 23. McKilvie, John, and Susannah Lyng.
1769, Apr. 8. McKim, Jane, and David Shields.
1763, June 1. McKinlay, William, and Mary Siplin.

1770, July 23. McKinley, Hugh, and Elizabeth Dunn.
1771, M'ch 28. McKinney, Mary, and Isaiah James.
1764, Nov. 11. McKinstry, John, and Elizabeth Carlisle.
1766, June 11. McKinstry, Samuel, and Martha Evans.
1767, July 14. McKinzey, Mary, and Thomas Lusk.
1774, Oct. 26. McKivvin, Mary, and Robert Walters.
1768, May   9. McKnight, Rebecca, and John Shields.
1748, Feb. —. McKnight, William, and Susannah Bond.
1775, May   22. McKone, Margaret, and Bryan Laughlan.
1770, Sep. 25. McKowan, George, and Catharine Adams.
1769, July 15. McLane, Daniel, and Martha Thorne.
1768, Oct. 20. McLaughlan, John, and Ann Lawrence.
1770, June 7. McLaughlan, Mary, and Daniel Ridge.
1774, Feb. 24. McLaughlan, Mary, and John Butler.
1772, Nov. 14. McLoughlan, Sarah, and William Jenkins.
1765, Oct, 19. McMackon, Daniel, and Ann Stinson.
1774, Nov. 24. MaMahon, Barnabas, and Ann Callahan.
1773, Oct. 6. McMahon, John, and Bridget McManis.
1773, Oct. 6. McManis, Bridget, and John McMahon.
1763, June 29. McMaster, Margaret, and Joshua Jones.
1744, M'ch —. McMekon, Hugh.
1766, Sep. 9. McMichael, Alexander, and Margaret Johnson.
1763, Oct. 12. McMichael, Elizabeth, and John Pogh.
1770, Nov. 8. McMichan, Samuel, and Jane McKee.
1760, July 9. McMicken, James, and Phebe Allis.
1764, Apr. 19. McMicken, Jane, and Archibald McCorkel.
1763, Apr. 27. McMillen, Thomas, and Jane Master.
1774, Dec. 31. McMinn, Thomas, and Mary Black.
1767, Sep. 1. McMullan, Ann, and Robert Conoly.
1775, July 3. McMullan, Mary, and Charles McIlherring.
1772, July 27. McMullan, Michael, and Margaret Collins.
1763, Sep. 19. McMullan, Sarah, and John Cain.
1776, M'ch 25. McMullan, Susannah, and William Linnard.
1766, Oct. 14. McMullen, Catharine, and Neal Leviston.
1766, Oct. 20. McMullen, Duncan, and Catharine Montgomery.
1766, Dec. 17. McMullen, Jane, and Gilbert Brown.
1765, Jan. 24. McMullen, Robert, and Margaret Davis.
1765, M'ch 1. McMullin, John, and Elizabeth Roades.
1769, Nov. 22. McMurtry, John, and Margaret Robinson.
1765, M'ch 15. McNair, Samuel, and Mary Man.
1763, May. 17. McNamer, Joseph, and Margaret Smiker.
1763, Jan. 5. McNamaray, Ann, and James McDaniel.
1746, Nov. —. McNare, Andrew, and Mary Jennings.
1772, April 11. McNeal, James, and Catharine Pollock.
1744, Aug. 2. McNeal, John.
1770, July 30. McNeal, John, and Elizabeth Miller.

1767, June 29. McNeal, John, and Rachel Howey.
1768, July 16. McNeal, Laughlan, and Ann Snowden.
1761, June 30. McNeal, Mary, and John McPatrick.
1772, Nov. 7. McNeal, Mary, and William Davis.
1762, Nov. 29. McNeal, Neal, and Elizabeth Steward.
1760, Oct. 15. McNealy, Andrew, and Martha Morrison.
1760, Aug. 26. McNealy, Margaret, and James Hughes.
1770, Aug. 21. McNealy, Martha, and Alexander Campbell.
1764, Dec. 22. McNeer, Ann, and John Vance.
1766, M'ch 12. McNeir, James, and Martha Keith.
1746, Feb. —. McNorth, Michael.
1761, Apr. 28. McNorth, Michael, and Ann Kirk.
1772, Dec. 4. McNought, James, and Mary Boyes.
1761, June 30. McPatrick, John, and Mary McNeal.
1772, Oct. 6. McPharland, Ann, and Robert Montgomery.
1770, Dec. 7. McPharlin, Mary, and John Murray.
1766, June 10. McPherson, Daniel, and Margaret Cails.
1743, Jan. 25. McPherson, James.
1767, May 15. McPherson, Margaret, and John Cumming.
1765, Jan. 8. McPherson, Margaret, and John McKichan.
1768, Jan. 23. McPherson, Mary, and Patrick Robertson.
1770, Jan. 13. McQuattiat, Margaret, and William Robinson.
1775, Apr. 1. McSeeny, Ann, and William Brown.
1767, Dec. 10. McSingley, Rebecca, and James Warden.
1744, Oct. —. McSparran, James. (See note.)
1745, June —. McSwame, James.
1773, Jan. 27. McSweeny, John, and Rachel Billow.
1773, June 10. McTaggart, Archibald, and Catharine Young.
1764, May 7. McVaughan, Susannah, and Charles Hart.
1774, Jan. 17. McVaugh, Edmund, and Elizabeth Taylor.
1745, May —. McVaugh, John.
1772, Dec. 18. McVeagh, Benjamin, and Parnel Humphreville.
1748, Apr. 13. McVeagh, Edmund, and Elizabeth Whartenoby.
1745, Jan. —. McVeagh. James.
1745, Sep. —. McWally, Alexander.
1764, June 27. McYoung, Elizabeth, and George Hackett.
1764, Nov. 28. McCarrel, John, and Margaret Garo.
1768, June 3. Mack, Robert, and Mary Potter.
1762, June 29. Mackeluff, Samuel, and Mary Darlington.
1774, Dec. 26. Mackey, Daniel, and Hannah Cracker.
1747, Nov. —. Mackintosh, John, and Margaret Sullivan.
1760, Dec. 6. Macky, Mary, and Robert Rawle.
1770, Nov. 5. Maclean, Charles, and Mary Lee.
1770, Oct. 15. Maclean, Elizabeth, and John Carnaghan.
1773, Dec. 14. Maclean, Laughlan, and Mary Lucas.
1770, Aug. 9. MacNamara, Mary, and Francis Burgess.

1772, Dec. 31. Macomson, Andrew, and Ann McClees.
1761, June 11. Macy, Deborah, and John Beaks.
1772, Jan. 18. Maddin, Ann, and John Coyl.
1773, Dec. 3. Maddin, Mary, and Hugh Quigley.
1770, May 1. Maddock, Hannah, and William Long.
1762, Jan. 15. Maddock, William, and Isabella Cahoone.
1774, Dec. 6. Maddox, Elizabeth, and John Harr.
1776, Apr. 30. Madeira, Christopher, and Elizabeth Neff.
1763, Feb. 22. Madera, Hannah, and Adam Slager.
1761, Jan. 7. Madlock, Patience, and John Watson.
1767, June 13. Maers, Ann, and Joseph Johns.
1743, M'ch 19. Magargit, Patrick.
1773, July 8. Magar, John, and Ann Harmonson.
1760, May 8. Magdalin, Christiana, and Joseph Cornelius.
1745, Aug. —. Magee, Alexander.
1776, Feb. 10. Magee, Margaret, and Isaac Willson.
1771, May 14. Magee, Mary, and John Ferguson.
1773, Jan. 16. Magee, Robert, and Hannah Gaa.
1762, Dec. 27. Magee, Susannah, and Elias Shepherd.
1774, Aug. 30. Magee, Thomas, and Elizabeth Allen.
1746, Aug. —. Magennis, Edward, and Rose Fullerton.
1767, July 25. Magrah, Thomas, and Hannah Doyle.
1774, Dec. 5. Magraw, Martin, and Elizabeth Ware.
1769, Feb. 4. Magraw, Hannah, and Hay King.
1762, Dec. 7. Mahanoy, William, and Mary Coyl.
1775, June 23. Mahar, Mary, and Archibald Dunn.
1743, July 15. Mahery, James.
1747, May —. Mahlen, Alice, and John Crosy.
1774, Dec. 19. Mahon, Lawrence, and Elizabeth Rosse.
1765, M'ch 14. Mahony, Anthony, and Hannah Collet.
1775, July 13. Main, Fergus, and Ann Kelum.
1767, Aug. 15. Main, Mary, and Samuel Hawke.
1761, Jan. 14. Main, Peter, and Elizabeth Justice.
1763, Jan. 27. Main, Rebecca, and Joseph Hulbert.
1773, June 17. Main, William, and Susannah Graham.
1746, Jan. —. Maine, Alexander.
1771, June 18. Maine, Elizabeth, and Anthony Nuss.
1772, Dec. 18. Mairns, Sarah, and Robert Jameson.
1770, Feb. 21. Mairs, Richard, and Martha Nash.
1776, Jan. 18. Malaby, Christiana, and Patrick Flynn.
1774, July 6. Malaby, Margaret, and Dennis Crohan.
1767, Jan. 21. Malaun, Mary, and Thomas Reed.
1772, Aug. 20. Malcolm, John, and Hannah Roberts.
1767, Oct. 3. Malcolm, Mary, and Moses Malcolm.
1767, Oct. 3. Malcolm, Moses, and Mary Malcolm.
1765, May 9. Malcolm, Robert, and Judith Abercrummey.

1762, Sep. 21. Malcom, Patrick, and Catharine McCall.
1760, June 25. Mallaan, John, and Margaret Stray.
1748, Sep. —. Mallaby, Margaret, and Francis Le Blan.
1770, Nov. 23. Mallice, Elizabeth, and Walter Manuel.
1761, Nov. 10. Mallpew, Margaret, and John Young.
1776, Feb. 3. Malone, Elenor, and Thomas Duncan.
1769, Apr. 24. Malone, Elizabeth, and Samuel Betson.
1764, Aug. 29. Malone, Letitia, and Enoch Morgan.
1765, Nov. 26. Malone, Mary, and William Kirk.
1763, Apr. 9. Maloney, Thomas, and Ann Church.
1765, Dec. 21. Manahon, Ann, and Andrew Hammon.
1748, June 16. Mandlin, Mary, and Woolrick Allen.
1775, Dec. 7. Mandlin, Miriam, and Jacob Plankinhorn.
1766, Aug. 5. Mange, Ernst, and Mary Sommer.
1743, Feb. 10. Mangridge, John.
1769, Nov. 2. Manington, Susannah, and James Sutton.
1759, Dec. 8. Mankin, Catharine, and Edward Hill.
1765, M'ch 15. Man, Mary, and Samuel McNair.
1762, Sep. 10. Mann, Elizabeth, and William Grimes.
1770, Nov. 23. Manuel, Walter, and Elizabeth Mallice.
1762, July 28. Manning, Elizabeth, and Benjamin, Rosbothon.
1765, Dec. 19. Mann, John, and Elizabeth McGlaughlin.
1765, Apr. 19. Mann, Lawrence, and Margaret Lumbarder.
1760, Aug. 5. Mannon, John, and Catharine Hinkle.
1762, Dec. 27. Mann, Peter, and Mary Zimmerman.
1744, Dec. —. Mann, Robert.
1768, June 14. Mann, William, and Rebecca Knight.
1747, June —. Manny, Francis, and Margaret Cox.
1761, Apr. 1. Manson, Margaret, and James Beynon.
1761, Sep. 7. Manson, Mary, and James Paine.
1761, Sep. 3. Manson, Sarah, and Edward Henry Church.
1772, May 27. Manuel, Elizabeth, and George Smith.
1772, Apr. 9. Many, Ann, and John Wood.
1744, Oct. —. Many, John Henry.
1774, Nov. 10. Many, John, and Sarah Lunt.
1748, Nov. 11. Many, Melchor, and Mary Colliday.
1747, Sep. —. Many, William, and Elizabeth Middleton.
1761, Apr. 15. Maolers, William, and Sarah Morgan.
1761, Apr. 6. March, Catharine, and Jacob Baker.
1773, Apr. 10. Marcker, George, and Margaret Stellwaggon.
1774, Oct. 18. Marclay, Benjamin, and Hannah Wentz.
1760, July 18. Marefield, Edward, and Sarah Walker.
1760, Oct. 21. Margaret, Mary, and George Godfrey.
1761, July 9. Margaret, Mary, and George Roose.
1762, May 24. Marin, Sarah, and James Brown.
1775, Jan. 14. Maris, Hannah, and Edward Hunter.

1767, Aug. 18. Maris, William, and Mary Nice.
1776, Apr. 11. Mark, John, and Eleanor Morrow.
1772, M'ch 28. Markle, Barbara, and John Smith.
1773, Dec. 13. Markoe, Abraham, and Elizabeth Baynton.
1768, Feb. 19. Marks, Elisha, and Sarah Smith.
1743, Dec. —. Marks, George.
1747, Feb. —. Marks, Rachel, and Alexander Graydon.
1760, Nov. 15. Marle, John, and Hannah Ash.
1770, Nov. 7. Marll, Thomas, and Lydia Reynolds.
1772, M'ch 19. Maroe, Prudence, and Jacob Rowand.
1746, Nov. —. Marple, Able, and Mary Hurt.
1773, Nov. 12. Marple, Benjamin, and Hannah Dungan.
1776, Apr. 11. Marple, David, and Hannah McClean.
1761, July 29. Marple, David, and Mary Martin.
1775, M'ch 8. Marple, Enoch, and Mary Corson.
1744, May 28. Marple, George.
1773, M'ch 17. Marple, Joseph, and Elizabeth Roberts.
1760, Feb. 5. Marriage, John, and Mary Busch.
1770, Sep. 3. Marriot, Anne, and Edward Cutbush.
1774, Oct. 8. Marriot, John, and Mary Marriot.
1774, Oct. 8. Marriot, Mary, and John Marriot.
1769, Jan. 5. Marriot, Rebecka, and William Workman
1763, M'ch 2. Marschar, Nicholas, and Margaret Halveston.
1770, May 23. Marsh, Agnes, and Nathaniel Philips.
1743, Sep. —. Marshal, John.
1773, Sep. 16. Marshall, Arthur, and Margaret Moore.
1768, Jan. 21. Marshall, Bathsheba, and Enoch Hughes.
1767, Jan. 21. Marshall, George, and Hannah Collings.
1762, Nov. 6. Marshall, Hannah, and Robert Priest.
1760, Sep. 18. Marshall, Isaac, and H. C. Hudman.
1765, Oct. 5. Marshall, Jacob, and Abigail Wood.
1764, Aug. 23. Marshall, Jane, and William Lindsay.
1768, M'ch 5. Marshall, John, and Hannah Baldwin.
1765, Feb. 21. Marshall, Joseph, and Mary Cox.
1763, M'ch 15. Marshall, Moses, and Eliza Reinhart.
1763, May 9. Marshall, Ralph, and Mary Winnimore.
1775, Jan. 24. Marshall, Ruth, and Richard Davis.
1769, Apr. 8. Marshall, Thomas, and Ann Cox.
1760, Oct. 21. Marshall, Thomas, and Mary Toot.
1770, Apr. 25. Marshall, William, and Hannah Ridge.
1760, Nov. 7. Marshall, William, and Jane Cummings.
1763, May 21. Marshall, William, and Margaret Bell.
1770, Nov. 24. Marshall, William, and Mary Fell.
1776, Jan. 19. Marsh, Edward, and Eleanor Smith.
1763, June 22. Marsh, James, and Mary Cummins.
1774, Nov. 20. Marsh, Joseph, and Eleanor George.

1761, July 4. Marsh, Joseph, and Sarah Bazelee.

1761, June 19. Mars, Negro, and negro woman Rose.

1764, Dec. 19. Marstetter, Frederick, and Susannah Schrack.

1748, M'ch 11. Martgridge, Elizabeth, and Thomas Leonard.

1775, July 1. Martin, Ann, and Lawrence Paul.

1772, Sep. 23. Martin, Anthony, and Ann Cline.

1766, Sep. 25. Martin, Anthony, and Mary Paine.

1770, June 8. Martin, Christopher, and Agnes Sneal.

1767, Oct. 31. Martindale, John Waters, and Catharine Child.

1746, Feb. —. Martin, Edmund.

1764, Nov. 26. Martin, Eleanor, and John Morton.

1769, Jan. 23. Martin, Eleanor, and Nicholas Fooss.

1763, Jan. 5. Martin, Elizabeth, and Patrick Russel.

1769, May 10. Martin, Elizabeth, and Robert Martin.

1767, Sep. 29. Martin, Frederick, and Mary Miller.

1775, Oct. 31. Martin, Hannah, and Abel Miller.

1766 Apr. 9. Martin, Hannah, and Thomas Francis.

1762, Apr. 26. Martin, James, and Deborah Williams

1773, June 23. Martin, James, and Margaret Jones.

1767, Jan. 14. Martin, Jane, and Alexander Bartram.

1761, Nov. 7. Martin, Jane, and Jerman Walker.

1746, May —. Martin, John.

1761, Sep. 5. Martin, John, and Ann Tate.

1765, May 8. Martin, John, and Elizabeth Bond.

1767, July 22. Martin, John, and Mary Raine.

1761, Oct. 21. Martin, John, and Mary Van Luviney.

1771, M'ch 18. Martin, John, and Rebecca Venaken.

1760, Sep. 25. Martin, Katharine, and William Halons.

1762, Apr. 27. Martin, Martha, and Samuel Rogers.

1761, July 29. Martin, Mary, and David Marpel.

1747, M'ch —. Martin, Mary, and David Smith.

1776, Jan. 5. Martin, Mary, and Peter Cane.

1761, July 28. Martin, Mary, and Peter Robert.

1761, Nov. 7. Martin, Randal, and Sarah Walker.

1769, May 10. Martin, Robert, and Elizabeth Martin.

1764, Apr. 5. Martin, Robert, and Jane Durrows.

1767, Oct. 8. Martin, Robert, and Mary Crowley.

1774, Dec. 1. Martin, Robert, and Rachel James.

1762, Dec. 10. Martin, Samuel, and Esther Morgan.

1767, July 24. Martin, Thomas, and Rebecca Morrison.

1766, M'ch 27. Martin, William, and Ann Leadbetter.

1760, Oct. 9. Martin, William, and Margaret Burton.

1748, Feb. —. Martlew, Peter, and Elizabeth Elder.

1762, Aug. 17. Martley, Doritey, and John Sauler.

1763, June 4. Mashawn, Ann, and Joseph Brooks.

1768, Dec. 1. Masho, Elizabeth, and Edward Dubbing.

1770, June 4 Maskell, Rachel. and Robert Collins.
1764, Sep.   5. Masmer, Elizabeth, and Alexander Murray.
1763, Jan. 26. Mason, Eleanor, and Edward Holwell.
1774, Nov.   7. Mason, George, and Catharine Simpson.
1774, Apr.   7. Mason, Hannah, and James Kaign.
1762, Apr.   6. Mason, John, and Doborah Stevens.
1764, Nov.   7. Mason, John, and Sarah Brown.
1770, Apr.   7. Mason, Mary, and Benjamin Morris.
1768, July 13. Mason, Mary, and David Potter.
1775, Feb.   1. Mason, Mary, and John Appowen.
1768, July 18. Mason, Matthew, and Mary Kion.
1768, Sep. 21. Mason, Rachel, and Jonathan Attmore.
1768, M'ch   7. Mason, Richard, and Letitia Tannagh.
1744, Apr. —. Mason, Samuel.
1760, Sep. 19. Mason, Sarah, and John Freeman.
1766, Oct. 25. Mason, Thomas, and Priscilla Syson.
1764, Oct. 11. Mason, William, and Sarah Thompson.
1763, Nov. 15. Massey, Charles, and Ann Prior.
1773, Dec. 27. Massey, Ebenezer, and Jane Claxton.
1764, Apr.   5. Massey, Eleanor, and George Sanderson.
1761, July   2. Massey, Frances, and Barnaby McClusky.
1771, Dec.   3. Massey, Mordecai, and Sarah Griffith.
1765, June 22. Massey, Phineas, and Susannah Battle.
1771, Jan.   5. Massey, Samuel, and Letitia Pryor.
1760, M'ch   6. Massey, Samuel, and Sarah Mifflin.
1760, M'ch   3. Massey, Wright, and Elenor Taylor.
1766, May   1. Massholder, Jacob, and Margaret Meyer.
1763, Apr. 27. Master, Jane, and Thomas McMillen.
1775, Sep. 30. Master, Joseph, and Elizabeth Young.
1762, Apr. 20. Master, Mary, and Christopher Rhinewald.
1773, Apr. 17. Masterson, Elizabeth, and John Daily.
1773, M'ch 16. Masterson, Elizabeth, and Thomas Slater.
1760, May   1. Mather, Jane, and Paul Jackson.
1746, May   —. Mathers, John.
1761, July 24. Mathers, John, and Ann Radford.
1770, Jan. 31. Mathers, Mary, and Edward Vernon.
1775, Oct.   2. Mathes, John, and Mercy Musgrove.
1768, Apr. 18. Mathew, Benjamin, and Diana Thomas.
1747, Sep. —. Mathews, Abraham, and Ann Lloyd.
1763, Sep.   5. Mathews, John, and Ann Chambers.
1763, Aug. 20. Mathews, John, and Martha Hughes.
1745, May   —. Mathews, Patrick.
1761, Sep. 28, Mathews, William, and Mary Lloyd.
1765, Jan.   8. Mathias, David, and Hannah Pugh.
1761, Jan.   8. Mathias, John, and Alice Thomas.
1771, Oct. 14. Matlack, Amos, and Hannah Trager.

1771, Nov. 27. Matlack, Elizabeth, and John Knox.

1773, Apr. 24. Matlack, Jonathan, and Hannah Waln.

1766, Nov. 26. Matlack, Seth, and Mary Shute.

1760, Dec. 20. Matlock, Titus, and Sarah Renshaw.

1770, May 4. Matson, Elizabeth, and John Patterson.

1775, Jan. 24. Matson, Mary, and Edmund McDaniel.

1762 Aug. 21. Matthew, Ann, and Michael Nief.

1774, Feb. 22. Matthew, Edward, and Eleanor Thomas

1769, Nov. 14. Matthew, Mary, and John Burton.

1768, Dec. 6. Matthew, Nathan, and Margaret Butler.

1769, Jan. 11. Matthews, Ann, and Jonathan Doil.

1769, M'ch 30. Matthews, Catharine, and Weldor Parsons.

1774, Sep. 6. Matthews, Hannah, and Casper Dull.

1775, Sep. 18. Matthews, Henry, and Deborah Knight.

1768, Feb. 17. Matthews, John, and Hannah North.

1772, May 2. Matthews, John, and Rachel Thomas.

1761, May 15. Matthews, Rose, and John Lindsay.

1774, Oct. 8. Matthew, Thomas, and Sarah Griffith.

1770, Nov. 27. Matthias, Mary, and Jonathan Evans.

1765, July 1. Mattingley, John, and Rebecca Jones.

1768, Oct. 29. Mauerlle, Conrad, and Mary Maxwell.

1767, Dec. 31. Maugridge, Ann, and William Snowden.

1761, Oct. 9. Mauk, Catharine, and John Hadley.

1762, Apr. 10. Mause, Charlotte, and Leonard Rost.

1775, Jan. 12. Maxwell, Amelia, and Richard Fortune.

1760, Sep. 23. Maxwell, Ann, and Matthias Wazenor.

1766, Nov. 12. Maxwell, Elizabeth, and Thomas Thompson.

1765, June 19. Maxwell, Hugh, and Margaret George.

1772, Jan. 1. Maxwell, Martha, and James Smith.

1768, Oct. 29. Maxwell, Mary, and Conrad Mauerlle.

1770, Dec. 19. Maxwell, Nathaniel, and Esther Carsan.

1762, Dec. 21. Maxwell, Rebecca, and James Pearson.

1771, Oct. 21. Maxwell, Robert, and Mary Cooper.

1743, May 27. Maxwell, William.

1764, Aug. 22. May, Andrew, and Mary Ball.

1762, May 21. May, Elizabeth, and John Brooke.

1773, Jan. 18. Mayer, Charles, and Margaret Wrench.

1767, May 21. May, George, and Deborah Cornman.

1768, M'ch 1. May Hannah, and Henry Moore.

1748, Nov. 11. Mayhew, John, and Rachel Haverd.

1761, June 8. May, John, and Isabella McCall.

1771, Aug. 26. May, John, and Mary Cobham.

1761, Nov. 6. Mayland, Deboro, and William Eldridge.

1767, Nov. 28. May, Margaret, and Joseph Drew.

1770, May 30. May, Mary, and Zacharias Nieman.

1766, Jan. 22. Maynard, William, and Ann Corson.

1769, Nov. 10. May, Sarah, and James Caruthers.
1760, Nov. 21. May, Susannah, and William Hughes.
1761, Apr. 20. May, Thomas, and Sarah Holland.
1761, Nov. 23. Mead, Catharine, and Thomas Fitzsimmons.
1763, Dec. 22. Mead, Mary, and Nicholas Nunns.
1761, Feb. 21. Meakson, Jane, and Adam Grier.
1775, Oct. 17. Means, James, and Jane Swinney.
1774, Dec. 3. Means, Margaret, and Joshua North.
1746, Feb. —. Mearns, Samuel.
1769, July 19. Mears, Eleanor, and John Stewart.
1771, Dec. 31. Mears, John, and Ann Gillis.
1748, Oct. 18. Meary, Catharine, and Erasmus Leaver.
1763, Jan. 10. Meas, James, and Isabella Hoops.
1765, Apr. 25. Megettigen, James, and Sarah Evans.
1768, M'ch 2. Meglone, Margaret, and Thomas Seal.
1746, Sep. —. Meirs, Hester, and Peter Hyneman.
1771, Sep. 21. Melchior, Elizabeth, and Jacob Shallus.
1772, Nov. 18. Melchior, Mary, and Francis Gasper Hasenclever.
1760, June 1. Melin, George, and Christiana Lyndmyre.
1774, July 27. Mendenhall, Noah, and Esther Stanley.
1766, Nov. 18. Menele, Catharine, and Joseph Ornado.
1767, July 2. Menge, John, and Catharine Wolfin.
1747, May —. Mennan, Samuel, and Mary Balwin.
1766, Nov. 10. Mentzger, Sarah, and John Lamburgh.
1748, Nov. 11. Menzie, James, and Eleanor Willins.
1773, Dec. 27. Meony, Hannah, and John Burrow.
1759, Dec. 1. Mercer, Ann, and William Richards.
1763, Nov. 12. Mercer, Nathaniel, and Anna Boys.
1772, Aug. 29. Merchant, Anna, and George Poff.
1761, Oct. 5. Merchant, Elizabeth, and Henry Galloway.
1774, Dec. 14. Merchant, James, and Eleanor Gready.
1747, June —. Merchant, John, and Ann Moses.
1775, Aug. 26. Merchant, Sarah, and Casper Gribble.
1776, Jan. 9. Mercley, Jacob, and Christiana Antes.
1773, June 1. Meredith, Anne, and Henry Hill.
1747, May —. Meredith, Ann, and Patrick Carthy.
1768, Jan. 13. Meredith, Daniel, and Mary Brown.
1765, M'ch 22. Meredith, Elizabeth, and George Climer.
1772, Dec. 5. Meredith, George, and Micah Bull.
1772, Apr. 1. Meredith, Hugh, and Mary Todd.
1776, Jan. 3. Meredith, Jane, and Benjamin Davis.
1771, Sep. 26. Meredith, John, and Mary Holton.
1772, May 19. Meredith, Samuel, and Margaret Cadwalader.
1765, Dec. 24. Meredith, Simon, and Ann Huff.
1766, Sep. 5. Mereton, John, and Sarah Midwinter.
1761, Sep. 19. Meridy, Ann, and Thomas Jones.

1744, July 21. Merriman, William.
1764, Oct. 6. Merriott, Elizabeth, and John Hutton.
1765, M'ch 20. Merris, Thomas, Jun., and Ann Butler.
1765, June 24. Merry, Esther, and John Cole.
1767, Feb. 4. Merryweather, Roger, and Martha Heatherington·
1765, May 26. Mertle, Catharine, and John Clements.
1763, M'ch 30. Mesfort, Casper, and Mary Seiglen.
1771, M'ch 21. Meskell, Margaret, and Middleton Heblethwaite.
1773, Jan. 6, Mesminger, Ann, and George Summers.
1747, May —. Messinger, Elizabeth, and John Miller.
1775, Apr. 13. Messner, Margaret, and James Farmer.
1774, Oct. 25. Meston, William, and Rebecca Justice.
1762, May 5. Mets, Elizabeth, and Abraham Hasselberg.
1770, Dec. 11. Mettlen, Elizabeth, and Isaac Williams.
1767, Apr. 23. Metz, Elizabeth, and John White.
1744, Oct. —. Metz, George.
1773, June 2. Metzger, George, and Elizabeth Hoff.
1762, Dec. 4. Metz, Jacob, and Rachael Henricks.
1762, Nov. 8. Mewhouse, Susannah, and Adam Walker.
1766, May 12. Meyer, Albert, and Barbara Strumbrey.
1766, May 1. Meyer, Margaret, and Jacob Massholder.
1766, Sep. 20. Meyer, Margaret, and Joseph Patton.
1768, Dec. 12. Meyer, Thomas, and Margaret Bloom.
1766, M'ch 26. Meyers, Deborah, and John Power.
1762, Feb. 18. Michael, (a negro belonging to Col. Byrd, and
Molly, a mulatto belonging to Mr. Beach.)
1761, Nov. 21. Micham, Sarah, and Richard Evanson.
1762, Dec. 10. Mickesner, John, and Ann Hutchison.
1761, Sep. 12. Middleton, Adam, and Westes Fulton.
1747, M'ch —. Middleton, Andrew, and Anable White.
1762, Apr. 28. Middleton, Edward, and Ann Griffith.
1760, Feb. 16. Middleton, Edward, and Susannah Lewis.
1747, Sep. —. Middleton, Elizabeth, and William Many.
1763, July 13. Middleton, Experience, and Benjamin Archer.
1761, Jan. 19. Middleton, James, and Mary Jones.
1764, July 7. Middleton, James, and Sarah Hill.
1773, Apr. 10. Middleton, John, and Elizabeth Anderson.
1770, M'ch 17. Middleton, John, and Mary Griffits.
1773, May 18. Middleton, Mary, and Nehemiah Cowgill.
1767, June 25. Middleton, Thomas, and Elizabeth Jenkins.
1776, June 15. Middleton, William, and Mary Milkger.
1767, Sep. 26. Midwinter, Elizabeth, and Thomas Crippen.
1766, Sep. 5. Midwinter, Sarah, and John Mereton.
1762, Sep. 20. Miers, George, and Lydia Hust.
1770, June 5. Mifflin, Esther, and Matthew Irwin.
1760, M'ch 6. Mifflin, Sarah, and Samuel Massey.

1770 Sep. 26. Mifflin, Sarah, and Turbut Francis
1760, Aug. 19. Milchant, Rebecca, and Felix Crishman.
1776, M'ch 29. Miles, Edward, and Sarah Wright.
1763, Sep. 3. Miles, Enos, and Sarah Pugh.
1772, Dec. 17. Miles, James, and Susannah Kigings.
1772, Feb. 29. Miles, John, and Mary Lewis.
1765, July 27. Miles, Margaret, and Thomas Paul.
1760, Aug. 30. Miles, Samuel, and Sarah James.
1769, Dec. 23. Miles, Thomas, and Hannah Corry.
1773, Sep. 10. Miley, Joseph, and Martha England.
1776, June 15. Milkger, Mary, and William Middleton.
1769, Jan. 28. Millar, Alexander, and Dorcas Logan.
1776, M'ch 28. Millard, Thomas, and Isabella Collett.
1769, Oct. 20. Millar, Elizabeth, and Joseph Sallsbagg.
1769, June 29. Millar, Henry, and Mary Hoffman.
1770, Jan. 23. Millar, Jane, and Archibald Jackson.
1769, Aug. 15. Millar, Mary, and William Moulder.
1775, Aug. 10. Millenber, Mary and Francis Swaine.
1774, M'ch 26. Millen, Elizabeth, and Thomas Shaw.
1775, Oct. 31. Miller, Abel, and Hannah Martin.
1764, July 17. Miller, Ann, and George Bigler.
1760, Dec. 19. Miller, Anthony, and Elizabeth Kemle.
1762, July 3. Miller, Catharine, and Frederick Renn.
1775, Oct. 31. Miller, Catharine, and John Ralston.
1768, Jan. 22. Miller, Catharine, and John Umsted.
1764, Nov. 22. Miller, Catharine, and Mark McCord.
1770, May 21. Miller, Edward, and Margaret Sherer.
1766, July 3. Miller, Eleanor, and Ezekiah Hutchinson.
1761, June 20. Miller, Elizabeth, and John Anderson.
1770, June 30. Miller, Elizabeth, and John McNeal.
1773, Apr. 1. Miller, Elizabeth, and William Robeson,
1775, Apr. 5. Miller, Frances, and Henry Zimmerman.
1770, Oct. 13. Miller, Frederick, and Catharine Rasbon.
1761, Aug. 13. Miller, George, and Mary Endt.
1762, July 28. Miller, Henry, and Sarah Roberts.
1764, Oct. 23. Miller, Hugh, and Frances Kilpatrick.
1763, Dec. 30. Miller, Jacob, and Mary Goodwin.
1767, Apr. 25. Miller, James, and Elizabeth Chappel.
1772, Sep. 2. Miller, James, and Mary Jacobs.
1764, Nov. 28. Miller, Jane, and Adam Kerr.
1763, Sep. 5. Miller, Jane, and Randall McKillup.
1747, May —. Miller, John, and Elizabeth Messenger.
1748, June 16. Miller, John, and Jane Gale.
1776, Jan. 13. Miller, John, and Mary Barker.
1743, Feb. 15. Miller, Jonathan.

1769, Oct. 31. Miller, Margaret, and Christian Frederick Foaring.
1767, Aug. 25. Miller, Margaret, and Christian Frederick Post.
1768, M'ch 3. Miller, Margaret, and James Davis.
1766, M'ch 26. Miller, Margaret, and Jonathan Hanson.
1774, Dec. 8. Miller, Margaret, and Patrick Duffy.
1764, Sep. 11. Miller, Martha, and Gilbert Grimes.
1764, Nov. 19. Miller, Martin, and Susannah Pechin.
1767, Sep. 29. Miller, Mary, and Frederick Martin.
1770, Sep. 1. Miller, Mry, and George Rilling.
1762, Jan. 12. Miller, Mary, and Jacob Baker.
1759, Dec. 17. Miller, Mary, and James Huay.
1775, Oct. 9. Miller, Mary, and Richard Lawrence.
1775, Nov. 16. Miller, Mary, and Thomas Bramall.
1765, Aug. 12. Miller, Mary, and Thomas Palmer.
1763, Apr. 11. Miller, Nicholas, and Hannah Reese.
1748, Sep. —. Miller, Patrick, and Susannah McClon.
1765, M'ch 19. Miller, Philip, and Catharine Yetten.
1774, Nov 21. Miller, Philip, and Effy Bryan.
1770, May 23. Miller, Philippine, and Henry Ash.
1762, Dec. 13. Miller, Philip Trucken, and Catharine Reese.
1772, July 16. Miller, Rachael, and John Gray.
1762, Aug. 17. Miller, Richard, and Jane Galley.
1761, M'ch 30. Miller, Robert, and Elizabeth Porter.
1772, Dec. 16. Miller, Robert, and Martha Black
1766, M'ch 29. Miller, Robert, and Mary Barclay.
1765, Aug. 30. Miller, Robert, and Prudence Phipps.
1770, M'ch. 26. Miller, Ruth, and William Turner.
1766, Sep. 3. Miller. Sarah, and John Boyd.
1761, Feb. 11. Miller, Sophia, and Henry Shueston.
1776. Jan. 22. Miller, Susannah, and Francis Bockius.
1767, June 5. Miller, Susannah, and John Quainter.
1773, June 2. Miller, Wigard, and Christiana Hesser.
1764. Feb. 7. Miller William, and Anna Maria Schofflet.
1761, M'ch 13. Miller, William, and Margaret Gold.
1760, Feb. 5. Miller, William, and Martha Turrance.
1775, Aug. 3. Millet, Nicholas, and Hannah Tremble.
1774, Apr. 20. Millington, Judith, and Samuel Smith.
1760, Sep. 18. Millin, William, and Catharine Kennedy.
1762, July 29. Mills, Alexander, and Ann Cenon.
1762, May 3. Mills, Francis, and Mary Pimple.
1767, Sep. 3. Mills, Thomas, and Eleanor Rowland.
1765, June 6. Mills, William, and Catharine Van Sciver.
1775, Feb. 2. Millward, George, and Elizabeth Ireland.
1747, Aug. —. Milner, James, and Elizabeth Davis
1748, June 16. Milnor, Martha, and Samuel Rockwell.

1775, M'ch 13. Milnor, Robert, and Martha Long.
1765, Aug. 28. Miloy, Margaret, and Samuel Galbraith.
1762, Aug. 21. Minanti, Daniel, and Mary Juvil.
1774, May 31. Mincuar, James, and Catharine Regan.
1760, Jan. 7. Ming, Dollore, and Sarah Colliday.
1747, Nov. —. Minshall, Samuel, and Jane Stanton.
1761, July 7. Minson, Rosinna, and Peter Oversting.
1763, June 3. Minsor, David, and Jean Gilmore.
1769, Aug. 29. Minton, Edward, and Mary McCann.
1770, June 16. Mintz, Christopher, and Barbara Glouse.
1773, Dec. 15. Mintz, William, and Elizabeth Coleman.
1764, Feb. 10. Mires, Sarah, and John Gallagher.
1775, Feb. 25. Miser, Philip, and Elizabeth Clingman.
1763, Jan. 15. Mitchel, Joshua, and Sarah Randal.
1773, July 22. Mitchell, Abraham, and Frances Gardiner.
1768, Nov. 29. Mitchell, Alexander, and Jane Cochran.
1766, Apr. 10. Mitchell, Alexander, and Mary Greenlaw.
1771, Sep. 13. Mitchell, Benjamin, and Susannah Willson.
1765, Oct. 29. Mitchell, Catharine, and Barbary McGarool.
1773, Dec. 9. Mitchell, Hannah, and John Johnson.
1743, Dec. —. Mitchell Henry.
1769, Apr. 24. Mitchell, Henry, and Martha Vanhorn.
1762, Dec. 18. Mitchell, Jane, and Andrew Caldwell.
1766, Aug. 15. Mitchell, Jane, and Thomas Shortle.
1774, Feb. 21. Mitchell, John, and Hannah Rudolph.
1762, May 18. Mitchell, John, and Mary Hoswell.
1767, Dec. 30. Mitchell, John, and Mary Pearson.
1747, Nov. —. Mitchell, Joshua, and Rebecca Davis.
1774, M'ch 17. Mitchell, Margaret, and Charles Hamilton.
1765, May 15. Mitchell, Margaret, and John Furgeson.
1765, Apr. 3. Mitchell, Mary, and Elijah Weed.
1773, Apr. 20. Mitchell, Mary, and John Emmes.
1771, June 20. Mitchell, Richard, and Hester Lazelier.
1763, M'ch 1. Mitchell, Richard, and Rachael Pierce.
1771, Nov. 11. Mitchell, Robert, and Margaret Hart.
1774, June 10. Mitchell, Samuel, and Anne Willet.
1774, Oct, 12, Mitchell, Sarah, and Heman Clark.
1772, Sep. 21. Mitchell, Sarah, and James Caldwell.
1770, Aug. 22. Mitchell, Thomas, and Mary Young.
1776, June 17. Mitchell, Thomas, and Rachel Pollin.
1765, Oct. 30. Mitchel, Richard, and Sarah Stevenson.
1744, July 21. Mitchel, Thomas.
1766, Dec. 24. Mitchener, Thomas, and Ann Billow.
1768, Jan. 25. Mock, Eilzabeth, and Daniel Burkhart.
1748, May 24. Mocky, Baraby.
1776, M'ch 7. Moffat, Ann, and Elijah Cozens.

1769, Dec.   4. Moffet, Thomas, and Sarah Willson.
1748, Nov. 11. Moffit, David, and Rachel Robinson.
1746, Nov. —. Moffitt, Elizabeth, and Michael Lisk.
1769, Apr. 13. Moiriam, Ezekiel, and Deborah Jobs.
1773, Oct. 21. Moland, William, and Hannah Noble.
1762, Apr. 12. Molley, Ann, and Darby Savage.
1766, June 14. Molley, Walter, and Mary Pawling.
1762, Feb. 18. Molly, (a mulatto, belonging to Mr. Beach.
                   Michael, a negro, belonging to Col. Boyer.)
1765, July   8. Money, John, and Margaret Smith.
1774, Nov. 26. Monger, Josiah, and Mercy Lynn.
1766, M'ch —. Monholland, Dennis.
1761, Nov. 13. Monk, Charles, and Hannah Clisston.
1765, Oct. 30. Monk, James, and Rebecca Prcie.
1746, Dec. —. Monny, Catharine, and John Roberts.
1773, Jan. 31. Montgomery, Ann, and John Shea.
1766, Oct. 20. Montgomery, Catharine, and Duncan McMullen.
1771, Jan. 19. Montgomery, Daniel, and Margaret McCleland.
1765, Aug.   4. Montgomery, Deborah, and John Grant.
1772, Oct. 10. Montgomery, Elizabeth, and John Rice.
1771, Feb.   4. Montgomery, Elizabeth, and Peter Taylor.
1767, Nov. 12. Montgomery, James, and Margaret Bowes.
1769, Aug. 30. Montgomery, John, and Jane Blaylock.
1767, Sep.   1. Montgomery, Jonathan, and Elizabeth Hawkin.
1763, July 15. Montgomery, Mary, and Henry Foster.
1772, Oct.   6. Montgomery, Robert, and Ann McPharland.
1767, Aug. 17. Montgomery, Robert, and Dorcas Armitage.
1766, Oct. 16. Montgomery, Susannah, and John Wilday.
1776, Feb.   1. Moode, Lydia, and Jacob Vanhorn.
1775, Aug.   7. Moore, Allen, and Hannah Gray.
1771, June   8. Moore, Anne, and Charles Lindsay.
1769, M'ch 21. Moore, Anne, and Christopher Rue.
1774, July 28. Moore, Ann, and Thomas Davick.
1763, M'ch 24. Moore, Anthony, and Mary Caswell.
1764, Feb. 18. Moore, Bartholomew, and Elizabeth Warner.
1764, Oct. 25. Moore, Charles, and Martha Lawrence.
1764, Nov. 10. Moore, Charles, and Martha Lawrence.
1760, Oct.   9. Moor, Edward, and Patience Hayes.
1771, Dec. 14. Moore, Edward, and Elizabeth Ramsower.
1773, Nov. 29. Moore, Edward, and Sarah Salisbury.
1773, Aug. 24. Moore, Eleanor, and Peter Stephens.
1772, Apr. 17. Moore, Elizabeth, and Charles Grugh.
1775, July   1. Moore, Elizabeth and Isaac Comley.
1760, Aug. 26. Moore, Elizabeth, and Matthew Pratt.
1769, M'ch   2. Moore, Elizabeth, and Robert Carson.

1767, May   4. Moore, Elizabeth, and Thomas Evans.
1763, Feb.   1. Moore, Elizabeth, and William Church.
1767, Aug. 11. Moore, Elizabeth, and William Gabb.
1768, Feb. 27. Moore, Frances, and Edward Sanders,
1765, July 18. Moore, George, and Rebecca Dobbins.
1772, June 17. Moore, Henry, and Hannah Jones.
1768, M'ch   1. Moore, Henry, and Hannah May.
1764, Apr.   7. Moore, Hester, and William Potts.
1744, Dec. —. Moore, Jathial.
1772, June   4. Moore, Jesse, and Susannah Lawrence.
1744, Oct. —. Moore, John. (See note.)
1747, Dec. —. Moore, John, and Jennet Herring.
1772, May   27. Moore, John, and Olive Wells.
1764, Dec.   3. Moore, John, and Rebecca Kenny.
1764, Dec. 21. Moore, Joseph, and Mary Kirkpatrick.
1773, Sep   16. Moore, Margaret, and Arthur Marshall.
1775, June 15. Moore, Margaret, and Gibbs Jones.
1776, June   4. Moore, Margaret, and John Roach.
1771, July 27. Moore, Margaret, and Joshua Ward.
1760, Oct. 21. Moore, Margaret, and Thomas Sivil.
1760, Dec. 11. Moore, Margaret. and William Salsbury.
1771, Aug.   8. Moore, Martha, and John Edwards.
1747, Dec. —. Moore, Martha, and Samuel Chapman.
1776, Jan. 13. Moore, Mary, and Adam Crisp.
1760, Aug. 11. Moore, Mary, and George Haetton.
1747, May   —. Moore, Mary, and James Delayo.
1768, June 25. Moore, Mary, and John Rees.
1767, Nov. 27. Moore, Mary, and William Johnson.
1763, Apr. 16. Moore, Matthew, and Ann Duff.
1763, July 26. Moore, Nathan, and Elizabeth Traygo.
1763, Nov. 28. Moore, Ralph, and Mary Dark.
1761. Apr. 18. Moore, Rebecca, and John Lindsey.
1761, Dec. 30. Moore, Robert, and Mary Dawson.
1768, Apr. 23. Moore, Samuel, and Martha Ritchey.
1771, June   6. Moore, Sarah, and Richard Davis.
1769, Apr. 20. Moore, Sarah, and Thomas Bateman.
1771, Sep. 23. Moore, Thomas, and Jane McDonald.
1764, Oct. 26. Moore, William, and Christiana Harding.
1769, Jan. 12. Moore, William, and Elizabeth Ball.
1767, M'ch 25. Moore, William, and Elizabeth Cox.
1765, June   8. Moore, William, and Elizabeth McFee.
1774, Oct. 15. Moore, William, and Mary Crager.
1761, May   11. Moorhead, James, and Lydia Jones.
1746, Dec. —. Moran, Mary, and Michael Farrel.
1772, Oct. 27. Moran, William, and Abigail Harlan.
1765, May   20. Morberry, Rebecca, and James Rice.

1766, M'ch 18. Moreland, Jane, and William Nichols.
1763, Aug. 20. Moreton, Eleanor, and Garret Boone.
1763, Nov. 12. Moreton, Elizabeth, and George Moreton.
1763, Nov. 12. Moreton, George, and Elizabeth Moreton.
1765, Sep. 7. Morgan, Abraham, and Ann Morgan.
1765, Sep. 7. Morgan, Ann, and Abraham Morgan.
1764, May 10. Morgan, Ann, and Thomas Bond.
1763, Feb. 11. Morgan, Ann, and Thomas Robins.
1748, Sep. —. Morgan, Cadwalader, and Lydia Cooper.
1772, Nov. 5. Morgan, Elizabeth, and Alexander Edwards.
1765, June 5. Morgan, Elizabeth, and Buckridge Sims.
1764, Aug. 29. Morgan, Enoch, and Letitia Malone.
1773, July 28. Morgan, Enoch, and Susannah Baily.
1762, Dec. 10. Morgan, Esther, and Samuel Martin.
1760, June 18. Morgan, Evan, and Mary Watkins.
1764, Oct. 18. Morgan, George, and Mary Baynton.
1768, June 16. Morgan, Grace, and Benjamin Carpenter.
1776, May 29. Morgan, Hannah, and James Balfour.
1771, Dec. 24. Morgan, Hannah, and John Bod.
1770, M'ch 27. Morgan, Isaac, and Sarah Davis.
1760, Oct. 30. Morgan, Jane, and Samuel Craig.
1744, Aug. 2. Morgan, John.
1765, Sep. 3. Morgan, John, and Mary Hopkinson.
1770, May 18. Morgan, John, and Sarah Hencock.
1761, Sep. 5. Morgan, Margaret, and Hugh Black.
1748, Feb. —. Morgan, Martha, and John Austin.
1763, Oct. 31. Morgan, Mary, and Arthur Burrows.
1772, Aug. 10. Morgan, Mary, and Benjamin Carpenter.
1770, Nov. 1. Morgan, Mary, and Erasmus Kelly.
1762, July 30. Morgan, Mary, and Frederick Warren.
1762, July 26. Morgan, Mary, and George David.
1760, Nov. 19. Morgan, Mary, and Joseph Watkins.
1774, Jan. 29. Morgan, Mary, and William Thomas.
1776, May 2. Morgan, Peter, and Rachel Gregory.
1768, June 10. Morgan, Rachel, and Thomas Long.
1774, Dec. 9. Morgan, Rebecca, and Griffith Jones.
1760, Aug. 23. Morgan, Richard, and Mary Jones.
1773, M'ch 6. Morgan, Sarah, and John Stewart.
1769, Dec. 20. Morgan, Sarah, and Joseph Johnson.
1761, Apr. 15. Morgan, Sarah, and William Maolers.
1768, June 6. Morgan, Thomas, and Mary Rittenhouse.
1748, Oct. 18. Moritz, William, and Hannah Beckman.
1770, Oct. 4. Morrell, John, and Jane Hall.
1775, June 7. Morrell, Sarah, and James Taylor.
1764, Feb. 6. Morrin, Elizabeth, and John Kopple.
1762, Jan. 23. Morris, Abraham, and Rachel Pew.

1775, M'ch 11. Morris, Alice, and Thomas Jones.
1761, M'ch 24. Morris, Andrew, and Rebecca Haines.
1767, May 8. Morris, Ann, and William James.
1770, Apr. 7. Morris, Benjamin, and Mary Mason.
1774, Oct. 20. Morris, Daniel, and Martha Lloyd.
1770, Apr. 2. Morris, Daniel, and Ruth Clews.
1770, Nov. 19. Morris, David, and Mary Ann Chew.
1769, M'ch 4. Morris, Eleanor, and Jonathan Supplee.
1776, M'ch 19. Morris, Enoch, and Mary Caldwell.
1766, June 2. Morris, Frances, and Andrew McGlone.
1764, M'ch 24. Morris, Grace, and Thomas Craig.
1771, M'ch 14. Morris, Hannah, and Jacob Evans.
1761, M'ch 9. Morris, Hannah, and James Rilph.
1775, Aug. 31. Morris, James, and Mary Derrick.
1772, M'ch 14. Morris, James, and Rosanna Cook.
1775, May 13. Morris, Jane, and Philip Kinsey.
1761, June 4. Morris, Jeremiah, and Daniel Jones.
1747, Nov. —. Morris, John, and Jane Goterd.
1760, May 16. Morris, John, and Sarah Ruston.
1760, May 10. Morris, Jonas, and Susannah Wells.
1767, Oct. 28. Morris, Lydia, and Thomas Shields.
1747, Nov. —. Morris, Margaret, and David Lewis.
1762, Nov. 16. Morris, Marian, and Robert Odling.
1762, May 29. Morris, Mary, and Blathwaite Jones.
1774, Apr. 28. Morris, Mary, and Thomas Evans.
1769, June 1. Morris, Mary, and William Bringhurst.
1769, May 4. Morris, Phebe, and Hugh Henry.
1770, Jan. 17. Morris, Rachel, and Joseph Dean.
1769, Feb. 27. Morris, Robert, and Mary White.
1763, M'ch 30. Morris, Sarah, and William Stanbury.
1774, Oct. 26. Morris, Stephen, and Margaret Coxe.
1764, M'ch 9. Morris, Susannah, and David Evans.
1767, May 28. Morris, Susannah, and Robert Russel.
1773, Oct. 18. Morris, William, and Anne Turner.
1762, Apr. 28. Morris, William, and Ann Griffith.
1763, Sep. 24. Morrison, Agnes, and Alexander Agen.
1760, June 18. Morrison, Ann, and David Wilson.
1772, Oct. 20. Morrison, Archibald, and Jane Dyer.
1761, July 13. Morrison, Charlotte, and Samuel Lyon.
1763, Sep. 15. Morrison, Jane, and John Dent.
1766, Sep. 3. Morrison, Jane, and William McIntosh.
1771, Aug. 17. Morrison, Jennet, and John McCullough.
1761, July 30. Morrison, John, and Frances Vallacut.
1774, July 26. Morrison, John, and Hannah Anderson.
1770, Oct. 6. Morrison, Margaret, and John Greenwood.
1760, Oct. 15. Morrison, Martha, and Andreas McNealy.

1767, July 24. Morrison, Rebecca, and Thomas Martin.
1762, Sep. 8. Morrison, Sarah, and Benjamin Hamilton.
1773, Nov. 27. Morrison, Thomas, and Deborah Ward.
1762, Feb. 16. Morrow, Ann, and Joseph Adams.
1776, Apr. 11. Morrow, Eleanor, and John Mark.
1763, June 27. Morrow, Jane, and Greger McGreger.
1771, Jan. 8. Morton, Hugh, and Anne Crozier.
1769, Apr. 15. Morton, Hugh, and Theodosia Howard.
1762, Nov. 18. Morton, Isaac, and Ann Brooks.
1762, Dec. 13. Morton, James, and Mary Wells.
1764, Nov. 26. Morton, John, and Eleanor Martin.
1775, Feb. 11. Morton, John, and Patience Siver.
1775, Dec. 26. Morton, John, and Sophia Sims.
1775, Jan. 14. Morton, Mary, and Charles Justis.
1773, Dec. 11. Morton, Sarah, and William Grantum.
1773, June 19. Morton, Sketchley, and Rebecca Taylor.
1761, Aug. 1. Morton, William, and Sarah Thompson.
1746, Sep. —. Mosely, Richard, and Ann Killcrease.
1775, Nov. 15. Mosely, Richard, and Ann Walker.
1772, Feb. 5. Moser, Catharine, and Charles Lewis Boehm.
1772, M'ch 5. Moser, Elizabeth, and Jacob Bunner.
1761, Dec. 8. Moser, George, and Dorothy Schocken.
1747, June —. Moses, Ann, and John Merchant.
1773, Jan. 23. Moss, John, and Catharine Drift.
1761, Apr. 13. Moostager, Moses, and Elizabeth Whitlock.
1774, Aug. 27. Motheral, John, and Margaret Cannon.
1769, May 1. Mott, Asher, and Ann Biles,
1765, May 15. Mott, Martha, and William Fenemore.
1768, Sep. 8. Mott, Ruth, and William Barnes.
1776, May 23. Mouch, Margaret, and Thomas Wright.
1772, Feb. 27. Moulder, Jemimah, and Robert Josiah.
1774, Apr. 28. Moulder, Mary, and George Bright.
1745, Aug. —. Moulder, William.
1769, Aug. 15. Moulder, William, and Mary Millar.
1766, Dec. 1. Mourning, Elizabeth, and William Smith.
1773, M'ch 24. Mouse, Catharine, and John Everhart,
1774, May 19. Mouse, Charles, and Mary Saddler.
1773, Dec. 7. Mouse, Daniel, and Mary Gilbert.
1767, July 16. Mouse, Elizabeth, and Adam Alberry.
1766, May 26. Mouser, Jacob, and Catharine Shedaker.
1776, Jan. 8. Mouse, Susannah, and Jasper Graff.
1762, July 12. Mousin, Charlotte, and Conrad Hays.
1770, Nov. 21. Moyer, John, and Anna Catharine Weltmonen.
1763, Apr. 28. Moyer, John, and Ann Duche.
1775, Jan. 4. Moyes, James, and Mary Laturn.
1775, June 28. Much, Jeremiah, and Catharine Fox.

1775, June 5. Muchlarein, Christiana, and William Stein.
1765, Jan. 10. Muhrell, James, and Martha Potter.
1761, Oct. 20. Mair, Elizabeth, and John Withers.
1746, July —. Mukins, Sarah, and George Custis.
1743, Jan. 13. Mulhalland, Dennis.
1765, Feb. 19. Mulladore, Barbara, and Henry Keign.
1768, Dec. 5. Mullan, Dennis, and Martha Porter.
1773, Sep. 28. Mullan Jonathan, and Mary Kite.
1776, May 2. Mullan, Owen, and Ann Lawrence.
1769, M'ch 30 Mullan, Sarah, and James Cooper.
1763, Oct. 3. Mullen, James, and Mary Hanes,
1761, June 29. Mullen, John, and Rachael Clarkson.
1765, Apr. 22. Mullen, Joseph and Elizabeth Donnally.
1764, Nov. 23. Mullen, Martha, and Joseph Woolman.
1764, Feb. 1. Mullendore, Anna Maria, and Frederick Gear-
               hart.
1775, Nov. 6. Mullet, John, and Ann Singleton.
1775, June 6. Mullins, James, and Ann Cassin.
1783, June 19. Mullock, Edward.
1767, Aug. 29. Mulloy, Mary, and August Hammerly.
1771, Feb. 16. Murchland, Elizabeth, and Sam'l McCrackin.
1774, Nov. 21. Murdoch, David, and Mary Lusher.
1772, July 11. Murdoch, John, and Sarah Whiteall.
1774, Sep. 1. Murdoch, Samuel, and Ann Lewis.
1770, Apr. 24. Murdock, Hannah. and Cornelius Sweers.
1768, Sep. 14. Murdock, Thomas, and Ann Sterrat.
1763, Jan. 31. Murdock, William, and Jane Brooks.
1763, May 19. Murfey, Ann, and John Duffey.
1769, June 21. Murfin, Thomas, and Anne Brooks.
1767, July 22. Murfin, William, and Elizabeth Brooks.
1766, Nov. 27. Murnix, Ann, and Thomas Jones.
1771, May 29. Murphey, Mary and Patrick Byrne.
1762, Aug. 5. Murphey, William, and Mary Aston.
1767, Nov. 26. Murphy, Daniel, and Sarah Humphreys.
1770, Dec. 4. Murphy, John, and Catharine Gillyan.
1772, Feb. 26. Murphy, John, and Mary Stephens.
1764, Nov. 23. Murphy, Margaret, and Dennis Dougherty.
1772, Nov. 4. Murphy, Sarah, and John Kreps.
1764, Sep. 5. Murray, Alexander, and Elizabeth Masmer.
1768, Apr. 7. Murray, Andrew, and Charity Humphrey.
1772, Dec. 28. Murray, Christiana, and James Johnston.
1764, Nov. 17. Murray, Edith, and Isaac Harris.
1769, June 29. Murray, Elizabeth, and Arthur Davids.
1766, Feb. 3. Murray, Elizabeth, and Elias Vanderlip.
1767, Aug. 17. Murray, Elizabeth, and James McCrackin.
1762, Sep. 20. Murray, Elizabeth, and John Rowney.

1770, May 31. Murray, Elizabeth, and Thomas Palmer
1770, Aug. 7. Murray, James, and Mary Glory.
1747, June —. Murray, Jane, and Thomas Bowlin.
1772, Apr. 13. Murray, John, and Elizabeth Syng.
1766, Dec. 16. Murray John, and Hannah Lindley.
1759, Dec. 26. Murray, John, and Margaret Hall.
1776, Apr. 8. Murray, John, and Martha Edgar.
1767, Apr. 24. Murray, John, and Mary McCoy.
1770, Dec. 7. Murray, John, and Mary McPharlin.
1767, Aug. 20. Murray, John, and Sarah Rankin.
1770, Nov. 3. Murray, Robert, and Hannah Sill.
1773, Nov. 3. Murray, Samuel, and Barbara Woolman.
1773, May 11. Murray, Simon, and Jane Cash.
1743, Feb. 3. Murray, Thomas.
1764, June 1. Murray, William, and Martha McIntire.
1743, July 23. Murrie, Thomas.
1771, Apr. 15. Murrin, Elizabeth, and Henry Litman.
1772, Jan. 11. Musfelden, Margaret, and Frederick Welpert.
1769, Nov. 25. Musgrove, Jane, and Thomas Owen.
1773, July 1. Musgrove, John, and Mary Sims.
1766, May 19. Musgrove, Mary, and Isaac Farr.
1775, Oct. 2. Musgrove, Mercy, and John Mathes.
1770, Jan. 10. Musgroves, Anne, and Charles Farguson.
1764, Nov. 23. Mushett, Thomas, and Sarah Trumble.
1745, June —. Myars, Peter.
1760, June 5. Myer, Elizabeth, and Frederick Fentle.
1775, Sep. 5. Myer, Henry, and Catharine Sweitzer.
1763, Jan. 3. Myer, Joseph, and Catharine Haegner.
1759, Dec. 1. Myer, Mary, and Christian Stimmer.
1772, Dec. 29. Myerly, Conrad, and Catharine Brandt.
1760, Feb. 11. Myersen, Elizabeth, and Jacob Hoover.
1775, Aug. 8. Myers, Benjamin, and Elizabeth George.
1768, Oct. 1. Myers, Elizabeth, and James Dickinson.
1769, Dec. 8. Myers, John, and Alice Slack.
1770, Feb. 16. Myers, Mary, and George Everard.

N.

1773, June 14. Nackervis, Paul, and Ann Nevill.
1747, Apr. —. Naclor, Rachel, and John Carvour.
1748, M'ch 11. Naest, Rachel, and John Roody.
1775, Oct. 9. Nagle, Charles, and Margaret Smith.
1776, Apr. 24. Nagle, Mary, and John Hooman.
1775, Nov. 25. Nagle; Mary, and William Stockton.
1773, Nov. 13. Naglee, Catharine, and John Lind.
1765, Sep. 11. Naglee, Henry, and Margaret Croston.
1744, Nov. —. Naglee, Jacob.

1770, Apr. 6. Naglee, Mary, and Jacob Ashmead.
1772, Nov. 4. Naglee, Thomas, and Hannah Belangee.
1769, June 27. Nail, Christian, and Elizabeth Taylor.
1761, June 3. Nail, Mary, and George Rute.
1772, July 13. Nailor, Jane, and John Shee.
1770, Feb. 21. Nash, Martha, and Richard Mairs.
1768, May 27. Nathan, Abram and Rachel Wilson.
1760, Sep. 2. Nathan, Lyon, and Eliazbeth Webb.
1764, Nov. 5. Naugle, Martha, and William Ennery.
1775, Dec. 15. Nauman, Daniel, and Mary Librich.
1761, May 6. Naylor, Lane, and Ann Vaughn.
1774, July 13. Neal, Ann, and John Wallace.
1768, Jan. 14. Neal, Daniel, and Margaret Brown.
1772, Jan. 1. Neal, Mary, and Daniel Stewart.
1744, Aug. —. Neal, Owen.
1769, Sep. 20. Nealson, William, and Mary Teany.
1772, Oct. 13. Neal, Thomas, and Ann O'Kill.
1772, Feb. 11. Neal, Thomas, and Margaret Bell.
1761, Oct. 29. Neans, Barnabas, and Elizabeth Burtholt.
1769, Sep. 25. Neave, Patrick, and Margaret Lublow.
1766, Jan. 27. Neave, Sarah, and William Baker.
1767, Nov. 11. Neb, Rebecca and Robert McBan.
1761, Jan. 29. Nebham, Hannah, and Rees Evans.
1765, Dec. 2. Needham, John, and Mary Jennings.
1766, May 17. Needom, Elizabeth, and Samuel Powel.
1762, July 10. Neeld, Elizabeth, and Samuel Jessip.
1772, May 14. Neeld, Richard, and Mary Belford.
1771, Jan. 22. Neely, Elizabeth, and Jacob Drake.
1775, July 3. Neels, Nicholas, and Mary Whitefield.
1766, June 20. Neely, William, and Elizabeth Thompson.
1774, Oct. 25. Nees, Adam, and Catharine Delabar.
1773, M'ch 15. Neff, Elizabeth, and Adam Baker.
1776, Apr. 30. Neff, Elizabeth, and Christopher Madeira.
1745, Nov. —. Negeley, John.
1746, M'ch —. Negle, Richard.
1765, Jan. 11. Neidolf, Jacob, and Susannah Rhine.
1764, Sep. 1. Neil, Elizabeth, and Michael Owner.
1748, July 13. Neil, Sarah, and Michael Hendrick.
1768, May 12. Neill, Martha, and Joseph Baker.
1772, Feb. 17. Neill, Sarah, and Robert Willson.
1764, M'ch 15. Neilson, Hugh, and Jane Thompson.
1776, Jan. 31. Neilson, Peggy, and Ezekiel Foreman.
1745, Feb. —. Neilson, Robert.
1770, May 30. Neiman, Zacharias, and Mary May.
1765, Apr. 10. Neiss, Catharine, and John Proudfoot.
1766, Mar. 18. Neiss, Mary, and Benjamin Davis.

1772, Aug. 15. Neithermark, Sarah, and John Garwood.
1766, May 23. Nell, Ann, and Peter Butler.
1768, June 7. Nelson, Alexander, and Mary Warnack.
1775, Dec. 5. Nelson, Andrew, and Mary McGinnis.
1765, Oct. 29. Nelson, Anna, and Henry Bernhold.
1764, June 9. Nelson, Ann, and John Wilson.
1774, Nov. 11. Nelson, Ann, and Samuel Anderson.
1774, Sep. 1. Nelson, Ann, and Thomas Creagh.
1771, Nov. 27. Nelson, Catharine, and Thomas Green.
1761, Nov. 30. Nelson, Eleanor, and Archibald McKessock.
1760, Sep. 11. Nelson, George, and Sarah Tomplinson.
1775, M'ch 14. Nelson, Margaret, and Francis Gilbert.
1773, May 17. Nelson, Margaret, and Joshua Cleaver.
1766, June 20. Nelson, Mary, and George Harding.
1769, July 13. Nelson, Mary, and John Barker.
1775, Apr. 20. Nelson, Mary, and Patrick Griffin.
1770, Nov. 28. Nelson, Nicholas, and Rebecca Plumber.
1763, Dec. 8. Nelson, Samuel, and Ann Scott.
1771, June 7 Nelson, Thomas, and Mary Williams.
1776, Feb. 16. Nelson, William, and Catharine Roberts.
1772, Apr. 27. Nerback, Anna, and Thomas Hyde.
1770, May 5. Nerry, Mary, and Charles Bowman.
1760, Dec. 4. Nesbitt, Margaret, and John Hall.
1748, M'ch 11. Nesen, Anna Maria, and John Ringer.
1764, Jan. 4. Nessmith, John, and Margaret Yerkis.
1772, Aug. 24. Neumannin, Margaret, and Thomas Britman.
1748, Sep. —. Nevell, Thomas, and Mary Davis.
1765, Oct. 31. Nevil, James, and Hannah Keen.
1773, June 14. Nevill, Ann, and Paul Nackervis.
1760, Oct. 24. Nevill, Thomas, and Mary Ann Hunt.
1766, Nov. 4. Nevin, Hugh, and Sarah Todd.
1771, Sep. 10. Nevling, Rev. John, and Catharine Stonematz.
1769, Feb. 18. Newall, Mary, and Benjamin Eastburn.
1747, June —. Newbald, William, and Margaret Coultas.
1771, June 27. Newberry, Mary, and Caleb Smedley.
1746, Oct. —. Newby, Elizabeth, and James Beard.
1774, Dec. 24. Newell, George, and Esther Blackledge.
1765, Aug. 14. Newland, Elizabeth, and Jonathan Rose.
1747, Aug. —. Newland, Mary, and Edward Shippen.
1772, Nov. 14. Newlin, Elizabeth, and Thomas Thorp.
1775, Nov. 28. Newman, Charles, and Ann Robeson.
1774, Aug. 23. Newman, Paine, and Mary Coates.
1769, Sep. 30. Newman, William, and Eleanor McGuire.
1746, Aug. —. Newmonim, Margaret, and Charles Witts.
1765, Oct. 16. Newton, Elizzabeth, and Isaac Durborow.
1761, Apr. 14. Newton, Elizabeth, and John Kelly.

1744, May —. Newton, Robert.
1745, Nov. —. Newton, Samuel.
1746, Nov. —. Nice, Arthur, and Mary Packer.
1767, Oct. 23. Nice, John, and Margaret Coffin.
1767, Aug. 18. Nice, Mary, and William Maris.
1767, Feb. 16. Nice, Susannah, and William Turner.
1761, Nov. 5. Nicholl, William, and Joanna Whaland.
1761, Aug. 19. Nichols, Esther, and Robert Patterson.
1761, M'ch 19. Nichols, Latitia, and James Thompson.
1762, Aug. 10. Nichols, Plesant, and William Vesey.
1762, Oct. 23. Nichols, Sarah, and Joseph Shute.
1772, Sep. 3. Nichols, William, and Brightwed Stout.
1766, M'ch 18. Nichols, William, and Jane Moreland.
1773, Apr. 28. Nicohlson, Ann, and William Mabury.
1760, Nov. 13. Nicholson, Archibald, and Alley McBride.
1760, July 22. Nicholson, Edward, and Sarah Vokins.
1762, May 22. Nicholson, Grace, and John Litte.
1768, May 26. Nicholson, Joseph, and Hannah Akin.
1771, Aug. 26. Nicholson, Mary, and Patrick Lyens.
1773, July 27. Nicholson. Rachel, and John Teis.
1763, Sep. 28. Nicholson, Ralph, and Mary Smith.
1767, Dec. 12. Nicholson, Ruth, and Jedidiah Allen.
1775, Dec. 28. Nicohlson, Sarah, and George Graff.
1763, Sept. 26. Nichoson, Sarah, and Samuel Pierce.
1769, Feb. 27. Nicholson, Sarah, and Thomas Snowden.
1773, May 24. Nicholson, Sophia, and Richard Eyres.
1771, July 23. Nicklin, Anna, and Francis Ravenhill.
1762, Aug. 21. Nief, Michael, and Ann Matthew.
1773, Feb. 12. Neiman, Zachariah, and Mary Bowler.
1764, June 28. Niles, Sarah, and Benjamin Watherington.
1767, Dec. 17. Niles, William, and Hannah Goodman.
1774, July 7. Nim, Martha, and Ralph Smith.
1763, July 27. Nimmen, George, and Jane Adams.
1748, July 13. Nise, Agnes, and Joseph Devit.
1746, Nov. —. Nitcullues, Arthur, and Mary Landerman.
1769, Oct. 31. Nithermark, Margaret, and Isaac Hendrickson.
1747, Apr. —. Nixon, Lea, and Garret Vanzant.
1748, Apr. 13. Nixon, Margaret, and Ephraim Leech.
1747, Jan. —. Nixon, Mary, and John Sutton.
1765, Apr. 5. Nixon, Sarah, and James Tomkins.
1776, June 18. Nixon, Thomas, and Mary Roberts.
1766, Oct. 30. Noarth, Hannah, and Isaac Lesesne.
1763, Feb. 9. Noble, Anthony, and Margaret Warnick.
1767, May 25, Noble, Anthony, and Sarah Bank.
1772, Dec. 4. Noble, David, and Anna Powell.
1772, Aug. 5. Noble, Edward, and Mary Roenun.

1773, June 9. Noble, Elizabeth, and Samuel Thomas.
1773, Oct. 19. Noble, Hannah, and William Moland.
1763, Apr. 5. Noblit, Lilley, and Joseph Hollen.
1765, Dec. 2. Noblitt, William, and Sarah Clinton.
1768, May 21. Noles, Rachel, and Richard Coarsen.
1764, Apr. 9. Norberry, Hannah, and Charles Roberts.
1783, June 11. Norbur, Heath.
1774, Feb. 14. Norcross, Uriah, and Ann Roswell.
1770, M'ch 8. Norie, Peter, and Margaret Campell.
1762, July 26. Norridge, Elizabeth, and John Slater.
1745, Aug. —. Norrington, Thomas.
1744, May —. Norris, Francis.
1774, May 11. Norris, Henry, and Ann Hill.
1766, Aug. 7. Norris, Joseph, and Hannah Wood.
1765, Apr. 26. Norris, Robert, and Hannah Gilbert.
1768, M'ch 5. Norris, Robert, and Margaret Long.
1761, Apr. 22. Norris, Sarah, and Samuel Forester.
1746, Nov. —. Norris, Thomas, and Catharine Steward.
1762, Aug. 31. Norris, Thomas, and Hannah Gilbert.
1766, M'ch 17. Norris William, and Ann Aubrey.
1764, Jan. 23. North, Elizabeth, and George Evans.
1768, Feb. 17. North, Hannah, and John Matthews.
1746, Dec. —. North, Jane, and John DeNyce.
1768, Jan. 9. North, John, and Elizabeth Hughes.
1775, Aug. 21. North, John, and Sarah Poole.
1747, Oct. —. North, Joseph, and Lydia Price.
1774, Dec. 3. North, Joshua, and Margaret Means.
1760, M'ch 3. Northrop, Rachel, and Joseph Ashton.
1773, Oct. 15. Northrop, Rachel, and Isaac Ashton.
1762, Aug. 25. Nortin, Jonathan, and Sarah Dod.
1761, M'ch 3. Norton, Elizabeth, and John Fluellen.
1769, Jan. 7. Norton, Elizabeth, and Paul White.
1763, Oct. 27. Nowla, Jemima, and Icahabod Higgins.
1763, Dec. 22. Nunn, Nicholas, and Mary Mead.
1762, May 10. Nuns, Ralph, and Margaret McIntosh.
1771, June 18. Nuss, Anthony, and Elizabeth Maine.
1746, July —. Nutt, Abraham, and Elizabeth Anderson.
1773, Sep. 30. Nuttle, Margaret, and Matthew Thompson.

O.

1774, Dec. 20. Oakman, Isaac, and Elizabeth Allen.
1767, Jan. 1. Oates, William, and Mary Tufft.
1776, June 7. Oat, Martha, and Daniel Green.
1760, June 9. Oblebee, Hannah, and John Davis.
1766, Nov. 1. O'Brian, Morto, and Elizabeth Bacon.
1765, Nov. 16. O'Bryan, Lewis, and Sarah Gilbert.

1775, Sep.   7. O'Daniel, Michael, and Eleanor Bryan.
1761, Sep.   17. Odenheimer, John, and Mary Riplee.
1772, June 11. Odenhaimer, Philip, and Catharine Utree.
1762, Nov. 16. Olding, Robert, and Marian Morris.
1763, Oct.   12. O'Donald, Jane, and Francis Ramsey.
1747, Jan.   —. Offinger, Catharine, and Samuel Channel.
1747, Jan.   —. Offinger, Mary, and David Haycott.
1747, Aug.   —. Ogden, Ann, and Robert Stone.
1769, July 13. Ogden, Ann, and Wiliam Siddons.
1769, Jan.   11. Ogden, William, and Mary Pinniard.
1770, June 21. Ogg, John, and Anne Pew.
1772, Oct.   7. Ogilby, Martha, and John Leacock.
1766, Apr.   10. Ogilby, William, and Sarah Davis.
1748, June 16. Ogle, Edward, and Margaret Howard.
1769, Oct.   10. Ogle, Susanah, and Gaspero Polumbo.
1771, May   27. O'Harra, John, and Sarah Jones.
1773, July   8. O'Haughan, Catharine, and Daniel Gillin.
1772, Oct.   13. O'Kill, Ann, and Thomas Neal.
1775, Oct.   12. O'Kill, Jane, and Rev. John Stuart.
1771, Jan.   17. Oldenburch, Daniel, and Mary Laversweiller.
1742, Dec.   28. Oliphant, Thomas.
1762, Dec.   27. Oliver, Ann, and John Devan.
1774, May   10. Oliver, Jane, and John Bower.
1775, Aug.   10. Oliver, John, and Edith Edes.
1765, M'ch 23. Oliver, John, and Mary Armstrong.
1772, July 15. Oliver, Joseph, and Susannah Banks.
1747, Feb.   —. Oliver, Thomas, and Elizabeth Donavon.
1775, May   25. Oliver, Walter, and Elizabeth Hall.
1767, Dec.   23. Olson, Thomas, and Mary Wood.
1761, Dec.   4. Omensetter, Barbara, and Christ Fisher.
1763, July 14. Omensetter, Sophia, and George Hite.
1760, Sep.   15. O'Miller, John, and Catharine Weisen.
1772, Nov. 10. O'Mullan, Catharine, and John Smith.
1772, Oct.   9. O'Neal, Barnabas, and Barbara Winter.
1774, Feb.   11. O'Neal, Daniel, and Elizabeth Welch.
1765, Jan.   1. O'Neal, James, and Sarah Green.
1765, Sep.   25. O'Neal, Jennett, and Robert Gregg.
1771, Apr.   15. O'Neal, John, and Susannah Johnston.
1772, Sep.   16. O'Neal, Rosana, and Israel Jenkins.
1768, Nov. 16. O'Neal, Sarah, and John Haines.
1773, June 17. O'Neil, Arthur, and Margaret Goff.
1774, Nov. 18. O'Neill, Henry, and Ann Campbell.
1745, June   —. Ord, George.
1767, Jan.   13. Ord, George, and Rebecca Lindmire.
1744, June 22. Ord, John.
1775, June   1. Ord, Martha, and William Webb.

1770, Dec. 11. Orffar, George, and Barbara Crousen.
1767, Dec. 11. Orin, Elizabeth, and John Room.
1770, May 31. Ormes, Jane, and William Keith.
1766, Nov. 18. Ornado, Joseph, and Catharine Menele.
1770, Dec. 6. Orrick, Matthias, and Martha Barr.
1764, Dec. 28. Osbern, Bridget, and John Howard.
1763, Sep. 12. Osborn, Margaret, and Robert Wilson.
1761, Aug. 3. Osborn, Margaret, and Tavenere Hamilton.
1775, May 4. Osborne, Catharine, and John Jameson.
1774, Aug. 8. Osborne, Elizabeth, and Patrick Conlay.
1775, May 17. Osborne, John, and Mary Christian.
1744, Aug. 13. Osborne, Jonas.
1767, Dec. 15. Osborne, William, and Sarah Bowde.
1767, Aug. 17. Osburn, Elizabeth, and Edward Beach.
1762, Apr. 29. Osburn, Elizabeth, and Henry Ireland.
1775, July 29. Osman, Marriam, and John Wood.
1776, Feb. 27. Osmon, John, and Elizabeth Sellers.
1760, Sep. 25. Othello, (a negro.)
1775, May. 22. Otis, James, and Charity Swailes.
1775, July 25. Otis, James, and Mary Conly.
1763, Sep. 19. Ott, Isaac, and Sarah Jones.
1774, Oct. 12. Ottinger, Dorothy, and Joseph Barge.
1765, M'ch 18. Ottinger, Hannah, and George Savage.
1772, Feb. 6. Otto, Bodo, Jun., and Catharine Schioughauser.
1766, Sep. 11. Otto, Bodo, and Maria Paris.
1764, May 26. Otto, Frederick, and Mary Withers.
1767, Oct. 24. Otto, Jacob, and Mary Whitehead.
1776, Apr. 9. Otto, John, and Catharine Hittner.
1765, Oct. 23. Otty, Abigail, and Michael Silb.
1764, Nov. 1. Overend, Martha, and Charles Kelly.
1764, Jan. 6. Overend, Thomas, and Martha Powell.
1770, Nov. 6. Overfelt, Sarah, and Moses Vancampen.
1745, Apr. —. Overin, Thomas.
1761, July 7. Oversting, Peter, and Rosinna Minson.
1773, Jan. 2. Overthrow, Elizabeth and James Pendlebury.
1745, Sep. —. Overthrow, Samuel.
1771, June 10. Owen, Anne, and Joseph Eastburn.
1776, Jan. 18. Owen, Ann, and Richard Clark.
1762, Jan. 1. Owen, Ebenezer, and Sarah Jones.
1770, Dec. 18. Owen, Elizabeth, and Jacob Godshalk.
1762, Sep. 14. Owen, Elizabeth, and Joseph Crispan.
1774, M'ch 22. Owen, Elizabeth, and Moses Lewis.
1745, July —. Owen, Hugh.
1762, Jan. 1. Owen, Rachael, and Gerrard Irwin.
1763, Jan. 18. Owen, Rachael, and Samuel Backman.
1744, Oct. —. Owen, Robert.

1769, Nov. 25. Owen, Thomas, and Jane Musgrove.
1776, May 22. Owens, Abel, and Isabella Davis.
1764, Sep. 1. Owner, Michael, and Elizabeth Neil.
1771, May 9. Oxley, Edward, and Margaret Steel.
1747, Feb. —. Oylers, Catharine, and Lewis Kadd.
1761, Apr. 14. Oyster, Hannah, and Peter Kiplinger.
1771, Apr. 26. Ozier, Elizabeth, and Richard Thompson.

P.

1776, Apr. 18. Packard, John, and Mary Barnes.
1746, Nov. —. Packer, Mary, and Arthur Nice.
1768, Oct. 25. Pack, James, and Mary Doack.
1764, Nov. 6. Page, Ann, and Thomas James.
1775, Apr. 24. Page, Thomas, and Catharine Bryan
1761. Sep. 7. Paine, James, and Mary Manson.
1745, June —. Paine, Joseph.
1766, Sep. 25. Paine, Mary, and Anthony Martin.
1767, Feb. 18. Paine, Mary, and John Chrystie.
1768, Nov. 28. Painter, Caroline, and Christian Young.
1762, Sep. 4. Painter, Doriley, and George Kellar.
1769, M'ch 2. Painter, Margaret, and John Howard.
1774, Sep. 26. Pake, John, and Jane Cobinger.
1763, Sep. 24. Palmer, Benjamin, and Esther Bidgood.
1772, M'ch 26. Palmer, Elizabeth, and Samuel Thomas.
1766, Sep. 3. Palmer, Elizabeth, and William Evitt.
1772, Apr. 9. Palmer, Hannah, and Ezekiel Letts.
1748, Oct. 18. Palmer, Jane, and James Penington.
1743, May 7. Palmer, John.
1766, June 14. Palmer, John, and Tacy Roberts.
1770, Dec. 26. Palmer, Jonathan, and Esther Roberts.
1764, Sep. 12. Palmer, Joyce, and Reuben Emerson.
1772, Jan. 2. Palmer, Margaret, and William McCulloch.
1765, Jan. 23. Palmer, Martha and Walker, Kerr.
1765, Aug. 24. Palmer, Richard, and Hannah Barclay.
1745, June —. Palmer, Thomas.
1770, May 31. Palmer, Thomas, and Elizabeth Murray.
1765, Aug. 12. Palmer, Thomas, and Mary Miller.
1774, Aug. 31. Palmer, Thomas, and Susannah Dubre.
1762, Apr. 1. Palmer, William, and Margaret Pew.
1773, Sep. 14. Pancoast, Ann, and Francis Robinson.
1770, May 17. Pancoast, Mary, and Aaron Hughes.
1763, Jan. 3. Pander, George, and Mary Steel.
1763, Sep. 20. Pane, Dilly, and William Peasely.
1772, June 20. Pannabicker, Peter, and Margaret Welker.
1776, Jan. 9. Pannybaker, John, and Dorothy Schombaugh.
1761, Jan. 30. Panton, Michael, and Veronique Verdiere.

1776, June 18. Paply, John, and Susannah Dewar.
1760, Oct. 11. Papy, Elizabeth, and Philip Travers.
1766, Sep. 11. Paris, Maria, and Bodo Otto.
1760, Apr. 15. Parham, Susannah, and Richard Parker.
1769, July 31. Parke, Cecelia, and Bertles Shee
1765, Dec. 4. Parker, Ann, and Alexander Gibbs.
1748, May 14. Paker, Benjamin, and Mary Briton.
1770, Dec. 3. Parker, Hannah, and John Thompson.
1745, Jan. —. Parker, Humphrey.
1772, Oct. 17. Parker, Jane, and James Alexander.
1748, Sep. —. Parke, Jane, and John Blakeney.
1769, Dec. 23. Parker, John, and Mary Lusk.
1745, Jan. —. Parker, Joseph.
1767, M'ch 5. Parker, Mary ,and Joseph Watkins.
1771, May 10. Parker, Mary, and Thomas Jones.
1767, Dec. 14. Parker, Peter, and Eliabeth Price.
1773, June 9. Parker, Rachel, and Benjamin Brownbash.
1768, Oct. 28. Parker, Rebecca, and James White.
1760, Apr. 15. Parker, Richard, and Susannah Parham.
1765, Sep. 11. Parker, Samuel, and Hannah George.
1773, M'ch 6. Parker, Susannah, and Asher Clayton.
1763, Aug. 31. Parker, William, and Hanna Call.
1771, June 19. Parkes, Elizabeth Isabella, and James Davis.
1773, June 18, Parkhill, Elijah, and Jane Long.
1748, Sep. —. Parkinson, John, and Mary David.
1747, Jan. —. Parkinson, Thomas, and Margaret Hall.
1767, M'ch 30. Parkison, James, and Ann Junkins.
1772, May 11. Parkison, Jane, and William Cowpland.
1772, Sep. 24. Parkison, Martin, and Elizabeth Henderson.
1759, Nov. 28. Parmel, Rachel, and Andros Edwards.
1745, M'ch —. Parmele, Charles.
1769, Oct. 11. Parmelly, Sarah, and Edward Thompson.
1763, Feb. 7. Parr, Mary, and William Crisp.
1776, Feb. 26. Parr, William, Esq., and Grace Dowell.
1761, Dec. 15. Parry, Caleb, and Elizabeth Jacobs.
1764, June 20. Parry, David, and Elizabeth Richards.
1761, July 23. Parry, Martha, and Richard Pearne.
1746, Oct. —. Parry, Mary, and George Smith.
1759, Dec. 12. Parry, Mary, and Joseph Francis.
1747, Aug. —. Parry, Sarah, and John Hall.
1769, Dec. 7. Parsell, David, and Anne Philips.
1761, May 2. Parsley, Sarah, and James Shankland.
1773, June 24. Parsons, Elizabeth, and James Thompson.
1762, Dec. 28. Parsons, George, and Mary Wamsley.
1772, Apr. 16. Parsons, Isaac, and Anstrus Shadowill.
1748, July 13. Parsons, John, and Susanna Adamson.

1761, Aug. 3. Parsons, Richard, and Jemiah Hibbs.
1769, M'ch 30. Parsons, Weldor, and Catharine Matthews.
1744, Dec. —. Parsons, William.
1768, Apr. 14. Paschall, Benjamin, and Ann Rudolph.
1761, Feb. 24. Paschall, Frances, and John Howell.
1768, M'ch 9. Paschall, Hannah, and Levi Hollingsworth.
1771, July 27. Paschall, John, Junior, and Rachel Smith.
1767, June 11. Paschall, Margaret, and John Hughes.
1771, June 13. Pass, Mary, and Paul Dawser.
1764, M'ch 3. Past, Catharine, and Jacob Faines.
1761, June 24. Past, Mary, and Owen Haflick.
1769, M'ch 17. Pastorius, Abraham, and Eleanor Leech.
1765, Oct. 18. Pastorius, Hannah, and William Connody.
1771, Nov. 28. Pastorius, Samuel, and Sarah Lincon.
1764, July 17. Patrick, Samuel, and Rebecca Gibbs.
1776, May 17. Patterson, Elizabeth, and John Cloud.
1746, June —. Patterson, Jane, and John Hall.
1747, Nov. —. Patterson, Jane, and Lotta Evans.
1774, Nov. 30. Patterson, John, and Ann Anderson.
1770, May 4. Patterson, John, and Elizabeth Matson.
1776, Feb. 21. Patterson, Malley, and William Taylor.
1768, Apr. 2. Patterson, Margaret, and Benjamin Griffey.
1760, Nov. 11. Patterson, Mary, and Archibald Gardner.
1761, Aug. 19. Patterson, Robert, and Esther Nichols.
1769, June 8. Patterson, Sarah, and John Reeves.
1760, M'ch 1. Patterson, Susannah, and William Hammond.
1768, M'ch 3. Patterson, Thomas, and Mary Brockden.
1764, Dec. 27. Patterson, William, and Susannah Williams.
1763, July 14. Patton, Jane, and James McGraugar.
1766, Sep. 20. Patton, Joseph, and Margaret Meyer.
1771, Aug. 19. Patton, Robert, and Elizabeth Sahler.
1767, Oct. 23. Paul, Anna, and Nicholas Kyser.
1764, June 21. Paul, Ann, and George Pepper.
1775, Oct. 2. Paul, Hannah, and Francis Young.
1775, Nov. 7. Paul, Hannah, and George Bewly.
1765, June 11. Paulhill, James, and Mary Geraud.
1747, Dec. —. Paulin, Witlock, and Mary Smith.
1763, Dec. 12. Paul, Jacob, and Jane Sutton.
1760, Nov. 26. Paul, James, and Hannah Kinderdine.
1775, July 1. Paul, Lawrence, and Ann Martin.
1770, Jan. 19. Paul, Peter, and Catharine Grubb.
1774, July 19. Paul, Richard, and Lydia Duche.
1762, Apr. 15. Paul, Susannah, and David Brown.
1776, M'ch 5. Paul, Susannah, and Revan Rakestraw.
1765, July 27. Paul, Thomas, and Margaret Miles.
1769, Feb. 25. Paul, William, and Alice Connell.

1760, Dec. 1. Pauston, Margaret, and John Fauntz.
1769, Dec. 7. Pawling, Henry, and Rebecca Bull.
1766, June 14. Pawling, Mary, and Walter Molley.
1764, Apr. 2. Paxton, Martha, and John Arney.
1768, Jan. 23. Paxton, Phineas, and Susannah Shaw.
1775, Sep. 12. Paxton, Thomas, and Elizabeth Randle.
1761, June 1. Paydon, Martha, and William Stinson.
1761, M'ch 21. Payne, Mary, and John Baccorth.
1748, June —. Pearce, Charles, and Ann Anstill.
1764, Nov. 29. Pearce, Daniel, and Rebecca McCoy.
1776, M'ch 5. Pearce, Henry Ward, and Rachel Relfe.
1748, June —. Pearce, Mary, and John Way.
1774 Dec. 15. Pearce, Richard, and Mary Kite.
1761, July 23. Pearne, Richard, and Martha Parry.
1746, Jan. —. Pears, John.
1768, May 3. Pearson, Abel, and Mary Bartholomew.
1765, M'ch 2. Pearson, Alice, and Benjamin Leedom.
1772, Nov. 30. Pearson, Ann, and James Sparks.
1760, Oct. 1. Pearson, Elizabeth, and George Goodwin.
1765, May 1. Pearson, Henrietta, and Charles Vineyard.
1762, Dec. 21. Pearson, James, and Rebecca Maxwell.
1768, Feb. 4. Pearson, John, and Hannah White.
1767, June 27. Peason, Joseph, and Mary Tuckniss.
1762, M'ch 1. Pearson, Margaret, and John Vanhorn.
1771, Nov. 25. Pearson, Martha, and Samuel Ash.
1767, Dec. 30. Pearson, Mary, and John Mitchell.
1765, July 9. Pearson, Mary, and William Symonds.
1771, May 22. Pearson, Mary, and William Thomas.
1773, May 1. Pearson, Munro, and Jane McCammon.
1764, Apr. 2. Pearson, Samuel, and Mary Wynn.
1763, Sep. 20. Peasely, William, and Dilly Pane.
1765, Apr. 3. Pechin, Christopher, and Christiana Bright.
1764, Nov. 19. Pechin, Susanna, and Martin Miller.
1745, Nov. —. Peck, William.
1745, Aug. —. Pederow, John.
1768, Nov. 26. Pedrick, Samuel, and Sarah Pedrick.
1768, Nov. 26. Pederick, Sarah, and Samuel Pedrick.
1772, Oct. 9. Peel, Ann, and Alexander Brown.
1767, Feb. 4. Peel, Catharine, and Jacob Hansberger.
1762, May 18. Peel, Grace, and William Dowell.
1774, Nov. 23. Peeling, Elizabeth, and John Cullam.
1773, Oct. 4. Peeling, George, and Elizabeth Howtin.
1743, May 23. Peel, John.
1765, Oct. 20. Peel, Mary, and Robert Field.
1771, May 16. Peirce, Anne, and Charles Fisher.
13—VOL. II.

1763, July 21. Peirce, John, and Rebecca Boore.
1764, July 16. Peirce, Levy, and Sarah Hillman.
1744, July 4. Peirce, Thomas.
1773, Nov. 3. Pemberton, John, and Alice Sutton.
1760, Sep. 6. Pemberton, Mary, and Enoch Flower.
1773, Jan. 2. Pendlebury, James, and Elizabeth Overthrow.
1774, Dec. 24. Peni, Ann, and Stephen Decator.
1748, Oct. 18. Penington, James, and Jane Palmer.
1745, June —. Penly, Edward.
1763, Dec. 24. Pennald, Edith, and William Beale, Junior.
1748, May 14. Pennall, Evan, and Elizabeth Powell.
1763, Oct. 27. Penebaker, Elizabeth, and Anthony Vanderslice.
1768, May 24. Pennebeker, Matthias, and Mary Custer.
1771, Apr. 17. Pennell, Elizabeth, and William Pennell.
1766, Nov. 27. Pennell, John, and Catharine Baton.
1765, Oct. 30. Pennell, Rebecca, and Thomas Walter.
1771, Apr. 17. Pennell, William, and Elizabeth Pennell.
1761, Apr. 13. Penner, Hannah, and Nathan Garnal.
1772, Dec. 5. Pennington, Charles, and Mary Beanor.
1770, Jan. 30. Pennington, John, and Mary Jemison.'
1763, Nov. 28. Pennington, Mary, and Isaac Smith.
1763, Feb. 26. Pennington, Paul, and Sarah Poole.
1744, June 20. Pennington, Thomas.
1761, Aug. 3. Pennington, William, and Mary Vickers.
1775, Jan. 9. Penn, Mary, and James Smith.
1762, Nov. 4. Pennock, Mary, and Joseph Yeates.
1767, Nov. 28. Pennyard, Matthias, and Dorcas Swinney.
1770, June 11. Pennyfeather, Dorothea, and Patrick Higgins.
1762, Oct. 23. Penny, Thomas, and Elizabeth Davis.
1764, Apr. 24. Penquite, Sarah, and Isaiah Walton.
1766, M'ch 15. Penrose, James, and Sarah Biddle.
1766, M'ch 25. Penrose, Mary, and Anthony Wayne.
1766, Apr. 3. Penrose, Samuel, and Ann Fleeson.
1767, Oct. 15. Penrose, Sarah, and Abram Robinson.
1764, M'ch 1. Penrose, Sarah, and Lester Falkner.
1774, May 26. Penty, William, and Ann Windkimer.
1764, June 21. Pepper, George, and Ann Paul.
1763, Nov. 28. Peppert, Sarah, and Frederick Grey.
1760, Dec. 24. Perkins, John, and Mary Lasy.
1772, May 13. Perkins, John, and Mary Woodward.
1766, Nov. 1. Perkins, Joseph, and Elizabeth Clare.
1766, Feb. 22. Perry, Elizabeth, and Adam Warburton.
1771, May 14. Perry, Elizabeth, and Robert Redhead.
1747, Nov. —. Perry, Jane, and Renier Lukins.
1746, June —. Perry, Sopher, and Elenor Joyner.
1760, Aug. 18. Pert, Elizabeth, and Benjamin Gilbert.

1765, May 1. Pesfer, Michael, and Elizabeth Simmon.
1748, May 14. Pessbear, Frederica, and Hannah Nicholas Burghard.
1765, Sep. 5. Peterkin, William, and Mary Braford.
1748, Oct. 18. Peters, Benjamin, and Dorothy Battin.
1747, Nov. —. Peters, Bridget, and Thomas Ellet.
1762, Apr. 24. Peters, Henry, and Elizabeth Ironfield.
1771, Aug. 8. Peters, Jacob, and Jane Jones.
1761, Nov. 11. Peters, Leah, and Henry Heist.
1772, Nov. 6. Peters, Margaret, and John McCullough.
1776, June 6. Peters, Mary, and Adam Lap.
1773, June 15. Peters, Mary, and Matthew Turner.
1773, Sep. 2. Peters, Moses, and Ruth Evans.
1767, Aug. 5. Peters, Mungrel, and Mary Evans.
1773, Apr. 13. Peters, Peter, and Sarah Bryan.
1743, Jan. 27. Peters, Rees.
1774, Feb. 16. Peters, Sarah, and George Thunn.
1744, June 20. Peterson, Andrew.
1774, Dec. 21. Peterson, Ann, and Thomas Coxe.
1774, July 14. Pettit, Elizabeth, and Edward Hines.
1770, June 21. Pen, Anne, and John Ogg.
1762, Jan. 23. Pen, Rachael, and Abraham Morris.
1768, July 9. Pen, Robert, and Mary Fullerton.
1772, Nov. 11. Peyton, William, and Mary Evans.
1747, May —. Pezoman, Catharine, and Charles Ewalts.
1766, Apr. 7. Phile, Daniel, and Elizabeth Evans.
1763, June 1. Philipinna, Margretta, and Nicholas Verkheiser.
1773, Oct. 4. Philips, Abigail, and Daniel McKay.
1772, July 13. Philips, Abigail, and Samuel McCormick.
1764, May 16. Philips, Anna, and William Campbell.
1769, Dec. 7. Philips, Anne, and David Parsell.
1773, Apr. 17. Philips, Catharine, and Nathan Sturgis.
1764, May 2. Philips, Charles, and Ann Jones.
1775, Oct. 27. Philips, Elijah, and Catharine Harvey.
1772, Oct. 31. Philips, Griffiths, and Ann Thomas.
1761, June 18. Pitt, William, and Cecily Frin.
1768, Aug. 1. Philips, John, and Christiana Bomin.
1762, Nov. 8. Philips, Jonathan, and Rachael Knight.
1773, Feb. 11. Philips, Joseph, and Elizabeth Johnston.
1773, Feb. 16. Philips, Letitia, and John Bissel.
1768, Aug. 17. Philips, Margaret, and Samuel Davis.
1746, Oct. —. Philips, Mary, and George Forster.
1747, Nov. —. Philips, Mary, and John Jones.
1770, May 23. Philips, Nathaniel, and Agnes Marsh.
1763, Sep. 5. Philips, Rachael, and James Berry.
1768, Jan. 13. Philips, Sarah, and William Harper.

1771, Aug. 29. Philips, Sybilla, and Jonathan Davis.
1743, May 24. Philips, Thomas.
1770, Feb. 21. Philips, William, and Abigail Taylor.
1764, Aug. 17. Philips, William, and Eleanor Cummins.
1760, July 18. Philipson, William, and Hannah Humphrey.
1774, Jan. 1. Phillaby, Ann, and Edward Bell.
1770, Apr. 3. Philler, Andrew, and Margaret Way.
1766, Apr. 9. Phillips, John, and Rebecca Pyewell.
1770, M'ch 28. Phillips, Joshua, and Sarah Davis.
1761, June 27. Phillis, Negro, and Negro Jack.
1762, June 10. Philmeyer, Margaret, and John Franks.
1746, June —. Philpot, John, and Ann Cuningham.
1747, M'ch —. Philpot, Phebe, and John Atkins.
1768, Nov. 4. Phillpot, Margaret, and Woodward Rawley.
1774, Oct. 19. Phipps, Elizabeth, and Aaron Allison.
1763, Dec. 12. Phipps, Esther, and Richard Crosby.
1763, Nov. 5. Phipps, Hannah, and George Aston.
1745, Aug. —. Phipps, John.
1748, Feb. —. Phipps, Mary, and Isaac Lewis.
1765, Aug. 30. Phipps, Prudence, and Robert Miller.
1771, May 27. Phipps, Sarah, and William Corbett.
1768, Aug. 17. Phyle, Dorothy, and George Heyl.
1745, Jan. —. Picke, John.
1770, May 11. Pickering, George, and Rebecca Channel.
1772, Apr. 9. Pickering, James, and Jane Casdrop.
1771, Feb. 6. Pickles, Sarah, and Benjamin Flower.
1767, M'ch 10. Pickworth, John, and Martha Holland.
1767, Oct. 28. Piercal, Dianna, and Thomas Kennety.
1770, Oct. 9. Pierce, Anne, and Charles Héwett.
1761, Sep. 30. Pierce, Hannah, and Caleb Buchan.
1761, Dec. 2. Pierce, James, and Hannah Way.
1760, Jan. 11. Pierce, John, and Margaret Wright.
1763, M'ch 1. Pierce, Rachel, and Richard Mitchell.
1763, Sep. 26. Pierce, Samuel, and Sarah Nicholson.
1768, Nov. 5. Piercy, Thomas, and Mary McClennon.
1744, Oct. —. Piles, Gabriel.
1772, Dec. 3. Piles, Mary, and Thomas Jann.
1761, Aug. 17. Pillager, Elizabeth, and Sebastian Heiler.
1769, Oct. 24. Pillager, John, and Rebecca Boyers.
1761, July 9. Pillages, Eve, and William Haslooch.
1760, Nov. 19. Pillet, Nathaniel, and Elinor Bankson
1764, Dec. 19. Pimley, Mary, and William McGlaughan.
1744, July 21. Pimm, John.
1761, Oct. 5. Pimple, Jacob, and Mary Stokes.
1762, Apr. 3. Pimple, Mary, and Francis Mills.
1744, M'ch —. Pine, Benjamin.

1772, Nov. 18. Pine, Elizabeth, and Matthew Whitehead.
1770, M'ch 22. Pine, John, and Elizabeth Broom.
1748, Sep. —. Pine, John, and Isabel Bruce.
1767, Oct. 7. Pine, John, and Rachel Burrow.
1773, Jan. 25. Pine, Sarah, and James Roberts.
1772, Oct. 6. Pines, Elizabeth, and William Bellamy.
1760 July 29. Pingard, Catharine, and John George.
1762, Feb. 27. Pinkerton, John, and Lydia Potts.
1770, Jan. 3. Pinkerton, William, and Anne Crosse.
1772, Feb. 29. Pinkstalk, Elizabeth, and George Wye.
1767, Apr. 2. Piniard, Eleanor, and John Sowder.
1769, Jan. 11. Pinniard, Mary, and William Ogden.
1764, May 4. Piper, Margaret, and William Kirkpatrick.
1774, June 6. Piper, Mary, and John Williams.
1773, Oct. 21. Pissant, Mary, and George Kurtz.
1747, Oct. —. Pitcairne, James, and Mary Rowoth.
1768, Oct. 25. Pitt, Ann, and John Koster.
1767, Jan. 29. Pitts, William, and Susannah Hillegas.
1772, June 13. Place, Frederick, and Ann Apple.
1775, Dec. 7. Plankinhorn, Jacob, and Miriam Mandlin.
1768, Apr. 6. Plankton, Peter, and Hannah Talkinton.
1760, June 24. Plaunyer, Elizabeth, and William Jacob Knight,
1775, Aug. 26. Pleasenton, Deborah, and Stephen Lewis.
1764, Feb. 16. Plimm, George, and Mary Shaw.
1748, June 16. Plins, George, and Mary Hastings.
1776, June 25. Pluck, George, and Catharine Wentz.
1775, Jan. 7. Puckrose, John, and Ann Lock.
1770, Nov. 28. Plumber, Rebecca, and Nicholas Nelson.
1761, Aug. 10. Plumer, Elizabeth, and Christian Vanhorn.
1764, M'ch 13. Plumley, Sarah, and Joseph Allen.
1762, M'ch 9. Plumley, Hannah, and James Grigg.
1762, M'ch 6. Plummer, William, and Jane Yardley.
1768, July 7. Plumsted, Mary, and James Willson.
1762, Aug. 13. Plumsted, Thomas, and Mary Coats.
1761, Aug. 11. Plum, John, and Catharine Waltrick.
1775, Feb. 2. Plunket, Alexander, and Mary Hoffman.
1774, Oct. 22. Plunket, Catharine, and Daniel Stonemotz.
1775, M'ch 28. Plunket, Robert, and Ann Dickinson.
1775, Nov. 1. Plunket, Sarah, and Henry Maag.
1764, Aug. 29. Poak, Isabella, and Alexander Jamison.
1763, Feb. 12. Poe, Martha, and Anthony Betting.
1772, Aug. 29. Poff, George, and Anne Merchant.
1763, Oct. 12. Pogh, John, and Elizabeth McMichael.
1764, Sep. 27. Pogue, John, and Catharine Porter.
1775, Jan. 25. Pogue, John, and Rachel Gilbert.
1759, Dec. 8. Poinyard, Martha, and John Taylor.

1772, Nov. 24. Poke, Robert, and Jane Crawford.
1773, Apr. 12. Polar, Peter, and Ann Studdin.
1761, Oct. 28. Poley, Samuel, and Isabella Winter.
1747, June —. Polgreen, Susannah, and Abram Hewlins.
1772, Sep. 11. Polim, William, and Rachel Hine.
1772, Sep. 8. Pollard, Elizabeth, and Daniel Cadden.
1765, Sep. 11. Pollard, William, and Mary Green.
1772, Apr. 11. Pollock, Catharine, and James McNeal.
1744, Sep. —. Polloy, George.
1767, M'ch 27. Polson, Jasper, and Agnes White.
1775, M'ch 17. Polton, Rachel, and Thomas Shaw.
1769, Oct. 10. Polumbo, Gaspero, and Susannah Ogle.
1769, Jan. 16. Pond, Hannah, and Josiah Shivers.
1760, Feb. 13. Poole, Catharine, and John Saxton.
1768, Apr. 20. Poole, Edward, and Mary Hair.
1764, July 2. Poole, James, and Hannah Keen.
1772, Dec. 3. Poole, Samuel, and Barbara Fandlin.
1775, Aug. 21. Poole, Sarah, and John North.
1763, Feb. 26. Poole, Sarah, and Paul Pennington.
1745, Aug. —. Poor, William.
1774, Apr. 30. Porpus, Mary, and Thurston Brown.
1770, Nov. 22. Port, Latitia, and Duddlestone Stocker Reese.
1764. Sep. 27. Porter, Catharine, and John Pogue.
1764, M'ch 30. Porter, Elizabeth, and Robert Miller.
1773, Oct. 13. Porterfield. Margaretta, and Alexander Douglass.
1765, Feb. 16. Porter, Jane, and James McCree.
1763, May 28. Porter, John, and Mary Shannon.
1761, Apr. 4. Porter, Lilly, and Andrew Willson.
1760, July 8. Porter, Lydia, and James Alexander.
1773, Sep. 21. Porter, Margaret, and William Bateman.
1768, Dec. 5. Porter, Martha, and Dennis Mullan.
1768, Sep. 28. Porter, Mary, and James Read.
1761, M'ch 16. Porter, Mary, and John Sales.
1766, Dec. 1. Porter, Richard, and Catharine Thecker.
1770, Aug. 31. Porter, Robert, and Elizabeth Watson.
1764, May 27. Porter, Robert, and Margaretta Lindsay.
1774, June 14. Porter, Stephen, and Mary Hart.
1746, Aug. —. Porter, Walker, and Sarah Hesselius.
1763, Jan. 6. Ports, Henry, and Catharine Cramrine.
1762, July 3. Poskell, John, and Mary Blanchfield.
1769, May 31. Posset, Nathan, and Mary Denny.
1767, Aug. 25. Post, Christian Frederick, and Margaret Miller.
1771, May 1. Post, Cornelius, and Mary Rees.
1768, July 13. Potter, David, and Mary Mason.
1747, June —. Potter, Levy, and Sarah Griffett.
1765, Dec. 23. Potter, Margaret, and Robert Bail.

1765, Jan. 10. Potter, Martha, and James Muhrell.
1761, Sep. 1. Potter, Mary, and Cornelius Hagan.
1768, June 3. Potter, Mary, and Robert Mack.
1764, Aug. 30. Potter, Matthew, and Jane Gillyatt.
1771, M'ch 23. Potts, Abigail, and William Coffing.
1762, May 24. Potts, Aquilla, and Martha Taylor.
1767, Jan. 10. Potts, David, and Mary Aris.
1766, Oct. 15. Potts, Deborah, and Caleb Hewes.
1774, Feb. 17. Potts, Elizabeth, and Andrew Kennedy.
1763, Sept. 10. Potts, Jacob, and Sarah Draper.
1764, Feb. 27. Potts, John, and Margaret Cormick.
1765, July 25. Potts, Joseph, and Meriam Kelly.
1762, Feb. 27. Potts, Lydia, and John Pinkerton.
1764, M'ch 14. Potts, Rebecca, and Nicholas Cox.
1772, Oct. 20. Potts, Samuel, and Sarah Fritts.
1764, Apr. 7. Potts, William, and Hester Moore.
1771, Jan. 4. Powel, Edward, and Mary Keyler.
1761, Apr. 29. Powel, George, and Mary Brunnery.
1769, Nov. 13. Powel, Hannah, and Thomas Warren.
1763, Mc'h 4. Powel, Margaretta, and William Johnson.
1770, Nov. 10. Powel, Martha, and Joseph Smith.
1767, Apr. 2. Powel. Rebecca, and Isaac Ashton.
1771, June 13. Powel, Samuel, and Elizabeth Coffin.
1766, May 17. Powel, Samuel, and Elizabeth Needom.
1765, Nov. 16. Powel, Sarah, and John Wilson.
1760, Sep. 1. Powel, Susannah and Edward Hanson.
1773, Dec. 27. Powel, Letitia, and David Jones.
1772, Dec. 4. Powell, Anna, and David Noble.
1745, Nov. —. Powell, David.
1748, May 14. Powell, Elizabeth, and Evan Rennall.
1769, Oct. . 2. Powell, George, and Hannah Ball.
1768, Oct. 26. Powell, Griffith, and Hannah Thomas.
1768, June 23. Powell, Isaac, and Sarah Rush.
1769, Nov. 2. Powell, John, and Sarah Willard.
1772, Oct, 17. Powell, Joseph, and Mary Ross.
1775, July 27. Powell, Letitia, and Joseph Webb.
1764, Jan. 6. Powell. Martha, and Thomas Overend.
1768, M'ch 31. Powell, Mary, and Douglass Ivory.
1763, Oct. 22. Powell, Ruth, and James Hudson.
1769, Aug. 5. Powell, Samuel, and Elizabeth Willing.
1770, Oct. 22. Powell, Thomas, and Mary Lee.
1765, Jan. 3. Powell, William, and Mary Thomas.
1744, June 12. Powelson, Peter.
1767, Dec. 24. Power, Alexander, and Mary Butterworth.
1760, Feb. 18. Power, Comfort, and William Scull.
1745, Aug. —. Power, John.

1766, M'ch 26. Power, John, and Deborah Meyers.
1761, July 30. Power, John, and Susan Reynolds.
1773, Dec. 9. Power, Joseph, and Anne Coleman.
1765, Aug. 12. Power, Susannah, and William Connor.
1775, May 17. Powers, Juliana, and Daniel Carroll.
1764, Nov. 29. Powlin, Sarah, and Patrick Willson.
1762, Aug. 31. Pratt, Ellenor, and Joseph Watkins.
1760, Aug. 26. Pratt, Matthew, and Elizabeth Moore.
1769, Feb. 13. Praul, Elizabeth, and Abraham Laren.
1766, Dec. 15. Prawl, Jane, and Arent Schuyler.
1762, Jan. 21. Prentice, John, and Priscilla Scull.
1771, Oct. 8. Prentice, Martha, and Hyman Saunders.
1773, Apr. 16. Presly, John, and Rosanna Henderson.
1760, Oct. 18. Preston, Elizabeth, and Robert Shepperd.
1770, M'ch 21. Preston, Hannah, and John Knowles.
1766, Sep. 1. Preston, John, and Catharine Cammel.
1743, M'ch 1. Preston, Joseph.
1776, Feb. 13. Preston, Manasseh, and Ann Ryan.
1765, Jan. 3. Preston, Mary, and George Baker.
1772, May 14. Preston, Richard Grafton, and Mary Lamb.
1748, Jan. —. Preston, Sarah, and Thomas William.
1766, June 4. Preston, William, and Elizabeth Scott.
1760, July 28. Preston, William, and Elizabeth Delavan.
1761. Dec. 31. Pretchard, Thomas, and Margaret Gunning.
1769, Dec. 30. Price, Anne, and Thomas Willson.
1743, M'ch 29. Price, Conrad.
1775, July 27. Price, Cornelia, and James Roshotham.
1747, June —. Price, Elizabeth, and Edward Smout.
1767, Dec. 14. Price, Elizabeth, and Peter Parker.
1773, May 1. Price, Elizabeth, and Samuel Purdy.
1746, Sep. —. Price, Eve, and Robert Hughes.
1766, Apr. 29. Price, Hannah, and Abraham Anderson.
1773, M'ch 10. Price, Hannah, and Samuel Carson.
1771, Dec. 18. Price, Hannah, and Samuel Davis.
1762, Sep. 1. Price, Hester, and James Craddock.
1744, Dec. —. Price, James.
1762, Oct. 9. Price, James, and Sarah Hendleston.
1761, M'ch 26. Price. Jane, and Robert Holland.
1760, Jan. 2. Price, Jeremiah, and Mary James.
1760, Dec. 29. Price, John, and Hannah Delaplaine.
1770, Nov. 19. Price, John Michael, and Anne Bowman.
1747, Aug. —. Price, John, and Sarah Jenkins.
1772, Dec. 28. Price, John, and Sarah Kentee.
1744, May —. Price, Joseph.
1770, Oct. 24. Price, Joseph, and Margaret Agnew.
1762, May 13. Price, Lewis, and Martha Pursell.

1747, Oct. —. Price, Lydia, and Joseph North.
1765, Oct. 30. Price, Rebecca, and James Monk.
1769, June 6. Price, Reese, and Hannah Roberts.
1744, Jan. —. Price, Robert.
1767, June 27. Price, Ruth, and George Thompson.
1744, Oct. —. Price, Samuel.
1771, May 30. Price, Sarah, and Abraham Evans.
1760, Oct. 30. Price, Sophia, and Charles Dougherty.
1745, May —. Price, William.
1769, Jan. 6. Price, William, and Elizabeth Woodward.
1773, June 28. Price, William, and Mary Allen.
1766, Oct. 4. Price, William, and Rebecca Jobs.
1747, June —. Prichard, Elizabeth, and Lewellin Davis.
1747, Sep. —. Prichard, Griffith, and Mary Jones.
1746, Apr. —. Prichard, James.
1768, June 10. Prichard, Joseph, and Judith Hughes.
1743, Sep. —. Prichard, Rees.
1775, July 25. Pricket, Mary, and Jacob Sharp.
1776, Jan. 31. Priest, George, and Phebe Evans.
1762, Nov. 6. Priest, Robert, and Hannah Marshall.
1765, Apr. 29. Prigg, Hannah, and Jacob Corse.
1747, June. —. Prigg, William, and Margaret Harper.
1769, Jan. 11. Prince, Elizabeth, and John Balson.
1773, May 18. Pringle, John, and Catharine Lake.
1763, Nov. 15. Prior, Ann, and Charles Massey.
1763, Dec. 6. Prior, Charles, and Margery Benson.
1764, Sep. 25. Prior, John, and Elizabeth Roberts.
1766, June 18. Prior, Samuel, and Elizabeth Gilbert.
1746, June —. Priscot, Harriet, and Thomas Lake.
1771, Jan. 31. Pritchard, Ann, and Gasper Guyger.
1760, Oct. 27. Pritchard, John, and Rachel Green.
1773, Dec. 1. Pritchard, Mary, and Alexander McCarragher.
1763, Nov. 23. Pritchard, William, and Isabella Gray.
1762, Nov. 18. Proby, Jacob, and Ann Steward.
1776, Feb. 19. Proctor, Francis, and Ann Henderson.
1766, Dec. 31. Proctor, Thomas, and Mary Fox.
1765, Aug. 20. Proctor, Joshua, and Margaret Green.
1774, Jan. 4. Proctor, Mary, and Nathan Jones.
1765, Apr. 10. Proudfoot, John, and Catharine Neiss.
1769, Aug. 31. Provost, David, and Sarah Boulton Loftus.
1744, Nov. —. Prugh, Thomas.
1776, Feb. 6. Pryer, Eleanor, and John Fitzpatrick.
1771, Jan. 5. Pryer, Laetitia, and Samuel Massey.
1768, Apr. 18. Pugh, Catharine, and Benjamin Davis.
1759, Dec. 19. Pugh, Daniel, and Rebecca Thomas.
1765, Jan. 8. Pugh, Hannah, and David Mathias.

1763, Nov. 9. Pugh, Henry, and Mary Jones.
1768, Oct. 29. Pugh, Hugh, and Mary Cyder.
1764, M'ch 27. Pugh, Jane, and Robert Evans.
1763, May 11. Pugh, Samuel, and Amy Evans.
1763, Sep. 3. Pugh, Sarah, and Enos Miles.
1761, Aug. 21. Pugh, Thomas, and Elizabeth Evans.
1774, Nov. 22. Pugh, Thomas. and Elizabeth Tresse.
1760, Oct. 30. Puligher, Daniel, and Rebecca Shea.
1772, Feb. 20. Pump, Nicholas, and Elizabeth Dutton.
1763, Nov. 24. Purcell, James, and Sarah Stewart.
1748, Sep. —. Purcell, William, and Margaret Kirby.
1747, Oct. —. Purce, Rachel, and William Davis.
1765, July 26. Purchess, Mary, and Henry Hill.
1762, Oct. 29. Purden, Fergus, and Abigail Little.
1762, Dec. 14. Purdon, John, and Mary Hutchinson.
1770, June 2. Purdy, Folliard, and Margaret Slack.
1765, May 14. Purdy, Mary, and John Ramsey.
1773, May 1. Purdy, Samuel, and Elizabeth Price.
1764, Apr. 20. Purfield, Andrew, and Sarah Farmer.
1772, Dec. 18. Pursell, Ann, and Thomas Rue.
1763, M'ch 1. Pursell, Jane, and John Scott.
1762, May 13. Pursell, Martha, and Lewis Price.
1776, June 29. Purser, Peter, and Jane Dugan.
1769, Apr. 25. Purviance, Juliana, and Isaac Hazlehurst.
1768, M'ch 23. Pyatt, Jane, and Thomas Roberts.
1774, Feb. 14. Pyatt, Sarah, and William Vanderman.
1761, Oct. 10. Pyewell, John, and Mary Garret.
1766, Apr. 9. Pyewell, Rebecca, and John Phillips.
1748, July 13. Pyles, Elizabeth, and Robert Ladner.
1770, Dec. 20. Pyles, John, and Mary Hall.
1770, Dec. 15. Pyles, Sarah, and Benjamin Woods.
1761, June 27. Pyne, Benjamin, and Elizabeth Edgar.
1772, Dec. 22. Pyot, James, and Rosanna Kearnes.
1748, Nov. 11. Pywell, Ann, and John Carson.

Q.

1767, June 5. Quainter, John, and Susannah Miller.
1760, Jan. 19. Quamany, John, and Rose Guinett.
1768, June 25. Quay, Mary, and Robert Slocombe.
1773, M'ch 6. Quee, John, and Susannah Kotman.
1767, Aug. 12. Quicksall, Newille, and Jacob Lowry.
1767, Oct. 10. Quig, Catharine, and James Huston.
1766, Jan. 3. Quigg, Ann, and Samuel Couch.
1773, Dec. 3. Quigley, Hugh, and Mary Maddin.
1766, May 26. Quigley, Isaac, and Jane Coleman.
1771, Apr. 16. Quimby, Phebe, and Ambrus Barcroft.

1744, Oct. —. Quin, Charles.
1765, Sep. 28. Quin, Francis, and Jane Kennedy.
1743, Dec. —. Quin, James.
1764, Dec. 10. Quin, Jane, and Patrick Archdearon.
1772, Nov. 25. Quin, Thomas, and Theodosia Harvey.
1746, July —. Quinn, Nicholas, and Esther Garwood.
1774, Dec. 6. Quirk, Mary, and Philip Gill.

R.

1770, M'ch 17. Rabhoore, John, and Sophia Collins.
1775, July 29. Race, Agnes, and Andrew McCormick.
1760, Nov. 3. Race, Elizabeth, and John Serett.
1773, Oct. 23. Raddon, William, and Frances Rudy.
1761, July 24. Radford, Ann, and John Mathers.
1746, Dec. —. Radley, Mary, and Thomas Jarrant.
1770, July 28. Rainbow, Michael, and Catharine Cook.
1770, Aug. 28. Rainbow, Peter, and Martha Thomas.
1767, July 22. Raine, Mary, and John Martin.
1769, July 11. Rainholt, Christiana, and James Bennet.
1776, M'ch 5. Rakestraw, Bevan, and Susannah Paul.
1775, Oct. 31. Ralston, John, and Catharine Miller.
1768, Apr. 8. Rambo, Alice, and Edward Roberts.
1747, June —. Rambo, Ann, and Jacob Lincoln.
1774, Jan. 15. Rambo, Ann, and Joseph Taylor.
1766, Nov 27. Rambo, Ann. and William Todd.
1762, Oct. 23. Rambo, Daniel, and Susannah Harvey.
1745, Apr. —. Rambo, Elias.
1760, Nov. 7. Rambo, Elizabeth, and Allen Kilheart.
1764, June 20. Rambo, Elizabeth, and David Davis.
1775, M'ch 30. Rambo, Elizabeth, and Isaac Worrell.
1773, Oct. 30. Rambo, Elizabeth, and Robert Binnington.
1748, Oct. 18. Rambo, Ezekiel, and Elizabeth Holstein.
1765, Jan. 16. Rambo, Jeremiah, and Sarah Rambo.
1764, June 16. Rambo, John, and Elizabeth Craton.
1772, June 16. Rambo, Mary, and Joseph Woodfield.
1772, Nov. 17. Rambo, Peter, and Ann James.
1765, Jan. 16. Rambo, Sarah, and Jeremiah Rambo.
1747, Feb. —. Rambo, ———, and the Swedish Minister.
1774, M'ch 7. Rambo, Tobias, and Margaret Faries.
1770, Oct. 30. Ramsay, Alexander, and Martha Dunbar.
1768, Dec. 6. Ramsay, James, and Honour Lee.
1774, Sep. 17. Ramsen, Michah, and Philip Siplay.
1763, Oct. 12. Ramsey, Francis, and Jane O'Donald.
1762, Dec. 14. Ramsey, Giles, and Mary Rice.
1766, Dec. 20. Ramsey, John, and Eleanor Henderson.
1765, May 14. Ramsey, John, and Mary Purdy.

1767, Apr. 9. Ramsey, Thomas, and Mary Hall.
1768, Dec. 2. Ramshaw, Benjamin, and Catharine Hutchinson.
1762, Aug. 12. Ramshear, Benjamin, and Elizabeth Champshear.
1771, Dec. 14. Ramsower, Elizabeth, and Edward Moore.
1760, Aug. 20. Ranbury, Mary, and William Furris.
1774, Feb. 26. Randall, James, and Pleasant Veasy.
1770, June 25. Randall, Thomas, and Hester Leech.
1762, Nov. 3. Randell, Elizabeth, and William Stoodell.
1766, June 16. Randell, Sarah, and James Kendall.
1775, Sep. 12. Randle, Elizabeth, and Thomas Paxton.
1774, June 18. Randle, George, and Sarah Brooks.
1746, M'ch —. Randle, John.
1775, M'ch 22. Randle, Mary, and Jonathan Harding.
1774, Aug. 23. Randle, Richard, and Mary Reed.
1763, Jan. 15. Randle, Sarah, and Joshua Mitchel.
1762, Feb. 18. Randolph, Benjamin, and Ann Brummage.
1744, Apr. —. Rankin, James.
1773, Apr. 26. Rankin, Jane, and Hugh Kidd.
1764, July 18. Rankin, Joseph, and Margaret Carson.
1767, Aug. 20. Rankin, Sarah, and John Murray.
1775, Nov. 25. Rankin, Sarah, and Robert Cornwall.
1775, Aug. 31. Ranstead, Elizabeth, and William Lewis.
1760, Aug. 7. Ranton, James, and Elizabeth Johnson.
1774, July 6. Rasberry, John, and Mary Fox.
1770, Oct. 13. Rasbon Catharine and Frederick Miller.
1771, May 20. Rash, Nicholas, and Judith Empson.
1770, Dec. 5. Ratcliff, Rebecca, and David Gladding.
1761, Sep. 25. Ratelis, James, and Garrat Glidding.
1769, Nov. 8. Ratten, Hannah, and Edward Hicks.
1771, July 23. Ravenhill, Francis, and Anna Nicklin.
1760, Dec. 6. Rawle, Robert, and Mary Macky.
1768, Nov. 4. Rawley, Woodward, and Margaret Phillpot.
1764, June 1. Rawlins, Benjamin, and Mary Dunnawin.
1748, Oct. 18. Ray, Matthew, and Sarah Harmen.
1765, Apr. 6. Read, Agnes, and William Conner.
1773, Jan. 26. Read, Ann, and Joshua Fanning.
1774, Dec. 22. Read Ann and Thomas Davison.
1763, Dec. 28. Read, Ann, and Thomas White.
1767, Aug. 26. Read, Charles, and Ann Branin.
1773, Jan. 5. Read, Collinson, and Mary McFunn.
1770, Nov. 27. Read, Henry, and Alice Turner.
1769, Aug. 24. Read, Hugh, and Mary Dowell.
1745, M'ch —. Read, James.
1764, Aug. 1. Read, James, and Elizabeth Cather.
1768, Sep. 28. Read, James, and Mary Porter.
1770, July 9. Read, James, and Susannah Currey.

1767, Dec. 11. Read, John, and Agnes Jones.
1763, Dec. 13. Read, John, and Jane Row.
1768, May   2. Read, John William, and Mary Lamany.
1762, July 10. Read, Margaret, and Joseph Edwards.
1767, Aug.   6. Read, Mary, and Philip Ross.
1764, Feb.   2. Read, Samuel, and Mary Wilder.
1761, Dec. 11. Read, William, and Elizabeth Chambers.
1762, Nov. 15. Reading, John, and Margaret Johnson.
1761, M'ch 18. Reading, Susan, and William Isaac.
1761, Aug. 10. Real, Catharine, and Charles Jones.
1773, Jan.   8. Reamer, Anna Margaret, and Jacob Baar.
1765, Oct. 30. Rearden, Ann, and Andrew Fitzsimmons.
1761, Nov. 11. Reckey, Mary, and John Darbyshire.
1766, Apr. 15. Redgrave, Ann, and John Taylor.
1769, M'ch   6. Redhead, Jonathan, and Catharine Carsonbury.
1771, May 14. Redhead, Robert, and Elizabeth Perry.
1771, June   5. Redman, Sarah, and Daniel Coxe.
1768, M'ch   3. Redman, Wallaston, and Catharine Clark.
1765, May 20. Redmond, Margaret, and John Bennet.
1773, Oct.   9. Redmond, Philip, and Hannah Kimmons.
1764, Aug.   8. Reed, Andrew, and Elizabeth Jenny.
1775, M'ch 18. Reed, Elizabeth, and John Seringar.
1769, June 20. Reed, Jane, and Joy Castle.
1748, Apr. 13. Reed, Jane, and William Allen.
1773, May   5. Reed, Leonard, and Elizabeth Fritz.
1774, Aug. 23. Reed, Mary, and Richard Randle.
1763, May 17. Reed, Sarah, and John Heath.
1767, Feb. 11. Reed, Thomas, and Jane Hill.
1767, Jan. 21. Reed, Thomas, and Mary Malaun.
1775, Dec. 19. Reed, William, and Mary Green.
1769, Nov.   6. Reeder, Benjamin, and Elizabeth Harvey.
1761, July 29. Reeder, George, and Catharine Keeler.
1766, Sep.   4. Reeney, Jane, and William Jones.
1743, Dec. —. Rees, Daniel.
1762, Oct. 14. Rees, Daniel, and Sarah Connely.
1773, Nov. 24. Rees, David, and Elizabeth Cobourn.
1770, Dec.   1. Rees, Eupharmia, and Joseph Gilbert.
1762, May 29. Rees, Elizabeth, and Isaac Lewis.
1748, Mc'h 11. Rees, Elizabeth, and Lewis Lewis.
1747, Nov. —. Rees, Hannah, and Samuel Jones.
1769, Feb. 28. Rees, John, and Jane Lindsay.
1768, June 25. Rees, John, and Mary Moore.
1771, May   1. Rees, Mary, and Cornelius Post.
1746, June —. Rees, Mary, and John Thaw.
1762, Dec. 13. Reese, Catharine, and Philip Truckenmiller.
1770, Nov. 22. Reese, Duddlestone Stocker, and Latitia Port.

1777, Aug. 22. Reese, Hannah, and Bowyer Brooke.
1763, Apr. 11. Reese, Hannah, and Nicholas Miller.
1774, Dec. 3. Reese, Mary, and Balthazar Emrick.
1763, Sep. 30. Reese, Melvin, and Violet Wilson.
1765, Oct. 25. Reese, Rachel, and John Salter.
1774, Oct. 12. Reeve, Elizabeth, and William Calvely.
1775, Dec. 18. Reeve, Nehemiah, and Ruth Small.
1743, June 11. Reeves, Benjamin.
1769, June 8. Reeves, John, and Sarah Patterson.
1760, July 23. Reeves, Stephen, and Elizabeth Edgecombe.
1774, May 31. Regan, Catharine, and James Mincuar.
1768, Oct. 7. Register, David, and Margaret Black.
1761, Nov. 11. Register, Hannah, and Joseph Edwards.
1748, M'ch 11. Reid, Thomas, and Margaret Davies.
1769, Sep. 1. Reily, Patrick, and Anne Brockington.
1764, Jan. 30. Reily, Ann, and Thomas Cahange.
1745, Oct. —. Reily, Charles.
1766, Oct. 1. Reily, Elizabeth, and Baltzer Cole.
1773, Apr. 22. Reily, Isaac, and Lydia Davis.
1747, Oct. —. Reily, John, and Mary Hillhouse.
1746, Feb. —. Reily, Joshua.
1765, Dec. 11. Reily, Mary, and Henry Burnet.
1765, Apr. 10. Reily, Sarah, and John Ross.
1763, M'ch 15. Reinhart, Eliza, and Moses Marshall.
1773, Oct. 1. Reinhart, John, and Barbara Wrax.
1775, Apr. 10. Reinhart, Nicholas, and Ann Stenner.
1760, Dec. 15. Reinholden, Garret, and Henry Smith.
1777, July 27. Reinholdt, Elizabeth, and Gilbert Carmack.
1770, July 30. Rienholdt George, and Mary Colbert.
1775, Aug. 10. Reinholdt, Mary Elizabeth, and Henry Wynkoop.
1761, June 16. Reinwalton, Susan, and David Grebble.
1776, M'ch 5. Relfe, Rachel, and Henry Ward Pearce.
1760, M'ch 3. Relf, John, and Rachel Francis.
1768, July 15. Relin, Rebecca, and John Kene.
1764, Apr. 14. Rell, John, and Elizabeth Winson.
1762, Apr. 22. Remberger, John, and Mary Bourim.
1773, Dec. 29. Remmey, Margaret, and John McPharland.
1770, Dec. 6. Renandet, Elizabeth, and John Deekman.
1776, Jan. 2. Rench, James, and Deborah Stubbs.
1769, M'ch 21. Rein, Christopher, and Anne Moore.
1762, July 3. Renn, Frederick, and Catharine Miller.
1763, Apr. 14. Renshaw, Elizabeth, and Isaac Janvier.
1768, June 16. Renshaw, Martha, and John Scott.
1774, Sep. 28. Renshaw, Rebecca, and Humphrey Williams.
1771, Apr. 16. Renshaw, Richard, Jr., and Anne Young.
1760, Dec. 26. Renshaw, Sarah, and Titus Matlock.

1764, Nov. 29. Rentzel, Hannah, and John Warner.
1762, Feb. 16. Replin, Juday, and James Reynolds.
1763, Aug. 5. Repson, Jacob, and Cleopha Seize.
1763, Oct. 5. Reser, Balser, and Catharine Colloby.
1764, Mc'h 28. Rew, Rachael, and Joseph Stackhouse.
1761, Nov. 19. Rey, George Michael, and Elizabeth Lyttle.
1770, M'ch 10. Reynolds, Anne. and Thomas Williamson.
1760, Sep. 17. Reynolds, Sarah, and Joseph Glascowstine.
1765, Sep. 14. Reynolds, Edward, and Mary Haney.
1762, Feb. 16. Reynolds, James, and Juday Replin.
1764, M'ch 16. Reynolds, James, and Mary Ross.
1763, Feb. 4. Reynolds, James, and Susannah Whitefield.
1763, July 16. Reynolds, Jane, and James Chapman.
1773, M'ch 23. Reynolds, John, and Charlotte Whittle.
1764, Sep. 24. Reynolds, John, and Elizabeth Alce.
1774, Jan. 1. Reynolds, John, and Sarah Gardner.
1770, Nov. 7. Reynolds, Lydia, and Thomas Marll.
1762, Feb. 25. Reynolds, Rush, and William Wills.
1761, July 30. Reynolds, Susan, and John Power.
1773, M'ch 19. Rhinehard, Henry, and Margaret Teaney.
1764, Feb. 20. Rhinehart, Catharine, and David Gable.
1765, Jan. 11. Rhine, Susannah, and Jacob Neidolf.
1762, Apr. 20. Rhinewald, Christopher, and Mary Master.
1765, M'ch 1. Rhoades, Elizabeth, and John McMullin.
1768, Nov. 22. Rhoads, Elizabeth, and George Lowra.
1773, Jan. 9. Rhoads, John, and Mary Thompson.
1762, May 1. Roads, Joseph, and Ann Jackson.
1772, April 9. Rhoads, Nathan, and Sarah Stradler.
1771, Apr. 9. Rhoads, Sarah, and Nathan Thomas.
1776, Apr. 24, Rhodes, John, and Hannah Lawther.
1743, Sep. —. Rhoofe, Jacob.
1771, Jan. 22. Riale, John, and Anne Rowland.
1766, Oct. 31. Rialt, Mary, and John Iwyer.
1771, Apr. 16· Rice, Edward, and Hannah Barcroft.
1772, Sep. 28. Rice, Elizabeth, and John Glayer.
1771, Sep. 21. Rice, George, and Eleanor Skelton.
1765, May 20. Rice, James, and Rebecca Morberry.
1772, Oct. 10. Rice, John, and Elizabeth Montgomery.
1772, M'ch 20. Rice, John, and Rachel Ball.
1765, Aug. 24. Rice, John, and Rachel Worthington.
1771, Aug. 22. Rice, Joseph, and Ann Currey.
1769, Apr. 4. Rice, Joseph, and Sarah Robbins.
1762, Dec. 14. Rice, Mary, and Giles Ramsey.
1772, July 23. Rice, Mary, and William Fians.
1769, May 13. Rice, Susannah, and Henry Fraley.
1776, Apr. 6. Rice, Thomas, and Penelope Justis.

1773, Feb. 9. Rich, Isaac, and Ruth Holton.
1761, May 27. Rich, Tamar, and John McCalla.
1775, Nov. 18. Richards, Charles, and Sarah Clark.
1764, June 20. Richards, Elizabeth, and David Parry.
1767, Aug 3. Richards, Ellis, and Machael Harbert.
1761, Sep. 10. Richards, John, and Alice Tuff.
1760, Oct. 21. Richards, Mary, and Jesse Chew.
1775, Sep. 4. Richards, Mary, and William Eachus.
1761, Dec. 17. Richards, Nathaniel, and Hannah Evans.
1769, June 19. Ricardson, David, and Anne McCasland.
1762, Jan. 7. Ricardson, Debrough, and Lewis Lewis.
1771, Feb. 5. Ricardson, Edmund, and Elizabeth Lycon.
1773, Nov. 13. Ricardson, Elizabeth, and Charles Hamilton.
1748, May 14. Richardson, Elizabeth, and Richard Busly.
1761, Feb. 10. Richardson, Elizabeth, and William Willman.
1773, Jan. 29. Richardson, Hannah, and Samuel Betson.
1774, Nov. 20. Richardson, Hannah, and Samuel Fairlamb.
1761, Oct. 7. Richardson, Jane, and William George.
1763, Apr. 1. Ricardson, John, and Hannah Darry.
1770, Sep. 27. Richardson, John, and Lydia Baker.
1773, Feb. 27. Richardson, Jonathan, and Margaret Howey.
1773, July 24. Richardson, Mary, and Michael Joseph Letellier.
1773, July 14. Richardson, Rachel, and Ephraim Jones.
1744, Apr. —. Richardson, Thomas.
1762, Apr. 29. Richards, Rachel, and Enoch James.
1747, Oct. —. Richards, Rebecca, and Theophilus Grew.
1770, June 4. Richards, Sarah, and Jacob Hughes.
1764, Apr. 18. Richards, Sarah, and Thomas Harrison.
1767, Apr. 22. Richards, Sarah, and William Connell.
1759, Dec. 1. Richards, William, and Ann Mercer.
1766, May 12. Richards, William, and Jane Baird.
1769, Dec. 16. Richey, Adam, and Rebecca Taylor.
1761, July 21. Richey, John, and Sarah Linn.
1774, June 14. Richi, Martha, and Abraham Hollis.
1745, June —. Richy, David.
1746, Dec. —. Richy, Margaret, and John Harper.
1760, Dec. 4. Rickets, Rose, and John Steward.
1772, June 26. Ricketts, Nathaniel, and Hannah Barthot.
1770, Sep. 8. Rickey, Alexander, and Hester Coates.
1766, M'ch 26. Rick, Mary, and Peter Adams.
1770, Dec. 3. Riddell, George, and Anne Freight.
1763, June 21. Riddle, James, and Jane Hall.
1770, June 7. Ridge, Daniel, and Mary-McLaughlan.
1770, Apr. 25. Ridge, Hannah, and William Marshall.
1770, Dec. 5. Ridge, John, and Sarah Britton.
1776, M'ch 26. Ridgeway, Allen, and Phebe Ridgeway.

1776, M'ch 26. Ridgeway, Phebe, and Allen Ridgeway.
1764, Feb. 15. Rife, George, and Elizabeth Hendricks.
1767, Aug. 10. Rifflin, Maria Sarah, and Edward Jones.
1771, Apr. 11. Rigger, Margaret, and James Leonard.
1746, Nov. —. Righter, George, and Elizabeth Cumree.
1773, M'ch 25. Righter, Hannah, and George Fetter.
1771, Sep. 12. Rigley, Joseph, and Rebecca Deacon.
1761, Oct. 7 Rill, Catharine, and Conrad Schiver.
1743, Dec. —. Rill, William.
1770, Sep. 1. Rilling, George, and Mary Miller.
1761, M'ch 9. Rilph, James, and Hannah Morris.
1775, June 7. Rinedollar, Mary, and Richard Ennis.
1760, M'ch 17. Ring, Conrad, and J. P. Brook.
1748, M'ch 11. Ringer, John, and Anna Maria Nesen.
1771, Jan. 19. Ringrose, John, and Margaret Crozier.
1772, July 8. Rinn, Mary and John Thomas.
1761, Sep. 17. Riplee, Mary, and John Odenheimer.
1760, July 5. Ripton, Mary, and William Appleton.
1772, Apr. 30. Risk, Charles, and Rebecca Boggs.
1771, M'ch 2. Ritchards, Susannah, and John Taney.
1762, Jan. 19. Ritchel, Catharine, and Aaron Hassard.
1764, Nov. 15. Ritche, Martha, and Thomas Kerr.
1768, Jan. 12. Ritche, Mary, and Alexander Searshill.
1768, Apr. 23. Ritchey, Martha, and Samuel Moon.
1763, Feb. 8. Ritchie, Elizabeth, and Daniel Ashton.
1772, May 23. Ritchie, Elizabeth, and Jacob Tyce.
1762, Dec. 23. Ritchie, Joseph, and Mary Handy.
1762, Nov. 24. Ritchie, Rachel, and William Skinner.
1771, Feb. 27. Ritchie, Robert, and Helena Smith.
1763, May 9. Ritchison, Elizabeth, and William Roberts.
1763, Nov. 23. Ritchison, Sarah, and John Thompson.
1770, Dec. 26. Rittenhouse, Benjamin, and Elizabeth Bull.
1772, Dec. 31. Rittenhouse, David, and Hannah Jacobs.
1768, June 6. Rittenhouse, Mary, and Thomas Morgan.
1761, Sep. 12. Rivercome, Justice, and Sarah Gibbs.
1775, Jan. 4. Rivers, Sarah, and John Cockshott.
1774, Jan. 25. Roach, Isaac, and Martha Schanlan.
1776, June 4. Roach, John, and Margaret Moore.
1766, Dec. 11. Roadt, Mary Eve, and Peter Warner.
1760, Nov. 10. Roak, Margaret, and Thomas Callender.
1769, Apr. 4. Robbins, Sarah, and Joseph Rice.
1761, July 28. Robart, Peter, and Mary Martin.
1769, June 24. Roberts, Abigail, and John Esserwine.
1770, May 31. Roberts, Anne, and John Griffins.
1770, Apr. 14. Roberts, Anne, and Nicholas Hugh.

14—VOL. II.

1747, Dec. —. Roberts, Ann, and Morris Groves.
1760, Sep. 3. Roberts, Bradford, and Ann Irish.
1776, May 11. Roberts, Catharine, and John Brooks.
1747, Dec. —. Roberts, Catharine, and Thomas Spergis.
1776, Feb. 16. Roberts, Catharine, and William Nelson.
1764, Apr. 9. Roberts, Charles, and Hannah Norberry.
1748, Aug. 15. Roberts, David.
1768, Apr. 8. Roberts, Edward, and Alice Rambo.
1774, M'ch 24. Roberts, Elizabeth, and Abel Thomas.
1769, Sep. 9. Roberts, Elizabeth, and Christopher Cornelius.
1772, M'ch 26. Roberts, Elizabeth, and Jacob Weiss, Jun.
1767, Oct. 1. Roberts, Elizabeth, and John Baker.
1764, Sep. 25. Roberts, Elizabeth, and John Prior.
1762, Sep. 20. Roberts, Elizabeth, and Joseph Keith.
1773, M'ch 17. Roberts, Elizabeth, and Joseph Marple.
1764, Nov. 1. Roberts, Elizabeth, and Samuel Indicot.
1760, Nov. 22. Roberts, Elizabeth, and Tunnis Titus.
1770, Dec. 26. Roberts, Esther, and Jonathan Palmer.
1774, M'ch 15. Roberts, Francis, and Ann Long.
1774, Aug. 2. Roberts, Hannah, and James Wills.
1772, Aug. 20. Roberts, Hannah, and John Malcolm.
1762, Nov. 25. Roberts, Hannah, and John Simpson.
1769, June 6. Roberts, Hannah, and Reese Price.
1772, Aug. 14. Roberts, Hannah, and Thomas Edwards.
1767, M'ch 21. Roberts, Jacob, and Mary Gill.
1770, Jan. 26. Roberts, James, and Mary Fuller.
1773, Jan. 25. Roberts, James, and Sarah Pines.
1775, Nov 25. Roberts, Jane, and Benjamin Sutch.
1746, Dec. —. Roberts, John, and Catharine Monny.
1761, May 12. Roberts, John, and Elizabeth Edwards.
1775, May 3. Roberts, John, and Hannah Larriall.
1765, June 26. Roberts, John, and Susannah Davis.
1764, Dec. 1. Roberts, Jonathan, and Ann Starr.
1761, July 31. Roberts, Joseph, and Mary Bark.
1762, Nov. 13. Roberts, Martha, and Anthony Bolton.
1774, Jan. 3. Roberts, Mary, and John Barrow.
1776, June 18. Roberts, Mary, and Thomas Nixon.
1760, July 31. Roberts, Mary. and William Sickle.
1748, July 13. Roberts, Mercy, and John Denton.
1743, June 27. Roberts, Phinehas.
1747, Feb. —. Roberts, Robert, and Margaretta Lucars.
1761, M'ch 11. Roberts, Ruth, and Jonathan Wells.
1761, M'ch 21. Roberts, Samuel, and Ann Jewell.
1763, M'ch 29. Roberts, Samuel, and Mary Eastburn
1762, July 28. Roberts, Sarah, and Henry Miller.
1763, Sep. 15. Roberts, Sarah, and Isaac Thomas.

1775, M'ch 16. Roberts, Susannah, and Lewis Thomas.
1769, July 24. Roberts, Tacey, and Benjamin Jones.
1766, June 14. Roberts, Tacy, and John Palmer.
1763, Apr. 23. Roberts, Thomas, and Jane Pyatt.
1762, Dec. 8. Roberts, Thomas, and Mary For.
1772, Apr. 4. Roberts, Timothy, and Mary James.
1763, May 9. Roberts, William, and Elizabeth Ritchison.
1760, July 23. Roberts, William, and Hannah Delavan.
1775, M'ch 29. Roberts, William, and Mary Towers.
1760, July 26. Roberts, William, and Rachel Griffiths.
1767, M'ch 9. Robertson, Daniel, and Mary McGloachlon.
1772, July 10. Robertson, Patrick, and Catharine Adams.
1765, Aug. 16. Robertson, Robertson, and Elizabeth Thomas.
1768, Jan. 23. Robertson, Patrick, and Mary McPherson.
1775, Nov. 28. Robeson, Ann, and Charles Newman.
1761, June 3. Robeson, John, and Martha Campbell.
1764, June 5. Robeson, Margaret, and Henry Robinson.
1772, Dec. 2. Robeson, Thomas, and Ann Talbert.
1773, Apr. 1. Robeson, William, and Elizabeth Miller.
1766, Sep. 6. Robinet, Rebecca, and Henry Dickson.
1775, Sep. 28. Robinet, Susannah, and Samuel Cannel.
1771, June 17. Robins, John, and Elizabeth James.
1768, Oct. 15. Robins, Joseph, and Jane Hoops.
1774, Feb. 17. Robins, Margaret, and Hastings Stackhouse.
1775, Oct. 25. Robins, Margaret, and John Scott.
1764, July 19. Robins, Mary, and Henry McAdams.
1768, Nov. 29. Robins, Mary, and William Taylor.
1773, July 19. Robinson, Abraham, and Rebecca Connoly.
1767, Oct. 15. Robinson, Abram, and Sarah Penrose.
1744, Jan. —. Robinson, Alexander.
1765, Apr. 23. Robinson, Alexander, and Ann Jameson.
1771, Oct. 12. Robinson, Ann, and William Lawrence.
1763, Jan. 24. Robinson, Barbara, and William Lawrence.
1775, Jan. 5. Robinson, Charles, and Ann Holsten.
1775, Feb. 3. Robinson, Daniel, and Margaret Thowtissel.
1764, Aug. 23. Robinson, Edward, and Phebe Colton.
1759, Dec. 21. Robinson, Elinor, and Samuel Gambies.
1763, Dec. 19. Robinson, Elizabeth, and George Kemble.
1773, Oct. 27. Robinson, Elizabeth, and Joseph Tyson.
1773, Sep. 3. Robinson, Elizabeth, and Nicholas Stackhouse.
1747, Sep. —. Robinson, Elizabeth, and William Jones.
1773, Sep. 14. Robinson, Francis, and Ann Pancoast.
1764, Sep. 6. Robinson, George, and Mary Harper.
1764, June 5. Robinson, Henry, and Margaret Robeson.
1766, Sep. 9. Robinson, Henry, and Rebecca Garrigues.
1764, Feb. 20. Robinson, James, and Jane McBrier.

1772, Jan. 21. Robinson, James, and Mary Davis.
1768, Nov. 10. Robinson, James, and Rachel Higgins.
1775, M'ch 31. Robinson, John, and Mary Comley.
1774, May 3. Robinson, Margaret, and Cornelius Hillman.
1760, Feb. 15. Robinson, Margaret, and John Johnston.
1769, Nov. 22. Robinson, Margaret, and John McMurtry.
1766, Apr. 16. Robinson, Mary, and John Cook.
1770, Dec. 6. Robinson, Mary, and Michael Chew.
1770, Apr. 23. Robinson, Mary, and Samuel Workman.
1765, Oct. 4. Robinson, Mary, and Thomas Downy.
1765, Oct. 1. Robinson, Mellesim, and James Walker.
1771, Nov. 28. Robinson, Priscilla, and Josiah Davis.
1748, Nov. 11. Robinson, Rachel, and David Moffit.
1766, Nov. 17. Robinson, Rebecca, and Luke Shield.
1769, Sep. 4. Robinson, Richard, and Elizabeth Coren.
1745, Sep. —. Robinson, Samuel.
1765, Oct. 26. Robinson, Samuel, and Mary Hufty.
1768, July 20. Robinson, Sarah, and Joseph Trotter, Junior.
1760, June 10. Robinson, Sarah, and William Woodhouse.
1760, Jan. 1. Robinson, Stanch, and Andrew Barton.
1775, July 10. Robinson, Susannah, and Daniel Shaw.
1768, Oct. 22. Robinson, Thomas, and Mary Hanson.
1767, Aug. 22. Robinson, William, and Elizabeth Taylor.
1760, Oct. 24. Robinson, William, and Margaret Castle.
1770, Jan. 13. Robinson, William, and Margaret McQuattiat.
1764, Dec. 5. Robinson, William, and Sarah Taylor.
1764, Sep. 24. Robins, Phebe, and Paul Jones.
1764, June 21. Robins, Samuel, and Hannah Evans.
1747, M'ch —. Robins, Sarah, and Thomas Hoodt.
1763, Feb. 11. Robins, Thomas, and Ann Morgan.
1773, Aug. 14. Robins, Thomas, and Sarah Campbell.
1760, M'ch 28. Robison, Jane, and John Love.
1763, Nov. 26. Robison, Thomas, and Mary Falkner.
1759, Dec. 1. Robotham, George, and Mary Burrows.
1767, Nov. 17. Robson, Aaron, and Jane Young.
1771, May 18. Rochaberger, Adam, and Catharine Hanson.
1748, June 16. Rockwell, Samuel, and Martha Milner.
1772, Dec. 7. Rockwell, Susannah, and George Goodwin.
1772, Feb. 19. Rode, Jacob, and Susannah Wrightman.
1771, Nov. 21. Rodgers, Elizabeth, and Daniel Griffith.
1775, Sep. 2. Rodgers, Hannah, and Bethrend Detchevery.
1763, May 12. Rodgers, Hannah, and William Kidd.
1776, Apr. 23. Rodgers, Jane, and William Anderson.
1783, June 11. Rodgers, John.
1783, June 21. Rodgers, John.
1770, Oct. 22. Rodgers, Margaret, and William Griffith.

1762, July 31. Rodin, William, and Ann Boardin.
1770, Oct. 18. Rodman, John, and Susannah Bonadiall.
1763, May 3. Rodman, Joseph, and Mary Allen.
1746, Aug. —. Roe, Ann, and John Kenoby.
1770, Oct. 30. Roe, Catharine, and John Stephens.
1769, Sep. 13. Roe, Hannah, and George Burden.
1766, M'ch 29. Roe, Jesse, and Rachel Cuspin.
1761, Aug. 6. Roe, Jesse, and Sarah Bowne.
1763, July 16. Roe, Roe, and James Brown.
1772, Aug. 5. Roenun, Mary, and Edward Noble.
1761, Nov. 5. Rogers, Eleanor, and Thomas Hockley.
1760, Aug. 20. Rogers, Hannah, and John Davis.
1766, Dec. 4. Rogers, Jane, and Matthew Hughes.
1771, Oct. 26. Rogers, John, and Elizabeth Laughran.
1748, Sep. —. Rogers, Margaret, and John McFarson.
1761, M'ch 23. Rogers, Margaret, and Joseph Kimble.
1773, Nov. 29. Rogers, Mary, and Andrew McGuire.
1770, Aug. 7. Rogers, Mary, and John Letetiere.
1746, Sep. —. Rogers, Mary, and Nathan Cook.
1762, Apr. 27. Rogers, Samuel, and Martha Martin.
1772, Apr. 8. Rogers, Samuel, and Mary Kearnes.
1773, Dec. 24. Rogers, Samuel, and Mary Kirkbridge.
1761, Dec. 11. Rogers, Thomas, and Mary Wilson.
1773, June 28. Rogers, William, and Hannah Gardiner.
1770, M'ch 19. Rohr, Susannah, and Anthony Haines.
1771, Oct. 12. Roker, Thomas, and Mary Crathorne.
1760, Oct. 24. Role, Martin, and Barbara Warner.
1769, Oct. 24. Roman, John, and Catharine Dittmars.
1763, June 14. Romeck Christiana, and John Beakler.
1768, Apr. 25. Roney, James, and Margaret Jamison.
1748, M'ch 11. Roody, John, and Rachel Naest.
1747, May —. Rooke, Thomas, and Mary Davis.
1770, Apr. 25. Rooke, Thomas, and Mary Johnston.
1767, Dec. 11. Room, John, and Elizabeth Orin.
1761, July 9. Roose, George, and Mary Margaret.
1770, Aug. 7. Roosen, Henry, and Jane Stauffer.
1764, Sep. 1. Rork, Abigail, and Morris Davis.
1775, July 27. Rosbotham, James, and Cornelia Price.
1783, June 16. Rosbothem, James.
1762, July 28. Rosbothom, Benjamin, and Elizabeth **Manning.**
1771, Aug. 2. Rose, Ann, and William Tharp.
1769, M'ch 4. Rose, Elizabeth, and Peter Jones.
1774, M'ch 3. Rose, James, and Mary Ward.
1765, Aug. 14. Rose, Jonathan, and Elizabeth Newland.
1764, Dec. 13. Rose, Mary, and John Dean.
1761, June 19. Rose, (negro woman,) and negro Mars.

1745, Sep. —. Rose, Peter.
1773, Jan. 29. Rose, Thomas, and Mary Brakell.
1747, M'ch —. Rosindell, Mary, and Richard Brookbank.
1763, June 8. Ross, Alexander, and Ann Daily.
1760, May 7. Ross, Ann, and John Welsh.
1768, July 7. Ross, Catharine, and Henry Gurney.
1763, Sep. 9. Ross, Eleanor, and Christopher Wray.
1763, Dec. 15. Ross, Esther, and Whitefield Smith.
1768, Dec. 8. Ross, John, and Clementina Crookshank.
1765, Apr. 10. Ross, John, and Sarah Reily.
1775, Nov. 7. Ross, Margaret, and William Cavel.
1764, M'ch 16. Ross, Mary, and James Reynolds.
1772, Apr. 1. Ross, Mary, and John Jameson.
1772, Oct. 17. Ross, Mary, and Joseph Powell.
1762, Dec. 31. Ross, Mary, and Mark Bird.
1745, Feb. —. Ross, Oneas.
1769, June 12. Ross, Philip, and Margaret Head.
1767, Aug. 6. Ross, Philip, and Mary Read.
1763, Oct. 21. Ross, Robert, and Eleanor McCrump.
1761, Sep. 9. Ross, Ruth, and Anthony Cadman.
1764, Apr. 24. Ross, William, and Esther Ferris.
1766, May 14. Ross, William, and Martha Stowe.
1774, Dec. 19. Rossel, Elizabeth, and Lawrence Mahon.
1774, Feb. 14. Roswell, Ann, and Uriah Norcross.
1762, Apr. 10. Rost, Leonard, and Charlotte Manse.
1762, Nov. 15. Roth, Philip, and Mary Stick.
1769, June 23. Rouch, Thomas, and Jane Goucher.
1762, July 19. Rouford, Rachael, and John Godlove.
1765, Sep. 2. Rousbaughan, Mary, and Frederick Hipple.
1748, Apr. 13. Rouse, Emanuel, and Mary Jackson.
1768, Oct. 31. Rouse, Mary, and John Walter.
1760, Jan. 4. Rouse, Mary, and William Gaa.
1773, Feb. 22. Rouse, Rachel, and William Hazlewood.
1768, July 12. Roush, Jacob, and Ann Deshler.
1763, Apr. 16. Routh, James, and Elizabeth Spear.
1774, Aug. 22. Row, Adam, and Susannah Welsh.
1772, M'ch 19. Rowand, Jacob, and Prudence Maroe.
1771, Feb. 13. Rowand, Joseph, and Rachel Cole.
1761, M'ch 16. Rowand, Sarah, and Joseph Browning.
1771, M'ch 30. Rowan, James, and Jane McConnell.
1770, May 9. Rowan, James, and Mary Shaw.
1774, May 8. Rowan, Mary, and Robert Lucas.
1743, Oct. —. Rowe, William.
1766, Apr. 19. Row, Hannah, and Michael McCall.
1763, Dec. 13. Row, Jane, and John Read.
1771, Jan. 22. Rowland, Anne, and John Riale.

1767, Sep. 3. Rowland, Eleanor, and Thomas Mills.
1773, Oct. 1. Rowland, James, and Elizabeth Barthurst.
1747, May. —. Rowland, John, and Ann Smith.
1774, May 5. Rowland, Mary, and Amos Davey.
1771, Aug. 15. Rowland, Mary, and John Jones.
1762, Sep. 20. Rowney, John, and Elizabeth Murray.
1747, Oct. —. Rowoth, Mary, and James Petcairne.
1747, M'ch —. Rox, Agnus, and Philip Woods.
1767, Aug. 6. Roxborough, Elizabeth, and Daniel Sutherland.
1763, Aug. 2. Roxby, George, and Mary Brown.
1762, Feb. 3. Royall, Margaret, and William Burnet.
1772, Jan. 3. Rudderow, Susannah, and William Hunter.
1775, Nov. 6. Ruden, Mary, and Paul Cruse.
1768, Apr. 14. Rudolph, Ann, and Benjamin Paschall.
1765, Oct. 28. Rudolph, Jacob, and Judith Yocum.
1769, Dec. 1. Rudolph, Thomas, and Deborah Wright.
1774, Feb. 21. Rudulph, Hannah, and John Mitchell.
1771, June 6. Rudulph, Zebulon, and Martha Syng.
1773, Oct. 23. Rudy, Frances, and William Raddon.
1775, Oct. 2. Rue, Anthony, and Catharine Huffty.
1775, Jan. 5. Rue, Catharine, and Isaiah Vanhorn.
1765, Oct. 3. Rue, Sarah, and Edward Hill.
1772, Dec. 18. Rue, Thomas, and Ann Pursell.
1774, Apr. 7. Rufcorn, Christian, and Margaret Jones.
1760, Dec. 3. Rumford, Jonathan, and Johana Holme.
1746, Dec. —. Rumsey, William, and Catharine Dennison.
1764, Feb. 16. Rumspeiger, Rosanna, and George Hugisheimer.
1768, Sep. 16. Rundle, Richard, and Lucretia Dungin.
1764, Jan. 4. Rupart, William, and Elizabeth McGarragy.
1744, Oct. —. Rupel, James.
1773, June 18. Ruper, William, and Ruth Walton.
1768, June 23, Rush, Elizabeth, and John Smith.
1774, Sep. 19. Rush, Elizabeth, and Robert Bethell.
1764, Jan. 2. Rush, Hannah, and James Curtain.
1766, Apr. 17. Rush, Hester, and Henry Alexander.
1743, June 2. Rush, John.
1770, May 3. Rush, Mary, and George Ingels.
1770, Aug. 2. Rush, Mary, and Joseph Tatem.
1761, Sep. 22. Rush, Rachel, and Angus Bowies.
1761, June 11. Rush, Rebecca, and Thomas Scamper.
1768, June 23. Rush, Sarah, and Isaac Powell.
1772, Sep. 14. Rush, William, and Catharine Showaker.
1775, Sep. 30. Rush, William, and Mary Stoneburner.
1775, Apr. 26. Rusk, John, and Catharine Strale.
1770, Aug. 1. Rusk, Samuel, and Christiana Gilbert.
1768, May 30. Rusk, William, and Susannah Willoughby.

1773, Nov. 27. Russel, Ann, and Hugh Smith.
1775, Jan. 7. Russel, Ann, and John Linch.
1765, Jan. 28. Russel, David, and Mary Grizzle.
1761, M'ch 7. Russel, George, and Sarah Eckleson.
1763, Jan. 18. Russel, Hannah, and James Love.
1764, Oct. 11. Russel, James, and Mary Brown.
1760, Oct. 28. Russel, Joseph, and Ann Edwards.
1769, Oct. 3. Russel, Letitia, and William Stewart.
1774, Aug. 19. Russel, Mary, and James Dempsey.
1763, Jan. 5. Russel, Patrick, and Elizabeth Martin.
1767, May 28. Russel, Robert, and Susannah Morris.
1747, Jan. —. Russel, Sarah, and Valentine Handlin.
1769, July 24. Russell, Alexander, and Jane Haines.
1768, Oct. 26. Russell, Allen, and Mary McCracken.
1768, Oct. 27. Russell, Barbara, and Thomas Camalin.
1771, Nov. 2. Russell, Elizabeth, and James Chaband.
1761, Feb. 24. Russell, Elizabeth, and Samuel Harral.
1762, June 2. Russell, James, and Rachael Dobins.
1770, Feb. 19. Russell, John, and Anne Crispin.
1762, Feb. 23. Rust, Elizabeth, and William Ayers.
1760, May 16. Ruston, Sarah, and John Morris.
1767, Feb. 17. Rute, Cornelius, and Mary Wiseman.
1761, June 3. Rute, George, and Mary Nail.
1762, Jan. 7. Rutherford, William, and Lillis Hunter.
1766, May 30. Ruth, Francis, and Elizabeth Taylor.
1768, Nov. 4. Rutter, Henry, and Catharine Cline.
1776, Feb. 13. Ryan, Ann, and Manasseh Preston.
1769, Sep. 21. Ryan, Dennis, and Agnus Arnold.
1743, Oct. —. Ryan, John.
1744, June 9. Ryan, Thomas.
1760, Nov. 20. Ryan, Patrick, and Catharine Callagher.
1765, Jan. 29. Ryan, Philip, and Ann Burk.
1769, Oct. 30. Ryans, Francis, and Rose Cook.
1775, July 22. Ryebolt, Philip, and Francis Tuckney.
1770, Dec. 6. Ryning, Mary, and Adam Taylor.
1763, Sep. 14. Ryon, Christine, and Jacob James.

S

1774, May 19. Saddler, Mary, and Charles Mouse.
1771, Apr. 26. Sadler, Susannah, and Charles Truckenmiller.
1748, Jan. —. Sage, Alexander, and Ann Dark.
1762, M'ch 31. Sagert, Gabriel, and Margaretta Telbin.
1771, Aug. 19. Sahler, Elizabeth, and Robert Patton.
1772, Apr. 9. Salen, Ann, and William Leib.
1765, Dec. 9. Salerin, Anna Margaretta, and Andrew Singheis.
1761, M'ch 16. Sales, John, and Mary Porter.

1767, Sep. 23. Salisbury, Ann, and William Shroudy.
1773, Nov. 29. Salisbury, Sarah, and Edward Moore.
1748, Oct. 18. Sallows, Elizabeth, and Joseph Beddom.
1769, Oct. 20. Sallsbagg, Joseph, and Elizabeth Millar.
1760, Dec. 11. Salsbury, William, and Margaret Moore.
1774, Dec. 29. Saltar, John, and Elizabeth Gordon.
1769, Nov. 29. Saltar, Lawrence, and Dorothy Gordon.
1765, Oct. 25. Salter, John, and Rachel Reese.
1774, May 2. Salts, Deborah, and Michael Stephens.
1771, Dec. 18. Sample, James, and Jane Anderson.
1760, Sep. 8. Sample, John, and Isabella Kaldazer.
1775, Feb. 3. Samuels, Mary, and Dean Timmons.
1762, Nov. 17. Sandelson, Robert, and Hester Kolleck.
1768, Feb. 27. Sanders, Edward, and Frances Moore.
1768, June 6. Sanders, James, and Margaret Hickman.
1764, Apr. 5. Sanderson, George, and Eleanor Massey.
1768, Oct. 27. Sandham, Matthias, and Rebecca Jackson.
1773, Oct. 16. Sandon, John, and Margaret Arnold.
1760, Sep. 1. Sands, Elizabeth, and Asaph Wilson.
1767, Feb. 3. Sands, Elizabeth, and Richard Clayton.
1774, Dec. 19. Sands, Mary, and John McDunnough.
1771, Nov. 27. Sands, Richard, and Elizabeth Bond.
1773, July 17. Sanky, Susannah, and William Langdon.
1760, June 27. Sant, Sarah, and Patrick Sinnott.
1763, June 30. Sarlix, Michael, and Anna Maria Fithing.
1771, Oct. 8. Sarnighausen, William, and Elizabeth Jenkins.
1760, Apr. 28. Sanup, Skinner, and Isabella Fairchild.
1771, Dec. 10. Saseman, Catharine, and Isaac Zimmerman.
1762, Feb. 18. Satter, John, and Rebecca Wilkinson.
1762, Aug. 17. Sauler, John, and Doritey Martley.
1769, Dec. 19. Saunder, Samuel, and Rachel Flower.
1773, Sep. 16. Saunders, Eleanor, and John Brown.
1771, Oct. 8. Saunders, Hyman, and Martha Prentice.
1760, Oct. 27. Saunders, John, and Elizabeth Thompson.
1767, Nov. 21. Saunders, Joseph, and Jane Iszard.
1764, Apr. 9. Saunders, Mary, and Richard Winter.
1762, M'ch 1. Saunders, Rebecca, and Giles Shippard.
1774, M'ch 26. Saunders, William, and Mary Camper.
1770, Aug. 18. Savage, George, and Jemima Harvey.
1769, Dec. 30. Savage, John, and Mary Coatham.
1762, Apr. 12. Savage, Darby, and Ann Molley.
1761, Oct. 15. Savage, Elizabeth, and James Davis.
1765, M'ch 18. Savage, George, and Hannah Ottinger.
1760, Dec. 17. Savage, Hannah, and John Barlow.
1743, Jan. 19. Savage, John.
1775, M'ch 4. Sawyer, Margaret, and Thomas Hall.

1760, Feb. 13. Saxton, John, and Catharine Poole.
1772, Oct. 23. Saylor, Beulah, and Samuel Loftus.
1763, Sep. 1. Sayre, Esther, and William Attlee.
1773, M'ch 16. Scallinger, Enous, and Sarah Cox.
1762, July 28. Scarisbrook, Maria Elizabeth, and John Gasper Stadler.
1768, Aug. 5. Scarsborough, Samuel, and Martha Conyer.
1770, M'ch 6. Scattergood, Sarah, and Matthew Bennet.
1761, June 11. Scamper, Thomas, and Rebecca Rush.
1774, Jan. 25. Schanlan, Martha, and Isaac Roach.
1766, Apr. 10. Schatfer, Mary, and Christopher Keigher.
1764, Oct. 15. Scheech, Erhard, and Margaretta Beckin.
1775, Apr. 29. Schriner, Mary, and George Shelley.
1764, M'ch 2. Schemberger, Maria, and William Hughes.
1761, Oct. 7. Schiver, Conrad, and Catharine Rill.
1772. Jan. 9. Schlosser, Mary Magdalen, and Jacob Frank.
1765, May 15. Schnack, Elizabeth, and George Lebrant.
1774, May 11. Schneider, Adam, and Margaret Dederick.
1770, Nov. 15. Schneider, Christian, and Anna Maria Johnson.
1772, May 5. Schneider, Henry, and Barbara Shockor.
1768, Feb. 22. Schneider, John, and Juliana Feyring.
1769, Feb. 17. Schneider, Nicholas, and Mary Dehaven.
1761, Dec. 8. Schocken, Dorothy, and George Moses.
1764, Feb. 7. Schofflet, Anna Maria, and William Miller.
1776, Jan. 9. Schombaugh, Dorothy, and John Pennybaker.
1770, Dec. 1. Schott, Barbara, and John Michael Berends.
1764, Aug. 10. Schrach, Hannah, and Reuben Ellis.
1764, Dec. 19. Schrack, Susannah, and Frederick Marstetter.
1772, Dec. 16. Schreck, Jacob, and Mary Elton.
1775, Feb. 28. Schreiner, Elizabeth, and John Baker.
1763, Apr. 4. Schriner, Elizabeth, and William Hamble.
1760, Jan. 3. Schriner, Nicholas, and Mary Gamper.
1767, Jan. 19. Schriver, Peter, and Mary Hinsman.
1773, Jan. 20. Schriver, William, and Elizabeth Hausman.
1763, Sep. 24. Schroyer, George, and Mary Stonemetz.
1767, May 4. Schlosser, Ernest, and Mary Hirman.
1775, M'ch 8. Schuler, John, and Elizabeth Antis.
1746, M'ch —. Schultz, Charles.
1776, Jan. 4. Schung, Peter, and Barbara Izard.
1774, Feb. 28. Schunk, Sarah, and Ludowick Ashenfelder.
1773, Dec. 11. Schuyler, Aaron, and Ann Wright.
1763, Dec. 1. Schweitzer, John Jacob, and Maria Elizabeth Blazer.
1775, Aug. 9. Scoby, Charles, and Elizabeth Black.
1761, M'ch 19. Scoghan, Ann, and John Beesly.
1744, Jan. —. Scot. James.

1746, Oct. —. Scot, James, and Mary Evans.
1745, June —. Scot, Matthew.
1748, June 16. Scot, Mary, and William Guy.
1767, July 4. Scott, Ann, and Adam Allyn.
1763, Dec. 8. Scott, Ann, and Samuel Nelson.
1769, Apr. 29. Scott, Ann, and Thomas McIlhose.
1769, May 24. Scott, Benjamin, and Mary Doan.
1762, Sep. 21. Scott, Catharine, and John Delap.
1767, Feb. 28. Scott, Elizabeth, and Abraham Gregory.
1766, June 4. Scott, Elizabeth, and William Preston.
1783, June 7. Scott, George.
1773, July 5. Scott, James, and Catharine Dorland.
1760, Jan. 15. Scott, James, and Elizabeth Holton.
1773, July 20. Scott, John, and Ann Dennis.
1763, M'ch 1. Scott, John, and Jane Pursell.
1775, Oct. 25. Scott, John, and Margaret Robins.
1768, June 16. Scott, John, and Martha Renshaw.
1763, Apr. 13. Scott, John, and Mary Dennison.
1776, Jan. 11. Scott, John, and Sarah Castle.
1768, Jan. 20. Scott, Joseph, and Hannah Lee.
1771, Dec. 19. Scott, Kesiah, and Robert Fitzgerald.
1774, M'ch 31. Scott, Mary, and John Gardner.
1764, Jan. 11. Scott, Matthew, and Elizabeth Thompson.
1761, Dec. 21. Scott, Samuel, and Amy Cozens.
1763, July 25. Scott, William, and Martha Springer.
1769, Aug. 2. Scotton, John, and Ruth Evans.
1746, M'ch —. Scotton, Samuel.
1762, Apr. 21. Scout, Elenor, and Abraham Sulphin.
1761, May 28. Scout, Elizabeth, and Matthew Donaway.
1772, Nov. 17. Scout, Elizabeth, and Nathan Gilbert.
1760, Apr. 17. Scull, Abigail, and Thomas Biddle.
1773, Aug. 12. Scull, Benjamin, and Elizabeth Berry.
1766, Oct. 1. Scull, Hester, and Joel Zane.
1760, Feb. 1. Scull, James, and Susannah Jennings.
1770, Nov. 29. Scull, John, and Mary Shoemaker.
1774, Sep. 12. Scull, Joseph, and Rebecca Whitman.
1767, Sep. 5. Scull, Martha, and Elizabeth Boys.
1747, Oct. —. Scull, Mary, and Joseph Wood.
1774, Dec. 10. Scull, Nicholas, and Ann Townsend.
1762, Jan. 21. Scull, Priscilla, and John Prentice.
1767, Apr. 1. Scull Susannah, and James Vansandt.
1760, Feb. 18. Scull, William, and Comfort Power.
1763, Oct. 25. Scull, William, and Jane Lodge.
1772, June 19. Scully, Thomas, and Mary Alricks.
1766, Dec. 15. Scuyler, Arent, and Jane Prawl.
1761, Sep. 8. Seal, John Christian, and Mary Smith.

1768, M'ch 2. Seal, Thomas, and Mary Meglone.
1745, M'ch —. Seall, John.
1763, May 25. Sealock, Thomas, and Susannah Cooper.
1766, June 19. Seans, Ann, and John Brown.
1744, Dec. —. Searfe, Timothy.
1762, Sep. 20. Sears, Elizabeth, and Christopher Anderson.
1768, Jan. 12. Searshill, Alexander, and Mary Ritch.
1767, Feb. 19. Seckel, Henry, and Christiana Lauderback.
1774, Jan.   4. Seckverns, Rebecka, and David Walton.
1764, June 26. Seddons, Mary, and John Johnson.
1775, Apr.   4. Seffrons, Elizabeth, and Frederick Gesting.
1763, M'ch 21. Segimund, Michael, and Margaret Shnaplein.
1772, Feb.   6. Schioughauser, Catharine, and Bodo Otto, Jun'r.
1765, Oct. 29. Seiburn, Catharine, and Geisbart Bogart.
1766, Feb. 28. Seicken, Jacob, and Catharine Starr.
1763, M'ch 30. Seiglen, Mary, and Casper Mesfort.
1763, Jan. 29. Seishols, Adam, and Elizabeth Fagan.
1763, Aug.   5. Seize, Cleopha, and Jacob Repson.
1769, Aug. 23. Sellar, Catharine, and Abraham Tustine.
1769, Jan. 13 Sellar, Peter, and Mary Tustin.
1776, Feb. 27. Sellers, Elizabeth, and John Osmon.
1775, M'ch 20. Sellers, Hannah, and Conrod Librant.
1762, Jan.   5. Sellers, William, and Sarah Bulley.
1764, Jan. 14. Sellows, Sarah, and Robert Sewell.
1768, Apr. 30. Selly, William, and Johanna Carnelly.
1770, Sep. 24. Semple, Mary, and John Johnston.
1766, Nov. 11. Senner, Francis, and Mary Harding.
1773, Jan.   7. Sent, Frederick, and Barbara Taylor.
1773, May   7. Sentzer, Mary, and George Henry, Junior.
1764, Nov. 16. Seren, Lewis, and Catharine Filgeren.
1760, Nov.   3. Serett, John, and Elizabeth Race.
1775, M'ch 18. Seringar, John, and Elizabeth Reed.
1764, Dec. 25. Sergeant, Isabella, and James Gibson.
1745, Aug.   —. Severing, Benjamin.
1775, Oct. 31. Sewell, Clement, and Cornelia Smith.
1764, Jan. 14. Sewell, Robert, and Sarah Sellows.
1764, Sep. 15. Sewel, Richard, and Ann Claxton.
1767, Dec. 16. Sewery, Jacob, and Elizabeth McCarty.
1772, M'ch 17. Seymore, Ann, and Nicholas, Egan.
1760, June 15. Seymore, Appollonia, and John Franks.
1772, Aug. 21. Seyoc, Benjamin, and Mary Holmes.
1772, May   18. Shadaker, Mary, and Thomas Carter.
1772, Apr. 16. Shadowill, Antrus, and Isaac Parsons.
1771, Jan. 14. Shafer, Jacob, and Mary Abreeken.
1771, Dec. 10. Shaffer, David, and Elizabeth Hay.
1770, Apr. 10. Shafford, Mary, and Ephraim Falconer.

1764, May 30. Shagney, John, and Margaret Jones.
1775, Sep. 2. Shallerin, Margaret, and Conrad Lombalter.
1773, Nov. 6. Shallus, Catharine, and Martin Fisher.
1771, Sep. 21. Shallus, Jacob, and Elizabeth Melchior.
1727, Nov. 16. Shaneholtz, Susannah, and Nicholas Chresoman.
1761, May 2. Shankland, James, and Sarah Parsley.
1746, Nov. —. Shankle, Sarah, and John Yodes, Junior.
1774, Feb. 10. Shannon, James, and Elizabeth Crawford.
1772, Oct. 1. Shannon, James, and Elizabeth Lane.
1775, Oct. 30. Shannon, Jane, an l Andrew Gallagher.
1774, Apr. 5. Shannon, John, and Agnes Dennison.
1774, Dec. 6. Shannon, Margaret, and James King.
1771, Oct. 25. Shannon, Mary, and Aaron Hunter.
1763, May 28. Shannon, Mary, and John Porter.
1761, M'ch 13. Shannon, Richard, and Hannah Howell.
1769, Feb. 17. Shannon, Robert, and Catharine Blazedell.
1761, Sep. 5. Shaoley, Thomas, and Mary Bailey.
1769, June 3. Sharald, Amy, and Atwood Cowman.
1743, Feb. 15. Sharp, Joseph.
1773, July 29. Sharpe, Rachel, and Abraham Wynkoop.
1775, July 25. Sharp, Jacob, and Mary Pricket.
1771, Jan. 5. Sharp, Mary, and Alexander Tod.
1761, Feb. 9. Sharp, Mary, and Benjamin Canons.
1775, Jan. 25. Sharp, Mary, and Daniel Hoff.
1771, Nov. 25. Sharp, Peter, and Ann Wright.
1766, Dec. 18. Sharpless, Ann, and John Andrew.
1773, Nov. 27. Sharpless, Nathaniel, and Elizabeth Wilkinson.
1762, June 14. Sharrald, Josiah, and Rachael Knight.
1776, Jan. 11. Shan, Elizabeth, and Godfrey Smith.
1760, Jan. 1. Shaner, Adam, and Margaret Boneringh.
1775, Apr. 1. Sharshwood, James, and Elizabeth Bradin.
1775, July 10. Shaw, Daniel, and Susannah Robinson.
1766, July 19. Shaw, John, and Agnes Ferguson.
1768, Apr. 5. Shaw, John, and Judith Barry.
1772, Apr. 27. Shaw, John, and Mary Comron.
1743, Apr. 25. Shaw, Jonathan.
1764, Feb. 16. Shaw, Mary, and George Plinn.
1770, May 9. Shaw, Mary, and James Roan.
1768, Oct. 20. Shaw, Mary, and James Sterling.
1744, May —. Shaw, Michael.
1771, Apr. 17. Shaw, Priscilla, and James Griffin.
1771, Dec. 11. Shaw, Samuel, and Sarah Abel.
1768, Jan. 23. Shaw, Susannah, and Phineas Paxton.
1764, Apr. 20. Shaw, Susannah, and Samuel Thomas.
1774, M'ch 26. Shaw, Thomas, and Elizabeth Millen.
1775, M'ch 17. Shaw, Thomas, and Rachel Polton.

1761, Feb, 3. Shaw, William, and Ann Crawford.
1761, M'ch 24. Shawton, Elizabeth, and Jacob Steer.
1747, Oct, —. Shea, Charles, and Elizabeth Cummins.
1763, July 4. Shea, Jeremiah, and Elizabeth Slator.
1776, Jan. 31. Shea, John, and Ann Montgomery.
1760, Oct. 30. Shea, Rebecca, and Daniel Puligher.
1773, July 1. Sheaff, William, and Barbara Sickle.
1767, May 11. Shearcross, Mary, and Joseph Volens.
1773, Oct. 1. Shears, Deborah, and John Hamilton.
1760, Oct. 30. Sheart, Jane, and Charles Hardin.
1744, May —. Shesale, John.
1765, Jan. 22. Shecon, Mary, and John Kerr.
1766, May 26. Shedaker, Catharine, and Jacob Mouser.
1768. Sep. 13. Shedaker, Sarah, and Robert Deacon.
1771, June 7. Shedaker, William, and Sarah Davis.
1764, Jan. 25. Shedd, John, and Agnes Smith.
1769, July 31. Shee, Bertles, and Cecilia Parke.
1770, Jan. 18. Shee, Catharine, and Alexander Thompson.
1772, July 13. Shee, John, and Jane Nailor.
1770, Apr. 14. Shee, Sarah, and Joseph Wright.
1765, May 15. Shee, Walter, and Ann Thompson.
1770, Aug. 11. Sheed, Elizabeth, and Mark McCamlin.
1772, Apr. 10. Sheed, George, and Mary Evans.
1768, Jan. 18. Sheed, William, and Isabella Waddel.
1747, Jan. —. Sheed, William, and Martha Coats.
1770, Jan. 25. Sheerman, Johanna, and John Vanhorn.
1747, Apr. —. Sheerwood, Sarah, and John Hinton.
1770, Aug. 23. Sheetz, Catharine, and Henry Kemmerer.
1760, Oct. 17. Sheffley, John, and Mary Griffiths.
1771, Oct. 11. Sheghan, Judith, and Jacob Stillwaggon.
1745, Nov. —. Sheiber, Baltzer.
1772, Sep. 21. Sheidle, Erhart, and Mary Deilman.
1760, July 22. Sheitz, George, and Catharine Dinsman.
1765, Dec. 28. Shell, Casper, and Anna Maria Behlin.
1763, Oct. 26. Shellcock, Sophia, and John Boley.
1766, Jan. 30. Shellenberg, John, and Mary Cookson.
1775, Apr. 10. Shelley, Deborah, and Robert Tempest.
1773, Sep. 10. Shelling, Margaret, and Thomas Castle.
1743, Nov. —. Shelly, John.
1744, Oct. —. Shelly Nathan.
1776, M'ch 11. Shelpshanks, Richard, and Ann Kidd.
1765, Apr. 22. Shenell, Joseph, and Esther Kinnersly.
1766, Feb. 6. Shepard, John, and Eleanor Creen.
1762, Dec. 27. Shepherd, Elias, and Susannah Magee.
1769, Sep. 1. Shepherd, Jemima, and Robert Bridges.
1775, Apr. 1. Shepherd, John, and Susannah Grace.

1768, July 25. Shepherd, Mary, and Job Butcher.
1763, M'ch 6. Shepherd, Matthew, and Jane Johnston.
1760, Oct. 18. Shepherd, Robert, and Elizabeth Preston.
1770, May 21. Sherer, Margaret, and Edward Miller.
1764, Jan. 23. Sherur, Rebecca, and John Vanderslice.
1773, Feb. 26. Sherlock, Bridget, and James Cronin.
1768, M'ch 30. Sherlock, Esther, and Samuel Williams.
1768, Aug. 13. Sherlock, Margaret, and John Burrows.
1747, Apr. —. Sherswood, George, and Ann Top.
1775, July 3. Sherwood, Ann, and Thomas Brown.
1770, M'ch 9. Shetzland, Adam, and Hannah Baker.
1774, Feb. 2. Shewell, Hannah, and Benjamin Gibbs.
1767, June 17. Shewell, Mary, and Isaac Hunt.
1766, Nov. 17. Shield, Luke, and Rebecca Robinson.
1766, Aug. 6. Shields, Ann, and Alexander McIntosh.
1769, April 8. Shields, David, and Jane McKim.
1762, Nov. 25. Shields, Elizabeth, and Levy Budd.
1775, Aug. 2. Shields, John, and Margaret Cannon.
1768, May 9. Shields, John, and Rebecca McKnight.
1772, Nov. 6. Shields, Mary, and John Ligget.
1775, May 11. Shields, Robert, and Hannah Jones.
1767, Oct. 28. Shields, Thomas, and Lydia Morris.
1769, Feb. 23. Shilly, Sarah, and Michael Dogharty.
1776, M'ch 5. Shimin, William, and Mary James.
1761, May 12. Shimmer, Samuel, and Elizabeth Johnson.
1774, Sep. 19. Shinkle, Mary, and Jacob Graff.
1776, M'ch 4. Shinn, George, and Sarah Kelly.
1766, Aug. 16. Shinn, Mary, and Richard Sinnett.
1762, M'ch 1. Shippard, Giles, and Rebecca Saunders.
1767, Sep. 26. Shippen, Abigail, and Edward Spence.
1774, Mar. 22. Shippen, Ann, and Robert Strettel Jones.
1760, Dec. 3. Shippen, Catharine, and Richard Wallin.
1747, Aug. —. Shippen, Edward, and Mary Newland.
1767, Sep. 23. Shippen, Susannah, and Samuel Blair.
1770, Oct. 3. Shippey, Frances, and William Claney.
1748, May 14. Shippy, ———, and ——— Bird
1765, Sep. 5. Shirley, Rosanna, and Thomas Bell.
1767, Sep. 5. Shivers, Elizabeth and Daniel Cozens.
1769, Jan. 16. Shivers, Josiah, and Hannah Pond.
1763, M'ch 21. Shnaplein, Margaret, and Michael Segimund.
1772, May 5. Shockor, Barbara, and Henry Schneider.
1769, July 12. Shockressy, Margaret, and Andrew Clayton.
1762, Dec. 23. Shoemaker, Benjamin, and Mary Felson.
1771, July 15. Shoemaker, Catharine, and Martin Shooster.
1762, Nov. 27. Shoemaker, Jacob, and Catharine Lee.
1771, Sep. 22. Shoemaker, Lana, and Nicholas Depui.

1747, Jun. —. Shoemaker, Margaret, and John Fotheringham.
1770, Nov. 29. Shoemaker, Mary, and John Scull.
1745, Aug. —. Shoemaker, Peter.
1761, M'ch 24. Shombaugh, Dorothy, and Isaac Snyder.
1771, July 15. Shooster, Martin, and Catharine Shoemaker.
1762, Apr. 14. Shores, Esther, and Charles Harrison.
1766, Aug. 15. Shortle, Thomas, and Jane Mitchell.
1772, Dec. 19. Short, Thomas, and Mary Brady.
1769, Dec. 19. Shotsland, Mary, and Alexander Brown.
1772, Dec. 9. Shoveler, Sturges, and Sarah Forrest.
1763, Jan. 26. Shovelin, Margaret, and Edward Collins.
1772, Sep. 14. Showaker, Catharine, and William Rush.
1776, M'ch 15. Shrack, Sarah, and Paul Kugler.
1773, Nov. 15. Shreve Israel, and Mary Cokley.
1772, Feb. 19. Shrigby, Priscilla, and Joshua Gilbert.
1768, Dec. 28. Shriver, Henry, and Margaret George.
1767, Sep. 23. Shroudy, William, and Ann Salisbury.
1746, Sep. —. Shryver, Elias, and Margaret Ingle.
1747, June —. Shubart, Ann, and Isaac January.
1761, Apr. 30. Shuck, Peter, and Hannah Lutzin.
1761, Feb. 11. Shueston, Henry, and Sophia Miller.
1775. July 22. Shuler, Catharine, and Frederick Antis.
1775, Oct. 21. Shulran, John, and Mary Irwin.
1770, Sep. 21. Shultz, Christopher, and Barbara Kyle.
1768, M'ch 4. Shultz, Conrad, and Catharine Kurtz.
1773, Jan. 29. Shultzer, Charlotte, and John Temple.
1770, Mc'h 21. Shunk, Barbara, and Simon Switzer.
1768, Nov. 17. Shunk, Margaret, and John Snyder.
1760, May 12. Shurman, Hannah, and John Horne.
1765, July 30. Shute, Ann, and John Cole.
1763, Aug. 17. Shute, Diana, and William Estlack.
1762. Oct. 23. Shute, Joseph, and Sarah Nicholas.
1768, May 19. Shute, Mary, and Hercules Courtney.
1746, Dec. —. Shute, Mary, and Isaac Lincon.
1766, Nov. 26. Shute, Mary, and Seth Matlack.
1764, July 13. Shute, William, and Edith Warner.
1745, Oct. —. Shutt, Philip.
1776, June 21. Sibbald, Jennet, and Dominick Joyce.
1764, Jan. 17. Sibert, Samuel, and Barbara Maag.
1773, July 1. Sickle, Barbara, and William Sheaff.
1766, Nov. 3. Sickle, Elizabeth, and Jacob Snyder.
1776, June. 8. Sickle, John David, and Mary Guyer.
1775, May 18. Sickles, Lawrence, and Barbara Chrissler.
1760, July 31. Sickle, William, and Mary Roberts.
1775, M'ch 4, Siddell, Joseph, and Mary Groom.
1764, Aug. 1. Sidders, Abigail, and Jonathan Abbett.

1772, Sep. 23. Siddon, Mary, and Christopher Binks.
1769, July 13. Siddons, William, and Ann Ogden.
1775, May 30. Sidell, Margaret, and Simon Barnet.
1775, Jan. 9. Sidle, Catharine, and George Michael Immel.
1775, Apr. 7. Sigler, Andrew, and Ann Howey.
1765, Oct. 23. Silb, Michael, and Abigail Otty.
1744, Nov. —. Sile, Joseph.
1770, Nov. 3. Sill, Hannah, and Robert Murray.
1776, Feb. 14. Silsby, Mary, and John Hunn.
1743, Apr, 9. Simcock, Benjamin.
1767, Feb. 21. Simcocks, Hannah, and Evan Evans.
1763, May 17. Simker, Margaret, and Joseph McNamar.
1765, May 1. Simmon, Elizabeth, and Michael Pesfer.
1769, July 14. Simmonds, Rachel, and Enoch Barret.
1771, Oct. 31. Simmons, Catharine, and Bethanath Hodgkinson.
1765, Oct. 11. Simmons, Leeson, and Hannah Watkins.
1746, July —. Simmons, Ruth, and Robert Williams.
1746, M'ch —. Simon, Jacob.
1746, Sep. —. Simon, Jacob, and Catharine Smith.
1760, Aug. 29. Simon, Joseph, and Barbara Thomas.
1761, Aug. 17. Simon, Sarah, and Thomas Hardly.
1761, June 25. Simonson, Mary, and David Davidson.
1760, Sep. 24. Simpson, Andrew, and Ann West.
1774, Nov. 7. Simpson, Catharine, and George Mason.
1768, Nov. 14. Simpson, Catharine, and Thomas Alexander.
1768, M'ch 24. Simpson, Gabriel, and Catharine Farrel.
1761, Nov. 30. Simpson, Hannah, and David Canthorn.
1775, Apr. 19. Simpson, Isabella, and John Bailey.
1762, Nov. 25. Simpson, John, and Hannah Roberts.
1747, Dec. —. Simpson, John, and Mary Wilcan.
1775, Jan. 5. Simpson, Rebecca, and James Kerr.
1775, Aug 1. Simpson, Samuel, and Mary Day.
1772, July 8. Simpson, Thomas, and Sarah Smith.
1769, June 19. Simpson, William, and Isabella Willson.
1763, Sep. 24. Sims, Andrew, and Sarah Chadwick.
1765, June 5. Sims, Buckridge, and Elizabeth Morgan.
1770, July 25. Sims, Mary, and Edward Fitzrandolph.
1761, May 7. Sims, Mary, and James Dennison.
1773, July 1. Sims, Mary, and John Musgrove.
1767, May 18. Sims, Sarah Woodross, and Benjamin Wynkoop.
1775, Dec. 26. Sims, Sophia, and John Morton.
1745, M'ch —. Sims, Zacharias.
1774, May 12. Sinclair, Deborah, and Anthony Wilkinson.
1767, Oct. 19. Sinclair, Jane, and James McClear.
1773, Jan. 14. Sinclair, Philip, and Margaret Stots.

1743, Oct. —. Sinclair, Thomas.

1770, Aug. 2. Singer, Elizabeth, and James Willson.

1765, Dec. 9. Singheis, Andrew, and Anna Margaretta Salerin.

1746, Apr. —-. Singleson, Thomas.

1775, Nov. 6. Singleton, Ann, and John Mullet.

1771, July 8. Singleton, Ann, and Samuel Coney.

1771, May 3. Singleton, Elizabeth, and Rev'd Morgan Edwards.

1767, M'ch 30. Sinlgeton, Elizabeth, and Thomas Tresse.

1762, July 8. Singleton, William, and Ann Barrents.

1762, Jan. 7. Singuar, Catharine, and John Weaver.

1766, Aug. 16. Sinnett, Richard, and Mary Shinn.

1771, Nov. 23. Sinnott, Mary, and Richard Broderick.

1760, June 27. Sinnott, Patrick, and Sarah Sant.

1768, Dec. 10. Sensfelder, Mary, and Zacharias Andreas.

1774, Sep. 17. Siplay, Philip, and Michael Ramsen.

1763, June 1. Siplin, Mary, and William McKinlay.

1760, Dec. 19. Sirl, Rebecca, and William Caster.

1768, Sep. 1. Sisk, James, and Jane Waggleton.

1746, Nov. —. Sisk, Michael, and Elizabeth Moffit.

1761, Feb. 14. Sisson. Mary, and James Coffee.

1769, Aug. 25. Sitfreet, John, and Mary Lavan.

1765, Feb. 11. Siver, Patience, and John Morton.

1760, Oct. 21. Sivil, Thomas, and Margaret Moore.

1783, June 22. Skellinger Jeremiah.

1771, Sep. 21. Skelton, Eleanor, and George Rice.

1765, June 19. Skelton, Mary, and Thomas Hunt.

1748, July 13. Skerret, James, and Susanna Warner.

1760, Dec. 24. Skickland, Miles, and Phebe Vanzant.

1760, Sep. 13. Skill, Samuel, and Patience Buckham.

1765, May 10. Skillen, Samuel, and Elizabeth, Towson.

1763, Dec. 27. Skillings, Willimine, and Marcus Hulings.

1765, May 16. Skilling, William, and Mary Blyth.

1766, July 21. Skillman, Mary, and William Fullerton.

1767, Nov. 7. Skillman, Thomas, and Mary Finney.

1760, Jan. 30. Skilton, Robert, and Ann Marshall.

1768, Sep. 8. Skinner, James, and Mary Butler.

1769, Apr. 14. Skinner, Mary, and David Griffin.

1765, Oct. 31. Skinner, Susannah, and William Finney.

1762, Nov. 24. Skinner, William, and Rachael Ritchie.

1764, Dec. 22. Skipsey, George, and Rachael Sutton.

1772, Feb. 24. Skipwith, Mary, and Michael Dersey.

1762, July 12. Skiverton, Francis, and Mary Lovegrove.

1769, July 29. Skrouse, Martha, and Martin Burry.

1761, Sep. 12. Skewiston, Francis, and Charlotte St. Leger.

1769, Dec. 8. Slack, Alice, and John Myers.

1765, Feb. 5. Slack, Cornelius, and Elizabeth Spear.

1770, Apr. 19. Slack, Elizabeth, and John Linley.
1774, Apr. 29. Slack, Jacob, and Elizabeth Straker.
1764. Oct. 24. Slack, Jane, and Bernard Vanhorn.
1770, June 2. Slack, Margaret, and Folliard Purdy.
1763, Feb. 22. Sleger, Adam, and Hannah Madera.
1767, Dec. 17. Slager, Jacob, and Elizabeth Tickleson.
1748, Sep. —. Slapler, Elizabeth, and Thomas Jackson.
1763, July 5. Slashman, Anna Margaretta, and George Godfrey Wilber.
1762, July 26. Slater, John, and Elizabeth Norridge.
1773, M'ch 16. Slater, Thomas, and Elizabeth Masterson.
1763, July 4. Slator, Elizabeth, and Jeremiah Shea.
1765, M'ch 20. Slator, Elizabeth, and Watson Younger.
1761, M'ch 18. Slaughter, Isaac, and Mary Hoffman.
1762, Oct. 16. Slaughts, Hannah, and Samuel Leidam.
1772, July 10. Sleighman, John Matthias, and Mary Williamson.
1771, Sep. 5. Sleigh, Sarah, and James Young.
1766, Oct. 29. Slicer, Hannah, and Abraham Tuley.
1761, M'ch 13. Slicks, John, and Elizabeth Hicks.
1763, Apr. 16. Slinton, Mary, and Samuel Lacon.
1761, Aug. 6. Sloan, John, and Margaret McFarlan.
1773, Sep. 15. Sloan, Timothy, and Alice Frazer.
1768, June 25. Slocombe, Robert, and Mary Quay.
1763, M'ch 8. Slogden, Robert, and Mary Willard.
1776, Apr. 22. Sloss, Rachel, and Henry Spees.
1776, M'ch 22. Slyder, Catharine, and Elias Verner.
1772, June 11. Slyhauff, Godfrey, and Rachel Herxe.
1759, Dec. 31. Small, Jane, and William Craig.
1775, Dec. 18. Small, Ruth, and Nehemiah Reeve.
1747, May —. Smallwood, John, and Mary Eures.
1747, Sept. —. Smallwood, John, and Mary Hart.
1762, July 12. Smallwood, John, and Rebecca Trump.
1766, Apr. 30. Smallwood, Margaret, and Robert Stiles.
1748, May —. Smallwood, Sarah, and James Terill.
1770, June 7. Smart, John, and Lydia Jones.
1775, Sep. 27. Smart, John, and Rachel Hlyder.
1770, Dec. 12. Smart, William, and Mary Vago.
1771, June 27. Smedley, Caleb, and Mary Newberry.
1773, May 13. Smick, Peter, and Eleanor Fitzgerald.
1773, May 3. Smick, Peter, and Mary Heide.
1776, Feb. 7. Smith, Abigail, and James Gottier.
1764, Jan. 25. Smith, Agnes, and John Shedd.
1770, Jan. 13. Smith, Anne, and Charles Young.
1761, M'ch 30. Smith, Ann, and James Smylie.
1764, July 31. Smith, Ann, and James Winter.
1747, May —. Smith, Ann, and John Rowland.

1748, Nov. 11. Smith, Ann, and Joseph Ball.
1761, Aug. 15. Smith, Catharine, and Abram Black.
1761, Sep. 21. Smith, Catharine, and Adam Talk.
1746, Sep. —. Smith, Catharine, and Jacob Simon.
1767, Feb. 2. Smith, Catharine, and James Beaty.
1766, June 14. Smith, Catharine, and James Sutter.
1766, Dec. 1. Smith, Catharine, and John Cahill.
1762, June 14. Smith, Catharine, and Matthias Folk.
1772, June 22. Smith, Catharine, and Stephen Bardon.
1771, July 18. Smith, Christian, and Ann Glassow.
1760, Jan. 11. Smith, Christian, and Godfrey Weltzet.
1760, June 30. Smith, Christopher, and Ann M. Brunner.
1775, Oct. 31. Smith, Cornelia, and Clement Sewell.
1761, Apr. 8. Smith, David, and Hannah Hibbs.
1747, M'ch —. Smith, David, and Mary Martin.
1776, Jan. 19. Smith, Eleanor, and Edward Marsh.
1775, Aug. 30. Smith, Eleanor, and Thomas Clifford.
1762, Feb. 15. Smjth, Eleanor, and William Davis.
1760, June 25. Smith, Elinor, and William Harper.
1767, Dec. 24. Smith, Elizabeth, and James Clements.
1746, Aug. —. Smith, Eliazbeth, and John Henry.
1760, Feb. 2. Smith, Elizabeth, and Joseph Gladney.
1748, Nov. 11. Smith, Elizabeth, and Thomas Joyce.
1760, Apr. 26. Smith, Ester, and John McEntíre.
1743, Dec. —. Smith, George.
1745, July. —. Smith, George.
1767, June 6. Smith, George, and Affa Drake.
1772, May 27. Smith, George, and Elizabeth Mannel.
1746, Oct. —. Smith, George, and Mary Parry.
1762, Sep. 20. Smith, George, and Sophia Doulbear.
1760, Aug. 1. Smith, George, and Susannah Wood.
1776, Jan. 11. Smith, Godfrey, and Elizabeth Sharr.
1761, Oct. 17. Smith, Grace, and Nicholas Lloyd.
1774, Apr. 8. Smith, Hannah, and Jacob Baker.
1762, Dec. 1. Smith, Hannah, and John Garretson.
1763, Feb. 21. Smith, Hannah, and William Cannaedy.
1771, Feb. 27. Smith, Helena, and Robert Ritchie.
1760, Dec. 15. Smith, Henry, and Garret Reinholden.
1773, Nov. 27. Smith, Hugh, and Ann Russel.
1764, Aug. 29. Smith, Humphrey, and Jane Wilson.
1763, Nov. 28. Smith, Isaac, and Mary Pennington.
1761, Jan. 15. Smith, Jacob, and Mary Pinder.
1744, Oct. —. Smith, James.
1761, M'ch 2. Smith, James, and Ann Lewis.
1760, Sep. 11. Smith, James, and Dorothy Boatman.
1760, June 7. Smith, James, and Margaret Fortion.

1772, Jan. 1. Smith, James, and Martha Maxwell.
1746, June —. Smith, James, and Mary Beason.
1775, Jan. 9. Smith, James, and Mary Penn.
1761, Dec. 29. Smith, Jane, and John Grimes.
1774, May 12. Smith, Jane, and John Smith.
1767, Aug. 5. Smith, Jane, and Thomas Jones.
1745, July —. Smith, John.
1748, Aug. 15. Smith, John.
1760, July 8. Smith, John, and Ann Wollax.
1776, M'ch 8. Smith, John, and Barbara Markle.
1762, Sep. 20. Smith, John, and Catharine Everly.
1772, Nov. 10. Smith, John, and Catharine O'Mullan.
1774, Jan. 4. Smith, John, and Cleary Wheeler.
1766, Aug. 4. Smith, John, and Deborah Waggoner.
1762, June 26. Smith, John, and Elizabeth Jones.
1768, June 23. Smith, John, and Elizabeth Rush.
1768, M'ch 24. Smith, John, and Jane McCaullay.
1774, May 12. Smith, John, and Jane Smith.
1775, Dec. 7. Smith, Johnston, and Mary Hannes.
1772, Jan. 31. Smith, Joseph, and Jane Beaks.
1770, Nov. 10. Smith, Joseph, and Martha Powel.
1760, Dec. 4. Smith, Joseph, and Philis Hilbo.
1770, Nov. 19. Smith, Judith, and Andrew Crawford,
1775, Oct. 9. Smith, Margaret, and Charles Nagle.
1765, July 8. Smith, Margaret, and John Money.
1764, Aug. 2. Smith, Martha, and William Hawskin.
1771, Oct. 15. Smith, Mary, and Henry McDowell.
1769, Nov. 11. Smith, Mary, and Jacob Goodshires.
1762, Aug. 24. Smith, Mary, and James Lenard.
1769, Apr. 24. Smith, Mary, and Jesper Beson.
1761, Sep. 8. Smith, Mary, and John Christian Seal.
1765, Dec. 2. Smith, Mary, and John Garlin.
1771, Oct. 12. Smith, Mary, and John Hall.
1763, Sep. 28. Smith, Mary, and Ralph Nicholson.
1775, Apr. 5. Smith, Mary, and Thomas Alexander.
1774, Dec. 22. Smith, Mary, and Thomas Genn.
1770, Feb. 21. Smith, Mary, and William Holton.
1747, Dec. —. Smith, Mary, and Witlock Paulin.
1773, Nov. 10. Smith, Nicholas, and Sarah Gabb.
1763, Apr. 12. Smith, Peter, and Susannah Whitstone.
1765, Apr. 29. Smith, Phebe, and George Kinsey.
1761, July 27. Smith, Rachel, and John Paschall, Junior.
1774, July. 7. Smith, Ralph, and Martha Nun.
1772, Aug. 27. Smith, Reuben, and Elizabeth Webb.
1745, Nov. —. Smith, Richard.
1762, Aug. 23. Smith, Richard, and Elizabeth Fister.

1762, Sep. 10. Smith, Robert, and Sarah Stewart.
1748, July 13, Smith, Robert, and Sarah Stilley
1766, Sep. 10. Smith, Robert, and Sarah Tucker.
1760, July 17. Smith, Samuel, and Abigail Canady.
1774, Apr. 20, Smith, Samuel, and Judith Millington.
1776, June 1. Smith, Samuel, and Magdalen Hayes,
1767, Aug. 27. Smith, Sarah, and Arthur Barker.
1768, Feb. 19. Smith, Sarah, and Elisha Marks.
1761, Nov. 21. Smith, Sarah, and Joseph Baird.
1772, July 8. Smith, Sarah, and Thomas Simpson.
1765, Jan. 12. Smith, Thomas, and Martha Lewis.
1763, Dec. 15. Smith, Whitefield, and Esther Ross.
1767, July 9. Smith, William, and Anna Zet.
1764, June 16. Smith, William, and Ann Bell.
1775, Nov. 27. Smith, William, and Ann Young.
1775, Aug. 11. Smith, William Drewet, and Margaret Stedham.
1764, Nov. 1. Smith, William, and Elizabeth Adams.
1766, Feb. 12. Smith, William, and Elizabeth Garrigues.
1764, Nov. 23. Smith, William, and Elizabeth Harper.
1766, Dec. 1. Smith, William, and Elizabeth Mourning.
1768, May 12. Smith, William, and Mary Chandler.
1771, Sep. 12. Smithers, James, and Rachel Bettertan.
1747, June —. Smout, Edward, and Elizabeth Price.
1761, M'ch 20. Smylie, James, and Ann Smith.
1770, June 8. Sneal, Agnes, and Christopher Martin.
1770, M'ch 17. Sneck, Catharine, and Casper Haas.
1746, Dec. —. Sneider, Elue Mary, and George Earnest.
1762, Aug. 20. Snodgrace, Rebecca, and John Watson.
1767, M'ch 4. Snodgrass, Margaret, and Matthew Law.
1761, M'ch 13. Snodgrass, Jane, and John Harvey.
1745, Oct. —. Snosh, William.
1768, Dec. 7. Snow, Elizabeth, and James Allenby.
1766, M'ch 26. Snow, John, and Mary Buffington.
1775, June 10. Snow, Mary, and Daniel Dolby.
1768, July 16. Snowden, Ann, and Laughlan McNeal.
1766, June 10. Snowden, Diley, and Benjamin Whitaker.
1763, M'ch 17. Snowden, Isaac, and Mary McCall.
1770, M'ch 22. Snowden, Jedediah, and Ann English.
1765, Apr. 20. Snowden, John, and Sarah Lefever.
1772, Aug. 10. Snowden, Joseph, and Sarah Harlin.
1772, Nov. 18. Snowden, Rachel, and William Davey.
1771, Oct. 12. Snowden, Samuel, and Hannah Gum.
1769, Feb. 27. Snowden, Thomas, and Sarah Nicholson.
1767, Dec. 31. Snowden, William, and Ann Maugridge.
1774, June 29. Snyder, Catharine, and John Hammer.
1768, Aug. 17. Snyder, Daniel, and Ann Berndollar.

1765, Jan. 9. Snyder, Elizabeth, and James Stuart.
1761, M'ch 24. Snyder, Isaac, and Dorothy Shombaugh.
1766, Nov. 3. Snyder, Jacob, and Elizabeth Sickley.
1770, May 9. Snyder, John, and Elizabeth Waggoner.
1768, Nov. 17. Snyder, John, and Margaret Shunk.
1769, Oct. 24. Snyder, Mary, and Christopher Jacoby, Jun.
1770, July 26. Snyder, Mary, and Nicholas Loughman.
1767, Dec. 8. Snyder, Sophia, and Henry Antis.
1768, Nov. 15. Snyder, Susannah, and John Kaps.
1775, Nov. 27. Sockman, Henry, and Christiana Brighdehen.
1765, Jan. 2. Somers, Isaac, and Elizabeth Davis.
1766, Aug. 5. Sommer, Mary, and Ernst Mange.
1748, Sep. —. Sommerour, Susanna, and Ulrick Yeakley.
1767, M'ch 18. Sommers, Elizabeth, and Adam Stricker.
1763, M'ch 30. Sotcher, Massey, and John Baldwin.
1775, Feb. 27. Souder, Sarah, and John Crann.
1760, May 12. Southwick, Mayham, and Grace Carson
1767, Apr. 2. Sowder, John, and Eleanor Piniard.
1771, June 29. Sowder, John, and Sarah Felton.
1773, Jan. 25. Sowder, John, and Mary Baker.
1771, Aug. 19. Sowder, Mary, and John Dunn.
1762, July 15. Spackman, Charles, and Elizabeth Gordon.
1761, Apr. 9. Spafford, Ann, and Nathaniel Galt.
1775, Apr. 15. Spangler, George, and Mary Schreiner.
1773, June 30. Spanton, Elizabeth, and George Way.
1775, June 7. Sparks, Dorothy, and Ebenezer Large.
1772, Nov. 30. Sparks, J. mes, and Ann Pearson.
1765, Feb. 5. Spear, Elizabeth, and Cornelius Slack.
1763, Apr. 16. Spear, Elizabeth, and James Routh.
1767, July 23. Spear, Esther, and John Wills.
1771, M'ch 4. Spear, George, and Alice Crosby.
1760, July 5, Spear, Jane, and John Burley.
1769, May 24. Spear, John, and Catharine Kelly.
1775, M'ch 18. Specht, John, and Catharine Knees.
1746, M'ch —. Specky, George.
1776, Apr. 22. Spees, Henry, and Rachel Slos.
1767, Sep. 26. Spence, Edward, and Abigail Shippen.
1762, Dec. 10. Spence, Peter, and Sarah Dixon.
1768, Sep. 22. Spencer, Ann, and John Kidd.
1769, July 28. Spencer, Brent, and Martha Thompson.
1746, Sep. —. Spencer, Diana, and Robert Finny.
1776, Feb. 7. Spencer, Esther, and John Tawzer.
1775, M'ch 23. Spencer, James, and Ann Coakley.
1746, Dec. —. Spencer, John, and Elizabeth Wilson.
1769, May 8. Spencer, Martha, and Berry Hartwell.
1768, Apr. 30. Spencer, Mary, and Robert Carson.

1771, Oct. 4. Spencer, Mary, and Thomas Lee.
1772, Sep. 15. Spencer, Nicohlas, and Martha Lee.
1747, Dec. —. Spencer, Rachel, and James McCullough.
1747, Dec. —. Spergis, Thomas, and Catharine Roberts.
1771, Oct. 17. Spicer, Abigail, and John Keble.
1764, Nov. 9. Spicer, Sylvia, and Samuel Jones.
1748, Sep. —. Spike, Jacob, and Susanna Allen.
1764, June 28. Spine, John, and Jane Godfrey.
1762, Dec. 7. Spoone, Dorothy, and Michael Hess.
1762, Nov. 19. Spring, Benjamin, and Letthea Chancellor.
1768, July 18. Springer, Barbara, and William Gordon.
1764, Feb. 18. Springer, Deborah, and William Beeby.
1763, July 25. Springer, Martha, and William Scott.
1770, Nov. 22. Sprogell, John, and Anne Crosstan.
1763, Feb. 1. Squirrell, Esther, and Thomas Carpenter.
1762, Aug. 31. Sreeve, Ann, and Elijah Weed.
1774, Feb. 1. Stackhouse, Elizabeth, and William Green.
1766, Jan. 25. Stackhouse, Esther, and Daniel Wright.
1774, Feb. 17. Stackhouse, Hastings, and Margaret Robins.
1764, M'ch 28. Stackhouse, Joseph, and Rachel Rew.
1773, Sep. 3. Stackhouse, Nicholas, and Elizabeth Robinson.
1762, Aug. 25. Stackhouse, Robert, and Susannah Hillings.
1764, Sep. 29. Stackhouse, Sarah, and John Sutton.
1768, Aug. 29. Staddleman, Elizabeth, and John Bonner.
1762, July 28. Stadler, John Gasper, and Maria Elizabeth Scarisbrook.
1765, M'ch 4. Stadtler, Christian, and Catharine Kurtzen.
1763, M'ch 12. Staets, Peter, and Elizabeth Dunning.
1770, Sep. 1. Stafford, Patrick, and Anna Harrae.
1748, Jan. —. Stagg, John, and Dorothy Crue.
1769, M'ch 2. Stagg, Susannah, and John Wilson.
1776, May 8. Staigner, Ludwick, and Leveace Anderholdt.
1768, May 17. Stainer, Solomon, and Margaret Carter.
1764, M'ch 13. Stall, John, and Frances Hyley.
1766, Sep. 3. Stall, Margaret, and Robert Dill.
1764, Feb. 15. Stamer, George, and Barbara Grayger.
1761, Jan. 21. Stamler, Michael, and Elizabeth Bamberger.
1774, Sep. 3. Stamp, Ann, and Philip Buck.
1763, M'ch 30. Stanbury, William, and Sarah Morris.
1768, June 17. Stancliff, John, and Elizabeth Dewey.
1746, Apr. —. Standley, George.
1770, Sep. 19. Standley, Sarah, and Godfrey Twells.
1745, Oct. —. Staneland, John.
1774, July 27. Stanley, Esther, and Noah Mendenhall.
1748, Sep. —. Stanley, William, and Elizabeth Fulton
1764, Nov. 7. Stanton, George, and Ann Tussey.

1747, Nov. —. Stanton, Jane, and Samuel Minshall.
1773, M'ch 4. Stark, John, and Ann Wade.
1764, Dec. 1. Starr, Ann, and John Roberts.
1766, Feb. 28. Starr, Catharine, and Jacob Seicken.
1762, Nov. 27. Starr, John, and Rebecca Cassey.
1765, Oct. 21. States, Isaac, and Tamar Tillyer.
1769, July 21. Statia, Rosanna, and Thomas Taylor.
1772, May 14. Statler, Mary, and William Dunten.
1763, Jan. 29. Stattleman, Michael, and Sarah Wynn.
1770, Aug. 7. Stauffer, Jane, and Henry Roosen.
1766, Aug. 18. St. Clair, Alexander, and Elizabeth Cammel.
1763, July 30. St. Clair, Elizabeth, and William McFarlin.
1761, Sep. 21. St. Clair, Magnus, and Catharine Young.
1744, Dec. —. Steaghers, Jacob.
1746, May —. Stebbs, Henry.
1744, June 27. Steele, Thomas.
1764, Oct. 2. Stedham, Elizabeth, and John Fouracres.
1747, June —. Stedham, Peter, and Isabel Jaquett.
1760, June 9. Stedham, Sarah, and John D. Honnuer.
1747, Dec. —. Stedman, Charles, and Ann Grome.
1775, Aug. 11. Stedman, Margaret, and Wm. Derwet Smith.
1761, July 16. Steel, Jannet, and David Hearn.
1771, May 9. Steel, Margaret, and Edward Oxley.
1762, June 24. Steel, Margaret, and John Flenthem.
1771, May 23. Steel, Margaret, and William Taylor.
1763, Jan. 3. Steel, Mary, and George Pander.
1770, Apr. 26. Steel, Thomas, and Mary Bathurst.
1763, May 17. Steele, William, and Mary Benset.
1748, Jan. —. Steen, Agnes, and Thomas Welhers.
1761, M'ch 24. Steer, Jacob, and Elizabeth Shawton.
1763, M'ch 2. Steer, Mary, and Miles Carpenter.
1769, Feb. 27. Steffer, Sophia, and Michael Taylor.
1767, Sep. 24. Stein, Catharine, and Christopher Honey.
1775, June 5. Stein, William, and Christiana Muchlarein.
1765, Apr. 18. Steinmetz, John, and Catharine Kepple.
1768, M'ch 26. Steinmetz, Susannah, and Jacob Swope
1762, Jan. 22. Stelle, Sarah, and Edward Yorke.
1773, Apr. 10. Stellwaggon, Margaret, and George Marcker.
1762, Nov. 13. Stemers, Margaret, and Benjamin Wallis.
1760, June 5. Stem, Frederick, and Hannah Temberman.
1744, Feb. —. Stemson, John.
1766, May 10. Stengis, Hannah, and George Featherhead.
1776, Apr. 10. Stenner, Anne, and Nicholas Reinhart.
1767, Dec. 9. Stenson, Mary, and James McGeshan.
1770, Apr. 14. Stephens, Catharine, and John Blake.
1773, M'ch 13. Stephens, Elizabeth, and Garret Vansant.

1761, Aug. 22. Stephens, Elizabeth, and John Britton.
1774, June 4. Stephens, Evan, and Jane Griffith.
1770, Oct. 30. Stephens, John, and Catharine Roe.
1776, June 18. Stephens, John, and Mary Lodge.
1772, Feb. 26. Stephens, Mary, and John Murphy.
1774, May 2. Stephens, Michael, and Deborah Salts.
1773, Aug. 24. Stephens, Peter, and Eleanor Moore.
1769, Jan. 16. Stephens, Rebecka, and John Craig.
1775, Nov. 29. Stephens, Sarah, and Benjamin Griffith.
1769, Feb. 6. Stephens, Walter, and Mary Christy.
1774, Dec. 27. Stephenson, Ann, and Edward Green.
1744, Apr. —. Stephenson, John.
1745, Aug. —. Sterliens, Stephens.
1768, Oct. 20. Sterling, James, and Mary Shaw.
1766, Sep. 16. Sterling, Margaret, and William Logan.
1763, Aug. 16. Sterner, Henry, and Catharine Krowle.
1768, Sep. 14. Sterrat, Ann, and Thomas Murdock.
1762, Sep. 6. Sterrat, Samuel, and Mary Keappock.
1774, Sep. 14. Sterret, Mary, and John Hensliff.
1783, June 20. Sterrett, Alexander.
1765, Sep. 26. Steuart, Alexander, and Ann Cummins.
1763, Jan. 10. Steuart, Andrew, and Margaret Bryant.
1762, Apr. 6. Stevens, Deborah, and John Mason.
1766, Feb. 8. Stevens, Elizabeth, and James Faries.
1776, Apr. 6. Stevens, Elizabeth, and Thomas Harris.
1764, Aug. 14. Stevens, Hannah, and Robert Brown.
1747, May —. Stevens, James, and Mary Swain.
1748, Aug. 15. Stevens, John.
1763, June 6. Stevens, John, and Sarah Stotehoff.
1773, Jan. 13. Stevens, Letitia, and Thomas Gardner.
1748, Oct. 18. Stenvenson, George, and Rebecca Dickinson.
1760, July 31. Stevenson, George, and Sarah Cannon.
1766, Oct. 22. Stevenson, Hugh, and Rebecca Craig.
1748, June 16. Stevenson, James, and Elizabeth Weldon.
1766, Dec. 18. Stevenson, Jennings, and Sarah Alexander.
1748, Nov. 11. Stevenson, John, and Mary Henderson.
1767, Dec. 2. Stevenson, Martha, and Thos. Thornborough.
1776, Jan. 24. Stevenson, Robert, and Elizabeth Deakin.
1765, Oct. 30. Stevenson, Sarah, and Richard Mitchel.
1783, June 3. Steward, Aaron.
1762, Nov. 18. Steward, Ann, and Jacob Proby.
1746, Nov. —. Steward, Catharine, and Thomas Norris.
1762, Nov. 29. Steward, Elizabeth, and Neal McNeal.
1746, Dec. —. Steward, James, and Hannah Godfrey.
1747, May —. Steward, Jane, and Robert Haines.
1774, Feb. 2. Steward, John, and Elizabeth Bustard.

1767, Mc'h 2. Steward, John, and Mary Jackson.
1760, Dec. 4. Steward, John, and Rose Rickets.
1768, Feb. 20. Steward, Mary, and Daniel Gorton.
1772, Jan. 1. Stewart, Daniel, and Mary Neal.
1769, May 4. Stewart, Eleanor, and Joseph McCoy.
1762, Dec. 18. Stewart, Elizabeth, and Benjamin Bastine.
1771, M'ch 13. Stewart, Elizabeth, and Edward Hanlin.
1765, Jan. 15. Stewart, Francis, and Jane Cammel.
1764, M'ch. 22. Stewart, George, and Parthenia Benton.
1768, Jan. 12. Stewart, Hugh, and Ruth Leonard.
1769, July 19. Stewart, John, and Eleanor Mears.
1775, Aug. 19. Stewart, John, and Sarah McIlvaine.
1773, M'ch 6. Stewart, John, and Sarah Morgan.
1770, M'ch 19, Stewart, Martha, and Henry Wilson.
1774, May 24. Stewart, Mary, and James Hunter.
1771, Oct. 29. Stewart, Mary, and Alexander Thompson.
1771, Nov. 12. Stewart, Rachel, and John Gugeny.
1763, Nov. 24. Stewart, Sarah, and James Purcell.
1762, Sep. 10. Stewart, Sarah, and Robert Smith.
1769, Oct. 3. Stewart, William, and Letitia Russel.
1762 Nov. 15. Stick, Mary, and Philip Roth.
1763 Aug. 19. Stiger, Elizabeth, and Thomas Huddleston.
1776 Feb. 21. Stiles, Henry, and Ann Banks.
1766, Apr. 30. Stiles, Robert, and Margaret Smallwood.
1763, Nov. 16. Stilla, John, and Mary Boys.
1763, Dec. 9. Stille, David, and Ann Dobson.
1762, Oct. 25. Stilley, Christiana, and Reynold Keen.
1762, M'ch 3. Stilley, Mary, and John Bird.
1761. Dec. 1. Stilley, Rachel, and Isaac Harman.
1778, Oct. 18. Stilley, Widow, and Samuel Austin.
1774, Oct. 31. Stillman, Andrew, and Hannah Bates.
1771, Oct. 11. Stillwaggon, Jacob, and Judith Shegan.
1769, Apr. 25. Stillwill, Richard, and Mary Larne.
1748, July 13. Stilly, Sarah, and Robert Smith.
1764, Dec. 11. Stilwell, Daniel, and Elisha Lupton.
1759, Dec. 1. Stimmer, Christian, and Mary Myer.
1763, Dec. 21. Stimson, John, and Rebecca Cox.
1765, Oct. 19. Stinson, Ann, and Daniel McMackon.
1771, Nov. 7. Stinson, Jane, and Jonathan Coates.
1765, Oct. 11. Stinson, Margaret, and Henry Gullen.
1766, Oct. 20. Stinson, Mary, and William Ismaster.
1747, Oct. —. Stinson, Sarah, and John Cole.
1765, M'ch 28. Stinson, Sarah, and Thomas Ellis.
1761, June 1. Stinson, William, and Martha Paydon.
1764, Nov. 10. Stinston, Sarah, and James Taggart.
1744, Feb. —. Stinton, Philip.

1761, Sep. 12. St. Leger, Charlotte, and Francis Skewiston.
1746, Oct. —. Stoaks, Sarah, and Gregory McCarty.
1748, Oct. 18. Stockard, John, and Elizabeth Collins.
1763, Oct. 10. Stockering, Anna Maria, and Peter Feiss.
1775, May 4. Stockford, Elizabeth, and William Kinnard.
1763, May 17. Stockhouse, Abel, and Hannah Breese.
1775, Nov. 25. Stockton, William, and Mary Nagle.
1762, Nov. 3. Stogdell, William, and Elizabeth Randell.
1769, Feb. 24. Stokeld, Conyers, and Mary Davenport.
1775, Apr. 27. Stokes, George, and Mary Warner.
1761, Oct. 5. Stokes, Mary, and Jacob Pimple.
1776, Feb. 24. Stone, Andrew, and Elizabeth Daniel.
1764, Nov. 11. Stone, Catharine, and Nicholas Bradollar.
1764, May 11. Stone, Catharine, and Peter Hardman.
1774, Dec. 12. Stone, Edward, and Dorothy Chilcot.
1761, Apr. 21. Stone, Elizabeth, and Peter Stoy.
1771, Oct. 24. Stone, Elizabeth, and William M. Barnet.
1770, Oct. 6. Stone, Gartree, and Isaac Larne.
1773, May 3. Stone, Jane, and Peter Kidd.
1760, Jan. 21. Stone, John, and Mary Walker.
1747, Aug. —. Stone, Robert, and Ann Ogden.
1748, M'ch 11. Stone, Sarah, and Isaac Taylor.
1765, May 15. Stoneburner, Hester, and William Woodrow.
1775, Aug. 30. Stoneburner, Mary, and William Rush.
1771, Sept. 10. Stonematz, Catharine, and Rev. John Nevling.
1770, M'ch 3. Stonematz, Margaret, and William Bell.
1768, Sep. 23. Stonemetz, Barbara, and Jacob Maag.
1764, July 26. Stonemetz, Frederick, and Priscilla Vanleer.
1776, May 21. Stonemetz, John, and Mary Foster.
1763, Sep. 24. Stonemetz, Mary, and George Schroyer.
1774, Oct. 22. Stonemotz, Daniel, and Catharine Plunket.
1774, Nov. 16. Stoop, Henry, and Susannah George.
1766, Sep. 4. Stoops, Mary, and Christopher Bumberry.
1763, Aug. 8. Stoops, Mary, and William Barber.
1768, May 12. Stoops, Sarah, and Andrew Tucker.
1761, Aug. 20. Storry, Mary, and John Gilbert.
1760, M'ch. 27. Story, Elizabeth, and John Green.
1765, Aug. 29. Story, Elizabeth, and William Adamson.
1763, June 6. Stotchoff, Sarah, and John Stevens.
1773, Jan. 14. Stots, Margaret, and Philip Sinclair.
1774, Dec. 21. Stots, Martha, and Joseph Wright.
1760, M'ch 28. Stroud, Peter, and Ann Firespack.
1764, Feb. 6. Stouder, Margaret, and Christian Taylor.
1772, Oct. 21. Stout, Abraham, and Mary Magdalena **Hartzell**.
1772, Sep. 3. Stout, Brightwed, and William Nichols.
1744, Dec. —. Stout, Cornelius.

1778, May 1. Stout, Elizabeth, and Elijah Crawford.
1775, Dec. 8. Stout, John Henry, and Margaret Calam.
1765, Sep. 20. Stout, Sarah, and Abraham Freid.
1743, Jan. 10. Stow, Charles.
1773, May 6. Stow, Charles, and Mercy Williard.
1766, May 14. Stowe, Martha, and William Ross.
1761, Apr. 21. Stoy, Peter, and Elizabeth Stone.
1772, Apr. 9. Stradler, Sarah, and Nathan Rhoads.
1774, Apr. 29. Straker, Elizabeth, and Jacob Slack.
1775, Apr. 26. Staley, Catharine, and John Rush.
1774, Sep. 5. Stratton, Elizabeth, and Esaias Hunt.
1771, June 22. Stratton, Elizabeth, and Grace Davidson.
1763, Sep. 3. Strawbridge, Jane, and Alexander McClean.
1761, June 1. Strawcutter, Mary, and Battice Ford.
1760, June 25. Stray, Margaret, and John Mallaan.
1746, June —. Street, Benjamin, and Elisah Collins.
1776, Feb. 3. Street, James, and Elizabeth Walton.
1747, Feb. —. Street, Joseph, and Rachel Jenkins.
1772, June 11. Street, Mary, and Robert Hamilton.
1761, Jan. 17. Streighkan, Mary, and William Eckhart.
1771, Jan. 21. Streper, John, and Deborah Levering.
1769, Nov. 4. Stretch, Catharine, and Thomas Burrow.
1770, M'ch 5. Stretch, Peter, and Sarah Howell.
1743, July 29. Stretch, Thomas.
1763, Apr. 13. Stretcher, Edward, and Elizabeth Davis.
1767, M'ch 18. Stricker, Adam, and Elizabeth Sommers.
1771, Sep. 18. Stricker, Mary, and John Heyl.
1766, M'ch 29. Strickland, Amos, and Mary Harding.
1760, Dec. 24. Strickland, Miles, and Phebe Vanzant.
1774, M'ch 8. Strimbek, John, and Elizabeth, Grace.
1775, Aug. 22. String, Peter, and Hannah Cole.
1774, Feb. 14. Strome, Eva, and Adolph Gillman.
1770, Jan. 13. Strong, Matthew, and Agnes Gerrard.
1774, Sep. 3. Strong, Sarah, and George Anderson.
1759, Dec. 22. Stroud, Deborow, and Stephen Harlin.
1763, Apr. 27. Stroud, Rachael, and William McCay.
1763, Sep. 14. Strout, Joseph, and Mary Keen.
1766, May 12. Strumbrey, Barbara, and Albert Meyer.
1768, Apr. 11. Strupe, John, and Rachel Kepharting.
1775, Dec. 14. Stuart, Eleanor, and James McDaniel.
1761, July 24. Stuart, Henry, and Sarah Garret.
1774, June 16. Stuart, James, and Ann Guy.
1765, Jan. 9. Stuart, James, and Elizabeth Snyder.
1762, July 15. Stuart, James, and Grace Bartly.
1761, Feb. 6. Stuart, James, and Margaret Henry.
1775, Oct. 12. Stuart, Rev'd John, and Jane O'Kill.

1764, Oct. 22. Stuart, Robert, and Margaret Warner.
1776, Jan. 2. Stubbs, Deborah, and James Rench.
1763, Aug. 30. Stubbs, William, and Deborah Johnson.
1766, Nov. 25. Stuber, Frederick, and Elizabeth Cook.
1761, Sep. 1. Studdert, John, and Deboro Harper.
1763, Apr. 12. Studdin, Ann, and Peter Polar.
1767, June 1. Studham, John, and Ann Ford.
1772, May 13. Stukesbury, William, and Susannah Thomas.
1766, Dec. 24. Stulberger, Mary, and Henry Faber.
1773, Apr. 17. Sturgis, Nathan, and Catharine Philips.
1774, May 2. Sturgus, Jesse, and Hannah Brooks.
1770, Jan. 2. Sturk, Rebecca, and Ebenezer Jones.
1762, Aug. 13. Stuttle, Margaret, and Nathaniel Holton.
1770, Dec. 10. Stutz, William, and Ozella Graffley.
1775, Aug. 1. Styber, Elizabeth, and Henry Lees.
1760, May 7. Styles, William, and Mary Brustrum.
1769, Oct. 31. Stytes, Daniel, and Lydia Cresse.
1760, Oct. 6. Suber, George, and Mary Talbert.
1764, Jan. 10. Suber, John, and Catharine Vanhorn.
1761, Apr. 25. Such, George, and Sarah Carver.
1771, Oct. 2. Suffrance, Elizabeth, and James Landee.
1744, Aug. 13. Sugar, Thomas.
1762, Aug. 5. Sullavon, James, and Ann Tanner.
1747, Dec. —. Sullevan, Dennis, and Margaret Lodges.
1769, Oct. 11. Sullivan, Andrew, and Martha McConnelly.
1769, Nov. 11. Sullivan, Anne, and Charles McIntire.
1775, July 3. Sullivan, Darby, and Catharine Cassey.
1747, Nov. —. Sullivan, Margaret, and John Mackintosh.
1762, Apr. 21. Sulphin, Abraham, and Elenor Scout.
1773, Nov. 1. Summer, Margaret, and Thomas Hayes.
1763, Apr. 28. Summers, Ann, and William Willet.
1773, Jan. 6. Summers, George, and Ann Mesminger.
1745, June —. Summers, John.
1775, Apr. 24. Sunlightner, Peter, and Elizabeth Wyle.
1746, June —. Suplee, Jacob, and Margaret Yocum.
1774, Aug. 3. Supplee, David, and Susannah Goodwin.
1774, Sep. 26. Supplee, John, and Sarah Thomas.
1769, M'ch 4. Supplee, Jonathan, and Eleanor Morris.
1775, Nov. 25. Sutch, Benjamin, and Jane Roberts.
1767, Aug. 6. Sutherland, Dan'l, and Elizabeth Roxborough.
1766, Nov. 27. Sutor, Ann, and George Clark.
1768, June 27. Sutor, Bridget, and Charles Tomkins.
1766, Nov. 27. Sutor, Isabella, and Magnus Carr.
1767, Jan. 8. Sutor, Jacob, and Catharine Helm.
1767, May 6. Sutor, Thomas, and Bridget Hunt.
1766, June 14. Sutter, James, and Catharine Smith.

1772, June — Sutter, James, and Elizabeth Whitton.
1776, May 16. Sutter, Peter, and Mary Cooke.
1769, May 11. Sutter, Peter, and Sarah Deacon.
1773, Nov. 3. Sutton, Alice, and John Pemberton.
1762, Apr. 8. Sutton, Bartholomew, and Deborah Doyle.
1761, Oct. 19. Sutton, Elizabeth, and William Bagnall.
1763, Dec. 12. Sutton, Jane, and Jacob Paul
1771, Oct. 24. Sutton, John, and Catharine Bloomfield.
1747, Jan. —. Sutton, John, and Mary Nixon.
1764, Sep. 29. Sutton, John, and Sarah Stackhouse.
1766, Sep. 16. Sutton, Martha, and Daniel Darrel.
1760, Aug. 11. Sutton, Mary, and Joseph Cox.
1774, Aug. 27. Sutton, Mary, and Sampson Clark.
1764, Dec. 22. Sutton, Rachael, and George Skipsey.
1769, Nov. 2. Suttor, James, and Susannah Mannington.
1775, May 22. Swailes, Charity, and James Otis.
1768, Apr. 26. Swain, Catharine, and John Armour.
Swain, David, and Rebecca Evans.
1747, May —. Swain, Mary, and James Stevens.
1743, July 22. Swain, Thomas.
1773, Dec. 3. Swaine, Alice, and Richard Costolo.
1774, Nov. 19. Swaine, Elizabeth, and Adam Depperwin.
1775, Aug. 10. Swaine, Francis, and Mary Millenber.
1760, Nov. 28. Swaine, John, and Rebecca Inglis.
1768, Apr. 2. Swan, Catharine, and Roger Flahavan.
1768, Dec. 29. Swan, Peter, and Elizabeth Taney.
1773, Apr. 8. Swanson, Hannah, and James Fowler.
1761, Sep. 1. Swanson, Sarah, and John Cribb.
1776, May 21. Swanton, George, and Sarah Eslick.
1774, M'ch 3. Swartzlander, Gabriel, and Salome Freed.
1761, Feb. 18. Sweatman, Ann, and Edward Williams.
1747, Feb. —. Sweedish, Minister, and ——— Rambo.
1770, Apr. 24. Sweers, Cornelius, and Hannah Murdock.
1765, Aug. 7. Sweetapple, William, and Mary Kennady.
1775, Sep. 5. Sweitzer, Catharine, and Henry Meyer.
1773, Apr. 15. Swift, Hester, and John Holmes, Junior.
1774, Feb. 19. Swift, Samuel, Junior, and Martha Ashton.
1783, June 16. Swim, John.
1761, Jan. 22. Swim, Mary, and Scipio Williams.
1767, Nov. 28. Swinney, Dorcas, and Matthias Pennyard.
1775, Oct. 17. Swinney, Jane, and James Means.
1767, Aug. 3. Swinney, Sarah, and Ralph Walmsly.
1770, M'ch 21. Switzer, Simon, and Barbara Shunk.
1768, M'ch 26. Swope, Jacob, and Susannah Steinmetz.
1768, M'ch 17. Syme, John, and Sarah Hoops.
1771, May 20. Symes, John, and Mary Forrest.

1765, July   9. Symonds, William, and Mary Pearson.
1772, Apr. 13. Syng, Elizabeth, and John Murray.
1762, Dec. 29. Syng, Esther, and Samuel Bunting.
1768, M'ch 24. Syng, George, and Elizabeth Bayne.
1766, June 26. Syng, George, and Hannah Hance.
1771, June   6. Syng, Martha, and Zebulon Rudulph.
1747, June —. Syng, Mary, and Thomas James.
1766, Oct. 25. Sysom, Priscilla ,and Thomas Mason.

T.

1772, Mc'h 13. Taber, Hannah, and John Young.
1763, Oct. 29. Tabor, Rebecca, and Samuel Brusster.
1771, Nov. 30. Taggart, Elizabeth, and William Bonham.
1764, Nov. 10. Taggart, James, and Sarah Stinston.
1773, July 30. Talbert, Ann, and John Logan.
1772, Dec. 2. Talbert, Ann, and Thomas Robeson.
1761, Dec. 5. Talbert, Dorothy, and George Chilleat.
1760, Oct. 6. Talbert, Mary, and George Suber.
1761, July 28. Talbert, Mary, and Thomas Talbert.
1761, July 28. Talbert, Rachel, and George Ingram.
1761, July 28. Talbert, Thomas, and Mary Talbert.
1748, Aug. 15. Tale, William.
1761, Sep. 21. Talk, Adam, and Catharine Smith.
1768, Apr. 6. Talkington, Hannah, and Peter Plankton.
1760, Dec. 2. Tallas, Jane, and Samuel Bartow.
1770, Sep. 13. Tallman, Augustine, and Margaret Bankson.
1766, Oct. 22. Tallman, George, and Mary Chambers.
1771, Oct. 30. Tallman, Mary, and Andrew Bankson.
1768, Dec. 29. Taney, Elizabeth, and Peter Swan.
1769, Oct. 24. Taney, Henry, and Susannah Hiley.
1771, M'ch 2. Taney, John, and Susannah Ritchards.
1762, Apr. 12. Tannacker, George, and Margaret Herger.
1768, M'ch 7. Tannagh, Letitia, and Richard Mason.
1762, Aug. 5. Tanner, Ann, and James Sullavon.
1763, Sep. 14. Tanner, Martha, and Christian Wheily.
1775, Nov. 9. Tanzer, Rebecca, and John Hanna.
1770, May 30. Tape Eleanor, and John Barter.
1764, Dec. 13. Tarras, John, and Maragret Josiah.
1764, Jan. 25. Tarrence, William, and Rebecca West.
1761, Apr. 20. Tarry, Rachel, and Isaac Wilson.
1761, Sep. 5. Tate, Ann, and John Martin.
1770, Aug. 2. Tatem, Joseph, and Mary Rush.
1765, Sep. 5. Tatlow, Rebecca, and Benjamin Bruster.
1772, Feb. 17. Tatnall, Susanna, and John Flinn.
1744, Sep. —. Tatnel, John.
1775, Jan. 4. Tatum, Mary, and James Moyes.

1771, Aug. 30. Tavers, Elizabeth, and William Guirey.
1761, Oct. 12. Tavey, Francis, and Hyd Harmer.
1761, Nov. 23. Tawson, Thomas, and Sarah Bickham.
1776, Feb. 7. Tawzer, John, and Esther Spencer.
1763, June 22. Taylor, Abigail, and Gerrard Vanhorn.
1770, Feb. 21. Taylor, Abigail, and William Philips.
1770, Dec. 6. Taylor, Adam, and Mary Ryning.
1762, June 23. Taylor, Ann, and William Colston.
1773, Jan. 7. Taylor, Barbara, and Frederick Sent.
1768, Feb. 24. Taylor, Barbara, and Jacob Dowdishle.
1773, Dec. 6. Taylor, Benjamin, and Mary Carver.
1772, May 23. Taylor, Benjamin, and Tade Wright.
1770, Aug. 29. Taylor, Casper, and Elizabeth Heynen.
1772, May 20. Taylor, Catharine, and Abraham Collins.
1764, Feb. 6. Taylor, Christian, and Margaret Stouder.
1746, Aug. --. Taylor, Daniel, and Letitia Freame.
1766, Dec. 2. Taylor, Eleanor, and Joseph Lewis.
1760, M'ch 3. Taylor, Elenor, and Weight Massey.
1769, June 27. Taylor, Elizabeth, and Christian Nail.
1774, Jan. 17. Taylor, Elizabeth, and Edmund McVaugh.
1766, May 30. Taylor, Elizabeth, and Francis Ruth.
1763, June 11. Taylor, Elizabeth, and John McClenaghan.
1767, Aug. 22. Taylor, Elizabeth, and William Robinson.
1743, Sep. —. Taylor, Francis.
1773, May 7. Taylor, George, and Catharine Bickley.
1776, M ch 27. Taylor, Hannah, and Amos Dillworth.
1763, Sep. 10. Taylor, Hannah, and Thomas Lepis.
1774, M'ch 5. Taylor, Hannah, and William Wilkinson.
1763, July 1. Taylor, Hester, and Isaac Garrigues.
1768, June 9. Taylor, Isaac, and Mary Edwards.
1763, Apr. 28. Taylor, Isaac, and Mary Lowry.
1748, M'ch 11. Taylor, Isaac, and Sarah Stone.
1761, Oct. 6. Taylor, Isaac, and Susanna Bowles.
1764, Oct. 10. Taylor, Israel, and Susannah Dougherty.
1761, May 27. Taylor, James, and Margaret Carter.
1760, Dec. 9. Taylor, James, and Rachel House.
1775, June 7. Taylor, James, and Sarah Morrell.
1774, July 11. Taylor, Jane, and William Harding.
1772, June 3. Taylor, John, and Ann Huston.
1766, Apr. 15. Taylor, John, and Ann Redgrave.
1762, Aug. 9. Taylor, John, and Isabella Barnhill.
1773, May 6. Taylor, John, and Jane Lockridge.
1774, Apr. 9. Taylor, John, and Margaret Kissler.
1759, Dec. 8. Taylor, John, and Martha Poinyard.
1774, Jan. 15. Taylor, Joseph, and Ann Rambo.

1771, Aug. 28. Taylor, Lizzie, and John Young.
1775, Feb. 11. Taylor, Llewellyn Joseph, and Sarah Carpenter.
1762, May 24. Taylor, Martha, and Aquilla Potts.
1771, Dec. 19. Taylor, Martha, and Robert Evans.
1772, Apr. 16. Taylor, Mary, and Abraham Garret.
1761, Jan. 22. Taylor, Mary, and Abram Johnson.
1763, Dec. 2. Taylor, Mary, and Edward Bingley.
1764, Jan. 21. Taylor, Mary, and John Heath.
1766, Sep. 30. Taylor, Mary Worrel, and Persifor Frazer.
1776, Jan. 17. Taylor, Matthias, and Elizabeth McIntire.
1769, Feb. 27. Taylor, Michael, and Sophia Steffer.
1771, Feb. 4. Taylor, Peter, and Elizabeth Montgomery.
1769, Dec. 16. Taylor, Rebecca, and Adam Richey.
1773, June 19. Taylor, Rebecka, and Sketchley Morton.
1783, June 16. Taylor, Samuel.
1766, Apr. 17. Taylor, Samuel, and Mary Bankson.
1764, Dec. 5. Taylor, Sarah, and William Robinson.
1769, July 21. Taylor, Thomas, and Rosanna Statia.
1760, July 19. Taylor, William, and Hannah Holland.
1776, Feb. 21. Taylor, William, and Malley Patterson.
1771, May 23. Taylor, William, and Margaret Steel.
1768, Nov. 29. Taylor, William, and Mary Robins.
1761, M'ch 18. Tay Mary, and Thomas Fell.
1773, M'ch 19. Teaney, Margaret, and Henry Rhinehard.
1769, Sep. 20. Teany, Mary, and William Nealson.
1773, July 27. Teis, John, and Rachel Nicholson.
1762, M'ch 31. Telbin, Margaretta, and Gabriel Sagert.
1748, Sep. —. Tell, Elizabeth, and Peserue Brown.
1760, June 5. Temberman, Hannah and Frederick Stem.
1743, Sep. —. Tempest, Robert.
1775, Apr. 10. Tempest, Robert, and Deborah Shelly.
1773, Jan. 29. Temple, John, and Charlotte Shultzer.
1744, Sep. —. Temple, Leonard.
1763, Jan. 18. Templer, Mary, and Philip Thomas.
1766, Apr. 11. Templin, Hannah, and Philip Lloyd.
1764, Feb. 28. Templin, Richard, and Elizabeth Erwin.
1769, July 31. Tenbrook, Catharine, and Samuel Harvey.
1766, July 9. Tennant, Charles, and Catharine Galbreath.
1766, Aug. 11. Tennant, Sarah, and Samuel Cheeseman.
1769, Apr. 14. Tennant, William, and Mary Down.
1769, Dec. 9. Tennis, Mary, and Charles Horton.
1748, May 14. Terrill, James, and Sarah Smallwood.
1768, Oct. 1. Terrapin, Philip, and Agnes Hare.
1745, July —. Terr, Joseph.
1763, July 9. Terry, David, and Grace Davis.
1768, Nov. 3. Terry, Ruth, and George Farland.

1772, Oct. 10. Terry, Thomas, and ——— Davis.
1763, Dec. 29. Terwin, Elizabeth, and Conrad Torn.
1774, Nov. 15. Test, Ann, and Samuel Kingsley.
1773, Nov. 2. Tested, Jacob Bentsen, and Catharine Edwards.
1770, Sep. 15. Test, Henry, and Rachel Iszard.
1770, May 31. Test, Jane, and Joseph Town
1775, Aug. 28. Test, Sarah, and Patrick Wright.
1768, Feb. 20. Tew, Elizabeth, and Jonathan Williams.
1761, Aug. 17. Thackary, Benjamin, and Mary Anderson.
1765, Sep. 5. Thacker, Joseph, and Ann Andrews.
1771, Aug. 2. Tharp, William, and Ann Rose.
1776, May 20. Thaw, Benjamin, and Hannah Ingle.
1746, June —. Thaw, John, and Mary Rees.
1766, Dec. 1. Thecker, Catharine, and Richard Porter.
1763, June 14. Thecker, Robert, and Catharine Clark.
1763, Aug. 23. Thiminger, Elizabeth, and George Kimly.
1760, Aug. 9. Thiss, Andrew, and Catharine Dibo.
1771, Aug. 27. Thoman, Anne, and John Wister.
1774, M'ch 24. Thomas, Abel, and Elizabeth Roberts.
1761, Apr. 18. Thomas, Abram, and Elizabeth Hackett.
1761, Jan. 8. Thomas, Alice, and John Mathias.
1769, Sep. 20. Thomas, Amos, and Ruth Bate.
1772, Jan. 15. Thomas, Amos, and Ruth Lloyd.
1770, Apr. 18. Thomas, Anne, and John Butcher.
1772, Oct. 31. Thomas, Ann, and Griffith Phillips.
1767, Apr. 15. Thomas, Ann, and Robert Haubert.
1747, Dec. —. Thomas, Ann, and Samuel Coster.
1761, Apr. 25. Thomas, Ann, and William Hirst.
1760, Aug. 29. Thomas, Barbara, and Joseph Simon.
1774, M'ch 10. Thomas, Benjamin, and Mary Walker.
1773, Jan. 21. Thomas, Benjamin, and Sarah Dyer.
1775, Jan. 17. Thomas, Daniel, and Sarah Britton.
1768, Apr. 18. Thomas, Diana, and Benjamin Matthew.
1774, Feb. 22. Thomas, Eleanor, and Edward Matthew.
1767, Dec. 12. Thomas, Elias, and Elizabeth Howell.
1772, Apr. 10. Thomas, Elizabeth, and Abiah Butler.
1768, M'ch 8. Thomas, Elizabeth, and Henry Haines.
1772, M'ch 12. Thomas, Elizabeth, and John Helm.
1765, Aug. 16. Thomas, Elizabeth, and Robert Robertson.
1772, Sep. 29. Thomas, Elizabeth, and William McGuire.
1770, Dec. 16. Thomas, Evan, and Elizabeth Wilmington.
1745, Aug. —. Thomas, Ezekiel.
1760, Aug. 20. Thomas, Frances, and John Custard.
1775, Apr. 8. Thomas, Hannah, and Cornelius Wynkoop.
1768, Oct. 26. Thomas, Hannah, and Griffith Powell.
1767, M'ch 5. Thomas, Hannah, and Jacob Johnson.

1769, Feb. 15. Thomas, Hannah, and Lawrence Allman.
1764, May 26. Thomas, Hazeel, and Juliana Thomas.
1775, May 6. Thomas, Isaac, and Mary Hammer.
1763, Sep. 15. Thomas, Isaac, and Sarah Roberts.
1772, Apr. 10. Thomas, James, and Mary Lewis.
1773, Nov. 11. Thomas, Jane, and Samuel Crozier.
1770, Feb. 9. Thomas, Jane, and Walter Dugan.
1746, June —. Thomas, Jane, and William Wallace.
1761, July 20. Thomas, Japeth, and Mary Drake.
1761, Oct. 29. Thomas, Jemima, and Jonathan Albertson.
1766, May 2. Thomas, Job, and Rebecca Bait.
1745, June —. Thomas, John.
1764, May 22. Thomas, John, and Jane Evans.
1761, May 20. Thomas, John, and Margaret Jenkins.
1763, Apr. 13. Thomas, John, and Mary Hansel.
1772, July 8. Thomas, John, and Mary Rinn.
1762, Sep. 6. Thomas, John, and Sarah Humphreys.
1764, Aug. 3. Thomas, Jonathan, and Jane Large.
1774, M'ch 30. Thomas, Jonathan, and Sarah Freeman.
1768, Jan. 9. Thomas, Joseph, and Jane Grier.
1764, May 26. Thomas, Juliana, and Hazeel Thomas.
1775, M'ch 16. Thomas, Lewis, and Susannah Roberts.
1771, May 22. Thomas, Manassah, and Elizabeth Evans.
1761, Aug. 14. Thomos, Margaret, and James Butler.
1768, May 7. Thomas, Margaret, and Joseph Huddleston.
1763, M'ch 11. Thomas, Margaret, and Richard Lewis.
1763, Feb. 24. Thomas, Margery, and Dougaldus Ged.
1775, June 1. Thomas, Martha, and John Brown.
1770, Aug. 28. Thomas, Martha, and Peter Rainbow.
1770, June 4. Thomas, Martha, and Richard Whitton.
1764, May 27. Thomas, Mary, and Edward Chew.
1761, May 8. Thomas, Mary, and James Davis.
1764, May 16. Thomas, Mary, and John David.
1762, Feb. 13. Thomas, Mary, and John Elliot.
1764, Dec. 12. Thomas, Mary, and Joshua Evans.
1770, June 4. Thomas, Mary, and Robert Whitton.
1761, Jan. 5. Thomas, Mary, and Thomas Austin.
1765, Jan. 3. Thomas, Mary, and William Powell.
1771, Apr. 9. Thomas, Nathan, and Sarah Rhoads.
1743, May 14. Thomas, Philip.
1763, Jan. 18. Thomas, Philip, and Mary Templer.
1765, Oct. 21. Thomas, Phineas, and Elizabeth Harper.
1766, M'ch 24. Thomas, Rachel, and Andrew Ashton.
1770, Oct. 18. Thomas, Rachel, and Barnabas Kendry.
1772, May 2. Thomas, Rachel, and John Matthews.
1759, Dec. 19. Thomas, Rebecca, and Daniel Pugh.

1775, Oct. 24. Thomas, Richard, and Sarah Hall.
1764, May 26. Thomas, Ruth, and William Griffiths.
1773, June 9. Thomas, Samuel, and Elizabeth Noble.
1772, M'ch 26. Thomas, Samuel, and Elizabeth Palmer.
1765, Nov. 28. Thomas, Samuel, and Mercy Collins.
1775, June 10. Thomas, Samuel, and Priscilla Evans.
1764, Apr. 20. Thomas, Samuel, and Susannah Shaw.
1774, Sep. 27. Thomas, Sarah, and Jeremiah Delany.
1767, Jan. 17. Thomas, Sarah, and John Hitchcock.
1774, Sep. 26. Thomas, Sarah, and John Supplee.
1760, Nov. 20. Thomas, Sarah, and Thomas Luptan.
1748, July 13. Thomas, Sarah, and William Weldon.
1764, Oct. 13. Thomas, Seth, and Martha Kirks.
1747, Aug. —. Thomas, Sidney, and John Jenkins.
1772, May 13. Thomas, Susannah, and William Stukesbury.
1764, Oct. 3. Thomas, Tacy, and John Chatham.
1772, Dec. 31. Thomas, Thomas, and Mary Dean.
1775, Nov. 18. Thomas, William, and Elizabeth Waters.
1774, Jan. 29. Thomas, William, and Mary Morgan.
1771, May 22. Thomas, William, and Mary Pearson.
1765, M'ch 14. Thomlinson, Benjamin, and Mary Isler.
1770, Jan. 18. Thompson, Alexander, and Catharine Shee.
1771, Oct. 29. Thompson, Alexander, and Mary Stewart.
1774, Nov. 14. Thompson, Ann, and Thomas Weir.
1765, May 15. Thompson, Ann, and Walter Shee.
1766, June 4. Thompson, Archibald, and Hannah Bartholomew.
1766, Apr. 12. Thompson, Archibald, and Sarah Hayes.
1762, Dec. 28. Thompson, David, and Mary Hutchison.
1769, Oct. 11. Thompson, Edward, and Sarah Parmely.
1766, Nov. 6. Thompson, Eleanor, and Frederick Lauderbrun.
1766, May 27. Thompson, Eleanor, and John Cummings.
1760, Oct. 27. Thompson, Elizabeth, and John Saunders.
1764, Jan. 11. Thompson, Elizabeth, and Matthew Scott.
1766, June 20. Thompson, Elizabeth, and William Neely.
1770, Dec. 27. Thompson, George, and Jane Hamilton.
1772, July 28. Thompson, George, and Rebecca Cash.
1767, June 27. Thompson, George, and Ruth Price.
1762, Feb. 6. Thompson, George, and Susannah Donavan.
1770, Nov. 20. Thompson, Hugh, and Hannah Welsh.
1773, June 24. Thompson, James, and Elizabeth Parsons.
1761, M'ch 19. Thompson, James, and Letitia Nichols.
1768, Feb. 15. Thompson, James, and Sarah Falconer.
1764, M'ch 15. Thompson, Jane, and Hugh Neilson.
1772, Jan. 16. Thompson, Jane, and Thomas Wiley.
1774, M'ch 26. Thompson, John, and Ann Garrett.
1770, Dec. 3. Thompson, John, and Hannah Parker.

1762, Feb. 17. Thompson, John, and Mary Huston.
1771, Nov. 15. Thompson, John, and Rebecca Gunning.
1766, Sep.   2. Thompson, John, and Ruth Legit.
1763, Nov. 23. Thompson, John, and Sarah Ritchison.
1766, May   8. Thompson, Joseph, and Sarah Hawkins.
1770, Feb. 20. Thompson, Margaret, and Nicholas Hollingshead.
1766, Apr. 23. Tompson, Margaret, and Robert Allison.
1769, July 28. Thompson, Martha, and Brent Spencer.
1776, Jan. 10. Thompson, Mary, and James Alexander.
1773, Jan.   9. Thompson, Mary, and John Rhoads.
1773, Sep   30. Thompson, Matthew, and Margaret Nuttle.
1776, M'ch 18. Thompson, Peter, and Martha Wharton.
1760, Feb. 12. Thompson, Rebecca, and William Derrock.
1771, Apr. 26. Thompson, Richard, and Elizabeth Ozier.
1769, Jan. 21. Thompson, Sarah, and Alexander Craig.
1763, Dec. 17. Thompson, Sarah, and Henry Butler.
1774, July 11. Thompson, Saran, and John Barr.
1764, Oct. 11. Thompson, Sarah, and William Mason.
1761, Aug.   1. Thompson, Sarah, and William Morton.
1767, Sep. 12. Thompson, Serene, and Joseph ——— (negroes.)
1766, Nov. 12. Thompson, Thomas, and Elizabeth Maxwell.
1771, May   7. Thompson, Thomas, and Margaret Wallace.
1775, Oct. 19. Thompson, William, and Elizabeth Campbell.
1745, Feb. —. Thomson, Andrew.
1745, June —. Thomson, James.
1746, June —. Thomson, James Steel, and Martha Lamplugh.
1746, Dec. —. Thomson, Joseph, and Ann Gelhard.
1747, June —. Thomson, Martha, and William Bubb.
1748, M'ch 11. Thomson, Robert, and Hannah Delaplain.
1775, June 20. Thomson, Sarah, and Francis Fox.
1744, May   —. Thomson, Thomas.
1773, Jan.   7. Thorn, Aaron, and Elizabeth Van.
1767, Dec.   2. Thornborough, Thomas, and Martha Stevenson.
1775, Oct. 11. Thornburn, Margaret, and Philip Henry.
1769, July 15. Thorne, Martha, and Daniel McLane.
1767, Nov. 24. Thornhill, Hannah, and Joseph Garner.
1764, May   30. Thornhill, Mary, and John Dewers.
1748, Oct. 18. Thornhill, Susanna, and David Dewer.
1760, May   6. Thornton, John, and Mary Hamilton.
1760, Dec. 24. Thornton, Jospeh, and Elizabeth Willet.
1772, Nov. 14. Thorp, Thomas, and Elizabeth Newlin.
1775, Feb.   3. Thowtissel, Margaret, and Daniel Robinson.
1762, May   11. Thrasher, Mary, and Peace Woodman.
1774, M'ch   5. Threlfal, Robert, and Elizabeth Braithwaite.
1774, Feb. 16. Thum, George, and Sarah Peters.
1767, Dec. 17. Tickleson, Elizabeth, and Jacob Slager.

1761, June   6. Thieft, Robert, and Mary Connaway.
1763, Apr. 27. Tilden, Anna, and John Bell.
1774, May   25. Tilghman, Edward, and Elizabeth Chew.
1743, Sep. —. Tilghman, James.
1772, M'ch 13. Till, Rebecka, and Simon Hufty.
1769, Oct. 28. Tillyer, Mary, and Thomas Beam, Jun.
1765, Oct. 21. Tillyer, Tamar, and Isaac States.
1775, Feb.   3. Timmons, Dean, and Mary Samuels.
1773, Sep.   1. Timmons, John, and Hannah Berry.
1774, Aug. 27. Tingle, Samuel, and Rebecca Bryan.
1769, June 28. Tinney, Elizabeth, and John Highle.
1764, June 13. Tinsmanin, Catharine, and Martin Holder.
1775, Nov.   1. Tipler, John, and Mary Doyl.
1743, Oct. —. Tipper, James.
1761, Aug.   7. Tippet John, and Dorothy Bethrat.
1771, May   14. Tisdale, Thomas, and Elizabeth Cresserin.
1764, M'ch 28. Titeem, Elizabeth, and John Cochan.
1773, Apr. 29. Tittermary, Letitia, and William Glover.
1745, Dec. —. Titus. "A Negro man."
1760, M'ch 25, Titus, Ann, and Joseph White.
1765, May   10. Titus, Elizabeth, and John Hellings.
1764, Jan. 14. Titus, Francis, and Margaret Wynkoop.
1761, Nov. 17. Titus, Jacob, and Hannah Kelly.
1770, Oct. 27. Titus, Samuel, and Deborah Feathers.
1775, Feb.   5. Titus, Sarah, and Jacob Vandegrift.
1760, Nov. 22. Titus, Tunnis, and Elizabeth Roberts.
1775, June   8. Tobin, Margaret, and Donald Conell.
1771, Jan.   5. Tod, Alexander, and Mary Sharp.
1770, June 30. Todd, Joseph, and Anne White.
1772, Apr.   1. Todd, Mary, and Hugh Meredith.
1748, Oct. 18. Todd, Mary, and John Corbet.
1766, Nov.   4. Todd, Sarah, and Hugh Nevin.
1762, May   4. Todd, Sarah, and John Finley.
1766, Nov. 27. Todd, William, and Ann Rambo.
1775, Nov. 11. Todd, William, and Hannah Davis.
1759, Dec. 22. Todman, John, and Rachel Young.
1761, Nov. 14. Toff, Jane, and Samuel Griffin.
1769, Dec.   9. Toland, Mary, and Thomas Lepper.
1763, Feb. 25. Tolbald, Mary, and Henry Williams.
1766, Sep. 17. Tomkin, Thomas, and Elizabeth Collister.
1764, M'ch 27. Tomkins, George, and Abigail Gilbert.
1768, June 27. Tompkins, Charles, and Bridget Sutor.
1748, Apr. 13. Tompkins, Elizabeth, and Nathan Warley.
1767, Apr.   1. Tompkins, Elizabeth, and William Bourk.
1765, Apr.   5. Tompkins, James, and Sarah Nixon.
1763, Apr. 26. Tompkins, Sarah, and Jacob Jones.

1762, Nov. 11. Tomland, Hugh, and Jane Brown.
1774, Nov. 5. Tomler, Isaac, and Ann Waggoner.
1743, June 13. Tomlinson, Benjamin.
1763, Sep. 13. Tomlinson, Ebenezer, and Ann Coggins.
1762, Apr. 19. Tomlinson, John, and Sarah Black.
1744, Sep. —. Tomlinson, Joseph.
1774, Oct. 8. Tomlinson, Thomas, and Phebe Carver.
1760, Sep. 11. Tomplinson, Sarah, and George Nelson.
1776, Apr. 24. Tonry, Patrick, and Margaret Kenan.
1775, Sep. 27. Tool, Mary, and Patrick Hare.
1747, Apr. —. Top, Ann, and George Sherswood.
1765, July 27. Topham, Daniel, and Mary Hope.
1763, Dec. 29. Torn, Conrad, and Elizabeth Terwin.
1770, June 6. Torr, John, and Hannah Brannin.
1761, Apr. 9. Torrons, John, and Jane Williams.
1747, May —. Torten, Andrew, and Susannah Cox.
1774, May. 27. Torton, Ann, and John Likens.
1761, Dec. 12. Tosst, Ann, and Henry Dorrel.
1747, Dec. —. Totten, Hannah, and Henry Dunn.
1745, May —. Totten, Joseph.
1775, M'ch 29. Towers, Mary, and William Roberts.
1746, M'ch. —. Towers, Robert.
1770, May 31. Town, Joseph, and Jane Test.
1772, Apr. 16. Towne, Benjamin, and Abigail Doughty.
1776, May 11. Towne, Benjamin, and Sarah Johnson.
1769, Feb. 14. Townshend, Margaret, and William Guy.
1774, Dec. 10. Townsend, Ann, and Nicholas Scull.
1768, June 6. Townsend, Elizabeth, and Peter Brusstar.
1766, Dec. 2. Townsend, Susannah, and Richard Lyndall.
1773, Sep. 10. Townsley, Joanna, and John Dorohue.
1765, May 10. Townson, Elizabeth, and Samuel Skillen.
1762, Mc'h 23. Toy, Eleanor, and Andrew Donaldson.
1766, June 12. Toy, Eleanor, and Robert Brewton.
1775, Oct. 2. Toy, Elizabeth, and Isaac Atkinson.
1776, M'ch 23. Toy, Hannah, and Timothy Cavener.
1748, May 14. Toy, James, and Patience Wallis.
1774, Apr. 15. Toy, William, and Mary Fitzsimmons.
1773, June 23. Trace, Elizabeth, and William Baths.
1773, Aug. 10. Trace, Peter, and Mary Weaver.
1771, Oct. 14. Trager, Hannah, and Amos Matlack.
1770, Dec. 22. Trapnel, Elizabeth, and Richard Barret.
1767, Mc'h 30. Trasse, Thomas, and Elizabeth Singleton.
1760, Oct. 11. Travers, Philip, and Eliazbeth Papy.
1763, July 26. Traygo, Elizabeth, and Nathan Moore.
1764, M'ch 26. Tree, Lambert, and Margaret Hamilton.
1771, Feb. 19. Treen, Henry, and Catharine Gallagher.

1775, Aug.   3. Tremble, Hannah, and Nicholas Millet.
1773, M'ch 16. Tremble, Thomas, and Hannah Brooks.
1743, May 17. Tremble, William.
1765, Jan. 10. Trent, Mary, and Silas Engles.
1774, Nov. 22. Tresse, Elizabeth, and Thomas Pugh.
1745, Sep. —. Treviller, James.
1761, May   7. Trigger, Ann, and Joseph Hunt.
1776, Feb. 10. Triggs, Jane, and David McFee.
1770, Nov. 26. Trimble, Eleanor, and Nicholas Young.
1745, Dec. —. Trimble, William.
1783, June 12. Trissler, Philip.
1774, June 10. Trist, Nicholas, and Elizabeth House.
1773, Dec. 17. Trites, Michael, and Elizabeth Grover.
1776, Feb.   7. Troth, Isaac, and Mary Assherton.
1768, July 20. Trotter, Joseph, Jr, and Sarah Robinson.
1748, Jan. —. Trotter, Spencer, and Margaret Welhany.
1776, Jan. 30. Troutman, Christian, and Elizabeth Foulckrod.
1771, Apr. 26. Truckenmiller, Charles, and Susannah Sadler.
1775, Apr. 17. Truckenmiller, John, and Susannah Bauer.
1769, June 22. Trumble, Francis, and Hannah Gardner.
1764, Nov. 23. Trumble, Sarah, and Thomas Mushett.
1762, July 12. Trump, Rebecca, and John Smallwood.
1760, Oct.   1. Trump, Sarah, and George, Bainhurst.
1768, May 11. Tucker, Andrew, and Sarah Stoops.
1770, Dec.   8. Tucker, Anne, and James White.
1765, Oct. 31. Tucker, Charity, and Robert Twales.
1760, Sep. 23. Tucker, Cornelius, and Ann Creighton.
1743, Oct. —. Tucker, Richard.
1765, Dec. 23. Tucker, Robert, and Mary Garret.
1766, Sep. 10. Tucker, Sarah, and Robert Smith.
1771, Oct.   2. Tucker, Stephen, and Ann Dupree.
1769, June 22. Tuckness, John, and Elizabeth White.
1775, July 22. Tuckney, Frances, and Philip Reybolt.
1767, June 27. Tuckniss, Mary, and Joseph Pearson.
1760, M'ch 3. Tader, Henry, and Elenon Dushane.
1761, Sep. 10. Tuff, Alice, and John Richards.
1773, Jan. 28. Tufft, Alice, and John Hickley.
1766, Dec.   8. Tufft, John, and Martha Gauff,
1767, Jan.   1. Tufft, Mary, and William Oates.
1764, Dec.   8. Tulet, John, and Catharine Weber.
1761, Oct. 29. Tuley, Abraham, and Hannah Slicer.
1760, Apr.   1. Tullerton, Margaret, and John Lemont.
1765, Jan. 15. Tull, James, and Mary Wood.
1764, Apr. 21. Turbury, Elizabeth, and Joseph Givin.
1764, May 10. Turk, John, and Ann Davis.
1770, Nov. 27. Turner, Alice, and Henry Read.

1768, June 10. Turner, Amelia, and John Brant.
1773, Oct. 18. Turner, Anne, and William Morris.
1767, Apr. 29. Turner, Ebenezer, and Ann Estleck.
1760, Dec. 16. Turner, Elizabeth, and James Baxter.
1770, Oct. 26. Turner, Jane, and William Vaghan.
1746, M'ch —. Turner, John.
1746, Aug —. Turner, John, and Mary Dagger.
1776, Feb. 19. Turner, John, and Mary Green.
1766, Apr. 7. Turner, Martha, and George Armstrong.
1766, Sep. 29. Turner, Mary, and John King.
1773, June 15. Turner, Matthew, and Mary Peters.
1762, Dec. 31. Turner, Peter, Junior, and Rebecca Bird.
1763, Sep. 6. Turner, Robert, and Mary McGlaughlin.
1772, July 9. Turner, William, and Abigail Anthony.
1770, M'ch 26. Turner, William, and Ruth Miller.
1767, Feb. 16. Turner, William, and Susannah Nice.
1760, Nov. 26. Turning, Eleazer, and Mary Colton.
1760, Feb. 5. Turrance, Martha, and William Miller
1764, Nov. 7. Tussey, Ann, and George Stanton.
1776, May 2. Tustin, Ann, and Edward Loder.
1769, Aug. 23. Tustine, Abraham, and Catharine Sellar.
1769, Jan. 13. Tustin, Mary, and Peter Sellar.
1761, Oct. 15. Twaits, Agnes, and James Chapman.
1765, Oct. 31. Twales, Robert, and Charity Tucker.
1761, Dec. 31. Tweddle, John, and Margaret McCroney.
1770, Sep. 19. Twells, Godfrey, and Sarah Standley.
1760, July 28. Twiner, Mary, and Thomas Buckley.
1765, Sep. 21. Twining, Sarah, and David Loofborough.
1764, Dec. 1. Twyer, Bridget, and James McGraw.
1775, June 23. Tybout, Esther, and John Fisher.
1771, May 18. Tyce, Andrew, and Rosin Blaze.
1772, May 23. Tyce, Jacob, and Elizabeth Ritchie.
1762, Feb. 3. Tynand, Thomas, and Mary Cally.
1772, Nov. 9. Tyrer, Thomas, and Catharine Willson.
1761, July 30. Tyshang, Peter, and Ann Kelson.
1775, Apr. 22. Tyson, Elizabeth, and Samuel Brown.
1773, Oct. 27. Tyson, Joseph, and Elizabeth Robinson.
1769, Aug. 21. Tyson, Richard, and Anne Atwell.

U.

1769, Sep. 14. Ublevy, Frederick, and Catharine Baltiwine.
1745 June —. Ulrick, Peter.
1773, Feb. 12. Ulrick, Rebecca, and Frederick Lauderburr.
1762, Sep. 14. Ummensetter, Jacob, and Elizabeth Beyer.
1772, Feb. 12. Umpstead, Abigail, and Samuel Hendricks.
1767, Sep. 19. Umstead, Catharine, and Enoch Wells.

1765, Feb.   1. Umstead, Harman, and Elizabeth Francis.
1768, Jan.   22. Umsted, John, and Catharine Miller.
1771, Sept. 14. Updegraff, Ann, and Jacob Clemens.
1773, Nov.   10. Updike, John, and Rebecca Wharton.
1765, June   26. Urch, James, and Mary Adams.
1776, Apr.   6. Usher, Ann, and George Henry.
1760, M'ch   18. Usher, Margaret, and James Hastings.
1774, Aug.   2. Ute, John, and Elizabeth Groce.
1772, June   11. Utree, Catharine, and Philip Odenhaimer.
1772, Oct.   15. Utre, Jacob, and Mary Gardner.

V.

1775, Oct.   31. Vackenhurst, Mary, and Andrew Lex.
1770, Oct.   26. Vaghan, William, and Jane Turner.
1770, Dec.   12. Vago, Mary, and William Smart.
1776, May   8. Valentine, Henry, and Sarah Buckin.
1761, July   30. Vallacut, Frances, and John Morrison.
1766, Oct.   8. Vallance, Nickolas, and Mary Williamson.
1764, May   1. Valtotten, Jacob, and Elizabeth Warner.
1773, Jan.   7. Van, Elizabeth, and Aaron Thorn.
1770, Oct.   24. Vananda, George, and Anne Dungan.
1774, M'ch   26. Vanartsdalen, Simon, and Joanna Hogleand.
1761, Jan.   7. Van Buskett, Andrew, and Rebecca Wankoop.
1776, Jan.   30. Van Buskirk, Andrew, and Mary Fetters.
1764, M'ch   15. Van Buskirk, Jacobus, and Mary Holleback.
1768, M'ch   26. Van Buskirk, Priscilla, and Peter Vanhorn.
1770, Nov.   6. Van Campen, Moses, and Sarah Overfelt.
1764, Dec.   22. Vance, John, and Ann McNeer.
1768, M'ch   7. Vance, John, and Martha Farmer.
1768, Nov.   21. Vance, John, and Mary Wood.
1771, May   21. Vancourt, Daniel, and Jane Austin.
1772, May   5. Vancourt, Elizabeth, and John Barnsley.
1768, Sep.   6. Vancourt, Sarah, and James Fulton.
1744, Jan.   —. Van Culm, Catharine, and Andrew Daibo.
1776, Feb.   15. Vandegrift, Amelia, and Thomas Beck.
1760, June   26. Vandegrift, Cornelius, and Elizabeth Vanzant.
1746, June   —. Vandegrift, Esther, and John Houton.
1760, Apr.   29. Vandegrift, Foleart, and Elizabeth Watson.
1763, June   16. Vandegrift, Garrard, and Sarah Delaplan.
1775, Feb.   5. Vandegrift, Jacob, and Sarah Titus.
1761, Apr.   16. Vandegrift, John, and Ann Walton.
1766, Sep.   27. Vandegrift, Nicholas, and Abigail Ward.
1772, Apr.   2. Vandegrift, Rebecca, and Henry Fagan.
1766, Feb.   3. Vanderlip, Elias, and Elizabeth Murray.
1774, Feb.   14. Vanderman, William, and Sarah Pyatt.
1772, Aug.   14. Vanderoof, Rachel, and Samuel Wallace.

1763, Oct. 27. Vanderslice, Anthony, and Elizabeth Pennebaker.
1764, Jan. 23. Vanderslice, John, and Rebecca Sherier.
1762, Oct. 12. Van Dike, Mary, and Jacob Wimmer.
1773, Aug. 25. Vanduff, Frederick, and Margaret Vanpalton.
1770, May 31. Vandyke, Cornelius, and Elizabeth Yerkes.
1766, Jan. 8. Vandyke, John, and Martha Huston.
1761, Aug. 10. Vanhorn, Christian, and Elizabeth Plumer.
1744, July 21. Vanhirst, Samuel.
1769, M'ch 4. Vanhorn, Abigail, and John Awlman.
1764, Aug. 24. Vanhorn, Bernard, and Jane Slack.
1764, Jan. 10. Vanhorn, Catharine, and John Suber.
1774, M'ch 7. Vanhorn, Catharine, and Ralph Crumbly.
1763, June 22. Vanhorn, Gerrard, and Abigail Taylor.
1775, Jan. 5. Vanhorn, Isaiah, and Catharine Rue.
1776, Feb. 1. Vanhorn, Jacob, and Lydia Moode.
1770, Jan. 25. Vanhorn, John, and Johanna Sheerman.
1762, M'ch 1. Vanhorn, John, and Margaret Pearson.
1768, May 25. Vanhorn, Margaret, and John Lazelere.
1769, Apr. 24. Vanhorn, Martha, and Henry Mitchell.
1768, M'ch 26. Vanhorn, Peter, and Priscilla Van Buskirk.
1764, June 11. Vanhorne, Christian, and Sarah Vanzant.
1772, Jan. 18. Vanhorne, Gabriel, and Mary Vansant.
1748, Nov. 11. Vanhorne, Lydia, and Thomas Collet.
1763, Jan. 4. Vankirk, Jacob, and Jane Hall.
1748, Apr. 13. Vankirk, Sarah, and Peter Johnson.
1744, July 21. Vanleer, Nathaniel.
1764, July 26. Vanleer, Priscilla, and Frederick Stonemetz.
1761, Oct. 21. Van Luviney, Mary, and John Martin.
1764, Sep. 10. Vanneman, Elizabeth, and Samuel Lench.
1776, M'ch 2. Vannosdon, Jane, and Garret Kouzer.
1773, Aug. 25. Vanpalton, Margaret, and Frederick Vanduff.
1773, Jan. 18. Vanpelt, Alice, and Zephania Lott.
1766, Nov. 12. Vanpelt, Joseph, and Charity Bennet.
1769, Feb. 14. Van Reed, Henry, and Anna Eastered.
1775, June 2. Van Reed, John, and Eve Yost.
1774, Aug. 23. Van Reed, Susannah, and Fred'k Kisselman.
1768, Aug. 27. Vansandt, Hannah, and Nathaniel Vansandt.
1767, Apr. 1. Vansandt, James, and Susannah Scull.
1768, Aug. 27. Vansandt, Nathaniel, and Hannah Vansandt.
1773, M'ch 13. Vansant, Garret, and Elizabeth Stevens.
1766, Oct. 22. Vansant, Herman, and Catharine Hogeland.
1768, Oct. 1. Vansant, James, and Rebecca Comley.
1773, Sep. 11. Vansant, Kesia, and Abraham Britton.
1772, Jan. 18. Vansant, Mary, and Gabriel Vanhorne.
1768, Jan. 9. Vansant, Rebecca, and Daniel Billew.
1761, M'ch 30. Vansickler, Richard, and Elizabeth Winecope.

1765, June 6. Vansciver, Catharine, and William Mills.
1764, Jan. 21. Vansciver, Jacob, and Esther Clare.
1767, Nov. 10. Vansickle, Mary, and Christopher Hilburn.
1760, June 26. Vanzant, Elizabeth, and Cornelius Vandegrift.
1747, Apr. —. Vanzant, Garret, and Lea Nixon.
1760, Apr. 30. Vanzant, Garret, and Rebecca Evans.
1744, May —. Vanzant, Nicholas.
1760, Dec. 24. Vanzant, Phebe, and Miles Strickland.
1764, June 11. Vanzant, Sarah, and Christian Vanhorne.
1769, Dec. 16. Vastine, Benjamin, and Catharine Heaton.
1759, Dec. 19. Vastine, Sarah, and Samuel Wilson.
1763, Feb. 19. Vaughan, Ann, and Charles Lyon.
1760, July 21. Vaughan, Elizabeth, and Daniel Greenough.
1764, Jan. 4. Vaughan, Isaac, and Jane Lawrence.
1744, Feb. —. Vaughan, John, and Elizabeth Hunt.
1764, Jan. 22. Vaughan, Mary, and George Daullis.
1774, Dec. 15. Vaughan, Sarah, and William Fling.
1761, May 6. Vaughn, Ann, and Lane Naylor.
1774, Feb. 26. Veasy Pleasant, and James Randall.
1763, Apr. 14. Venable, Robert, and Diana, (negroes.
1771, M'ch 18. Venaken, Rebecca, and John Martin.
1744, Oct. —. Venaman, Tobias.
1761, Jan. 30. Verdiere, Veronique, and Michael Panton.
1771, Feb. 6. Verity, Jacob, and Jennet Blair.
1763, June 1. Verkheiser, Nicholas, and Margaretta Philipinna.
1776, Mar. 22. Verner, Elias, and Catharine Slyder.
1770, Jan. 31. Vernon, Edward, and Mary Mathers.
1762, June 5. Vernon, Robert, and Phebe Hart.
1775, Jan. 23. Vernor, Jacob, and Sarah McDaniel.
1760, Feb. 13. Vershon, Felix, and Ameron Butler.
1762, Aug. 10. Vesey, William, and Pleasant Nichols.
1762, Oct. 9. Vestine, Hannah, and Samuel Graham.
1769, Nov. 14. Vicary, John, and Mary Harvey.
1761, Aug. 3. Vickers, Mary, and William Pennington.
1761, Oct. 9. Vickery, Elizabeth, and John Willis.
1762, April 6. Vickery, Samuel, and Rebecca Lumley.
1783, June 16. Vincent, Alexander.
1765, May 1. Vineyard, Charles, and Henrietta Pearson.
1770, Apr. 28. Vinnest, Mary, and John Lovell.
1763, Aug. 2. Vivers, Margaret, and Richard White.
1765, Apr. 24. Vogdas, Jacob, and Elizabeth Hampton.
1760, July 22. Vokins, Sarah, and Edward Nicholson.
1767, May 11. Volans, Joseph, and Mary Shearcross.
1763, Aug. 10. Vore, Gideon, and Mary Adams.
1766, Oct. 9. Voto, Sarah, and Samuel Jackson.

W.

1776, Apr. 18. Wack, Casper, and Mary Leydey.
1768, Jan. 18. Waddel, Isabella, and William Sheed.
1768, Oct. 1 Waddington, Richard, and Mary Hartley.
1765, Oct. 17. Wade, Andrew, and Susannah Ackles.
1773, M'ch 4. Wade, Ann, and John Stark.
1763, Aug. 11. Wade, James, and Rebecca Weaver.
1770, Jan. 30. Wager, John, and Sarah Harper.
1771, Oct. 31. Wager, Philip, ahd Mary Keller.
1774. Nov. 5. Waggoner, Ann, and Isaac Tomler.
1766, Aug. 4. Waggoner, Deborah, and John Smith.
1770, May 9. Waggoner, Elizabeth, and John Snyder.
1773, June 22. Waggoner, John, and Elizabeth Levan.
1765, Dec. 20. Waggoner, Margaret, and Christian Kremer.
1772, Apr. 10. Waggoner, Mary, and Conrod Carl.
1765, May 7. Wagstaff, Thomas, and Hannah Leech.
1745, Nov. —. Wagstaffe, James.
1744, Nov. —. Waillon, Andrew.
1762, Aug. 3. Wain, Michael, and Elizabeth Hall.
1744, July 21. Wainwright, Jonathan.
1743, Oct. —. Wakefield, John.
1766, Dec. 10. Wakefield, Thomas, and Elizabeth Willard.
1746, Oct. —. Walder, Frederick, and Elizabeth Brenneman.
1747, Aug. —. Waldrick, James, and Mary Ford.
1762, Nov. 8. Walker, Adam, and Susannah Mewhouse.
1775, Nov. 15. Walker, Ann, and Richard Mosely.
1766, Dec. 8. Walker, Catharine, and Benjamin Devo.
1775, Nov. 15. Walker, Elizabeth, and John Adams.
1761, Oct. 29. Walker, Hannah, and Jacob Hultzheimer.
1769, Dec. 20. Walker, Hannah, and Joseph Keegan.
1765, Oct. 1. Walker, James, and Melissim Robinson.
1761, Nov. 7. Walker, Jerman, and Jane Martin.
1774, M'ch 10. Walker, Mary, and Benjamin Thomas.
1773, May 27. Walker, Mary, and John Lyne.
1760, Jan. 21. Walker, Mary, and John Stone.
1772, June 16. Walker, Mary, and Thomas Clayton.
1760, July 1. Walker, Peter, and Sarah Webb.
1769, May 6. Walker, Robert, and Ann Maag.
1764, Aug. 1. Walker, Robert, and Isabella Hughes.
1747, Aug. —. Walker, Samuel, and Agnes Lloyd.
1764, Dec. 11. Walker, Samuel, and Elizabeth Derringer.
1760, July 18. Walker, Sarah, and Edward Marefield.
1773, June 17. Walker, Sarah, and Jacob Willson.
1761, Nov. 7. Walker, Sarah, and Randal Martin.
1771, Sep. 25. Walker, Sarah, and Thomas Hammitt.

1772, Sep. 16. Walker, Thomas, and Margaret Hoops.
1767, June 27. Walker, Thomas, and Martha Dickson.
1760, Nov. 19. Wallace, Jane, and Robert Hutchinson.
1774, July 13. Wallace, John, and Ann Neal.
1773, Apr. 27. Wallace, Joseph, and Elizabeth Weaver.
1775, Jan. 19. Wallace, Joseph Jacob, and Elizabeth Lukens.
1773, Aug. 3. Wallace, Joshua Maddox, and Tace Bradford.
1771, May 7. Wallace, Margaret, and Thomas Thompson.
1774, July 7. Wallace, Mary, and Robert Richardson Cross.
1775, M'ch 17. Wallace, Robert, and Margaret Kenney.
1746, Aug. —. Wallace, Samuel, and Elizabeth Baird.
1774, Apr. 11. Wallace, Samuel, and Jemima Dean.
1772, Aug. 14. Wallace, Samuel, and Rachel Vanderoof.
1769, July 3. Wallace, Susannah, and Samuel Baker.
1771, Sep. 27. Wallace, Thomas Edward, and Sarah Dennis.
1746, June —. Wallace, William, and Jane Thomas.
1761, M'ch. 3. Walling, John, and Sarah Heaton.
1763, June 2. Wallington, Timothy, and Mary Honey.
1760, Dec. 3. Wallin, Richard, and Catharine Shippen.
1762, Nov. 13. Wallis, Benjamin, and Margaret Stemers.
1772, M'ch 11. Wallis, Elizabeth, and William Barker.
1767, May 15. Wallis, Jane, and John Wallis.
1767, May 15. Wallis, John, and Jane Wallis.
1763, Dec. 14. Wallis, Mary, and Jacob Kinnard.
1748, Apr. 13. Wallis, Patience, and James Toy.
1761, Nov. 27. Wallis, Robert, and Lilley George.
1770, M'ch 1. Wallis, Samuel, and Lydia Hollingsworth.
1771, Feb. 12. Wall, John, and Hannah Flower.
1762, May 29. Wall, Martha, and Edward Hare.
1761, Sep. 30. Wall, Mary, and James Brown.
1745, Nov. —. Walls, Robert.
1766, Dec. 24. Wall, Thomas, and Mary Dowthait.
1747, June —. Walm, Mary, and Joseph Brown.
1767, Aug. 23. Walmsly, Ralph, and Sarah Swinney.
1760, May 29. Walner, Katharine, and John Ellick.
1748, Sep. —. Walner, Martha, and Joseph Ferguson.
1773, Apr. 24. Waln, Hannah, and Jonathan Matlack.
1743, May 17. Walpole, Robert.
1776, May 13. Walsh, Richard, and Catharine Haas.
1768, Oct. 31. Walter, John, and Mary Rouse.
1764, Aug. 1. Walter, Mary, and Adam Weidner.
1774, May 4. Walters, Mary, and John Williams.
1774, Oct. 26. Walters, Robert, and Mary McKivin.
1771, Feb. 7. Walters, William, and Catharine McCarty.
1765, Oct. 30. Walter, Thomas, and Rebecca Pennell.
1761, Apr. 16. Walton, Ann, and John Vandegrift.

1773, June 16. Walton, Boaz, and Mary Assheton.
1762, Dec. 24. Walton, Boaz, and Rebecca Leech.
1761, Sep. 1. Walton, Daniel, and Sarah Gilbert.
1774, Jan. 4. Walton, David, and Rebecca Secverns.
1776, Feb. 3. Walton, Elizabeth, and James Street.
1764, Apr. 24. Walton. Isaiah and Sarah Penquite.
1761, Apr. 13. Walton, Joshua, and Jane Wyrel.
1760, May 23. Walton, Katherine, and Thomas Clark.
1761, M'ch 11. Walton, Martha, and William Griffith.
1761, Apr. 23. Walton, Mary, and Peter January.
1761, M'ch 14. Walton, Massee, and William Walton.
1771, Oct. 19. Walton, Rachel, and Joseh Boucher.
1773, June 18. Walton, Ruth, and William Ruper.
1761, M'ch 14. Walton, William, and Massee Walton.
1761, Aug. 11. Waltrick, Catharine, and John Plum.
1763, Feb. 9. Warnick, Margaret, and Anthony Noble.
1772, Oct. 15. Wane, Ann, and William Hayman.
1761, Jan. 7. Wankoop, Rebecca, and Andrew Van Buskett.
1766, Feb. 22. Warburton, Adam, and Elizabeth Perry.
1766, Sep. 27. Ward, Abigail, and Nicholas Vandegrift.
1772, May 28. Ward, Ann, and Benjamin Ward.
1772. May 28. Ward, Benjamin, and Ann Ward.
1773, Nov. 18. Ward, Deborah, and Thomas Morrison.
1762, Apr. 15. Ward, Elizabeth, and James Wilkins.
1767, Dec. 10. Warden. James, and Rebecca McTingley.
1762, May 8. Ward, George, and Rachel Wilkers.
1771, July 27. Ward, Joshua, and Margaret Moore.
1775, Nov. 25. Ward, Lewis, and Robert Lily.
1774, M'ch 3. Ward, Mary, and James Rose.
1762, May 5. Ward, Mary, and Samuel Buzby.
1769, May 29. Ward, Mary, and Thomas Carter.
1764, Nov. 21. Ward, Mary, and Thomas Willson.
1769, Dec. 28. Ward, Phebe, and Joel Clarke.
1762, Oct. 23. Ward, Thomas, and Mary Cambell.
1768, Sep. 21. Ware, David, and Ann Barber.
1774, Dec. 5. Ware, Elizabeth, and Martha Magraw.
1768, Sep. 24. Ware, Mary, and Thomas Hilldrup.
1748, Apr. 13. Warley, Nathan, and Elizabeth Tomkins.
1768, June 7. Warnock, Mary, and Alexander Nelson.
1760, Oct. 24. Warner, Barbara, and Martin Role.
1764, July 13. Warner, Edith, and William Shute.
1764, Feb. 18. Warner, Elizabeth and Bartholomew Moore.
1764, May 1. Warner, Elizabeth, and Jacob Valtotten.
1765, Aug. 28. Warner, George, and Barbara Crips.
1764, Nov. 29. Warner, John, and Hannah Rentzel.
1774, Dec. —. Warner, Joseph, and Ann Greesbury.

1748, Sep. —. Warner, Margaret, and Nichols Knight.
1764, Oct. 22. Warner, Margaret, and Robert Stuart.
1775, Apr. 27. Warner, Mary, and George Stokes.
1765, Dec. 14. Warner, Mary, and John West.
1766, Dec. 11. Warner, Peter, and Mary Eve Roadt.
1748, July 13. Warner, Susannah, and James Skerret.
1747, Feb. —. Warner, Swan, and Sarah Hastings.
1765, Sep. 12. Warnick, Sarah, and Prisley Blackston.
1748, Jan. —. Warren, Elizabeth, and Matthew Cummins.
1762, July 30. Warren, Frederick, and Mary Morgan.
1748, Aug. 15. Warren, Robert.
1769, Nov. 13. Warren, Thomas, and Hannah Powel.
1761, July 23. Warrick, Jacob, and Elizabeth Fluellen.
1760, Jan. 24. Warrington, Jonathan, and Ann Knight.
1773, Oct. 6. Warwick Elizabeth, and Samuel Holmes.
1760, Nov. 22. Washington, Isaac, and Martha Carver.
1774, Sep. 25. Wasseman, Sophia, and Abraham Fox.
1762, Jan. 23. Waterman, James, and Lea Willson.
1747, Oct. 4. Waterman, Phineas, and Mary Johnston.
1772, Nov. 21. Waterman, Thomas, and Hannah Inglis.
1763, Sep. 8. Water. Peter, and Ann Fust.
1767, M'ch 28. Waters, Eleanor, and John Briton.
1775, Nov. 18. Waters, Elizabeth, and William Thomas,
1762, Sept. 1. Waters, Mary, and Amberus Bearding.
1765, Oct. 14. Waters, Rachel, and Benjamin Griffith.
1769, Nov. 15. Waters, Sarah. and William Dewees.
1764, June 28. Watherington, Benjamin, and Sarah Niles.
1764, M'ch 13. Watherington, William, and Esther Hommer,
1776, M'ch 16. Watkins, Ann, and Isaac Jones.
1765, Oct. 11. Watkins, Hannah, and Leeson Simmons.
1775, M'ch 21. Watkins, Jane, and Robert Coxe.
1762, Aug. 31. Watkins, Joseph, and Ellenor Pratt.
1760, Nov. 19. Watkins, Joseph, and Mary Morgan.
1767, M'ch 5. Watkins, Joseph, and Mary Parker.
1775, May 3. Watkins, Margaret, and John Dillon.
1760, June 18. Watkins, Mary, and Evan Morgan.
1767, July 3. Watkins, William, and Ann Fisher.
1775, June 8. Watson, Abigail, and John Wood.
1763, Sep. 10. Watson, Alice, and John Henderson.
1766, Aug. 5. Watson, Ann, and Edward Hunt.
1770, Nov. 5. Watson, Anne, and John Hayward.
1765, July 1. Watson, Ann, and John Groves.
1760, Apr. 29. Watson, Elizabeth, and Foleart Vandegrift.
1770, Aug. 31. Watson, Elizabeth, and Robert Porter.
1764, Aug. 1. Watson, Elizabeth, and Samuel Dugan.

1776, May 16. Watson, Elizabeth, and Samuel Fletcher.
1773, Nov, 18. Watson, Isaac, and Elizabeth Ballard.
1746, Nov. —. Watson, Jane, and Patrick, Willie.
1761, Jan. 30. Watson, John, and Eleanor Ball.
1765, May 9. Watson, John, and Mary Carpenter.
1761, Jan. 7. Watson, John, and Patience Madlock.
1762, Aug. 20. Watson, John, and Rebecca Snodgrace.
1768, Jan. 28. Watson, Richard, and Elizabeth Hillings.
1743, July 23. Watson, Thomas.
1761, Dec. 2. Watson, William, and Margaret Boggs.
1767, June 8. Watson, William, and Patience Adam.
1762, Feb. 17. Wattkins, James, and Comfort Griffin.
1776, May 21. Watts, Adam, and Mary Cockran.
1764, May 21. Watts, Elizabeth, and Thomas Felwell.
1762, Nov. 26. Watts, John, and Rachel Watts.
1762, Nov. 26. Watts, Rachel, and John Watts.
1767, M'ch 10. Watts, Stephen, and Frances Assheton.
1772, Apr. 14. Watts, Stephen, and Martha Eaton.
1773, June 30. Way, George, and Elizabeth Spanton.
1761, Dec. 2. Way, Hannah, and James Pierce.
1748, June 16. Way, John, and Mary Pearce.
1770, Apr. 3. Way, Margaret, and Andrew Philler.
1764, Oct. 6. Way, Robert, and Catharine Gandawit.
1766, M'ch 25. Wayne, Anthony, and Mary Penrose.
1773, May 28. Wayne, Elizabeth, and David Wilkin.
1774, June 1. Wayne, Hannah, and James Justice.
1775, Nov. 11. Wayne, Mary, and Samuel French.
1760, Sep. 23. Wazenor, Matthias, and Ann Maxwell.
1761, Nov. 28. Wear, Jane, and Francis Lockart.
1762, Nov. 29. Weatherby, Samuel, and Sarah Bremar.
1773, July 20. Weatherby, Whitehead, and Sarah Jones.
1775, July 21. Weaver, Catharine, and Daniel Lester.
1773, Apr. 27. Weaver, Elizabeth, and Joseph Wallace.
1762, Jan. 7. Weaver, John, and Catharine Singuar.
1764, June 9. Weaver, Martha, and John Jackson.
1773, Aug. 10. Weaver, Mary, and Peter Trace.
1763, Aug. 11. Weaver, Rebecca, and James Wade.
1763, Aug. 11. Weaver, Rosinna, and John Aglee.
1776, Apr. 6. Weaver, Susannah, and Jacob Lutes.
1760, Sep. 2. Webb, Elizabeth, and Lyon Nathan.
1772, Aug. 27. Webb, Elizabeth, and Reuben Smith.
1764, Dec. 8. Webber, Catharine, and John Tulet.
1760, Dec. 27. Webb, John, and Margaret Lington.
1775, July 27. Webb, Joseph, and Letitia Powell.
1760, July 1. Webb, Sarah, and Peter Walker.
1775, June 1. Webb, William, and Martha Ord

1743, Dec. —. Webster, George.
1761, Nov. 4. Webster, Lewis, and Sarah Freeman.
1770, Jan. 30. Webster, Mary, and John Johnston.
1769. M'ch 16. Webster, Samuel, and Margaret Adams.
1748, Aug. 15. Weckward, Samuel.
1762, Aug. 31. Weed, Elijah, and Ann Sreeve.
1765, Apr. 3. Weed, Elijah, and Mary Mitchell.
1768, Jan. 12. Weed, George, and Elizabeth Dickinson.
1747, Nov. —. Weeks, Sarah, and Henry Woodward.
1762, Aug. 26. Weeton, Enos, and Catharine Lissa.
1764, Aug. 1. Weidner, Adam, and Mary Walter.
1764, Oct. 9. Weidner, David, and Johanna Wummeldors.
1763. Oct. 24. Weiley, Ann, and Peter Hunt.
1768, May 11. Weir, Mary, and Robert Flack.
1774, Nov. 14. Weir, Thomas, and Ann Thompson.
1760, Sep. 15. Weisen, Catharine, and John O. Miller.
1760, May 28. Weiser, Samuel, and Judith Levan.
1773, July 26. Weising, Catharine, and Henry Hattman.
1772, M'ch 26. Weiss, Jacob, Junior, and Elizabeth Roberts.
1765, Jan. 7. Welch, Annis, and John Hiser.
1774, Feb. 11. Welch, Elizabeth, and Daniel O'Neal.
1776, Jan. 17. Welch, James, and Margaret Wiley.
1761, M'ch 24. Welch, James, and Rose Farrel.
1770, Aug. 18. Welch, Robert, and Susannah Bradford.
1770, M'ch 10. Welch, Valentine, and Catharine Graff.
1770, July 19. Welch. Valentine, and Phebe Graff.
1772, M'ch 2. Welcome, Joseph, and Elizabeth Ford.
1769, June 17. Welden, Joseph, and Mary Kenton.
1748, June 16. Weldon, Elizabeth, and James Stevenson.
1748, July 13. Weldon, William, and Sarah Thomas.
1748, Jan. —. Weldon, William, and Sarah Whealy.
1748, Jan. —. Welhany, Margaret, and Spencer Trotter.
1748, Jan. —. Welhers, Thomas, and Agnes Steen.
1772, June 20. Welker, Margaret, and Peter Pennabicker.
1767, Nov. 19. Wellden, Ann, and Jonathan Frump.
1772, July 4. Wellman, William, and Elizabeth Ames.
1746, June —. Wells, Ann, and James Collins.
1770, July 21. Wells, Cowley, and Phebe Jackson.
1767, Sep. 19. Wells, Enoch, and Catharine Umstead.
1768, Dec. 12. Wells, Hester, and Stephen Aires.
1746, Dec. —. Wells, James.
1746, Dec. —. Wells, Jane, and Anthony Woodcock.
1747, Feb. —. Wells, Jehosheba, and Joseph Bryan.
1743, June 2. Wells, John.
1761, M'ch 11. Wells, Jonathan, and Ruth Roberts.
1768, Aug. 2. Wells, Mary, and Edward Gottier.

1762, Dec. 13. Wells, Mary, and James Morton.
1772, May 27. Wells, Olive, and John Moore.
1773, May 19. Wells, Peter, and Jeremiah Davis.
1774, Feb. 23. Wells, Peter, and Margaret Crozius.
1746, Nov. —. Wells, Peter, and Susannah Bocke.
1759, Dec. 6. Wells, Rebecca, and Charles Cox.
1770, Aug. 15. Wells, Richard, and Martha Curry.
1761, Oct. 31. Wells, Sarah, and Henry Grubb.
1760, May 10. Wells, Susannah, and Jonas Morris.
1772, Jan. 11. Welpert, Frederick, and Margaret Musfelden.
1766, Sep. 11. Welsh, Casper, and Mary Bacer.
1768, Dec. 5. Welsh, Elizabeth, and Henry Domineck.
1770, Nov. 20. Welsh, Hannah, and Hugh Thompson.
1769, Oct. 25. Welsh, James, and Jane Chandler.
1760, May 7. Welsh, John, and Ann Ross.
1761, Apr. 7. Welch, Luke, and Jane White.
1772, Sep. 18. Welsh, John, and Catharine Kennedy
1771, Feb. 17. Welsh, Mary, and Richard Hartley.
1774, Aug. 22. Welsh, Susannah, and Adam Row.
1770, Nov. 21. Weltmonen, Anna Catharine, and John Moyer.
1760, Jan. 11. Weltzet, Godfrey, and Christiana Smith.
1763, May 9. Wenhimore, Mary, and Ralph Marshall.
1761, Nov. 7. Wenn, Hester, and William Griffitts.
1773, Nov. 16. Wentworth, William, and Lydia Hinton.
1774, Sep. 15. Wentz, Abraham, and Sophia Wentz.
1768, June 2. Wentz, Barbara, and Francis Hainick.
1776, June 25. Wentz, Catharine, and George Pluck.
1766, Apr. 28. Wentz, Elizabeth, and John Coleston.
1774, Oct. 18. Wentz, Hannah, and Benjamin Marclay.
1770, June 22. Wentz, Jacob, and Barbara Alsentz.
1771, July 3. Wentz, Mary, and Gerart Hoot.
1774, Sep. 15. Wentz, Sophia, and Abraham Wentz.
1771, Apr. 19. Wertman, Adam, and Barbara Earhottin.
1760, Sep. 24. West, Ann, and Andrew Simpson.
1763, Jan. 31. West, Charles, and Mary Lee.
1761, Oct. 8. West, Elizabeth, and Joshua Hill.
1760, May 22. West, James, and Susannah Hurst.
1776, Apr. 10. West, John, and Hannah Kitheart.
1765, Dec. 14. West, John, and Mary Warner.
1762, July 29. West, John, and Phebe Hutchinson.
1775, Sep. 27. West, Joseph, and Elizabeth Lawrence.
1761, May 20. West, Lucretia, and Job Barton.
1767, May 26. West, Mary, and Elijah Anderson.
1747, Nov. —. West, Nathaniel, and Elizabeth Evans.
1772, Apr. 22. West, Phebe, and Abner Bradfield.
1765, Jan. 25. West, Rebecca, and William Tarrence.

1767, M'ch 28. West, Richard, and Sarah Hammon.
1745, June —. West, Samuel.
1774, Aug. 16. West, Sarah, and John Hugg.
1748, M'ch 11. West, Sarah, and Rees Howell.
1768, M'ch 17. West, Thomas, and Mary Kithcart.
1760, May 5. Western, William, and Ann Janivier.
1772, Apr. 1. Weston, Benjamin, and Sarah Lawwell.
1770, May 1. Weston, William, and Anne Davis.
1745, Sep. —. Wetherby, William.
1762, July 21. Wetley, Henry, and Mary Daugan.
1761, Nov. 5. Whaland, Johanna, and William Nichols.
1764, Nov. 19. Whaland, Thomas, and Margaret Burkhart.
1744, Nov. —. Whaly, Hugh.
1748, Apr. 13. Whartenoby, Elizabeth, and Edmund McVeagh.
1771, Apr. 21. Wharton, Carpenter, and Elizabeth Davis.
1772, M'ch 10. Wharton, Charles, and Jemima Edwards.
1761, June 24. Wharton, John, and Rebecca Chambers.
1776, M'ch 18. Wharton, Martha, and Peter Thompson.
1768, Apr. 14. Wharton, Phebe, and John Hanna.
1773, Nov. 10. Wharton, Rebecca, and John Updike.
1774, Dec 6. Wharton, Thomas, Jr., and Elizabeth Fishbourn.
1762, Nov. 4. Wharton, Thomas, and Susannah Loyd.
1748, Oct. 8. Whealey, Sarah, and John Williams.
1748, Jan. —. Whealy, Sarah, and William Weldon.
1759, Dec. 22. Wheat, Abigail, and Adam Hope.
1774, Jan. 5. Wheeler, Cleary, and John Smith.
1764, Jan. 16. Wheeler, Eleanor, and John Baker.
1765, Nov. 26. Wheeler, Samuel, and Ann Flower.
1763, Sep. 14. Whiley, Christian, and Martha Tanner.
1763, Oct. 19. Whiley, Sarah, and Jacob Williams.
1766, June 10. Whitaker, Benjamin, and Dilley Snowden.
1774, May 27. White, Abner, and Jane McCrea.
1774, Oct. 7. White, Agnes, and Barefoot Brunston.
1767, M'ch 27. White, Agnes, and Jasper Polson.
1747, M'ch —. White, Anable, and Andrew Middleton.
1770, June 30. White, Anne, and Joseph Todd.
1776, June 3. White, Barbara, and Philip Ardla.
1773, M'ch 18. White, Catharine, and Daniel Burchardt.
1762, Sep. 25. White, Daniel, and Hannah Barber.
1765, M'ch 20. White, Elizabeth, and Andrew Boon.
1769, June 22. White, Elizabeth, and John Tuckness.
1760, June 28. White, Elizabeth, and Thomas Allison.
1773, Nov. 15. White, Esther, and Nathaniel Huddleston.
1768, Sep. 8. White, Hannah, and Bernard Fearis.
1768, Feb. 4. White, Hannah, and John Pearson.
1770, Dec. 8. White, James, and Anne Tucker.

1747, June —. White, James, and Ann Wilcox.
1768, Oct. 28. White, James, and Rebecca Parker.
1747, Aug. —. White, Jane, and John Anderson.
1761, Apr. 7. White, Jane and Luke Welch.
1760, Jan. 23. White, John, and Dareus McCorkle.
1767, Apr. 23. White, John, and Elizabeth Metz.
1775, July 15. White, John, and Jane Cleland.
1760, May 6. White, John, and Margaret Hamilton.
1769, Apr. 26. White, Jonathan, and Elizabeth James.
1760, M'ch 25. White, Joseph, and Ann Titus.
1765, June 8. White, Joseph, and Sarah Headley.
1769, June 23. White, Josiah, and Catharine McCool.
1761, Oct. 30. White, Lidya, and Henry Forst.
1761, July 14. White, Margaret, and David Hamilton.
1771, Aug. 5. White, Martha, and Abraham Bennet.
1775, Dec. 26. White, Martha, and John Keiter.
1771, Sep. 10. White, Mary, and Isaac Harris.
1774, Dec. 6. White, Mary, and James Baker.
1766, July 30. White, Mary, and Philip Cline.
1769, Feb. 27. White, Mary, and Robert Morris.
1768, Aug. 1. White, Mary, and William Edwards.
1769, Jan. 7. White, Paul, and Elizabeth Norton.
1769, Sep. 1. White, Peter, and Barbara Care.
1747, May —. White, Peter, and Elizabeth Coole.
1775, Aug. 26. White, Rebecca, and John Kreiser.
1763, Aug. 2. White, Richard, and Margaret Vivers.
1768, M'ch 17. White, Sarah, and Moore Furman.
1763, Dec. 28. White, Thomas, and Ann Read.
1760, Oct. 1. White, Thomas, and Margaret Conrad.
1773, Feb. 10. White, William, and Mary Harrison.
1771, Aug. 12. White, William, and Sarah Kinnard.
1772, July 11. Whiteall, Sarah, and John Murdock.
1771, Jan. 24. Whitebread, Anne, and William Bellamy.
1763, Jan. 8. Whitebread, George, and Sarah Lees.
1760, Dec. 19. Whitebread, Hannah, and Rowland Ellis.
1770, Apr. 26. Whitebread, Mary, and John McDaniel.
1775, July 3. Whitefield, Mary, and Nicholas Neels.
1768, Oct. 5. Whitefield, Rachel, and Thomas Maain.
1760, May 2. Whitefield, Sarah, and George, Fenny.
1763, Feb. 4. Whitefield, Susannah, and James Reynolds.
1769, Nov. 18. Whitehead, Margaret, and John Atkinson.
1767, Oct. 24. Whitehead, Mary, and Jacob Otto.
1764, Aug. 6. Whitehead, Mary, and Michael Cressap.
1772, Nov. 18. Whitehead, Matthew, and Elizabeth Pine.
1746, M'ch —. Whitehead, Robert.
1762, Jan. 13. Whitehead, Thomas, and Mary Huffman.

1744, M'ch —. Whitely, Anthony.
1776, May 7. Whiteman, Elizabeth, and George Wood.
1774, Aug. 15. Whiteman, Jacob, and Elizabeth Barge.
1776, May 18. Whiteman, Jacob, and Sarah Keissler.
1761, Apr. 13. Whitlock, Elizabeth, and Moses Mostager.
1776, M'ch 21. Whitman, Catharine, and William Davis.
1774, Sep. 12 Whiteman, Rebecca, and Joseph Scull.
1762, Apr. 5. Whitman, Richard, and Elizabeth Whitton.
1770, Apr. 28. Whitpaine, Anne, and Thomas Forrest.
1776, M'ch 13. Whitpaine, William, and Sarah Cassell.
1763, Apr. 12. Whitstone, Susannah, and Peter Smith.
1773, M'ch 23. Whittle, Charlotte, and John Reynolds.
1772, June 8. Whiton, Elizabeth, and James Sutter.
1762, Apr. 5. Whitton, Elizabeth, and Richard Whitman.
1770, June 4. Whitton, Richard, and Martha Thomas.
1770, June 4. Whitton, Robert, and Mary Thomas.
1770, Apr. 28. Whitton, Thomas, and Anne Finney.
1767, Oct. 19. Whitton, William, and Arody Hammitt.
1760, June 19. Whorley, Edmund, and Sarah Wright.
1769, May 29. Wickersham, Amos, and Elizabeth Hays.
1761, M'ch 21. Wickoff, Cornelius, and Lamakeer Crousen.
1775, M'ch 8. Wickward, Rachel, and Richard Brown.
1762, July 9. Widdifield, John, and Elizabeth Hyman.
1770, July 7. Wier, Mary, and James Barker.
1772, May 7. Wiggfall, Samuel, and Rachel Baulby.
1772, Feb. 19. Wightman, Susannah, and Jacob Rode.
1766, Sep. 13. Wigmire, Bridget, and William Dunn.
1767, M'ch 28. Wigmore, Ann, and William Carncross.
1745, Oct. —. Wigmore, John.
1766, Apr. 14. Wigton, John, and Margaret Cochran.
1764, June 30. Wikenerin, Catharine, and John Adam Cripps.
1766, Jan. 8. Wikoff, Isaac, and Martha Cox.
1769, M'ch 30. Wikoff, Peter, and Altha Cox.
1772, Dec. 2. Wikoff, Peter, and Catharine Kreusen
1747, Dec. —. Wilcan, Mary, and John Simpson.
1768, May 17. Wilcocks, Alexander, and Mary Chew
1747, June —. Wilcox, Ann, and James White.
1761, Sep. 2. Wilcox, Mary, and Simon Guert.
1768, Apr. 18. Wild, Joseph, and Margaret Johnson.
1768, Dec. 7. Wild, Michael, and Rachel Bourdmanning.
1765, Jan. 1. Wild, William, and Elizabeth Barry.
1765, M'ch 13. Wildee, John, and Mary Jones.
1764, Feb. 2. Wilder, Mary, and Samuel Read.
1763, May 16. Wildman, Mary, and Henry Cordrey.
1760, Nov. 19. Wildmire, John, and Mary Lightmenen.
1744, Aug. 13. Wildon, James.

1770, Oct. 4. Wiles, Sarah, and Thomas Cheeseman.
1776, Jan. 25. Wiles, William, and Ann Hyder.
1776, Jan. 17. Wiley, Margaret, and James Welch.
1772, Jan. 16. Wiley, Thomas, and Jane Thompson.
1768, Oct. 17. Wilkie, John, and Hannah Adams.
1773, May 28. Wilkin, David, and Elizabeth Wayne.
1761, July 15. Wilkins, Adda, and Nathan Fawset.
1762, Apr. 16, Wilkins, James, and Elizabeth Ward.
1762, June 28. Wilkins, Thomas, and Mary Jaggard.
1773, Aug. 21. Wilkins, William, and Elizabeth Axford.
1761, June 30. Wilkins, Zuba, and Isaac Lane.
1772, Aug. 6. Wilkinson, Amos, and Mercy Carpenter.
1774, May 12. Wilkinson, Anthony, and Deborah Sinclair.
1763, Aug 8. Wilkinson, Daniel, and Sarah Boned.
1764, July 30. Wilkinson, Elizabeth, and James Creag.
1746, Dec. —. Wilkinson, Eliazbeth, and John Jones.
1773, Nov. 27. Wilkinson, Elizabeth, and Nathaniel Sharpless.
1762, July 10. Wilkinson, Margaret, and Peter Barndollar.
1746, Oct. —. Wilkinson, Mary, and James Haselton.
1773, Sep. 25. Wilkinson, Rebecca, and David Harrow.
1762, Feb. 18. Wilkinson, Rebecca, and John Sutter.
1763, Apr. 7. Wilkinson, Robert, and Elizabeth Clark.
1743, June 10. Wilkinson, Thomas.
1763, Nov. 24. Wilkinson, Thomas, and Mary Craft.
1774, M'ch 5. Wilkinson, William, and Hannah Taylor.
1760, May 8. Wilkirs, Rachel, and George Ward.
1776, Aug. 6. Will, Christopher, and Sarah Keiser.
1769, M'ch 30. Will, William, and Anna Clampffer.
1764, July 4. Will, William, and Barbara Culp.
1774, Aug. 6. Willard, Alice, and Ambrose Bartlett.
1763, Sep. 17. Willard, Ann, and Joseph Jenkins.
1766, Dec. 10. Willard, Elizabeth, and Thomas Wakefield.
1763, M'ch 8. Willard, Mary, and Robert Slogden.
1773, May 6. Willard, Mercy, and Charles Stow.
1769, Nov. 2. Willard, Sarah, and John Powell.
1766, Oct. 16. Wilday, John, and Susannah Montgomery.
1774, June 10. Willet, Anne, and Samuel Mitchell.
1766, June 24. Willet, Catharine, and Joshua Comly.
1760, Dec. 24. Willet, Elizabeth, and Joseph Thornton.
1764, Feb. 29. Willet, John, and Elizabeth Hough.
1766, M'ch 18. Willet, Walter, and Martha Harding.
1763, Apr. 28. Willet, William, and Ann Summers.
1747, Apr. —. William, Theophilus, and Catharine Griffy.
1761, Aug. 13. Williams, Ann, and William Cornelland.
1769, July 5. Williams, Catharine, and William Bathkill.
1761, Dec. 8. Williams, Catharine, and William Dunwick.

1762, Apr. 26. Williams, Deborah, and James Martin.
1766, Dec. 1. Williams, Deborah, and John David.
1766, Aug. 13. Williams, Edward, and Abigail Lloyd.
1761, Feb. 18. Williams, Edward, and Ann Sweatman.
1747, Apr. —. Williams, Edward, and Catharine Brady.
1748, Sep. —. Williams, Edward, and Mary Brown.
1772, May 29. Williams, Eleanor, and John Dalrymple.
1772, June 17. Williams, Elias, and Hannah Zane.
1771, Apr. 22. Williams, Elizabeth, and Andrew Forsyth.
1774, Dec. 3. Williams, Elizabeth, and Ezekiel Abbot.
1771, M'ch 26. Williams, Elizabeth, and George Gordon.
1762, May 11. Williams, Elizabeth, and Patrick Davis.
1775, July 15. Williams, Elizabeth, and Samuel Clinton.
1762, Aug. 13. William, Elizabeth, and Thomas Gibson.
1761, June 20. Williams, Elizabeth, and William Boirs.
1763, June 17. Williams, Enoch, and Hannah Grey.
1771, Oct. 21. Williams, George, and Mary Hutchinson.
1769, Dec. 5. Williams, Hannah, and John Forst.
1763, Oct. 22. Williams, Hannah, and Thomas Jones.
1772, June 3. Williams, Hannah, and William McCullough.
1744, Apr. —. Williams, Henry.
1763, Feb. 25. Williams, Henry, and Mary Tolbald.
1764, Feb. 9. Williams, Hugh, and Louisa Grew.
1774, Sep. 28. Williams, Humphrey, and Rebecca Renshaw.
1770, Dec. 11. Williams, Isaac, and Elizabeth Mettlen.
1774, Oct. 19. Williams, Isaac, and Mary Eaton.
1774, Nov. 2. Williams, Jacob, and Elizabeth Hampton.
1763, Oct. 19. Williams, Jacob, and Sarah Wiley.
1763, Oct. 1. Williams, James, and Mary Francis.
1761, Apr. 9. Williams, Jane, and John Torrons.
1748, June 16. Williams, John, and Ann Edwards.
1769, Jan. 4. Williams, John, and Hester John.
1771, Oct. 31. Williams, John, and Mary Ann Dobbins.
1770, Nov. 26. Williams, John, and Mary Evy.
1761, Sep. 2. Williams, John, and Mary Kenty.
1774, June 6. Williams, John, and Mary Piper.
1774, May 4. Williams, John, and Mary Walters.
1748, Oct. 18. Williams, John, and Sarah Whealey.
1768, Feb. 20. Williams, Jonathan, and Elizabeth Tew.
1771, June 12. Williams, Joseph, and Eleanor Kilmagh.
1762, Dec. 13. Williams, Joseph, and Elizabeth Labour.
1761, Feb. 4. Williams, Joseph, and Mary Cannady.
1766, Nov. 5. Williams, Kissander, and Paul McCarty.
1771, Feb. 1. Williams, Margaret, and John Iliff.
1774, M'ch 24. Williams, Mary, and John Little.
1769, Nov. 2. Williams, Mary, and Richard Backhouse.

1771, June   7. Williams, Mary, and Thomas Nelson.
1763, Oct.   6. Williams, Oliver, and Rose McDaniel.
1776, Jan. 24. Williams, Phebe, and Peter Duffy.
1773, Sep. 22. Williams, Rachel, and Abiah James.
1769, Jan. 25. Williams, Rebecca, and William James.
1746, July —. Williams, Robert, and Ruth Simmons.
1767, Oct. 24. Williams, Ruth, and John Hoff.
1768, M'ch 30. Williams, Samuel, and Esther Sherlock.
1762, May   19. Williams, Sarah Ann, and Samuel Flower.
1768, June 11. Williams, Sarah, and David Worthington.
1770, Nov.   7. Williams, Sarah, and Isaac Forsyth.
1760, Aug.   7. Williams, Sarah, and William Huston.
1761, Jan. 22. Williams, Scipio, and Mary Swim.
1764, Dec. 27. Williams, Susannah, and William Patterson.
1774, Nov. 11. Williams, Thomas, and Ann Johnston.
1748, Jan. —. Williams, Thomas, and Sarah Preston.
1760, Dec. 18. Williams, William, and Agnus Debtford.
1767, Apr. 10. Williams, William, and Lucy Fisher.
1775, June   6. Williamson, Benjamin, and Elizabeth Larimore.
1743, May   18. Williamson, Charles.
1773, Aug. 31. Williamson, David, and Ann McCullough.
1767, Dec.   9. Williamson, Hannah, and Samuel Yardly.
1763, Jan.   1. Williamson, Hannah, and Thomas Lawrence.
1743, Aug. 27. Williamson, James.
1776, Feb.   1. Williamson, Jeremiah, and Lydia Josiah.
1763, Aug.   9. Williamson, Jesse, and Sarah Briton.
1774, Nov.   2. Williamson, John, and Mary Williamson.
1772, July 10. Williamson, Mary, and John Matthias Sleighman.
1774, Nov.   2. Williamson, Mary, and John Williamson.
1766, Oct.   8. Williamson, Mary, and Nicholas Vallance.
1765, Apr. 10. Williamson, Mary, and Peter Bell.
1775, Aug. 15. Williamson, Robert, and Hannah Hamilton.
1770, M'ch 10. Williamson, Thomas, and Anne Reynolds.
1762, M'ch 13. Willibe, Henry, and Susannah Lickle.
1746, Nov. —. Willie, Patrick, and Jane Watson.
1762, Feb.   8. Willing, Ann, and Tench Francis.
1769, Aug.   5. Willing, Elizabeth, and Samuel Powell.
1775, Nov. 15. Willing, Margaret, and Robert Hare.
1763, June   9. Willing, Thomas, and Ann McCall.
1748, Nov. 11. Willins, Elenor, and James Menzie.
1769, Apr. 29. Williot, John, and Rebecca Clark.
1761, Oct.   9. Willis, John, and Elizabeth Vickery.
1771, Oct. 29. Willis, Samuel, and Elizabeth Lukens.
1761, Feb. 10. Willman, William, and Elizabeth Richardson.
1770, M'ch   6. Willock, Henry, and Catharine Kill.
1759, Dec.   6. Willoughby, Henry, and Cradle Lusherton.

1768, May 30. Willoughby, Susannah, and William Rusk.
1774, Aug. 12. Wills, James, and Hannah Roberts.
1767, July 23. Wills, John, and Esther Spear.
1746, Apr. —. Wills, Noah.
1762, Feb. 25. Wills, William, and Rush Reynolds.
1772, Nov. 11. Willson, Alexander, and Mary Kennedy.
1761, Apr. 4. Willson, Andrew, and Lilly Porter.
1772, Nov. 9. Willson, Catharine, and Thomas Tyrer.
1764, Apr. 10. Willson, Charles, and Rebecca Freak.
1767, Aug. 25. Willson, Elizabeth, and Daniel Hathorn.
1775, Nov. 27. Willson, Elizabeth, and John Chatham.
1772, Apr. 23. Willson, Francis, and Mary Armstrong.
1764, Nov. 1. Willson, George, and Elizabeth Adams.
1770, M'ch 19. Willson, Henry, and Martha Stewart.
1771, Feb. 7. Willson, Hugh, and Letitia Conn.
1776, Feb. 10. Willson, Isaac, and Margaret Magee.
1769, June 19. Willson, Isabella, and William Simpson.
1773, June 17. Willson, Jacob, and Sarah Walker.
1768, M'ch 17. Willson, James, and Ann Harbert.
1770, Aug. 3. Willson, James, and Elizabeth Singer.
1768, July 7. Willson, James, and Mary Plumsted.
1772, July 1. Willson, Joseph, and Margaret Windram.
1772, Apr. 9. Willson, Judith, and John Hamble, Junior.
1762, Jan. 23. Willson, Lea, and James Waterman.
1776, M'ch 5. Willson, Martha, and James Hamilton.
1769, Oct. 4. Willson, Matthew, and Isabella Bodley.
1764, Nov. 29. Willson, Patrick, and Sarah Powlin.
1770, July 3. Willson, Robert, and Rachel Armstrong.
1772, Feb. 17. Willson, Robert, and Sarah Neill.
1769, Dec. 4. Willson, Sarah, and Thomas Moffit.
1770, Oct. 20. Willson, Sarah, and William Household.
1763, M'ch 1. Willson, Solomon, and Sarah Coffin.
1771, Sep. 13. Willson, Susannah, and Benjamin Mitchell.
1769, Dec. 30. Willson. Thomas, and Anne Price.
1769, June 17. Willson, Thomas, and Catharine Catan.
1764, Nov. 21. Willson, Thomas, and Mary Ward.
1770, Oct. 12. Wilmer, Lambert, and Mary Barker.
1760, Aug. 7. Wilmingham, Mary, and Herman Huevelston.
1770, Dec. 16. Wilmington, Elizabeth, and Evan Thomas.
1743, Apr. 26. Wilmington, John.
1763, July 5. Wilber, George Godfrey, and Anna Margaretta Slashman.
1768, Apr. 28. Wilson, Ann, and John Brown.
1760, Sep. 1. Wilson, Asaph, and Elizabeth Sands.
1745, Jan. —. Wilson, David.
1745, Aug. —. Wilson, David.

1760, June 8. Wilson, David, and Ann Morrison.
1766, Dec. 2. Wilson, Elizabeth, and James Calhoun.
1746, Dec. —. Wilson, Elizabeth, and John Spencer.
1764, July 17. Wilson, Gabriel, and Sarah Brintnell.
1763, Aug. 12. Wilson, George, and Martha Craig.
1761, Apr. 20. Wilson, Isaac, and Rachel Tarry.
1745, July —. Wilson, James.
1746, June —. Wilson, James. and Mary McCall.
1764, Aug. 29. Wilson, Jane, and Humphrey Smith.
1764, Nov. 1. Wilson, Jane, and John Bourns.
1746, Dec. —. Wilson, Jane, and Stephen Durham.
1760, Aug. 13. Wilson, Jane, and William Haslet.
1764, June 9. Wilson, John, and Ann Nelson.
1761, Sep. 29. Wilson, John, and Grace Lippenket.
1762, Apr. 10. Wilson, John, and Jane Wright.
1760, Feb. 25. Wilson, John, and Mary Conner.
1773, Aug. 20. Wilson, John, and Otilla Ludwick.
1765, Sep. 10. Wilson, John, and Sarah Doughty.
1765, Nov 16. Wilson, John, and Sarah Powell.
1769, M'ch 2. Wilson, John, and Susannah Stagg.
1763, Dec. 24. Wilson, Joseph, and Mary Cooper.
1773, Dec. 2. Wilson, Margaret, and Benjamin Griffith.
1773, Nov. 10. Wilson, Martin, and Elizabeth Bate.
1748, June 16. Wilson, Mary, and Arthur Latimore.
1767, June 25. Wilson, Mary, and James Dougherty.
1748, June 16. Wilson, Mary, and John Dixon.
1768, Dec. 6. Wilson, Mary, and Jonathan Beere.
1761, Dec. 11. Wilson, Mary, and Thomas Rogers.
1768, May 27. Wilson, Rachel, and Abram Nathan.
1763, Sep. 12. Wilson, Robert, and Margaret Osborn.
1762, Apr. 17. Wilson, Robert, and Margaret Pew.
1767, Nov. 12. Wilson, Samuel, and Ann Clark.
1759, Dec. 19. Wilson, Samuel, and Sarah Vastine.
1763, Sep. 30. Wilson, Violet, and Melvin Reece.
1773, M'ch 29. Wilson, William, and Mary Hughes.
1762, Oct. 12. Wimmer, Jacob, and Mary Van Dike.
1769, Oct. 26. Wincheles, Elizabeth, and John Fullerton, **Junior.**
1748, Apr. 13. Windell, John, and Rebecca Bay.
1774, May. 26. Windkimer, Ann, and William Penty.
1772, July 1. Windram, Margaret, and Joseph Willson.
1767, June 20. Winecoop, Mary, and George Hogeland.
1761, M'ch 31. Winecope, Eliazbeth, and Richard **Vansickler.**
1775, Aug. 17. Winemore, Philip, and Elizabeth **Finley.**
1767, Apr. 15. Wing, John, and Sarah Hubbs.
1776, M'ch 9. Winn, Phebe, and John Adams.

1772, Feb. 10. Winn, Sarah, and James Hall.
1770, June 7. Winnimore, Susannah, and James Lees.
1764, Apr. 14. Winson, Elizabeth, and John Rell.
1760, July 8. Winter, Ann, and Robert Lewton.
1772, Oct. 9. Winter, Barbara, and Barnabas O'Neal.
1760, Feb. 20. Winter. Elizabeth and Michael Fisher.
1761, Oct. 28. Winter, Isabella, and Samuel Poley.
1764, July 31. Winter, James, and Ann Smith.
1761, Oct. 21. Winter, John, and Margaret Bell.
1768, Apr. 25. Winter, John, and Mary Barret.
1764, Feb. 8. Winter, John, and Mary Cox.
1764, Apr. 9. Winter, Richard, and Mary Saunders.
1768, May 28. Winterton, Rebecca, and James Coffee.
1767, July 27. Wisebaugh, Mary, and Jacob Binder.
1767, Feb. 17. Wiseman, Mary, and Cornelius Rute.
1760, May 5. Wister, Daniel, and Lowry Jones.
1762, July 8. Wister, Hannah, and John Doyle.
1771, Aug. 27. Wister, John, and Anne Thoman.
1761, Oct. 20. Withers, John, and Elizabeth Muir.
1764, May 26. Withers, Mary, and Frederick Ott.
1775, Sep. 21. Withey. James, and Sarah Claypoole.
1747, May —. Wittatue, Sarah, and Valentine Kygher.
1762, Nov. 24. Witton, Mary, and Jeremiah Dungan.
1746, Aug. —. Witts, Charles, and Margaret Newmonim.
1745, Apr. —. Wivell, Edward.
1747, May —. Woelaston, Joshua, and Priscilla Jones.
1768, Sep. 1. Woggelom, Jane, and James Sisk.
1774, M'ch 21. Woglom, Peter, and Jane Fletcher.
1759, Dec. 22. Wolfall, Charles, and Sarah Garrigus.
1772, July 2. Woef, Mary, and George Kidd.
1765, July 11. Wolferdin, Ann, and Jacob Kaufman.
1766, Apr. 10. Wolfganger, Sarah, and George Couser.
1767, July 2. Wolfin. Catharine, and John Menge.
1760, July 8. Wollax, Ann, and John Smith.
1764, Sep. 27. Wolley, Sarah, and William Drewry.
1773, Feb. 13. Wolohon, John, and Sarah Hammitt.
1762, Dec. 28. Womsley, Sarah, and George Parsons.
1764, Dec. 27. Won, Rebecca, and Christian Kensley.
1765, Oct. 5. Wood, Abigail, and Jacob Marshall.
1766, Oct. 10. Wood, Elizabeth, and Farlan McFarlan.
1763, Nov. 3. Wood, Elizabeth, and Thomas Bishop.
1774, July 18. Wood. Elizabeth, and William Ledlie.
1776, May 7. Wood, George, and Elizabeth Whiteman.
1747, M'ch —. Wood, Hannah, and Abel Lodge.
1766, Aug. 7. Wood, Hannah, and Joseph Norris.
1768, Apr. 30. Wood, Hermoine, and Jacob Hall.

1765, Oct.   9. Wood, Isaac, and Elizabeth Howell.
1762, Apr.   3. Wood, Isaac, and Margaret McDowel.
1766, Dec. 18. Wood, James, and Chlotilde Haggerty.
1746, Jan.   —. Wood, Jeremiah.
1775, June   8. Wood, John, and Abigail Watson.
1772, Apr.   9. Wood, John, and Ann Many.
1771, Oct. 26 Wood, John, and Mary Cannon.
1766, Aug. 13. Wood, John, and Mary Kinsey.
1775, July 29. Wood, John, and Merriam Osman.
1747, Oct.   —. Wood, Joseph, and Mary Scull.
1768, Nov.   3. Wood, Margaret, and Curtis Clay.
1765, Jan. 15. Wood, Mary, and James Tull.
1771, Nov.   1. Wood, Mary, and John Campbell.
1768, Nov. 21. Wood, Mary, and John Vance.
1776, Jan. 13. Wood, Mary, and Samuel Branson.
1767, Dec. 23. Wood, Mary, and Thomas Olson.
1767, Dec. 22. Wood, Priscilla, and Daniel Billen.
1761, May   27. Wood, Rachel, and Joseph McClane.
1765, Feb. 25. Wood, Rebecca, and Isaac Dodge.
1760, Aug.   1. Wood, Susannah, and George Smith.
1774, Nov. 10. Wood, Susannah, and Thomas Elton.
1767, Nov. 12. Wood, Thomas, and Mary Hughes.
1765, Jan. 30. Wood, Thomas, and Rebecca Yerkes.
1762, Sep. 20. Wood, William, and Margaret Boyce.
1775, Aug.   7. Wood, William, and Mary Goveren.
1770, Dec. 15. Woods, Benjamin, and Sarah Pyles.
1763, M'ch   3. Woods, John, and Hannah Churchman.
1747, M'ch   —. Woods, Philip, and Agnus Rex.
1769, Jan. 16. Woodward, Elizabeth, and William Price.
1769, Apr. 26. Woodbridge, Samuel, and Sarah Beardin.
1746, Dec.   —. Woodcock, Anthony, and Jane Wells.
1766, M'ch 10. Woodcock, Catharine, and Michael Clogg.
1748, Oct. 18. Woodell, Stacey, and Rachel Likens.
1772, June 16. Woodfield, Joseph, and Mary Rambo.
1760, June 10. Woodhouse, William, and Sarah Robinson.
1762, May   11. Woodman, Peace, and Mary Thrasher.
1765, May   15. Woodrow, William, and Hester Stoneburner.
1773, July 15. Woodside, Hannah, and William M'Ilhenny.
1747, Nov.   —. Woodward, Henry, and Sarah Weeks
1760, Nov. 21. Woodward, John, and Ann Jolley.
1772, May   13. Woodward, Mary, and John Perkins.
1763, Apr.   9. Woodward, William, and Elizabeth Dunklit.
1760, Apr. 14. Woolard, James, and Frances Brittain.
1769, Aug.   8. Woolf, Andrew, and Eve Criles.
1772, Sep. 23. Woolland, Suannah, and Matthias Burch.
1771, May   29. Woollis, Nicholas, and Hannah Haycock.

1773, Nov. 3. Woolman, Barbara, and Samuel Murray.
1764, Nov. 23. Woolman, Joseph, and Martha Mullen.
1744, Feb. —. Woolston. Jeremiah.
1760, Aug. 7. Woorel, Ezekiel, and Ann Kinsey.
1770, Apr. 23. Workman, Samuel, and Mary Robinson.
1769, Jan. 5. Workman, William, and Rebeck Marriot.
1774, Dec. 15. Worknot, Martin, and Catharine Lutsen.
1774, Feb. 28. Worknot, Martin, and Elizabeth Farrell.
1760, M'ch 5. Work, Patrick, and Jennel Galbreath.
1765, Jan. 15. Work, Robert, and Jane Cochran.
1775, Apr. 17. Wormington, John, and Ann Collet.
1745, June —. Wormley, Hatten.
1767, Jan. 15. Wormley, Mary, and Joseph Ledru.
1767, M'ch 12. Wormly, Mary, and John William Hoffman.
1771, Nov. 6. Worn, Philip, and Mary Heyl.
1743, Oct. —. Worral, Jacob.
1769, May 11. Worrall, Demas, and Elizabeth Collum.
1747, Oct. —. Worral, Mary, and William Henderson.
1775, May 24. Worrell, Esther, and Philip Kirk.
1775, Feb. 25. Worrell, Hannah, and James Howes.
1775, M'ch 30. Worrell, Isaac, and Elizabeth Rambo.
1767, Apr. 20. Worrell, Rebecca, and Joseph Bell.
1746, Sep. —. Worthington, Abram, and Lydia Driver.
1768, June 11. Worthington, David, and Sarah Williams.
1767, Jan. 24. Worthington, Joseph, and Mary Carver.
1765, Aug. 24. Worthington, Rachel, and John Rice.
1770, Sept. 20. Worthington, Sarah, and William Kemble.
1745, Oct. —. Wosdell, William.
1773, Oct. 1. Wrax, Barbara, and John Reinhart.
1763, Sep. 9. Wray, Christopher, and Eleanor Ross.
1773, Jan. 18. Wrench, Margaret, and Charles Mayer.
1773, Dec. 11. Wright, Ann, and Aaron Schuyler.
1771, Nov. 25. Wright, Ann, and Peter Sharp.
1762, July 26. Wright, Anthony, and Hanah Albright.
1763, Feb. 19. Wright, Anthony, and Hannah Hobbs.
1766, Jan. 25. Wright, Daniel, and Esther Stackhouse.
1769, Dec. 1. Wright, Deborah, and Thomas Rudolph.
1761, Jan. 15. Wright, Elizabeth, and Dennis Callahan.
1771, M'ch 20. Wright, Elizabeth, and Samuel Hines.
1763, Oct. 31. Wright, George, and Mary Edwards.
1748, Aug. 15. Wright, Henry.
1762, Apr. 10. Wright, Jane, and John Wilson.
1743, June 8. Wright, John.
1774, Feb. 28. Wright, John, and Ann Agnes Carr.
1774, Dec. 21. Wright, Joseph, and Martha Stots.
1770, Apr. 14. Wright, Joseph, and Sarah Shee.

1771, Nov. 28, Wright, Leonard, and Sabian Bower.
1771, May 30. Wright, Letitia, and John Hutchinson.
1761, Dec. 28. Wright, Lydia, and John Eyre.
1760, Jan. 11. Wright, Margaret, and John Pierce.
1761, Feb. 14. Wright, Mary, and James Kelly.
1761, Jan. 8. Wright, Mary, and Manuel Eyre.
1765, Aug. 29. Wright, Mary, and Peter Helm.
1775, Aug. 28. Wright, Patrick, and Sarah Thest.
1746, Sep. —. Wright, Rebecca, and Elias Hughes.
1760, June 19. Wright, Sarah, and Edmund Whorly.
1776, M'ch 29. Wright, Sarah, and Edward Miles.
1764, M'ch 10. Wright, Sarah, and Jacob Burd.
1772, May 23. Wright, Tade, and Benjamin Taylor.
1776, May 23. Wright, Thomas, and Margaret Mouch.
1769, June 14. Wright, Thomas, and Martha Hays.
1771, Aug. 2. Wright, William, and Elizabeth Bartram.
1772, May 25. Wright, William, and Isabella Bullock.
1763, May 9. Wrighter, Ann, and Aaron Levering.
1765, Sep. 10. Wrighter, Mary, and Enoch Levering.
1774, Sep. 23. Wrigley, Francis, and Catharine McGrath.
1764, Oct. 9. Wummeldors, Johanna, and David Weidner.
1772, Feb. 29. Wye, George, and Elizabeth Pinkstalk.
1775, Apr. 24. Wvle, Elizabeth, and Peter Sunlightner.
1773, July 29. Wynkoop Abraham, and Rachel Sharp.
1767, May 18. Wynkoop, Benjamin, and Sarah Wooddrop Sims.
1775, Apr. 8. Wynkoop, Cornelius, and Hannah Thomas.
1775, Aug. 10. Wynkoop, Henry, and Mary Elizabeth Reinholdt.
1772, M'ch 10. Wynkoop, Jacob, and Hannah Cleaver.
1764, Jan. 14. Wynkoop, Margaret, and Francis Titus.
1764, Apr. 2. Wynn, Mary, and Samuel Pearson.
1773, Jan. 29. Wynn, Sarah, and Michael Stattleman.
1761, Apr. 13. Wyrel, Jane, and Joshua Walton.
1746, Oct. —. Wyse, John Jacob, and Rebecca Coxe.
1771, July 1. Wyson, Franey, and James Davis.
1747, Aug. —. Wyson, Mary, and George Boardman.
1765, May 9. Wyven, Mary, and John Kensinger.

Y.

1765, Jan. 7. Yarborough, Elizabeth, and James Irwin.
1764, July 19. Yard, Mary, and Joseph Horsing.
1762, M'ch 6. Yardley, Jane, and William Plummer.
1767, Dec. 9. Yardley, Samuel, and Hannah Williamson.
1760, Jan. 30. Yarnal, William, and Mary Charce.
1770, Sep. 25. Yarnall, Sarah, and Collins McCleaster.
1744, Oct. —. Yarnell, Thomas.
1748, Sep. —. Yeakley, Ulrick, and Susannah Sommerour.

1764, Oct. 6. Yeates, Agnes, and Richard Carter.
1775, Apr. 6. Yeates, Ann Elizabeth, and John Downey.
1762, Nov. 4. Yeates, Joseph, and Mary Pennock.
1771, Sep. 28. Yeates, Mary, and Anthony Fortune.
1768, June 3. Yeates, Mary, and John McCoy.
1760, Dec. 23. Yeates, Mary, and Jonathan Dillon.
1761, Sep. 21. Yeingtin, Susannah, and John Hildebrand.
1760, May 29. Yeo, Margaret, and Edward Giles.
1775, Jan. 11. Yercas, Sarah, and Robert Grant.
1772, M'ch 7. Yerkes, Anthony, and Mary Harper.
1764, Jan. 4, Yerkes, Margaret, and John Nessmith.
1765, Jan. 30. Yerkes, Rebecca, and Thomas Wood.
1772, Dec. 12. Yerkus, Deborah, and Samuel Ayres.
1770, May 31. Yerkus, Elizabeth, and Cornelius Vandyke.
1770, Apr. 14. Yerkus, Elizabeth, and John Huffdale.
1773, Sep. 23. Yerkus, Herman, and Mary Clayton.
1769, Aug. 30. Yerkus, John, and Anne Coffin.
1774, Apr. 20. Yerkus, Sarah, and Thomas Bower.
1765, M'ch 19. Yetten, Catharine, and Philip Miller.
1765, Feb. 26. Yetter, Christopher, and Margaret Hart.
1769, July 12. Yeumans, John, and Elizabeth Heatcorn.
1771, Nov. 7. Yoacum, Andrew, and Sarah Grant.
1767, Sep. 23. Yocom, Abram, and Rebecca Harris.
1768, Feb. 20. Yocom, Ann, and Samuel How.
1748, Feb. —. Yocum, Deborah, and Casper Bussard.
1765, Jan. 2. Yocum, Eleanor, and John Ingles.
1765, Oct. 28. Yocum, Judith, and Jacob Rudolph.
1768, June 29. Yoder, Ann, and Jacob Kolb.
1746, Nov. —. Yoder, John, Junior, and Sarah Shankle.
1762, Dec. 7. Yoder, Peter, and Eve Levan.
1746, June —. Yocum, Margaret, and Jacob Suplee.
1774, May 5. Yokee, Margaret, and John Cartwright.
1764, May 30. York, Thomas, and Margaret Forbes.
1765, M'ch 4. Yorke, Andrew, and Eleanor Coxe.
1762, Jan. 22. Yorke, Edward, and Sarah Stille.
1768, July 13. Yorkson, Francis, and Alexander Hale.
1760, Oct. 21. Yort, Mary, and Thomas Marshall.
1774, July 4. Yosset, Mary, and John Cronin.
1775, June 2. Yost, Eve, and John Reed.
1771, Apr. 16. Young, Anne, and Richard Renshaw, Junior.
1775, Nov. 27. Young, Ann, and William Smith.
1773, June 10. Young, Catharine, and Archibald McTaggart.
1760, Sep. 21. Young, Catharine, and Magnus St. Clair.
1770, Jan. 13. Young, Charles, and Anne Smith.
1768, Nov. 28. Young, Christian, and Carolina Painter.

1767, Apr. 28. Young, Christopher, and Rebecca Heissel.
1762, Sep. 10. Young, Elizabeth, and Benjamin Johnson.
1760, Oct. 19. Young, Elizabeth D., and Jacob Hibbs.
1775, Sep. 30. Young, Elizabeth, and Joseph Master.
1762, May 13. Young, Elizabeth, and Patrick McClean.
1775, Oct. 2. Young, Francis, and Hannah Paul.
1760, Dec. 2. Young, George, and Jane McDaniel.
1764, Jan. 14. Young, George, and Rosanna Hoffman.
1762, Nov. 3. Young, Grace, and Isaac Fish.
1767, Dec. 11. Young, Hannah, and Barzillai Haines.
1770, Jan. 5. Young, James, and Mary Kerr.
1771, Sep. 5. Young, James, and Sarah Sleigh.
1767, Nov. 17. Young, Jane, and Aaron Robson.
1764, Dec. 21. Young, John, and Christiana Heassley.
1772, M'ch 13. Young, John, and Hannah Taber.
1771, Aug. 28. Young, John, and Lizzie Taylor.
1760, Nov. 10. Young, John, and Margaret Mallpew.
1762, May 6. Young, John, and Mary Ann Bedford.
1773, Nov. 18. Young, Joseph, and Eleanor Argyle.
1772, Aug. 5. Young, Llewellyn, and Adriana Llewellyn.
1772, Feb. 6. Young, Margaret, and James Doughty.
1771, Nov. 1. Young, Mary, and George Kelly.
1770, Aug. 22. Young, Mary, and Thomas Mitchel.
1776, Jan. 19. Young, Mary, and William Kennedy.
1770, Nov. 26. Young, Nicholas, and Eleanor Trimble.
1765, June 13. Young, Nicholas, and Mary Double.
1759, Dec. 22. Young, Rachel, and John Todman.
1771, Apr. 2. Young, Samuel, and Elizabeth Ecroyad.
1768, Nov. 25. Young, Sarah, and Nicholas Hood.
1774, Dec. 26. Young, Susannah, and Michael Loots.
1762, Dec. 20. Young, Susannah, and William Clark.
1775, May 27. Young, Thomas, and Barbara Clingman.
1745, June —. Young, William.
1762, May 5. Young, William, and Rebecca Flower.
1770, July 2. Younger, Sarah, and Peter Kurtz.
1765, M'ch 20. Younger, Watson, and Elizabeth Slator.
1760, May 17. Younkonan, Michael, and Eliza Allman.

Z.

1775, Nov. 8. Zahan, Martin, and Elizabeth Derringen.
1772, June 17. Zane, Hannah, and Elias Williams.
1766, Oct. 1. Zane, Joel, and Hester Scull.
1773, Jan. 14. Zantzinger, Adam, and Susannah Keppele.
1767, M'ch 24. Zerban, Wenden, and Catharine Bacon.
1767, July 9. Zet, Anna, and William Smith.
1766, Oct. 30. Zeinining, Mary, and Adam Gilbert.

1775, Jan. 13. Zigler, Jacob, and Esther Buchwater.
1760, Dec. 3. Zimmerman, Catharine, and Joseph Gross.
1773, Jan. 12. Zimmerman, George, and Margaret Hensman.
1774, Apr. 5. Zimmerman, Henry, and Frances Miller.
1771, Dec. 10. Zimmerman, Isaac, and Catharine Sasseman.
1762, Dec. 24. Zimmerman, Mary, and Peter Mann.
1772, Oct. 5. Zimmerman, Rebecca, and John Eshinbaugh.
1762, June 10. Zugterin, Jacobina, and Philip Hyle.

ADDENDA.

[The Editors are indebted to Charles R. Hildeburn, of Philadelphia,
for the following supplement to, and corrections of, the foregoing records. The Roman numerals refer to:—

    I. Records of Christ Church, Philadelphia.
    II. Records of First Presbyterian Church, Philadelphia.
    III. Records of Presbyterian Church, Abington, Montgomery Co.
    IV. Records of Trinity P. E. Church, Oxford.
The date given is, with the exception of those names italicized, that
of the marriage.]

A.

Date of Marriage.	Names.	Where Married.
1745, Jan. 2.	Abbett, Lydia, and George McCall.	I.
1746, Jan. 4.	Adams, Comfort, and George Duisburgh.	I.
1746, Jan. 16.	Adamson, Philip, and Frances McCready.	I.
1744, Jan. 9.	Alberdine, *Mary Elizabeth, and John Valentine Graft.	II.
1744, M'ch 26.	Allen, John, and Mary Butcher.	I.
1743, Dec. 26.	Allen, Patrick, and Margaret Marshall.	I.
1743, Jan. 15.	Allen, Sarah, and Andrew Bankson.	I.
1744, May 28.	Allent, Ulrich, and Barbara Christie.	II.
1743, Apr. 9.	Ambler, Nathaniel, and Mary Cooke.	I.
1744, Aug. 2.	Anderson, Anne, and John Morgan.	II.
1745, July 25.	Anderson, Hannah, and William Denormandie.	I.
1743, M'ch 18.	Anderson, John, and Mary Barr.	II.
1743, Jan. 26.	Anderson, Lawrence, and Abigail Ingram.	I.
1743, Dec. 12.	Annis, William, and Susannah Tuttle.	I.
1743, Nov. 12.	Angel, Rebecca, and Patrick Bourne.	I.
1743, Jan. 11.	Armitage, Enoch, and Barbara Baltes Spiner.	III.
1745, Sep. 5.	Armstrong, Mary, and Alex. McWally.	II.
1743, Oct. 21.	Ashton, Isaac, and Sarah Renshaw.	IV.
1744, May 16.	Ashton, Thomas, and Rebecca Cotman.	I.
1745, July 9.	Atkinson, Mary, and Daniel Bankson.	II.
1744, Nov. 12.	Austin, John, and Susanna Davis.	II.

B.

1745, May 2.	Baird, Thomas, and Anne Cormont.	I.
1743, Jan. 15.	Bankson, Andrew, and Sarah Allen.	I.

Date of Marriage.		Names.	Where Married.
1745, July	9.	Bankson, Daniel, and Mary Atkinson.	II.
1742, May	7.	Bankson, Deborah, and John Palmer.	I.
1743, Oct.	11.	Bankson, Peter, and Sarah Linn.	I.
1745, Jan.	21.	Barker, Benjamin, and Catharine Trussel.	I.
1745, Aug.	27.	Barney, Valentine, and Marg. McMahon.	I.
1743, M'ch	18.	Barr, Mary, and John Anderson.	II.
1743, M'ch	31.	Barstler, Catharine, and Conrad Price.	I.
1744, May	31.	Bartholomew, Andrew, and Elizabeth Beeks.	I.
1743, Jan.	11.	Bay, Thomas, and Rebecca Robinson.	I.
1743, July	27.	Beaman, William, and Anne Jeans.	
1744, Apr.	6.	Beaton, Daniel, and Mary Griffith.	II.
1743, Feb.	3.	Beck, Jeoffrey, and Lydia Philips.	II.
1744, May	31.	Beeks, Elizabeth, and Andrew Bartholomew.	I.
1745, Oct.	19.	Bell, Thomas, and Barbara Morgan.	II.
1743, Apr.	6.	Bell, William, and Lydia Edgar.	II.
1745, Apr.	24.	Benezet, Daniel, and Elizabeth North.	I.
1783, June	1.	Berry, Martin, and Sophia Edwards.	I.
1783, June	19.	Bickerton, Leah, and Edward Mullock.	I.
1745, Jan.	14.	Bidding, Henry, and Ruth Reese.	II.
1745, Sep.	19.	Bingham, William, and Mary Stamper.	I.
1743, Sep.	5.	Blackman, Henry, and Ann Crawford.	II.
1743, Oct.	22.	Blair, Ann, and James Tipper.	I.
1744, M'ch	25.	Bolithe, John, and Mary Hutchins.	I.
1762, Dec.	13.	*Bonrem, Mary, and John Remberger.*	
1743, Apr.	9.	Boon, Elizabeth, and Benjamin Simcock.	I.
1748, Aug.	18.	Boor, Mary, and David Lynn.	I.
1743, Jan.	19.	Boore, Joseph, and Elizabeth Paxton.	III.
1745, Nov.	14.	Boude, Elizabeth, and John Nigely.	I.
1743, Nov.	12.	Bourne, Patrick, and Rebecca Angel.	I.
1743, May	17.	Bowen, Eleanor, and Robert Walpole.	I.
1745, July	6.	Bower, Sarah, and James Wilson.	II.
1745, Oct.	19.	Boyd, Hugh, and Elizabeth Hunter.	II.
1743, Oct.	23.	Bradley, George, and Mary Harrison.	I.
1743, Feb.	5.	Bright, Anthony, and Jane Hobart.	I.
1744, May	18.	Brittin, Mary, and Nicholas Vanzant.	III.
1744, Apr.	27.	Broderick, Jane, and John Ellis.	I.
1743, May	15.	Brooks, Jane, and Robert Newton.	II.
1744, Sep.	15.	Brown, Elizabeth, and James Dean.	II.
1745, Feb.	5.	Brown, John, and Mary Oliver.	II.
1744, Oct.	27.	Brown, Thomas, and Elizabeth Fisher.	I.
1743, Nov.	24.	Brownyard, Hannah, and John Ingram.	I.
1744, Jan.	30.	Bryson, Walter, and Sarah McKenny.	II.

Date of Marriage.	Names.	Where Married.
1746, May 2.	Buchanan, James, and Eleanor Smith.	II.
1748, *May* 14.	*Burd, James, and Sarah Shippen.*	
1743, Aug. 26.	Burden, Joseph, and Mary Haeftis.	II.
1743, Oct. 14.	Burk, Anne, and John Lindsay.	II.
1743, May 18.	Burk, Mary, and Charles Williamson.	I.
1745, Sep. 19.	Burn, Mary, and John McCollum.	II.
1744, M'ch 26.	Butcher, Mary, and John Allen.	I.
1765, *July* 27.	*Butterfoss, Barbara, and Peter Care.*	
1744, Feb. 11.	Byrn. Daniel, and Katharine Williams.	II.

C.

1745, Sep. 18.	Cain, Roger, and Elizabeth Welsh.	II.
1763, *Nov.* 5.	*Cameron, Elizab'h, and Menan Kennard.*	
1743, June 2.	Camp, Wilmouth, and John Rush.	I.
1747, M'ch 7.	Campbell, Thomas, and Tabitha Storke.	I.
1743, Dec. 3.	Carlisle, Hannah, and Daniel Rees.	II.
1745, June 20.	Caroll, Ann, and George Hawkins.	II.
1743, May 2.	Carpenter, John, and Sarah Driver.	II.
1743, Dec. 10.	Carpenter, Joshua, and Orange Johnson.	I.
1744, May 31.	Carpenter, William, and Elizabeth Cummins.	I.
1743, June 11.	Carr, Elizabeth, and Thomas Wilkinson.	I.
1744, May 28.	Carter, Stephen, and Mary Manny.	II.
1745, Dec. 16.	Carty, Thomas, and Ann Haimer.	II.
1744, June 5.	Cassel, Nicholas, and Mary Fretwell.	I.
1783, June 11.	Chamberlain, Benjamin, and Elizabeth Foreman.	I.
1745, Nov. 28.	Chancellor, David, and Mary Greenless.	II.
1743, Dec. 16.	Chew, Nathaniel, and Anna Gibbons.	II.
1744, May 28.	Christie, Barbara, and Ulrich Allent.	II.
1745, June 25.	Clampfert, Margaret, and Peter Ulrick.	I.
1745, May 14.	Clarke, Henry, and Ann Jones.	I.
1746, Feb. 2.	Claypoole, George, and Mary Morris	I.
1743, Oct. 20.	Cole, Elizabeth, and John Wakefield.	I.
1743, Feb. 12.	Coleman, Mary, and Joseph Sharp.	I.
1744, Aug. 23.	Collings, Elizabeth, and Thomas Sugar.	I.
1745, Apr. 20.	Collins, Abraham, and Rachel Ring.	I.
1745, Aug. 17.	Collins, Charles, and Bridget Harney.	II.
1745, June 6.	Collins, Rebecca, and John Field.	II.
1745, Sep. 14.	Colly, Susanna, and David Wilson.	II.
1744, Apr. 4.	Comeron, Daniel, and Martha Smith.	I.
1745, May 20.	Connelly, Michael, and Anne Clingman.	II.
1744, Oct. 10.	Connely, Deborah, and Henry Elwes.	I.
1744, Sep. 8.	Conyers, Joseph, and Mary River.	I.
1745, Feb. 15.	Cook. Margaret, and John Jewers.	I.
1743, Apr. 9.	Cooke, Mary, and Nathaniel Ambler.	I.

Date of Marriage.	Names.	Where Married.
1745, June 25.	Coombe, Jane, and James Thompson.	I.
1744, July 14.	Cooper, Edward, and Sarah Preson.	l.
1745, M'ch 6.	Corbetz, Christopher, and Elizabeth Ruby.	II.
1745, May 2.	Cormont, Anne, and Thomas Baird.	I.
1744, May 16.	Cotman, Rebecca, and Thomas Ashton.	I.
1743, Nov. 30.	Couch, William, and Ruth Jones.	II.
1744, Sep. 8.	Cranfield, Michael, and Sarah Warren.	I.
1743, Sep. 5.	Crawford, Ann, and Henry Blackman.	II.
1746, Apr. 5.	Crawford, Peter, and Elizabeth Lowder.	l.
1744, Oct. 18.	Crookshank, Alex., and Rebecca Hudson.	I.
1745, June 17.	Cross, Mary, and David Richey.	IV.
1743, June 11.	Cross, Westema, and Ann Hamilton.	II.
1744, May 31.	Cummins, Elizabeth, and Wm. Carpenter.	I.
1743, Apr. 11.	Cummins, Jane Elizabeth, widow, and Rev. Robert Jenney.	I.
1744, Oct. 10.	Cunningham, Ann, and John Freeston.	I.
1744, Feb. 6.	Cunningham, William, and Priscilla Owen, widow.	I.
1744, Oct. 1.	Curtis, Jane, and George Metz.	I.
1744, May 19.	Cuthbert, Thomas, and Ann Wilkinson.	I.

D.

1744, M'ch 24.	Daily, Eleanor, and Andrew McBroom.	II.
1744, May 28.	Daily, Mary, and Robert Fleming.	II.
1745, Nov. 14.	Danks, Jane, and William Peck.	II.
1743, Aug. 20.	Davey, Hugh, and Elizabeth Woodrop	I.
1783, June 16.	Davis, Elizabeth, and James Rosbottom.	I.
1745, Aug. 8.	Davis, Myrick, and Sarah Miles.	I.
1746, M'ch 4.	Davis, Nathaniel, and Hannah Martin.	II.
1744, Dec. 23.	Davis, Robert, and Margaret O'Neal.	l.
1744, May 19.	Davis, Sarah, and John Sheasle.	I.
1744, Nov. 12.	Davis, Susannah, and John Austin.	II.
1743, Feb. 28.	Davis, William, and Esther Owen.	I.
1747, June 13.	Daws, George Vincent, and Ann Fling.	I.
1744, Sep. 15.	Dean, James, and Elizabeth Brown.	II.
1743, June 16.	Deigner, Peter, and Christian Smith.	I.
1745, July 22.	Dell, Peter, and Susannah Dounett.	II.
1764, Oct. 9.	*Denning, Catharine, and James Jackson.*	
1743, Jan. 20.	Dennis, Elizabeth, and Joseph Savage.	I.
1745, July 25.	Denormandie, William, and Hannah Anderson.	I.
1743, Nov. 3.	Dewees, William, and Rachel Haste.	III.
1743, July 16.	Dexter, Mary, and Lambert Emmerson.	I.
1744, May 19.	Doraugh, James, and Mary Taylor.	II.
1745, Jan 17.	Douglass, Eleanor, and John Pick.	**I.**

Date of Marriage.	Names.	Where Married.
1745, July 22.	Dounett, Susannah, and Peter Dell.	II.
1743, May 28.	Dowell, William, and Mary Domms.	I.
1746, Feb. 4.	Down, Robert, and Anne Sharp.	I.
1743, June 16.	Dowthwaite, Sam'l, and Mary Wilkinson.	I.
1746, Feb. 18.	Doyle, Rebecca, and Joshua Reily.	II.
1745, Aug. 2.	Dugdale, Mary, and Alexander Magee.	III.
1746, Jan. 4.	Duisburgh, George, and Comfort Adams	I.
1744, July 16.	Dunkin, Mary, and Joseph Durborrow.	I.
1744, May 8.	Dugan, Mary, and Michael Shaw.	II.
1748, Aug. 27.	Dunn, Susannah, and William Tate.	I.
1744, July 16.	Durborrow, Joseph, and Mary Dunkin.	I.
1745, Aug. 3.	Dutton, Sarah, and John Power.	II.
1744, July 28.	Dyor, Sarah, and Thomas Mitchell.	I.
1743, May 2.	Driver, Sarah, and John Carpenter.	II.

E.

1745, Oct. 10.	Easly, Isabel, and Charles Reily.	II.
1743, Apr. 6.	Edgar, Lydia, and William Bell.	II.
1744, Aug. 16.	Edge, John, and Sarah Felton.	II.
1744, Dec. 18.	Edwards, Anne, and Thomas Lewis.	II.
1746, Jan. 18.	Edwards, John, and Elizabeth Saunders.	I.
1783, June 1.	Edwards, Sophia, and Martin Berry.	I.
1748, June 16.	*Elleson, Margaret, and Charles Gilfoy.*	
1744, Nov. 24.	Elliot, Martha, and Joseph Sill.	I.
1744, Apr. 27.	Ellis, John, and Jane Broderick.	I.
1745, May 31.	Ellis, John, and Elizabeth Price.	I.
1745, Sep. 8.	Ellis, Richard, and Sarah Harris.	I.
1744, Oct. 10.	Elwes, Henry, and Deborah Connely.	I.
1743, July 16.	Emmerson, Lambert, and Mary Dexter.	I.
1745, M'ch 3.	Ennis, Elizabeth, and Charles Parmale.	I.
1743, May 28.	Enoch, Gertrude and William Maxwell.	III.
1745, Apr. 24.	Evans, Anne, and Ebenezer Evans.	I.
1745, Dec. 9.	Evans, Anne, and Evan Jones.	I.
1745, Apr. 24.	Evans, Ebenezer, and Anne Evans.	I.
1743, Sep. 7.	Evans, Eleanor, and Rees Prichard.	II.
1745, June 6.	Evans, Jane, and Thomas Palmer.	II.
1744, Jan. 21.	Evans, Lewis, and Martha Hoskins.	I.
1743, Aug. 18.	Evans, Mary, and Benjamin Gilbert.	III.
1744, M'ch 29.	Evans, Simon, and Elizabeth Sloan.	III.
1748, Aug. 17.	Evans Thomas and Eleanor Rees.	I.
1746, May 20.	Evanson, Nathaniel, and Elizabeth Palmer.	I.
1744, June 2.	Eve, Oswald, and Anne Moore.	I.

F.

Date of Marriage.	Names.	Where Married.
1743, May 19.	Farrell, James, and Jane Heath.	II.
1743, Oct. 26.	Farrey, John, and Isabella Finton.	I.
1748, Aug. 15.	Farrington, Elizabeth, and John Stevens,	I.
1745, June 6.	Field, John, and Rebecca Collins.	II.
1745, May 9.	Finney, John, and Amelia Lindsey.	I.
1743, Oct. 8.	Finnyman, Martha, and Richard Tucker.	I.
1743, Oct 26.	Finton, Isabella, and John Farrey.	I.
1760, M'ch 28.	*Firespach, Ann, and Peter Stroud.*	
1744, Oct. 27.	Fisher, Elizabeth, and Thomas Brown.	I.
1744, Sep. 1.	Fisher, Thomas, and Mary Watson.	II.
1744, Feb. 12.	*Fitzpatrick, Daniel, and Catharine Lee.*	
1745, June 22.	Fleming, Joseph, and Mary Sullivan.	II.
1744, May 28.	Fleming, Robert, and Mary Daily.	II.
1743, Oct. 15.	Fletcher, Alice, and William Hutchinson.	II.
1744, May 30.	Fletcher, John, and Sarah Jones.	II.
1747, June 13.	Fling, Ann, and George Vincent Daws.	I.
1745, Nov. 15.	Folwell, Mary, and Samuel Newton.	II.
1744, Feb. 5.	Ford, Elizabeth, and Thomas Grant.	I.
1745, May 27.	Fordham, Mary, and Patrick Matthews.	II.
1783, June 11.	Foreman, Elizabeth, and Benjamin Chamberlain.	I.
1744, M'ch 26.	Fox, John, and Catharine, Roche.	I.
1748, Apr. 15.	Fox, Thomas, and Anne Woodward.	I.
1743, Sept. 30.	Francis, Anne, and James Tilghman.	I.
1774, M'ch 3.	*Frede, Salome, and Gabriel Swartzlander.*	
1744, Oct. 10.	Freeston, John, and Ann Cunningham.	I.
1744, June 5.	Fretwell, Mary, and Nicholas Cassel.	I.
1744, Dec. 1.	Fulford, Richard, and Elizabeth Grimes.	II.
1760, Aug. 20.	*Ferris, William, and Mary Ranbury.*	
1743, M'ch 27.	Fusman, Elizabeth, and Meredith Jones.	I.

G.

1745, Sep. 30.	Gardner, Mary, and Peter Rose.	I.
1743, July 11.	Garwood, William, and Martha Johnson.	I.
1745, June 1.	Gaw, Mary, and Joseph Totten.	II.
1743, July 10.	Gibbons, Henry, and Elizabeth Cooke.	II.
1743, Dec. 16.	Gibbons, Anna, and Nathaniel Chew.	II.
1764, M'ch 27.	*Gilbert, Abigail, and George Tompkins.*	
1743, Aug. 18.	Gilbert, Benjamin, and Mary Evans.	III.
1748, June 16.	*Gilfoy, Charles, and Margaret Elleson.*	
1744, Apr. 10.	Gilpin, Thomas, and Susannah Boyes.	II.
1783, June 25.	Godshalt, Elizabeth, and Andrew Howard.	II.
1743, Apr. 25.	Goldy, Joseph, and Margaret Wells.	II.

Date of Marriage.	Names.	Where Married.
1744, Dec. 31.	Goodin, John, and Deborah West.	II.
1745, Oct. 15.	Goodin, Mary, and John McCormick.	I.
1744, Jan. 28.	Goodin, Phœbe, and William Hawkins.	I.
1744, Jan. 9.	Graft, John Valentine, and Mary Elizabeth Alberdine.	II.
1744, Feb. 5.	Grant, Thomas, and Elizabeth Ford.	I.
1744, Sep. 13.	Green, Pyramus, and Mary Morris.	I.
1745, Nov. 28.	Greenless, Mary, and David Chancellor.	II.
1743, Feb. 10.	Gregory, Elizabeth, and John Maugridge.	I.
1747, Apr. —.	Griffey, Catharine, and Theophilus Williams.	
1744, Apr. 6.	Griffith, Mary, and Daniel Beaton.	II.
1744, Dec. 10.	Griffith, Mary, and Timothy Scarfe.	II.
1744, Aug. 3.	Griffith, Rachel, and David Lewis.	II.
1747, May —.	Groover, Mary, and William Kenton.	
1744, Dec. 1.	Grimes, Elizabeth, and Richard Fulford,	II.
1743, Oct. 24.	Guery, Judith, and Patrick McDonagh,	I.
1745, June 15.	Guttier, Hannah, and Matthew Scot.	I.
1743, Nov. 11.	Grymes, Michael, and Elizabeth Smith.	II.

H.

1745, Dec. 16.	Haimer, Anne, and Thomas Carty.	II.
1743, May 23.	Hainey, Elizabeth. and John Peel.	I.
1744, M'ch 15.	Haliday, James, and Judith Harris.	II.
1743, Oct. 24.	Hall, John, and Mary Hugg.	I.
1743, June 11.	Hamilton, Ann, and Westema Cross.	II.
1744, Jan. 25.	Hancock, Thomas, and Susannah Symons.	I.
1743, Sep. 8.	Harcomb. Hannah, and Hugh Hodge.	II.
1745, Aug. 17.	Harney, Bridget, and Charles Collins.	II.
1744, July 30.	Harris, Ann, and Samuel Vanhist.	I.
1744, M'ch 15.	Harris, Judith, and James Haliday.	II.
1745, Sep. 8.	Harris, Sarah, and Richard Ellis.	I.
1743. Oct. 23.	Harrison, Mary, and George Bradley.	I.
1746, Apr. 17.	Harrison, Mary, and Noah Wills.	I.
1743, May 14.	Harry, Lydia, and Philip Thomas.	I.
1745, July 6.	Hartley, Benjamin, and Rachel Coats.	I.
1745, M'ch 23.	Hartshorne, Jas., and Catharine McCreagh.	I.
1745, Sep. 19.	Hassell, Elizabeth, and Alex. Huston.	I.
1743, Nov. 3.	Haste, Rachel, and William Dewees.	III.
1745, June 24.	Haughmy, Barbara, and Joseph Paine.	II.
1743, Aug. 17.	Haven, John, and Elizabeth Potts.	II.
1745, June 20.	Hawkins, George, and Ann Carroll.	II.
1744, Jan. 28.	Hawkins, William, and Phœbe Goodin.	I.
1745, Nov. 14.	Hayhurst, William, and Rebecca Searle.	I.
1746, Feb. 8.	Headon, Catharine, and Edmund Martin.	II.

Date of Marriage.	Names.	Where Married.
1743, Aug. 26.	Heaftis, Mary, and Joseph Burden.	II.
1743, May 19.	Heath, Jane, and James Farrell	II.
1746, Feb. 26.	Hertzel, Judith, and George Stucky.	I.
1744, Oct. 16.	Heselius, Elizabeth, and Samuel Price.	I.
1744, Oct. 4.	Hill, Hugh, and Mary Hoodt.	I.
1743, Feb. 5.	Hobart, Jane, and Anthony Bright.	I.
1743, Sep. 8.	Hodge, Hugh, and Hannah Harcomb.	II.
1745, May 30.	Hoffety, Mary, and William Price.	I.
1744, Oct. 4.	Hoodt, Mary, and Hugh Hill.	I.
1744, Aug. 29.	Hooper, Margaret, and John Hyat.	I.
1745, Nov. 16.	Hopewell, John, and Deborah Sharp.	II.
1745, Sep. 4.	Hopman, Peter, and Mary Painter.	II.
1743, July 2.	Horner, Thos. and Elizabeth Waterman.	I.
1744, Jan. 21.	Hoskins, Martha, and Lewis Evans.	I.
1743, Dec. 14.	Houda, Anna Maria, and George Marks.	II.
1783, June 25.	Howard, Andrew, and Eliza'th Godshalt.	II.
1744, Aug. 9.	Howard, John, and Sarah Moet.	I.
1745, May 27.	Howel, Jane, and James McSwain.	I.
1746, April 3.	Howell, Rachel, and James Prichard.	II.
1744, Oct. 18.	Hudson, Rebecca, and Alexander Crookshank.	I.
1743, Oct. 24.	Hugg, Mary, and John Hall.	I.
1744, Dec. 5.	Hughes, Martha, and William Parsons.	II.
1745, Jan. 13.	Hughes, Morgan, and Ann Stephens.	I.
1744, Jan. 25.	Hughes, William, and Elizabeth Thomas.	II.
1761, Sep. 21.	*Hildebrand, John, and Susanna Yeington.*	
1745, Oct. 26.	Hunter, Elizabeth, and Hugh Boyd.	II.
1744, June 13.	Hurley, Mary, and Peter Powelson.	I.
1745, Sep. 19.	Huston, Alexander, and Elizabeth Cassell.	I.
1744, M'ch 25.	Hutchins, Mary, and John Bolithe.	I.
1743, Oct. 15.	Hutchinson, William, and Alice Fletcher.	II.
1744, Aug. 16.	Hyat, Ann, and Jonas Osburn.	I.
1744, Aug. 29.	Hyat, John, and Margaret Hooper.	I.
1743, Sep. 1.	Hynes, Rachel, and Robert Tempest.	I.

I.

1761, Apr. 2.	Inglis, Mary, and Julines Herring.	I.
1743, Jan. 26.	Ingram, Abigail, and Lawrence Anderson.	I.
1743, Nov. 24.	Ingram, John, and Hannah Brownyard.	I.
1745, June 22.	Irwin, Margaret, and George Ord.	II.

J.

1764, Oct. 9.	*Jackson, James, and Catharine Denning.*	
1743 July 27.	Jeans, Anne, and William Beaman.	I.
1745, Feb. 15.	Jewers, John, and Margaret Cook.	I.

Date of Marriage.	Names.	Where Married.
1744, May 9.	Jodon, Francis, and Martha Roberts.	II.
1743, July 11.	Johnson, Martha, and William Garwood.	I.
1743, Dec. 10.	Johnson, Orange, and Joshua Carpenter.	I.
1744, M'ch 29.	Johnston, Hannah, and Samuel Mason.	I.
1745, M'ch 10.	Jones, Ann, and John Scull.	I.
1745, May 14.	Jones, Ann, and Henry Clarke.	I.
1744, Aug. 18.	Jones, Catharine, and Owen Neal.	II.
1745, Aug. 22.	Jones, Elizabeth, and Benjamin Levering.	I.
1745, Aug. 14.	Jones, Evan, and Diana Thomas.	I.
1745, Dec. 9.	Jones, Evan, and Anne Evans.	I.
1744, May 9.	Jones, Hannah, an l Joseph Price.	I.
1743, Feb. 13.	Jones, Isaac, and Frances Strettell.	I.
1743, Aug. 20.	Jones, John, and Sarah Price	I.
1745, Nov. 14.	Jones, Martha, and Patrick Rowney.	I.
1743, M'ch 27.	Jones, Meredith, and Elizabeth Fusman.	I.
1743, Nov. 30.	Jones, Ruth, and William Couch.	II.
1744, May 30.	Jones, Sarah, and John Fletcher.	II.

K.

1743, July 9.	Karnes, David, and Marg. Ovington.	I.
1746, Apr. 23.	Keen, Matthias, and Mary Murray.	II.
1743, May 11.	Keley, William, and Susannah Woods.	I.
1763, Nov. 5.	Kennard, Meenan, and Elizabeth Cameron.	
1745, June 3.	Kennedy, Hannah, and Richard Kennedy.	I.
1747, May —.	Kenthon, William, and Mary Groover	
1745, June 3.	Kennedy, Richard, and Hannah Kennedy.	I.
1745, Aug. 6.	Keys, Mary, and Stephen Stephens.	I.
1744, Sep. 13.	Knowles, John, and Mary Wilkinson.	IV.
1745, Oct. 10.	Kollock, Magdalen, and Jasper McCall.	I.
1746, Jan. 23.	Kollock, Philips, and Hester Leach.	I.

L.

1748, Aug. 2.	Lawrence, Giles, and Sarah Thomas.	I.
1745, Apr. 20.	Leacock, Susannah, and James Read.	I.
1746, Feb. 18.	Leadbeater, Geo., and Catharine Thomas.	I.
1774, Feb. 12.	Lee, Catharine, and Daniel Fitzpatrick.	
1746, Jan. 23.	Leech, Hester, and Philip Kollock.	I.
1745, Jan. 3.	Leech, Sarah, and Æneas Ross.	I.
1743, Feb. 12.	Le Gay, Jacob, and Mary Weyman.	I.
1743, Oct. 6.	Legay, Ruth, and John Marshall.	I.
1746, Apr. 23.	Leipencout, Jacob, and Grace Rudrow.	I.
1746, Apr. 9.	Leipencout, Mary, and George Standley.	I.
1743, Dec. 17.	Lenellen, Elizabeth, and George Webster.	I.
1745, Aug. 22.	Levering, Benjamin, and Elizabeth Jones.	I.
1744, Aug. 3.	Lewis, David, and Rachel Griffith.	II.

Date of Marriage.	Names.	Where Married.
1746, M'ch 20.	Lewis, George, and Mary McGwyer.	II.
1743, Aug. 26.	Lewis, Henry, and Rachel Powel.	I.
1746, Dec. 18.	Lewis, Thomas, and Anne Edwards.	II.
1745, May 9.	Lindsey, Amelia, and John Finney.	I.
1743, Oct. 14.	Lindsey, John, and Anne Burk.	II.
1743, Oct. 11.	Linn, Sarah, and Peter Bankson.	I.
1743, May 28.	Lister, Adam, and Ann Watts.	I.
1746, M'ch 26.	Little, James, and Martha McConnell.	II.
1765, *Sep.* 21.	*Loofborough, David, and Sarah Twining.*	
1746, Apr. 5.	Lowden, Elizabeth, and Peter Crawford.	I.
1743, May 27.	Lownes, Mary, and Thomas Phillips.	I.
1748, Aug. 8.	Lynn, David, and Mary Boor.	I.

M.

Date of Marriage.	Names.	Where Married.
1744, M'ch 24.	McBroom, Andrew, and Eleanor Daily.	II.
1745, Jan. 2.	McCall, George, and Lydia Abbett.	I.
1745, Oct. 10.	McCall, Jasper, and Magdalen Kollock.	I.
1743, Jan. 29.	McCall, Samuel, and Ann Searle.	I.
1745, Sep. 19.	McCollum, John, and Mary Burn.	II.
1746, M'ch 26.	McConnell, Martha, and James Little.	II.
1745, Oct. 15.	McCormick, John, and Mary Goodin.	I.
1746, Jan. 16.	McCready, Francis, and Philip Adamson.	I.
1745. M'ch 23.	McCreagh, Catharine, and James Hartshorn.	I.
1743, Oct. 23.	McCullough, Mary, and John Ryan.	I.
1743, Oct. 24.	McDonagh, Patrick, and Judith Guery.	I.
1748, Aug. 15.	McGee, Elizabeth, and Henry Wright.	I.
1746, M'ch 20.	McGwyer, Mary, and George Lewis.	II.
1746, Feb. 11.	McKenny, John, and Bridget Sullivan.	I.
1744, Jan. 30.	McKenny, Sarah, and Walter Bryson.	II.
1744, M'ch 24.	McMahon, Hugh, and Agnas Norton.	I.
1745, Nov. 14.	McMahon, Jane, and Richard Smith.	I.
1745, Aug. 27.	McMahon, Margaret, and Valen. Barney.	I.
1744, Aug. 2.	McNeal, John, and Elizabeth McNealus.	II.
1744, Aug. 2.	McNealus, Elizabeth, and John McNeal.	II.
1745, May 27.	McSwain, James, and Jane Howel.	I.
1745, June 27.	McVaugh, John, and Mary Poynter.	II.
1745, Jan. 1.	McVeagh, James, and Rebecca Worrell.	II.
1745, Sep. 5.	McWally, Alex., and Mary Armstrong.	II.
1745, Aug. 2.	Magee, Alexander, and Mary Dugdale.	III.
1744, June 20.	Maherty, Margaret, and And. Peterson.	II.
1743, Feb. 10.	Mahery, James, and Mary Smith.	I.
1743, Dec. 20.	Malowny, Mary, and James Quin.	I.
1744, May 28.	Manny, Mary, and Stephen Carter.	II.
1743, Dec. 14.	Marks, George, and Ann Maria Houda.	II.

Date of Marriage.	Names.	Where Married.
1743, Oct. 6.	Marshall, John, and Ruth Legay.	I.
1743, Dec. 26.	Marshall, Margaret, and Patrick Allen.	I.
1746, Feb. 8.	Martin, Edmund, and Catharine Headon.	II.
1743, M'ch 1.	Martin, Elizabeth, and Joseph Preston.	I.
1746, M'ch 4.	Martin, Hannah, and Nathaniel Davis.	II.
1746, May 31.	Martin, John, and Elizabeth Thomas.	II.
1744, June 23.	Mason, Anne, and John Ord.	I.
1745, July 18.	Mason, Catharine, and George Smith.	I.
1744, M'ch 29.	Mason, Samuel, and Hannah Johnston.	I.
1743, July 24.	Mather, Margaret, and Thomas Watson.	I.
1744, July 21.	Matlack, Mary, and John Pim.	II.
1745, May 27.	Matthews, Patrick, and Mary Fordham.	II.
1743, May 28.	Maxwell, William, and Gertrude Enoch.	III.
1744, Oct. 1.	Metz, George, and Jane Curtis.	I.
1745, Aug. 8.	Miles, Sarah, and Myrick Davis.	I.
1744, July 28.	Mitchell, Thomas, and Sarah Dyer.	I.
1744, Aug. 9.	Moet, Sarah, and John Howard.	I.
1744, June 2.	Moore, Anne, and Oswald Eve.	I.
1744, Dec. 11.	Moore, Salatial, and Esther Williams.	II.
1745, Oct. 19.	Morgan, Barbara, and Thomas Bell.	II.
1744, Aug. 2.	Morgan, John, and Anne Anderson.	II.
1742, Dec. 29.	Morgan, Mary, and Thomas Oliphant.	I.
1744, May 23.	Morris, Francis, and Mary ———.	II.
1744, Sep. 13.	Morris, Mary, and Pyramus Green.	I.
1746, Feb. 2.	Morris, Mary, and George Claypoole.	I.
1745, Aug. 17.	Morton, Mary, and Thomas Norrington.	I.
1745, Aug. 3.	Moulder, Wm., and Hannah Smallwood.	I.
1745, June 25.	Moyer, Peter, and Mary Wagener.	II.
1783, June 19.	Mullock, Edward, and Leah Bickerton.	I.
1746, Apr. 23.	Murray, Mary, and Matthias Keen.	II.
1744, July 4.	Murrey, Isabell, and Thomas Peirce.	II.

N.

1744, Feb. 5.	Naylor, Mary, and Jeremiah Woolston.	II.
1744, Aug. 18.	Neal, Owen, and Catharine Jones.	II.
1747, Feb. —.	Neisman, Rev. Gabriel, and Margaret Rambo.	I.
1745, Nov. 14.	Nigely, John, and Elizabeth Boude.	I.
1744, May 15.	Newton, Robert, and Jane Brooks.	II.
1745, Aug. 17.	Norrington, Thomas, and Mary Morton.	I.
1745, Apr. 24.	North, Elizabeth, and Daniel Benezet.	I.
1744, M'ch 24.	Norton, Agnas, and Hugh McMahon.	I.

O.

1744, Dec. 23.	O'Neal, Margaret, and Robert Davis.	I.
1742, Dec. 29.	Oliphant, Thomas, and Mary Morgan.	I.

Date of Marriage.	Names.	Where Married.
1745, Feb. 5.	Oliver, Mary, and John Brown.	II.
1745, June 22.	Ord, George, and Margaret Irwin.	II.
1744, June 23.	Ord, John, and Anne Mason.	I.
1744, Aug. 16.	Osburn, Jonas, and Anne Hyat.	I.
1743, July 9.	Ovington, Margaret, and David Karnes.	I.
1745, June 7.	Owen, Hugh, and Sarah Williams.	II.
1744, Feb. 6.	Owen, Priscilla, and Wm. Cunningham.	I.

P.

Date of Marriage.	Names.	Where Married.
1745, June 24.	Paine, Joseph, and Barbara Haughmy.	II.
1745, Sep. 4.	Painter, Mary, and Peter Hopman.	II.
1743, May 7.	Palmer, John, and Deborah Bankson.	I.
1744, Sep. 12.	Palmer, Rebecca, and Leonard Temple.	II.
1746, May 20.	Palmer, Elizab'h, and Nathaniel Evanson.	I.
1745, June 6.	Palmer, Thomas, and Jane Evans.	II.
1745, Jan. 16.	Parker, Humphrey, and Tamer Scot.	II.
1745, Feb. 23.	Parker, Joseph, and Elizabeth Smith.	II.
1745, M'ch 3.	Parmale, Charles, and Elizabeth Ennis.	I.
1744, Dec. 5.	Parsons, William, and Martha Hughes.	II.
1743, Jan. 19.	Paxton, Elizabeth, and Joseph Boore.	III.
1744, June 20.	Pearce, Mary, and Thomas Pennington.	I.
1745, Nov. 14.	Peck, William, and Jane Danks.	II.
1745, Aug. 17.	Pedrow, John, and Mary Starn.	I.
1743, May 23.	Peel, John, and Elizabeth Hainey.	I.
1744, July 4.	Peirce, Thomas, and Isabell Murrey.	I.
1772, *June 20.*	*Pennabicker, Peter, and Margaret Welker.*	
1744, June 20.	Pennington, Thomas, and Mary Pearce.	I.
1744, June 20.	Peterson, And'w, and Margaret Maherty.	II.
1743, Feb. 3.	Philips, Lydia, and Jeoffrey Beck.	II.
1743, May 27.	Philips, Thomas, and Mary Lownes.	I.
1745, Jan. 17.	Pick, John, and Eleanor Douglas.	I.
1744, July 21.	Pim, John, and Mary Matlack.	II.
1744, M'ch 2.	Pine, Benjamin, and Hannah Stokes.	I.
1745, Aug. 1.	Poor, William, and Catharine White.	I.
1743, Aug. 17.	Potts, Elizabeth, and John Haven.	II.
1743, Aug. 26.	Powel, Rachel, and Henry Lewis.	I.
1745, Nov. 23.	Powell, David, and Susannah Williamson.	II.
1744, June 13.	Powelson, Peter, and Mary Hurley.	I.
1745, Aug. 3.	Power, John, and Sarah Dutton.	II.
1745, June 27.	Poynter, Mary, and John McVaugh.	II.
1744, July 14.	Preson, Sarah, and Edward Cooper.	I.
1743, M'ch 1.	Preston, Joseph, and Elizabeth Martin.	I.
1743, M'ch 31.	Price, Conrad, and Catharine Barstler.	I.
1745, May 31.	Price, Elizabeth, and John Ellis.	I.
1744, Dec. 21.	Price, James, and Mary Eyre.	I.

Date of Marriage.	Names.	Where Married.
1744, May 9.	Price, Joseph, and Hannah Jones.	I.
1744, Jan. 13.	Price, Robert, and Eve Souder.	II.
1744, Oct. 16.	Price, Samuel, and Elizabeth Heselius.	I.
1743, Aug. 20.	Price, Sarah, and John Jones.	I.
1745, May 30.	Price, William, and Mary Hoffety.	I.
1746, M'ch 17.	Prichard, Hannah, and Robert Whitehead.	I.
1746, Apr. 3.	Prichard, James, and Rachel Howell.	II.
1743, Sep. 7.	Prichard, Rees, and Eleanor Evans.	II.

Q.

1743, Dec. 20.	Quin, James, and Mary Malowny.	I.

R.

1747, Feb. 6.	Rambo, Margaret, and Rev. Gabriel Neisman.	I.
1760, Aug. 20.	*Ranbury, Mary, and William Ferris.*	
1744, Apr. 11.	Rankin, James, and Katherine Rue.	II.
1745, Apr. 20.	Read, James, and Susannah Leacock.	I.
1743, Dec. 29.	Reed, Florinda, and George Smith.	I.
1743, Dec. 3.	Rees, Daniel, and Hannah Carlisle.	I.
1748, Aug. 17.	Rees, Eleanor, and Thomas Evans.	I.
1762, Dec. 13.	*Reese, Catharine, and Philip Truckenmiller.*	
1745, Jan. 14.	Reese, Ruth, and Henry Bidding.	II.
1743, Dec. 31.	Register, Sarah, and James Scot.	II.
1745, Oct. 10.	Reily, Charles, and Isabell Easly.	II.
1746, Feb. 18.	Reily, Joshua, and Rebecca Doyle.	II.
1762, Apr. 22.	*Remberger, John, and Mary Bonrem.*	
1743, Oct. 21.	Renshaw, Sarah, and Isaac Ashton.	IV.
1747, M'ch —.	*Rex, Agnus, and Philip Woods.*	
1744, Apr. 9.	Rice, Sarah, and Henry William.	I.
1745, June 17.	Richey, David, and Mary Cross.	IV.
1745, Apr. 20.	Ring, Rachel, and Abraham Collins.	I.
1744, Sept. 8.	River, Mary, and Joseph Conyers.	I.
1744, May 9.	Roberts, Martha, and Francis Jodon.	II.
1743, June 27.	Roberts, Phineas, and Ann Winn	II.
1743, July 30.	Robins, Anne, and Thomas Stretch.	I.
1743, Jan. 11.	Robinson, Rebecca, and Thomas Bay.	I.
1744, M'ch 26.	Roche, Catharine, and John Fox.	I.
1783, June 16.	Rosbottom, James, and Elizabeth Davis.	I.
1745, Sept. 30.	Rose, Peter, and Mary Gardner.	I.
1745, Jan. 3.	Ross, Æneas, and Sarah Leech.	I.
1745, Nov. 14.	Rowney, Patrick, and Martha Jones.	I.
1743, Oct. 17.	Rowe, William, and Ann Taylor.	I.
1745, M'ch 6.	Ruby, Elizab'h, and Christopher Corbetz.	II.

Date of Marriage.	Names.	Where Married.
1746, Apr. 23.	Rudrow, Grace, and Jacob Leipencout.	I.
1744, Apr. 11.	Rue, Katharine, and James Rankin.	II.
1743, June 2.	Rush, John, and Wilmouth Camp.	I.
1743, Oct. 23.	Ryan, John, and Mary McCullough.	I.

S.

1746, Jan. 18.	Sanders, Elizabeth, and John Edwards.	I.
1743, Jan. 20.	Savage Joseph, and Elizabeth Dennis.	I.
1744, Dec. 10.	Scarth, Timothy, and Mary Griffith.	II.
1743, Dec. 31.	Scot, James, and Sarah Register.	II.
1745, June 18.	Scot, Matthew, and Hannah Guttier.	I.
1745, Jan. 16.	Scot, Tamer, and Humphrey Parker.	II.
1745, M'ch 10.	Scull, John, and Ann Jones.	I.
1743, Jan. 29.	Searle, Anne, and Samuel McCall.	I.
1745, Nov. 14.	Searle, Rebecca, and William Hayhurst.	I.
1745, Nov. 16.	Sharp, Deborah, and John Hopewell.	II.
1743, Feb, 12.	Sharp, Joseph, and Mary Coleman.	I.
1746, Feb. 4.	Sharpe, Anne, and Robert Down.	I.
1744, May 2.	Shaw, Michael, and Mary Dungan.	II.
1744, May 19.	Sheasle, John, and Sarah Davis.	I.
1748, May 14.	Shippen, Sarah, and James Burd.	
1744, June 27.	Siddon, Deborah, and Thomas Steele.	II.
1744, Nov. 24.	Still, Joseph, and Martha Elliott.	I.
1743, Apr. 9.	Simcock, Benjamin, and Elizab'h Brown.	I.
1768, Sept. 1.	*Sisk, James, and Jane Woggelom.*	
1761, Sept. 12.	*Skwiston, Francis, and Catharine St. Leger.*	
1744, M'ch 29.	Sloan, Elizabeth, and Simon Evans.	III.
1745, Aug. 3.	Smallwood, Hannah, and Wm. Moulder.	I.
1743, June 16.	Smith. Christian, and Peter Deigner.	I.
1746, May 2.	Smith, Eleanor, and James Buchanan.	II.
1743, Nov. 11.	Smith, Elizabeth, and Michael Grymes.	II.
1745, Feb. 23.	Smith, Elizabeth, and Joseph Parker.	II.
1743, Dec. 29.	Smith, George, and Florinda Reed.	I.
1745, July 18.	Smith, George, and Catharine Mason.	I.
1745, July 27.	Smith, John, and Mary Thomas.	I.
1744, Apr. 4.	Smith, Martha, and Daniel Comeron.	I.
1743, July 15.	Smith, Mary, and James Mahery.	I.
1745, Nov. 14.	Smith, Richard, and Jane McMahon.	I
1744, Jan. 13.	Souder, Eve, and Robert Price.	II.
1748, Aug. 28.	Spencer, Elizabeth, and Robert Warren.	I.
1743, Jan. 11.	Spiner, Barbara Baltes, and Enoch Armitage.	III.
1744, M'ch 31.	Spruce, Grissel, and John Stephenson.	I.

19—Vol. II.

Date of Marriage.	Names.	Where Married.
1761, Sept. 12.	St. Leger, Charlotte, and Francis Skwiston.	
1745, Jan. 21.	Stackhouse, Elizab'h, and David Wilson.	I.
1745, Sept, 19.	Stamper, Mary, and William Bingham.	I.
1746, Apr. 9.	Standley, George, and Mary Lipencout.	I.
1745, Aug. 17.	Starn, Mary, and John Pedrow.	I.
1746, May 22.	Stebbs, Henry, and Elizabeth Williams.	II.
1744, June 27.	Steele, Thomas, and Deborah Siddons.	II.
1744, Feb. 6.	Stemson, John, and Mary Timerman.	I.
1745, Jan. 13.	Stephens, Ann, and Morgan Hughes.	I.
1745, Aug. 6.	Stephens, Stephen, and Mary Keys.	I.
1744, M'ch 31.	Stephenson, John, and Grissel Spruce.	I.
1748, Aug. 15.	Stevens, John, and Elizabeth Farrington.	I.
1745, June 22.	Stockdal, Prudence, and John Thomas.	II.
1744, M'ch 2.	Stokes, Hannah, and Benjamin Pine.	I.
1747, M'ch 7.	Storke, Tabitha, and Thomas Campbell.	I.
1744, Dec. 2.	Stout, Cornelius, and Rebecca Till.	I.
1743, Jan. 11.	Stow, Charles, Jr., and Lydia Strowing.	I.
1743, July 30.	Stretch, Thomas, and Ann Robins.	I.
1743, Feb. 13.	Strettell, Frances, and Isaac Jones.	I.
1760, M'ch 28.	Stroud, Peter, and Ann Firespach.	
1743, Jan. 11.	Strowing, Lydia, and Charles Stow, Jr.	I.
1746, Feb. 26.	Stuckey, George, and Judith Hertzell.	I.
1744, Aug. 23.	Sugar, Thomas, and Elizabeth Collings.	I.
1746, Feb. 11.	Sullivan, Bridget, and John McKenny.	I.
1745, June 22.	Sullivan, Mary, and Joseph Fleming.	II.
1743, July 22.	Swain, Thomas, and Elizabeth Corbet.	I.
1774, Mar. 3.	Swartzlander, Gabriel, and Salome Freed.	
1744, Jan. 25.	Symons, Susannah, and Thos. Hancock.	I.

T.

1748, Aug. 27.	Tate, William, and Susannah Dunn.	I.
1743, Oct. 17.	Taylor, Ann, and William Rowe.	I.
1744, May 19.	Taylor, Mary, and James Doraugh.	II.
1743, Sept. 1.	Tempest, Robert, and Rachel Hynes.	I.
1744, Sept. 12.	Temple, Leonard, and Rebecca Palmer.	II.
1746, Feb. 18.	Thomas, Catharine, and Geo. Leadbetter.	I.
1745, Aug. 14.	Thomas, Diana, and Evan Jones.	I.
1744, Jan. 25.	Thomas, Elizabeth, and William Hughes.	II.
1746, May 31.	Thomas, Elizabeth, and John Martin.	I.
1745, June 22.	Thomas, John, and Prudence Stockdal.	II.
1745, July 27.	Thomas, Mary, and John Smith.	I.
1743, May 14.	Thomas, Philip, and Lydia Harry.	I.
1748, Aug. 2.	Thomas, Sarah, and Giles Lawrence.	I.
1744, May 2.	Thompson, Mary, and Thomas Thomson.	II.
1745, June 25,	Thomas, James, and Jane Coombe.	I.

Date of Marriage.		Names.	Where Married.
1744, May	2.	Thompson, Thomas, and **Mary** Thompson.	II.
1743, Sept.	30.	Tilghman, James, and Anne Francis.	I.
1744, Dec.	2.	Till, Rebecca, and Cornelius Stout.	I.
1744, Feb.	6.	Timmerman, Mary, and John Stemson.	I.
1743, Oct.	22.	Tipper, James, and Ann Blair.	I.
1764, *M'ch*	27.	*Tompkins, George, and Abigail Gilbert.*	
1744, Sept.	20.	Tomlinson, Joseph, and Elizabeth Wortington.	II.
1743, May	28.	Tomms, Mary, and William Dowell.	I.
1745, June	1.	Totten, Joseph, and Mary Gaw.	II.
1762, *Dec.*	13.	*Truckenmiller, Philip, and Catharine Reese.*	
1745, Jan.	21.	Trussel, Catharine, and Benjamin Barker.	I.
1743, Oct.	8.	Tucker, Richard, and Martha Finnyman.	I.
1743, Dec.	12.	Tuttle, Susannah, and William Annis.	I.
1765, *Sept.*	21.	*Twining, Sarah, and David Loofborough.*	

U.

1745, June	25.	Ulrick, Peter, and Margaret Clampfert.	I.

V.

1744, July	30.	Vanhist, Samuel, and Ann Harris.	I.
1744, May	18.	Vanzant, Nicholas, and Mary Brittin.	III.

W.

1745, June	25.	Waggener, Mary, and Peter Moyer.	II.
1744, June	9.	Waine, Elizabeth, and Thomas Bryan.	I.
1743, Oct.	20.	Wakefield, John, and Elizabeth Cole.	I.
1746, May	24.	Walmsley, Grace, and Benjamin Herbert.	I.
1743, May	17.	Walpole, Robert, and Eleanor Bowen.	I.
1748, Aug.	28.	Warren, Robert, and Elizabeth Spencer.	I.
1744, Sept.	8.	Warren, Sarah, and Michael Cranfield.	I.
1743, July	2.	Waterman, Elizabeth, and Thomas Horner.	I.
1744, Sept.	1.	Watson, Mary, and Thomas Fisher.	II.
1743, July	24.	Watson, Thomas, and Margaret Mather.	I.
1743, May	28.	Watts, Ann, and Adam Lister.	I.
1743, Dec.	17.	Webster, George, and Elizabeth Lewellin.	I.
1743, Apr.	25.	Wells, Margaret, and Joseph Goldy.	II.
1745, Sept.	18.	Welsh, Elizabeth, and Roger Cain.	II.
1772, *June*	20.	*Welker, Margaret, and Peter Pennabicker.*	
1744, Dec.	31.	West, Deborah, and John Goodin.	I.
1743, Feb.	12.	Weyman, Mary, and Jacob Le Gay.	I.
1745, Aug.	1.	White, Catharine, and William Poor.	I.
1746, M'ch	17.	Whitehead, Robert, and Hannah Pritchard,	I.
1744, May	19.	Wilkinson, Anne, and Thomas Cuthbert.	I.

Date of Marriage.	Names.	Where Married.
1743, June 16.	Wilkinson, Mary, and Samuel Dowthwaite.	I.
1744, Sept. 13.	Wilkinson, Mary, and John Knowles.	IV.
1743, June 11.	Wilkinson, Thomas, and Elizabeth Carr.	I.
1746, May 22.	Williams, Elizabeth, and Henry Stebbs.	II.
1744, Dec. 11.	William, Esther, and Salathial Moore.	II.
1744, Apr. 9.	William, Henry, and Sarah Rice.	I.
1745, Oct. 15.	Williams, Jane, and William Wosdel.	I.
1744, Feb. 11.	Williams Katherine, and Daniel Byrn.	II.
1747, April —.	*Williams, Theophilus, and Catharine Griffy*	
1743, May 18.	Williamson, Charles, and Mary Burk.	I.
1745, Nov. 23.	Williamson, Susannah, and David Powell.	II.
1746, Apr. 17.	Wills, Noah, and Mary Harrison.	I.
1743, Apr. 26.	Wilmington, John, and Mary Leech.	I.
1745, Jan. 21.	Wilson, David, and Elizabeth Stackhouse.	I.
1745, Sept. 14.	Wilson, David, and Susanna Colly.	II.
1745, July 6.	Wilson, James, and Sarah Bower.	III.
1768, Sept. 1.	*Woggelom, Jane, and James Sisk.*	
1743, Aug. 20.	Woodrop, Elizabeth, and Hugh Davey.	I.
1747, M'ch —.	*Woods, Philip, and Agnus Rex.*	
1743, May 11.	Woods, Susannah, and William Keley.	I.
1748, Aug. 15.	Woodward, Anne, and Thomas Fox.	I.
1744, Feb. 5.	Woolston, Jeremiah, and Mary Naylor.	II.
1745, Jan. 1.	Worrell, Rebecca, and James McVeagh.	II.
1744, Sep. 20.	Worthington, Elizabeth, and Joseph Tomlinson.	
1745, Oct. 15.	Wosdel, William, and Jane Williams.	I.
1748, Aug. 15.	Wright, Henry, and Elizabeth McGee.	I.

Y.

1761, *Sept.* 21. *Yeington, Susanna, and John Hildebrand.*

PENNSYLVANIA MARRIAGE LICENSES, 1742–1748.

[The following lists of Marriage Licenses, issued between 1742 and 1748, are copied from the original License Book, in which are also recorded those for "Public Houses, Indian Traders and Pedlars, Vessels Registered [Thomas Graeme, Naval Officer], and Fines." Between December of 1742 and May 1746, only the names of the male applicants are of record, but between 1746–1748, both are entered. The fee for a Marriage License was £1., and the clergymen who purchased them in quantity, "to be accounted for," are the Reverend Messrs. Backhouse, Currie, Pugh, Becket, Ross and Tranberg.]

1742–3.
December
28. Tho. Olephant   31. Elisha Boss

January.
1. Enoch Armitage
7. William James
10. Charles Stow
    Thomas Bay
13. Dennis Mulholland

15. Henry Bankson
18. Joseph Boore
19. Joseph Savage
25. James McPherson
26. Lawrence Anderson
27. Rees Peters
29. Sam¹ McCall

February
1. Geoffrey Beck
3. Tho⁰ Murray
4. Auth⁰ Bright
    Thomas Hunt
10. John Maugridge
15. Isaac Jones

15. Joseph Sharpe
    Jacob Legay
    Jonathan Miller
16. Joshua Henzey
28. William Davis

March

1. Joseph Preston
3. John McClure
8. John Lease
18. John McCullough
19. Patrick Magargit

19. John Anderson
26. Meredith Jones
28. Benjamin Loxley
29. Conrad Price

April

5. John Holmes
6. William Bell
9. Nathan Ambler
9. Benj. Simcock
9. Joseph Goldy

9. Joseph Gardner
9. Peter Hoffman
25. Jonathan Shaw
26. John Wilmington

May

3. John Carpenter
4. Peter George
6. William Holland
7. John Pulmers
11. William Kelley
14. Philip Thomas
17. William Tremble
17. Robert Walpole
18. Charles Williamson
19. James Farrel

23. John Peel
24. Barnaby Mocky
24. Thomas Philips
27. William Maxwell
27. John Guest
27. John Williams
27. Mary Griffin
27. Adam Lister
27. William Dowell

June

2. John Rush
2. John Wells
2. John Berry
8. John Wright
10. Tho' Wilkinson
11. Joseph Love
11. Westeura Cross

11. Benj. Reeves
13. Sam. Dowthwaite
13. Benj. Tomlinson
16. Peter Deizner
22. John Bowler
27. Phinchas Robert
30. Magnus Falconer

July

1. David Karnes
1. Francis Duncan
2. Thomas Homer
5. Sam. Knowles
11. Henry Gibbons
16. Lambert Emerson
16. Wm Garwood

15. James Mahery
22. Thomas Swain
23. Tho' Watson
23. Thomas Murrie
27. Wm Beaman
29. Tho' Stretch

August

16. Benjamin Gilbert
17. John Haven
20. Sam' Harper
20. Hugh Davie

20. John Jones
24. Henry Lewes
26. Joseph Barden
27. James Williamson

September

Robert Tempest
Rees Prichard
Hugh Hodge
James Collum
Francis Taylor
Henry Blackman
Peter Cheesman

Martin Flinn
John Marshal
Jacob Rhoofe
Jacob Backman
Isaac Larue
James Tilghman

October

Jacob Worral
Thomas Farmer
Peter Bankson
Richard Tucker
John Lindsay
Thomas Sinclair
Wm Hutchinson
Wm Rowe
James Allison

John Wakefield
James Tipper
George Bradley
Isaac Asheton
John Torrey
John Ryan
John Hall
Patrick McDonagh

November

Blaithwaite Jones
Henry Dewees
John Shelby
Robert Lowry

John Ingram
Patrick Bourne
Wm Couch
Michael Grimes

December

Daniel Rees
Wm Rill
Henry Mitchell
Wm Annis
Tho˙ Bourne
George Webster

Joshua Carpenter
Nathan: Chew
Patrick Allen
James Quin
George Smith
Geòrge Marks

1743–4.

January.

James Scott
Charles Lyon
John Valentine Graff
Robert Price
Alexander Robinson
Wm Cunningham
Richard Ellis

Lewis Evans
Tho˙ Hancock
Wm Hughes
Wm Hawkins
Walter Bryson
Joshua Bispham

February

Jeremiah Wollston
Philip Stinton
Daniel Bourne

Thomas Gant
John Stemsen
Robert Ball

March

Benj. Pine
Anthony Whitely
James Haliday
Henry Gray
John Allen

John Fox
Andrew McBroom
Hugh McMekon
John Bolitho

April

Samuel Mason
Simon Evans
Timothy Griffith
Ludowick German
John Stephenson
Thomas Richardson
Daniel Courdon

John Campbell
Daniel Beaton
James Rankin
Henry Williams
Thomas Gilpin
Jacob Banksen
John Ellis

May

Thomas Battus
Andrew Bartholomew
Thomas Thomson
Michael Shaw
Thomas Johnson
Joseph Price
Francis Jodon
John Catharinger
Nicholas Vanzant
28. Robert Fleming
28. Jonathan Darell
28. George Marple
28. Henry Gayner
28. Ulrich Allen

John Shearle
James Doraugh
Tho' Cuthbert
Stephen Carter
Thomas Ashton
Robert Newton
John Dungan
Francis Norris
31. William Carpenter
31. Oswald Eve
31. John Fletcher

June

5. Nicholas Cassell
7. Wᵐ Baldwin
9. Thomas Bryan
11. William Freeman
12. Peter Powelson
20. Thomas Pennington

20. Andrew Peterson
26. James Chipman
John Locke
22. John Ord
27. Thomas Steele

July

4. Thomas Pierce
4. Peter Jones
21. John Pemin
William Merriman
Edward Cooper
Nath' Vanleer
Joseph Durborow

James Gregory
George Harding
Jonathan Wainwright
Thomas Mitchell
Samuel Vanhist
Samuel Bramhill
Joseph Finley

August

John McNeal
David Lewis
John Morgan
John Howard
13. John Elder
Jonas Osborne

Owen Neal
James Welden
Thomas Sugar
Thomas Fisher
John Hyat

September

David Chambers
Michael Cranfield
Pyre Green
John Tatnel
James Dean
Abel James
Leonard Temple
Joseph Conyers

Daniel Harrison
John Holl
John Knowles, Jr.
Michael Loup
Jos. Tomlinson
Samuel Cheesman
George Pottery
John Irwin

October

George Metz
Hugh Hill
Christopher Ottinger, Jr.
John Freeston
Henry Elwes
Wm Harris
Alex. Cruckshank

Samuel Price
James Smith
Charles Quin
Gabriel Piles
Andrew Cock
Thomas Brown
John Henry Mang

November

Richard Ellis
Wm Londerman
Joseph Carter
John Austin
Robert Owen
James Russel
James Larrymore
Thomas Prugh

Joseph Sill
Andrew Waillore
George Fudge
Jacob Naglee
Hugh Whaly
Matthias Cline
Oliver Low
Edward Chairman

December

Cornelius Stout
Richard Fulton
Ralph Dunn
William Parsons
Jacob Steaghers
Timothy Scarfe

Robert Mann
Sathial Moore
James Price
Thomas Lewis
Robert Davis
John Goodin

1745.

January.

Francis Holton	David Wilson
James McVeagh	John Picke
John Crows	Morgan Hughes
Humphry Parker	Henry Bitting
Benjamin Barker	

February

George McCall	John Jewers
Daniel Benezet	Robert Neilson
Aneas Ross	John Harrison
John Brown	Andrew Thomson
John Dodson	Joseph Parker

March

Christopher Corbetz	John Scull
Charles Parmele	Peter Grant, Sen'
Zachray Sims	James Hartshorn
Ralph Dracord	James Read

April

Elias Rambo	John Asheton
Robert Dawson	Joseph Black
Edward Wivell	Eleazer Evans
Tho' Overin	Dan McCleane
Abram Collins	Warwick Coates

May

John Finney	Patrick Matthews
Thomas Baird	John Buckley
Joseph Totten	John Ellis
Jenkin Williams	Wm Price
Michael Conolly	John McVeagh

June

John Field
William Young
Edward Penly
Niels Jones
Samuel West
Thomas Palmer
John Summers
Richard Jugs
Richard Kennedy
Sam' Holmes
William Lane
Peter Ulrich
James Thomson
Stephen Early

Joseph Paine
Peter Myers
Joseph Fleming
John Thomas
George Hawkins
George Ord
Matthew Scott
David Ricky
John Abraham De
Normandy
Hatton Wormley
W^m McCalla
James McSwaine

July

William Poor
Hugh Bowes
Alexander Magee
Myrick Davis, Jr.
Evan Jones
Thomas Norrington
Charles Collins
John Pederow
David Wilson
Benj. Levering

William Moulder
John Power
Stephen Stephens
Richard Hall
John Adam Heer
Valentine Barney
Peter Engle
John Phipps
Ezekiel Thomas
Peter Shoemaker

September

Richard Ellis
Peter Hopman
William Wetherby
John McCollum
Roger Cain
Samuel Robinson
James Treviller

Peter Rose
Stephen Early
Alexander Huston
Samuel Overthrow
William Bingham
Alex. McWatty

October

Gaspar McCall	Wm Gregory
Wm Snook	Mathew Gleaves
Charles Reily	Thomas Ball
Wm Wosdell	Hugh Boyd
Jno. McCormick	Jno. Staneland
Philip Shutt	Jno. Wigmore
Hugh McGlome	

November

Wm Hayhurst	John Hopewell
David Chancellor	Baltzar Sheibert
James Wagstaffe	Patrick Rowny
John Buxon	Richard Smith
Samuel Davis	Robert Wall
Daniel Powell	William Peck
Samuel Newton	John Negeley
Andrew Cowen	Joseph Junton
Alex. Williamson	John Duncan
William Sample	

December

Robert Irwin	Christopher Green
Thomas Carty	William Trimble
Ebenezer Doughty	Evan Jones
John Adams	A negro man Titus

1746.

January.

John Edwards	George Duysbrugh
Nicholas Gilbert	Alexander Mame
Jeremiah Wood	Wm Logan
John Pears	Evan Edwards
Philip Kollock	George Claypoole
Philip Adamson	

February

George Leadbetter
James Wells
Joseph Johnson
Michael McNorth
Robert Down

Samuel Mearns
Peter McKenny
Edmund Martin
Joshua Reily
Michael Israel

March

Dennis Monholland
Nathaniel Davis
Richard Negle
Jacob Simon
Thomas James
Robert Towers
Samuel Scotton
George Stucky

Robert Whitehead
George Lewis
Charles Schultz
James Litle
John Turner
John Randle
John Berwick

April

James Prichard
Peter Crawford
Noah Wills
George Standley

Peter Howard
Jacob Leipencutt
Mathias Keen
Thomas Singleton

May

Hugh Brisben
Nathaniel Evanson
Benj. Harbert
John Mathers

Sebastian Felty
John Martin
Henry Stebbs
James Buchanan

PENNSYLVANIA MARRIAGE LICENCES, 1742–1748.

1746.

June.

Zachariah Barr—Jane Griffin
John Thaw—Mary Rees
John Hall—Jane Patterson
James Boggs—Catherine Knobles
William Wallace—Jane Thomas
John Comoby—Susanna Bound
Walter Brown—Hannah Bailey
James Steele Thomson—Martha Lamplugh
John Houton—Esther Vandegrift
James Smith—Mary Beaser
Sopher Perry—Elinor Joyner
Arthur Hyger—Barbara Guyger
Benjamin Street—Elizabeth Collins
James Collum—Ann Wells
James Wilson—Mary McCall
James Cowper—Rebecca Edwards
Jacob Supplee—Margaret Yocum

July.

Thomas Dodd—Sarah Belless
Robert Williams—Ruth Simmons
Alexander Chambers—Ann Fox
George Custis—Sarah Makins
Nicholas Quinn—Esther Garwood
Hugh Cain—Sarah Klainhoof
James Devereux—Esther James
James Channell—Rebecca Key

John Philpot—Ann Cunningham
William Forest—Sarah Hall
Thomas Lake—Harriet Prescot
Jonathan Beber—Mary Artis
Abram Nutt—Eliz. Anderson

August.

Edward Magenness—Rose Fullerton
Daniel Taylor—Laetitia Fream
Charles Witts—Margaret Newmonim
John Henry—Elizabeth Smith
John Hutchins—Ann Hawkins
Samuel Wallace—Eliz. Baird
John Celtres—Frances Dukemanear
Walter Porter—Sarah Hesselius
John Turner—Mary Dagger
John Knobs—Ann Roe

September.

Abram Worthington—Sydia Driver
Robert Finny—Diana Spencer
Peter Hyneman—Hester Meirs
Elias Hughes—Rebecca Wright
Elias Shryoer—Margaret Ingle
Robert Hughes—Eve Price
Wm. Killpatrick—Eliz. Frederick
Dan. Dupuy—Eleanor Dylander
Jacob Simon—Catharine Smith
Nathan Cook—Mary Rogers
Joseph Johnson—Rachel Trego
Richard Mosely—Ann Kilirease
John Rowan—Margaret Hill

October.

Jonathan Arnold—Eliz. McCollock
James Beard—Eliz. Newby
George Smith—Mary Parry

Nathan Dyke—Sarah Johnson
Frederick Walder—Eliz. Brenneman
John Crook—Beata Hoffman
George Foster—Mary Philips
James Hasleton—Mary Wilkinson
Joseph House—Elizabeth Fitzwater
William Clark—Buleah Coats
John Jacob Weiss—Rebecca Coxe
Gregory McCartey—Sarah Stoaks
James Scott—Mary Evans

November and December.

John Annis—Mary Hollin
John Gibbons—Barbara Beegle
Andrew McNare—Mary Jennings
Michael Sish—Elizabeth Moffit
John Yoder, Jr.—Sarah Shankles
Hugh Liney—Eliz. Bessat
Peter Wells—Susanna Brock
Jno. Armstrong—Rebecca Armstrong
Stephen Lewis—Hannah Jones
George Righter—Eliz. Cumres
Abel Marple—Mary Hart
John Chares—Jane Coffin
Thomas Norris—Catherine Steward
Patrick Wellie—Jane Watson
Stephen Carpenter—Rebecca Collins
Arthur Nitcullues—Mary Sanderman
Anthony Nue—Mary Packer
Henry Krier—Margaret Cody
John Roberts—Catherine Monny
John Harper—Margaret Richy
William Rumsey—Catherine Dennison
John Jones—Eliz. Wilkinson
John Spencer—Eliz. Wilson
George Ernest--Elice Mary Sneeder
Anthony Woodcosh—Jane Wells

Thomas Tarrant—Mary Radley
George Heap—Mary Jacobs
Michael Farrel—Mary Moran
John de Nyce—Jane North
James Steward—Hannah Godfrey
Joseph Thomson—Ann Gilliard
Isaac Lincon—Mary Shute
Nicholas Craypeel—Margaret Feyhelyn
Stephen Durham—Jane Wilson

1747.

January.

Thomas Parkinson—Margaret Hall
Sam. Channel—Catherine Ottinger
Francis Garrigues—Mary Knowles
John Sutton—Mary Nixon
Conrad Bower—Philipina Keylwein
Andrew Dalbo—Catherine Van Culin
William Shead—Martha Coats
Valos Handln—Sarah Russel
David Haycott—Mary Ottinger

February.

Alexander Graydon—Rachel Marks
Doughty Jones—Hannah Gardner
Robert Roberts—Margaret Lucans
John Vaughan—Eliz. Hunt
George Londer—Jane Cowe
Swan Warner—Sarah Hastings
Joseph Street—Rachel Jenkins
Joseph Bryan—Jehosheba Wells
Lewis Kadd—Catherine Oyler
William Kelly—Susannah Leonard
Thomas Oliver—Eliz. Donovon
The Swedish Minister—Rambo

March.

Philip Woods—Agnes Rea
Thomas Hoodt—Sarah Robins
Jon. Hugh—Eleanor McClellan
Jacob Beesens—Catherine Alberson
Richard Dennis—Hannah Coates
Jno. Atkins—Phoebe Philpott
Andrew Middleton—Anabel White
Francis Kelly—Eliz. Hoy
William Davis—Martha Jemmison
David Smith—Mary Martin
Richard Brookbank—Mary Rosmiddle
Richard Barret—Mary Evanson
Alexander Crookshank—Cicelly Brumbre
Henry Copp—Susannah Lamplugh
Joseph Brown—Ann Bessy
Abel Lodge—Hannah Wood

April.

Griffy Evans—Eleanor Edwards
Theophilus William—Catherine Griffy
Robert Heaton—Ann Cowans
John Cowans—Rachel Nailor
Edward Williams—Catherine Brooks
John Hinton—Sarah Sheerwood
Garret Van Zandt—Lea Nixon
George Sharswood—Ann Top
Matthew Jackson—Agnes Finley

May.

Alexander McBride—Ann Dixon
Thomas Rooke—Mary Davis
James Stevens—Mary Swain
Patrick Carthy—Ann Meredith
Charles Ewall—Catherine Pesoman

Andrew Torben—Susannah Cox
Jno. Smallwood—Mary Ewres
Jno. Crosly—Alice Mahlon
William Kenton—Mary Groover
Peter White—Eliz. Coole
Henry Harp—Eliz. Higgenbottom
John Holton—Bretty Helm
Joshua Wolleston—Priscilla Jones
Jno. Miller—Eliz. Messenger
Robert Haines—Joice Steward
William McIlvaine—Ann Emerson
James Delap—Mary Moore

June.

Samuel Mennan—Mary Baldwin
John Rowland—Ann Smith
Jacob Good—Elizabeth Freame
Valentine Kygher—Sarah [?]
Isaac January—Ann Shubart
Jacob Duche—Esther Bradley
William Prigg—Margaret Harper
William Bull—Martha Thompson
James Benezet—Ann Hasell
James White—Ann Wilcox
Allen McClean—Jane Irwin
Peter Stedham—Isabel Jaquett
James Lindsay—Mary Boardman
Abram Heulins—Susannah Polgreen
Francis Manny—Margaret Cox
Levy Potter—Sarah Griffitt
Thomas Betty—Hannah Forbes
George Vincent Daws—Ann Fling
David Boyers—Eliz. Byers
George Howell—Sarah Garrigues
John Merchant—Ann Moses
Lewellin David—Eliz. Prichard

July.

James Murray—Th. Bawlin
Edward Smout—Elizabeth Price
James Collins—Eliz. Bredin
Jacob Lincoln—Ann Rambo
Frederick Becker—Christ. Lozareen
Joseph Brown—Mary Waln
John Hunt—Mary Ann Butler
Thomas James—Mary Syng
John McCalla—Jane Harrison
William Newbold—Margaret Coultas
Stephen Anthony—Sus. Boerman
John Fotheringham—Margaret Shoemaker

August.

Edward Shippen—Mary Newland
James Milner—Eliz. Davies
Samuel Walker—Agnes Lloyd
Edmund Brodrick—Mary Cahoon
Patrick Corbit—Ann Donavan
Robert Stone—Ann Ogden
John Anderson—Jane White
George Boardman—Mary Weyser
John Jenkins—Sidney Thomas
John Price—Sarah Jenkins
James Waldrich—Mary Ford
John Hall—Sarah Parry

September.

Andrew Geary—Susannah Bateman
Abraham Matthews—Ann Lloyd
William Jones—Elizabeth Robinson
William Many—Eliz. Middleton
———— Ingram—Sarah Johnson
Griffith Prichard—Mary Jones
John Smallwood—Mary Hart
Adam Lyn—Eleanor Jones

October.

Joseph Friend—Rebecca Eyre
Patrick Carrighan—Margaret Douglass
Theophilus Grew—Rebecca Richards
John Riley—Mary Hillhouse
Jonathan Brooks—Rebecca Hager
Joseph Wood—Mary Scull
Charles Shea—Elis. Cummins
Alexander Guthrie—Mary Albright
William Edwards—Isabel Chalmler
William Henderson—Mary Worrall
William Davis—Sarah Stinson
Isaac Billew—Rachel Britton
Thomas Primmen—Eliz. Edwards
James Pitcairn—Mary Rowoth
Joseph North—Lydia Price

November.

*Nathaniel Graham—Susannah Dinsdale
*Peter Jacquet—Elizabeth Jacquet
*Peter Haston—Margaret Hedges
*David Lewis—Margaret Morris
*Thomas Ellet—Bridget Peters
*John Bord—Ann Bryant
John Morris—Jane Goterd
Thomas Hill—Eliz. McClellan
Samuel Minshall—Jane Stanton
Henry Woodward—Sarah Weeks
Joshua Mitchels—Rebecca Davis
Renier Lukins—Jane Perry
Nathaniel West—Eliz. Evans
James Kappock—Mary Emmerson
John Jones—Mary Philips
Samuel Byers—Eliz. Calwell

---

* These licences were returned by Pastor Peter Tranberg.

John Mackintosh—Margaret Sullivan
Samuel Jones—Hannah Rees
Lot Evans—J. Patterson
Adam Burk—Margaret Allen
Thomas Eggar—Eliz. Ellis
William Gray—Eliz. Jones

December.

Thomas Sturgis—Catherine Roberts
Thomas Baldridge—Ann Bell
James Curry—Agnes Cunningham
Isaac Hughes—Rebecca [?]
Anthony McCue—Lydia Lloyd
James Conrad—Jane Hatfield
Witlock Paulin—Mary Smith
John McFarland—Rachel Coburn
Samuel Coster—Ann Thomas
James McCollough—Rachel Spence
Joseph Warner—Ann Greesbury
Samuel Chapman—Martha Moore
John Benton—Eliz. Chevalier
Dennis Sullivan—Margaret Lodge
Morris Gwin—Ann Roberts
Moses Kenton—Mary Leed
William Ghiselm—Rebecca Buchston
Christopher Finny—Martha Dibbins
Jno. Simpson—Mary Wilson
John Moore—Jennet Hering
Henry Dunn—Hannah Totten
Charles Stedman—Ann Grame [Græme]

PENNSYLVANIA MARRIAGE LICENSES, 1742-1748.

1748.

January.

Spencer Trotter—Margaret Williams
James Adams—Sarah Jones
Mathew Cummins—Eliz. Warren
Thomas Ely—Sarah Dicks
Richard Custard—Eliz. Brownback
Thomas Withers—Agnes Steen
George Allen—Mary Harding
John Stagg—Dorothy Crue
William Browning—Abigale Custard
William Weldon—Sarah Whealy
Thomas Williams—Sarah Preston
Alexander Sager—Ann Dant
John Arts—Eliz. Gratehouse
David Hall—Laycock Grebig

February.

John Austin—Martha Morgan
Richard Addis—Susanna Haslet
Isaac Lewis—Mary Phipps
William McKnight—Susanna Bond
Caspar Bussard—Deborah Yocum
Joseph Lane—Mary Bobkin
Thomas Dilks—Rhody Langly
Peter Martlew—Elizabeth Elder

March.

Anthony Adamson—Dorothy Haines
Rees Howel—Sarah West

John Evans—Sarah Denny
Thomas Kennard—Mary Ecoff
Lewis Lewis—Elis. Rees
John Roody—Rachel Naeff
John Ringer—Anna Maria Nesen
Henry Craffs—Mary Fowler
Thomas Leonard—Eliz. Martgridge
Robert Thomson—Hannah Delaplaine
William Davison—Esther Deverik
Isaac Taylor—Sarah Stone

April.

George David—Eliz. James
Edmund McVeagh—Eliz. Whartenby
Thomas Reid—Margaret Davies
Balthaser Kreamer—Eliz. Gerrard
Henry Harrison—Mary Aspden
Daniel Cavanaugh—Hannah Demsey
William Allen—Jane Reed
Peter Johnson—Sarah Vankirk
John Wendell—Rebecca Bay
Emanuel Rouse—Mary Jackson
John Blakely—Eliz. Barkley
Nathan Warley—Eliz. Tomkins
Ephraim Leech—Mary Nixon
Robert Jenny—Jane Eliz. Cummins (Gratis)

May.

———Bird— ———Shippy
John Davis—Agnes Darrough
Evan Pennall—Elizabeth Powell
Nicholas Burghard—Hannah Frederica Pessbear
William Davis—Sarah Davis
Swan Justis—Mary Jones
Richard Busby—Eliz. Richardson
James Ferice—Sarah Smallwood

William Ellis—Rebecca Collins
James Toy—Patience Walles
Benjamin Parker—Mary Briton
Hugh McClones—Rachel Banes
James Charlesworth—Ann Crimp
David Cumming—Sarah Jobson

June.

John Dixon—Mary Wilson
John Wilson—Ann Edwards
George Plosis—Mary Hastings
William Guy—Mary Scot
Woolrick Allen—Mary Mandlin
John Hamilton—Margaret Hamilton
Tristram Davis—Isabel Jamison
John Miller—Jane Gale
Samuel Rockwell—Martha Milner
Arthur Latimore—Mary Wilson
*John Way—Mary Pearce
*Edward Ogle—Margaret Howard
*Charles Gilfoy—Margaret Ellison
*James Stevenson—Eliz. Weldon
*James Carson—Mary Espy
*Charles Pearce—Ann Austill

July.

Michael Hendrick—Sarah Neil
John Denton—Mercy Roberts
William Allison—Mary Pennington
Robert Ladner—Elizabeth Pyles
Joseph Devit—Agnes Nise
David Griffith—Hannah Emmit
Thomas Boncher—Mary Farell
Samuel Crispin—Sarah Barnet

* Returned by Pastor Tranberg.

Robert Smith—Sarah Stilly
James Skerret—Susanna Warner
William Weldon—Sarah Thomas
William Henderson—Celia Frewin
John Parsons—Susanna Adamson

August.[*]

Samuel Wickward
Henry Wright
John Stevens
John Smith
John Caruthers
Thomas Evans
Archibald Christie
James Berney
David Roberts
William Tate
Thomas Fox
David Davis
Giles Lawrence
David Lynn
Anthony Palmer
Robert Warren

September.

Morris Evan—Mary Buchan
Cadwalader Morgan—Lydia Cooper
Ulrich Teakley—Susanna Sommerour
John Blakeney—Jane Parker
John Pine—Isabel Bruce
William Purcell—Margaret Kirkby
William Fowler—Susanna Jones
Thomas Nevill—Mary Davis
Nicholas Knight—Margaret Warner
William Stanley—Eliz. Fulton

---

[*] Mr. Peters has not entered the names of the women for this month.

James Bailey—Rebecca Davis
Patrick Miller—Susanna Molton
Edward Williams—Mary Brown
Leonard Herman—Barbara Keupler
Joseph Ferguson—Martha Walmer
Jacob Spike—Susanna Allen
James Bodine—Sarah Bessonet
Francis Le Blan—Eliz. Till
Jno. McFarson—Margaret Rogers
Jno. Parkinson—Mary Daniel
Thomas Parkman—Eliz. Stapler

October.

William Moritz—Hannah Berkman
Dennis Dyer—Abigal Edwards
John Corbet—Mary Todd
Mathew Ray—Sarah Harmer
Solomon Hilliard—Jane Buckley
David Dewer—Susanna Thornhill
Peter Harper—Eve Deel
Stacey Woodall—Rachel Likens
John Williams—Sarah Whealey
Erasmus Leaver—Catherine Meary
James Boyse—Mary Grimes
Joseph Beddow—Eliz. Sallows
Jno. Stockerd—Eliz. Collins
Jonathan Case—Eliz. Durborow
George Stevenson—Rebecca Dickinson
James Penington—Jane Palmer
Benjamin Peters—Dorothy Battin
Ezekiel Rambo—Eliz. Holstein
Samuel Austin—Widow Stilley

November.

John Carson—Ann Pywell
William Falkner—Abigal Harcott

Joseph Bates—Anna Smith
Jno. Mayhew—Rachel Harverd
Thomas Collet—Lydia Van Horn
James Menzie—Elinor Willing
Nicholas Hicks—Christ. Alburtson
Melchior Meng—Mary Colliday
David Moffit—Rachel Robinson
Thomas Joyce—Eliz. Smith
John Hevenson—Mary Henderson
Isaac Milner—Hannah Fischer
George Smith—Anna Margaret Bauman
Jonathan Carmalt—Elizabeth Stenton

PENNSYLVANIA MARRIAGE LICENSES, ISSUED BY GOVERNOR JAMES HAMILTON, 1748–1752.

BY HELEN JORDAN.

[In the Manuscript Department of the Historical Society of Pennsylvania is an interesting old account book,—"The Honourable James Hamilton Esq. his account current with Richard Peters,"—which contains Marriage, Public House, Pedlar, Horse Jockey, Indian Trader, and Insurance Licenses ; Passports, and Ship Registers, issued between 1748 and 1752. The Reverends Backhouse, Ross, Currie, Acrelius, and Schlatter appear to have been the favorite clergymen of that day. It is also of record that the Governor paid pew rent at Christ Church £8. annually ; that from 1749–1752 he subscribed £50. per annum to the Assembly ; and that he made a donation of £50. to the Academy.

The following List of Marriage Licenses is not included in those printed in Pennsylvania Archives, Second Series, Vol. II.]

Aaron, Moses, and Elizabeth Buller, 1752, January 3.
Abbot, Mary, and Benjamin Browning, 1751, March 23.
Abevan, Jane, and James Much, 1751, April 20.
Adams, James, and Martha Henry, 1749, June 7.
Adams, James, and Elizabeth Watson, 1751, October 16.
Adridge, Elizabeth, and George Charm, 1751, May 27.
Agin, Tobias, and Elizabeth Rupertson, 1752, February 29.
Aken, Margaret, and Jacob Ebald, 1749, October.
Alaire, Alexander, and Elizabeth Palmer, 1749, October.
Alberson, Ruloff, and Mary Coates, 1749, April.
Albertson, Jane, and William Egerton, 1749, December.
Albertson, William, and Elizabeth Cambell, 1752, April 1.
Alexander, William, and Marg^t Dunn, 1751, September 4.
Alexander, Hezekiah, and Mary Sample, 1752, June 12.
Allarue, Anna, and Jacob Subers, 1748, January 17.
Allen, Richard, and Elizabeth Boore, 1748, January 3.
Allen, Margery, and Ralph Smith, 1749, April 22.

Allenby, Mary, and Peter Revell, 1748, November.
Anderson, Patrick, and Hannah Martin, 1748, November.
Anderson, Jane, and Isaac Arthur, 1749, January.
Anderson, John, and Martha McFarland, 1749, May.
Anderson, Andrew, and Susannah Bellows, 1751, February 2.
Anderson Isaac, and Edith Shull, 1751, April 16.
Anderson, Mary, and James Woodside, 1751, October 26.
Anderson, Ann, and Anthony Martin, 1752, May 26.
Andover, Joseph, and Mary Reames, 1751, July 1.
Anmin, Barbara, and Michael Dyade, 1748, November.
Annis, Samuel, and Sarah Pearson, 1750, August.
Annis, Susannah, and Robert Lindsay, 1751, December 13.
Annis, Ann, and Josiah Davenport, 1751, December 13.
Appowen, Samuel, and Hannah Cocks, 1749, March.
Armitage, Mary, and Thomas Dunn, 1751, August 24.
Armstrong, Eleanor, and John Clarke, 1751, November 11.
Arnold, Mark, and Elizabeth Lawrence, 1750, September.
Arrell, William, and Elizabeth Norwood, 1749, March 25.
Arrell, Richard, and Christian Davies, 1749, July.
Arthur, Isaac, and Jane Anderson, 1749, January.
Ash, Henry, and Rebecca Leach, 1749, March 25.
Ashmead, Ann, and Samuel Potts, 1751, October 9.
Ashton, Richard, and Lydia Bell, 1749, March 31.
Ashton, Isaac, and Mary Hall, 1749, June 16.
Asprell, Mary, and Leonard Humphries, 1752, May 4.
Atkinson, Barbara, and Thomas Davis, 1749, August.
Atkinson, John, and Jane Jones, 1751, June 6.
Atwood, William, and Mary Penry, widow, 1751, March 16.
Ayres, John, and Catharine Humsted, 1750, July.

Badcock, Hannah, and John Evans, 1751, November 15.
Bailey, John, and Jane Watkins, 1749, March.
Bailey, Ann, and Hugh Smith, 1751, June 25.
Bain, Mary, and Jago Henry, 1748, February 25.
Bainbridge, Sarah, and Francis Hall, 1748, February 11.
Baker, Mary, and Isaac Howell, 1751, April 17.

Baker, Hannah, and Israel Davies, 1751, April 26.

Ball, Abigail, and Peter Gilbert, 1749, June 16.

Ballard, Rebeccah, and Joseph Cox, 1749, December.

Bainbridge, Mary, and Thomas Gorden, 1751, October 16.

Bane, Mary, and Richard Jerrard, 1751, May 18.

Banfield, Thomas, and Ruth Mandlin, 1750, May.

Bankson, Deborah, and John Lord, 1751, June 8.

Barkley, James, and Mary Marner, 1749, April 19.

Barnhill, Abraham, and Catharine Kemping, 1749, October.

Barnhill, John, and Sarah Craig, 1750, December.

Barney, Thomas, and Elizabeth Palmer, 1749, July.

Barr, Zachariah, and Martha Camron, 1749, March.

Barr, Jane, and Thomas Ross, 1751, June 20.

Barry, Garret, and Margaret Morris, 1750, August.

Bartholomew, John, and Elizabeth Bostein, 1749, October 30.

Bartholomew, Benjamin, and Ann Davis, 1752, February 15.

Bartholomew, Thomas, and Elizabeth Towne, 1750, December.

Bartholomew, Mary, and Philip Thomas, 1751, December 28.

Bartholt, Melchior, and Mary Slaughter, 1750, June.

Bartleston, Susannah, and Jacob Rittenhouse, 1749, July.

Barton, Thomas, and Susannah Cooke, 1750, November.

Bastick, John, and Elizabeth Fearns, 1752, March 26.

Batho, George, and Mary Wattlebaum, 1752, July 20.

Balter, Aneas, and Ann Mason, 1750, November.

Battin, Samuel, and Rachel Martin, 1749, January.

Beake, Thomas, and Christiana Boss, 1749, May.

Beal, Deborah, and Thomas Rambo, 1748, March 18.

Beatty, Joseph, and Katharine Conolly, 1751, July 11.

Beaver, Dewalt, and Sybylla Steinbruner, 1751, June 15.

Beene, Elizabeth, and James Strowde, 1749, July.

Behme, John, and Elizabeth Carter, 1748, November.

Bele, George, and Katharine Gainer, 1751, July 22.

Bell, James, and Agnes Mathews, 1749, January.

Bell, Lydia, and Richard Ashton, 1749, March 31.

Bell, Isaiah, and Margaret Jones, 1749, August.
Bell, Elizabeth, and George Nicholson, 1751, November 1.
Bell, Joseph, and Margaret Stevens, 1752, July 13.
Bellows, Susannah, and Andrew Anderson, 1751, February 2.
Bener, Gertrude, and Adam Smith, 1750, October 1.
Benne John, and Elizabeth Pites, 1752, January 27.
Bennet, Abraham, and Mary Harrison, 1749, March.
Bennet, John, and Christiana Soddem, 1751, September 24.
Bennet, Daniel, and Mary Felton, 1751, November 18.
Bennet, Eleanor, and Isaac Bennett, 1752, July 21.
Bennett, Isaac, and Eleanor Bennet, 1752, July 21.
Bensall, Charles, and Sarah Ingle, 1748, January 18.
Bernhart, Hans George, and Susannah Catharine Sichlin, 1751, October 17.
Bettson, John, and Mary Connor, 1749, December.
Biddle, Michael, and Rachel Scull, 1749, March.
Bissert, Elizabeth, and Adam Shoub, 1752, July 29.
Black, William, and Ann Wethers, 1749, March.
Blackfan, Sarah, and Richard Wood, 1751, November 7.
Blake, Robert, and Hannah Hartley, 1749, April.
Blake, Hannah, and John Dougherty, 1749, April.
Blake, Thomas, and Elizabeth Jones, 1749, October.
Bland, Elias, and Hannah Stamper, 1752, June 22.
Bloome, John George, and Phoebe Fleeken, 1752, June 1.
Blythe, Martha, and William Cinneer, 1751, May 17.
——— ———, and Malachia Bonham, 1751, July 19.
Bonham, Malachia, and ——— ———, 1751, July 19.
Bond, Joseph, and Elizabeth Donaldson, 1748, November.
Bonsell, Samuel, and Margaret House, 1748, November.
Boogart, Gisbert, and Elizabeth Vannest, 1749, October.
Boone, Elizabeth, and John Turner, 1749, March.
Boore, Elizabeth, and Richard Allen, 1748, January 3.
Boss Christiana, and Thomas Beake, 1749, May.
Bostein, Elizabeth, and William Bartholomew, 1749, October 30.
Bowen, Hannah, and Evan Evans, 1749, May.
Bowen, Elizabeth, and Thomas Rodger, 1751, June 27.

Bowes, Rachel, and John Sayre, 1751, April 6.

Bowes, Sarah, and Thomas Smith, 1752, March 9.

Boyd, Patrick, and Margaret Eaton, 1749, March.

Boyd, Ann, and William Weldon, 1749, April 27.

Boyd, Hannah, and Samuel Spencer, 1751, April 10.

Boyer, Margaret, and Jacob Duremont, 1751, November 20.

Boyse, Sebastian, and Mary Marshtellon, 1748, January 23.

Braddock, Ann, and Thomas Campbell, 1751, May 28.

Brading, Elizabeth, and William McGee, 1749, November.

Bradley, William, and Ann Rigg, 1751, October 29.

Brand, ———, and Dr. John Kearsley, 1748, November.

Brand, Martin, and Mary Gardner, 1751, September 25.

Brandley, Katharine, and Leonard Freily, 1752, May 6.

Brandon, Maria, and John Brant, 1751, July 5.

Branson, Elizabeth, and Lynford Lardner, 1749, October.

Brant, John, and Maria Brandon, 1751, July 5.

Breading, Robert, and Mary Cammell, 1749, July.

Bredin, Robert, and Eleanor Roan, 1750, August.

Breintnall, Rebecca, and Edward Weyman, 1751, July 4.

Breintnall, Martha, and James Lowther, 1752, May 11.

Brenner, Caspar, and Catharine Easterling, 1751, December 17.

Brian, Cornelius, and Mary Roberts, 1749, May.

Bruch, Thomas, and Elizabeth Brooks, 1752, May 28.

Bringhurst, Sarah, and George Palmer, 1749, January.

Bringhurst, John, and Mary Finney, 1749, March.

Brodricks, Honour, and Bernard McCosker, 1750, June.

Brooks, George, and Margaret Montgomery, 1751, February 9.

Brooks, Elizabeth, and Thomas Bruch, 1752, May 28.

Brown, Jane, and Henry Tisdale, 1749, April 18.

Brown, Thomas, and Elizabeth Draper, 1749, June.

Brown, Gustavus, and Elizabeth Harper, 1751, June 5.

Brown, Andrew, and Jane McFarlin, 1751, April 13.

Brown, Joseph, and Martha Hutchinson, 1751, May 11.

Browne, Jane, and John Crawford, 1750, July.

Browning, Benjamin, and Mary Abbot, 1751, March 23.

Bryley, Catharine, and Thomas Childs, 1751, November 11.
Buchanan, James, and Mary Dean, 1752, May 5.
Buckman, Isaac, and Mary Hillborn, 1751, November 18.
Budd, Levi, and Elizabeth Edge, 1749, December.
Buffington, Peter, and Hannah White, 1750, July.
Bull, Elizabeth, and Thomas Rossiter, 1751, April 18.
Buller, Elizabeth, and Moses Aaron, 1752, January 3.
Bunting, Joseph, and Esther Powel, 1751, October 28.
Burk, Alice, and Patrick Farril, 1750, October 1.
Burkloe, Samuel, and Mary Evans, 1749, March.
Burley, Alice, and John Simmons, 1749, March.
Burns, Elizabeth, and Thomas Darling, 1748, November.
Burton, Joseph, and Patience Burton, 1751, December 13.
Burton, Patience, and Joseph Burton, 1751, December 13.
Burton, Anthony, and Mary Hough, 1752, February 12.
Butler, Benjamin, and Elizabeth James, 1748, February 2.
Button, Jacob, and Margaret Klein, 1752, January 7.
Byrn, Elizabeth, and William Woodcock, 1749, March.

Cadge, Margaret, and William Parr, 1750, August.
Cahn, Hannah, and Charles Hamderson, 1749, December.
Calwell, David, and Mary Davies, 1749, July.
Callwell, Marg^t, and William Williamson, 1751, September 3.
Camron, John, and Mary Castle, 1748, November.
Camron, Martha, and Zachariah Barr, 1749, March.
Cameron, Thomas, and Sarah Yao, 1749, August.
Cameron, Sarah, and George Dor, 1751, December 11.
Cambell, Elizabeth, and William Albertson, 1752, April 1.
Cammell, William, and Sarah Perkins, 1749, March.
Cammell, Mary, and Robert Breading, 1749, July.
Cammell, Elizabeth, and Thomas Lacky, 1749, October.
Campbell, Edward, and Mary Lawrence, 1748, February 2.
Campbell, James, and Elizabeth Gaw, 1749, July.
Campbell, Thomas, and Ann Braddock, 1751, May 28.
Carberry, Mary, and John Cox, 1749, May.
Carew, George, and Elizabeth Sinclair, 1751, April 11.
Carey, Mary, and George Hardin, 1749, November.

Carr, Jonathan, and Deborah Robinson, 1748, February 24.
Carr, Mary, and Thomas Fisher, 1751, April 8.
Carrear, Abraham, and Ann Senington, 1749, May.
Carrell, Rachel, and Robert Stewart, 1752, May 30.
Carry, Thomas, and Margaret McMullar, 1752, January 8.
Carson, John, and Sarah McMurray, 1750, December.
Carter, Elizabeth, and John Behme, 1748, November.
Carter, Joseph, and Ann Micklehenny, 1749, April.
Carter, Mary, and John Preston, 1752, June 1.
Cartmell, Sarah, and Thomas Herbert, 1750, September.
Carvell, Thomas, and Rebecca Harris, 1749, December.
Carty, Patrick, and Jemima Pue, 1749, November.
Cash, Rebecca, and Andrew Doz, 1748, November.
Cassell, Susanna, and Edward Drinker, 1752, July 2.
Castle, Mary, and John Camron, 1748, November.
Castle, Ann, and Nathaniel Donnell, 1749, May.
Cather, Mary, and Andrew Lowry, 1751, January 15.
Catringer, John, and Katharine Kelly, 1749, April.
Canthen, Mary, and Francis Hardin, 1749, April 8.
Chambers, Ann, and Patrick Jones, 1749, January.
Chambers, Mary, and James Claypole, 1750, September.
Chancellor, Eliz., and Alexander Stedman, 1749, May.
Chandler, Susanna, and Thomas Coates, 1752, March 30.
Charlesworth, John, and Mary Wood, 1749, December.
Charlton, William, and Isabella Taylor, 1748, January 21.
Charm, George, and Elizabeth Adridge, 1751, May 27.
Childs, John, and Hannah Gisselin, 1748, March 16.
Childs, Thomas, and Catharine Bryley, 1751, November 11.
Cinneer, William, and Martha Blythe, 1751, May 17.
Clair, Barbara, and Elias Toy, 1751, March 1.
Clarke, Hannah, and Francis Lewis, 1749, January.
Clark, Ann, and William Hayes, 1751, February 13.
Clarke, Robert, and Bridget Savoy, 1751, July 17.
Clarke, John, and Eleanor Armstrong, 1751, November 11.
Clarke, Mary, and William Davis, 1751, November 18.
Clarkson, John Levirnus, and Rachel West, 1749, March.
Clampter, William, and Elizabeth Rees, 1750, May.

Claud, Robert, and Magdalen Peterson, 1749, November.

Claud, Jeremiah, and Eedy Hartin, 1750, May.

Claypole, James, and Mary Chambers, 1750, September.

Clements, Elizabeth, and John Ogg, 1748, March 17.

Cliff, George, and Esther Hervey, 1751, April 23.

Clowser, Peter, and Elizabeth Spedin, 1750, June.

Coat, Thomas, and Ann Tyson, 1749, December.

Coats, Thomas, and Hannah Pugh, 1748, February 11.

Coats, Rebecca, and Thomas Shute, 1748, March 21.

Coats, Rebecca, and Thomas Shute, 1749, May.

Coates, Mary, and Ruloff Alberson, 1749, April.

Coates, Abraham, and Susannah Wallace, 1750, June.

Coates, Thomas, and Susanna Chandler, 1752, March 30.

Cobourne, Job, and Sarah Moore, 1750, May.

Cochran, Samuel, and Elizabeth Newton, 1751, February 28.

Cocks, Hannah, and Samuel Appowen, 1749, March.

Cogell, Mary, and James Neale, 1749, April.

Cole, Mary, and James Hunter, 1751, November 12.

Coleman, Rebecca, and Thomas Stamper, 1749, May.

Coleman, Elizabeth, and Samuel Fisher, 1749, June 15.

Coleman, Joseph, and Mary Johnson, 1752, April 2.

Colgan, William, and Susannah Heath, 1749, January.

Collet, Mary, and John Daniel, 1748, November.

Collins, Susanna, and Andrew Tates,. 1748, November.

Collins, Andrew, and Mary Saunders, 1748, November.

Comfort, Robert, and Eleanor Tomlinson, 1751, August 22.

Connor, Mary, and John Bettson, 1749, December.

Conolly, Katharine, and Joseph Beatty, 1751, July 11.

Conquergood, William, and Katharine Murray, 1751, November 9.

Conradin, Margaretta, and Conrad Reaver, 1750, August.

Cook, Rose, and Dennis Ferrell, 1748, November.

Cook, Jonathan, and Margaret Miles, 1749, May.

Cooke, Susannah, and Thomas Barton, 1750, November.

Coomb, Ann, and Zachariah Vanleewenigh, 1748, February 25.

Coombe, Mary, and Stephen Harris, 1749, May.

Cooper, Mary, and Samuel Kirk, 1751, April 3.
Cooper, Hannah, and John Mickle, 1752, July 25.
Coopes, James, and Hannah Hibbs, 1750, September.
Cuppock, James, and Catharine Pugh, 1752, July 8.
Corbet, Ann, and James Freeman, 1749, April.
Coren, Isaac, and Ruth Jones, 1751, July 6.
Cornock, William, and Alice Griffith, 1751, September 14.
Cotman, Hannah, and James Treherne, 1751, April 15.
Couch, Daniel, and Phœbe Pollard, 1750, December.
Cox, William, and Mary Francis, 1749, April.
Cox, Samuel, and Elizabeth Spronce, 1749, May.
Cox, John, and Mary Carberry, 1749, May.
Cox, Joseph, and Rebeccah Ballard, 1749, December.
Cox, Jacob, and Martha Rambo, 1750, December.
Cox, Israel, and Christiana Horton, 1751, April 6.
Craig, John, and Isabel Miller, 1749, September.
Craig, Sarah, and John Barnhill, 1750, December.
Craig, Robert, and Ann Grear, 1751, October 16.
Crawford, Ann, and Jacob Souder, 1749, October.
Crawford, John, and Jane Browne, 1750, July.
Crawford, Archibald, and Margaret Wigton, 1750, December.
Creux, Henry, and Margaret Garner, 1749, September.
Crispin, Silas, and Martha Miles, 1749, January.
Croker, Deborah, and Bowman Hunlohe, 1751, November 26.
Cropp, Christian, and Catharine Suber, 1751, April 16.
Crosier, Elizabeth, and Swan Justice, 1751, November 29.
Crosley, Elizabeth, and William Malin, 1748, February 1.
Cummings, James, and Sarah Logan, 1751, June 3.
Cunningham, William, and Elizabeth West, 1748, February 13.
Cunningham, Redmond, and Martha Ellis, 1749, January.
Cuthbert, Rebecca, and William Noblett, 1752, June 16.

Dalbo, Gabriel, and Mary Emson, 1751, November 18.
Dalby, Richard, and Ann Williams, 1750, August.
Daniel, John, and Mary Collet, 1748, November.

Darling, Thomas, and Elizabeth Burus, 1748, November.
Darlington, Robert, and Jannet Macky, 1751, January 29.
Davenport, Josiah, and Ann Annis, 1751, December 13.
Davids, John, and Sarah Harper, 1751, February 28.
Davies, Abigal, and Evan Lloyd, 1748, November.
Davies, Christian, and Richard Arrell, 1749, July.
Davies, Israel, and Hannah Baker, 1751, April 25.
Davies, Mary, and John ———, 1752, April 28.
Davies, Mary, and David Calwell, 1749, July.
Davies, Priscella, and George Warral, 1752, April 27.
Davies, Samson, and Sarah Miles, 1752, May 20.
Davies, Steven, and Mary Morgan, 1752, May 18.
Davis, William, and Letitia Price, 1751, April 26.
Davis, Abel, and Sarah Griffith, 1752, January 10.
Davis, Ann, and Benjamin Bartholomew, 1752, February 15.
Davis, Ann, and John Pickle, 1749, March 31.
Davis, Ellis, and Mary Jones, 1749, September.
Davis, Hannah, and Michael Pugh, 1749, September.
Davis, Hannah, and Benjamin Van Horn, 1749, June 8.
Davis, Isaac, and Mary Griffith, 1752, March 18.
Davis, Isabella, and John Scott, 1752, March 7.
Davis, James, and Joan Lloyd, 1752, May 1.
Davis, Jonathan, and Susanna Jenkins, 1748, March 4.
Davis, James, and Mary Spooner, 1751, July 2.
Davis, Jane, and Patrick Fenning, 1751, August 15.
Davis, John, and Mary Prichard, 1749, March 29.
Davis, Katharine, and John Mather, 1751, May 27.
Davis, Margaret, and John Griffith, 1749, December.
Davis, Margaret, and Foster Parks, 1749, September.
Davis, Rachel, and Andrew Flood, 1751, June 24.
Davis, Rees, and Olive Head, 1751, October 19.
Davis, Samuel, and Martha Pricket, 1749, April.
Davis, Samuel, and Margaret Rowen, 1752, January 27.
Davis, Sarah, and William Douglass, 1749, March.
Davis, Thomas, and Barbara Atkinson, 1749, August.
Davis, William, and Mary Clarke, 1751, November 18.
Dawson, Mary, and George Morrison, 1751, August 6.

Dawson, Mary, and Alexander Ore, 1749, December.

Dawson, Rosamond, and Charles Green, 1752, May 18.

Day, Abigail, and William Thomas, 1751, January 17.

Day, John, and Martha Forest, 1750, November.

Deacon, Thomas, and Jane Ore, 1749, December.

Dean, Mary, and James Buchanan, 1752, May 5.

Dean, Mary, and Joseph Wharton, 1751, April 23.

Deer, Dorothy, and Simon Treisbach, 1752, April 7.

Delbick, Daniel, and Eve Helering, 1751, November 7.

Dennis, Elizabeth, and Joseph Graseberry, 1740, November.

Depue, Ann, and Daniel Shoemaker, 1751, March 14.

Dindsey, Mary, and John Lawdon, 1749, September.

Dixon, Robert, and Frances Killpatrick, 1748, March 17.

Dixon, Thomas, and Rebecca Greenman, 1751, October 19.

Donaldson, Elizabeth, and Joseph Bond, 1748, December.

Donaldson, Hugh, and Mary Dermley, 1751, May 15.

Donaldson, Joseph, and Sarah Wilkinson, 1751, August 1.

Douglass, William, and Sarah Davis, 1749, March.

Donnell, Nathaniel, and Ann Castle, 1749, May.

Doran, Ann, and Patrick Kelly, 1749, January.

Dorvill, Joseph, and Ann Shackleton, 1748, November.

Dougherty, John, and Hannah Blake, 1749, April.

Dowding, Elizabeth, and John Faris, 1749, July.

Dowlin, Paul, and Elizabeth Williams, 1750, October 15.

Downe, John, and Barbara Smith, 1751, August 24.

Doyle, Edward, and Hannah Eaton, 1751, December 11.

Doyle, John, and Sarah Wood, 1751, November 19.

Doyle, Prudence, and James Wilson, 1752, February 1.

Doz, Andrew, and Rebecca Cash, 1748, December.

Drain, John, and Jane Ross, 1750, October 25.

Drapers, Elizabeth, and Thomas Brown, 1749, June.

Drinker, Edward, and Susanna Cassell, 1752, July 2.

Drinker, Edward, and Susanna Williams, 1749, November.

Dubois, Jonathan, and Helena Wynkoop, 1751, November 15.

Duffield, Edward, and Katharine Parry, 1751, June 10.

Dulton, Isaac, and Mary Wright, 1750, October 13.

Dulton, James, and Hannah Price, 1751, January 5.

Dunbar, Eleanor, and Patrick Gordon, 1749, March.

Duncan, Hannah, and Thomas Worthington, 1751, April 20.

Dungan, Deborah, and Benjamin Stevens, 1751, August 28.

Dunn, Gartright, and Thomas Greenwood, 1748, November.

Dunn, Marg^t, and William Alexander, 1751, September 4.

Dunn, Thomas, and Mary Armitage, 1751, August 24.

Dunning, Mary, and William Goforth, 1750, December.

Duremont, Jacob, and Margaret Boyer, 1751, November 20.

Dyado, Michael, and Barbaro Annien, 1748, November.

Dyer, Elizabeth, and James Dyer, 1751, February 23.

Dyer, James, and Elizabeth Dyer, 1751, February 23.

Eader, Ann, and Samuel Scolly, 1749, January.

Eastburne, Hannah, and Joseph Hossay, 1752, July 17.

Easterling, Catharine, and Caspar Brenner, 1751, December 17.

Eaton, Hannah, and Edward Doyle, 1751, December 11.

Eaton, Margaret, and Patrick Boyd, 1749, March.

Ebald, Jacob, and Margaret Aken, 1749, October.

Eberolt, Jacob, and Susanna Opdegrass, 1751, May 31.

Eckles, George, and Susannah Holmes, 1750, October 6.

Edgar, John, and Mary Owen, 1748, December.

Edge, Elizabeth, and Levi Budd, 1749, December.

Edgil, Rebecca, and Samuel Mifflin, 1750, August.

Edinburg, Catharine, and Lawrence Walter, 1749, November.

Edwards, John, and Mary Newman, 1751, September 25.

Egerton, William, and Jane Albertson, 1749, December.

Elizabeth, Mary, and Christopher Schiemel, 1750, December.

Ellett, Elizabeth, and Robert ———.

Elliot, Hannah, and William Mann, 1748, January 21.

Ellis, Martha, and Redmond Cunningham, 1749, January.

Elton, John, and Mary Hart, 1749, March.

Emson, Mary, and Gabriel Dalbo, 1751, November 18.

Evans, Abner, and Sarah Thomas, 1751, March 16.

Evans, Alice, and Joseph Lunn, 1751, November 26.

Evans, Eleanor, and Robert Evans, 1751, May 16.

Evans, Elizabeth, and Samuel Roberts, 1751, April 25.
Evans, Evan, and Hannah Bowen, 1749, May.
Evans, Evan, and Priscilla Waterman, 1750, May.
Evans, Fanny, and Charles Ford, 1751, December 21.
Evans, Hannah, and Jonathan Martin, 1751, March 23.
Evans, Hannah, and Rowland Parry, 1750, July.
Evans, James, and Elizabeth Lloyd, 1750, May.
Evans, John, and Hannah Badcock, 1751, November 15.
Evans, John, and Ann Williams, 1751, November 20.
Evans, Mary, and Samuel Burkloe, 1749, March.
Evans, Morris, and Lettice Morris, 1750, May.
Evans, Robert, and Eleanor Evans, 1751, May 16.
Evans, Sarah, and John Jones, 1749, December.
Evans, Sarah, and Thomas Martin, 1751, December 20.
Evans, Simeon, and Rebecca Gudgeon, widow, 1749, April.
Evans, William, and Martha Huff, 1751, September 11.
Ewing, Andrew, and Elizabeth Tupy, 1749, September.
Ewing, Elizabeth, and Thomas Wills, 1749, September.
Ewing, John, and Sarah Yates, 1749, March.
Eyers, Mary, and Jasper Scull, 1749, January.

Faber, John, and Rebecca Wells, 1749, August.
Fallet, William, and Dorcas Peisley, 1749, March.
Fannimore, Richard, and Hannah Horner, 1749, July.
Faries, Jane, and Robert Ferguson, 1749, April 13.
Faris, John, and Elizabeth Dowding, 1749, July.
Farril, Patrick, and Alice Burk, 1750, October 1.
Farron, John, and Hannah Tisdel, 1752, July 22.
Fausman, Benjamin, and Margt Troy, 1749, May.
Faust, Anthony, and Elizabeth Fisher, 1749, April 28.
Fearns, Elizabeth, and John Bastick, 1752, March 26.
Felton, Mary, and Daniel Bennet, 1751, November 18.
Fenby, John, and Margaret Longwell, 1749, May.
Fend, Elizabeth, and Christian Lehman, 1751, April 23.
Fenning, Patrick, and Jane Davis, 1751, August 15.
Ferguson, Robert, and Jane Fareis, 1749, April 13.
Ferrell, Dennis, and Rose Cook, 1748, November.

Field, Robert, and Rachel Mayberry, 1749, March.

Finney, Mary, and John Bringhurst, 1749, March.

Finnimore, Joshua, and Rebecca Pearson, 1749, May.

Fish, Mary, and John Hamilton, 1750, October 20.

Fisher, Deborah, and James Williams, 1751, December.

Fisher, Elizabeth, and Anthony Faust, 1749, April 28.

Fisher, Margaret, and Robert Fleming, 1752, April 15.

Fisher, Samuel, and Elizabeth Coleman, 1749, June 15.

Fishes, Thomas, and Mary Carr, 1751, April 8.

Fitszymmonds, William, and Honour Spencer, 1752, January 22.

Fitz Summons, Mary, and Dennis Sullivan, 1749, September.

Fitzgerald, Mary, and James Kirke, 1749, March.

Fitzrandolph, Edward, and Mary Lownes, 1752, April 15.

Fleming, Robert, and Margaret Fisher, 1752, April 15.

Flemming, Robert, and Mary Cummell, 1750, August.

Flood, Andrew, and Rachel Davis, 1751, June 24.

Floyd, John, and Mary Latham, 1750, June.

Fontasket, Christian, and Barbara Merg, 1750, November.

Ford, Ann, and John Sadler, 1749, October.

Ford, Bridget, and Patrick Gayher, 1750, September.

Ford, Charles, and Fanny Evans, 1751, December 21.

Ford, John, and Sarah Ann ———, 1748, January 9.

———, Sarah Ann, and John Ford, 1748, January 9.

Ford, William, and Elizabeth Price, 1748, November.

Fordham, Elizabeth, and Stephen Shewell, 1750, May.

Forest, Martha, and John Day, 1750, November.

Forten, Elizabeth, and Benjamin Wiley, 1749, October.

Foster, Mary, and John Long, 1750, August.

Foster, Mary, and Daniel Street, 1752, April 8.

Foster, Mary, and Isaiah Vansant, 1749, March.

Foster, Salathiel, and Mercy Kerle, 1749, November.

Foster, Sarah, and William Tillyer, 1749, April.

Fox, Elizabeth, and William Henry, 1750, October 13.

Fox, George, and Mary Woods, 1751, August 3.

Francis, Elizabeth, and John Lawrence, 1749, April.

Francis, Margaret, and John Towers, 1749, May.

Francis, Mary, and William Cox, 1749, April.
Francis, Thomas, and Susannah Turner, 1751, February 25.
Francy, Susanna, and Emanuel Roderick, 1751, March 5.
Frazier, ———, and ——— ———, 1751, June 27.
Freeman, James, and Ann Corbet, 1749, April.
Freid, Philip, and Reginia Penering, 1749, April 10.
Freily, Leonard, and Katharine Brandley, 1752, May 6.
Furnace, Susannah, and Edward Young, 1749, July.

Gaa, Sarah, and Thomas Cameron, 1749, August.
Gainer, Katharine, and George Bele, 1751, July 22.
Gardiner, Abraham, and Sarah Hollwell, 1749, March.
Gardner, John, and Hannah Howard, 1751, August 13.
Gardner, Mary, and Martin Brand, 1751, September 25.
Gardner, William, and Rebecca Mathews, 1749, March.
Gardner, William, and Elizabeth Tatnall, 1749, April.
Garner, Margaret, and Henry Creux, 1749, September.
Gaunt, Zebulon, and Esther Woolman, 1750, November.
Gaw, Elizabeth, and James Campbell, 1749, July.
Gayher, Patrick, and Bridget Ford, 1750, September.
Gibbins, James, and Mary Miller, 1750, August.
Gilbert, Jane, and Felix Leonard, 1749, May.
Gilbert, Lucretia, and John Thomas, 1752, March 2.
Gilbert, Peter, and Abigail Ball, 1749, June 16.
Gill, John, and Rachel Key, 1749, October.
Gisselin, Hannah, and John Childs, 1748, March 16.
Glascow, Jane, and Anthony Pritchard, 1751, August 28.
Goforth, William, and Mary Dunning, 1750, December.
Good, Ezekiel, and Jane Monleky, 1748, November.
Gordon, Alexander, and Mary Pender, 1749, June 24.
Gordon, Lewis, and Mary Jenkins, 1749, January.
Gordon, Patrick, and Eleanor Dunbar, 1749, March.
Gordon, Thomas, and Mary Bambridge, 1751, October 16.
Gorsuch, Hannah, and Thomas Jones, 1751, December 21.
Graham, Mary, and William Graham, 1751, March 27.
Graham, William, and Mary Graham, 1751, March 27.
Grandam, Jane, and Simeon Warner, 1749, April.

Grantham, Charles, and Magdalen Hendrickson, 1749, August.

Grautum, Margaret, and Thomas Thompson, 1751, March 18.

Graseberry, Joseph, and Elizabeth Dennis, 1749, November.

Grasshold, Dorothy, and Michael Holling, 1749, August.

Graysbury, James, and Mary Norwood, 1750, September.

Grea, Mathias, and Barbara Taylor, 1752, April 4.

Grear, Ann, and Robert Craig, 1751, October 16.

Greathouse, William, and Barbara Statzin, 1749, March.

Green, Charles, and Rosamond Dawson, 1752, May 18.

Green, Thomas, and Ann Lewis, 1749, April 5.

Greenman, Rebecca, and Thomas Dixon, 1751, October 19.

Greenwood, Thomas, and Cartright Dunn, 1748, December.

Griffin, Elizabeth, and George Rankin, 1750, December.

Griffith, Abram, and Catharine Lewellin, 1752, June 20.

Griffith, Alice, and William Cornock, 1751, September 14.

Griffith, John, and Margaret Davis, 1749, December.

Griffith, Mary, and Isaac Davis, 1752, March 18.

Griffith, Sarah, and Abel Davis, 1752, January 10.

Grimes, Richard, and Mary Hamilton, 1748, February 14.

Groff, Jos., and Anna Katherina Hoffing, 1748, March 21.

Grogan, James, and Hannah Walsh, 1750, August.

Gudgeon, Rebecca, widow, and Simeon Evans, 1749, April.

Guilhott, Mary, and James Shirley, 1749, July.

Guthry, Ann, and Joseph, 1752, March 9.

Hair, Benjamin, and Elizabeth Simpson, 1751, September 21.

Haley, Honour, and John Williams, 1748, March 7.

Hall, Alice, and Richard Parsons, 1749, October.

Hall, Elizabeth, and John Petty, 1748, February 2.

Hall, Francis, and Sarah Bainbridge, 1748, February 11.

Hall, Jane, and Alexander Stuart, 1752, June 16.

Hall, Mary, and Isaac Ashton, 1749, June 16.

Hamderson, Charles, and Hannah Calve, 1749, December.

Hamilton, Charles, and Jane Urbain Voyer, 1749, June 7.

Hamilton, John, and Mary Fish, 1750, October 20.

Hamilton, Margaret, and John Leacock, 1749, October.

Hamilton, Martha, and Henry Roberts, 1751, October 17.
Hamilton, Mary, and Richard Grimes, 1748, February 14.
Hamilton, Thomas, and Margaret Twining, 1749, January.
Hancock, Mary, and Richard Moore, 1748, February 27.
Hannah, and Quako, negroes, 1748; January 27.
Hanns, Mary, and Clotworthy Reed, 1751, July 2.
Hardie, Robert, and Elizabeth Rogers, 1752, May 28.
Hardin, Francis, and Mary Cauthen, 1749, April 8.
Hardin, George, and Mary Carey, 1749, November.
Harding, Elizabeth, and Peter Hodgson, 1749, March.
Harding, Elizabeth, and Henry Knight, 1748, November.
Harding, Margᵗ, and Abram Skinner, 1751, November.
———— Captⁿ, and Sarah Hargrave, 1749, October.
Hargrave, Sarah, and Captn. ————, 1749, October.
Harman, Ann, and James McDowell, 1751, August.
Harper, Ann, and Moses Wells, 1749, April 26.
Harper, Elizabeth, and Gustavus Brown, 1751, June 5.
Harper, James, and Ann McKees, 1750, November.
Harper, John, and Sarah Wells, 1750, October 20.
Harper, Rose, and Randal Mitchell, 1751, December 11.
Harper, Sarah, and John Davids, 1751, February 28.
Harriet, Anderson, and Mary Warnick, 1749, October.
Harry, John, and Rachel Saul, 1751, July 27.
Harry, Mary, and James Sparkes, 1751, June 3.
Harry, Sarah, and Amos Roberts, 1750, October 6.
Harris, Joseph, and Margaret Miller, 1751, October 25.
Harris, Rebecca, and Thomas Carvell, 1749, December.
Harris, Rebecca, and George Owen, 1751, May 4.
Harris, Stephen, and Mary Coombe, 1749, May.
Harris, Susanna, and Moses Marshall, 1751, June 18.
Harrison, Mary, and Abraham Bennet, 1749, March.
Harrol, Elizabeth, and John Rambo, 1748, March 21.
Hart, Mary, and John Elton, 1749, March.

PENNSYLVANIA MARRIAGE LICENSES, ISSUED BY GOVERNOR JAMES HAMILTON, 1750–1752.

BY HELEN JORDAN.

Hart, Neal, and Mary Kale, 1750, October 3.

Hart, William, and Ann McCreary, 1749, July.

Hartin, Eedy, and Jeremiah Claud, 1750, May.

Hartley, Ann, and Wm. Heuehman, 1752, June 3.

Hartley, Hannah, and Robert Blake, 1749, April.

Harvey, Benjamin, and Margaret Lawdirmae, 1751, April 13.

Harvey, Priscilla, and James Murphy, 1751, August 13.

Haugh, Michael, and Eve Stegarin, 1749, April.

Havelfinger Katharine, and John Rees, 1752, May 9.

Hawkins, Phobe, and Howell Morgan, 1750, September.

Hawkins, Rachel, and Edward Turner, 1751, August 17.

Hawks, William, and Margaret Pollard, 1751, August 23,

Hayes, Elizabeth, and Thomas Welsh, 1750, September.

Hayes, Nicholas, and Alice Hunter, 1751, November 18.

Hayes, William, and Ann Clark, 1751, February 13.

Hazard, Elizabeth, and Theophilus Wiley, 1752, June 26.

Head, Olive, and Rees Davis, 1751, October 19.

Head, Samuel, and Mary Woeneldorfe, 1848, November.

Heath, Susannah, and William Colgan, 1749, January.

Helering, Eve, and Daniel Delbick, 1751, November 7.

Hellings, Sarah, and Samuel Testin, 1751, November 29.

Helmer, Mary, and George Masters, 1752, July 4.

Helmes, Andrew, and Alice Wilkins, 1752, January 11.

Hemphill, James, and Elizabeth Wells, 1750, December.

Hendrickson, Magdalen, and Charles Grantham, 1749, August.

Heuehman, Wm., and Ann Hartley, 1752, June 3.

Henry, Margt., and Hugh McMelon, 1751, September 28.

Henry, Margaret, and John Miller, 1752, March 18.

Henry, Martha, and James Adams, 1749, June 7.

Henry, William, and Elizabeth Fox, 1750, October 13.

Herbert, Thomas, and Sarah Cartmell, 1750, September.

Heron, Mary, and Humphrey Mersden, 1751, November 8.

Hervey, Esther, and George Cliff, 1751, April 23.

Hewlings, Lawrence, and Abigail Wallace, 1749, August.

Hibbs, Hannah, and James Coopes, 1750, September.

Hicks, Mary, and John Searle, 1748, February 16.

Hiddings, Henry, and Mary Wym, 1752, March 23.

Hillborn, Mary, and Isaac Buckman, 1751, November 18.

Hillman, John, and Rachel Test, 1750, June.

Hodgson, Peter, and Elizabeth Harding, 1749, March.

Hoffing, Anna Katherina, and Jos. Groff, 1748, March 21.

Hoffman, Rebecca, and Thomas Pedrick, 1751, November 16.

Holgas, Mary, and William Whittenham, 1751, February 9.

Holland, Samuel, and Elizabeth Scull, 1749, December.

Holliday, Henry, and Elizabeth Rue, 1751, January 15.

Holliday, Juliana, and Placius Daniel McCauel, 1751, November 4.

Holling, Michael, and Dorothy Grasshold, 1749, August.

Hollingsworth, Jacob, and Susannah Justice, 1749, March.

Holloway, Hannah, and James Waring, 1749, January.

Holloway, Margaret, and Peter Morstris, 1751, October.

Hollowback, Matthias, and Elizabeth Yodern, 1750, October 2.

Hollwell, Sarah, and Abraham Gardiner, 1749, March.

Hollyday, Elizabeth, and John Sitch, 1751, December 19.

Holmes, Susannah, and George Eckles, 1750, October 6.

Holt, Rebecca, and Joseph Walton, 1752, January 14.

Hood, John, and Elizabeth Silus, 1749, December.

Hood, Jonathan, and Mary Hood, 1748, December.

Hood, Mary, and Jonathan Hood, 1748, December.

Horner, Hannah, and Richard Fannimore, 1749, July.

Horton, Christiana, and Israel Cox, 1751, April 6.

Hossay, Joseph, and Hannah Eastburne, 1752, July 17.

Hough, Mary, and Anthony Burton, 1752, February 12.

House, Margaret, and Samuel Bonsell, 1748, December.

House, Mary, and Morris Morgan, 1749, December.
How, Mary, and Jacob Stadler, 1751, August 6.
Howard, Hannah, and John Gardner, 1751, August 13.
Howard, Rebecca, and John Lewillin, 1751, March 20.
Howell, Isaac, and Mary Baker, 1751, April 17.
Howell, Sarah, and Thomas Rowland, 1750, October 31.
Hudson, Deborah, and Jesse Price, 1748, December.
Huff, Martha, and William Evans, 1751, September 11.
Huffty, David, and Dorothy Willard, 1751, April 16.
Hufty, Phoebe, and Abraham Vandegrift, 1749, August.
Hughes, Edward, and Elizabeth Williams, 1749, September.
Hughes, Isaac, and Lydia Weldon, 1748, December.
Hughes, Robert, and Abigail McGee, 1751, November 1.
Hughes, Samuel, and Elizabeth Raine, 1751, April 17.
Hultenstein, Jacob, and Maria Sevan, 1749, April.
Hulton, James, and Mary Weeks, 1749, April 20.
Humphries, Charles, and Marg^t. Parry, 1749, August.
Humphries, Leonard, and Mary Asprell, 1752, May 4.
Humphries, Richard, and Dinah Wheat, 1749, April.
Humsted, Catharine, and John Ayres, 1750, July.
Hunloke, Bowman, and Deborah Croker, 1751, November 26.
Hunter, Alice, and Nicholas Hayes, 1751, November 18.
Hunter, James, and Mary Cole, 1751, November 12.
Huston, Wm., and Mary McDowell, 1749, September.
Hutchinson, Martha, and Joseph Brown, 1751, May 11.
Huysler, John Peter, and Annie Writtenhausen, 1749, June 12.
Iddings, Elizabeth, and James Lewis, 1752, March 23.
Ingels, Joseph, and Mary James, 1749, April.
Ingle, Sarah, and Charles Bensall, 1748, January 18.
Ihnis, William, and Hannah Koppock, 1752, March 7.
Ireson, William, and Elizabeth Stewart, 1749, July.
Irwin, Margaret, and Isaiah King, 1749, October 25.
Isburg, Peter, and Hannah Over, 1750, August.
Jackson, William, and Abigail Styles, 1752, March 11.
Jago, Henry, and Mary Bain, 1748, February 25.

James, Elizabeth, and Benjamin Butler, 1748, February 2.
James, Mary, and Joseph Ingels, 1749, April,
James, Mary, and Thomas Treviller, 1749, April.
Jarret, Jane, and Mathias Nethermark, 1751, June 14.
Jennings, Rebecca, and Richard Price, 1751, October 7.
Jenkins, Charles, and Elizabeth Quantrall, 1752, June 13.
Jenkins, Jenkin, and Elizabeth Thomas, 1748, December.
Jenkins, Mary, and Lewis Gordon, 1749, January.
Jenkins, Susanna, and Jonathan Davis, 1748, March 4.
Jerrard, Richard, and Mary Bane, 1751, May 18.
Jessop, Abraham, and Alice Pedrix or Pederick, 1749,
    August.
John, David, and Catharine Roberts, 1752, March 12.
Johnson, Elizabeth, and James Whitton, 1751, January 3.
Johnson, Isabella, and Philip Stevens, 1749, September.
Johnson, John, and Mary Wills, 1752, April 11.
Johnson, Joshua, and Ann Panyard, 1750, September.
Johnson, Mary, and Joseph Coleman, 1752, April 2.
Johnson, Mary, and Joseph Steward, 1749, March.
Johnson, Milby, and Teny Simson, 1749, October.
Johnson, Sarah, and William Price, 1749, March.
Johnston, Robert, and Elizabeth Mitchell, 1750, October 11.
Jolly, Charles, and Catherine Mayberry, 1752, January 8.
Jones, Daniel, and Mary Smith, 1751, November 19.
Jones, Derrich, and Jane Muckleroy, 1752, June 17.
Jones, Elizabeth, and Thomas Blake, 1749, October.
Jones, Griffith, and Catharine Prichard, 1749, July.
Jones, Jane, and John Atkinson, 1751, June 6.
Jones, John, and Sarah Evans, 1749, December.
Jones, John, and Mary Morford, 1749, September.
Jones, John, and Sarah Morris, 1751, January 19.
Jones, John, and Mary Nettle, 1751, December 4.
Jones, Margaret, and Isaiah Bell, 1749, August.
Jones, Mary, and Ellis Davis, 1749, September.
Jones, Patrick, and Ann Chambers, 1749, January.

PENNSYLVANIA MARRIAGE LICENSES, ISSUED BY GOVERNOR JAMES HAMILTON, 1748–1752.

BY HELEN JORDAN

Jones, Ruth, and Isaac Coren, 1751, July 6.

Jones, Samuel, and Jane Kinderdine, 1751, August 6.

Jones, Samuel, and Rachel Thomas, 1751, August 19.

Jones, Thomas, and Hannah Gorsuch, 1751, December 21.

Jones, William, and Ann Moss, 1749, May.

Jordan, Jeremiah, and Mary Lewis, 1749, April 26.

Jugran, Susanna, and Abraham Lawrence, 1751, April 13.

Justice, Catharine, and William Penloon, 1751, November 18.

Justice, John, and Amy Morton, 1750, November.

Justice, Susannah, and Jacob Hollingsworth, 1749, March.

Justice, Swan, and Elizabeth Crosier, 1751, November 29.

Kale, Mary, and Neal Hart, 1750, October 3.

Kalm, Peter, and Anna Maria Sweman, widow, 1749, December.

Kaufman, Joseph, and Katharinia Waterin, 1750, May.

Kearsley, Dr. John, and ——— Brand, 1748, December.

Keen, Daniel, and Elizabeth McCarty, 1752, January 7.

Kelles, William, and Catharine Nash, 1749, November.

Kelly, Catharine, and John Catringer, 1749, April.

Kelly, John, and Rebecca Sutton, 1752, April 10.

Kelly, Patrick, and Ann Doran, 1749, January.

Kemping, Catharine, and Abraham Barnhill, 1749, October.

Kennedy, Samuel, and Susannah Montgomery, 1750, June.

Kerle, Merey, and Salathiel Foster, 1749, November.

Key, Rachel, and John Gill, 1749, October.

Killpatrick, Frances, and Robert Dixon, 1748, March 17.

Kimpson, Samuel, and Susanna Thoman, 1750, May.

Kinderdine, Jane, and Samuel Jones, 1751, August 7.

King, Isaiah, and Margaret Irwin, 1749, October 25.

Kinsey, Katherine, and William Pritchard, 1750, June.

Kinsley, Catharina, and Henry Reichart, 1752, June 5.

Kinzlee, Jacob, and Catharine Konering, 1749, October.

Kirk, Samuel, and Mary Cooper, 1751, April 3.

Kirke, James, and Mary Fitzgerald, 1749, March.

Klein, Margaret, and Jacob Button, 1752, January 7.

Knight, Henry, and Elizabeth Harding, 1748, December.

Knight, Peter, and Elizabeth Wilkinson, 1752, June 20.

Koch, Catharine, and John McEvers, 1750, June.

Koch, widow of Peter Koch, and ———— McEvert, 1749, April.

Konering, Catharine, and Jacob Kinzlee, 1749, October.

Koppoch, Hannah, and William Junis, 1752, March 7.

Kristman, Henry, and Mary Eliz. Schmeltzer, 1749, May.

Krowser, Barbara, and John Lort, 1749, March 30.

Kuhl, Mary, and Edward Scot, 1749, September.

Kyser, Mathew, and Katharine Midwinter, 1750, November.

Lacky, Thomas, and Elizabeth Cammell, 1749, October.

Lampleigh, Mary, and Richard Mopely, 1751, May 24.

Lang, Thomas, and Elizabeth Sinclair, 1749, November.

Lardner, Lynford, and Elizabeth Branson, 1749, October.

Lasberry, William, and Sarah Paul, 1749, October.

Latham, Mary, and John Floyd, 1750, June.

Lawdirmae, Margaret, and Benjamin Harvey, 1751, April 13.

Lawdon, John, and Mary Dindsey, 1749, September.

Lawrence, Abraham, and Susanna Jugran, 1751, April 13.

Lawrence, Elizabeth, and Mark Arnold, 1750, September.

Lawrence, John, and Elizabeth Francis, 1749, April.

Lawrence, Margaret, and Davis Malin, 1751, February 21.

Lawrence, Martha, and Jenkins Price, 1751, January 19.

Lawrence, Mary, and Edward Campbell, 1748, February 2.

Lawrenson, Olive, and George Logan, 1751, April 15.

Lea, John, and Christiana Trusse, 1749, March.

Leacock, John, and Margaret Hamilton, 1749, October.

Lee, John, and Catharine Stille, 1752, July 1.

Lee, Mary, and Patrick Wall, 1749, November.

Leech, Rebecca, and Henry Ash, 1749, March 25.

Leech, William, and Elizabeth Moor, 1751, September 4.

Lehman, Christian, and Elizabeth Fend, 1751, April 23.

Leidheisser, George, and Anna Margaret Paven, 1751, June 19.

Lenington, Ann, and Abraham Carrear, 1749, May.

Leonard, Felix, and Jane Gilbert, 1749, May.

Leonard, Judah, and Thomas Lyneall, 1749, December.

Lessell, Mary, and Samuel Shaw, 1751, October 26.

Levin, Sebastian, and Susannah Schreider, 1751, May 8.

Lewes, Isaiah, and Mary Thomas, 1751, April 26.

Lewillin, John, and Rebecca Howard, 1751, March 20.

Lewis, Ann, and Thomas Green, 1749, April 5.

Lewis, Francis, and Hannah Clarke, 1749, January.

Lewis, James, and Elizabeth Iddings, 1752, March 23.

Lewis, Jane, and Isaac Warner, 1752, June 20.

Lewis, John, and Sarah Tatum, 1752, July 31.

Lewis, Martha, and James Shannan, 1752, March 25.

Lewis, Mary, and James McClure, 1751, August 28.

Lewis, Mary, and Jeremiah Jordan, 1749, April 26.

Lidnerd, Charity, and John Wheatley, 1751, August 6.

Linckom, Hester, and Patrick Tonin, 1748, February 2.

Lindsay, James, and Elinor Ronalson, 1748, January 10.

Lindsay, Robert, and Susanna Annis, 1751, December 13.

Lindsay, Jane, and Thomas Wilson, 1751, April 24.

Lisle, Hannah, and Robert Steele, 1751, December 14.

Littell, Jane, and Robert Shannon, 1749, September.

Little, Lawrence, and Bridget Peacking, 1749, October.

Lloyd, Elizabeth, and James Evans, 1750, May.

Lloyd, Evan, and Abigal Davies, 1748, December.

Lloyd, Joan, and James Davis, 1752, May 1.

Lockhart, Robert, and Jane McFarson, 1749, November.

Logan, George, and Olive Lawrenson, 1751, April 15.

Logan, Sarah, and James Cummings, 1751, June 3.

Long, Andrew, and Mary Smith, 1752, January 3.

Long, John, and Mary Foster, 1750, August.

Long, Sarah, and John Robinson, 1752, May 25.

Longwell, Margaret, and John Fenby, 1749, May.

Lòrd, John, and Deborah Bankson, 1751, June 8.

Lowry, Andrew, and Mary Cather, 1751, January 15.

Lowry, George Henry, and Catharine Penering, 1749, May.

Lownes, Mary, and Edward Fitzrandolph, 1752, April 15.

Lowther, James, and Martha Breintnall, 1752, May 11.

Lubers, Jacob, and Anna Allarue, 1748, January 17.

Lunn, Joseph, and Alice Evans, 1751, November 26.

Lyneall, Thomas, and Judah Leonard, 1749, December.

McBride, Daniel, and Jennet McCracken, 1751, October 29.

MacCall, Magd^n, and John Swift, 1749, May.

McCall, Robert, and Catharine Mulica, 1750, May.

McCammin, Elizabeth, and Alexander Parkes, 1751, April 9.

McCauel, Placius Daniel, and Julianna Holliday, 1751, November 4.

McCarty, Elizabeth, and Daniel Keen, 1752, January 7.

McCay, Wm., and Rebecca Smith, 1750, May.

McClean, Michael, and Rachel Patterson, 1749, May.

McClean, William, and Mary Stalker, 1749, May.

McClure, James, and Mary Lewis, 1751, August 28.

McCoskerr, Bernard, and Honour Brodricks, 1750, June.

McCoy, James, and Elizabeth Wilson, 1752, May 9.

McCracken, Jennet, and Daniel McBride, 1751, October 29.

McCracken, Martha, and Jeremiah Smith, 1750, October 13.

McCreary, Ann, and William Hart, 1749, July.

McCreight, Margaret, and John Mathews, 1752, May 14.

McCullough, Ann, and Peter Peel, 1751, November 30.

McDonnel, Isabel, and Bryce McFall, 1749, September.

McDowell, James, and Ann Harman, 1751, August 14.

McDowell, Mary, and Wm. Huston, 1749, September.

McDowell, Samuel, and Ann Saunders, 1749, September.

McDurmant, Margaret, and John Mann, 1749, April.

McEvers, John, and Catharine Koch, 1750, June.

McEvert, ———, and ——— Koch, widow of Peter Koch, 1749, April.

McFall, Bryce, and Isabel McDonnel, 1749, September.

McFarland, Martha, and John Anderson, 1749, May.

McFarlin, Jane, and Andrew Brown, 1751, April 13.

McFarson, Jane, and Robert Lockhart, 1749, November.

McGee, Abigail, and Robert Hughes, 1751, November 1.

McGee, William, and Elizabeth Breading, 1749, November.

McGittighan, Bryan, and Ann Toomy, 1751, November 4.

McNealus, Isabel, and John Standeland, 1751, February 16.

McIlvain, John, and Mary Roman, 1750, May.

McKee, Margaret, and William Sittington, 1752, January 15.

McKees, Ann, and James Harper, 1750, November.

McKinley, Eliz., and John McKorkle, 1749, December.

McKinley, Mary, and Samuel Muckledoff, 1751, June 18.

McKnight, Margaret, and John Peel, 1750, July.

McKorkle, John, and Eliz. McKinley, 1749, December.

McMehon, Hugh, and Marg^t Henry, 1751, September 25.

McMim, Jane, and William Sherlock, 1750, October 8.

McMullan, Margaret, and Thomas Carry, 1752, January 8.

McMurray, Sarah, and John Carson, 1750, December.

Macky, Jannet, and Robert Darlington, 1751, January 29.

Maddon, Mary, and John Wallace, 1749, August 19.

Mann, W^m, and Hannah Elliot, 1748, January 21.

Malin, Davis, and Margaret Lawrence, 1751, February 21.

Malin, W^m, and Elizabeth Crosley, 1748, February 1.

Mandlin, Ruth, and Thomas Banfield, 1750, May.

Mann, John, and Margaret McDurmant, 1749, April.

Marres, Mary, and James Barkley, 1749, April 19.

Marren, Jane, and Peter White, 1749, November.

Marshall, Joseph, and Rachel Scot, 1749, November.

Marshall, Moses, and Susanna Harris, 1751, June 18.

Marshtellon, Mary, and Sebastian Boyse, 1748, January 23.

Martin, Anthony, and Ann Anderson, 1752, May 26.

Martin, Hannah, and Patrick Anderson, 1748, December.

Martin, Jonathan, and Hannah Evans, 1751, March 23.

Martin, Rachel, and Samuel Battin, 1749, January.

Martin, Susannah, and Edward Milner, 1751, February 13.
Martin, Thomas, and Sarah Evans, 1751, December 20.
Mason, Abraham, and Catharine Wyne, 1750, November.
Mason, Ann, and Oneas Balter, 1750, November.
Mason, William, and Mary Wood, 1752, May 28.
Masters, George, and Mary Helmer, 1752, July 4.
Mather, John, and Katherine Davis, 1751, May 27.
Mathews, Agnes, and James Bell, 1749, January.
Mathews, Edward, and Agnes Pummin, 1750, October 25.
Mathews, John, and Margaret McCreight, 1752, May 14.
Mathews, Rebecca, and William Gardner, 1749, March.
Mathews, Thomas, and Rachel Young, 1752, May 18.
Mathias, David, and Susannah Packer, 1749, January.
Mayberry, Catherine, and Charles Jolly, 1752, January 8.
Mayberry, Rachel, and Robert Field, 1749, March.
Mayer, John, and Ann Sheed, 1751, December 12.
Meredith, Mary, and Thomas Riley, 1751, March 11.
Merek, Susannah, and Samuel Smith, 1749, May.
Merg, Barbara, and Christian Fontasket, 1750, November.
Mersden, Humphry, and Mary Heron, 1751, November 8.
Mickle, John, and Hannah Cooper, 1752, July 25.
Micklehenny, Ann, and Joseph Carter, 1749, April.
Middleton, Martha, and Abraham Wilson, 1750, November.
Midwinter, Katharine, and Mathew Kyser, 1750, November.
Mifflin, Samuel, and Rebecca Edgil, 1750, August.
Miles, Ann, and Samuel Thomas, 1751, February 17.
Miles, Hannah, and William Ogburn, 1748, December.
Miles, Margaret, and Jonathan Cook, 1749, May.
Miles, Martha, and Silas Crispin, 1749, January.
Miles, Sarah, and Samson Davies, 1752, May 20.
Miller, Isabel, and John Craig, 1749, September.
Miller, John, and Margaret Henry, 1752, March 18.
Miller, Margaret, and Joseph Harris, 1751, October 25.
Miller, Mary, and James Gibbins, 1750, August.
Milligin, Philip, and Sarah Vaughan, 1748, January 30.

PENNSYLVANIA MARRIAGE LICENSES, ISSUED BY GOVERNOR JAMES HAMILTON, 1748–1752.

BY HELEN JORDAN.

Millis, Robert, and Osly Montgomery, 1751, August 16.
Milner, Edward, and Susannah Martin, 1751, February 18.
Mitchell, Ann, and Edward Snead, 1752, June 1.
Mitchell, Elizabeth, and Robert Johnston, 1750, October 11.
Mitchell, Randal, and Rose Harper, 1751, December 11.
Mitchell, Thomas, and Ann Philips, 1749, March.
Monleky, Jane, and Ezekiel Good, 1748, December.
Montgomery, John, and ———— ————, 1751, January 2.
————, ————, and John Montgomery, 1751, January 2.
Montgomery, Margaret, and George Brooks, 1751, February 9.
Montgomery, Osly, and Robert Millis, 1751, August 16.
Montgomery, Susannah, and Samuel Kennedy, 1750, June.
Moor, Elizabeth, and William Leech, 1751, September 4.
Moore, Ann, and James Wilkinson, 1752, April 23.
Moore, John, and Mary Simpson, 1751, August 15.
Moore, Richard, and Mary Hancock, 1748, February 27.
Moore, Sarah, and Job Cobourne, 1750, May.
Moore, Susanna, and Christopher Smith, 1751, July 5.
Moorland, Ann, and James Watson, 1749, May.
Mopely, Richard, and Mary Lampleigh, 1751, May 24.
Moreton, John, and Hannah Painter, 1751, February 8.
Morford, Mary, and John Jones, 1749, September.
Morgan, Howell, and Phobe Hawkins, 1750, September.
Morgan, Mary, and Steven Davies, 1752, May 18.
Morgan, Mordecas, and Mary Pugh, 1749, July.
Morgan, Morris, and Mary House, 1749, December.

Morgan, Samuel, and Katharine Sprogel, 1751, March 12.

Moriarty, Sylvester, and Hannah White, 1752, April 13.

Morris, Garret, and Jane Reading, 1748, December.

Morris, Jane, and Joseph Yeates, 1750, December.

Morris, Lettice, and Morris Evans, 1750, May.

Morris, Margaret, and Garret Barry, 1750, August.

Morris, Sarah, and John Jones, 1751, January 19.

Morrison, George, and Mary Dawson, 1751, August 6.

Morstris, Peter, and Margaret Holleway, 1751, October 1.

Morton, Amy, and John Justice, 1750, November.

Moss, Ann, and William Jones, 1749, May.

Much, James, and Jane Abevan, 1751, April 20.

Muckledoff, Samuel, and Mary McKinley, 1751, June 18.

Muckleroy, Jane, and Derrick Jones, 1752, June 17.

Mulford, Sarah, and George Spafford, 1748, January 30.

Mulica, Catharine, and Robert McCall, 1750, May.

Mullan, Harriet, and Edward Tow, 1752, February 15.

Murphy, James, and Priscilla Harvey, 1751, August 13.

Murray, Andrew, and Susannah Weaver, 1751, August 25.

Murray, Katharine, and William Conqueryood, 1751, November 9.

Myers, Catharine, and George Smith, 1749, September.

Nash, Catharine, and William Kelles, 1749, November.

Neale, James, and Mary Cogell, 1749, April.

Nelson, Katharine, and James Power, 1751, August 19.

Nelson, Rebecca, and Archibald Torenes, 1750, November.

Nethermark, Lucas, and Margaret Webb, 1749, March.

Nethermark, Mathias, and Jane Jarret, 1751, June 14.

Nettle, Mary, and John Jones, 1751, December 4.

Newman, Mary, and John Edwards, 1751, September 25.

Newton, Elizabeth, and Samuel Cochran, 1751, February 28.

Nicholson, George, and Elizabeth Bell, 1751, November 1.

Noblett, William, and Rebecca Cuthbert, 1752, June 16.

Norris, Mary, and Wm Ranberry, 1749, December.

North, Elizabeth, and George Plymm, 1749, November.

Norwood, Elizabeth, and William Arrell, 1749, March 25.

Norwood, Mary, and James Graybury, 1750, September.
Ogburn, William, and Hannah Miles, 1748, December.
Ogg, John, and Elizabeth Clements, 1748, March 17.
Olipheal, Ann, and David Thomson, 1751, May 16.
Oor, George, and Sarah Cameron, 1751, December 11.
Opdergrass, Susanna, and Jacob Eberolt, 1751, May 31.
Opdegraaf, Susannah, and George Waas, 1751, November 20.
Ore, Alexander, and Mary Dawson, 1749, December.
Ore, Jane, and Thomas Deacon, 1749, December.
Ottaghan, Catharine, and Oliver Ottaghan, 1750, August.
Ottaghan, Oliver, and Catharine Ottaghan, 1750, August.
Over, Hannah, and Peter Isburg, 1750, August.
Owen, George, and Rebecca Harris, 1751, May 4.
Owen, Mary, and John Edgar, 1748, December.

Packer, Susannah, and David Mathias, 1749, January.
Paen, Hannah, and Ralph Walker, 1749, April 1.
Painter, Hannah, and John Moreton, 1751, February 8.
Palmer, Elizabeth, and Alexander Alaire, 1749, October.
Palmer, Elizabeth, and Thomas Barney, 1749, July.
Palmer, George, and Sarah Bringhurst, 1749, January.
Panyard, Ann, and Joshua Johnson, 1750, September.
Parker, Ann, and Michael Paul, 1750, November.
Parkes, Alexander, and Elizabeth McCammin, 1751, April 9.
Parks, Foster, and Margaret Davis, 1749, September.
Parr, William, and Margaret Cadge, 1750, August.
Parry, Katharine, and Edward Duffield, 1751, June 10.
Parry Marg^t., and Charles Humphries, 1749, August.
Parry, Rowland, and Hannah Evans. 1750, July.
Parsons, Hannah, and James Worrall, 1749, October.
Parsons, Richard, and Alice Hall, 1749, October.
Paschal, Hannah, and John Stow, 1751, April 6.
Pass, John, and Judith Smith, 1751, July 17.
Pastorius, Ann, and John Wynn, 1748, March 1.
Patterson, Rachel, and Michael McClean, 1749, May.
Paul, Michael, and Ann Parker, 1750, November.

Paul, Sarah, and William Lasberry, 1749, October.

Paven, Margaret Anna, and George Seidheisser, 1751, June 19.

Peacking, Bridget, and Lawrence Little, 1749, October.

Pearson, John, and Elmer Walpole, 1750, November.

Pearson, Rebecca, and Joshua Finnimore, 1749, May.

Pearson, Sarah, and Samuel Annis, 1750, August.

Pederick or Pedrix, Alice, and Abraham Jessop, 1749, August.

Pedrake, Thomas, and Christian Stedamy, 1750, May.

Pedrick, Thomas, and Rebecca Hoffman, 1751, November 16.

Peel, John, and Margaret McKnight, 1750, July.

Peel, Peter, and Ann McCullough, 1751, November 30.

Peele, Sarah, and Thomas Riche, 1751, December 18.

Penering, Catharine, and George Henry Lowry, 1749, May.

Penering, Reginia, and Philip Freid, 1749, April 10.

Pennington, Elizabeth, and William Swan, 1751, August 12.

Penry, Mary, widow, and William Atwood, 1751, March 16.

Perkins, Sarah, and William Cammell, 1749, March.

Peterson, Magdalen, and Robert Claud, 1749, November.

Petty, John, and Elizabeth Hall, 1748, February 2.

Pender, Mary, and Alexander Gordon, 1749, June 24.

Philips, Ann, and Thomas Mitchell, 1749, March.

Philips, Rebecca, and Erasmus Stevens, 1749, March.

Pickle, John, and Ann Davis, 1749, March 31.

Pites, Elizabeth, and John Beane, 1752, January 27.

Pleadwell, Sarah, and John Priest, 1751, June 5.

Pleeken, Phoebe, and John George Bloome, 1752, June 1.

Peisly, Dorcas, and William Fallet, 1749, March.

Plymm, George, and Elizabeth North, 1749, November.

Pocklington, Marg^t., and Peter Stelly, 1749, April 17.

Pollard, Margaret, and William Hawks, 1751, August 23.

Pollard, Phoebe, and Daniel Couch, 1750, December.

Poole, Hannah, and Thomas Williams, 1751, April 10.

Porter, James, and Marg^t. Smith, 1751, September 7.

Potts, Samuel, and Ann Ashmead, 1751, October 9.

Ponloon, William, and Catharine Justice, 1751, November 18.
Powel, Esther, and Joseph Bunting, 1751, October 28.
Powell, Hannah, and Charles Spateman, 1752, June 8.
Power, James, and Katharine Nelson, 1751, August 19.
Power, William, and Ellinor Thomson, 1749, July.
Preisbach, Simon, and Dorothy Deer, 1752, April 7.
Preston, John, and Mary Carter, 1752, June 1.
Price, Elizabeth, and William Ford, 1748, December.
Price, Hannah, and James Dutton, 1751, January 5.
Price, Jenkins, and Martha Lawrence, 1751, January 19.
Price, Jesse, and Deborah Hudson, 1748, December.
Price, Letitia, and William Davies, 1751, April 26.
Price, Richard, and Rebecca Jenings, 1751, October 7.
Price, William, and Sarah Johnson, 1749, March.
Prichard, Catharine, and Griffith Jones, 1749, July.
Prichard, Mary, and John Davis, 1749, March 29.
Priest, John, and Sarah Pleadwell, 1751, June 5.
Prisgy, Mary, and George Wells, 1749, December.
Pritchard, Anthony, and Jane Glascow, 1751, August 28.
Pritchard, William, and Katherine Kinsey, 1750, June.
Pricket, Martha, and Samuel Davis, 1749, April.
Pue, Jemima, and Patrick Carty, 1749, November.
Pugh, Catharine, and James Coppock, 1752, July 8.
Pugh, Hannah, and Thomas Coats, 1748, February 11.
Pugh, Mary, and Mordecas Morgan, 1749, July.
Pugh, Michael, and Hannah Davis, 1749, September.
Pugh, Thomas, and Margaret Tucker, 1752, July 1.
Pummell, Mary, and Robert Flemming, 1750, August.
Pummin, Agnes, and Edward Mathews, 1750, October 25.

Quako, and Hannah, negroes, 1748, January 27.
Quantrall, Elizabeth, and Charles Jenkins, 1752, June 13.

Raine, Elizabeth, and Samuel Hughes, 1751, April 17.
Rambo, Gunnar, and Susanna Rambo, 1752, April 13.
Rambo, John, and Elizabette Harrol, 1748, March 21.
Rambo, Martha, and Jacob Cox, 1750, December.

Rambo, Susanna, and Gunnar Rambo, 1752, April 13.
Rambo, Thomas, and Deborah Beal, 1748, March 18.
Ranberry, W^m., and Mary Norris, 1749, December.
Rankin, George, and Elizabeth Griffin, 1750, December.
Reading, Jane, and Garret Morris, 1748, December.
Reames, Mary, and Joseph Andover, 1751, July 1.
Reaver, Conrad, and Margaretta Conradin, 1750, August.
Redman, John, and May Sobers, 1751, April 15.
Reed, Clotworthy, and Mary Hanns, 1751, July 2.
Rees, Elizabeth, and Wm. Clampter, 1750, May.
Rees, John, and Katharine Havelfinger, 1752, May 9.
Reichart, Henry, and Catharina Kinsley, 1752, June 5.
Reily, Ann, and Edward Vaughn, 1752, April 18.
Reiner, Katherine, and Henry Schneider, 1751, December 14.
Renshaw, Thomas, and Elizabeth Shute, 1752, April 1.
Rettenhouse, Jacob, and Susannah Bartleston, 1749, July.
Revell, Peter, and Mary Allenby, 1748, December.
Riche, Thomas, and Sarah Peele, 1751, December 18.
Richey, Edward, and Mary Shannan, 1751, June 4.
Rickey, Elizabeth, and James Rickey, 1750, December.
Rickey, James, and Elizabeth Rickey, 1750, December.
Rigg, Ann, and William Bradley, 1751, October 29.
Riley, Thomas, and Mary Meredith, 1751, March 11.
Roan, Eleanor, and Robert Bredin, 1750, August.
Roberts, Amos, and Sarah Harry, 1750, October 6.
Roberts, Ann, and William Roberts, 1751, February 21.
Roberts, Catharine, and David John, 1752, March 12.
Roberts, Henry, and Martha Hamilton, 1751, October 17.
Roberts, John, and Hannah Warner, 1752, April 1.
Roberts, Mary, and Cornelius Brian, 1749, May.
Roberts, Samuel, and Elizabeth Evans, 1751, April 25.
Roberts, William, and Ann Roberts, 1751, February 21.
Robinson, Deborah, and Jonathan Carr, 1748, February 24.
Robinson, John, and Sarah Long, 1752, May 25.
Roderich, Emanuel, and Susanna Francy, 1751, March 5.
Rodger, Thomas, and Elizabeth Bowen, 1751, June 27.
Roe, Hannah, and John Steers, 1749, March.

Rogers, Elizabeth, and Robert Hardie, 1752, May 28.
Roman, Mary, and John McIlvaine, 1750, May.
Ronalson, Elinor, and James Lindsay, 1748, January 10.
Roof, Jacob, and Elizabeth Speece, 1749, July.
Ross, Gertrude, and Thomas Tell, 1752, June 6.
Ross, Jane, and John Drain, 1750, October 25.
Ross, Thomas, and Jane Barr, 1751, June 20.
Rossiter, Thomas, and Elizabeth Bull, 1751, April 18.
Rowen, Margaret, and Samuel Davis, 1752, January 27.
Rowland, Thomas, and Sarah Howell, 1750, October, 31.
Rudolph, Tobias, and Rebecca Weaver, 1751, October 8.
Rue, Elizabeth, and Henry Holliday, 1751, January 15.
Rundle, Daniel, and Ann Tripe, 1751, May 6.
Rupertson, Elizabeth, and Tobias Agin, 1752, February 29.
Rush, Joseph, and Rebecca Sincox, 1750, September.
Russel, Thomas, and Eliz. Wallace, 1748, February 7.
Ryall, George, and Mary Worley, 1749, May.

Sadler, John, and Ann Ford, 1749, October.
Sample, Mary, and Hezekiah Alexander, 1752, June 12.
Saul, Rachel, and John Harry, 1751, July 27.
Saunders, Ann, and Samuel McDowell, 1749, September.
Saunders, Ann, and Isaac Stratton, 1751, April 25.
Saunders, Mary, and Andrew Collins, 1748, December.
Savage, Hannah, and Lewes Walker, 1750, December.
Savoy, Bridget, and Robert Clarke, 1751, July 17.
Sayre, John, and Rachel Bowes, 1751, April 6.
Schaemel, Christopher, and Mary Elizabeth, 1750, December.
Schmeltzer, Mary Eliz., and Henry Kristman, 1749, May.
Schneider, Henry, and Katherine Reiner, 1751, December 14.
Scholar, William, and Teresia Wheeler, 1751, August 8.
Schreider, Susannah, and Sebastian Levin, 1751, May 8.
Scolly, Samuel, and Ann Eader, 1749, January.
Scot, Edward, and Mary Kuhl, 1749, September.
Scot, Rachel, and Joseph Marshall, 1749, November.
Scott, John, and Isabella Davis, 1752, March 7.

Scull, Elizabeth, and Samuel Holland, 1749, December.
Scull, Jasper, and Mary Eyers, 1749, January.
Scull, Rachell, and Michael Biddle, 1749, March.
Searle, John, and Mary Hicks, 1748, February 16.
Seth, James, and Ann Wilkinson, 1750, October 10.
Sevan, Maria, and Jacob Hultenstein, 1749, April.
Sewellin, Catharine, and Abram Griffith, 1752, June 20.
Shackleton, Ann, and Joseph Dorvill, 1748, December.
Shannan, James, and Martha Lewis, 1752, March 25.
Shannan, Mary, and Edward Richey, 1751, June 4.
Shannon, Mary, and George Smith, 1750, August.
Shannon, Robert, and Jane Littell, 1749, September.
Shaw, Joseph, and Sarah Watts, 1751, February 28.
Shaw, Samuel, and Mary Lessell, 1751, October 26.
Sheed, Ann, and John Mayer, 1751, December 12.
Sherlock, William, and Jane McMim, 1750, October 8.
Sherrin, Sarah, and Nicholas Ward, 1748, December.
Shewell, Stephen, and Elizabeth Fordham, 1750, May.
Shirley, James, and Mary Guilhott, 1749, July.
Shoab, Adam, and Elizabeth Bissert, 1752, July 29.
Shoemaker, Daniel, and Ann Depue, 1751, March 14.
Shoemaker, John, and Mary White, 1752, April 13.
Shovel, Elizabeth, and William Williams, 1752, March 10.
Shull, Edith, and Isaac Anderson, 1751, April 16.
Shute, Elizabeth, and Thomas Renshaw, 1752, April 1.
Shute, Thomas, and Rebecca Coates, 1749, May.
Shute, Thomas, and Rebecca Coates, 1748, March 21.
Sichlin, Susannah Catharine, and Hans George Bernhart,
    1751, October 17.
Silus, Elizabeth, and John Hood, 1749, December.
Simpson, Elizabeth, and Benjamin Hair, 1751, September 21.
Simpson, Elizabeth, and Thomas Thompson, 1749, June 6.
Simpson, Mary, and John Moore, 1751, August 15.
Simson, Teny, and Milby Johnson, 1749, October.
Sinclair, Elizabeth, and George Carew, 1751, April 11.
Sinclair, Elizabeth, and Thomas Lang, 1749, November.

Sinclair, Joseph, and Barbara Vanhist, 1748, February 6.
Sincox, Rebecca, and Joseph Rush, 1750, September.
Sitch, John, and Elizabeth Hollyday, 1751, December 19.
Sittington, William, and Margaret McKee, 1752, January 15.
Skinner, Abram, and Marg^t Harding, 1751, November.
Slaughter, Mary, and Melchior Bartholt, 1750, June.
Smith, Adam, and Gertrude Bener, 1750, October 1.
Smith, Barbara, and John Downe, 1751, August 24.
Smith, Christopher, and Susanna Moore, 1751, July 5.
Smith, George, and Mary Shannan, 1750, August.
Smith, George, and Catharine Myers, 1749, September.
Smith, Hugh, and Ann Bailey, 1751, June 25.
Smith, James, and Hannah Watts, 1749, March.
Smith, Jeremiah, and Martha McCracken, 1750, October 18.
Smith, Judith, and John Pass, 1751, July 17.
Smith, Marg^t, and James Porter, 1751, September 7.
Smith, Mary, and Daniel Jones, 1751, November 19.
Smith, Mary, and Andrew Long, 1752, January 3.
Smith, Ralph, and Margery Allen, 1749, April 22.
Smith, Rebecca, and Wm. McCay, 1750, May.
Smith, Samuel, and Susannah Merek, 1749, May.
Smith, Thomas, and Sarah Bowes, 1752, March 9.
Snead, Edward, and Ann Mitchell, 1752, June 1.
Sobers, May, and John Redman, 1751, April 15.
Sodden, Christiana, and John Bennet, 1751, September 24.
Son, John, and Elizabeth Weakley, 1749, October.
Sort, John, and Barbara Krowser, 1749, March 30.
Sonder, Jacob, and Ann Crawford, 1749, October.
Spafford, George, and Sarah Mulford, 1748, January 30.
Sparkes, James, and Mary Harry, 1751, June 3.
Spateman, Charles, and Hannah Powell, 1752, June 8.
Spedin, Elizabeth, and Peter Clowser, 1750, June.
Speece, Elizabeth, and Jacob Roof, 1749, July.
Spencer, Honour, and William Fitszymmonds, 1752, January 22.
Spences, Samuel, and Hannah Boyd, 1751, April 10.
Spicker, Katharine, and Garret Winkop, 1751, June 5.

Spooner, Mary, and James Davis, 1751, July 2.

Sprogel, Katharine, and Samuel Morgan, 1751, March 12.

Spronce, Elizabeth, and Samuel Cox, 1749, May.

Stadler, Jacob, and Mary Stow, 1751, August 6.

Stalker, Mary, and William McClean, 1749, May.

Stamper, Hannah, and Elias Bland, 1752, June 22.

Stamper, Thomas, and Rebecca Coleman, 1749, May.

Standiland, John, and Isabel McNealees, 1751, February 16.

Statzin, Barbara, and William Greathouse, 1749, March.

Stedamy, Christian, and Thomas Pedrake, 1750, May.

Stedman, Alexander, and Eliz. Chancellor, 1749, May.

Steele, Robert, and Hannah Lisle, 1751, December 14.

Steers, John, and Hannah Roe, 1749, March.

Stegarin, Eve, and Michael Haugh, 1749, April.

Steinbruner, Sybylla, and Dewalt Beaver, 1751, June 15.

Stelly, Peter, and Marg^t Pocklington, 1749, April 17.

Stevens, Benjamin, and Deborah Dungan, 1751, August 28.

Stevens, Erasmus, and Rebecca Philips, 1749, March.

Stevens, Margaret, and Joseph Bell, 1752, July 13.

Stevens, Philip, and Isabella Johnson, 1749, September.

Steward, Joseph, and Mary Johnson, 1749, March.

Stewart, Elizabeth, and William Ireson, 1749, July.

Stewart, Robert, and Rachel Carrell, 1752, May 30.

Stille, Catharine, and John Lee, 1752, July 1.

Stow, John, and Hannah Paschal, 1751, April 6.

Stratton, Isaac, and Ann Saunders, 1751, April 25.

Street, Daniel, and Mary Foster, 1752, April 8.

Street, Rachel, and Thomas Testin, 1751, March 19.

Strowde, James, and Elizabeth Beene, 1749, July.

Stuart, Alexander, and Jane Hall, 1752, June 16.

Styles, Abigal, and William Jackson, 1752, March 11.

Styles, Henry, and Elizabeth Williams, 1749, October.

Suber, Catharine, and Christian Cropp, 1751, April 16.

Sullivan, Dennis, and Mary FitzSummons, 1749, September.

Sutton, Rebecca, and John Kelly, 1752, April 10.

Swaghouser, Conrad, and Margaret Ulrick, 1751, March 19.

Swan, William, and Elizabeth Pennington, 1751, August 12.

Sweman, Anna Maria (widow), and Peter Kalm, 1749, December.

Swift, John, and Magd^n MacCall, 1749, May.

Tates, Andrew, and Susanna Collins, 1748, December.

Tatnall, Elizabeth, and William Gardner, 1749, April.

Tatum, Sarah, and John Lewis, 1752, July 31.

Taylor, Barbara, and Grea Matthias, 1752, April 4.

Taylor, Isabella, and Wm. Charlton, 1748, January 21.

Tell, Thomas, and Gertrude Ross, 1752, June 6.

Test, Rachel, and John Hillman, 1750, June.

Testin, Samuel, and Sarah Hellings, 1751, November 29.

Testin, Thomas, and Rachel Street, 1751, March 19.

Thomas, David, and Mary Walton, 1750, May.

Thomas, Elizabeth, and Jenkin Jenkins, 1748, December.

Thomas, John, and Lucretia Gilbert, 1752, March 2.

Thomas, Mary, and Isaiah Lewes, 1751, April 26.

Thomas, Owen, and Mary Wilson, 1750, July.

Thomas, Philip, and Mary Bartholomew, 1751, December 28.

Thomas, Rachel, and Samuel Jones, 1751, August 19.

Thomas, Samuel, and Ann Miles, 1751, February 13.

Thomas, Sarah, and Abner Evans, 1751, March 16.

Thomas, William, and Abigail Day, 1751, January 17.

Thompson, Thomas, and Margaret Grantrum, 1751, March 18.

Thompson, Thomas, and Elizabeth Simpson, 1749, June 6.

Thomson, David, and Ann Olipheal, 1751, May 16.

Thomson, Ellionar, and William Power, 1749, July.

Thomson, Susanna, and Samuel Kimpson, 1750, May.

Thorington, Abigail, and John Wegery, 1750, June.

Tillyer, William, and Sarah Foster, 1749, April.

Timmons, John, and Alice Burley, 1749, March.

Tisdale, Henry, and Jane Brown, 1749, April 18.

Tisdel, Hannah, and John Farron, 1752, July 22.

Tomin, Patrick, and Hester Linckom, 1748, February 2.

Tomkins, Hannah, and John Weldon, 1751, May 17.
Tomlinson, Eleanor, and Robert Comfort, 1751, August 22.
Toomy, Ann, and Bryan McGittighan, 1751, November.4.
Torenes, Archibald, and Rebecca Nelson, 1750, November.
Tow, Edward, and Harriet Mullan, 1752, February 15.
Towers, John, and Margaret Francis, 1749, May.
Towne, Elizabeth, and Thomas Bartholomew, 1750, December.
Toy, Elias, and Barbara Clair, 1751, March 1.
Treherne, James, and Hannah Cotman, 1751, April 15.
Treviller, Thomas, and Mary James, 1749, April.
Tripe, Ann, and Daniel Randle, 1751, May 6.
Troy, Margt, and Benjamin Fausman, 1749, May.
Trusse, Christiana, and John Lea, 1749, March.
Tucker, Margaret, and Thomas Pugh, 1752, July 1.
Tupy, Elizabeth, and Andrew Ewing, 1749, September.
Turner, Edward, and Rachel Hawkins, 1751, August 17,
Turner, John, and Elizabeth Boone, 1749, March.
Turner, Susannah, and Thomas Francis, 1751, February 25.
Twining, Margaret, and Thomas Hamilton, 1749, January.
Tyson, Ann, and Thomas Coat, 1749, December.

Ulrich, Margaret, and Conrad Swaghouser, 1751, March 19.

Vandegrift, Abraham, and Phoebe Hufty, 1749, August.
Vanhist, Barbara, and Joseph Sinclair, 1748, February 6.
Van Horne, Benjamin, and Hannah Davis, 1749, June 8.
Vanleewenigh, Zachariah, and Ann Conul, 1748, February 25.
Van Lewening, Ann, and Samuel Webster, 1749, January.
Vannest, Elizabeth, and Gisbert Boogart, 1749, October.
Vansant, Isaiah, and Mary Foster, 1749, March.
Vaughan, Sarah, and Philip Milligin, 1748, January 30.
Vaughn, Edward, and Ann Reily, 1752, April 18.
Voyer, Jane Urbain, and Charles Hamilton, 1749, June 7.

Waas, George, and Susannah Opdegraaf, 1751, November 20.

Waggstaffe, Richard, and Sarah Yarnall, 1751, November 12.

Wall, Patrick, and Mary Lee, 1749, November.

Wallace, Abigail, and Lawrence Hewlings, 1749, August.

Wallace, Eliz., and Thomas Russel, 1748, February 7.

Wallace, John, and Mary Maddon, 1749, August 19.

Wallace, Susannah, and Abraham Coates, 1750, June.

Walker, Lewes, and Hannah Savage, 1750, December.

Walker, Ralph, and Hannah Pam, 1749, April 1.

Walpole, Eleanor, and John Pearson, 1750, November.

Walsh, Hannah, and James Grogan, 1750, August.

Walter, Lawrence, and Catharine Edinburg, 1749, November.

Walton, Jacob, and Jane Walton, 1751, March 27.

Walton, Jane, and Jacob Walton, 1751, March 27.

Walton, Joseph, and Rebecca Holt, 1752, January 14.

Walton, Mary, and David Thomas, 1750, May.

Ward, Nicholas, and Sarah Sherrin, 1748, December.

Ward, Ruth, and William Ward, 1750, November.

Ward, William, and Ruth Ward, 1750, November.

Waring, James, and Hannah Holloway, 1749, January.

Warner, Arnold, and Rachel Warner, 1749, March.

Warner, Hannah, and John Roberts, 1752, April 1.

Warner, Isaac, and Jane Lewis, 1752, June 20.

Warner, Rachel, and Arnold Warner, 1749, March.

Warner, Simeon, and Jane Grandam, 1749, April.

Warnick, Mary, and Anderson Harriet, 1749, October.

Warrel, George, and Priscilla Davies, 1752, April 27.

Waterin, Katherinia, and Joseph Kaufman, 1750, May.

Waterman, Priscilla, and Evan Evans, 1750, May.

Watkins, Jane, and John Bailey, 1749, March.

Watson, Elizabeth, and James Adams, 1751, October 16.

Watson, James, and Ann Moorland, 1749, May.

Wattlebaum, Mary, and George Batteo, 1752, July 20.

Watts, Hannah, and James Smith, 1749, March.

Watts, Mary, and Robert Wood, 1750, December.

Watts, Sarah, and Joseph Shaw, 1751, February 28.

Weakley, Elizabeth, and John ——, 1749, October.

Weaver, Rebecca, and Tobias Rudolph, 1751, October 8.

Weaver, Susannah, and Andrew Murray, 1751, August 25.

Webb, Margaret, and Lucas Nethermark, 1749, March.

Webster, Samuel, and Ann Van Lewening, 1749, January.

Weeks, Mary, and James Hutton, 1749, April 20.

Wegery, John, and Abigal Thorington, 1750, June.

Weldon, John, and Hannah Tomkins, 1751, May 17.

Weldon, Lydia, and Isaac Hughes, 1748, December.

Weldon, William, and Ann Boyd, 1749, April 27.

Wellin, Elizabeth, and John Wyatt, 1750, August.

Wells, Elizabeth, and James Hemphill, 1750, December.

Wells, George, and Mary Prisgly, 1749, December.

Wells, Moses, and Ann Harper, 1749, April 26.

Wells, Rebecca, and John Taber, 1749, August.

Wells, Sarah, and John Harper, 1750, October 20.

Welsh, Thomas, and Elizabeth Hayes, 1750, September.

Wermley, Mary, and Hugh Donaldson, 1751, May 15.

West, Elizabeth, and Wm. Cuningham, 1748, February 13.

West, Rachel, and John Levinus Clarkson, 1749, March.

Wethers, Ann, and William Black, 1749, March.

Weyman, Edward, and Rebecca Breintnall, 1751, July 4.

Wharton, Joseph, and Mary Dean, 1751, April 23.

Wheat, Dinah, and Richard Humphries, 1749, April.

Wheatley, John, and Charity Lideard, 1751, August 6.

Wheeler, Teresia, and William Scholar, 1751, August 8.

White, Hannah, and Peter Buffington, 1750, July.

White, Hannah, and Sylvestor Moriarty, 1752, April 13.

White, Mary, and John Shoemaker, 1752, April 13.

White, Peter, and Jane Marren, 1749, November.

Whittenham, William, and Mary Holgas, 1751, February 9.

Whitton, James, and Elizabeth Johnson, 1751, January 3.

Wigton, Margaret, and Archibald Crawford, 1750, December.

Wiley, Benjamin, and Elizabeth Torten, 1749, October.

Wiley, Mary, and David Wilson, 1752, July 27.

Wiley, Theophilus, and Elizabeth Hayard, 1752, June 26.

Wilkins, Alice, and Andrew Helmes, 1752, January 11.

Wilkinson, Ann, and James Seth, 1750, October 10.

Wilkinson, Elizabeth, and Peter Knight, 1752, June 20.

Wilkinson, James, and Ann Moore, 1752, April 23.

Wilkinson, Sarah, and Joseph Donaldson, 1751, August 1.

Willard, Dorothy, and David Huffty, 1751, April 16.

Williams, Ann, and Richard Dalby, 1750, August.

Williams, Ann, and John Evans, 1751, November 20.

Williams, Elizabeth, and Paul Donlin, 1750, October 15.

Williams, Elizabeth, and Edward Hughes, 1749, September.

Williams, Elizabeth, and Henry Styles, 1749, October.

Williams, James, and Deborah Fisher, 1751, December 7.

Williams, John, and Honour Haley, 1748, March 7.

Williams, Susanna, and Edward Drinker, 1749, November.

Williams, Thomas, and Hannah Poole, 1751, April 10.

Williams, William, and Elizabeth Shovel, 1752, March 10.

Williamson, William, and Marg^t Callwell, 1751, September 3.

Wills, Mary, and John Johnson, 1752, April 11.

Wills, Thomas, and Elizabeth Ewing, 1749, September.

Wilson, Abraham, and Martha Middleton, 1750, November.

Wilson, David, and Mary Wiley, 1752, July 27.

Wilson, Elizabeth, and James McCoy, 1752, May 9.

Wilson, James, and Prudence Doyle, 1752, February 1.

Wilson, Mary, and Owen Thomas, 1750, July.

Wilson, Thomas, and Jane Linsay, 1751, April 24.

Winkop, Garret, and Katharine Spicker, 1751, June 5.

Womeldorfe, Mary, and Samuel Head, 1748, December.

Wood, Mary, and John Charlesworth, 1749, December.

Wood, Mary, and William Mason, 1752, May 28.

Wood, Richard, and Sarah Blackfan, 1751, November 7.

Wood, Robert, and Mary Watts, 1750, December.

Wood, Sarah, and John Doyle, 1751, November 19.

Woodcock, William, and Elizabeth Byrn, 1749, March.

Woods, Mary, and George Fox, 1751, August 3.

Woodside, James, and Mary Anderson, 1751, October 26.

Woolman, Esther, and Zebulon Gaunt, 1750, November.

Worley, Mary, and George Ryall, 1749, May.

Worrall, James, and Hannah Parsons, 1749, October.

Worthington, Thomas, and Hannah Duncan, 1751, April 20.

Wright, Mary, and Isaac Dutton, 1750, October 13.

Wright, Susanna, and Nathan Yearsley, 1752, January 11.

Writtenhausen, Annie, and John Peter Huysler, 1749, June 12.

Wyat, John, and Elizabeth Wellin, 1750, August.

Wym, Mary, and Henry Hiddings, 1752, March 23.

Wyne, Catharine, and Abraham Mason, 1750, November.

Wynkoop, Helena, and Jonathan Dubois, 1751, November 15.

Wynn, John, and Ann Pastorius, 1748, March 1.

Yarnall, Sarah, and Richard Waggstaffe, 1751, November 12.

Yates, Sarah, and John Ewing, 1749, March.

Yearsley, Nathan, and Susanna Wright, 1752, January 11.

Yeates, Joseph, and Jane Morris, 1750, December.

Yodern, Elizabeth, and Mathias Hollowback, 1750, October 2.

Young, Edward, and Susannah Furnace, 1749, July.

Young, Rachel, and Thomas Mathews, 1752, May 18.

LIST OF MARRIAGE LICENSES ISSUED IN THE SECRETARY'S OFFICE
FROM AUGUST 1755 THROUGH APRIL 1759

These marriage licenses, entered in the MS Cash Book of Richard Peters, Provincial Secretary, in the Historical Society of Pennsylvania, for the period from August 1755 through April 1759, are in addition to those "Names of Persons for whom Marriage Licenses were issued in the Province of Pennsylvania, Previous to 1790," as printed in the *Pennsylvania Archives*, 2nd Series, Volume II. They follow in time those licenses listed in "Pennsylvania Marriage Licenses, 1742-1748," and "Pennsylvania Marriage Licenses Issued by Gov. James Hamilton, 1748-1752," as published in the *Pennsylvania Magazine of History and Biography*, Volumes XXXIX (1915), 176 ff., and XXXII (1908), 71 ff., respectively.

August 1755

William Erdelheit & Marie Foghten	1, 5, 0
David Evans and Letitia Thomas	1, 5, 0
Joseph Griffitts & Esther Ryan	1, 5, 0
William Keen & Ann Chillingsforth	1, 5, 0
Archibald Hector and Violet	1, 5, 0
Thomas Coates & Marcy Rachford	1, 5, 0
Joseph Canny & Rebecca Brown	1, 5, 0
John Ferguson & Eliz. Palmer	1, 5, 0
John Val. Claudius & Sopⁿ. Heinigen	1, 5, 0
Robert Fulton & Eleanor Wyncoop	1, 5, 0
Joseph Wood & Ann Dixon	1, 5, 0
Thomas Sands & Sarah Duncan	1, 5, 0
Jonas Hopman & Eleanor Cobb	1, 5, 0
Richard Coles & Mary Rigdon	1, 5, 0
	14 – £17,10, 0

September 1755

John Dunn & Jane Landy	1, 5, 0
Joseph Collins & Diana Pricket	1, 5, 0
Edw. Drinker & Elis: Franks	1, 5, 0
Issackar Davids & Elisa: Nailor	1, 5, 0
Benj:ⁿ Lukens & Alice Cadwalader	1, 5, 0
Jn° Hayes & Ann Valentine	1, 5, 0
William Carr & Mary Robinson	1, 5, 0
Day Branson & Chrⁿ. Anderson	1, 5, 0
James Spotswood & Cat: Linsey	1, 5, 0
Edwᵈ. Smith & Hañah Brown	1, 5, 0
Robt. Scott & Margaret Fox	1, 5, 0
Robt. Jones & Elis: McCullough	1, 5, 0
Thomas Watkins & Mary White	1, 5, 0
Thos. Sylvester & Ann Horditch	1, 5, 0
	14 – £17,10, 0

Marriage Licenses Issued in the Secretary's Office

George Smith & Catherina Clair	1, 5, 0
Richard Morris & Susanna Rush	1, 5, 0
Joseph Stamper & Sarah Maddox	1, 5, 0
William Dickinson & Elis: Delipplin	1, 5, 0
John Stamper & Catherine Simmons	1, 5, 0
John Hemphill & Elis: Powel	1, 5, 0
William Brown & Ann Davis	1, 5, 0
Benj^a. Bond & Rose Miller	1, 5, 0
David Fulton & Elis Yerkas	1, 5, 0
John Patrick & Ab: Hockley	1, 5, 0
Benj.^{a} Chamberlain & Elis: Messer	1, 5, 0
Evan Stevens & Elisabeth Jemmison	1, 5, 0
Joseph Cammell & Susanna Holgate	1, 5, 0
John Cooper & Winneford Linch	1, 5, 0
Thomas Calvert & Mary Howard	1, 5, 0
William Long & Elisabeth Henderson	1, 5, 0
Richard Smith & Abigail Pinguet	1, 5, 0
	17 – £21, 5, 0

November 1755

Robert Smith & Jane Laghrin	1, 5, 0
George Kast and Barbara Keigerin	1, 5, 0
Rich^d. Dungworth & Sus^a. Melvin	1, 5, 0
James Lacey & Mary Jones	1, 5, 0
Richard Banks & Mary Lindsay	1, 5, 0
Hugh Shaw & Margery Hough	1, 5, 0
Timothy Carell & Elis. Mary Cleeter	1, 5, 0
John Morris & Barbara Mitchel	1, 5, 0
Paul Roberts & Ann Williams	1, 5, 0
Wm. Snoddy & Jane Montgomery	1, 5, 0
James McMullan & Marg^t. Green	1, 5, 0
Samuel Brown & Mary Buchannan	1, 5, 0
James Marshall & Jane Lindsay	1, 5, 0
Wm. Masden & Eleanor VanBushkirk	1, 5, 0
	14 – £17,10, 0

December 1755

Bernard Vandegrift & Jane Vanhorn	1, 5, 0
John Barnes & Hannah Phipps	1, 5, 0
Joshua Jones & Hannah Vansant	1, 5, 0
Ephraim Jenkins & Mary Delahanty	1, 5, 0
John Lloyd & Mary David	1, 5, 0
Jno. Buckingham & Jane Bennett	1, 5, 0
Jacb: Deñinfelt & Anna Marisin	1, 5, 0
Richard Platt & Ann Johnston	1, 5, 0
William Wilson & Elis. Dabbins	1, 5, 0

Samuel Morris & Rebecca Wistar 1, 5, 0
John Maly & Katherine Walker 1, 5, 0
Andrew Knoxe & Isabel White 1, 5, 0
John Strickland & Mary Grogan 1, 5, 0
Peter Hunter & Mary Emler 1, 5, 0
John Cloyd & Sarah Bartholomew 1, 5, 0
John Lowder & Martha Vastine 1, 5, 0
John Linsey & Mary Lacey 1, 5, 0
Jacob Ingle & Barbara Witmer 1, 5, 0
Thomas Cheyne & Mary Taylor 1, 5, 0
Joseph Lukens & Sarah Powel 1, 5, 0
Joseph Hulins & Elis Valleygase 1, 5, 0
                                          21 – £26, 5, 0

January 1756

Richard Palmer & Phoebe Jones 1, 5, 0
Robert Levers & Mary Church 1, 5, 0
Robert Sanford & Marg^t. Haddeck 1, 5, 0
Richard Howison & Mary Edwards 1, 5, 0
John Bunting & Ann Saunders 1, 5, 0
William Davison & Christiana Bowman 1, 5, 0
Anthony King & Sarah Gardner 1, 5, 0
Peter Ax & Elis Nise 1, 5, 0
William Griffiths & Phoebe Thomas 1, 5, 0
Joseph Kelly & Jane Ladely 1, 5, 0
Nat^l. Current & Reb^a. Dwight 1, 5, 0
John Coburn & Hannah Muro 1, 5, 0
Robert Richardson & Reb^a. Townsend 1, 5, 0
Abel Moore and Hannah Hibbard 1, 5, 0
William Jones & Katherine Henry 1, 5, 0
James Barton & Mary Archer 1, 5, 0
Alexander Magee & Mary Conyers 1, 5, 0
                                          17 – £21, 5, 0

February 1756

Rich^d. Renshaw & Isab^a. Irwin 1, 5, 0
Ellis Price & Sarah Osborne 1, 5, 0
Nicholas Williams & Cat. Bilderback 1, 5, 0
Francis Stickley & Mary Elis: Sheafer 1, 5, 0
William Green & Mary Miller 1, 5, 0
Howel Griffith & Elis: Pugh 1, 5, 0
Mathew Davis & Eleanor Wilson 1, 5, 0
Thomas Bowen & Esther Jones 1, 5, 0
John Church & Elis: Jenkins 1, 5, 0
Charles Tonking & Eleanor Stiles 1, 5, 0
Stephen Yerkes & Rebecca Whitesides 1, 5, 0
Joseph Bickerson & Sarah Maddock 1, 5, 0
Samuel Hart & Marg^t. Hasslett 1, 5, 0
                                          13 – £16, 5, 0

Marriage Licenses Issued in the Secretary's Office

March 1756

Thorne Farmer and Eliz. Hyder	1, 5, 0
George Bail & Hannah Murdock	1, 5, 0
Alex. (blank) & Sarah Holland	1, 5, 0
George Brook & Sarah Herbert	1, 5, 0
Elias Yerkes & Rebecca Foster	1, 5, 0
Jacob Stonemetz & Dorothy Finklering	1, 5, 0
Isaac Davis & Sophia North	1, 5, 0
Thos. Francis & Sarah Cornock	1, 5, 0
Archibald Barron & Eliz Rouen	1, 5, 0
William Coopeland & Martha Shiffers	1, 5, 0
Thomas Cornock & Marg. Edwards	1, 5, 0
Wm. Anderson & Mary Ladely	1, 5, 0
	12 – £15, 0, 0

April 1756

Dennis Conrad & Eliz McFall	1, 5, 0
Jacob Colliday & Fronica Walter	1, 5, 0
Daniel Broadhead & Elizab. Depui	1, 5, 0
Robert Akin & Martha Hueston	1, 5, 0
John Wood & Ann Cooper	1, 5, 0
Daniel Lawrence & Sarah Wheat	1, 5, 0
David Williams & Ann Thomas	1, 5, 0
William Warden & Mary Rice	1, 5, 0
Paul Custard & Margaret Malone	1, 5, 0
Nathan Spencer & Hannah Luffberry	1, 5, 0
Isaac Kirk & Mary Tyson	1, 5, 0
Jacob Kirkerner & Sarah Thomas	1, 5, 0
Miche. Little & Durboro Williams	1, 5, 0
John Jones & Ann Fairris	1, 5, 0
John Leedham & Ruth Strickland	1, 5, 0
John Felton and Ann Hurst	1, 5, 0
Wm. Tonkin and Martha Brown	1, 5, 0
Wm. French & Eliz Brown	1, 5, 0
Charles Day & Ann Clark	1, 5, 0
Thomas Trickett & Catherine Ash	1, 5, 0
Tho. James Smith & Christine Beaks	1, 5, 0
John Gary & Eliz Beverage	1, 5, 0
Richd. McBride & Susana. Harron	1, 5, 0
James McGill & Mary Wells	1, 5, 0
Robert Todd & Eliz. McFarlin	1, 5, 0
Henry Duff & Ann Pickle	1, 5, 0
	£32,10, 0

Samuel Johnson & Jemima Langley	1, 5, 0
Joseph Hough & Mary Tomkin	1, 5, 0
Abrām Larew & Else Vandergrift	1, 5, 0
Cornelius Stevens & Mary Pugh	1, 5, 0
Jacob Rebato & Mary Adams	1, 5, 0
David Henderson & Lydia Hesselius	1, 5, 0
John Thomas & Sarah Humphrey	1, 5, 0
Jacob Furstz & Ann Krafts	1, 5, 0
John Sees & Cat. Gosner	1, 5, 0
Banjᵃ. Powers & Grace Cadwallader	1, 5, 0
William Plumer & Eliz. Richardson	1, 5, 0
Henry Schneider & Ros. Neunan	1, 5, 0
Robᵗ. Tomkins & Eliz. Huff	1, 5, 0
Andrew Nox & Marth. Dicken	1, 5, 0
David McElwaine & Eliz. Graydon	1, 5, 0
Francis Hogg & Ab. Smith	1, 5, 0
	£20, 0, 0

Joseph Granger & Eliz. Bright	1, 5, 0
Daniel Doan & Sarah Dyer	1, 5, 0
Geo: Kerr & Mary Morgan	1, 5, 0
Mich. Everly & Marg. Bratt	1, 5, 0
Thoᵍ. Cotteringer & Marg. Facundus	1, 5, 0
Ebenezer Call & Marg. Thompson	1, 5, 0
John Cox & Sarah Edgell	1, 5, 0
David Davis & Johanᵃ. Cranquit (?)	1, 5, 0
William Fleming & Mary Polyard	1, 5, 0
Joseph Farre & Sarah Dilliplain	1, 5, 0
Wm. McDaniel & Jane Gray	1, 5, 0
Tho: Cookson & Martha Miller	1, 5, 0
	£15, 0, 0

Jacob Polyard & Eliz: Price	1, 5, 0
Atwood Cowman & Mary Morgan	1, 5, 0
Geo: Thomas & Martha Jones	1, 5, 0
John McCarty & Marg. Fitzgerald	1, 5, 0
John Ruxby & Ann Davis	1, 5, 0
John Dark & Mary Kees	1, 5, 0
James Leech & Deborʰ: Tomlinson	1, 5, 0
Jacob Hollingshead & Mary Hollingsh:ᵈ	1, 5, 0
Jacob Masonex & Mary Justice	1, 5, 0
Humphrey Smith & Mary Calhoone	1, 5, 0
James Tomlinson & Barbara Brown	1, 5, 0
William Wagstaff & E. Bailey	1, 5, 0
	£15, 0, 0

Marriage Licenses Issued in the Secretary's Office

August 1756

Thomas Henderson & Eliz:ᵃ Cookson	1, 5, 0
John Keegan & Elizᵃ Hudson	1, 5, 0
Hugh Williams & Dorothy Read	1, 5, 0
Randell Wilson & Marg. Montgomery	1, 5, 0
Geo: Atkinson & Cat. McGinnes	1, 5, 0
Philip Herple & Maria Overpicker	1, 5, 0
Wm. Warner & Mary Hoskins	1, 5, 0
David Brooks & Mary Hunt	1, 5, 0
John Jones & Hannah Richardson	1, 5, 0
John Stenton & Margt. Cuningham	1, 5, 0
William Clever & Mary Knight	1, 5, 0
Geo: Shoemaker & Ann Rettinhous	1, 5, 0
Thomas West & Mary Combs	1, 5, 0
Benj: Ward & Eliz. Pearcy	1, 5, 0
Thomas Mathias & Eliz. Jones	1, 5, 0
Samuel Wynn & Marg. Comb	1, 5, 0
Tobias Leahy & Jane Williams	1, 5, 0
Geo. Bishop & Mary Haws	1, 5, 0
Ezekiel Shepperd & Cat. Hill	1, 5, 0
Wm. Jones & Sarah Gauff	1, 5, 0
David Strang and Judith Lock	1, 5, 0

September 1756

Joseph Mather & Eliz: Bearge	1, 5, 0
John Kaiter & Rebecca Lace	1, 5, 0
Tho. Alex:ᵃ Sherlock & Marg.ᵗ Miller	1, 5, 0
Ceaser Gislin & Eliz: Rankin	1, 5, 0
Andrew Steel & Marg.ᵗ Culbertson	1, 5, 0
Thomas Smith & Jane Rubee	1, 5, 0
James Johnson & Sarah Smith	1, 5, 0
Benj: Jackson & Martha Hughes	1, 5, 0
James Cope & Elinor Minchim	1, 5, 0
Samuel Martin & Mary Smith	1, 5, 0
Isaac Shoemaker & Mary Duffil	1, 5, 0
Henry Cole & Alce Dunlap	1, 5, 0
George Smith & Mary Ball	1, 5, 0
Abel Reece & Catharine Davis	1, 5, 0
Dan. Carter & Eliz. Adams	1, 5, 0
Casper Roan & Bar. Boydler	1, 5, 0
	£20, 0, 0

October 1756

Geo: Crush & Maudelin Shimble	1, 5, 0
Joseph Ward & Eliz: Reece	1, 5, 0
Humphrey Jones & Mary Roberts	1, 5, 0
Dan. Etteng & Cat: Fenning	1, 5, 0
James Evans & Marg. Doyle	1, 5, 0

John Tiggs & Susannah Reice	1, 5, 0	
George Claypool & Mary Parkhouse	1, 5, 0	
Jo: Claypool & Mary Wilkinson	1, 5, 0	
Henry Comley & Rach: Strickland	1, 5, 0	
Sam. Worrel & Elianor Worrel	1, 5, 0	
Sam. Shaw & Mary Hall	1, 5, 0	
Peter Valleau & Eliz. Cole	1, 5, 0	
John Francis & Ann Williams	1, 5, 0	
Thomas Tapper & Rebecca Dilks	1, 5, 0	
	£17,10, 0	

Novemb.ʳ 1756

Wm. Ballard & Ann McCullough	1, 5, 0	
Tho.ˢ Mathers & Mary Paterson	1, 5, 0	
Benj: Walton & Cat. Williamson	1, 5, 0	
Sam. Cooke & Graham Kearny	1, 5, 0	
Geo: Brown & Susañah Harlin	1, 5, 0	
Jnº. Saunders & Cat. Weaver	1, 5, 0	
Luke Scanlan & Martha McKnight	1, 5, 0	
Samuel James & Esther Morris	1, 5, 0	
Charles Steward & Sarah Lawell	1, 5, 0	
Morgan Flaharty & Rose Sullivan	1, 5, 0	
Tho˟. Eastwick & Marg: Bullock	1, 5, 0	
Joseph Skirm & Sus: Coleman	1, 5, 0	
Hance Boone & Mary Urin	1, 5, 0	
Wm. Hardcastle & Ann Sculley	1, 5, 0	
Tho: Liwen & Elianor Dodd	1, 5, 0	
Jacob Mechlin & Mary Zim̄erman	1, 5, 0	
	£20, 0, 0	

Decemb. 1756

Joseph Martindale & Marg. Conolly	1, 5, 0	
John Gogin & Cath. O'Brian	1, 5, 0	
Chas. Moore & Rebecca Pratt	1, 5, 0	
John Henderson & Ann Talbot	1, 5, 0	
Thomas King & Susan: Coats	1, 5, 0	
Andrew Oliphant & Ann Hughes	1, 5, 0	
Jnº. Williamson & Jane Newton	1, 5, 0	
Antho: Harle and Ann Valentine	1, 5, 0	
Jonathan Dilworth & Ann Peters	1, 5, 0	
Wm. Byer & Mary Boyer	1, 5, 0	
Em. Woodbee & Jane Linkhorne	1, 5, 0	
James Turner & Eliz: Macky	1, 5, 0	
Dan. Mackent & Sarah Pastorius	1, 5, 0	
Wm. Ramsey & Mary Hall	1, 5, 0	
Wm. Anderson & Ann Custurd	1, 5, 0	
John Buchannan & Avesratler Rakes	1, 5, 0	
Hugh Thompson & Margᵗ. Morgan	1, 5, 0	
Wm. Smith & Marg. Preston	1, 5, 0	
	£22,10,	

Marriage Licenses Issued in the Secretary's Office

January 1757

1	Enoch Evans & Mary Evans	1, 5, 0
6	John Blackford & Ann Hunter	1, 5, 0
5	John Fry & Milicent Oneal	1, 5, 0
8	Joseph Ingles & Mariam Field	1, 5, 0
13	Isaac Course & Eliz: Stillee	1, 5, 0
17	Ired Irwin & Eliz. Martin	1, 5, 0
18	Philip Cloyn & Mary Fetzer	1, 5, 0
29	John Gilham & Abigal Woodward	1, 5, 0
P22	Charles Meredith & Mary Chappel	1, 5, 0
26	Conrad Shultz & Barbara Swackhart	1, 5, 0
do.	Luke Williams & Martha Hartley	1, 5, 0
do.	Thoˢ. Wynn & Margᵗ. Coulson	1, 5, 0
do.	Thoˢ. Lonon & Sarah Gramer	1, 5, 0
29	James Frisby & Sarah Noxon	1, 5, 0
Pdo.	William Francis & Sarah Walton	1, 5, 0
Pdo.	Richᵈ. Howell & Eliz: Jones	1, 5, 0

£20, 0, 0

February 1757

1	Levy Trump & Catherine Palmer	1, 5, 0
4	Geo: Andreas & Barbara Deil	1, 5, 0
	John Rees & Susannah Richards	1, 5, 0
5	Ryneer Vanderslice & Mary Umsted	1, 5, 0
7	Fred Shaltz & Roseanna Fustring	1, 5, 0
10	John Hannis & Mary Glover	1, 5, 0
10	Rob. Grimes & Marg. Holland	1, 5, 0
12	Medan Martin & Ann Ludon	1, 5, 0
21	John Rees & Sophia Kuman	1, 5, 0
21	Philip Halbert & Hannah Preston	1, 5, 0
28	James Moffit & Tubia Allen	1, 5, 0

£13,15, 0

March 1757

John Harrison & Mary McCoy	1, 5, 0
John Britt & Mary McConnel	1, 5, 0
James White & Jane Price	1, 5, 0
Josiah Harper & Sushanna Way	1, 5, 0
Henry Caswell & Mary Daily	1, 5, 0
Benj: Eastburn & Mary Walton	1, 5, 0
Wm. Bowman & Eliz. Hart	1, 5, 0
Wm. Davis & Abigal Scull	1, 5, 0
Geo. Passach & Mary Rutter	1, 5, 0
Thomas Sewell & Racˡ: James	1, 5, 0
Walter Batt & Sarah Davis	1, 5, 0
Thos Derrock & Ann Thompson	1, 5, 0
Wm. O'Brien & Kat. Williams	1, 5, 0
Cornelius Vancamp & Winfred Depu	1, 5, 0
Wollore Meng & Marg: Jones	1, 5, 0

Benj. Peel & Eliz Madden 1, 5, 0
James Downey & Ann McCormack 1, 5, 0
Sam. Stackhouse & Mary Hays 1, 5, 0
Wm. Robinson & Hannah Nagle 1, 5, 0
                                                      £23,15, 0

April 1757

Geo. Hall and Jane Campbell 1, 5, 0
Nath. Russel & Mary Lacy 1, 5, 0
Abr^m. Harding & Rachel Wilson 1, 5, 0
Nath: Thomas & Eliz: Mather 1, 5, 0
Jacob Hugg & Hannah Wells 1, 5, 0
Geo. Young & Mary Cloud 1, 5, 0
Mich: Klingman & Eliz: Mellerin 1, 5, 0
Joseph Price & Mary Jones 1, 5, 0
James Warner & Zebella Battle 1, 5, 0
John Short & Sarah Newport 1, 5, 0
David Greenlow & Mary Henderson 1, 5, 0
Peter Keyser & Hannah Levering 1, 5, 0
Wm. Douglass & Mary Price 1, 5, 0
Thomas Turbet & Eliz. Crawford 1, 5, 0
Daniel Craig & Eliz. Caruthers 1, 5, 0
Geo: Bryon & Eliz. Smith 1, 5, 0
James Worrel & Mary Stuart 1, 5, 0
Dan. Lukin & Eliz: Read 1, 5, 0
Peter Kirby & Catharine Millard 1, 5, 0
Lawrence Stuart & Jean Neally 1, 5, 0
John Gordon & Hannah Dunbar 1, 5, 0
                                                      £26, 5, 0

May 1757 (no entries)

June 1757

Richard Wright & Abig. Wigerly 1, 5, 0
Nath. Pelly & Sarah Cooper 1, 5, 0
Jn° Butler & Martha Coleman 1, 5, 0
Jo: Askaw & Eliza: Colever 1, 5, 0
Silas Prior & Letitia Brockdon 1, 5, 0
Robert Robertson & Eliz: Grislin 1, 5, 0
Benja: Ellis & Sarah Bates 1, 5, 0
Abel Dungan & Gainer Lukins 1, 5, 0
Jn° Morrison & Eliza Duke 1, 5, 0
Jacob Reinno & Catherine Gaue 1, 5, 0
Jn° Wagg & Mary Loweay 1, 5, 0
Job Walton & Catherine McVaugh 1, 5, 0
                                                      £15, 0, 0

Marriage Licenses Issued in the Secretary's Office

July 1757

Joseph George & Ann George	1, 5, 0
William Wood & Martha Gwinnap	1, 5, 0
Thomas Pennrose & Ann Dowdon	1, 5, 0
William Smith & Mary Maid	1, 5, 0
Edw: Green & Eliz: White	1, 5, 0
Joseph Todd & Martha McCavers	1, 5, 0
Jnº Philip Dehause & Leonore Rine	1, 5, 0
James Lee & Mary Worrel	1, 5, 0
	£10, 0, 0

August 1757

Thomas Hazelber & Brideᵉ. Miles	1, 5, 0
Nathan Fletcher & Eliz: Fling	1, 5, 0
Martin Welch & Jane McGraugh	1, 5, 0
James Andreas & Ann Luttin	1, 5, 0
John Dunken & Mary Drinker	1, 5, 0
William Wallace & Ruth Miller	1, 5, 0
James Kelly & Mary Knox (?)	1, 5, 0
Joseph Morrison & Mary Stuart	1, 5, 0
John Woods and Jane Carley	1, 5, 0
Arthur Bennet & Elinor Knowles	1, 5, 0
David Arnold & Naomia Jones	1, 5, 0
William McGlathry & El: Jolly	1, 5, 0
Collin McSwinna & Ann Lockard	1, 5, 0
Edward Belford & Jnº Askin	1, 5, 0
Jonat: Wood & Judith Samuels	1, 5, 0
Josiah Chattin & Mary Miller	1, 5, 0
Richard Airs & Eliz: Brownin	1, 5, 0
John Losk & Mary Karson	1, 5, 0
William West & Mary Hodge	1, 5, 0
John Anderson and Mary Wilson	1, 5, 0
Thoˢ Dukemiñer & Lidia Holmes	1, 5, 0
Bryan Younger & Elizabeth Deykin	1, 5, 0
Samuel Crook & Mary Heady	1, 5, 0
Richard Hudson [crossed out]	
John Matlack & Ann Furguson	1, 5, 0
Robert Crocket & Mary Middleton	1, 5, 0
	£31, 5, 0

September 1757

1	John Welch and Frances Bullard	1, 5, 0
2	Edward Croston & Ann Forbes	1, 5, 0
2	John Avergaste & Rebecca Felty	1, 5, 0
5	Henry Dawkins & Percilla Wood	1, 5, 0
8	Benjᵃ: Condy & Eliz: Lathberry	1, 5, 0
13	Jaˢ. Dicknson & Sarah Allen	1, 5, 0
13	John King & Cath: Daulton	1, 5, 0
17	George Lay & Honor Kellin	1, 5, 0

21	Benjamin Molton & Cath: Shellock	1, 5, 0
	Benj:ᵃ Chew and Eliz: Osweld	1, 5, 0
26	William Stoy & Eliz: Maus	1, 5, 0
28	Alexander Boggs & Margᵗ. Lloyd	1, 5, 0
29	John Chappel & Martha Duffel	1, 5, 0
do.	Isaac Jones & Mary Harper	1, 5, 0
		£17, 0, 0

October 1757

4	John Gillard & Mary Farrel	1, 5, 0
do.	Joseph Shute & Sarah Patterson	1, 5, 0
5	John McCally & Mary Craig	1, 5, 0
7	Robert Robson & Jane Haley	1, 5, 0
do.	Peter Witmer & Sarah Shitzer	1, 5, 0
8	Isaac Lefever & Deb: Midwinter	1, 5, 0
11	John Gibson & Ann Ball	1, 5, 0
13	John Bishop & Mary Marshall	1, 5, 0
do.	Anthony May & Mary Kalket	1, 5, 0
14	Chichester Reynolds & Marg:ᵗ Wodward	1, 5, 0
15	James Adams & Sarah Davis	1, 5, 0
18	John Adams & Jane Fairest	1, 5, 0
18	Arnold Baily & Mary Cunningham	1, 5, 0
18	John Kaiser & Rebecca Lukens	1, 5, 0
18	Edward Clerk & Mary Howard	1, 5, 0
20	John Boyd & Agnes Jones	1, 5, 0
20	Chas. Lawrence & Rach: Moulder	1, 5, 0
25	Thoˢ. Griffith & Mary Littlejohn	1, 5, 0
29	Wm. Palmer & Susannah Wiley	1, 5, 0
29	Job Whatson & Margᵗ Johnson	1, 5, 0
29	Wm. Rees & Martha Thomas	1, 5, 0
29	Ephraim Caldwell & Cath. Carmickle	1, 5, 0
		£27,10, 0

November 1757

4	Joseph Kelly & Marg: Woods	1, 5, 0
do.	Phineas Koone & Elizᵃ: Rush	1, 5, 0
do.	James Barker & Dorothy Camby	1, 5, 0
8	Leonard Herman & Eliz: England	1, 5, 0
do.	John Hough & Olive Rogers	1, 5, 0
9	James Brockington & Ann Oney	1, 5, 0
11	David Smith & Elizᵃ Roxborough	1, 5, 0
14	Robert Smith & Deborah Myers	1, 5, 0
16	Terrence McMaken & Elizᵃ Dodds	1, 5, 0
19	James Mathew & Susanna Sheppard	1, 5, 0
do.	Philip Mendenhall & Mary Jones	1, 5, 0
23	Thomas Blacklidge & Mary Pitts	1, 5, 0
26	George Kennard & Mary Hurley	1, 5, 0
28	Wm. Fitzgareld & Ann Ryan	1, 5, 0

29	Nath: Newlin & Jane Woodward	1, 5, 0
do.	Samuel Watson & Mary Johnston	1, 5, 0
30	Thomas Smith & Hannah Hastings	1, 5, 0
do.	John David & Elizabeth Ware	1, 5, 0
do.	Benj:ᵃ Rambo & Rachel Reeves	1, 5, 0
do.	John Hickman & Marg: Kennedy	1, 5, 0
do.	John Poultney & Jane Harding	1, 5, 0

£26, 5, 0

December 1757

1	John White & Mary Stalcop	1, 5, 0
	Peter Plom and Mary Schrider	1, 5, 0
	John Wildman and Mary Tomlinson	1, 5, 0
	Thomas Haines and Eliz:ᵃ Haines	1, 5, 0
2	John Cumming and Jane Pursex (?)	1, 5, 0
	Neal Mathews and Eliz: McCalley	1, 5, 0
	James Young and Margᵗ: Patten	1, 5, 0
	Joshua Carpenter and Eliz:ᵃ Davis	1, 5, 0
	Abrām Zimmerman & Marg: Berger	1, 5, 0
	Randel Morgan and Amy Chew	1, 5, 0
	Mich: Magra and Ann Reardon	1, 5, 0
	Wm. Moore & Sarah Lloyd	1, 5, 0
	Archib: Gillaspy & Lydia Cook	1, 5, 0
	John Armstrong & Margᵗ. McHenry	1, 5, 0
	Jonathan Cox & Hannah Parker	1, 5, 0
	Jnᵒ Kirkpatrick & Rachel Lewis	1, 5, 0
	John Logan and Rachel Flood	1, 5, 0
	John Chabaud & Ann Turner	1, 5, 0
	John Read and Margᵗ. Hannis	1, 5, 0
	Wm. Beir and Sarah Dilworth	1, 5, 0
	Garret Sickles & Eliz: Burklow	1, 5, 0
	Benj.ᵃ Lownsberry & Ann Young	1, 5, 0
	Hugh Low & Catherine Yozen	1, 5, 0
	Jnᵒ. McConnel & Martha Levy	1, 5, 0

£30, 0, 0

January 1758

4	Michael Milberger & Eliz: Schlattern	1, 5, 0
5	Richard Lovelock and Ann Fell	1, 5, 0
7	George Dowell and Sarah Griffith	1, 5, 0
11	George Kidd and Sarah Lehigh	1, 5, 0
12	Jacob Dubree and Hannah Davis	1, 5, 0
do.	John Parry and Eliz:ᵃ Ledru	1, 5, 0
13	John Fogle and Margᵗ. Fogell	1, 5, 0
16	John Williams and Ann Baker	1, 5, 0
17	Simon Guest and Agness Salkell	1, 5, 0
18	Wm. Free and Marg.ᵗ Jones	1, 5, 0
20	Henry Bragg & Susannah Moon	1, 5, 0
24	John Hainey and Catherine Penner	1, 5, 0

27	John Warner & Edith Jackson	1, 5, 0
27	Thomas Powell & Liticia Steward	1, 5, 0
30	Negro Tom. & Stockers' Woman	1, 5, 0
		£18,15, 0

February 1758

2	Edmund Physick and Abigail Syng	1, 0, 0
	James Davis and Massey Chew	1, 5, 0
3	Jacob Rush and Hannah Myers	1, 5, 0
4	John Wilson and Rose Hall	1, 5, 0
	John Paul and Mary Paul	1, 5, 0
8	Derick Krozen and Mary Bennel	1, 5, 0
11	David Thomas and Agnes Anderson	1, 5, 0
13	John Kennedy and Marg.ᵗ Walker	1, 5, 0
	Joseph Ashmead & Lydia Whiteman	1, 5, 0
18	George Abington & Sarah Wilson	1, 5, 0
18	P. Fred: Mouse and Frances Heap	1, 5, 0
do.	John Richardson & Lucy Brown	1, 5, 0
21	Michael Smith and Ann M. Tadren	1, 5, 0
	Thomas Brown and Ann Breton	1, 5, 0
27	Daniel McDaniel & Sarah Cummings	1, 5, 0
do.	Benja: Fordham & Elishiba Shed	1, 5, 0
		£19,15, 0

(No entries for March through June, 1758)

July 1758

1	John Stone and Deborah Godfrey	1, 5, 0
3	Anthony David and Mary Gandowen	1, 5, 0
5	William Sims and Mary Brookbank	1, 5, 0
?6	Paul Troy and Lettice Maxwell	1, 5, 0
8	Thomas Rees and Ann Thomas	1, 5, 0
17	John Johnson and Sarah Pritchard	1, 5, 0
19	William Hicks and Francis Jeykill	1, 5, 0
20	James Lighton and Jane Anderson	1, 5, 0
	Donald Monroe and Catherine Kisoada	1, 5, 0
21	Peter Fadley and Susannah Nise	1, 5, 0
22	Wm. Young and Grace Price	1, 5, 0
25	Jonathan Roberts and Margaret Locky	1, 5, 0
	George Teeter Bougher & Ellenor Hollobock	1, 5, 0
	Benj:ᵃ Ford & Sarah Clayton	1, 5, 0
20	Thomas Fitzsimmons & Catherine Meade	1, 5, 0
26	Wm. Barnhill & Isabella Barnhill	1, 5, 0
	James Harvey & Grace Birrett	1, 5, 0
2	Henry Bryan & Margaret Allison	1, 5, 0
		£22,10, 0

Marriage Licenses Issued in the Secretary's Office

August 1758

2	John Bond and Margaret Allen	1, 5, 0
do.	David Seers and Elizabeth Pametie	1, 5, 0
3	Thomas Atkins and Hannah Rutter	1, 5, 0
5	Abram Long and Mary Gikens	1, 5, 0
do.	Jn° Hartshorne and Sarah Shelva	1, 5, 0
8	Peter Koocker and Susannah Stedleman	1, 5, 0
9	Joseph Allen and Mary Hutton	1, 5, 0
do.	David Davis and Jane Harry	1, 5, 0
9	Jeremiah Baker and Ruth Boneham	1, 5, 0
11	Alex.ª Rutherford and Katherine Stuart	1, 5, 0
12	John Boyd and Eliz.ª Sullivan	1, 5, 0
do.	Ambrose Leipscum & Eliz:ª Furguson	1, 5, 0
16	William Moore and Rachel Wright	1, 5, 0
19	John Sheerman and Margᵗ. Skittlton	1, 5, 0
	John Hassel & Alce Each	1, 5, 0
	George Pierce and Mary Hill	1, 5, 0
23	Cornelius Newkirk and Mary Miller	1, 5, 0
	Thomas Grew and Lovisa Parvin	1, 5, 0
	Abraham Newkirk and Yockamintie Enoch	1, 5, 0
	Thomas Russel and Margaret Atkins	1, 5, 0
24	Thomas Lowry and Mary McKnight	1, 5, 0
	Charles Gorge and Ann Amberson	1, 5, 0
	Jonathan Paul and Sarah Young	1, 5, 0
26	John Martin and Abigail Barker	1, 5, 0
30	Isaac Chandler and Ester Chandler	1, 5, 0
31	Jonathan Davis and Mary Nailer	1, 5, 0
		£32,10, 0

September 1758

3	Jacob Powell & Susannah Cerl	1, 5, 0
4	Mathias Shits & Catherine Pyfer	1, 5, 0
5	Geo: Henry Heft & Cath: Poth	1, 5, 0
6	Robᵗ. Clerk & Rebecca Sherrard	1, 5, 0
7	John Adams & Cornelia England	1, 5, 0
do.	John White and Margaret Gregg	1, 5, 0
do.	Abraham Gibbon & Sarah Thomas	1, 5, 0
9	Patrick Wolf & Elizabeth Edwards	1, 5, 0
do.	Henry Punner & Elizabeth Spencer	1, 5, 0
12	William Preston & Barbara Heisler	1, 5, 0
18	William Magsun & Mary Hutchins	1, 5, 0
19	Benjamin Fuller & Rebecca Stamper	1, 5, 0
	Richard Meek & Grace Dart	1, 5, 0
	John Harvey [crossed out]	
	James Cannan & Mary Bedford	1, 5, 0
	Joseph Bevan & Isabella Wilson	1, 5, 0
	John Sayre & Mary Bowes	1, 5, 0
	Abraham Bickley & Mary Sewell	1, 5, 0

Thomas Bryant & Mercy Cook 1, 5, 0
Joseph Graham and Eliz: Lacy 1, 5, 0
John Sawyer & Elizabeth Thomas 1, 5, 0
Henry Stilfield & Marg.ᵗ Nailer 1, 5, 0

£26, 5, 0

October 1758

4	Augustine Bartholomew & Mʳ Russell	1,	5,	0
6	Edward Murphy & Mary Beech	1,	5,	0
7	John Dungan and Ann Thomas	1,	5,	0
9	Peter Capes and Mary Banks	1,	5,	0
10	Andrew Patterson & Elizᵃ Caruthers	1,	5,	0
do.	Samuel Harper and Ann Powell	1,	5,	0
10	Francis Harris and Elizᵃ. Peel	1,	5,	0
do.	William Hussey & Elinor Hanlon	1,	5,	0
11	John Robinson & Ann Elexander	1,	5,	0
13	Jonathan Humphreys & Ann Moore	1,	5,	0
do.	Thomas Barnes & Eliz.ᵃ Carr	1,	5,	0
17	John Thompson & Dorothy McKean	1,	5,	0
19	Andrew Hedge & Sarah Griffin	1,	5,	0
21	Thomas Mullen and Ann Bowles	1,	5,	0
24	John McDonnough & Roseabella Hasselton	1,	5,	0
26	Henry Flood and Eliz.ᵃ Fitchet	1,	5,	0
do.	John Sander and Sarah Stevens	1,	5,	0
27	Benj.ᵃ Conrand & Marg.ᵗ Richardson	1,	5,	0
do.	James Plunket & Sarah Slay	1,	5,	0
28	John Stout and Anna Dottama	1,	5,	0

£25, 0, 0

November 1758

David Aldridge and Sarah Chew 1, 5, 0
James Baily and Elizabeth Ham 1, 5, 0
Lewis Thomas and Susannah Evans 1, 5, 0
William Ashton and Catharine Easterly 1, 5, 0
George Bender and Barbara Foucht 1, 5, 0
Archibald Little & Susannah Lee 1, 5, 0
Owen Roberts and Mary Finley 1, 5, 0
John Gregory and Ann Miller 1, 5, 0
Christian Merkle & Juliana Gest 1, 5, 0
William Lukins & Hannah Tyson 1, 5, 0
Richard Winter & Ann Peal 1, 5, 0
Alexander McConnel & Martha Wilson 1, 5, 0
Joseph Roberts & Martha Taylor 1, 5, 0
Thoˢ. Forster and Mary Tillyer 1, 5, 0
Matthew Potter and Mary Smith 1, 5, 0
James Steel & Martha Canby 1, 5, 0
John McNeal and Mary Taylor 1, 5, 0
Joseph Rush and Elizabeth Hilton 1, 5, 0

Marriage Licenses Issued in the Secretary's Office

Samuel Davis and Esther Watkins	1, 5, 0
John Mercer and Elizabeth Miller	1, 5, 0
Randell Morgan & Martha Wilson	1, 5, 0
Christian Zachrighter and Maudlin Whatmenin	1, 5, 0
George Ketterer & Mary Stump	1, 5, 0
Daniel Thompson & Hannah Lyttejohn	1, 5, 0
Peter Mark & Ann Coleston	1, 5, 0
	£31, 5, 0

(*No entries for December 1758 through March 1759*)

April 1759

8	Thomas Vaughan & Prudence Jones	1, 5, 0
do.	John Dickey & Mary Hessing	1, 5, 0
do.	Henry Dougherty & Ann Edgar	1, 5, 0
4	Thomas Patterson & Eliz. Wells	1, 5, 0
do.	George Bridges & Margaret Sims	1, 5, 0
do.	William Hayes & Ann Hoge	1, 5, 0
do.	Benjamin Boore & Ann Cook	1, 5, 0
11	James Simpson & Ennis McCalvie	1, 5, 0
13	Joseph Elwell and Margaret Couey	1, 5, 0
17	Tobias Yearger & Catherine Singer	1, 5, 0
do.	Israel Hewlings & Jane Sharp	1, 5, 0
do.	Alexander Mcpherson & Mary Furguson	1, 5, 0
18	Mathew Adams & Mary Glenn	1, 5, 0
do.	Peter Erwin & Christiana Simmons	1, 5, 0
do.	Nicholas Rambo & Martha Sharp	1, 5, 0
19	George Kearst & Eliza Kelback	1, 5, 0
20	John Richards & Jennet Rees	1, 5, 0
	Cuffe and Letitia	1, 5, 0
21	John Galley and Jane Carr	1, 5, 0
24	David Potts and Alce Schull	1, 5, 0
25	Benjamin Patten & Jañet Giffen	1, 5, 0
do.	William Thorne & Eliz\u1d43. Clifton	1, 5, 0
27	Charles Nichols & Elianor Pinyard	1, 5, 0
28	Philip Murphy & Marg. Arnold	1, 5, 0
do.	George Bowman & Eliz: Myrin	1, 5, 0
30	Joseph Vandegrift & Eliz: Williamson	1, 5, 0
		£32,10, 0